This is, I believe, the first endeavor to set down the whole and true story of the motion picture. I have been in contact with the author's researches through his years of preparation and I am aware of an unrelenting effort at exact fact. A high degree of detailed accuracy has been attained. Ramsaye's theories, opinions and deductions are his own.

Thos A Edison.

THOMAS A. EDISON, inventor of the motion picture film, the
camera and the Kinetoscope — the technological foundation of the art of the motion picture.

A MILLION AND ONE NIGHTS

A HISTORY OF THE MOTION PICTURE THROUGH 1925

TERRY RAMSAYE

A TOUCHSTONE BOOK
Published by Simon & Schuster, Inc.
NEW YORK

First Touchstone Edition, 1986

Published by Simon & Schuster, Inc.
Simon & Schuster Building
Rockefeller Center
1230 Avenue of the Americas
New York, New York 10020

TOUCHSTONE and colophon are registered trademarks of
Simon & Schuster, Inc.

Manufactured in the United States of America

10 9 8 7 6 5 4 3 2 1 Pbk.

Library of Congress Cataloging in Publication Data

Ramsaye, Terry, 1885–1954.
    A million and one nights.

    (A Touchstone book)
    Includes index.
    1. Moving-pictures—United States—History.
2. Silent films—History and criticism. 3. Cinematography
—History. I. Title.
PN1993.5.U6R35   1986   791.43'09   86-3685
ISBN 0-671-62404-0 Pbk.

A NOTE ON THE NEW EDITION

When A Million and One Nights *was first published in 1926, it was hailed as "the first complete source book on the motion picture" and its author, Terry Ramsaye, as "the first authentic film historian." The intervening years have established* A Million and One Nights *as a classic, standard work on the history of the motion picture from the beginning through 1925. The contents of this edition are identical with those of the original two-volume edition.*

—THE PUBLISHERS

PREFACE

This history is a tale for its own sake. Many, and perhaps most, of the facts presented in these pages will be found to be new or at variance with the generally accepted traditions and writings of the motion picture.

The recorded annals and expressions pertaining to the screen broadly considered fall, often precipitately, into two classifications; those written to serve special interests within the industry or other partisan purposes and the observations of writers remotely external to the world of the motion picture.

Late in 1920 James R. Quirk, the editor-publisher of *Photoplay Magazine*, recognizing the lack of any coherent and authenticated record of the rise of the motion picture commissioned me to undertake the preparation of a series of twelve articles covering the subject. The preliminary survey of the field indicated so much material that the series was extended to thirty-six installments running for three years in the magazine. However, even this extraordinary editorial endurance did not permit a complete presentation of the ever unfolding story with its tempting new vistas beckoning for exploration. Now two years more have been devoted to completing some of the more important researches and a recasting of the entire mass of material in the light of the progressive developments.

The enthusiastic approval of the endeavor by Mr. Quirk and access to the extensive records and files of *Photoplay* have been important to the continuance of the researches subsequent to the completion of the magazine serial version.

Because of the strong coloration of individual and special

interest in much of the writing concerning the screen, it is necessary to state that there is nothing in this narrative especially in behalf of any person or concern in anywise related to the art or industry.

My contact with the motion picture began in 1913 when I was a member of the staff of *The Chicago Tribune*, functioning between the editorial and circulation departments. This led to connections, in sequence, with a number of motion picture corporations and ramifications of their sometimes peculiar enterprises. In 1920, upon undertaking the labors of this history, I abandoned all corporation connections and started afield with a free hand. In this five-year period my occasional services to the motion picture have been as a free-lance consultant on specific business problems or editorial aspects of individual productions for various and competing concerns. Within the domain of the motion picture I have neither friendships nor enmities of sufficient weight to influence the telling of this story.

The material for this history has been gleaned practically in its entirety from original sources, first through my personal contacts within the industry and secondly by research in previously unpenetrated strata of record. It early became apparent that nothing offered, either by prior publication or from the contemporary personal recollections of persons involved, could be finally accepted or interpreted without painstaking checks and verifications. With but an inconsiderable number of exceptions, every living person among those mentioned in this history has been interviewed, some of them many times, while the correspondence, accounts and archives in general of others have been examined in detail. The records of the several hundred litigations of the thirty years of patent and commercial wars have yielded much of the material strangely ignored by prior writers. Also for reasons, which become apparent in the body of the story, an extensive fabric of erroneous tradition, with some strands of deliberate distortion of the record, has had to be unravelled. The work has been complicated and prolonged by the continuous provocation of the existing possibility of uncovering every exact moment and affair of bearing on the subject—an enslaving condition which condemns me to an eternal sense of dissatisfaction and incompleteness.

The situation which finds a majority of the leading figures in the history of the screen yet alive, and frequently active, has presented me with both opportunities and problems not common to historians comfortably insulated by the centuries, with their subjects safely reduced to graveyard mould.

This endeavor has been aimed at determining with some accuracy the place of the motion picture in the contemporary world and tracing the steps by which it has arrived at this place.

The literature of the motion picture is mostly yet to be written. Many aspects of the art appear to call for intensive examination and record. It has been possible, in the compression of this memorandum of quarter of a million words, no more than slightly to indicate the high lights of the evolution of narrative styles and technique by the picture makers and the parallel education of the screen audience in the hieroglyphs and vernacular of screen narration.

The innumerable and complex racial, political, and geographical relations and reactions in which the screen has been importantly involved are yet to be explored. Largely the psychology of the motion picture is still awaiting an investigator. Not even a small part of the important technological developments within the film and the camera have been adequately recorded for the public.

A slight, tentative beginning of screen discussion and appraisal was made by Vachel Lindsay in his "Art of the Moving Picture" published about 1916. It was largely a rhapsody from the viewpoint of a poet sitting in a Springfield, Illinois, theatre, capable for its day and pleasant, but neither professing nor possessing penetration. A step significant and indicative of the analytical screen literature to come has been accomplished in "Pictorial Beauty on the Screen" by Victor Oscar Freeburg, Ph. D. It is the most effective discussion of dramatic film technique yet brought forth.

In the field of periodical publication some pregnant discussions of the motion picture have come from Julian Johnson and Ralph Block, both picture production executives, and from Gilbert Seldes, John Farrar, Burton Roscoe, Robert Sherwood and others among the professional critics, in the main as incidental side glances from their concerns with other arts and literature. A school of motion picture criticism is evolving with a deliberation which seems tedious beside the racing progress of the pictures. This probably results from the fact that nearly all those who know anything about the motion picture, as well as some who do not, are busy making them.

This history has necessarily concerned itself exclusively with the motion picture of the theatre screen, which, while the obviously dominant florescence of the art, represents only one of its functions.

It has seemed advisable, even in its incompleteness, to get this record into the safekeeping of the printed word now, in view of the imminent passing of the pioneers and the ephemeral character of much of the important source material. Conditions revealed by these researches indicate a large opportunity of service for a motion picture museum.

For an adequate listing of the persons to whom I am indebted for coöperation and access to important records the reader might well be referred to the entire array of names in the index, but because of their generosity of attention I wish to especially acknowledge the courtesies of Thomas A. Edison, the late Norman Charles Raff, Thomas Armat, William Kennedy Laurie Dickson, C. Francis Jenkins, Jeremiah J. Kennedy, Robert W. Paul, Cecil Hepworth, Charles Urban, Louis and Auguste Lumière, Henry Norton Marvin, George Kleine, Frank L. Dyer, Jacques A. Berst, Robert Cochrane, John R. Freuler, Edwin S. Porter, Fred Hawley, J. Stuart Blackton, W. W. Hodkinson, Lewis J. Selznick and Adolph Zukor. Acknowledgement is also due to the assistance of Betty Shannon Ramsaye, who has been associated with my labors of inquiry, and to Walter B. Pitkin of Columbia University, through whom the fruits of related but yet unpublished researches in some other fields have been made available.

Twenty-one years ago Charles I. Blood, city editor of *The Kansas City Times*, called me, a timid novitiate, to the desk for my first assignment.

"There has been a shooting in the West Bottoms," he said. "Go find out who did it, when he did it, why he did it and who he did it to—and that will be a story."

That is what I have endeavored to do for the motion picture.

T. R.

New York, May 1, 1926.

FOREWORD

THE ART AND ITS AUDIENCE

Here is a news story. It endeavors to cover the birth of a new art—the motion picture.

For the first time in the history of the world, so far as the author has been able to discover, an art has sprouted, grown up and blossomed in so brief a time that one person might stand by and see it happen.

The motion picture has occurred, or perhaps has been committed, in the presence of a reporter, who has been busy the while, taking notes and interviewing the possibly innocent bystanders.

The motion picture is a genuine art. It is genuine in that it is strictly popular, appealing to and serving the multitudes.

This art has grown out of simple, elemental wishes. The forms which it has taken are the products of now well recognized human traits. Like all the great arts its appeal is based on a few primitive, and therefore universal, instincts and mechanisms in man. Sex and combat are the chief instincts. The eye is the principal mechanism.

The motion picture is the great common denominator of the arts.

Like all great arts, the motion picture has grown up by appeal to the interests of childhood and youth.

The average life of the savage who began the arts of the dance, the song and the picture was not more than fifteen years. Men were old at twenty. Women were withering hags at eighteen. A person of fifty was a Methusaleh.

The intelligence tester tells us that the effective age of the average American mind today is about fourteen. That is old enough for all practical purposes, the most important of which is reproduction. Nature is not wasteful, so why make us older? More elaborated older minds are, measured by the commonalty, accidental freaks like paper-shell pecans and navel oranges.

The insurance tables indicate that we die at age 58 now, on the average, anyway. Even this longevity has been attained for so tiny a period in history that it is of no moment. The human race has always been young. It is a world of distinctly young ideas.

The song, the dance and the picture have sprung from minds essentially juvenile and adolescent. Our arts are the product of the slow, inevitable process of trial and error in serving mass tastes down the ages. Art has been distilled and filtered through the likes and dislikes, the acceptances and the rejections, of the billions of our ancestors. The experiences, sex life and outlook of those billions have been those characteristic of the eighteen-year-old boy and girl. The world and all its arts are the property of the adolescents.

Classic art, which means popularly accepted art, is adolescent to the core.

Classic art is a flowing tapestry, woven in the same unvarying patterns by the same young weavers from the beginning to today. The colors are softened, blended and perfected by glamor as the fabric stretches back in the perspective of time into history, tradition and mythology. Where the weaving is fresh in the Loom of Now we see the same colors, fresh, raw and garish in today's headlines and tonight's movies.

But the figures of this tapestry's pageant are all one merry company, members of the immortal race of Personified Desires: Diana, Aphrodite, Sappho, Dido, Helen of Troy, Hercules, Jason, Ulysses, Solomon, Salome, Cyrus, Alexander,

Cleopatra, Cæsar, Richard Cœur d'Lion, Robin Hood, Nell Gwyn, Elizabeth, Marie Antoinette, Romeo and Juliet, Paul and Virginia, Dick and Ben Turpin, Joan of Arc, Ivan-the-Terrible, Lief-the-Lucky, Columbus, Pocahontas, Priscilla, George Washington, Napoleon, Daniel Boone, Kit Carson, Coal Oil Johnny, Buffalo Bill, Jesse James, Lydia Pinkham, John L. Sullivan, Eugene Sandow, Bushman and Bayne, Pickford, Theda Bara, Fairbanks, Gloria Swanson, Tom Mix, Sarah Bernhardt, Gyp-the-Blood, Cecil Rhodes, Edison, Roosevelt, Harry Houdini, Morgan-the-elder, Beatrice Fairfax, Thomas Meighan, Jack Dempsey and Rudolph Valentino.

The motion picture reveals all of the art processes of all the ages. In the swift history of the films we see the entire evolution of art, compressed and oversped on the screen of Time. The motion picture is itself a tabloid picture of the evolving eternity behind us.

An art is born before our eyes, just as these very movies have shown us in stop-motion pictures the butterfly emerging from the cocoon. We see it struggle limply forth, dry its glamorous wings, and fly—with all its gay, gaudy spirit of youth, strong as youth is strong, weak as youth is weak.

And—butterfly like, the service of this gossamer winged art of flitting shadows is mostly in pollenizing the blossoms of the Wish, be they ragweeds of commonalty or roses of culture. Ragweeds are more abundant than roses.

The scholars, the historians, the cloistered critics of the colleges, all seeing the older arts down the cooler vistas of the ages, see them detached from their origins. Inevitably they see them all wrong. You can not know the nut unless you know the tree. You can not know the tree unless you know the soil. The motion picture is close to the soil.

A silly sanctity surrounds the standard, accepted, classic and traditional views of art. Each of the arts is surrounded by its priests and temple dancers. They chant mummeries which pass for lore and scream for the blood of heretics.

All of the arts and all the industries are products of the same forces. In the adventure of these pages we shall identify these forces, for the motion picture, in sex, fight, ambition and fear, in the plots and hopes of promoters, actors, publishers and politicians, and in the yearning, wishing millions who pay the box office tolls where they see the sign hanging out: "Dreams for Sale."

Our bold inquiry will take us into unfrequented byways of personality. Because they have been so fortunate, or so daring, as to involve themselves in the loving, hating, plotting, rioting flamboyances of the motion picture's growth, some hidden phases and motives in the lives of the people of the screen must be winnowed and measured here. It is a characteristic incident of the racing development of the art which brings the writing of this history while a majority of the makers of screen history are yet alive.

Most history is autopsy. This one is vivisection.

If this is to be history it must pursue its investigations with the same impartial, critical interest as if the demi-gods, the idols and the kings and queens of the screen empire were at one with the dust of ancient Egypt, instead of dusting up and down Fifth avenue and Sunset boulevard. We must be free to be as frank about Mary Queen of Hollywood as about Mary Queen of Scots. We must be open in treatment no matter which Charles-the-Great comes into our story. Adam, Aristotle and Adolph must be on a parity here. There is only a little matter of dates between them anyway.

CONTENTS

CONTENTS

CONTENTS

xvii

CONTENTS

CONTENTS

CONTENTS

CONTENTS

CONTENTS

CONTENTS

CONTENTS

CONTENTS

CONTENTS

CONTENTS

CONTENTS

CONTENTS

CONTENTS

xxx

CONTENTS

CONTENTS

Kent, sales manager extraordinary—Gloria Swanson blooms—The evolution of the vertical trust in the soil-to-nuts cycle—Putting the presentation into the can with the film—A birthday present to W. S. Hart, Jr.—And a pair of baby's shoes on Zukor's desk.

ILLUSTRATIONS

ILLUSTRATIONS

ILLUSTRATIONS

THE PREHISTORY OF THE SCREEN

In the public mind and in the consciousness of many of its students the motion picture seems a magic thing, born yesterday and of full growth this morning. But magic and miracles always fade in the light of information. It is the vastness of what we do not know which creates the great astonishments.

To the investigator who will pursue the facts through a maze of obscurities, one of the most interesting aspects of the screen is its belated arrival. The motion picture was a great deal overdue many, many centuries ago.

It is the very fact of the tardiness of the arrival of the screen which has resulted in this apparently miraculous growth and flowering into the magnitude which enables it to claim position among the leading industries of the world: This development has thus far occupied slightly more than three decades. To many the time seems even shorter, since there is a natural but erroneous tendency to think of the motion picture as having begun its career at the moment of the individual discovery.

If from the dark depths of the forest you transplant a stunted, struggling little tree, dwarfed and light-starved, out into a favorable soil and a place in the sun, its pent energies and deep primeval powers will shoot it into an amazingly rapid growth, a fevered redemption of the lost years. It is so with the motion picture.

He who will have the patience to follow this growth of the motion picture will find it too, like the tree, clearly an organism, following organic law in its development. The living picture will be found following that law with the unrelenting persistence that marks the growth of all living things, from yeast mold to races.

It is only by this recognition of the organic character of the motion picture and its consequent interrelation to all of the organism of mankind and society that it can be truly understood. Critics and forecasters, academic, professional and commercial, are continually committing themselves to error, and to the swift exposures of those errors, because of their failure to see the screen as one of the strands of the yarn of life, with an infinity behind and ahead.

The motion picture is as irresistible as the life stream behind it. It persists as a fundamental expression of that stream. Men and their movements which appear to control it are merely riding on its surface for their hour, and their operations are little more than evidences of the currents below. They who think they are the creators and masters of the motion picture are its servants.

The motion picture may be called the last-born offspring of the parent impulse of all the arts of expression, which are seeking to transmit to and infect others and ourselves with an impression of things and emotions.

The motion picture is the realization of the age-old Wish of the world.

This is not said in glorification of the picture, but is offered as fact based on all of the significance of Wishing.

Wishing has made the race, and with it the growing thing that has flowered on the screen. Nothing but desire has ever forced expression, and all of the expressions of art, recognized and unrecognized, are efforts, partially successful, to attain the objects of the Wish.

There is ample scientific authority for the assertion that in the beginnings of the human race wishes preceded communication and language—probably by some millions of years.

Man is the most wishful thing on the face of the earth. Simpler organisms await pure propinquity, chance, and the casual opportunities of natural supply to gratify their Wishes. As we ascend the biologic scale of intelligence we see increasing provision for the gratification of the Wish: from plants dependent on the happenings of a single spot and oysters feeding on what the tides may bring, to roaming beasts of prey and on to bees in the hive, a community gone insane with communism and the business of foresight and provision. Up at the top of the scale is man, the supreme go-getter of them all.

Out of the power and experience of the Wish man early found that some things were highly pleasurable. They delivered satisfaction to his assorted senses. Of those things and events he wanted more and ever more. He observed, presumably, that every time these things occurred he got the same pleasant sensations, the same emotional or sensory kick. Then, impatient of waiting for these pleasant things to happen of their own accord, came the impulse to push ahead and make them happen.

Man sought to repeat the pleasant event. That impulse to seek started it all. This probably began long before he became anything that we would call Man. But that was the desperate beginning of everything. That was the coming of the serpent into the garden, call it sin or intelligence as you will.

It took memory to know that the repetition of the event would bring a repetition of the pleasure. Memory thus came to seek the repetition of the pleasure by the re-creation of the event.

That dawning ability to re-enjoy by re-creation of the event of pleasurable memory was the beginning of knowledge. Perhaps it is a tribute to the antiquity of the strongest Wish of all that the Biblical phrase "to have knowledge of" is impregnated with the same duality of meaning that has come into the word "kiss" in some of the pungent fiction of the current period.

It is a rather fair presumption that it relates at least to that of which the race had its first knowledge. The serpent, you know, is quite as authentically an emblem of Wisdom as of the Devil.

Out of the Wish, his blazing and gnawing desires, man evolved expression, communication, and all of his arts. Research has traced the steps of that evolution; it shows that the ego of man makes him want to know himself.

That ego is the very soul of both the arts and the sciences. Man in his own profession and his own recreation. The chief of his desires, the keenest of his Wishes, the greatest of his recreations is the business of re-creating himself biologically and his emotional adventures in memory and its art forms.

This explains delightfully the inexorable persistence and dominance of the love story in the fiction of stage and screen and printed word. It is the one idea which dominates everywhere all the time, in ink, in celluloid, in paint and bronze and marble. It is what the saxophone says. Beauty and art, for the majority, are inseparable from sex.

The crab-apple of Eden and the orange of Hollywood are undoubtedly fruit of the same tree.

The evidences gathered by the students of language among the surviving and extinct primitives indicate that expression begins with signs of pantomime; that is, it begins with drama in its simplest form. When man set out to re-create events and to communicate, his own body was the first medium to fall under his control. His hands and arms were his first instruments. By gesture he could contrive to make another recognize something of the character of the idea impelling the imitative or suggesting postures and movements. A Chippewa Indian boy at play can thus make you see a bear, or a moose, very clearly. The simulative "chicken dance" of the Blackfeet, a pantomimic representation of the courtship of the prairie chicken performed by the braves before the admiring squaws, is an elaboration of the same idea passed into ritual.

This is the simplest form of telling. It is, in so far as possible, a very literal and actual re-creation of the event. The simple idea is "I will be as nearly a bear as I can, and then he will see the bear as I saw it." It is, note this, an effort to make a living picture, a motion picture, the medium of making the appearance of the event occur again.

But signs and pantomime have limitations of both scope and time. Despite an amazing ingenuity of pantomimic expression there are many things so remote from the possible action of the pantomimist that he cannot conveniently say them with his gestures and grimaces. Duration also is an element. The thing said in pantomine is said and gone. It does not continue to be said. The pantomimic picture fades as fast as it is created.

To escape these limitations man sought a more convenient and capable method of expression, a more enduring re-creation of the event for his own memory and for the benefit of others. It was thus that graphic art, the business of making pictures, was born into the service of the Wish.

Prehistoric troves have left to us some of those remotely early expressions, messages in image. The cave man seems to have wanted to say "bear" and "woman" rather often. They must have been ideas much on his mind—the thing that wished him and the thing that he wished, both delicious dangers. He began to sculpture his ideas of "bear" and "woman" in plastic mud, and presently to scratch representations of them on stone, on slabs of bone and ivory. It was, presumably, quite a step from sculpture which definitely sought to re-create the object in all of its external aspects in three dimensions to the relative abstraction of drawing which endeavors a three dimensional message in a single plane.

A vast new liberty came with this new method of telling, this new method of re-creation of the object or event by sculpture and drawing. It was no longer necessary to stay on the spot and pantomine the message. More could be said, and it would stay said for quite a while.

But this son of Pithecantropus discovered that art is long and time is fleeting. We can fancy him dropping his flint stylus in weariness and sighing that "the pictures are only in their infancy."

Communication grew impatient of the pace of the cave artists. It doubtless developed that there were many bears and many women to be discussed, and many things to be said of them. Continuing consideration of Things and Places and a developing recognition of Time and Space brought a complexity of emotions and ideas. Mud images and wall pictures could not keep up with the flow of thought and things to be said. The primitive man became a better thinker and more ardent expresser than an artist. In time he got to the point he could no longer say it all with pictures on a rock.

Man has been forced ever and ever to seek a greater facility for his re-creations.

The re-creation of the event is but a service of man's memory, an aid to summoning up at will and living again emotions enjoyed. By art man lives in the Past, the Present, and the Future all at once. His anticipations are but projections of memories, tinted by heart's desire. It is the peculiar, and perhaps only, especial beneficence of creation that man forgets the unpleasant. The pleasant he tries to re-create that he may re-live it, and that is art.

Efforts at re-creation for this service of the emotional desire began in ancient ritual in the simple form of complete re-enactment. To achieve the desired same result the whole thing was done over, be it the hunt, the battle, or the harvest. But art evolved a trifle, and a process of abridgment evolved into re-creation by symbolic acts, briefer cues to memory. Memory and imagination were growing. This method of re-creation by symbolic acts is in common survival today: witness the rites of the Eucharist, the pantomimic dances, and pageantry.

The progression from re-creation of the event by the complete act to re-creation by symbolic act is illustrated by a significant reversion. In Mexico a zealous sect, the Flagellantes, has been given to a complete re-enactment of the Christ legend, so literal as to include the actual crucifixion of the honored actor. The Passion Play of Oberammergau is itself only a somewhat less sanguinary re-creation by the complete act. The practise of the church, we see, has evolved from the literal ancient ritual to the symbolic drama of the altar of to-day.

When the re-creation of the event has a distinct purpose of utility, as for instance in the rain dance of the Hopi tribe, or in the cannibalistic hope involved in the doctrine of transubstantiation, we call it ritual. When the re-creation becomes more remotely symbolical, and at the same time loses its direct purpose of readily recognizable utility, we call it art.

The Dionysia of the ancient Greeks began as a sort of corn dance in furtherance of the crops. They evolved into a whole set of Athenian theatrical rituals. Then they became the Roman Bacchanalia, and to-day survive as the cute little May Pole dance, merely something pretty for the ornamentation of the Sunday school picnic. Also the juice of the corn is still a considerable factor in modern dancing. A great deal of the motion and emotion come out of the same bottle for the irrigation of the Wish. We still serve the old god Dionysius with fidelity. His name is with us yet, administered as "Denis" at the christening font. The roots of art are in ritual and the roots of ritual are in the tall grass. The cornfield waves forever. "All flesh is grass" quoth Isaiah. When the eccentric

Nebuchadnezzar betook himself to the pasture on all fours—after vitamin B, no doubt—he was, perhaps, not so crazy as Daniel presumed.

These rituals and their evolutions are, however, but by-pass channels of expression in re-creative effort, and are significant to us here only because of their very definite pictorial character.

Returning to our primitive picture-making man, we find him ever reaching for more facile media for his swelling flood of ideas, his picture-crowded mind.

For ages he struggled on with his picture making, his pantomime and ritual, and an evolving vocal language, growing words while sound and the action marched side by side. This was expression but not record. The service of memory requires record.

Out of this grew the profession of remembering, the function of the bards and minstrels. Here were born the sagas and the songs of Homer. Sound had been infected of meaning by association with events and their pictorial re-creations by pantomime and ritual. Now the event was being photographed on the memories of the professional rememberers, by translation into sound. The mnemonic need brought cadence and meter and rhythm to aid. Rhymes for remembering began. We use the same devices to-day: "Thirty days hath September, April, June, and November. . . ." There is something in the motion of the meter wave that keeps the memory on the path, just as the bicyclist keeps his equilibrium by moving forward. So poetry and music came to join in the function of remembering and telling; always the re-creating, the picturing of the event. They contributed motion and emotion.

All of these professional rememberings seem to depend for their very survival upon falling into the metrical wave motion of song and chant. The great epic of ancient India, the Mahabharata, is believed to have begun as prose, a tale of the affairs of the brothers Pandu and Dhritarashtra and their many sons. The family boast grew into an encyclopedia of India after it became metrical. It reached at last total of 100,000 distichs or couplets, being eight times as big as the Iliad and the Odyssey put together. The jingle kept it going. The prose writer sometimes comes to a stop, but the poet's metrical momentum overcomes all frictions. A prose novelist can be terminated by shooting, while a poet's refrain is picked up and carried on by his successors and assigns forever.

We must recognize a significant identity in the rhythmic quality of the dance as evolved ritual and the rhythm element of song, chant and verse serving the same Wishes. Poetry is made of dancing words, in measures that may be tripped by either foot or tongue. The beating syllabic feet of verse are indeed just sound-pictures of the motion, pointing again most precisely at the intrinsically pictorial character of language. The rhythmic movement of dance and song are identical for the identical purposes of memory, and apparently the memory is one and the same function whether it is to govern the feet or the tongue. Memory rhythm controls both ends in behalf of the middle. And memory lives in motion.

A sharply defined illustration of the motion control of memory is afforded in a parlor memory trick in vogue some years past. The memory performer essayed to repeat rapidly in succession the names of anywhere from twenty-five to fifty articles in the precise order in which they were stated to him. This was readily accomplished by the expedient of mentally building a pictorial action sequence, no matter how absurd, involving the articles as they were named to him. Thus if the series began "shingle, stove, chair," the memory scenario might run "shingle jumps into stove, stove sits in chair, etc., etc." When called upon to repeat the list the performer merely retraced the action of his motion scenario and picked up the articles in sequence.

Thus it appears that memory lives in mental motion pictures.

This motion pictorial element is even more astonishingly revealed in the memory feats which are incidental to the work of Gay MacLaren, dramatic recital artist. Her unique performances consist in giving entire plays, in the voices and actions of all of the members of the casts, attaining a high degree of stage illusion. Her repertoire includes some eighteen plays, and she sometimes adds two a season. The process of acquisition requires merely that she see five performances of the play as a member of the audience. No conscious memory effort enters into the process. The essence of the feat appears to be a recording of the stage picture, a function of what is termed her "camera mind." With only a setting of a table and two or three chairs, she reproduces that entire stage picture down to the most inconsiderable detail of action, by the sheer perfection of pantomimic reproduction of that action.

Any of these eighteen plays, many of them full three hours in length and including perhaps fifteen or twenty characters, is available in Miss MacLaren's memory at an instant's notice. The entire play with its infinity of pantomimic details and rapid fire of spoken parts, so essential to the multiple character delineations, flows on through a single personality with all the ribbon like continuity of a film. Her memory is a motion picture.

This element of motion is eternally of the vastest importance. It is the life. Only the motion, the actitation, persists. Trees die, the forest lives forever. Men and nations perish, but the race itself goes on. It is only the on-and-on movement that makes language an instrument of living man. All living and all that purports to reflect living must partake of and participate in this motion. There are a myriad evidences, some interesting because of their remoteness.

It is deeply significant that practically all modern psychologists agree that man cannot even think without some muscular motion. They agree that motion is an integral part of thinking, and not a mere aid to it. Some creative workers are notorious for the motion by-play which attends their efforts. They stalk and storm and gesticulate.

You cannot think without movement, be it ever so tiny, of some muscle somewhere in your throat, eye, ear, neck or arm. It must not be taken from this that ear-flapping is an index of intelligence. The moves tend, in some way, to realize the thing you have in mind. When you think "julep" your mouth waters and you swallow. Walter B. Pitkin of Columbia University in a lecture before a group of writers remarked that if it were given to us to be able to see interpretively every motion that a man made we should be able to tell what he was thinking about. The poker face is a defensive recognition of this principle. Four of a kind tends to generate telltale motions, and the royal flush often spreads to the face.

This motion quality of language re-creation of events is exemplified in the evolution of headline English in the daily newspapers. When the dynamic journalism commonly attributed to Hearst came into being it evolved a principle of head-writing which is briefly: "Do not write labels; put it in the active voice, present or future tense if possible. Get a verb in the head. Make it slam. Always get the today angle."

The event which occurred in the vicinity of midnight and which has been covered by the morning papers is mentioned in the hectic afternoon edition rewrites as "early to-day." The event may have occurred yesterday or a week ago, but the headline of its first presentation is active, present progressive; "Famous Beauty Shoots Near Husband," or "Airship Rams Submarine." The effort is continually to picture the event as going on at the instant before the reader's eyes.

This kinetic, motion-pictorial journalism consists outstandingly of the endeavor always to say a thing the most effective and immediate way. Its only use for yesterday is to give today a sharper taste and to-morrow a keener anticipation. It is the writing of the people, by the people, and for the people. Circulations are the indicators. Its essence is this same principle: a picture of movement, always on and on.

The hunger for movement is the root of all manner of aspects of our civilization, many more tangible than the recognized arts of expression—the one-step and fox trot, the merry-go-round, the swing, the rocking chair, shoot-the-chutes, all the park rides, the motor car. Let a man invent a new movement, and the world will reward him as it has Ford, Wrigley, Rockefeller and Eastman. A good movement is priceless.

This motion accompaniment of thought enters conspicuously into the chewing gum habit, which succeeds so well in filling what would be otherwise total vacua. The jaw motion of chewing gum is close kin to the little movements which seek to realize the wish-laden thought. Being such a close associate of thought it can by easy transfer be made to take its place. It can be observed at its best in an East Side dance hall where jaw and foot operate in utter synchronism with the orgiastic pulsations of the music. Chewing gum at a penny a stick got aboard the great human principle of motional emotion and won millions for its purveyors. The Liggett & Myers Tobacco Company tried to ride the same principle with its attempt of some years past to popularize edible tobacco with the slogan evolved by the late Richard A. Foley, reading: "The Men who Chew are the Men who Do." It failed because tobacco contains too little chew movement and too much marksmanship for urban populations.

We are going and going, where or nowhere makes no matter if we but *go*.

All this movement may seem no more than the dance of the midges where the sunbeam shafts through the birches over the trout pool, but it seems that much—life.

The static philosopher under the Bo tree seeks the perfect peace of All-Knowledge and finds it Oblivion. There are only the Quick and then the Dead. That is arrival. Motion is the be all and end all. The going is the life.

It was, and yet is, the business of the sagas to preserve the continuity of the race, reminding it that it *came* and that it is *going*—on and on and on.

Down in the Society Islands the profession of remembering survives with tribal reverence and honors for the old woman entrusted with the chanted annals of their people. Investigators have related instances in which these librarians of the race have recited lines of royal genealogy purporting to trace a thousand generations. For the identical purpose similar functionaries, usually old squaws, exist in most of the North American Indian tribes and among the Esquimaux.

So sound, by virtue of its pictorial meaning in words, became the memory cue, the light for the screen of recollection. More and more the burden of the re-creation of the event was shifted from the clumsy process of re-enactment to swift processes of visual imagination. The artist became author and sidestepped through language, making the listener mentally draw his own picture.

Sound by words became the medium of picture transmission in this wise, by translation first of the act into the significant sounds or words, and then again by translation back into the act in the mind of the listener. The process suggests the analogy of the translation of voice into the electrical wave and back to the voice again, as in the telephone and radio. Both are conversions of basically pictorial conceptions into transmissible media.

Sound and word made the brain, in an indirect sense, photosensitive.

This business of expression was and is tremendously difficult and complex. Picture making went on and grew in association with sound, just as pantomime did. Ideas in word-sounds had companions in idea-pictures. By a gradual, tedious metamorphosis, by generalization, degeneration and formalization the pictures became symbols for the associated sounds. When the pictures were divorced from their pure pictorial meaning and wedded to the sound they, by that step, became an alphabet.

The alphabet gave a tremendous impetus to the business of communication. It vastly shortened the process of re-creation of events, but added complication to complication by putting yet another pair of transformers in the circuit. The process was now from act to sound to alphabet, and then back down the line again through eye and mind from alphabetical word to the re-creation of the act on the screen of the mind.

But the artist communicator, as a writer of words, had no longer to trouble about accurate representations of his bear or woman. He could indicate everything swiftly with a few formal strokes, signs for the sounds which were signs for the pictures.

This pictorial ancestry of the alphabet is most readily established by examination into the writings of the ancients. And in fact, nearly the whole history of the human arts of expression is preserved for our examination in the archaic human islands that remain here and there in the sea of modern civilization. Among the living remnants of the ages in remote tribes and un-evolved peoples we can study the trend of the arts of expression with just as much assurance as we may study the ice age where it lingers still in the islands of prehistoric time frozen on the mountain glaciers.

In some of the simpler forms of the sign language of the American Indian we can see how intensely pictorial were the beginnings. Two fingers straddling the edge of the other hand signifies a man on a horse. To hammer on an open hand with the clenched fist means stone. The right arm bent and slightly raised forward with the hand closed and knuckles upward signifies old man. The derivation of the sign becomes apparent the moment that the hand clutches a supporting staff and completes the picture.

It is, of course, the most common knowledge that the written language of the Chinese to-day remains not at all an alphabet but a system of just such signs, pictures, simplified and formalized on paper with a brush. The Chinese ideographs are the persistence of a pictorial language in a state of arrested development.

In the most ancient of Chinese inscriptions the strictly pictorial origins of their written language is evidenced. By comparison with modern forms of the same characters we can observe the trends of formalizations in behalf of speed and the limitations of the writers' tools, brush, ink and paper. The first writings were with a firm stylus, more readily controlled in detail than the brush.

	Ancient	Modern
Sun		
Moon		
Mountains		
Child		

Horse　馬

Fish　魚

The next tiny step, showing the origin of derived compounds and the beginning of the sort of elaboration which has carried the language of the scholars of all races so far from the primitive concrete images, is indicated in such characters as theses:

	Ancient	Modern
Bright (sun and moon)		明
Forest (a group of trees)		林
Obstruction (A tree or bit of wood in doorway)		閑
East (Sun seen through a tree)		東

The Chinaman has stuck to the pictorial side of the ideograph to the bitter end, an interesting fact in view of the more recent anthropological notion that he is perhaps the purest and simplest survival of original man.

Out of the dusty yellow lore of ancient China comes a significant proverb: "One hundred tellings are not so good as one seeing." It is the axiomatic statement of the purpose of telling, to enable—by re-creation of the event—the seeing.

"One hundred tellings are not so good as one seeing." It is the lament of an eye-minded world.

Again in the ancient Persian, the tongue of the Rubaiyat of Omar's pleasant despair, we find the same famed proverb: "When will hearing be like seeing?"

We have it in the English, "Seeing is believing," and in the Americanese of "I'm from Missouri, show me."

The next step in the continuity of development is to be found in the transition of the Egyptian hieroglyphics or picture writings into the arbitrary forms of alphabet as we know alphabets in our common use of to-day. A most effective example of how pictures came to be letters in written words is afforded in the hieroglyphic representation of the name of Cleopatra. This comes to us from a period when the hieroglyphic language had reached its highest development, with some four thousand years of recorded Egyptian culture behind it.

 Here is the name of Cleopatra, as it appeared within the cartouche or circumscribing line which denoted the royal Shield. The characters read from right to left.

Now analyzing the name we discover the conversion of pictographs into phono-graphs or sound symbols.

An angle or knee		In Egyptian, or Coptic, *Kne* supplies the sound of **K**
A lion		.... *Labo* gives the sound of **L**
A reed		.... *Aak* supplies the sound of **A** or **E**
A noose		.... Of unknown name, supplies the sound of **O**
A mat		.... *Pu* supplies the sound of **P**
An eagle		.... *Ahom* supplies the sound of **A** (broad)
A hand		.... *Tot* supplies the sound of **T**
A mouth		.... *Rho* gives the sound of **R**
An eagle		.... *Ahom* supplies the sound of final broad **A**

Again, as we examine the Hebrew alphabet, one of the several successors to the hieroglyphic, we discover the continuing processes of evolution. In the Egyptian the picture became a sound, and in the Hebrew the picture signs for the sound are simplified into nearly arbitrary forms, still with a tinge of the picture in them. The first letter of the Hebrew alphabet, in its older forms, is plainly the head of the ox, a conventionalization from the same source as the great sculptures of the winged bulls on the palaces of Babylon. The animal concerned, zoölogical history now asserts, was really identical with the Wisent, lingering yet in parts of Germany and Russian, and a close relative of the American Bison. This wild ox was abundant in western Asia in Sumerian days and appears on many cylinder seals and Summerian inscriptions. The later Babylonians and Assyrians adopted the figure although the animal likely had disappeared from the region. The Assyrian character for "bull" was the triangle representing the broad face of the wild ox, with a pair of horns projecting. It was almost exactly our own letter "A" drawn upside down. The early Hebrew term for bull was *alphu*, expressed by the Assyrian sign. In turn evolved the Hebrew-Phœnician *aleph*, denoted by the same character inverted, then came the Greek *alpha* and now the Roman "A".

If you chance ever to have seen a big bison bull leading his herd and heading into a storm on the Alberta prairie, or thundering on the charge at a foe, it is easy to understand how he got himself up at the front of all the alphabets, no matter how much it may offend to admit that our language begins with simple, pure bull. The wild bull was the first fact alike in the lives of the Sumerian hunters and the American Indian.

So it comes that in the Hebrew the alphabet begins with the picture of *Aleph*, the ox, the initial sound of which it conveys; while the second letter represents a house or tent, *Beth*, and gives its initial sound "B" to the letter. And so onward, *Ghimel*, represented by the neck of the camel and carrying the sound of its initial to the character, and *Daleth*, representing a door and sounding like "D."

The Hebrew alphabet, starting *Aleph, Beth, Ghimel, Daleth,* or A, B, C, D, is really a succession of pictures, Ox, Tent, Camel, Door. Our very word Alphabet, combined of the first two letters of the Greeks, *Alpha* and *Beta*, is an abridgment or partial pictorial re-creation of the alphabet, which points the way of the process of pictorial re-creation. When folk of the commonalty speak of the "A-B-C's" they are falling back on a more strictly literal re-creation in preference to the use of the slightly abstracted name-symbol of the adopted word "Alphabet." Alphabet is too far from the picture of the letters for some minds.

The process of alphabet derivation from pictures is strikingly shown in reverse in the pictorial nursery alphabet books and their jingles:

"A is for Apple so big and so round,
B is for Bunny . . ."

To aid the infantile mind over the bump of abstraction in the conception of symbols the sub-primer of the nursery backs down the road to get a running start from the plane of simple familiar pictures.

So we see that written language and alphabets have come out of what really has been a striving for living pictures, reduced to shorthand by practical necessity of expediency.

So much has the word come into the go-getting service of the Wish that Alfred Binet, pioneer intelligence tester, chose power over words as his yardstick twenty or more years ago.

It is to be anticipated that biologists may raise the fact that the sense of hearing is older than sight—which presumably is a consequence of the origin of life in the waters of the ancient murky seas, where the vibrations received as sounds were more available than light, the medium of sight impression. Perhaps eye-mindedness, which paved the way for the motion picture, began as the silts settled out of the ancient seas and the clouds of the primordial sky cleared. The Fundamentalists may find in Genesis: ". . . and darkness was on the face of the deep. And God said, Let there be light, and there was light."

—lvi—

When and where light became available evolution seems to have hastened to make it serve. Hearing must necessarily be as slow as the sound wave. Sound travels at about 1100 feet a second in the air at the surface of earth. Light under the same condition travels about 186,000 miles a second. Light is nearly 900,000, or close to a million, times as fast as sound. The organism, seeking to be informed about who was coming to eat him up, turned toward the faster line of communication. Seeing had an advantage over hearing about as great as getting the ringside news hot off the radio as against reading about it in a weekly newspaper.

The language of sounds acquired the pictorial value of gesture and pantomime and further pictorial concepts beyond the power of mere pantomime. So our words are picture laden vehicles. With eye-mindedness came the language as we know it now. This frozen gesture-picture language, precious gift of the ages of experience, became venerated and sacred, a subject of worship like the Classical Chinese. Nothing less than the zeal of religion can explain the purists' ardent defense of their ancient orthodoxies of honored usage.

Progress and elaborations of civilization are driving even the educated Chinese to the use of Pidgin English to express concepts beyond their old ideographs. A related evolution, not so acutely marked, is indicated when Marguerite E. DeWitt, Authors' League of America, writes in *American Speech:* "We speak twentieth century English and approximately write that of Chaucer's day."

If hearing had embodied the refinement of definition and the capacity for swift, precise information of the external world the human race might have evolved as strictly ear-minded rather than eye-minded. But hearing lacks just that quality of nicety and scope. The sight component was necessary to make the language talk.

But in this long-ago quest the development of communication by a falling back on hearing was an alternative of expediency. It would have been hardly more complex, but much less convenient, to have chosen to address the sense of touch as the alternative avenue. In the blind who read Braille we see the thing done.

In Braille reading the mind, through the tactile nerves, receives pictorial impressions just as truly as the normal person receives them from the abstractions of the printed word for the eye and of the spoken word for the ear.

Thus we find languages clearly elaborated for three of the senses, sight, hearing, and touch. Only a lack of refinement and range, and perhaps a lack of the necessity, prevents a similar elaboration of language or picture symbols for the smell-taste sensory combination. And no one of experience will deny that, by association, aromas have their power to awaken pictorial images, from the stockyards of Chicago to the fields of new mown hay.

The facility of the translations involved becomes so great that it is a common place instead of a wonder. We have piled translation upon translation without end in this transmission of pictures. The reporter observes the event, be it the ball game, prize fight, fire, or flood and converts it into words, either written or dictated straight to the telegraph operator, who receives them by eye or ear and translates them into dots and dashes, a mere wave rhythm in the electric pulse on the wire. And in the craft of the telegrapher a whole new system of abstractions appear in the coding abbreviations. The reporter may write or dictate "shot and instantly killed," but the operator sends "s-a-i-k."

The telegraph sounder converts the pulse of the sending current back into the sounds of the dots and dashes and another operator receiving writes them into letters and words. The words may then be printed, as they come, or again translated into Braille in a newspaper for the seeing fingers of the blind. In any event the process is one of communicating a picture from one mind's eye to another through the complications of media which strive to overcome both distance and time.

The process is even more strikingly exemplified in some of the so called "sensational" newspapers when a staff artist in the publication office, perhaps hundreds of miles from the event, takes the words from the wire as the basis for a strip of progressive pictures and diagrams to show how it happened. This is really just pictorial pre-digestion of the words, ready made translation, prepared for consumers believed by the editor to require this assistance in, or substitute for, the process we call "reading." It should be called simple rather than sensational journalism. It is sensational only in that it offers a short-cut to the ultimate sensation in the receiving mind. He who calls it "yellow journalism" confesses the snobbery of his impatience at what is to him an annoying proclamation of the obvious. The fundamental effort is at understanding, differing in no basic quality, moral, ethical or mental, from the drawings which accompany a patent application on a new washing machine.

Radio transmission of photographs now attained, and the efforts at similar transmission of motion pictures now in progress, are but a part of the same process, a striving to transfer the labors of translation from mind to the genii of electricity and machines.

Trying to communicate with words we are ever in a struggle with the faults of their translation into mental pictures. "Don't you *see* what I mean?" we implore as the words begin to limp. By illustration, simile, metaphor and parable we try to fortify the picture message of the words.

Just as the complexities of society and thought outgrew the pictures on the cave walls, the processes of algebra and calculus outgrew the capacities and facilities of simple arithmetical numbers. Then symbols, partial re-creations, or essences, came to take their place. Mere convenience led the mathematicians to the adoption of the ready-made symbols from the Roman and Greek alphabets. A B C and X Y Z became handy intruments for the demonstration of pure abstract principle shorn of confusing, hampering and concrete finite quantities and relations. The step from numbers, say 4, 5, 7, to A B C in algebra is after all just such a step as the child makes in arithmetic when he can add bare, bald numbers instead of the familiar problems of "How many red apples will John have?" in the primary textbooks.

The progression from the concrete picture to the abstract thought is nearly identical in every form of expression. This places the motion picture in a most significant light.

In the evolution of the alphabet from the original impulse to picture, to re-create the event, to make a living and therefore moving picture of it, we see the liberation of thought, communication and expression from the tediousness of graphic art. And with this liberation it is obvious that there was a progression from the concrete to the abstract and from Things to Ideas. Here at once in this consideration of affairs archaic we discover the fundamental character and limitation of the art of the motion picture. And it may be to the point to remark that with this thought in mind the student of the motion picture will perhaps be able more clearly to evaluate some of the curious internal struggles of the art of the motion picture on the screen of to-day.

The strivings of the abstract against the walls of the concrete are often in evidence on the screen. These strivings have resulted in such significant and curious experiments as D. W. Griffith's *Intolerance*. *Intolerance* was a box office failure because of the discomfort which it caused in the minds of its patrons. The picture did not please a sufficient number of persons in relation to its cost.

Intolerance registered in the mass mind only as a stupendous miscellany of something, now Babylon, now medieval France, now barbaric modern America, the whole considerably shot up with excitement. The concrete happenings were not generalized into illustrations of the abstract principle of intolerance. Tillie-the-Toiler in the orchestra seat with her boy-friend did not see the individual gripped by fetish, ritual and intolerance. She saw the King of Babylon having a swell time interrupted by the hardboiled guy Cyrus. She saw that there was a rough night in Paris on the eve of St. Bartholomew. She saw that Mae Marsh in the young mother rôle was having a hellofa tough time while John Law was framing to hang Bobby Harron. And that is all that Tillie saw. She was peevish because Mr. Griffith kept mixing these stories up. For Tillie, these stories had nothing to do with each other.

Allusion, simile, and metaphor can succeed in the printed and spoken word as an aid to the dim pictorial quality of the word expression. The motion picture has no use for them, because it itself is the event. It is too specific and final to accept such aids. The only place that these verbal devices have on the screen is in support of the sub-title or legends, which need support indeed in their contrasted weakness of words beside the pictures. *Intolerance* was a giant metaphor. The public saw it just as it sees the Pyramids of Egypt, without an interest in history, or the Grand Canyon of the Colorado, without an interest in geology.

This incapacity of the eye-minded public for attention to even the tiniest abstraction or breaking away from simple pictorial movement is a trait as old as the world. The art of letters has become accepted only as the result of the most tremendous effort and necessity.

Most of mankind is still illiterate. The art of reading and writing is remote centuries ahead in the development of the millions of the majority. In these proud United States with their high degree of literacy the publishers estimate that there are only about six million potential buyers and readers of any reasonably intelligent book or of magazines of such a moderate intellectual standard as that of *The Saturday Evening Post*.

The race of man was so loath to engage in the mental labor of learning letters, so wedded to the easy re-creation of events by the ritual and picture, that for very long periods the business of reading and writing was delegated to priests and slaves. Learning of abstract letters was in the nature of dirty work, too hard and tedious to torture the hours of the wealthy. The idea is embodied in the modern by-word, "Brains are cheap."

The evolution of the alphabet and a facile written language produced an increasingly wide and deep channel for the processes of thought and communication. It was the liberation of thought from the literal thralldom of the picture which gave the written word its higher intellectual power. But it was only the vaster greater convenience of word writing as against laborious picture making which made the written word the main channel of recorded expression.

When word-writing liberated expression from the picture, writing became the main stream. Graphic art, the business of pictures, was robbed of its major importance. It has since remained an incidental, meandering system of trickles, brooks, and rivulets sometimes paralleling the big river of expression in written words.

Every now and then one of these little creeks of graphic art is swelled into a pool by the wallowings and splashings of some sufferer trying to convey abstract ideas with pictures. A fuss of no importance always results from trying to blow a twenty horsepower whistle with a five horsepower boiler.

A vast deal of most profound foolishness about painting and sculpture has grown out of just such efforts and splashings. Every now and then we get all wet from the spray of such things as Cubism, Vorticism, and Futurism. The result is always muddy water.

It is apparent that, when the alphabet evolved from pictures to open the way for abstract communication, thought began to escape from just Things and the simple emotions concerned only with Things. But the whole population did not follow in that escape. The majority did not jump off the concrete bank of pictures into the abstract river of words. They did not want to swim. They stayed on the assured soil of just Things. They are still sitting by the river, making small use of the alphabet and looking at pictures of Things, mostly bears and women.

Beside our metaphorical river of expression, at a spot somewhere in the vicinity of the place where the abstract alphabet broke out at the side of the concrete dam of pictures, we can pick up that particular line of trickles in the old main channel which will lead us down to the motion picture of to-day.

Let us consider written language as the off-shoot which became the greater stream for the current of ideas, leaving the now less important and obscured course of graphic art and picture making to go on its way with a diminished freight of thought. Drawing, painting, and sculpture survived and continued down the centuries, developing at times and borrowing back on occasion some refinement of ideas from the rushing new current of the written word and its abstract powers.

Every one used words and language, while a relatively few atavistic artists maintained and built upon the tradition of the picture-writer of the old home cave. They are still doing it. Doubtless it is this atavistic character of graphic art which accounts for certain matters of long hair, smocks, and Illustrators'

Balls—a subject slightly outside of our chosen segment of the universe.

Meanwhile the picture still retained its power, and words, for the masses, had only the power of the pictures in them. The picture was yet to have its day—and that is our screen history.

The process by which the cave picture became the written language tended to carry the business of expression off into heights of abstraction a good way beyond the original intent. The language, in fact, has gone so far that it is largely out of reach of the infantile public, as we have noted concerning the book market. For the masses the word is but a make-shift of unpleasant tediouness still. Therein is the secret of the golden kingdom of the screen.

Now what Mr. Og was trying to do for Mr. Ug back there in the cave was to give him, by drawing on the wall, a complete re-creation of the event; in other words, a life size, natural color, stereoscopic, talking motion picture. He was seeking to project into Mr. Ug's osseous consciousness the image which he had enjoyed, and he was trying to do it with a picture on the wall. It is a choice idea to dally with:

Adam Og presents
EVA EGG
in
THE FIG TREE
A mastodonic drama

Adam Og sought re-creation of effect by a representation of the complete act. He wanted to give Mr. Ug an identical thrill. He still does.

Drifting down the by-waters of graphic art, we can pick up significant examples of the effort all the way tending and striving toward this same life size, natural color, stereoscopic, talking motion picture—the compete re-creation. And incidentally, in technical terms, we have potentially arrived at just that. Motion pictures variously containing each of those qualities have been made for some years. No important scientific problem prevents them from being combined. But many artistic and commercial problems stand in the way.

The records of the past are rich with the rudimentary efforts at the motion picture idea. For so many centuries that even the Chinese have lost count, elaborate shadow plays have been a part of the art lore of various of the old Asiatic peoples, and they survive yet in Siam. Little silhouettes mounted on sticks for manipulation before a lamp or candle are used to enact a shadow marionette show upon the wall. These silhouettes are often exquisitely executed bits of craftsmanship in elaborate sets which include both the characters and the scenery for rather complicated shadow drama.

In Java a considerable folk art of shadow play survives and flourishes. A large cloth screen is erected between the audience and the sun. Back of this screen the manipulators of the drama move silhouettes of half life size which cast their shadows through the cloth. The "cast" of one of these long shadow plays is often a huge pile of hundreds of silhouette figures, depicting pantomimic phases of action and related to each other just as the succeeding steps of a strip comic cartoon in our daily press. This shadow drama of Java has its formalized rubber stamp types of villains, hero, heroines, mothers-in-law and the like, evolved precisely as we have them in the melodrama of the stage and more conspicuously on our screen.

Shadow plays of silhouettes variously created can be found in the tradition of every civilized people. No doubt they have the common ancestor of the shadow mimicry of nursery walls, whereby ages of mothers have entranced and quieted bawling young Adams with fascinating silhouettes cast by deft hands in suggestion of the braying donkey, the champing wolf, and the barking doggie—motion pictures in their simplest form.

Countless other pictorial efforts from progressive frieze reliefs on temples, depicting the triumphal return of the king from the war and hunt, down to the painted cycloramas of the Battle of Gettysburg are expressions of the same idea, the effort to re-create the event to be pleasurably remembered.

All art is pervaded by this single purpose, a living motion story of thrill and glory and pleasure. Consider narrative sculpture from the mud images of the prehistoric troglodytes to now; miles upon miles of life size history in stone left by the Cambodian kings, the countless classic arches from Trajan's biographical and Dacian boasts at Benevento to Napoleon's Arc du Carrousel proclaiming the triumphs of 1805, and the Robert E. Lee-Old South saga Borglumed into the face of Stone Mountain in Georgia, U. S. A. 1925. We still say it with rocks.

Chisel and brush have continued paddling down the river of expression, but failing ever behind the written word. Two factors put the plastic and graphic arts behind: first; mere mechanical facility, and second, also most importantly, their weakness as compared with the power of the word to convey motion. The word is pictorially weak, but it moves. The active verb is the soul of the language. It is the vitalizing current that sweeps the word onward. The infinitive is our tie to the infinite. The statue and the painting can only say *was*. The word can say *is*, and luring us on it can promise *to be*. The race wants to *is* and *is* onward, continually being *to be*.

The graphic art, the original simple picture making process of event re-creation, light starved and thwarted in its growth, waited down the ages, and after the ages through the measured centuries, for this catalytic essence of life—the vital gift of motion.

When motion came to vivify the picture it was armed for the conquest of the world of concrete expression, already vacated by the advancing fore-fringe of the abstract words. Words were born as pictures, but among the erudite minorities they had gone on to another plane of concept.

Motion made the picture a language instead of a sign: made it the fundamental language it set out to be in the beginning. Motion made the picture move from *was* to *is* and to *to be*. The tedious translations were swept away. No longer in concrete communication was it necessary for the communicator to struggle to convert his pictorial concepts into symbols of sounds or symbols of alphabet form to endow them with motion and give them transmission. No longer was it necessary for the listener to receive with the ear that jumble of rapid sounds and translate it in terms of pictures and motion for the mind's eye.

Motion in the picture cut out the transformers in the language expression circuit. The mind could now get its emotion juice from the re-created event direct. The transformer losses were eliminated. The juice was stronger, purer. The line noises, the static and squeals and howls of word perversion and attenuation, were gone. Automatic, photographic record supplied in full authenticity what before the individual had to conjure up for himself out of bits of memory and by really stupendous feats of intellectualization.

In this the motion picture is not a thing apart, but only functioning with the whole effort of the evolving thing we call life. In the re-creation of events for the re-enjoyment of emotions the film brings just such a short cut directness as the whole of scientific industry is seeking in every phase of human concern. Science has remade the world by bringing about the marvel of work done without human labor. It has eliminated the complications of costly muscle power and has substituted a similar but cheaper organic re-action in the coal-steam-electricity institution. Now again science seeks another set of eliminations, another series of direct lines, in super-power, solar power and radio power transmission, and again in fixation of atmospheric nitrogen and synthetic foods. Art and industry are laboring alike, and by very like steps, for one and the same service— the pleasant titillation of the five senses of the human animal and that sixth product of those five factors which is euphemistically called the soul.

To pursue the parallel to its last extreme step, one may say that just as electricity may be called the one fundamental energy so we may call the motion picture the one fundamental art. Of course the exponents of the status quo with investments, emotional and intrinsic, in the attenuated, specialized and derived arts may be expected to scorn such a view of the screen. It is always so of authority which bases itself on tradition. The authority of painting, sculpture, literature and music have a great deal in common with the divine right of kings and similar conventions.

Probably the most remarkable property of the motion picture as an art medium has been neglected or undiscovered by the scholars and critics. This is its unparalleled ability to superimpose emotional stimuli. In this the screen is alone and supreme. With the incredible swiftness of light it can throw its dramatic "kicks" one after another into the eye consciousness attaining a cumulative effect which is tremendous as measured against any one of its components. In all of the other media, as in painting, sculpture and the stage drama, only one punch can be delivered at a time. Sheer mechanics make this inescapable. But optical mechanics permit the motion picture to build the spectator to a pitch of dramatic feeling and then shower blow upon blow and climax upon climax upon him before the effect of the first has subsided. Reaching for this facility the stage has at times resorted to complications of machinery with but the most casual success. But the motion picture dramatist attains the result with absurd ease by the trifling expedient of splicing block and film cement. Only music can approximate the flow of the film, but music is a conveyor of mood, not a narrator. The film is specific, primitive, actual, faster than life and twice as natural.

It is this rapid fire capacity to superimpose dramatic tensions to a new depth of intensity which tends to compel attention to any motion picture no matter how trivial. It may all be of no importance whatever, but we are held because while something is continually happening something else also is always in the process of being about to happen. We may scoff and scorn the meager, trite content of the picture, but someway we sit and see it through, riding its monotony rocking-chair fashion, while if the same tawdry art were presented to us on the stage we would walk out, and if in a book we would throw it under the radiator. The film has the spell of continuity and speed.

A pleasant coincidence of opinion is discovered in Barbara Low's article on the limitation of the cinema's value in education, in the *Contemporary Review* (London), November, 1925, in which, after citing Ferenczi's statement of the "period of unconditional omnipotence" and the "belief in magic gesture" of child development, she observes:

> It is surely clear that the cinema entertainment must gratify this "magic omnipotence wish" more than any fairy tale, any novel, picture or drama can possibly do—and does so independently, to a large extent, of the theme of the film. It is the *method* which brings about so vividly the sense of wish fulfillment. It is the cinema's business to show all problems solved, all doors opened, all questions answered: it must simplify and arbitrarily select, which is one way of making the spectator feel his wishes are fulfilled, since real life is complex, unselective, often baffling our curiosity, and rarely offering solutions to our problems.

The sages and the Homeridæ come in the film can, bottled right at the spring.

—lxix—

The film is the primordial art, freed and empowered. For eons the picture on the wall could only say "bear" and "woman." Now endowed with motion it can say "There goes the bear," and more joyously still "Here comes the woman."

The yearnings of Adam Og and his friend Ug can now be satisfied, and Eva Egg may have her career.

The ancient cosmic itch is being scratched at last.

The motion picture appeals to the savage in us all. Yes, even to the Great Ape within us, crouching back, wondering and fearing, in the shadows cast by the fires of daring thought.

The motion picture does what man tried to do when he invented language. It fulfills the strivings of a million million years!

In the twilighted theatre, lulled with music's emotional and motional rhythms, we see our day-dream wishes ethereally materialized before us at the screen's window, which opens on the land of heart's desire. Without painstaking thought or effort it comes and rolls on and on and on.

The motion picture is the Prayer Wheel of the Wish.

CHAPTER ONE

FROM ARISTOTLE TO PHILADELPHIA, PA.

Now begins the world's most human story—the history of the motion picture. It is a tale as old as creation, and as new as tomorrow morning's paper.

For the first time in the history of civilization we can see the complete flowering of an art form in a single generation. Within thirty years, the motion picture has progressed from the sleeping germ of the age-old wish to the effulgent blossoming of the universal screen of today. Never before in all the ages has this happened. The beginnings of the stage are lost in obscure antiquity. The art of the printed book is half a millennium. Painting and music have come to us out of the remote unknown. All these are the fruit of patient endless time. But many, perhaps a majority of the readers of this page can remember when there were no motion picture films.

The men who saw the birth of sculpture, painting, and drama were mouldering in the sleep of the ages when the Redwoods came to clothe the Sierras, when Cheops planned his Pyramid. But the first men to see a motion picture on a film are yet alive, and with a hearty prospect of seeing many another. There is no parallel in all human experience.

But the motion picture is young only as the bud upon the tree is young. Under them both are roots deep in endless time. The motion picture is a bud that has flowered. To see and know rightly this flowering of the films we shall start our inquiry back down this branch of the tree of expression.

Here Romance and Science come blithely down the centuries

—1—

bringing us the art of the screen and pictures that live. Among their retainers we shall find philosophers, savants and priests, gamblers, adventurers and cut-throats, noblemen, gentlemen and commoners, wise men and fools—all of the motley of life. This is the chapter of the savants.

The coming of the motion picture was inevitable. For ages it existed only in man's desire. It has been attained because of that age old wish for the re-creation of events attended by emotions of pleasure.

When in that dim long ago, the leaders of thought laid down their fears of the whimsy of Gods and took up a hope in law and a reasonable universe, progress began toward the myriad attainments of the modern era. Among these we may importantly number the motion picture.

So long ago and so obscurely were the first discoveries on the path to the screen made that it would be futile to search for them. Aristotle in ancient Greece it was who first wrote down the observation that even a square hole in a shutter illumined by the sun cast a circular spot of light against the wall of a darkened room. He was only mildly curious about it. Natural science in his day consisted of noting oddities. Others of equal antiquity observed that the stone twirled by the slinger and the glowing light of a rapidly whirled firebrand both presented apparently continuous circles to the eye.

In those two primitive phenomena were hidden all of the secrets of the motion picture. That hole in the wall of a chamber in Hellas was the pinhole aperture which cast a true image of the sun, and that darkened room was in truth a camera. The circles described by the whirling stone of the Balearic slinger and the firebrand were demonstrations of the principle of the persistence of vision.

Doubtless many a curious scholar in the succeeding centuries saw various puzzling phenomena of light and images, but not until we arrive at so recent a milestone as the Italian Renaissance do we find recorded glimmerings of the beginning of the service of optics to art.

Somewhat hazy tradition credits the invention of a device known as the *camera lucida* to Leone Battista Alberti, a roistering, rejoicing artist of Florence.

Alberti may of course have been only among the first to use the apparatus. It was a prismatic arrangement by which a reduced virtual image of an object could be apparently cast on a drawing board, making it convenient for tracing outlines. Alberti was so versatile and so infinitely busy with the prodigious activities of the period that he probably welcomed such a labor-saving device. It is related of him that he astonished all Florence with his feats of strength and skill. He could, so history solemnly states in dignified Latin, make a standing jump over any man's head. Also he could stand in an aisle of the Cathedral of Florence and toss a coin so high in the air that it could be heard to tinkle against the vaulted roof above. He was the Fairbanks of Florence.

The unborn motion picture's destiny hovered through the fifteenth century about Florence. It was the remote, heroic year of 1452 when gay Ser Pero, the notary, having indulged in amorous dalliance with a comely peasant girl Catarina, found himself the father of a most vociferous and promising son, duly christened Leonardo.

Now this Leonardo da Vinci became all kinds of a man, artist, architect, decorator, engineer, scientist, and author.

One of Leonardo's concerns was expressed in a pursuit of the most realistic results possible on the canvas of painting. He wanted to make the picture absolutely re-create the event, to make it happen again before the eyes of the spectator. His literal aims are reflected in a passage of his *Trattato Della Pittura*, where he writes:

—3—

I have seen a portrait so like that the favorite dog of the original took it for his master and displayed every sign of delight; I have also seen dogs bark at painted dogs and try to bite them; and a monkey make all sorts of faces at portraits of his own kind; I have seen swallows on the wing attempt to settle on iron bars painted across painted windows of painted houses.

In all of which Leonardo was doubtless nature-faking, but he was definitely stating the desire for a living picture.

This quest of reality made Leonardo pursue the secrets of life endlessly. He stood by execution yards to observe and sketch the expressions and gestures of poor creatures on their way to their doom. He littered his studio with gruesome bodies for dissection that he might learn the mysteries of muscle-controlled expression. He took life apart in search of secrets that should make his canvases live.

This search after the means of re-creating the event sent Leonardo, some centuries early, very directly in pursuit of the camera of to-day. Among Leonardo's experiments was an investigation of the laws of perspective by placing a glass plate between the eye and the object, and noting thereon where the lines of sight cut the plane of the glass.

Then, too, Leonardo observed that if he cut a small circular hole in a shutter of a darkened room there would be an image on the wall opposite, showing in detail the building or landscape outside in the full light of the sun. This room was in reality the *camera obscura*, used by artists for centuries after, and it was indeed too the camera of to-day, lacking yet only the sensitized film or plate. If Leonardo had had the chemical means of coating the glass plate of his experiments in perspective and catching thereon the image he found on the wall of his room, he would have had photography, which in a nameless unconscious way he was seeking.

It had not apparently come to Leonardo that there was a

possibility of pictures in motion. But he was after a strict recording of nature in the picture, up to the fact of motion. He hoped to suggest life by a frozen moment of it, a still photography in which the skill of hand and eye performed functions of photo-chemistry yet undiscovered.

Leonardo's search after reality in art, his hunger for convincing pictures, made him seek every emotional aid. Vasari wrote of Leonardo that he employed musicians to play for Mona Lisa while she sat as his model. Doubtless there was a laughing up the sleeve among Leonardo's contemporaries at such a fanciful extravagance. Stepping lightly over time and space to the Biograph studio in Los Angeles in 1913-4, four centuries after Leonardo, we find D. W. Griffith employing an orchestra to make Blanche Sweet emotional before the camera recording *Judith of Bethulia.* Griffith's contemporaries laughed and scorned.

In Leonardo we have seen the artist beginning to use science consciously as an aid to capturing a moment of the event, a picture. The urge of art was strong indeed in his day. Art was the particular subsidized servant of authority and the Church. It was the great medium of propaganda, the medium of re-creating emotions by re-creating events. Painting marched side by side with pageantry and ritual. It was about the year 1500, only half a century after Gutenburg and Fust began printing from type. Dramatic ritual and the graphic arts were much more important then, before the printing craft loosed the modern flood of words upon the world. What was to be said to the masses had to be said in pictures. That is still largely true, but not for lack of words.

For a full two centuries after the coming of printing from type and the rising tide of books the pictorial art remained unchanged, losing ground in the unequal race with words. The picture was fast and firmly immobile, as immobile as the wood or canvas upon which it was painted. Before the art of the picture could hope for a share in the living fluidity of the word's ability to state motion it had to be freed, loosened from the wall.

Just about two hundred years from the invention of the printing press and a century and a half after Leonardo's prime, the picture began reaching for this new freedom which lay still centuries ahead. One evening in 1640 Athanasius Kircher invited nobles and wealthy citizens of Rome to a remarkable first night showing at the Jesuit College. Kircher desired to present for the consideration of the rich and the mighty the first model of his *Magia Catoptrica*, or magic lantern. Nowadays the same thing is done with similar pomp and to the same purpose by motion picture producers presenting their wares at private previews in the Ritz-Carlton.

Kircher's show consisted of a few crudely painted slides depicting devils, demons and skeletons. Death, Evil, and the Devil were important factors in the life of that day, when the principal emotion useful for the control of the multitudes was fear. Kircher chose the Devil for his star quite as naturally as the motion picture maker of to-day reaches for Cinderella in some guise, purveying the positive appeals of hope and sex instead of the negative emotion fear.

The slide shadows on the wall filled the audience of ignorant nobles and the wealthy climbers of Rome with amazement and delight. There were plaudits for Kircher. This inventor of the magic lantern was a German from the ancient community of Geiss, known to a more modern day as Hesse Cassel, the territory which later contributed the Hessians to the war of the American Revolution.

Kircher the Jesuit has told at length in his book, published in 1646 under the title of *Ars Magna Lucis et Umbræ* (The

Great Art of Light and Shade), about this magic lantern. This ancient volume has been brought to light by Will Day of London, an able authority and collector of motion picture archives. Kircher's lantern had a lamp, reflector, and a lens, just as the magic lantern of to-day has.

Kircher also illustrated in this volume a method of changing from picture to picture by the use of a revolving drum. His drum shows pictures of the radiant sun, the head of a lion, and the head of an ass. He was really getting dangerously near the motion picture idea. His pictures were painted on glass.

Kircher's magic lantern progressed from that day as fast as illuminants improved and lens makers evolved their craft. This was not really so long ago, when one reflects that the Pilgrims had become well established in Massachusetts by that date and that Southampton, Long Island, was thriving in Indian trade and the pursuit of "whayles and other greate fish."

Through Kircher we see the pictures become liberated from the immobility of paint and canvas. The ingenuous Jesuit began with his *Magia Catoptrica* to make pictures of light and shade. They were not yet, in his crude hand-drawn slides, truly mobile in a pictorial sense but they contained that inherent possibility. His pictures in light and shadow were a step back toward the fluidity of motion in nature's pictures presented direct to the eye from the object, also seen only in terms of light and shade.

Picture making on the wall was ready and waiting now to receive motion.

The striving after literal motion recreations of events continued with every conceivable sort of presentation. One of the most ingeniously elaborate of them is set forth in a play-bill of 1811 recently found in London. It reads:

Sanger's Mechanical Collection of Alabaster Figures and Moving Wax Work, now exhibiting in this town for — days only. The proprietor, in offering this truly moral, elegant and truly scientific exhibition to the notice of a discerning public, states, without fear of contradiction, that this expensive production of years of hard study and perseverance has been ultimately crowned with success. He thus fearlessly invites the patronage of all good members of society, as the aim, object and end of his endeavors have been to please the old and instruct the young; teaching them to look from nature to nature's cause. The first enclosure contains a splendid lifelike representation of Moses striking the rock, or the Children of Israel in the Wilderness. Moses is seen at the head of the Israelites standing on a rock near Mount Horeb. The just proportion and mechanical movement of this figure surpasses everything of the kind that has hitherto been attempted. Moses is seen to raise his arm and strike the rock, from whence water appears to flow. The speculation of the eye and movement of the mouth, as if inviting the people to drink from the waters that are gushing from the rock. To the left is Aaron, with an intelligent smile upon his countenance, as he gazes on the stream which slakes the thirst of the great multitude. The whole of these beautiful figures will be set in motion by the aid of mechanical ingenuity. The movement of the limbs, the rolling of the eyes, and heaving of the chests of men, women, and children, taken altogether give it a life-like representation of what has in reality taken place, as we are bound to believe, according to the records of sacred history.

One is particularly delighted to note that these living wax works so handsomely registered the heaving of the chest. Chest heaving has become a prime essential of modern screen drama.

Not until nearly two hundred years after Athanasius Kircher and his lantern show, did scientific investigation begin determined pursuit of the mysterious principles of the appearances of motion, leading toward the motion picture. These scientific beginnings held no relation to showmanship, then apparent.

It was at the end of the first quarter of the last century when one Peter Mark Rôget of London began to make certain observations filled with motion picture portent. This Rôget is scientifically most important and historically little known. His name, shorn of every vestige of personality, survives among the tools of the writer's craft in the title of Rôget's Thesaurus, the word book.

As one might suspect from the doubly impressed Christianity of his christening in honor of two apostles, Rôget was a minister's son. His father was John Rôget, formerly of Geneva, pastor of the French Protestant church in Threadneedle street, London. His mother was a sister of Sir Samuel Romilly, and to her gallant British biographers have credited Peter Mark's heritage of mind. Their authority for this does not appear. The precocious youth was graduated from the medical school of the University of Edinburgh at the age of 19.

Rôget became a physician. It was doubtless a choice of mere practicality. The practice of medicine was, bear in mind, well near the only earning career open to a scientifically minded man of that day.

Rôget was interested in everything within the scope of science. He became an expert on water supply. He rioted in mathematics. He invented a logarithmic slide rule for rapid calculating and as a result was elected a fellow of the Royal Society of Great Britain, becoming its secretary. He lectured on "The Laws of Sense and Perception" before the Royal College of Physicians and spent three earnest years on the study of the "external senses." He was eagerly interested in the problem of the manner in which the human mind becomes conscious of the outside world.

It was therefore inevitable that Rôget should have engaged in researches bearing on the principles of vision, and that his findings should now be seen as uncovering various laws underlying the yet undreamed motion picture. Further it is intensely significant, bearing immediately on the principle of event re-creation and the identity of picture and language that Rôget was so aggressively interested in mere words that he made the compilation of his classic Thesaurus the valedictory labor of his declining years. Clearly the word and the picture, the impression of the "external sense" of sight were intimately related in his mind.

The star of motion picture destiny, always traveling westward in the course of the race, reached England with Rôget. One day while he was engaged in his inquiry into the affairs of the external senses he chanced to glance from his study window to note the approach of a vehicle. It was only a baker's cart and Rôget hurriedly turned back to his papers. But, as he turned away, the line of his vision swept past the interferences of the slats of a Venetian blind. Through the slitted apertures the scientist caught the impression that the cart was proceeding by jerks. He saw it, despite its rapid motion, momentarily at rest in each slit, and, through each successive opening, he saw it in a different phase of motion.

Rôget had previously placed a great deal of confidence in his eyes. This was something to be investigated at once. In 1824, a century ago, Rôget appeared before the Royal Society to read a paper entitled "Persistence of Vision with Regard to Moving Objects."

This matter of seeing and its new problems might well have been expected to intrigue the interest of Sir John Herschel, who had seen so much. In Charles Babbage's "Passages from the Life of a Philosopher" we can find the story of how a thought from Herschel contributed to the progress of the motion picture idea. Sir John sat toying with a shilling. He ventured that it was "possible to see both sides of the coin at once," and proceeded to demonstrate by spinning the coin on the table.

blending the image of the face of the shilling with that of the obverse.

Babbage mentioned the incident to his friend Dr. William Henry Fitton, a geologist, chemist, and physician. The next day Dr. Fitton had evolved a demonstrating device. It was a little disc of cardboard with strings attached to twirl it. On one side was a drawing of a bird, on the other a cage. When the disc was revolved between the strings, the bird appeared in the cage.

Then it appears that another doctor came confusingly into the course of history. John Ayrton Paris, M.D., with Cambridge and Edinburgh behind him and all manner of scientific interests in "natural philosophy" and materia medica, began in some way the commercial manufacture of the little device, and it acquired the altogether alarming name of the Thaumatrope. Dr. Paris rather takes the credit of the thing in his work entitled "Philosophy in Sport made Science in Earnest." If there was such conflict of testimony about the parentage of this trivial ancestor of the motion picture in 1826, what may we expect of today?

Meanwhile the initial studies of Dr. Rôget, embodied in his paper before the Royal Society, set other minds at work.

The great Michael Faraday made an inquiry based on the curious appearances of the wheels of the baker's cart seen through a Venetian blind. Faraday constructed machines which revolved various arrangements of cogs and spokes, revolving at different speeds. He found, as he set forth in the Journal of the Royal Institute of Great Britain, that the impression of rest could come from combinations of motions, that rapid movement could be made to appear from slow moving and that an impression of backward movement might result from actual forward motion. Every spectator of the motion picture of today has seen some of these same manifestations

—11—

in the eccentricities of wagon wheels which turn backwards on the screen, while the vehicle goes forward. Faraday studied movements on a system of wheels.

Over on the Continent Dr. Joseph Antoine Ferdinand Plateau, then a youth of thirty among grey-bearded scientists, began work on this notion of "the persistence of vision" at the University of Ghent in Belgium. Almost simultaneously, Dr. Simon Ritter von Stampfer at Vienna in Austria engaged in similar investigations.

It was the next year after the publication of Faraday's observations that Plateau and Stampfer almost at the same time, but independently of each other, arrived at the first devices in the world for seeing pictures in simulated motion. By coincidence their devices were identical in all respects. Both placed pictures of phases of motion, handmade drawings of course, on the rim of a disc and viewed them through slits in another disc, blackened on the viewing side, and revolving on the same axis with the picture disc. If the eye were placed in proper position and the pair of discs were twirled, the successive pictures appeared before the eye as of a continuous series. The smaller the slits the sharper the pictures appeared; the blurring motion was also lessened. This was the world's first motion picture machine, devised in the year 1832, in Ghent and Vienna.

Up to this time and point, the study of motion had not been aimed directly at the making of living pictures. Herschel, Rôget, and Faraday worked only on the bare bones of abstract principle. Plateau and Stampfer with little dancing figures on their discs began to give humanity to the principle.

The motion picture had been born, but it was yet dependent for the making on the handwork of an artist. The images for the little disc machines had to be made in the only way that pictures could be made, through the fallible eye and limited hands of the artist.

Stampfer gave his picture machine the horrendous name of the Stroboscopic Disc, while Plateau called his the Phenakisto-scope.

Over many years and in the face of tragedy Plateau carried on his experiments and researches in seeing. Through the very weeks in which he evolved the device which blazed the way to motion picture seeing for the world's millions the light of his eyes was fading into the dark of utter blindness. He who would see so much paid the price of his sight.

In 1829 Plateau went out of his laboratory and gazed at the midday sun for twenty unblinking seconds. He wanted to see more of the great lamp of the universe, source of all seeing, than any one had seen before. When he turned to go back to his desk and note what he had seen the black of night was about him. In a few days he recovered his sight. But for fourteen years it waned, and in 1843 flickered out forever. Through the twilight and on into the dark Plateau, seeing through the eyes of others and their words, carried on and gave to the world works on vision that are landmarks of scientific history.

After a time Plateau changed the name of his Phenakisto-scope to the Fantoscope. A coloration of life was coming to the motion picture. It had been as abstract as X Y Z of algebra, but now it was called "phantom-seeing," related as closely to life as ghosts and phantoms.

Plateau in the concoction of what we may call cast and scenario for his Fantoscope chose the same star as did Athanasius Kircher, the Jesuit inventor of the magic lantern two hundred years before—namely, the Devil. How the Devil does persist in motion pictures! Plateau's Fantoscope showed

"Le Diable Soufflant"—The Devil Blowing up Fire. Kircher's painted lantern slides could only show a portrait of the Devil, but Plateau's Devil was in action. Even Hell is improved by science.

Science was to remain yet another half a century the sole custodian and agency of motion picture destiny. In Vienna, the city of Stampfer, Lieutenant Baron Franz von Uchatius, of the Second Regiment of Artillery in the Austrian Army, became interested in the science of implements of war, especially ballistics and metallurgy. He, like the rest, wanted to see more accurately.

In 1853 he wedded the magic lantern inherited from Kircher and the Stroboscopic Discs of Stampfer, thereby projecting the pictures on the wall. Only one eye at a time could see the pictures of the Stroboscope and the Fantoscope, but many eyes could simultaneously see the Uchatian pictures on the wall.

Now projection and the fluid freedom of light-painting had come to the motion picture. It still awaited the chemical genii of photography to make the pictures.

William George Horner of Bristol, England, son of a minister, a school master and mathematician, gave the little dancing pictures of the Fantoscope a more popular application by mounting them on the inside of a slitted cyclinder, which revolved on a stand. It was an adaptation of mere convenience as a parlor novelty. This Horner described in the *Philosophical Magazine* under another irritating name, the Dædaleum. In 1860 one Desvignes, a Frenchman, patented an evolution of this device, and it received the name of the Zoetrope, or Wheel of Life. The favorite subject consisted of drawings of a galloping horse. The Zoetrope can still be found in European toy shops of to-day. It took the embryonic motion picture out of the laboratory to an eye hungry world.

Now for a while the progress of the motion picture stood still, waiting for a better and more facile recording of motion than could be had through the eye and the hand of the artists.

Even before 1800 there had been beginnings in photo-chemistry. Observers were noting that substances faded or darkened in the light. With opaque stencils they began to make patterns on surfaces coated with fading substances. These, of course, were mere shadows, and could not be called pictures any more than Kircher's magic lantern shadows cast by devils painted on glass. The image-forming lens, the artificial eye, did not enter into the process. Neither were the sun painted patterns permanent. It was found in time that one of the best substances for this light stenciling was a solution of certain salts of silver. In 1819 Sir John Herschel, the same who twirled the shilling and gave us the Thaumatrope, found that sodium thiosulphate would dissolve silver chloride. That was, in popular terms, the discovery of what we buy at the druggist's kodak counter as "hypo," the same being hyposulphite of sodium. This hypo takes the unaffected silver salts out of our negatives and makes them permanent; therefrom the amateur photographer's term of "fixing."

The history of photography is a long long trail down which we may not detour for very many steps. But it is most interestingly important to take note as we go of Daguerre, notable in our day because his name has been given to those treasured old pictures of our great-grandfathers and mothers, prim in their stocks and laces, known as Daguerreotypes. He was quite a person, this M. Louis Jacques Mandé Daguerre, painter, manager of the Diorama, and member of the Legion of Honor.

M. Daguerre was artistically, and perchance in other more human ways, very much like Leonardo. As a painter he wanted not what we have come to call interpretive art, but literal re-creations of the event. He was after the fundamental picture telling of the caveman, the one art form that has al-

—15—

ways been popular and always will be popular. Daguerre tried to paint the place so that you thought you were there. One of his feats was the painting of a background setting for an altar which seemed to make the church open on a vast fairyland garden. Daguerre was a super-scene painter, with a brush dipped in saccharine. The Diorama was Daguerre's commercial pictorial show, just such an affair as the Cyclorama of the Battle of Gettysburg.

Daguerre wanted a camera just as earnestly and for the same reasons as Leonardo did. He wanted to re-create the event better than the frailties of memory, eye and hand would permit. But the camera was closer now. Chemistry was about to give memory a silver-salted record to take down the pictorial message of Leonardo's *camera obscura*.

On December 14, 1829, Daguerre, the artist, and M. Joseph Nicephore Niépce, "landowner of Chalons-sur-Mere," entered into a contract aimed at evolution of the photographic art.

Photography did evolve, and Daguerre attained the ability to make light record its images through a lens on a treated metal plate. He required exposures of long duration, respectable fractions of an hour.

Through the efforts of many men photographic processes and materials improved. Operations were simplified, and the exposures shortened until only a matter of a few seconds were required to impress the image on the photographic emulsion coating of the plate.

The year 1860 had come, and with it the wet plate process of photography, still used by engravers. The destiny of the motion picture was now moving westward in its following of the course of empire. In Philadelphia in that year Coleman Sellers, the head of a mechanical engineering business and withal an inventor of the successful sort, put himself at the problem of making pictures live and move.

Sellers posed his small sons. Coleman, Jr., pounded away at some amateur carpentry while Horace rocked in a little chair beside him. Sellers had a difficult time keeping his wet plates wet while he changed from pose to pose of the successive steps of the action, and invented a glycerine bath to keep the plates alive. He did not photograph motion, because he had no device fast enough, physically or chemically, but he built up, step by step, a synthetic cycle of movement by poses considered representative instants of the motion. This was doing photographically just what the artists had done when they drew the pictures for the Wheel of Life.

Sellers made his pictures stereoscopic, with an ordinary twin-lensed camera. He mounted the successive prints on a sort of paddle-wheel device in which they could be viewed by looking down on them through a stereoscope, while the paddle-wheel was turned by hand. At the proper rate of speed an impression of motion resulted.

Sellers named his machine the Kinematoscope and patented it February 5, 1861. It is interesting to note that he recognized that a period of rest in the presentation of each picture, to permit it to register in the eye, was necessary. He did not embody a stop device for that purpose, but achieved the result in a degree because on his paddle-wheel machine the picture moved away from the spectator in the direction of the line of sight and remained in view practically until the next took its place.

When he named his machine the Kinematoscope, Sellers launched a word that was far to overshadow his own slight fame and long outlive his invention. This was the first appearance of Kinema, which spread the world and in every language means motion picture. We shall encounter kinema and its derivatives often.

With the Sellers machine the motion picture had caught up

with the progress of photography and stood waiting for it to make way.

The principles of the motion picture that was to be were rather well recognized now. Within three years of the patenting of the Sellers device in the United States a somewhat visionary experimenter in France, Louis Arthur Ducos du Hauron, obtained a patent there, in the application for which he wrote:

> My invention consists in substituting rapidly and without confusion to the eye, not only of an individual but when so desired a whole assemblage, the enlarged images of a great number of pictures when taken instantaneously and successively at very short intervals. . . . The observer will believe that he sees only one image, which changes gradually by reason of the successive changes of form and position of the objects which occur from one picture to the other. Even supposing that there be a slight interval of time during which the same object was not shown, the persistence of the luminous impression upon the eye will fill this gap. There will be as it were a living representation of nature and the same scene will be reproduced upon the screen with the same degree of animation. . . . By means of my apparatus I am enabled especially to reproduce the passing of a procession, a review of military manœuvers, the movements of a battle, a public fête, a theatrical scene, the evolution or the dances of one or of several persons, the changing expression of countenance, or, if one desires, the grimaces of a human face; a marine view, the motion of waves, the passage of clouds in a stormy sky, particularly in a mountainous country, the eruption of a volcano. . . .

This stated in anticipation the motion picture. M. Ducos never got beyond the idea on paper, filed April 25, 1864.

After Sellers the development of the picture lingered yet a while in Philadelphia. Henry Renno Heyl of Columbus, Ohio, a designer and inventor of machinery, removed to Philadelphia in 1863, destined to have a share in the evolution of the motion picture. Heyl was highly skillful in mechanical principles.

He devised special machinery for the working of paper and wire stitching of books and pamphlets. He became the original patentee of the now commonly used wire-stitched paper box, used by the haberdashers, florists, and department stores.

The program announcement of the "Ninth Entertainment of the Young Men's Society of St. Mark's Evangelical Lutheran Church, Philadelphia, to be given at the Academy of Music by O. H. Willard, Esq., on Saturday evening February 5, 1870, in aid of the library fund," contains the following paragraph concerning the first exhibition of a picture device invented by Heyl:

THE PHASMATROPE

This is a recent invention, designed to give various objects and figures upon the screen the most graceful and lifelike movements. The effects are similar to those produced in the familiar toy called the Zoetrope, where men are seen walking, running, and performing various feats in most perfect imitation of real life. This instrument is destined to become a most valuable auxiliary to the appliances for illustration, and we have the pleasure of having the first opportunity of presenting its merits to an audience.

The Heyl machine carried thin glass positive pictures, mounted radially on a wheel, which carried and exposed them intermittently to the light ray of the magic lantern. This machine had a shutter and a ratchet and pawl intermittent mechanism which produced all of the mechanical effects necessary to the proper projection of pictures, even by today's standards. The making of the pictures was by just such a process of successive poses as Sellers had used. Heyl and a dancing partner were photographed in six positions of the waltz at O. H. Willard's studio at 1206 Chestnut street, Philadelphia.

The six pictures were made on negatives *carte de visite* size, and were reduced in printing to positives on glass a little larger than a postage stamp, and rather close to the size of the image on the modern film. Each of the pictures was printed three times, to supply eighteen images to fill the wheel. Hence each revolution of the Phasmatrope gave three turns of the waltz. The operator synchronized the picture to the orchestral music at the entertainment and gave the audience of 1,600 persons a profound sensation. The entertainment included also a wheel picture of an acrobatic performance. The receipts for the show were $850.

Just what direct personal contact there may have been between the Sellers effort and the work of Heyl is not certain. Charles C. Heyl of Germantown, son of the inventor and heir to the Phasmatrope, recalls that his father became a member of the Franklin Institute and was for thirty years a member of its board of directors. There the elder Heyl and Sellers became intimate friends.

Through the Heyl device the problem of showing motion pictures had now come nearer to a satisfactory solution than the making of them. The screen was waiting for the laggard camera to catch step by attaining the ability to photograph objects in motion, not mere timed poses.

Heyl was apparently the first to project photographic pictures. But because of the limitations of photography his motion was entirely synthetic. The Sellers device was an evolution of the Zoetrope, which in turn had developed from the Plateau-Stampfer Stoboscopic Disc machine. And farther back Lt. von Uchatius had projected the Stroboscopic pictures on a screen, very much as Heyl projected photographs later.

The next step was to come from a far place and unexpected sources.

CHAPTER TWO

MUYBRIDGE IN MYTH AND MURDER

Again the star of the motion picture's destiny moves westward, now to California. It is still four decades before the first camera clicked in Hollywood.

We have come to Muybridge and his tradition. We shall examine into the tale of a tale which by constant repetition has become the supreme classic reference of all motion picture history. It is the screen's accepted first chapter of Genesis, growing in authority and weight down the years.

For at least twenty years every writer and every speaker on the annals of the motion picture has repeated with increasing assurance the time-worn story of the race horse pictures with which the late Eadweard Muybridge has been so orthodoxly credited with fathering the motion picture. Thereby the story has taken to itself the greatness of great names and the backing of high authority.

But the supreme classic is supremely wrong. Muybridge, in a word, had nothing to do with the motion picture at all; and, in truth, but a very small part, if any, in the creative work of the hallowed race horse incident.

The principal necessity for discussing the Muybridge story here is not his part in the background of the motion picture itself, but the overwhelmingly distorted shadow of his fame.

The reader familiar with the long told story of common acceptance will find now and again glints of the stuff from which the Muybridge myth has been constructed, along with here and there evidences of how it came to grow into the fabric of tradition.

—21—

Our California of the Seventies was a newly preëmpted Promised Land with a rising culture of the logical sort to follow the hurly-burly of the actively romantic days of the gold rush of '49. The land was in the hands of a coterie of industrial pioneers of the type always designated by friendly biographers as "empire builders." California was the distinctly empirical property of a group typified and headed by Collis P. Huntington, Charles Crocker, Governor Leland Stanford and James R. Keene, names written conspicuously across Pacific Coast history. They were the Rockefellers, Morgans and Goulds of their domain, the United States from the Sierras to the sea. The Southern Pacific railway, and its components and subsidiaries, were at once the symbol and instrument of their dominion.

From the dimmest dawn of history down to the gasoline age, from Attila to Henry the Ubiquitous, the conquerors have come a-horseback. The fast horse was through the ages the best servant of man's fight against time and distance. In this day, when the horse is hardly more than a living fossil, racing survives by the force of fetich, still glamored with the title of "the sport of kings."

Horseflesh was, therefore, still a utility as well as a diversion in the seventies. The horse was a considerable and imposing fact in the lives and interests of those ducal builders of empire in the great open spaces of the West.

Governor Leland Stanford owned an imposing racing stable and was a breeder of fast horses. He had a deal of knowledge and definite opinions concerning the horse. It was his solemn and somewhat lone assertion that at various gaits a horse at full speed took all of his four feet off the ground at once. The horse was as provocative of conversation and argument then as the motor car is now.

James R. Keene and Frederick MacCrellish were among those who differed with Stanford's notion most vigorously.

There is no knowing how long they may have argued about it, but eventually in '72 the day came when the last word was "I'll bet you."

It was a right princely bet, too, being in the sum of $25,000, good California gold. The traditional story always refers to it as a wager, gaining thereby some flavor of antiquity and a savor of extra gentility.

More recently, since the name of Stanford has become immortalized by a university and laureled by time, one or two distinguished chroniclers writing for local consumption have sought to cast over the race horse matter a Puritan aura by firmly asserting in limpid accents that Governor Stanford never at any time or place indulged in betting. Let us observe that the worthy governor owned many race horses with great pride in their speed and that this was the California of 1872, when and where men were men, etc. The circumstantial evidence is as definite as that surrounding a darky in a melon patch.

The wager may have closed the argument, but it did not settle the issue. Somebody had to prove something. Governor Stanford started out to do it. He wanted to be able to show conclusively what the feet of the race horse did in action. It was necessary to have ocular proof in hand—in other words, a picture. Up to that moment pictorial art had been purely a servant of communication and evolved esthetics. Now it was called upon to take a brass tacks, scientific assignment. Artists and sculptors through the centuries had accepted the pictorial tradition so typically expressed in the antique *Balbi* in the Neopolitan museum. Stanford did not agree with the artists. He had to find picture making that was untrammeled of opinion, able to record rather than to fancy. This inevitably meant resort to photography.

Stanford cast about and presently employed this Eadweard Muybridge, a San Francisco photographer. Muybridge was locally known for his work in making various photographs for the U. S. Coast Survey. He had been sent to Alaska to make photographs by way of supplying official answer to the cry of "Seward's Folly" raised at the purchase of the territory for seven millions from Russia in 1867. It is probable in the light of both the political and industrial interests of Stanford that this was the source of his acquaintance with the photographer.

Muybridge worked with the wet plate process, which was then still the best available method of recording the image cast by a lens. Stanford sent him to Sacramento in '72 to try for pictures which would show the gait of the horse. This was an attempt at making snapshots, a daring conception in that day. Muybridge worked with the ordinary stand camera of the period. It was loaded with a plate freshly sensitized in a black tent darkroom on the spot. Then this plate was exposed as a horse was driven past the camera.

Photographic manuals indicate that the briefest practical exposure was then about one-twelfth of a second. That was about one half as rapid as the action of the common Brownie camera used by children and novices today. Such a long exposure could not record rapid motion close to the camera. A trotting horse registered in a blur on the plate.

Muybridge inevitably failed and was about ready to give up.

Stanford was disappointed but still eager for the pictorial proof which he was sure would confirm his opinion in the matter of the motion of the horse. Perhaps Keene was chaffing him a bit, too.

A sudden, and previously unexplained interruption now appears in all of the scientific and popular accounts of Muybridge's work. The solemn records of the journals and the archives of libraries and universities leave some five years of Muybridge's life accounted for by saying "when he returned to San Francisco five years later . . ." You may search the libraries of San Francisco, Philadelphia, New York, Paris and London in vain. There is an ample and abundantly erroneous literature of his labors in two or three languages. But there is no recorded word there of the lost years, and those years hold the secret chapters of the highest drama in the life of the man whom a careless world calls "the grandfather of the motion picture."

Stowed deep in the dust of the records of an obscure country court house is a file of tape bound papers which supplies the key. The file jacket reads:

THE PEOPLE OF THE STATE OF CALIFORNIA
vs.
EADWEARD MUYBRIDGE

Those old papers in their faded legal blue jackets take us back to the black day of October 17, 1874, when the lost years began. Muybridge was at work over his plates in the darkroom of the photographic establishment of Bradley & Rulofson in San Francisco. The status of his connection with that concern is not clear. He may have been, and likely was, an employe on a piece work basis. A lawyer called on Muybridge who was a defendant in a suit for $100, the bill of one Mrs. Susan Smith, midwife. She had attended Mrs. Muybridge at the birth of a child a short time before. The child was born while Muybridge was at Sacramento, and now Mrs. Muybridge was away on a visit to the Dalles in Oregon. It was typical of Muybridge's carelessness with his financial affairs that the bill should have been unpaid. There must however have been some other factor. Muybridge was resisting payment.

A hint came from the lawyer that Mrs. Smith knew something about Mrs. Muybridge. If she were not paid there was to be vengeance. Muybridge, aflame, went to Mrs. Smith, who told a tale of domestic perfidy.

One Major Harry Larkyn, the midwife said, had brought Mrs. Muybridge to her house for confinement, and there had been love scenes with the new born babe between them. Mrs. Smith elaborated with stories of visits by Mrs. Muybridge to Larkyn's quarters, with a touch about a veil and shawl left behind. Muybridge refused to believe. Mrs. Smith countered by giving her lawyer letters from Mrs. Muybridge in Oregon, discussing Larkyn in tender terms and enclosing a picture of the baby with the name "Harry" written on the back. It would appear, too, that Mrs. Muybridge was hiding from Larkyn, for there were advertisements in the personal columns of the San Francisco and Portland papers through which he had tried to communicate with her.

This Major Larkyn was an Irishman of English culture and an adventurer. He had in a year served on several San Francisco newspapers and was now with the *San Francisco Stock Report*. He was of the dashing sort, handsome with the glamor of a whisper of noble lineage. He was a familiar of the merry life of San Francisco, hail fellow and often met.

Mrs. Flora Muybridge was, the records tell us, twenty-three and a rare beauty, petite, plump and blue-eyed.

Muybridge was forty-seven, given to moods of gloom and eccentricity.

Also it was California, golden and provocative.

Now this seventeenth of October the lawyer came with the papers, the letter, Judas-sweet, and the picture of the child. The name "Harry" was scribbled on the back of the photograph.

Muybridge, emerging from the darkroom, squinted against the glare of outer light and regarded these documents of his despair.

From among his effects in the workshop he snatched a revolver and dashed into the hall. He had been marked as curious at the Bradley & Rulofson establishment because of some phobia which would not let him use the elevator. This day he dashed into the car and descended. In the hall below William Rulofson encountered Muybridge and sought to calm him. Muybridge poured out his trouble and declared he was going to see Larkyn, whom he knew to be at Calistoga. Rulofson parleyed, hoping to delay Muybridge until the last boat had gone. The dock was twelve squares away from the Rulofson galleries in Montgomery street. Four minutes to the sailing hour Muybridge broke away, running. He made it.

When the boat docked that evening Muybridge walked ashore and presently went about the streets of Calistoga on his quest. Calistoga was a way station on romance road. There where the warm sulphur waters bubbled up at the foot of Mount St. Helena, Sam Brannan, locally known as "the great and only," had come from New York and built a resort, named in token of his native Saratoga. Up these same streets one Robert Louis Stevenson came one day, not long after the time of this chapter, and went up the mountain with his bride to write "The Silverado Squatters."

Major Larkyn and his light o' love had been there, too.

Now vengeance entered, in sequel, with the outraged personality of Eadweard J. Muybridge. Larkyn was, he learned, at the Yellow Jacket mine, seven miles distant.

It was eleven that night when a liveryman deposited Muybridge at the house where Larkyn was stopping.

Muybridge shouted a call for Larkyn.

Larkyn came to the door and peered out into the dark.

"I can't see you," he answered.

"My name is Muybridge—here is a message from my wife."

The message was a shot from Muybridge's revolver.

Larkyn clapped his hands to his heart and turned back into

the house. In half a minute he was dead. Muybridge, following Larkyn in, was disarmed and sent away that night to the jail at Napa City, the county seat.

The affair was the sensation of the year in Napa county. Shootings were common enough, but not affairs so dramatically involving beauty, love and high pitched romance.

Sam P. Davis, a reporter for the *San Francisco Chronicle* and a friend of Larkyn, came to minister last attentions, and write the story. Davis was a brother of Robert H. Davis, now one of the famous among New York's magazine editors, whose recollections furnished the first clue to this chapter of our history.

Four months later, February 3, 1875, Muybridge was called to trial in the Napa City courthouse. The hearing occupied two days. The defense relied on asylum officials to support a temporary insanity plea. That was before the alienist had been invented. The evidence revealed that Muybridge had been injured in a stage coach runaway accident in July 1860, while crossing the continent on his way to England. He had lain long ill with injuries to his head, at Fort Smith, Arkansas, and months after was treated in England by the famous Sir William Gull. Doubtless Muybridge's injuries were genuine enough, since it appears the Southern Overland Stage Company settled with him for $2,500 when he returned to California. Many reputable citizens testified to the change that the accident had wrought in Muybridge's mental character and conduct.

The streets about the little brick courthouse in Brown street were crowded with wagons and ponies and the courtroom overflowed through the open doors into the halls that afternoon when Wort W. Pendegast of counsel for the defense made his plea to the jury of hard faced pioneers. Pendegast had come into the Napa Valley from Kentucky, bringing with him the ability for courtroom oratory which was the special gift of the land of

EADWEARD MUYBRIDGE as he appeared in the
years of his fame at the University of Pennsylvania.

The Napa Daily Register.

PUBLISHED EVERY AFTERNOON.

SATURDAY, FEB. 6, 1875.

"NOT GUILTY."

End of the Muybridge Trial.

BRILLIANT SPEECH OF SENATOR PENDEGAST.

The Prisoner Overpowered with Emotion.

FRIDAY, Feb. 5, 1875.

AFTERNOON SESSION.

Court convened at 1 P. M. Jury called and found all present.

The Court began by announcing that it had concluded to admit evidence of prisoner's condition of mind subsequent to the killing, with privilege to defense to rebut. Defense recalled J. M. McArthur. Was in Muybridge's company most of the time after the killing, till he took him to Calistoga: noticed his deportment.

[Pendegast interrupted by a request to exclude witnesses.]

Appearance and deportment was exceedingly cool and deliberate; observed nothing unusual; neither after arrival at Calistoga was appearance unusual: was cool and collected. As as instance of coolness, said Muybridge poured out a drink very steadily when they all drank together on their arrival at Calistoga: when I took his pistol from him he was steady, nerved and cool. Cross-examination—He was unusually cool. Conduct that of any man under ordinary circumstances; conduct was unusual under the circumstances. Don't think I told him "keep cool" or testified to that statement.

and Muybridge was brought in to receive it. It was "We the jury, find the defendant not guilty."

OVERPOWERED WITH JOY.

On hearing his acquittal, Mr. Muybridge was so overcome with his emotions as to fall into a paroxysm similar to that which had seized him on the memorable 17th of October, when he heard of his wife's infidelity. He fell upon Mr. Pendegast and wept, and went into convulsions. He was removed to the offices of his counsel, and Dr. Boynton sent for. By the time of that gentleman's arrival, however, he had so far recovered as to be out of the need of medical aid, and rapidly regained his wonted composure.

He is now a free man and has received the congratulations of a multitude of friends. He leaves tonight for San Francisco, where, so confident was he of acquittal that he had an engagement to dine with a friend tomorrow.

SPEECH OF HON. W. W. PENDEGAST.

Rejoiced that there were some points in the case that were not controverted and upon which all agreed. I agree with Judge Stoney that the prisoner at the bar is guilty of murder in the first degree, or he is guilty of nothing. Either send him from the Court-room a free man, or send him to the scaffold. He deserves absolute freedom, or he deserves death. Between the two ye are the judges. No controversy as to the killing or its attendant circumstances. Admit that Muybridge took the life of Harry Larkyns, and that he took it in no self-defense. Do not wish to bring Larkyns from his bloody grave; am willing that he should sleep there till the resurrection morn.

How *The Napa Daily Register*, of Napa City, California, reported the acquittal of Muybridge — the day that his five mysterious years began.

bourbon and blue grass. He was tall and lank and solemn. His voice poured out with the emotion of a great organ.

Pendegast laid the statutes aside and invoked the "unwritten law." His address to the jury is a tradition of the Napa County bar. Pendegast's oratory was interrupted by rounds of applause. He pulled out the tremolo, the vox humana and all the rest of the stops on the organ. After thundering a philippic of vengeance and justice "above the law," Pendegast dropped to a softened plea carefully pitched to hush the courtroom into churchly silence.

"I can not ask you," he said, "to send this man forth to family and home—he has none. Across the arch of his fireplace where once were written the words Home—Wife—Child—Content and Peace, there now appears as a substitute for all, in black letters, placed there by the destroyer, the single awful word "Desolation." But I do ask you to send him forth free—let him take up the thread of his broken life and resume that profession on which his genius has shed so much lustre, the profession which is now his only love. Let him go forth into the green fields, by the bright waters, through the beautiful valleys and up and down the swelling coast, and in the active work of securing shadows of their beauty by the magic of his art, he may gain surcease of sorrow, and pass on to his end in comparative composure."

The jury was charged and retired for deliberation in late afternoon. Hours passed and the disappointed crowd went away for supper, as the jurors had theirs sent in. Meanwhile argument and balloting continued.

Ballot after ballot was taken. Always the vote was "Not guilty—11, guilty—1."

Old Sam Newcomer was foreman of the jury. He was one of the oldest settlers of the valley. He had come for gold and he stayed to be a rancher. He was tall and gaunt and spare.

He wore a white moustache and a goatee, grandee fashion. He was a type of the covered wagon era.

Newcomer and ten fellow jurymen raged and cursed at W. T. Commary, the twelfth man, voting "Guilty."

Commary was a hardy determined person, too. He was a carpenter. Strangely enough, in the light of his decision, he had a young and beautiful wife, quite as fair as she who had cost Larkyn his life. They lived in Napa City near the courthouse.

Argument and oaths were unavailing with Commary.

"He's as guilty as hell and you know it," he insisted. "The law is the law. Every man here knows he's guilty."

Midnight came. Twelve cots were moved into the jury room.

As the twelve good men and true sat pulling off their boots, Newcomer called for another ballot. "Not guilty—11, guilty —1."

They blew out the oil lamps and went to bed, cursing.

Newcomer lay still, staring up at the dark ceiling. On the cot next to him was Commary.

Soon the heavy breathing and snoring of ten tired men filled the room. Two men tense beyond sleep lay still in the dark.

It must have been near two o'clock in the morning when Newcomer sat up on the edge of his cot facing Commary. Commary sullenly grunted. Newcomer spoke low, but clearly.

"Listen to me Commary. You've knowed me for a long time." Newcomer waited. Commary was looking hard at him.

"I reckon I have, Sam Newcomer."

"Well Bill, you've never seen me pray. It's a long time since I ever said a prayer, Bill. But I'm going to say one now."

Newcomer stopped to let Commary think. Then he went on.

"And Bill, I'm a-going to pray to God that while you're locked up here in this jury room some —— gets your wife!"

Newcomer waved in gesture toward Commary's home.

Then the foreman of the jury slipped to his knees and buried his face in his hard hands on the edge of Commary's cot. Minutes of silence passed with him there kneeling. Commary stared hard into the night.

In silence Newcomer got up and went back to bed.

The earliest rooster in Napa City was crowing and it was still dark when Commary reached over and nudged Newcomer. Newcomer seemed to be very deep in sleep. Commary got up and shook him.

"Sam, let's take another ballot," he whispered.

Newcomer got up and searched his clothes for a match. He went softly about and lighted the lamps. He called the sleeping jurymen. Sockfooted and shirt-tailed they sat up.

"Boys" Newcomer began gently. "Sometimes the day makes a difference in the way men see things. We don't any of us feel the same about things. It's way after midnight now. It's another day. Let's take a ballot."

The jurymen resented their awakening and they glowered again at Commary who continued his silence under their abuse.

"I'm foreman of this jury and there's going to be another ballot." Newcomer insisted. Again they balloted, cursing Commary the while.

"Not guilty—12."

They called the bailiff and reported that they had a verdict. The judge came and the jury filed in. Then Wall Kennedy, the jailer, brought Muybridge up from below.

The ceremony of acquittal was soon over and Muybridge left the courtroom free. Commary hurried home.

Soon all Napa City was awake with the sensation. Muybridge departed and for the next five years none of those who had known him knew where he had gone. He was the while, crushed in gloom, living on a hinterland ranch property of Leland Stanford. Mrs. Muybridge vanished after the trial and today no trace remains of her subsequent career.

Wall Kennedy, the jailer who set Muybridge free, deserves a special paragraph in history for another and more cheerful reason. Kennedy was a spinner of handsome pioneer yarns. It was his pride that he was the most able liar on the west slopes of the Sierras. A young photographer named Frank Bacon appeared in Napa City and opened a gallery. He and Kennedy became pals. Bacon never tired of Kennedy's yarns, particularily the jailer's tale about when "I drove a swarm of bees across the Rocky Mountains in the winter of '51 an' never lost a bee."

Bacon and his wife had a flair for amateur theatricals. They appeared occasionally at entertainments at the nearby Soldiers' Home at Yountsville, where Bacon gathered other bits of lore from the veterans of the wars.

This is where Frank Bacon got his character of "Lightnin' Bill Jones" and that bee story with which he conquered Broadway many and many a year later.

The endless intricate intertwinings of the strands of destiny ordained that some forty years ahead this photographer-actor, Bacon, in the fame of his declining years, should engage in the first experimental mating of the motion picture and the radio. Not long before Bacon's death, Watterson R. Rothacker, a Chicago producer, experimentally presented a picture of Bacon in a theatre, while the actor in a distant projection room viewed a synchronized copy of the picture and radiocast his lines to the theatre audience.

Napa City is just Napa now. But the town is still proud of memories of Muybridge and Pendegast and Bacon and Stevenson. The story of Newcomer and Commary remains something of a lawyer's jury room secret still. It was told long after by Newcomer to Raymond Benjamin, the young new district attorney of Napa County. Now Benjamin offices in San Francisco, and sits in councils as chairman of the Republican state committee of California.

The Larkyn shooting was the only aggressive act of Muybridge's life. It was the product of his only great emotional crisis, the one scarlet splash of a drab personality. He was pronouncedly of the recessive type as indicated by all ordinary conduct and by the whole record of his technical career.

San Francisco had forgotten the drama of Calistoga when the photographer emerged from his retirement and appeared there again to equip himself to resume his effort at horse pictures for Stanford. In those five years the chemistry of photography had developed. Emulsions now permitted exposures of only a tiny fraction of the time required to make a picture in 1872. The photographic plate was now fast enough to record the movements of a speeding horse. But the camera and its operator were not.

Muybridge snapped away at the Stanford horses with bizarre results, suggestive of the work of some of our present kodak amateurs. Now and then Muybridge caught as much as the nose of a horse on his plate. Seeking to correct the timing of his exposure he would next, perhaps, get a nicely recorded image of the tail just as the trotter passed out of the picture.

After endless attempts, hundreds in number, by sheer chance Muybridge got about four pictures which had some possible significance. One of them somewhat indistinctly showed a horse with all of his feet off the ground. The rest caught differing phases of the gait.

Governor Stanford prized these costly pictures. He kept them by him at his desk and when affairs of state or the Central Pacific were not too demanding, he toyed with the pictures of the gait, trying to arrange them in a logical, progressive sequence. But the pictures were not all of the same stride or even of the same horse. They were indicative but not conclusive.

This was tantalizing. Stanford decided that if one camera could catch the horse at the top of his stride with all his feet off the ground, a row of cameras could perhaps show by steps just how the horse picked up his feet and put them down again. That would indeed settle the question and add importantly to the lore of the horse.

Stanford instructed Muybridge to try firing a whole volleying broadside of cameras. Expense was no object with the horse issue at stake.

Muybridge pursuant to instructions tried a row of cameras. He had more difficulty trying to expose them in a proper sequence than he had had in trying to snap one camera at the right instant. A line of strings attached to the shutters was stretched across the track. The horse driven past was expected to snap the strings and make pictures of himself as he progressed. But strings are subject to many influences of variation. They stretched. They shrank. They jarred the cameras. They frightened the horses. They did everything but work.

Stanford, with now a greater investment and a keener interest than ever, waxed impatient.

There were men in the railroad service who could do things. The performance of the impossible was well near a daily occurrence in the stupendous engineering work of the railway technicians of those pioneer days in the coastal and mountain country.

Stanford talked of his problem to Arthur Brown, chief engineer of maintenance. Brown had under him a staff which was laying down engineering precedent for all the world. Remote from the facilities of the East these California railroaders were used to relying on their own resources. They progressed boldly to the attainment of things that men more burdened with lore and precedent would not have attempted.

Brown suggested to Stanford that John D. Isaacs, a most inventive young man on the engineering staff, be entrusted to the undertaking. Isaacs was a graduate of the University of Virginia in the class of '75. He brought to his work an unusual fitness and a scientific training much beyond the ordinary scope of the technical men of industry in that day. He is interesting as a Virginian, too, since the sons of that state were ultimately to figure so conspicuously in the evolution of the motion picture.

Isaacs, it chanced, was also an advanced amateur photographer. He had cameras imported from France and quite an assembly of the other apparatus which the complex photography of the time required. He was also abreast of the progress reported from eastern and European researchers.

Stanford knew Isaacs and approved the assignment.

Isaacs learned what had been done and the results. He diagnosed the Stanford problem as a proposition in the abstract recording of motion and set to work to solve it in the laboratory instead of on the race track. His first efforts were made with attempts to picture a rolling wheel taken from an old switch engine in the shop yards at Oakland. The engine wheel was a logical scientific choice, since knowledge of its predetermined motions enabled a check on the results.

The principal problem concerned, now that the plates were fast enough, was in the matter of shutter action and the timing of the shutter releases, with relation one to another.

Exposures as brief as one two-thousandth part of a second were attained by shutters snapped open and shut by heavy rubber bands with a one hundred pound pull. This was apparently the adoption of a method patented in England by one Thomas Skaife in 1856.

This settled, the question now was how to set the cameras off one after another at precisely the proper instants. Isaacs recalled having read the year before, in '76, an article in the *Scientific American* describing an electric bell, newly invented in Europe. He decided that here was a clue to a method of electrical control for the camera shutters. This promised to be much more reliable and accurate than any rigging of strings. Isaacs had considerable technical familiarity with the little then known of electrical possibilities. He decided to apply the bell ringing device, operated by an electro-magnet, to the shutter releases of the cameras. He drew up a design and the mechanisms were constructed by Paul Seiler of San Francisco, electrical authority of the region.

That was the day before rubber tires and the wheels of racing sulkies were steel shod. Isaacs worked out a system of electrical contacts with wire stretched at intervals across a measured section of the Stanford race track at the governor's Palo Alto stud farm. As the sulky swept past the wheels closed the circuits successively and the magnetic releases set off the cameras.

This worked with entire success. It was a satisfactory method for photographing a trotting horse driven from a sulky, but not for the running horse with no vehicle to supply the contacts. This led to the application of a chronographic machine with a metal cylinder carrying projecting pins like the cylinder of a Swiss music box. When the machine was set in motion as the horse entered the section covered by the cameras, the pins one after another closed contacts controlling the cameras for successive exposures. This permitted the making of a series of "instantaneous" photographs of any object passing the cameras, whether it touched the ground or not, even a pigeon in flight.

Stanford was excited and delighted with the results.

The battery of the cameras, first five and then twelve in

JOHN D. ISAACS, former chief engineer of the Southern Pacific railway, who devised the chronophotographic machines which made Muybridge famous.

A Classic Specimen of the animal locomotion pictures made by Eadweard Muybridge, using the device evolved by John D. Isaacs for Leland Stanford in the California experiments of the '70's. — Observe the cross-section pattern of the background, which is only visible where the horse's shadows prevented over-exposure.

number for the earlier work, was increased to twenty-four. They were mounted under an open shed with their lenses centered exactly twelve inches apart. They bore across the track against a white background forty feet long carrying spaced vertical black lines exactly opposite the camera lenses, and with a movable board before it bearing horizontal black lines on a white ground and four inches apart as they rose from the level of the track. These lines enabled the effect of photographing an animal in movement on a sheet of cross section paper. This was a characteristic piece of engineering practice natural to Isaacs. By reference to the lines it was possible to say with considerable exactness where each hoof of a horse was with reference to the track at any instant of exposure.

Measured by today's photographic standards the quality of the pictures was rather low. They were ordinarily little more than silhouettes, but sufficient.

The photographic equipment was now complete for its purpose. Isaacs' job was done. He went back to his railroad engineering. He had big important things to do, now that Stanford's whimsical interest had been served. Isaacs dismissed the whole affair as a task done. Muybridge stayed to operate the device and make endless series of pictures of every animal that could be led, driven, or shooed past the cameras.

It was a scientific episode to Isaacs. To Muybridge it was a career.

The work at Palo Alto continued for several years. Stanford took a large pride in the pictures. The stellar series showed his famous "Occident," one of the most highly valued horses of the Stanford stables.

Expenditures mounted up until Stanford had invested something like $40,000 in his horse pictures. The Stanford picture making continued until about 1881. Taking the pictorial products which Muybridge made with Isaacs' device, Stanford turned them over to Dr. J. D. B. Stillman for analysis and interpretation. Stillman elaborated an exhaustive study of the locomotive movements of the horse. He announced most sensationally that there was no such thing as what was conceived by artists as the gallop.

A pretentious volume, exhaustively and expensively illustrated with heliotype gelatine process reproductions of the original photographs, was issued. The title page of the work reads:

> The Horse in Motion, as shown by Instantaneous Photography, with a study of animal mechanics founded on anatomy and the revelations of the camera, in which is demonstrated the theory of quadrupedal locomotion—by J. D. B. Stillman, A.M., M.D. Executed and published under auspices of Leland Stanford. James R. Osgood & Company, Boston 1882. Copyright 1881 by Leland Stanford.

Governor Stanford went about on his travels exulting and showing the photographs of his horses. It was a good story for a sportsman to tell and it was backed by photographic evidence. From a café in Paris the story of the pictures was wafted to the studio of Jean Louis Meissonier, a genre and historical painter. Meissonier's work was remarkable for its microscopic detail. His miniatures have long been world famed. Optical facts were of first importance to Meissonier. The artist, having some independent notions of his own on the observation and recording of motions, was having heated debates with his confrères in the studios of Paris, even as Stanford had had with the horsemen at his clubs in San Francisco. Meissonier was believing his own excellent eyes, and traditional authority was scolding him for it bitterly.

Meissonier was just such another scientist at heart as Leonardo, who was eternally abandoning his remunerative commissions and half-done paintings to pursue some elusive object of research. In Meissonier we see a reiteration of the identical interest in the phenomena of sight. Leonardo had yearned toward a record of the image cast by the *camera obscura*. Meissonier was reaching for the slow motion camera's analysis of action which has come to us within the last few years.

Meissonier went in haste to interview Governor Stanford and to inspect the photographs. He spent hours over the pictures, examining their every aspect minutely. The embattled artist found elements of vindication. He asked for the authorship of the photographs and learned that Muybridge was the photographer. It was natural that Stanford should think of Muybridge the photographer, represented by the physical photographs in hand, rather than of Isaacs whose connection was with the more abstract method of getting the pictures. Meissonier urged that Stanford send Muybridge to France.

The year following Meissonier introduced Muybridge at a private gathering attended by the invited elect of the creative workers of Paris. Among those mentioned in the records of that affair were Alexander Dumas, Steinheil, Detaille, Dr. Mallez and Goupil. The pictures, recording horses, dogs, and deer in action were shown in ordinary photographic prints passed about from hand to hand.

The pictures were provocative in the extreme. There was violent debate and some scoffing. The centuries of museum sanctified art were not to be overturned in a moment by a handful of photographs made by a visiting stranger from the wild remoteness of some place called California. Bear in mind that the camera was not yet established as an instrument of scientific verity. These artists could guide brush and pencil at will. They suspected something of the kind from the photographer. The photographs were not, in the circumstances, in the nature of final proof. The camera could be wrong!

But Meissonier had other resources. He was going to prove that even though these pictures did show the horse in positions disagreeing with tradition he could synthesize the actual movement from them. Muybridge had brought with him the trot and the gallop, taken apart. Messionier now proposed to put them together again. The final proof was therefore to be that these disputed parts could be combined into an undisputed whole. If the optical combination of the unfamiliar positions resulted in the familiar effect the case was made.

An instrument already existed available for this purpose. It was the projecting Zoetrope. Remember that Franz von Uchatius had made such a machine many years before and that it had been variously improved upon, especially in the work of Henry Renno Heyl in Philadelphia.

Meissonier had a series of the Stanford horse pictures converted into transparencies and applied to the projecting zoetropic machine. It seems that this step was rather an immediate following of some aspects of the work of M. Emile Reynaud in France in 1877. Reynaud had created a sensation of a sort with a new kind of shadow show given in a theatre in Paris. He projected from behind the screen, with bands of animated paintings and drawings on translucent material. Probably he used waxed or varnished fabrics and paper. He attempted to supplant the drawings with photographs, but failed for photographic reasons. He was exceedingly close to the modern motion picture idea. He called his machine the Praxinoscope.

The zoetropic device with the Stanford-Isaacs-Muybridge pictures applied is found emerging into records as the Zoopraxiscope, signifying that Meissonier had put the animals of Muybridge's photographic Zoo into the Praxinoscope.

The machine consisted of a revolving glass disc on which the transparencies were mounted, with an opaque shutter disc with slots corresponding to the pictures revolving in the opposite direction. With a light source behind the glass disc and a projecting lens in front of the shutter, the controlled coincidence of picture and shutter opening on the line of illumination permitted a glimpse of a phase of motion to be cast on the screen, only to be supplanted at once by another. The optical results were wonderful then, but distressing to consider in the light of today's screen.

Obviously Muybridge had nothing to do with the evolution of this device. Its use was in the nature of a coincidental repetition of the Stanford affair. Stanford, in an argument, had sought record of an instant of motion and employed Isaacs to show Muybridge how to catch it. Meissonier, in a similar controversy, wanted to prove the record of that instant by making it fit back into the motion and took the Zoetrope to do it. In both instances Muybridge was functioning in a detailed part.

The zoetropic projection of the horse pictures gave Meissonier the best of the argument. He could make the seemingly impossible and awkward appearing hoof positions fit into the gait. It was a sensation in art and science.

This was Muybridge's first contact with a motion picture idea.

Now the photographer from California was acclaimed and on the road to greatness. He hastened to London in his native England to bask in glory. He lectured with large profundity and tooting astuteness before the Royal Institution. John D. Isaacs, busy railroading in faraway California read about it and grinned.

When in the ardor of his new pride Muybridge later brought a suit against Governor Stanford, seeking added credits, Isaacs was asked to give testimony. His deposition terminated the action.

A horseman's argument had made Muybridge a photographer of motion. An artist's argument had shown him synthesis of motion.

There is no evidence that Muybridge had ever before thought of the work in any possible relation to a motion picture.

Everything that developed such a relation was, for the photographer at Palo Alto, the sheerest coincidence. He was engaged solely in stopping the horse on the plate, by methods handed to him for the purpose.

Fame was to overtake Muybridge just as wealth overtook the Boer farmer who was using a giant Kimberly diamond for a door weight when a mining expert called. Meissonier and the scientists of France knew what the photographs of the race horse meant, and used them. Even then their significance was only partly apparent to Muybridge. All the rest of his days he used his pictures in exactly that same way without further elaboration of methods or principles.

Among those who held a special interest in the Muybridge pictures was Dr. E. J. Marey, a French physicist and founder of Marey Institute. Marey's most important observation was that the Muybridge pictures, being taken from successive points of view by successive cameras, gave the impression of a horse standing in one spot kicking the landscape past him. Marey wanted, in his study of the now bubbling issue of motions, to get pictures taken from a single point of view, as observed by the eye.

As investigation will show, Marey's subsequent work did not follow the Muybridge pattern, as often related, but rather that of Janssen, an astronomical observer who in 1874 evolved a sort of photographic pistol or revolver, which took successive pictures of a transit of Venus on a single plate, through one lens.

One may fancy that Muybridge found himself a little dizzy with this sudden acclaim and attention from persons in high station. The career of Muybridge up to this point had not been marked by extraordinary energy or ambition. Also he was past the creative age.

But by the next year Muybridge had caught his balance and was riding his new fame with aplomb. When he returned to the United States he was wearing a handsomely effulgent halo of genuine imported European recognition.

The University of Pennsylvania invited Muybridge in, offering facilities for continued work in the recording of motion, all this as an adjunct to the research work of various other departments. Muybridge became the photographer to a university instead of a race track. Otherwise the conditions of 1872 in California obtained.

The assignment was congenial to the unaggressive Muybridge, with its easy assurance of a comfortable berth and interesting associations. He was a picturesque person, with a great shock of hair and a long patriarchal beard, artistically stained with tobacco. In that distant time, nearly a half century ago, when cigarettes were the essence of sin, Muybridge smoked them incessantly. He chronically wore tattered clothes and his hat was invariably full of holes.

Muybridge was a pictorial acquisition for the University of Pennsylvania in a double sense. He became one of the notables of the campus, where he photographed all manner of animals in motion, including the varsity track team.

The fame of the university photographic expert grew and he was much in circulation among scientific groups and such gatherings as those of the Franklin Institute, a technical society of note. There he met Coleman Sellers and Henry Renno Heyl.

A Philadelphia friend remarks of Muybridge: "We never heard of the interesting story of the dramatic affair in San Francisco. When he was in this city Muybridge always allowed it to be understood that he was a bachelor. This permitted a certain freedom of action which he evidently enjoyed."

In February, 1886, Muybridge visited Edison in New Jersey. The Muybridge tradition in Philadelphia relates that he sought Edison with the idea of combining the phonograph with the Zoopraxoscope to produce talking pictures. It makes a handsome paragraph, but it does not fit the unaggressive Muybridge pattern.

"Muybridge came to my laboratory to show me some pictures of a horse in motion that he had taken in California," says Edison. "But nothing was said about the phonograph."

It seems to have been only a call aimed at recognition from the famous Edison. Muybridge was a lion hunter.

Muybridge continued his work at the University of Pennsylvania for about ten years, concluding in 1893 when the university entered an exhibit of his pictures at Zoopraxographical Hall at the Columbian Exposition in Chicago. The exhibit included showings of the pictures on the Zoopraxoscope. This instrument at the World's Fair, ten years after the Paris episode which launched the Muybridge career, was practically identical with the machine Meissonier had used. In his ten great years Muybridge had contributed nothing in progress toward the screen of today. He left the motion picture exactly where he found it—on the projecting zoetrope of Paris.

This fact alone is a sufficient measure of his work.

He used devices which were made for the work on which he was primarily an incidental employe and he applied them to the work in the routine manner of the ordinary operator. Whatever there was of progress in the machine shown at the World's Fair, at the close of Muybridge's active career, we have seen as the contributions of such earlier workers as Uchatius, Sellers and Heyl.

This is not to be taken as a disparagement of Muybridge or

his work, but as an evaluation. Retrospection has conjured up for him anticipations which he did not hold. He took not one step beyond Meissonier's idea.

Muybridge has left behind a tiny volume which is the most revealing document of his life. It was issued by him near the close of his active work, apparently to gather all of his glories into one scintillating heap. It is a little book bound in black cloth, lettered with gold, staggering under the title of "Descriptive Zoopraxography—or the Science of Animal Locomotion." It contains a most euphemistic legend, only slightly pinned to fact, about his California labors. It infers, for example, that the entire initiative of the horse picture experiments was his. It recites in pride the whole array of Muybridge's lecture dates, following the recognition of Meissonier, and tops the list with his appearance before an audience including Huxley, Gladstone, Tyndall, Lord Tennyson and the Prince and Princess of Wales. This was the occasion of his address on "The Science of Animal Locomotion in its Relation to Design in Art," before the Royal Institute of Great Britain in 1882. Muybridge went drunk with great names in his little book. He devoted some twelve pages to reproducing the signatures of great men who subscribed to an issue of reproductions of his pictures of motion studies made at the University of Pennsylvania. Among these signatures appear: "C. Vanderbilt, U. S. Grant, John Ruskin, Rutherford B. Hayes, Phil Sheridan" and some hundreds of other notables of the time. There is a distinct pleasure in observing that the hero of the saga of "Sheridan's Ride" should have contributed so handsomely to the man made famous by photographing a fast horse. The subscription price of the de luxe versions of Muybridge's work ranged from one hundred to five hundred dollars. The complete set occupies eight volumes each as large as the ordinary newspaper file.

Muybridge was an old man when he retired. He returned

to England and lived at Kingston-on-Thames. He died in 1904. Most subsequent writings have described him as a British scientist who went to California for the specific purpose of picturing Stanford's horses, and have attributed to him impulses which in truth were external influences. He was entirely a creation of events.

John D. Isaacs, who contributed the only element of invention embodied in the photography of Muybridge, rose in the technical world, but never again did his career impinge upon the evolution of the motion picture. He was but twenty-seven years of age when he worked out the electrical shutter control and timing device used at Palo Alto. He became especially well known among transportation engineers for his large scale work. He was the designer of the railway car ferry Solano which plied the waters of San Francisco bay, a craft of precedent-making dimensions and performances. He evolved sensational bridge truss designs utilizing the great timbers available in the California forests, and when those forests began to vanish he became a pioneer in methods of timber preservation and special treatments as exemplified by the creosoting process.

Isaacs stayed in the railway service in San Francisco until about 1906, when the Harriman mergers became effective. He then went to Chicago to be consulting engineer to the Harriman system. The government's dissolution of the Harriman system sent him back west to the Southern Pacific, in the service of which he in turn removed to New York still at his post as the head of the engineering staff, the dean of American transportation engineers. The Muybridge myth grew up outside the pale of Isaacs' attention. The facts of Palo Alto were forgotten until the investigations for this history led the author over the long trail across the continent and fifty years of time, reaching Isaacs, then retired, in 1924 at his summer home on Cape Cod.

Within the ten years in which Muybridge was engaged at the

University of Pennsylvania there were various widely scattered experimental efforts with the photography and presentation of motion. All of them, by distortions similar to those of the Muybridge legend, have been cited at various times as the true and only progenitors of the motion picture art.

Wallace Goold Levison of Brooklyn, New York, was an able scientific amateur photographer in the early eighties. He became acquainted with Muybridge and photographed him with a homemade magazine hand camera in the outdoor studio at the University of Pennsylvania. Levison, like Marey in France, developed an interest in making photographic records of motion from a single point of view, instead of down a row of cameras as in the Muybridge method. Levison contrived an apparatus which might roughly be described as a photographing Zoetrope in that it moved photographic plates on a wheel in sequence behind a lens and shutter, instead of using a sequence of cameras which could not, obviously, occupy the same position. Levison's work became of record when on June 13, 1888, he read a paper before the Brooklyn Academy of Photography and again on February 16, 1891, when he appeared before the New York Academy of Sciences.

In England about 1885 the late William Friese-Greene displayed some pictures of successive phases of motion made on a single glass plate after the Marey method, in the window of his photographic shop in the Piccadilly district of London. By 1889 Friese-Greene and an associate, Evans, had tinkered a bit with a plan of using a sensitized tape in a highly complex mechanism. They were following upon Reynaud's Praxinoscope idea. The Friese-Greene-Evans device had no more significance or practical value than the Praxinoscope of 1877.

The same years found Louis Aime Augustin LePrince, a native of France, working on similar devices in England. The LePrince idea finally reached a conception of a pair of parallel strips of sensitized paper or equivalently flexible material, which were to travel alternately, step by step past two lenses, one above the other. This was reducing the process to one machine instead of the many used in the Isaacs-Muybridge process, and more nearly to one point of view. LePrince, while living temporarily in New York, took out an American patent, No. 376,247, issued in 1886. He returned to Great Britain where another patent was issued January 10, 1888.

These were both merely paper patents. LePrince did not accomplish what patent authorities call "a reduction to practice." His work is therefore a part of the tentative background of motion picture effort.

The work of LePrince was terminated by his disappearance. In the early autumn of 1890 LePrince returned to France to visit a brother living near Paris. On the afternoon of September 16, 1890, LePrince went to the village railway station to go to Paris. He boarded the train. He was never seen again so far as his friends and relatives were able to discover. Ordinary motives for a voluntary disappearance of the sort were lacking.

Some well meaning British patriots occasionally write letters to the papers claiming all motion picture honors for LePrince, and telling in circumstantial details of showings of motion pictures he projected in the early '80s.

But the interesting fact is that LePrince's machine was successfully demonstrated, for the first and only time, ten years after he vanished. It was a bit of expert trickery and manipulation by Joseph Mason, a mechanician and special witness put on the stand by the American Mutoscope & Biograph Company in an effort to attack the priorities of Thomas A. Edison, in the early patent battles in New York.

The LePrince machine used was a working model constructed for the purpose from his patent specifications. It took its pictures from two points of view, which would have resulted in a vibrating image. Mason placed his subject against a black velvet curtain, thus avoiding a background to betray relative positions, then tediously hand registered each frame of the LePrince negative in the printing process, to center the wabbling figure. The optically fraudulent result looked like a vindication for the LePrince claims. It was not, and the facts of the manipulation definitely indicate the inability of LePrince to have made a successful picture, even if he had had materials.

The half-conscious struggle toward the screen had now narrowed down to the mechanics of the camera. Progress had been brought nearly to a standstill by the mechanical limitations of the heavy, fragile glass plate of photography. A new material was necessary to free the methods of recording motion from the conceptions anchored to the glass plate camera.

But the art of the living picture had traveled a long way since Leonardo's strivings and since Athanasius Kircher's lantern show of 1640 in Rome. We have traced the impulse from artist to priest to scientist and back to the artist. Now the scientists and inventors were at their innings again. The hour of the film was coming, almost on the next tick of the clock.

CHAPTER THREE

IN THE HOUSE OF THE WIZARD

W E are come now down the path of many years until we stand at the threshold of the House of the Wizard. It is a place deep with awesome mystery and legends of Magic. It is said that strange deeds are done here at strange hours. Here weird lights burn and men toil like gnomes in their cave of the night while God-fearing people are asleep.

Within this place is a wonder trove. Here are, they say, rows upon rows of canisters, bottles, jars and flasks containing curious liquids and powders, crystals, metals, drugs and all manner of substances from the far places of the earth. The black ones might even conceal skulls and reptiles. There are padlocks and chains about, and dark places where the honest light of day never shines. Here are humming, whirring, screaming machines, some of them running endlessly and spitting sparks the color of Fiddlers' Green, which is seven miles south of Perdition.

It is a place of dark Sorceries. Here abides a man who hath a familiar spirit about Things, a worker in the Black Art, which, being rare, is called Common Sense. He who is the master of this place is possessed of twain Devils, one Thought and the other Energy. It is a little Island of Intelligence, located for the while in the city which is called Newark in the state which is called New Jersey.

It is 1886, Anno Domini. May the saints preserve us! We enter.

This is the laboratory of Thomas Alva Edison. He is already known as the Wizard of Menlo Park, who has given to the world the dynamo, the incandescent lamp, the telephone transmitter and the phonograph.

The people call him Wizard because they love magic and mystery, hoping against hope that here is a royal road to All Desire. They believe that Principles and the truth about Things and Machines are invented.

All great inventions are greeted as objects of virgin birth, discoveries sprung of inspiration. The popular impression is that the inventor takes smart devices out of his mind as a prestidigitator lifts the long eared rabbit out of the tall silk hat. Hard work, persistence and patience, the bravery of him who walks in the dark alone, the tedious facts of evolution, conscious and unconscious, all these are distasteful and painful to contemplate for the Many. Therefore the fact of effort is ignored, and the fiction of wizardry and miracle is substituted.

Edison was working in this year of 1886 in his laboratory at Newark, busily completing improvements and perfections of the phonograph while waiting the completion of his new establishments at West Orange.

The phonograph had been worked out rather to his liking in the late months of that year. While he had been tinkering along on it, the notion came to Edison that he would like to give it eyes as well as ears. He dallied with the idea of a machine which recorded and transmitted not only the sound but the sight. He felt that it was a somewhat whimsical notion, but that, if it were done, it would be the completion of the phonograph. Eyes have always meant more than ears to Edison—and to every one else since the first sun-up of primeval day. He was, we see, in agreement with the Chinese in their adage, "One hundred tellings are not so good as one seeing."

If Edison appraised this notion at all he thought it trivial. His work was the work of big things, machines and methods that dealt with power, dynamos, batteries, lights that men might see to work, ore crushers, cement mills, giant rolls, and the like. His play was of the little things like the phonograph. This picture machine-phonograph was something to be done when another playtime came.

With the phonograph out of his way for the while, Edison's mind turned again toward a problem that had been long bedeviling him—the magnetic separation of various ores. Smelters were wasteful. He wanted a better way.

It was time to add to his staff of assistants, too. He was inclined to bring in a young fresh mind. He looked about. Over in his electrical plant in New York was a bright English youth, William Kennedy Laurie Dickson. Dickson was young enough and fresh enough, too.

Dickson's job with Edison was a dream come true. While in his teens at home in England Dickson had become fascinated with the published stories of the wonders achieved by "The Wizard of Menlo Park" in New Jersey in that far U. S. A. Dickson took to Edison with all of the fervor with which other ·youngsters of his age worshipped the dime novel glories of "Deadwood Dick" and "Frank Merriwell."

Young Dickson wrote a letter of application to Edison, offering his small assistance in the business of wizarding the wonders of the laboratory. Edison gave him a grave and solemn reply, stating that he was not contemplating any additions to his staff and advising the young man to stay at home in England.

Whereupon Dickson did precisely the proper thing. He sailed for America, bringing along Edison's letter and various of his own papers to show that he was a research worker, too. He presented himself, and Edison's letter opposing his coming, at the Edison plant.

Edison looked the boy over with a twinkle in his eyes.

"Well, since you have come, you'd better get to work," Edison decided, pointing to the interior of his shop.

This was in 1881. Two years later Dickson, rising in Edison's esteem, was put in charge of an electrical testing department in the plant which was located in the old Roach shipbuilding establishment in Goercke street in downtown New York. It is of incidental interest that in his electrical work for Edison this young Dickson walked along the borderland of the unknown realm of the radio. Dickson made the galvanometer tests for Edison relating to what Sir William Preece later called "the Edison effect" incidental to the operation of the incandescent electric light.

In a patent application filed by Edison November 15, 1883, he stated:

> I have discovered that if a conducting substance is interposed anywhere in the vacuous space within the globe of an incandescent lamp, and said conducting substance is connected outside of the lamp with one terminal, preferably the positive one, of the incandescent conductor, a portion of the current will, when the lamp is in operation, pass through the shunt current thus formed, which shunt includes a portion of the vacuous space within the lamp. This current I have found to be proportional to the degree of incandescence of the conductor or candlepower of the bulb.

That lamp was the forerunner of the radio tube of today. Edison was interested in possibilities, but he was so overworked that he never continued his experiments with "the Edison effect." His notes and Dickson's galvanometer test readings went into his note books to repose there, mere memoranda of unscaled peaks in the vast world of the Wizard's explorations.

Now in 1886 Dickson was mature and twenty-four. He was absorbedly busy in his work of putting the electric light and telephone wires of New York City underground. An order from Mayor Grant was sweeping the forests of poles from the avenues to save Manhattan from being buried in the wires of its communication.

When Edison called Dickson to join him in his private research laboratory, the young Englishman attained the supreme wish of his ambitions.

Edison gave his new assistant two major assignments, researches aimed at magnetic separation of ores, and, as occasion permitted, an endeavor to construct a combination apparatus for seeing and hearing. This latter was, Dickson says, "to combine Mr. Edison's phonograph with a practical zoetropic moving figure device."

Edison was in some degree familiar with what had been done in the direction of the motion picture. He had available the scientific reviews, and he read them. He watched the Germans especially, and a remarkable zoetrope device invented by Ottomar Anschütz came to his attention. Anschütz, like the rest, used photographic plates on a wheel. But he cleverly illuminated each successive phase of motion with a flash of light from a Geissler tube. The Geissler tube was chosen as a light source because of the rapidity with which its glow is produced and quenched. It gave enough light for direct vision, but not enough for projection on a large screen. This machine, heavy and complicated, saw some slight commercial amusement service in Berlin, Paris and London under the charming name of the Tachyscope.

Edison talked his own ideas over with Dickson while the ore process work went on. Late the next year, 1887, Edison set Dickson to work with experiments aimed at putting eyes into the phonograph.

Edison's thought of the phonograph and the motion picture were inseparable. He thought of the picture as the completion that would give the phonograph a new significance. We shall find the phonograph idea in control through all of Edison's motion picture efforts as an inventor.

And here it is interesting to record that, in applying some years before for patents covering the phonograph, Edison's claims covered both cylinder and disc talking machines. Also that, owing to a minor technicality, the patent office held up the disc claims while allowing the cylinder patents. This seemed of little importance to the inventor.

"No matter," said Mr. Edison, when advised to modify the disc applications to conform to the patent office requirements, "the disc phonograph will never amount to anything, anyway."

Every one knows what happened as a result of that slip. It empowered competition that won millions on the Edison idea. Technically the disc phonograph is probably inferior in a number of respects to the cylinder machine. But there were commercial reasons to arise that outweighed the technical factor in the exploitation of the phonograph. Edison's mistake was not a scientific error, but a commercial one.

All this is important here, because in time we shall see the same sort of a judgment in relation to the motion picture. Tremendous consequences were involved.

It is with no surprise that we find that Edison first set Dickson at the effort to make pictures on what was practically a phonograph cylinder. A little drum was coated with photographic emulsion and was put to recording motion under a tiny camera just as the phonographic cylinder coated with wax records sound under a diaphragm controlled needle.

Dickson had hardly more than got under way with this when it was discovered that while the phonograph record must needs run continuously the picture drum had to be stopped intermittently to permit the recording and perhaps the seeing of the pictures.

This might have been foreseen if enough attention had been given the work that had already been done on the persistence of vision and the illusions of motion. But it was characteristic of the Edison plant to accept little of the work of others lest it be contaminated with errors.

Edison decided that it would be necessary to make about forty pictures a second in order to get a perfect motion record. Trial and commercial practice have proven since that sixteen a second are sufficient, but Edison still views that as a commercial degradation of the picture.

In time Edison and Dickson contrived to get a cylinder picture-recording camera that did start and stop forty-eight times a second. The little pictures on the cylinders were hardly as large as the end of a dance program lead pencil. They were photographed in spirals around the cylinder, just like the spiral sound wave records of the phonograph.

Edison was being controlled with extraordinary persistence by that phonograph idea. From a little scratch in the wax cylinder he could fill the ear with sound. From an almost equally tiny record he was determined to fill the eye with pictures viewed through a microscope over the little cylinder.

Together Edison and Dickson got this cylinder motion picture machine to work well enough to know that it did not offer an important probability of success.

The labor got tedious and trying. The workshop vapored of high tension. This playtime job was getting serious.

Edison, who had made machines that crushed five ton boulders into dust like clods in the hands of a gardener, was all but stumped by a silly little device for making pictures that would dance.

For hours he would sit in abstraction, scratch pad in hand, puzzling over the picture. He sketched out one notion after another, discarding as rapidly as the thoughts grew, tossing the crumpled drawings away. There was a lot of tugging at his left eyebrow in that peculiar nervous mannerism of the inventor's moods of concentration.

Presently a better notion would come, a swift moment of rough drawing, and then Dickson would get instruction to "try this."

And the rough sketches would be formally pasted into the Edison experiment record books on the motion picture, and the work started.

Edison stuck to his task with grim tenacity.

He was making very little progress. He drew, without stint, upon the reservoirs of his energy, which, though apparently unlimited, seemed prodigal even to those who knew his appetite for work.

The cylinder machine would make pictures, but they were exceedingly poor pictures. Again and again, after each defeat, the attack was renewed with unabated ardor.

The first acting for the motion pictures took place before that absurd little phonograph that was trying to be a camera.

And the first actor was Fred Ott, a mechanic and member of the staff, chosen because he was the jester of the works. There were two Otts on the staff, John F. and Fred. And since Fred was the first of all motion picture actors, it is perhaps an obligation to history to set down how he happened there.

A number of years before, when Edison's labors were concentrated on the third floor of a little frame building in Newark, John F. Ott, a mechanic, wandered into the room where Edison was working over a machine, disheveled and stained of shop dirt. Ott did not know Edison, and it probably would have been of no importance to him if he had.

"What do you want?" Edison asked without looking up.

"Work."

"Can you make this work?" Edison pointed to a heap of junk in a corner.

"Yes."

"Are you sure?"

"You needn't pay me if I don't."

Ott started in. He did not know what the machine was and he did not ask foolish questions. He tinkered until it was all in one piece. It proved to be a dynamo, the first he had seen. He made it work.

That job brought the Otts into the Edison organization and the historic beginnings of the motion picture. Fred Ott was the merry one. He laughed the loudest at Edison's funny stories and had some of his own.

Ott, first of all film stars, has officially told his own story of how he behaved before the camera on those historic occasions. The authenticity of this is guaranteed, under the oath of Ott, sworn as a witness in the case of Thomas A. Edison vs. The American Mutoscope and Biograph Company, in equity No. 8289, before the day of picture press agents.

"I had a white cloth wound around me and then a little belt to tie it in around the waist so as not to make it too baggy—look like a balloon—and then tied around the head; and then I made a monkey of myself."

So the motion picture was born in slapstick comedy, staged in that solemn laboratory. Many a little cylinder full of the gyrations of the monkey-shining Mr. Ott was recorded. Those were "the follies of 1888."

Edison was meanwhile puzzling considerably over photographic matters. Some place in Germany some one was making microscopic pictures of people and buildings, mounting them in tiny tubes with a speck of a lens to magnify them. They became popular toys. And the little pictures, no bigger than a pin head, were perfect. But never could the researchers find just how they were made.

At last the cylinder motion picture was abandoned. There must be a bigger picture, which meant other methods, Edison decided.

Edison did not concern himself with glass plates as the other experimenters had. It is Edison's great characteristic to have what seems to many an instinctive knowledge and discernment concerning materials. He did not have to go up against the limitations of heavy fragile plates in order to recognize them.

The next step was the great one. From John Carbutt, a maker of photographic materials, Dickson obtained some heavy celluloid sheets coated with a photographic emulsion. Carbutt was trying to supplant breakable glass with tough celluloid for general photographic purposes. Only very short bands or strips of this material were obtainable. A new picture device was made with a stop motion and shutter to open the lens and expose the band step by step eight or ten times a second. The stop motion was primitive indeed, just an escapement like that on the balance wheel of a watch, working on notches along the upper edge of the celluloid strip.

By this time the plant at West Orange had been completed and over there Room Five of Edison's private laboratory building was dedicated to the motion picture, and kept locked by night and by day. Workmen came and went on call to do their little parts with various machines. Only Edison and Dickson had access at will. It was the beginning of a profound secrecy about the motion picture which continued for many and many years after there were no secrets to be kept.

Fred Ott and a fellow worker, C. H. Kayser, were the members of the general laboratory staff most often called in for mechanical assistance in the building of the successive experimental machines. The stand of an old Singer sewing machine became the pedestal upon which the tentative mechanisms got their try-outs.

The notches on the top of the celluloid band gave way to a line of perforated holes, and the stop motion device became a Geneva cross and spur wheel which engaged the film by jerks, one jerk per revolution of the wheel. Longer bands were sought by cementing strips cut from the Carbutt celluloid plates together end to end.

Then when Dickson found that the bands did not run very steadily he added another row of perforations at the bottom. This was exceedingly close to the motion picture film of to-day. But the celluloid was heavy, and it was in awkwardly short lengths.

One enduring thing, the present world's standard of size in motion picture photography, was established in these experiments on the slabs of Carbutt celluloid. Every motion picture made today is photographed precisely to the same scale as those monkey-shining pictures of Fred Ott. The motion picture was measured before it was really born.

Edison's subsequent experiments, his perfected machines and those of the competitors and successors who came after, all in due time, adopted the same standard.

Several motion picture experts and inventors have published elaborate accounts of how they set the world's standard gauge for the films. Presumably they are unaware that pictures of that gauge have been in existence for about thirty-nine years. It was all decided in Room Five, even down to the four little perforations which stand at each side of each tiny frame of the motion picture.

A better vehicle for the pictures had to be found. Experiments were made with strips made of thin coatings of collodion, the same sort of stuff called liquid court-plaster, with which one paints a wounded finger. The collodion strips were rough in texture and fragile, but they were good enough to demonstrate the principle.

Now we have come to the late summer of the year of 1889.

Down from Rochester, New York, came word to Edison that George Eastman, the kodak maker, had achieved a thin, flexible film base for photographic emulsions. Eastman was trying to solve the problem of "roller photography." Glass plates were impractical for a popular instrument. Eastman wanted a machine without cumbersome plate holders and fragile glass. He was trying to get photography for the amateur down to a mere press-the-button operation. He had achieved a half-way satisfactory result with rolls of paper coated with a detachable emulsion. But the kodaks had to be sent back to the Rochester plant to be unloaded and to have the pictures processed. This was too complicated. A new material was to be the answer.

Back of this quest is another involved history, too long for more than a glimpse here. An interesting overlapping of the old graphic art and the new one yet to be born was involved in the genesis of film. The scene of the beginning was the studio of John McDougall in Newark, father of Walt McDougall, *New York World* cartoonist. McDougall was a photographer and a painter of miniatures. Celluloid had been newly invented. McDougall was interested in it, not as a photographic base but as a substitute for ivory in the painting of his tiny portraits.

McDougall's studio, three floors up, in Broad street, was a rendezvous for many creative minds, among them George Inness and Thomas Moran, painters, and Thomas Dunn English, the author of "Ben Bolt." This group of talkers and chess players included the Rev. Hannibal Goodwin, rector of the House of Prayer, a fashionable Newark church. Goodwin had a flair for amateur chemistry, and in the attic of the rectory still standing in Newark one may see the acid stains on the walls of his workshop.

Goodwin gave some interested attention to the celluloid sheets on which McDougall painted. He began to tinker with the then new zinc etching process of making printing plates. This led him into etching photography and resulted in his invention of a film base to take the place of glass plates in the camera. The film was not celluloid but a related nitrocellulose compound. May 2, 1887, Goodwin applied for a patent.

Eastman, struggling with the problems of stripping emulsion bearing surfaces from his paper kodak rolls, also hit upon a material resulting from the drying of a varnish made of wood alcohol and "soluble cotton" painted on glass. It was flexible, transparent and tough, answering his kodak purposes perfectly. This appears to have been discovered early in 1889. Now about August 1, of that year, Eastman put in operation a small plant, his Court Street factory, where the film was made on a table, a hundred feet long and covered with sheets of plate glass cemented together.

When Eastman filed his claims in the U. S. Patent office he was found to be in interference with Hannibal Goodwin and a complex line of controversy ensued. The Goodwin Camera & Film Company passed to the control of the Anthony & Scoville Company, later the Ansco, which in 1902 brought an infringement suit against Eastman. Eleven years more were to pass before the action ended, and while it pended Goodwin died. Although not a part of the motion picture wars, the Goodwin-Eastman suit exerted some dramatic influences on the destiny of the embattled screen.

Having heard of the new Eastman film Edison dispatched Dickson to Rochester for information and a sample. The first

EDISON'S FIRST MOTION PICTURE machine, when he set out to record action on a cylinder akin to his phonograph — at right, a section of a cylinder motion picture record in 1888.

GEORGE EASTMAN, whose solution of the kodak's problem of "roller photography" with film in 1889 produced the material which Edison needed for the motion picture.

Edison purchase memorandum remitting for a prior delivery of the first motion picture film in the world is still in the files of the Eastman Kodak Company at Rochester, under date of September 2, 1889.

Edison now examined the Eastman film in Room Five.

"That's it—we've got it—now work like hell."

With that material in hand, Edison knew that the solution of the picture puzzle was but a matter of details. There were no important difficulties ahead now. Edison began to think more about the phonograph and other things then. He felt relieved.

Edison interests abroad needed the stimulus of some personal attention and there was time for even a bit of a joy ride. So it came that, after leaving a mass of instructions in Room Five, he said good-bye to West Orange. When the palatial *La Burgoyne* sailed from New York on the third of August, 1889, Edison stood at the rail waving good-bye toward the dock, clutching a miniature phonograph, delivered at the last moment, under his arm.

That was the year of the Paris Exposition. Edison had a hundred-thousand-dollar exhibit of his works there, centered about the marvels of his incandescent electric light. Edison took a look at the Eiffel Tower, sundry titled persons and some art galleries of note now that the subject of pictures was interesting him.

Europe did not excite Edison very much. In a letter home he shrewdly observed that the much-lauded old masters of the galleries seemed to depend for their value on the rarity of them and the long purses of collectors. To his eyes the old art was dead. And well it might be!

If in all the world there was a man with a right to smile at the labors of Leonardo, Rubens, Hals, Rembrandt, Goya and all those re-creators in paint, that man was Thomas Alva Edison, with his secret of Room Five. He was destined to be at once their heir and their successor—the picture maker to a new and faster age.

Edison had put a blazing electric light into Athanasius Kircher's *Magia Catoptrica* of two hundred and fifty years before, and now he was about to put the essence of life into its shadows on the wall.

Dickson was back home in the House of the Wizard, following instructions to "work like hell." Word came from him that he had something to show his chief.

CHAPTER FOUR

IT MOVES!—OCTOBER 6, 1889

EDISON sailed again, from Havre, having enough of Europe and eager for home and the workshops at West Orange. He walked ashore on the familiar soil of New Jersey on the bright Sunday morning of October 6, 1889, and went directly to the laboratories to look things over.

There was a surprise in store for the Wizard of Orange. The sanctuary of Room Five, dedicated to the problem of the motion picture, had been moved.

For weeks before Edison's departure Dickson had been asking for bigger quarters. "Don't need it," Edison decided.

With Edison over the sea, Dickson had been able to prevail on his good friend Charles Batchelor, left in charge of Edison plant affairs, to authorize a special photographic building. It was duly erected in September, 1889, at a total cost of $516.64. The movies were beginning to run into money, even before they moved much.

Dickson proudly led his chief into this new building, inwardly trembling a bit at his audacity at having it built and struggling at the same time to suppress elation at what he had to show.

Up in the dark attic of the building was the triumphant mystery, the motion picture machine with the destiny of a world industry and the solution of the problem of the ages in it.

Precisely what it was that Dickson showed Edison on this occasion remains an issue between their differing testimonies. The reader may arrive at his own conclusions, after considering the evidences.

In a book on the life of Edison, written by William Kennedy Laurie Dickson and Antonia Dickson, published in 1895, with a foreword of approval from Edison, occurs this paragraph:

> . . . The crowning point of realism was attained on the occasion of Mr. Edison's return from the Paris Exposition of 1889, when Mr. Dickson himself stepped out on the screen, raised his hat and smiled, while uttering the words of greeting, "Good morning, Mr. Edison, glad to see you back. I hope you are satisfied with the kineto-phonograph."

In this statement Dickson is quite explicit in setting forth that there was a projected picture on a screen—and, what is less important, that it was synchronized with a phonograph record, making a talking picture.

One must, however, measure these glowing words with a certain cautious recognition of the enthusiasm of some inventive craftsmen. Dickson, like many another zealous workman, has at times written of his anticipations in terms that declare them already attained. This is exemplified in another booklet from his pen published in 1896 in which, discussing the new marvel of screen pictures, he says: "Projected stereoscopically the results are even more realistic, as those acquainted with that class of phenomena may imagine, and a pleasing rotundity is apparent which in ordinary photographic displays is conspicuous by its absence." One would imply that Dickson had achieved stereoscopic projection. But thirty years have passed without a satisfactory attainment of the result he described in 1896.

And as for that day of Edison's return from Paris in 1889, subsequent events will prove that any picture projection that may have been attained then was far indeed from a solution of the screen problem.

The time was coming when this priority of projection from film was to be an all important issue in a war of patent litigation, and yet in spite of that, but under complicated conditions, Edison did not claim it when the time came.

Edison took the stand in his own behalf in an action against the American Mutoscope & Biograph Company, about eleven years later, and this paragraph from Dickson's book was read to him as part of a question.

"There was no screen," was Edison's dry answer.

In considering this answer, however, one must weigh also the fact that when it was made, Dickson's interests and Edison's no longer coincided. Dickson, by events to which we shall come in time, had become aligned with the defendant Biograph concern.

We shall also come upon the fact that for commercial reasons Edison did not for years after believe that the motion picture should be projected on the screen. He opposed the making of a projection machine from the beginning, and adhered to his position until, in effect, the motion picture business had been taken away from him.

It seems reasonably certain that Dickson had two demonstrations for Edison, one an attempt at a projector throwing a picture on the screen, and the other a little black box with a hole in it into which one peered through a lens directly at the speeding film. The probabilities are that Edison found the projected picture imperfect and unpleasantly inadequate and that the peep show machine gave to his eye a more immediately satisfactory result. Swift decisions firmly held are also characteristic of Edison's work.

Anyway, Edison certainly did pin his faith and fortunes on the peep show.

Dickson now, after the lapse of thirty-five years, in the face of all of the claims and controversies, remains insistent that the projection of a picture was attained in the Edison laboratories by him as early as 1888.

In a letter to the author of this history, under date of May 4, 1924, written from Boulogne-sur-Mer, France, Dickson, after describing the preliminaries, says:

> . . . The results of this work led next to the endeavor to synchronize the phonograph with this machine and project on to a screen 8' x 10'—which would have been more of course if the studio had been larger.
>
> We often projected without the phonograph, and these tests or exhibits were made before many witnesses and scientists. The synchronization was remarkably good, as the phonograph motor governed the film stop-motion device, which made it impossible for one to get ahead or behind the other. This was done electrically from an auxiliary commutator on the phono-motor.
>
> The taking camera was used to project all our pictures, or rather a duplicate machine. The taking sprocket wheel slipped off and a very slightly smaller one substituted to allow for the slight but perceptible shrinkage of the positive film—otherwise the perforations in film would not match the sprockets.
>
> So we have it that we projected in 1888 (end) with or without the phonograph, and to make money, as then thought, a nickel in the slot machine was put out by the hundreds to pay for these experiments. . . .

There is no equivocation about Dickson's flat assertion of projection in 1888 and 1889.

It becomes significant, too, to quote a direct statement of Edison, made in a marginal notation on a draft of this manuscript in December, 1921, in which he wrote, dealing with another issue:

> The facts are that Dickson and I had a machine projecting on a screen 5 ft. square at the time we were making peep machines. . . .

Seeking to settle this small but interesting point once and for all the author in June, 1924, addressed a special inquiry to Edison. In the course of his reply Edison said:

I am very sure that we projected motion pictures on the screen before we stopped making the peep hole machine. One of the peep hole machines was changed so that it would project a picture about twelve inches square. Then a large screen was made and the camera was used. This screen was five feet square. Geneva stop was probably badly made, as the picture was quite unsteady. . . . I can not remember the case where I said there was no screen. If I made any such answer, I certainly misunderstood the question.

It is thus certain that the Edison plant had some sort of projection inside of the six years before the motion picture went on the screen for the public.

It was inevitable that Edison, following upon his phonograph experiences, should consider the recorder also an instrument of reproduction, and in an obscure and abandoned patent application, No. 403,535, involving the stereoscopic picture idea, filed immediately following his camera patent, one discovers a paragraph discussing the camera as a projector, in 1891.

The date of this Edison projection, as between 1889 and '91, does not matter. It was the first in the world anyway, no matter how imperfect or unsatisfactory it may have been.

The outstanding fact was that Edison did not put the picture on the screen for the public because he did not want to, and did not consider it profitable to do so.

External influences were, after a while, coming to make Dickson ardently anxious to project. Much of subsequent screen history traces to that.

The motion picture was going to insist on the birth of the screen. The wish of the race, seen in the struggles of Leonardo, Athanasius Kircher, Daguerre and their successors down the years, was not to be denied, even by the Wizard.

In Dickson's writings of 1895, in his subsequent utterances

and testimonies, one acutely familiar with the detailed movement of events in the early day of the motion picture can discover evidences of a struggle. It is obvious that Dickson is
and has been for some three decades torn by a fast sense of
loyalty to Edison and an internal desire to assure himself, and
appear, as nearly as might be, the creator of the motion picture. No man could have been more circumspect in the form
of his expressions than Dickson, constantly proclaiming Edison's priorities, while alongside and under the proclamation one
is never allowed to forget that Dickson also labored in Room
Five.

In this suppressed issue between Edison and Dickson the
basic facts are clear at least this far: the fundamental ideas
were Edison's, while the details of execution were worked out
by their combined efforts. No one, not even the men themselves, can say which of them it was who solved the most of the
detailed problems. That is, at best, hardly more than a
quibble. The motion picture was one of the problems which
Edison assigned to himself and his staff.

It would be most unfair to assume from this that Edison has
ever by any gesture or expression sought to minimize the value
of Dickson's work. To the contrary he has, of record, given
Dickson decided recognition. In the foreword of a quaint
booklet on their labors, issued in 1896, we find reproduced in
Edison's own penmanship and over his signature:

> I believe that in coming years by my work and that of Dickson,
> Muybridge, Marié and others who will doubtlessly enter the field
> that grand opera can be given at the Metropolitan Opera House at
> New York without any material change from the original, and
> with artists and musicians long since dead.

One notes also that there was the vision of the screen in that
paragraph, too, but Edison saw it much farther ahead in the
future than it was in fact. He was thinking how slowly indeed

(A) Early Edison efforts when the first films ran through the camera horizontally.

(B) The first motion picture film order, from Edison to Eastman reading:

Eastman Dry Plate Co.   Sept. 2nd '89

Dear Sir: —

Enclosed please find sum of $2.50 P.O.O. due you for one roll Kodak film for which please accept thanks — I shall try same today & report . . . it looks splendid — I never succeeded in getting this substance in such straight long pieces.

Sincerely yrs.
W. K. L. Dickson

P.S.—Can you coat me some rolls with your highest sensitometer — please answer

KINETOSCOPE No. 1, built by Edison in 1889,
when the fifty-foot films ran on a spool bank,
long before the reel was born.

the public had taken to the telephone, the typewriter and many other new services of invention. Edison did not and could not know that the motion picture was really but the realization of the oldest effort of the race of man—the visual re-creation of events, therefore far from being new in the sense of devices serving younger desires.

The Edison peep show machine was christened the Kinetoscope, and the camera wherewith the pictures were made was the Kinetograph. The Kinetoscope was a simple mechanism operated by a battery impelled electric motor by which the film, approximately fifty feet in length, was run between an electric light and a rapidly revolving shutter which exposed the picture by flashes to the viewing lens into which the spectator peered. The film was wound in an endless loop over a series of small rollers, known as a spool bank. The reel of today and methods of handling it were unborn. In the peep show machine the film ran continuously.

Because of the small area of the film to be illuminated, the tremendous loss of light incurred by the necessary shutter action could be suffered without losing the picture. The shutter opening had to be small to make the movement of the film so slight as not to blur the image for the eye as it raced past the lens. And at the same time the light had to be so intense that the impression of each little flash lasted until the next revolution of the shutter exposed the next image of the film.

The motion picture on the screen in terms of something approaching the perfected projection of to-day, the mechanical basis of the film art as we know it, lay still some years ahead on that day when Edison landed back in New Jersey to see the fruit of the labors in Room Five.

But the great vital step had been taken. The Edison labors had brought the camera up to the ability to record motion.

The Kinetograph camera took its motion pictures in true records of motion, on strips of film as much as fifty feet in length, sixteen images to the foot. In the work of Sellers, Heyl and the Isaacs experiments the making of a motion record of the screen had been held to the limitations of the still camera, awkwardly and ineffectively applied to the problem of motion. Sellers and Heyl posed their pictures in what they thought were instants of motion. The Isaacs method used by Muybridge required a tremendous battery of cameras. The Edison Kinetograph with its running film fifty feet long did perfectly what would have been imperfectly done in eight hundred poses of the Sellers or Heyl pictures or by eight hundred cameras controlled by the Isaacs method.

It is important to note this limitation of length to fifty feet. The reel of motion pictures of to-day is approximately one thousand feet in length, and many pictures have been presented in twelve such reels, or two and a quarter miles of film. This limitation to fifty feet existed because the camera operated with jerky, intermittent motion as it stepped the film past the lens. These jerks against the weight of the film had to overcome the inertia of the roll at each jerk. If the film was much longer than fifty feet the jerk would break it.

But for a while this fifty feet was ample. The motion picture was just beginning to speak, and one syllable of fifty feet was enough. As soon as the need came this trivial mechanical obstacle was immediately overcome, and by agencies which made a deal of screen history, as we shall observe.

Meanwhile, mark you well this Edison peep show Kinetoscope. Every strand in the thread of motion picture destiny runs through it. It is the inescapable link between the gropings of the past and the attainments of the present. Every motion picture machine, every motion picture enterprise, every motion picture personality, screen star or magnate of the screen theatre, can be traced to some connection growing out of the little black box that Edison dubbed the Kinetoscope. This is one of the absolute facts of the history of the motion picture. It must be stated most positively, in view of the hundred and one contrary and unfounded assertions of other claimants.

It is provable that there is not now and never has been subsequent to the year 1888 any motion picture film machine whatsoever of any relation to the screen art of today that is not descended by traceable steps from the Kinetoscope.

So at last in the year 1889 we have come to the solution of the motion picture problem. Edison had done again what he had done so often before and has done so often since. He had taken a laboratory endeavor, confusedly picking its slow way through the tedious mazes of evolution, and led it quickly across the final step into practical workable fact. In the motion picture he had done what in varying degrees he had done with the dynamo, the telephone, and the typewriter. His has been the magic touch of matter-of-fact practicality. He makes dreams come true by making things work. Therefore he is the Wizard.

For a considerable time yet after this homecoming in '89, the motion picture was to stand aside while Edison concerned him-self with other things which he felt to be more important, es-pecially the phonograph.

The Kinetoscope and its solution of the problem of the ages made no very deep impress on Edison. Like other wonders worked out and pigeonholed in his laboratory, it could wait. The secret of the radio was already sleeping there among the pigeonholes, never to be awakened in West Orange.

The phonograph was the thing at the moment. Edison wanted that established first, before he offered the seeing ma-chine which was to supplement the ear message of the hearing machine.

This concentration of Edison's interest on the hearing ma-chine, the phonograph, brings a psychological reflection. Edi-son was growing deaf. Therefore the wish-to-hear kept him laboring on the device which was to give a new hearing to all the world. One remembers the parallel in the work of Ferdinand Plateau of Ghent, slowly growing blind and fighting through the deepening shadows of his twilight to give the world a new seeing.

In these men the Wish, accented by their infirmities, is per-sonified. Each hungered most for the thing he was losing. Here in their labors we see the creative power of the Wish, the will for gratification which makes Man the supreme go-getter. It is a thrilling coincidence that Edison, building upon the seeing efforts of Plateau, brought to realization the blind man's

Wish as an adjunct to his own materialization of the deaf man's Wish. Edison wanted the motion picture only as an accessory to the phonograph.

The phonograph was going out to the newly founded trade. Slot machine parlors, where one might drop a nickel, put the tubes to his ears and hear the band play, were springing up in the cities. Out in the lesser places entertainers soon were taking to the road with phonograph entertainments. The phonograph was a sensation.

Among those early day itinerant phonograph entertainers was the late Lyman Howe of Wilkes-Barre, Pa. On a circuit through the smaller towns of his territory Howe gave phonograph entertainments in connection with Ladies' Aid Societies and church boards, dividing the profits with the churches. He was pioneering for a motion picture business of renown, but he little suspected it then.

At about the same time over in Paris, an enterprising Frenchman heard about the wonderful Edison phonograph that had come to London. He was busy, but he had a young friend, one Charles Pathé, who had little to do. He pressed a bundle of francs in Pathé's hand and told him to go to London and get one of those talking machines. It was natural indeed that there should be a market for talking machines in France, the home of conversation. M. Pathé came back with a phonograph, and it was a vast success. He made more trips to London, this time on his own account, and built up a phonograph business that survives yet. But more important still to Pathé, he established a contact with the genius of Edison and the greater thing to come.

There were scientific whisperings about and wee bits of news of the Edison kinetograph and the kinetoscope, camera and viewing machine, in a few publications meanwhile. *Harper's Weekly*, in the issue of June 13, 1891, came out with a two-page spread on the subject of the invention, discussed in glowing words.

Meanwhile Edison came to the opinion that after all secrecy could hardly protect his invention much longer, and so August 24, 1891, he made application for a United States patent.

At this time it was suggested to Edison, as a matter of routine at least, that perhaps application should also be made for foreign patents, including France and England.

"How much will it cost?" Edison asked casually.

"Oh, about $150."

Edison waved the suggestion aside. "It isn't worth it."

In this one sees a striking parallel to his attitude toward the disc phonograph patents, repeated here with the motion picture.

Of course there was, again, a modifying element in the situation. It had been Edison's experience that the more patents he took out abroad the more he lost. Foreign patents sometimes have an effect of advertising possibilities to infringers and pirates.

But if Edison, on that day in August of 1891, had said "Yes," he might have put himself in a position to get many millions of dollars in the foreign field, and have changed the whole course of European and American screen history.

What Edison thought of the peep show Kinetoscope, as compared with the projected picture, is indicated by the fact that his patent application concerned itself with the peep show machine only. He ignored the screen possibilities.

Putting aside considerations of Edison's neglect of his prospects and rights, the sum total of his failure to patent even the Kinetoscope abroad undoubtedly was ultimately to make for the earlier progress of the motion picture art. It left borrowers and improvers of his idea abroad free to go ahead when their time came.

After this application for a patent was filed Dickson went on, intermittently, with experimentation in the little photographic building at West Orange.

The project remained rather inactive. Dickson now and then made pictures and tried out films. The Eastman researchers at Rochester were striving for better quality, nearer and nearer to the ideal requirements of the Edison experiments. Both were making progress. Now and then samples of another kind came from the Anthony-Scoville concern, working with the formulas of the Rev. Hannibal Goodwin. Eastman's stock was preferred.

The Kinetoscope was, then, not on Edison's mind for long at a time. It was something that he might show a favored friend among those who so often came to the haunts of the "wizard" looking for wonders. But there were other things more vital pressing on the busy scientist's attention. His interests were growing steadily in many directions and business, as personified by his various departmental and business managers, was urging and demanding attentions of him that he would doubtless rather have given to the laboratory. The phonograph business was in trouble. Then, too, this Kinetoscope was after all a toy. It was not a part of Edison's view of the larger scheme of things, the world where power, electricity, and light were battling to conquer new continents of development and bring natural forces to the service of man.

It is simple enough now to look back and smile at Edison thus casually neglecting the institution that was within a quarter of a century to prove the only real rival the printing press has ever known. It is very simple looking back—but in that day Edison saw farther ahead in the motion picture than any other man in the world, even though he saw hardly at all.

This Kinetoscope, it must be borne in mind, was not the motion picture as we know it now, but only its immediate ancestor, the little moving picture in a box into which one person at a time could look.

And by reason of his preoccupation with other things, or his indifference to it, or some of both, this was nearly as far as Edison was to go with the motion picture as an inventor.

There is no knowing how long the Kinetoscope, with the secret of the living picture locked in it, might have slept in the Edison laboratories if it had not by chance been exposed to eyes alert for commercial opportunity. Business, the simple desire to make money, was soon to become a force in the evolution of the picture, just as it has always been the driving factor of all those activities which embroider our civilization with Things.

Among those who went to West Orange on occasion to visit the Wizard was Thomas Lombard of the North American Phonograph Company, formed to exploit Edison's phonograph for commercial uses as a dictating machine to take the place of the stenographer. Lombard saw the Kinetoscope with its marvel of living pictures and became vastly interested. He prevailed upon Edison to contemplate an agreement for the exploitation of this device at such time as it might be ready for the market.

The motion picture was about to be thrust upon the world for the next stage of its evolution.

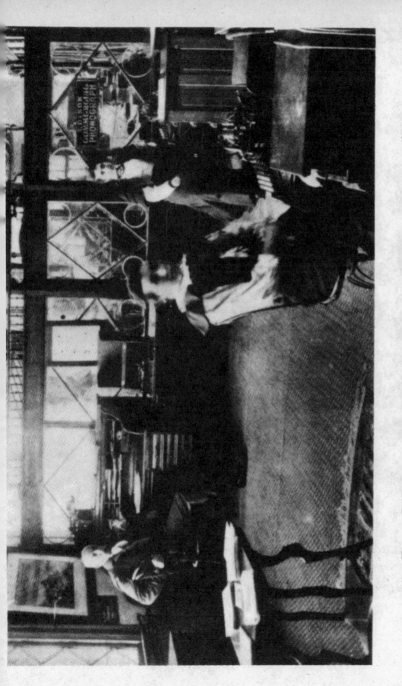

Thomas R. Lombard — at left — the first man to see commercial opportunity in the motion picture machine he had discovered in Edison's laboratory — Pictured here in the office of the World's Fair exhibit of the Edison phonograph in 1893, awaiting the Kinetoscopes which never arrived.

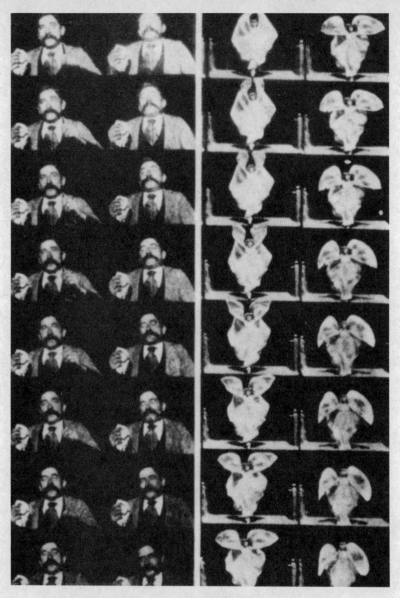

FRED OTT'S SNEEZE, the first close-up ever made, photographed by W. K. L. Dickson at the Edison "Black Maria" studio—at right—Annabelle-the-Dancer in the *Serpentine*, pictured by Edison for the Kinetoscope.

CHAPTER SIX

WONDERS OF THE WORLD'S FAIR

WE have come down to the year of 1891, the eve of the four hundredth anniversary of the landing of Columbus. Mighty preparations were in progress for the great Columbian Exposition in Chicago. By a somewhat indirect route Columbus, an accredited discoverer of America, became posthumously also an agency in the discovery of the empire of the screen. Let us trace the chain of events and men.

John Boyd Thatcher of New York, one time governor and a person of social and political prominence in that day, was chosen chairman of the Awards Committee of the Columbian Exposition. Frank R. Gammon, who had been interested in the introduction of the phonograph, became Thatcher's chief assistant in this weighty matter of medals and ribbons of the World's Fair awards. Thomas R. Lombard was much engaged in giving the phonograph an impressive display at the Fair.

Lombard was still filled with enthusiasm about the living pictures of the Kinetoscope, showing Fred Ott at his monkeyshines and W. K. L. Dickson lifting his hat. Lombard talked often and earnestly to Gammon and in turn to Norman Charles Raff of Canton, Ohio, brother-in-law of Gammon.

Raff, young and aggressive, had recently come out of a colorful experience in the mining fields of the Southwest. He was born on the main street of destiny.

Only a year or so before he had a finger in the shaping of the early steps of a great unborn romance of oil. Raff was sleeping in a room back of his bank in a little corrugated iron shack on a dusty hillside in remote Arizona when deep in the night he was aroused by a rapping and summons. He lighted his lamp with some trepidation and invited his caller to enter. He was Charles R. Canfield, then a prospector wandering among the hope holes of the desert.

"I'm busted and I can't get any more powder or grub on credit," Canfield explained. "But I've hit the color, and it looks good. I haven't any other security, but I've got to have a hundred dollars."

Raff looked him over and opened the strong box. The next day the strike came, and Canfield christened his mine "The Comstock" after the Comstock lode of classic fame. Three hundred thousand dollars in gold out of that hole went East through Raff's bank in the next month. Canfield sold out and, with a lawyer friend, from down the gulch, Edward L. Doheny, went on west to California, where they invested Comstock gold in a livery stable. A farmer with a load of black and odorous mud on his wagon put up there for the night. Doheny and Canfield smelled the mud and bought the farm for $2,500. The well they drilled became the Gray Goose, the most famous in all the California oil fields.

Raff had seen enough of the whims of chance in the West to make him willing to listen to Lombard's glowing words of promise about the new and yet unknown Edison marvel, the living pictures.

"You ought to go down and see him about it," Lombard insisted. Raff went.

This Norman C. Raff of '93 was a vastly impressive person of most dignified mien, older then by far than he ever was after. He registered at the Waldorf and strode Fifth avenue in an elegant otterskin great-coat, purchased in San Francisco. The otter coat was thrill and pride of the Avenue the day of its entry. And since the financier, yet in his early twenties, camouflaged his youth behind a heavy beard of the design affected by French statesmen, he was suspected of being a foreign nobleman, incognito. The genial greeter behind the Waldorf's registration desk made bold to call the visitor from the West "Count," and the name stuck. It went rippling up and down the Avenue as the otter coat passed in review.

Then when Mrs. Raff heard an echo of this rumor concerning the Count of Canton, the otter coat went into the mothballs. The same Norman C. Raff until his death at Orlando, Fla., in 1925, came on occasion from his home in Canton, Ohio, to stop a while at the Waldorf-Astoria.

Raff went over the Hudson and the meadows of Jersey in those days of '93 to see the Wizard of Orange and his amazing picture machine. Negotiations between Edison and Raff for the rights of sale for the Kinetoscope resulted, followed by the formation of the Kinetoscope Company, including Raff, Lombard and Gammon.

The Columbian Exposition was about to open and they were eager to introduce their wondrous machine there. It was the prime opportunity to plant the seed of a national and world distribution.

But Edison had supplies of neither machines nor film pictures for them. He promised to rush them through. The opening of the Fair in Chicago was delayed and it seemed possible that a battery of Kinetoscopes could be ready.

The first day of February, 1893, a studio for picture making was completed at a cost of $637.67. It was the world's first motion picture studio. Nothing like it had ever been seen before. Also nothing like it has ever been seen since. This studio was swung bridge fashion from a pivot post. William Kennedy Laurie Dickson spoke of it as "The Kinetographic Theatre." The rest of the Edison staff called it the "Black Maria." It took its name from the current patois for the patrol wagon, a somber vehicle more familiar to the generality of folks in those quaint days when well liquored persons preserved the custom of trying to go home. The Black Maria was designed to permit the swinging stage to follow the light of the sun. The sincere whole-hearted photography of that primal day demanded maximum contrast. The performer stood in the full glare of the little sunlit stage, against a shadow-boxed background as black as Sunday night in a coal mine. The resulting picture was hard and sharply defined, like a jig saw pattern. Blending middle tones and aerial perspective were undreamed refinements of the art to come many labored years ahead.

Now for the first time in the history of the world a demand for motion picture talent arose. The studio had to have somebody to photograph. Mary Pickford was not born yet and Charles Chaplin was only three years old.

Fred Ott, the home talent comedian of the Edison staff, who had posed for the camera through the years of experimental work, was called to the stage.

Ott rejoiced in a handsome moustache of the magnificent Texas pattern, with symphonic curves. Ott was robust, cheery and abundant. His sneeze was the pride of the Edison works. He could, and did, sneeze louder than any other white man born east of the Rockies.

Dickson placed Ott before the camera, stepped to the starting switch and ordered the star to sneeze. Nothing occurred.

The first studio property man was then and there sent out to acquire the first of all motion picture accessories—a box of snuff.

The snuff did not work, so they tried pepper. Ott's sneeze refused to ignite. They doubled the dose and mixed snuff and pepper. Again failure. Ott coughed, choked, gagged and melted into tears, but sneeze he could not. They struck the set and called it a day. The next day it worked.

Following the picturing of the sneeze Ott was photographed at a desk, while a mischievous office boy slipped up behind him and shook a pepper box. This was the embryo of scenario construction, the first screen gag, the first invented motivation of a sequence. Here also was the first close-up.

Dickson was cameraman, director and laboratory staff. Acts from the variety shows of those pre-vaudeville days supplied most of the material for the first Kinetoscope productions. Here again the motion picture was following phonograph precedent. The phonograph was taking the song hits of the music halls and variety theatres out to the arcades and phonograph parlors, popular brands of canned goods for a low priced patronage. The motion picture set out in the identical path, taking its material from the same source to purvey them to the same market.

As with the dawn of graphic art in the paleolithic age the motion picture first concerned itself mightily with animals. The Black Maria super-productions of the season of 1893–4 pictures conspicuously Professor Batty's troupe of trained bears, monkey acts, cats and trained dogs. Then infallibly true to primitive pattern it turned from bears to women, picturing the famous dancers of the day. The list of the first films includes Mae Lucas, solo dancer of *A Gaiety Girl*, a current stage hit playing at Daly's theatre in New York, the famous Annie Oakley, famed as *Little Sure Shot* of Buffalo Bill's Wild West show, a Sioux Indian dance and Colonel William Cody, (Buffalo Bill himself), Mme. Bertholdi, a contortionist, Eugene Sandow, the strong man, a slapstick barbershop scene, a Chinese laundry scene, two cock fights, a tooth extracting operation in which Dr. Colton, first to administer gas, demonstrated, and a bit from Hoyt's *Milk White Flag*, a contemporary stage success. All these pictures were fifty feet or less in length.

Most of those in this dramatic motley of the first to face the film camera are dead, among them the mighty Sandow, and

Buffalo Bill with his brave Sioux ghost dancers. Others are scattered and remote from their beloved Broadway. Mae Lucas, the hit of George Edwards' girl show, went from the season's success of '94 at Daly's theatre on a world tour of the company. When this chapter was written she was Mrs. B. L. Rhodes of Norfolk, Virginia, and Annie Oakley, still *Little Sure Shot* after thirty years, was operating a shooting school for society folk at Asheville in North Carolina.

A letter written by Mrs. Rhodes, the Mae Lucas of '94, gives some evidence that Edison was a bit of a crafty impresario, in spite of his scientific abstractions.

"Mr. Edison came to a performance of the *Gaiety Girl* at Daly's in September," says Mrs. Rhodes. "He saw a performance, came back stage, and requested that the 'Carnival Dancers,' Maggie Crosland, Lucy Murray—both since dead—and I, dance for him before his Kinetoscope. He stated that he had been able to produce pictures of people walking about and had reached the stage where he would like to attempt the picture of a person in rapid motion."

The speed capacity of Edison's camera had been amply demonstrated months before, but it was a neat idea to impress these stage folks with their opportunity to serve the wizardry of science.

The dancers consulted their traveling manager, J. A. E. Malone, about this weighty matter, and he in turn cabled George Edwards, the London manager of the show. The great name of Edison won and the next Sunday he sent carriages in which the dancing girls were driven to Orange to pose at the Black Maria.

There is a thrill of discovery in finding in the early correspondence a letter which tells of photographing "Miss Ruth Dennis" for the Kinetoscope. This was five years before that day in 1899 when she went with faltering courage to the stage

The Edison "Black Maria," the first motion picture studio in the world, built to make pictures for the peep show Kinetoscope — the studio revolved to follow the sunlight.

MAE LUCAS — Now Mrs. B. L. Rhodes of Norfolk, Virginia — at left, and her dancing partner in the *Gaiety Girls* at Daly's Theatre in New York in 1894, when Miss Lucas went to dance for the Edison Kinetoscope.

door of the old Republic theatre to seek Belasco and won a tiny dancing part in *Zaza* despite the fact she was from Brooklyn and had freckles. She is now Ruth St. Denis, and world famous. Her motion picture of '94 went to the public labelled with one word: "Dance."

The World's Fair at Chicago opened and closed again before the first Kinetoscopes and films were ready. It has been stated repeatedly by all of the writers of screen beginnings that the Edison peep show pictures were shown at the Columbian Exposition, and several pioneers have recollected and described the machines and the fair building in which they say they saw them in Chicago. But these statements are none the less incorrect. The Kinetoscopes were not yet completed. Raff was in Chicago waiting for them.

There were, however, a number of devices at the Fair which showed how closely the motion picture was crowding its way forward toward a part in the world's affairs. Among them was the Zoopraxoscope projecting Muybridge photographs from glass plates, including the famous running horse of the Palo Alto race track. Ottomar Anschütz's complicated electrical Tachyscope mentioned in an earlier chapter was also on display, operating as a slot machine. The Tachyscope gave one the joy of observing one of Herr Hagenbeck's best elephants waddle across a bit of the Tier Garten. But these picture machines, presented as sensational novelties of the day, had already been left behind in the march of motion picture progress.

The Muybridge and Anschütz pictures were merely casual bits of marvel among the thousand and odd marvels of the Fair. A few thousands saw the show in Zoopraxographical Hall where the Muybridge machine displayed jerky pictures of animal movements, the walk of the racoon, the wrinkling of a hog's skin, the beating heart of a dog, and the pace of a man afflicted with locomotor ataxia. It was highly scientific but no forerunner of *The Birth of a Nation* or *The Covered Wagon*.

The only result of the Muybridge showing was a neat certificate of honor from John Boyd Thatcher's Award Commission, reading:

> The photographs made by Mr. Edward Muybridge, under the auspices of the University of Pennsylvania, show with great elaboration and precision the locomotion and movements of animals, including man.

The Award Commission could little anticipate that its own secretary, Frank R. Gammon, was about to engage in the movement which would give the world a new art and language, born of a better execution of the idea in Zoopraxographical Hall.

By merest chance the Anschütz Tachyscope, itself just as far removed as the Muybridge device from any important part in the evolution of the motion picture art, came by this showing to have a bearing on history yet to be made.

Among the visiting, sight-seeing thousands in Chicago was Thomas Armat, a young man of cavalier stock, from Richmond, Virginia. He was engaged somewhat in real estate in the office of a cousin in Washington, D. C., but his heart was in scientific affairs. More especially he was interested in electricity and its application to traction. A brother, J. Hunter Armat, was with him. In a booth under an Illinois Central overhead crossing near the entrance of the fairgrounds, J. Hunter Armat came upon the sideshow of the Anschütz Tachyscope. He dropped a nickel and peeked. A moment later he looked up in excitement.

"Here, Tom, take a look at this thing—it's a wonder."

Thomas Armat invested a nickel in a glimpse of the Hagenbeck elephant.

"If you could connect that up with a magic lantern, it would make quite a show," Thomas Armat remarked as they turned their steps toward the Midway. It was a passing thought, due to reoccur later with large consequences to the motion picture.

Those were the happy days of long ago. The *Christopher Columbus*, the first whaleback leviathan of the Great Lakes, was making daily trips carrying wondering thousands. The famous Palmer House, resplendent in massive Victorian grandeurs with its lavish magnificence of a bar room paved with silver dollars, was the social capital, crest-stamped with the authority of having housed the Spanish Infanta. Mrs. Potter Palmer was the ascendant and right royal queen of all society west of the Hudson river and north of Louisville, entertaining royalty amid the plaudits of press and populace.

Rails and telegraph wires were webbing the open spaces of the continent. The last feeble Indian wars were being fought out with the meandering, unruly remnants of the red buffalo hunters of the plains. It was the day of sweeping skirts, when ladies had no legs whatever, and women had nothing else. In the theatres it was the great era of tragic drama, remarkable minstrelsy successes, and a great deal of most haughty and elevated opera and concert.

While the World's Fair went on, Norman C. Raff and his associates in the Kinetoscope Company waited impatiently for the shipment of machines from West Orange. But they were not forthcoming. Edison had more important things to do than to hurry up this trivial toy of the living picture.

Early the next spring, too late for the Fair, the first lot of Kinetoscopes was ready for shipment. The first ten of the peep show machines were shipped across the Hudson to Andrew M. Holland of Holland Brothers, who had come down from Ottawa, Ontario, to be the eastern agents of the Kinetoscope Company. Raff kept his headquarters in Chicago for the time, presumably because Thomas R. Lombard's interests centered there in the Investment Syndicate Company, 501–3 Chicago Stock Exchange. Lombard was the president of that concern.

The ten machines reached Holland Brothers on April 6, 1894, and on April 14 their Kinetoscope Parlor, the first of the hundreds to be scattered over the world, opened at 1155 Broadway, New York City.

Edison had now gone into the motion picture business. The industry of the films began then and there, 1155 Broadway, on April 14, 1894. There is a spot that might well be marked by a tablet of bronze.

By this time Edison had invested, according to his cost accounting, a total of precisely $24,118.04 in the motion picture business, between 1887 and April 1, 1894. He sold Kinetoscopes to Raff's concern at $200 each. They retailed at from $300 to $350.

Holland Brothers' Kinetoscope Parlor offering "the Wizard's latest invention" was a Broadway sensation. Long cues of patrons stood waiting to look into the peep hole machines and see the pictures that lived and moved. The front of the establishment was garnished with an illuminated electric dragon with fiery eyes. That was, of course, the symbol stamp of Edison wizardry supreme.

Early in May another shipment of Kinetoscopes and films went to Chicago, where Raff opened a peep show parlor in the Masonic Temple building, then Chicago's prided skyscraper. The machines stood banked in a row. The spectator paid his twenty-five cents admission, and passed down the line to peer into the peep holes, while an attendant switched on the machines one after another. Presently Edison supplied a nickel-in-the-slot attachment which eliminated the man at the switches.

The account books of this enterprise in the Masonic Temple

indicate that it was operated for a time by a subsidiary exhibition concern known as the International Novelty Company.

The articles of incorporation of the International Novelty Company repose among the archives of the State of Iowa, forgotten relics of the world's second motion picture corporation and the large hopes of remote investors of the long ago. It was the first day of September 1894 when Clara Cox of Omaha in the County of Douglass and the State of Nebraska affixed her notarial seal and attest to the fact that the incorporators of this half million dollar concern admitted their signatures to be "their voluntary act and deed." Erastus A. Benson, a prairie capitalist rejoicing in the dignity of Omaha's Benson Block building, Frank W. Carmichael, and O. C. Redick were the incorporators.

There is something dramatically forlorn about this picture company out on the wild Missouri, declaring that "it shall continue for fifty years," while "the principal place of transacting business of this corporation shall be in the City of Council Bluffs, County of Pottawattamie and State of Iowa."

Not many years before Council Bluff's major claim to fame had been as a terminus where one crossed the river to reach the Union Pacific's new steel trail over the Great American Desert. Here was the happy hunting ground of the "green goods men" with their facsimile greenbacks and their handsome gold bricks. Here was the rendezvous of lucky miners from the Black Hills and the Dakotas, and of the "road agents" who rode on their trails.

Now for one fleet moment Council Bluffs added the motion picture to its lore. But Council Bluffs held more promise of becoming a scenario than a film center. Its only claim for screen fame now is as the home of Harry Langdon, comedian. Before the year of 1895 was out the International Novelty Company had faded from view.

The purpose of the Kinetoscope Company was not primarily to conduct peep show parlors but to sell territorial rights on the business of the machines. The motion picture, born of Edison's phonograph efforts, was now following the pattern of his phonograph merchandising.

It became apparent that national distribution would have to be from New York. Broadway was then as now the amusement capital of the world. So Norman C. Raff removed his offices from the Masonic Temple building in Chicago to the Postal Telegraph building in New York. He ventured a six-months lease.

The territorial rights on the Kinetoscope began to sell, but meanwhile the company reserved for itself the most promising spots—in today's parlance, the metropolitan "first runs." They had parlors now in operation in New York and Chicago. They opened, on June 20, 1894, a parlor in San Francisco in conjunction with the phonograph parlor conducted there by Peter Biagacilupi, and another on June 26 on the Boardwalk in Atlantic City in connection with the Columbia Phonograph Company's phonograph parlor. In October and November they gave temporary exhibitions in Washington and Baltimore.

The motion picture film had made its début—in a peep show. From this day on, the motion picture was to follow a continuous line of development. The days of faltering steps and the lapses of intermittent effort were over. The spawn of the Kinetoscope was now being flung to the world.

CHAPTER SEVEN

BLACK'S PRE-FILM PICTUREPLAY

WHILE the motion picture was progressing with mincing steps in the peep show Edison Kinetoscope the sheer force of the evolution of expression presented the world with an interesting paradox—the birth of the photoplay upon the screen.

Bear in mind that the motion picture film had not yet reached the screen. Most emphatically the film did not yet even contemplate the screen.

And yet now came the screen photoplay.

This event of 1894 seems quite as remarkable as though the apple had come into being before the tree.

But if a paleontological botanist came upon a fossil apple in the apparently more ancient strata of the club-mosses he would dig deeper and eventually find the tree, revising the evolutionary time table as he dug. There are no accidents in evolution, no apples before the tree.

So now as we pick up our apple of the photoplay of '94, we must consider the roots and relics of expression discussed in the section devoted to the Pre-history of the screen. We shall find that this paradoxical photoplay which reached the screen before the film came is after all a most material substantiation of our view of the motion picture as an organic growth.

The agent of this curious new expression form, the pre-film photoplay, was Alexander Black, the same Alexander Black who is today best known as a novelist.

Black became the inventor, or rather the discoverer, of the photoplay in the years of 1893–4 in precisely the same period in which Edison was building the peep show machines which introduced the film picture to the public in Kinetoscope parlors.

It would have simplified the problem of the narrator and eased the tension of attention for the reader if the Black photoplay had actually antedated the Kinetoscope instead of paralleling it. But in its own complex way the work of Black had its roots far back of the Kinetoscope film and its fruits far ahead of it.

Black's movement toward the picture story on the screen began with his interest in the ordinary still camera, then a decidedly new and very novel device from the viewpoint of the public. The art of photography was only beginning to emerge from the professional laboratory into a general instrument of expression. Hand cameras, astonishing instruments "without legs," which could be carried about and used without a tripod, had just come into being in the early Nineties. It was discovered that actual photographs of all manner of everyday events, even to such astonishing things as snapshots of persons on the streets, could be made. The word snapshot was born of that day.

Every invention of wide public application finds its interpreters, just as the screen has created the motion picture critic and as radio has created an army of technical journalists of the broadcasting art. Alexander Black became the authoritative writer and speaker on the new wonders of the camera in the early Nineties.

Black was an enthusiastic amateur photographer, and his photography crept into his writing. He wrote for the newspapers and magazines about the wonders of photography and the delights of the new sport of snapshooting. We can probably with justice indict him as a progenitor of the race which the humor of two decades ago called "Kodak fiends."

The writing led Black, as the popular photographic authority, to the lecture platform. He addressed marvelling audiences of the time from the lyceum stages of the East, under the auspices of Major Pond, with a lecture entitled "Ourselves as Others See Us." It was, naturally, illustrated with stereopticon lantern slides of snapshots made by Black and other amateurs. He went gunning with his camera up and down the highways and byways of New York and spread the pictorial pelts of his prey upon the limelight screen.

That was so long ago that one could then get a good cigar for five cents, and the milk-shake was the prevailing drink for women and children.

But this business of snapshooting and lecturing on it was, after all, an incident for Black. He was primarily a writer, a teller of tales. Photography was only a subject. It was something that he wrote and talked about. Inevitably he began to see in it the possibility of making it say something for itself.

Many of the Black snapshots which he projected on the screen for his lecture were pictures of action, frozen moments of motion. In other words, they gave glimpses of something in the process of happening. They were therefore, like any other picture, tiny fragments of the event, specks of drama.

This fact began to become apparent to Black as night after night his slides followed each other through the stereopticon and marched across the screen as he spoke. It chanced that in classifying his slides to give his lecture satisfactory order, he found that almost automatically there was a tendency for pictorial story sequences to develop on the screen. He put his pictures of Wall Street magnates together, his Fifth Avenue belles together, and his Bowery bums together. He had plenty of the tramp pictures. A sleeping tramp on a park bench was easy and interesting game for the camera hunter.

In fancy, the lecturer saw glints of plot in those accidental picture sequences among the tramps. Little snatches of dramatic events seemed to be taking place, with the story run-

ning along with an entire disregard of the change of the person
of the actor in every successive scene. The automatic logic of
the plot suggestion prevailed over the continual change of personnel.

There is no evidence that this property of narrative continuity became apparent to Black's audiences attending *Ourselves
as Others See Us*. It presumably was only apparent to him
because of his extreme familiarity with the material. This
familiarity made the slides no longer so much pictures of indi-
viduals to him as type symbols and phases of action. Therefore the mind of the lecturer was ready to deal with them as
dramatic alphabet blocks from which it seemed he might build
stories.

In the spring of 1894 Black had the notion clearly in mind
and set forth on a most ambitious project. He proposed making a long sequence of photographic slides presenting a sequen-
tial story, involving many persons and many scenes of action.
He was entirely familiar with what had been accomplished by
the attempts at the motion picture on glass plates by such devices
as Heyl's Phasmatrope and the French Praxinoscope used by
Muybridge.

Black had followed the work of Muybridge as an obvious
matter of technical interest. He was in the audience when
Muybridge addressed the Oxford club of Brooklyn in 1889.
It was an occasion made painfully memorable by a misunderstanding.

Following his usual exhibition of running horses and sundry
scientific studies of motion, Muybridge presented on his "Zoopraxiscope" a picture of a dancing girl in a costume which in-
terfered neither with her movements nor the vision of the audience. The stumbling of an usher or some similar mishap
made a noise in the back of the house. Some one hissed for
silence. Muybridge hastily assumed that the hiss was for his

dancing girl picture. He stopped the show and harangued that staid Oxford club audience on the purity of art and the divinity of the human form. Every hair of his patriarchal beard was aquiver with righteous and scientific wrath. Muybridge gathered fervor as he progressed. When he had relieved the verbal pressure, the dancing girl flickered on the screen again before an audience which sat in a silence which seemed to eddy about in blizzardy drifts. The occasion was a triumph for science and art, but not for cordiality.

The glass plate pictures presented by Muybridge gave a jerky brief vision which had neither the duration nor quality which Black sought. Also the Edison Kinetoscope pictures were no aid, being locked in a peep show where they might be viewed by but one person at a time.

However much his acquaintance with those two devices may have encouraged Black he was none the less sent pioneering for a new process all his own.

Black aimed at an expression method which should be made up of still pictures projected by the ordinary stereopticon and spoken words or lines delivered from the stage. The totality of effect he sought was simply the telling of a story by a blend of words and pictures. He hoped that between the two components of word and picture he would convey an impression of dramatic action.

Black arrived at a rate of four slides a minute for his presentation. The plan was to make the pictures successively blend into one another in the dissolving stereopticon, avoiding an optical "jar" as much as possible. Each picture represented a step forward in the action. The pictures were carefully registered always to present every still object in the view in precisely the same position, while only the moving actors were shown in altered attitudes. There could, of course, be no hope of depicting rapid motion. Black chose, in such instances, to picture the moments before and after the swift action involved. For example, the villain might stand menacing the hero with an upraised dagger, while the next slide would show the victim of the stab in a heap on the floor. The spoken obligato from the stage had to carry across the imagined stroke of the stabbing.

All of Black's artist friends assured him that what he proposed was entirely impossible. This made it worth trying.

Black set about preparing an outline of his photographic story. He called it a "picture play," having to invent a name for something that had never existed before. The term lived then only so long as his project. A dozen years later "picture play" was re-invented and made a part of motion picture parlance.

In outlining in written notes his first picture play idea, Black wrote some fourteen thousand words. The first picture play brought with it, we see, a most considerable first scenario as well. It contemplated a full evening's entertainment, or full "feature length" in the language of the modern motion picture.

The story of this picture play was built about the adventures of a girl reporter, designated as *Miss Jerry*, the rôle which gave title to the piece.

By mid-summer the actual photographic work began, with Black officiating at the camera, being simultaneously author and director as well. In that pioneer endeavor he encountered most of the problems which were to complicate the technique of photoplay production in the films evolved many a year later. The production ran into some hundreds of exposures and the work covered many weeks.

Miss Blanche Bayliss, whose face was then familiar to the admirers of the drawings of A. B. Wenzell, had the rôle of *Miss Jerry*. Black was after realism with vast sincerity and having laid down a newspaper story involving notables he insisted on having them. He had written Chauncey M. Depew and his office at Grand Central Station into the play. Extensive explanations were required when the world's first photoplay director asked Depew to pose for and with *Miss Jerry*. Depew had never heard of a pictureplay, nor had any one else in all the wide world. Black's largest difficulty was to tell what he was doing. Depew either understood or surrendered to avoid misunderstandings. At any rate there were no precedents against it, so he posed. These slides undoubtedly became the medium of the only public appearances in which Depew did not make a speech.

Outdoor scenes were pictured with a hand camera, while the indoor scenes, or sets as we know them now, were made at the Carbon Studio at 5 West 16th street, the private studio and gallery of James Lawrence Breese, a patron of the arts and friend of the enterprising Black. There was considerable confusion over "props" and costumes, registered in the piece and then, until the last moment, forgotten in the new scenes. There was the ever constant peril that the heroine would appear at the door in one dress and emerge into the room in another, a common oversight of the film drama later.

Problems in illumination akin to those of the motion picture of to-day were worked out with the use of arc lights, reflectors and diffusing screens. The film drama did not arrive at those refinements of photographic technique until it had acquired the experience of years, but the very first photoplay had them.

The locations of the picture ranged from polite Fifth Avenue to the depths of the slums of Cherry Hill. Unforeseen events reshaped the story on the spot, and the photoplay grew by itself under the hand of the maker. Black evolved a directorial method of improvised speeches calculated to make his cast act and react, just as the modern director bullies and cajoles his stars.

The cast included William Courtenay, in the rôle of hero,

and Ernest Hastings, as the polished villain. Both won stage fame later.

Miss Jerry had its first night, or preview showing, at the Carbon Studio on the night of October 9, 1894. It was presented with elaborate musical accompaniment by John Hyatt Brewer, composer. The audience included William Dean Howells, Edmund Clarence Stedman, Frank R. Stockton, Brander Matthews, and many other celebrities in literature and art. The play ran for two hours. Howells commented that it was too long. Black cut it to an hour and a half, and Howells approved.

Dr. Seth Low saw *Miss Jerry* at the première. "How do you move the figures and keep the pictures still?" he asked. Then Black knew that he had indeed created an illusion of motion.

Miss Jerry went to the lyceum stage and appeared for the delectation of the cognoscenti through the East, including presentations from the Emerson platform at Concord, Mass., and in Boston. Edward Everett Hale approached Dr. Black with mock annoyance after the Boston performance.

"It is so inevitable," remarked Hale, "that I am chagrined that I did not think of it myself."

As the Kinetoscope parlors were now invading the principal cities in the autumn of '94 much of the editorial comment of the press anticipated an application of the film to the Black idea, when Edison should achieve the screen.

This might well have influenced Edison, the father of the film. It might also just as well have influenced Black, the father of the photoplay. It did neither. The point is interesting. Nowhere else in the field of human endeavor can we find so clearly defined that thin line between art and science. Edison was science. Black was art. Between them they held in their separated hands the ingredients of the *aqua regalis*, that universal solvent of expression—the story telling motion picture film. Only time and tedious experience could bring the two elements together into the flowing menstruum of the modern screen.

That process of alchemy which we are tracing in this history perhaps will give the reader a new view of the identity of art and science, twin odalisques in the harem of the Wish. Similar fusions are continually taking place about us. The sum total of them makes up what we are pleased to call the progress of civilization. The deeper we dig the more it seems that this progress consists only of new and better ways to scratch the same old cosmic itches.

Miss Jerry gave Black a new vocation for several seasons. He became known to the lyceum circuits as "the picture-play man." Imitators sprang up using simulative names, like "picture drama" and "picture comedy." It appears they feared copyright restrictions, which in fact did not exist.

The success of *Miss Jerry* impelled Black to an even more pretentious effort for his second season. The new pictureplay was entitled *A Capital Courtship*, with scenes laid in Washington. Black was rather aware of the box office value of notables. The story included Grover Cleveland, the president, and, afterward, President McKinley, Thomas B. Reed, speaker of the House of Representatives, and Sir Julian Pauncefote, the British ambassador. Black put his camera under his arm, went to Washington and got them. He had quite a time trying to tell Grover Cleveland what a pictureplay was. When Cleveland at last comprehended that it was proposed to show him signing a bill, he searched his desk for an actual bill which awaited signature. No make-believe paper would do. The president was something of a literalist, too.

On the whole *A Capital Courtship* was as much of a success as *Miss Jerry*. But the second picture contained a snow scene which seems to have been unsuccessful. William J. Baer, later a celebrated painter of miniatures, appeared in *A Capital Courtship* and attended its première. When the snow scene reached its crisis Baer remarked:

"The only way Black could have made that snow more original would have been by having it fall upward."

Black continued his pictureplays on the lyceum stage, but refused to be interested when B. F. Keith, the Boston variety magnate, sought to have the pictureplays presented at his theatres. This may strike the reader of to-day as a blunder, but Black understood the limitations of his device much better than Keith did. In his own words, Black "insisted that his plays were essentially a lyceum rather than a theatrical feature and chose to avoid general audiences that would look for livelier dramatic elements." That, however, is only Black's own gentle way of admitting that the illusion of his photoplays, with their four images a minute and interlarded word imagery of spoken lines, depended upon intellectualizations by the audience. It would have been courting failure to have taken a chance before the lowbrow audiences of the variety houses. The Black pictureplay made the audience work, even if unconsciously, to fill the gaps in the motion record. The limitation resulting from this necessity is obvious. The distinction is as sharp as between wit and slapstick. Variety and its successor, vaudeville, evolved for audiences with small power of concentrated attention. The pictureplay had to supply ready made attention before it could reach the millions.

Black has retrospectively named his process "the slow movie." It was in fact a motion picture in which the eye received the minimum of cues to keep the mind in the desired emotion path. Imagination had to fill the long gaps in the visual record. The film drama of to-day presents four times as many images a second as Black gave in a minute. A total of 960 frames of film images now go on the screen in the same time that the pictureplay of '94 presented four slides. The modern screen thereby supplies ready-made imagination, and requires relatively almost no imaginative or intellectual abilities for its observation.

Black's pictureplay was really just a somewhat grotesque bud of the tree of expression. Black, the story teller, by coincidence was also a photographer. He was a great deal more of a story teller than an inventor. The result was the application of the camera and photography as it then existed to the best possible approach to the synthetic re-creation of an event. It was obviously identical in its basic character with the prior efforts in graphic and pictorial expression all the way from Leonardo to Daguerre. Had Black been less of a story teller and more of an inventor he would probably have labored toward the evolution of better picture machinery instead of his curious utilization of the stereopticon. But he would probably not have given us *Miss Jerry*, which was a stupendous piece of pioneering. It is a mere incidental misfortune that so far as the motion picture was concerned the pioneering was wasted by a failure to see what Black had done.

It was a full ten years before the motion picture, coming to the screen as we shall see only a year later, tediously evolved out of expensive labored experience a photoplay which appreciated the principles which Black developed in a few weeks. The inventors who gave us the screen as a means of saying had nothing to say. So long as they controlled it, it remained dumb.

Black's stereopticon pictureplays were unrecognized forecasts of the age of screen sagas to come. He carried the still camera up to the limit of its possibilities of story telling and the re-creation of events.

It may appear surprising that when the motion picture film

reached the screen Black made no effort to bring it to the service of his idea. That is to be explained by a whole group of reasons. The first screen pictures were, as we shall note at their arrival in ensuing chapters, inadequate vehicles for story telling because of their brief duration and feeble quality. Their audience was a class to which Black had no message. And Black was moving on to more serious effort in other phases of expression.

It is of significance, in our understanding of the relation between the motion picture and expression, that Black's major activity of to-day is as the editor of a newspaper syndicate. This editorship in turn concerns itself largely with spirited pictorial art, in which Black is a high authority. This is not bare coincidence, but is rather another evidence of the fundamental identity and pictorial character of all forms of expression, more especially as between the picture and the word in modern newspapering. The syndicate which Black serves is Newspaper Feature Service, a Hearst enterprise and an accessory to the graphically dynamic journalism of the Hearst school.

The outward form of Black's effort is apparently changed, but in fact he is still telling stories and purveying emotions with pictures, just as in the days of *Miss Jerry* in '94.

The development of the stereopticon slide for the illustration of incidental song numbers for vaudeville and motion picture theatres attained an elaboration approaching in a degree the Black pictureplay. The song slides reached their peak of development about 1908. The production of series of slides often entailed considerable dramatic staging, travel for backgrounds and casting and costuming.

When Charles K. Harris made his slide series for *"Linda, Can't You Love Your Joe?"* he sent a photographer into Alabama and Tennessee for settings and real southern darkies. As many as sixty persons appeared in the ensemble scenes.

In 1907 Harris' song *The Best Thing in Life* was in effect song-and-picture drama in three acts, using twenty-eight slides, with scenes ranging from a club room interior to Madison Square in a snowstorm. *Hello Central, Give Me Heaven* was illustrated with scenes from a Chicago Telephone exchange. Here was a word-and-hieroglyph art evolving concurrently with the motion picture.

CHAPTER EIGHT

TWO GALLANTS FROM VIRGINIA

AMONG the young men who passed up and down the Broadway of '94 in quest of their diversions were Grey and Otway Latham, brothers and beaux gallant from Old Virginia.

The Lathams were handsome blades of the dashing type which fits the romantic picture of the South that was, graceful land of languor and luxury, of jasmine bowered, white columned verandas looking out on spacious lawns and vistas of ancient live oaks.

Grey and Otway Latham were born perhaps a century after their proper period into an era of alien work-a-day spirit. Economic exiles from the land of the julep and the fox hunt, they were now a part of the rising turmoil of Manhattan, the metropolis of the work-cursed Yankee.

They were sons of a distinguished Southerner, Woodville Latham of the Lathams of Northcliffe, Virginia. To the history of the motion picture he has been obscurely known as Professor Latham, but in the annals of the Old South he is pridefully named as Major Latham, sir!

Mostly, Major Latham's family hopes had gone down with many another Southern pride at the surrender of Lee at Appomattox Court House. Major Latham, as well became his traditions, had served the Confederacy and its lost cause ably, first as a major of artillery in the field and then as the executive officer of the great Southern arsenal at Columbus, in Georgia.

Before the war Major Latham had been devoted to the sciences, especially the study of chemistry. He had wealth and

—104—

OTWAY LATHAM   MAJOR WOODVILLE LATHAM   GREY LATHAM

Two blithe young Virginians, who with their father made the first effort to put the motion picture on the screen commercially, with romantic, adventurous and tragic consequences.

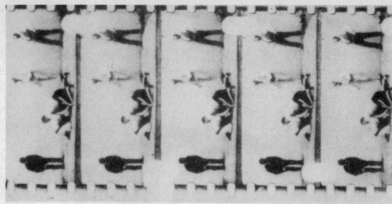

LATHAM RELICS — at left — Michael Leonard, who posed for the first screen fight made for Latham's special edition of Edison's Kinetoscope — above — one of Latham's Pantoptikon's, first projector — at right — Latham Eidoloscope film of 1895, exact size.

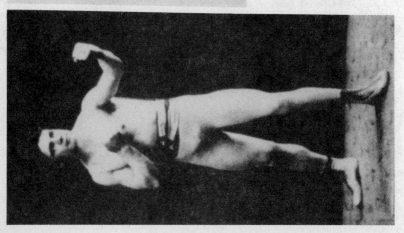

leisure and an introspective bent. He was one of fifteen heirs of Woodville Latham, the elder, to share in the inheritance of ruined estates in the sad aftermath of the War of the Rebellion. Even so, he had a competency to be supplemented by the earnings of a commercial application of his scientific pursuits. With the war behind him, business beckoned to the Major. The Baltimore & Ohio lines invited him to become the resident engineer in charge between Pittsburgh and Chicago. This would have meant going into the North. It may have been the Southerner in him, or mayhap the scholar, which made him reject this appointment to take the chair of chemistry and physics at the University of West Virginia, at a professor's salary. Financial pressure increased.

Latham's three sons, Percy, Grey and Otway were young collegians now, members of the Major's classes. They were learning the merry life and acquiring expensive tastes. They were handsome, high strung and headstrong. The world was theirs and they took it.

Major Latham found he could not keep pace with the growing demands upon him and with considerable reluctance abandoned his professorship with its pleasant retirements in collegiate halls and laboratories to plunge into business.

With the remnants of his fortune Major Latham established his sons in a drug business in Nashville, Tennessee, and himself set out to engage in dealings in real estate.

After all, his sons were young with the world all ahead of them and the Major was ready to sacrifice himself and his scholarly, cloistered life to them and the aggressive new era of after-the-war.

But fortune was unkind alike to the sons' drug business and the Major's real estate efforts, which had taken him variously to Chattanooga and St. Louis. Percy and Grey and Otway were still playboys, with no heart for business. And the Major would rather have been back in his study or over the bench in his laboratory deep in test tubes and valencies.

In the year of the Kinetoscope we discover Grey and Otway Latham in New York, drawn toward the maelstrom of the new economic era—and gay Broadway. They had swiftly gone through the assets of their drug concern in Tennessee and were now employes, Grey with the drug house of Parke, Davis & Company, Otway with the Tilden Drug Company. Otway had established a friendship with Samuel J. Tilden, Jr., nephew of the celebrated Samuel J. Tilden, one time governor of New York and Democratic candidate for the presidency of the United States, defeated by a Republican recount of the ballots of 1876.

Major Latham, now in failing health, had followed on to New York with his sons and was living with them at the Hotel Bartholdi, at the corner of Broadway and Twenty-third street, still hopefully advising them and promising himself an upturn in the rapidly ebbing tide of Latham fortunes. He had with him a handful of his books, reliquaries and symbols of the life he had put behind him, following the service of his sons and their flaming youth. The old habits of the library and laboratory followed him and through the long hours of the night he sat still desultorily pursuing his researches with the clangor of Broadway in his ears and the lights of Madison Square Garden across the park flashing in front of his window. He hoped to re-establish himself in this alien soil and time.

Now came another Southern youth, Enoch Rector, who had been a classmate of the Latham brothers under their father at the University of West Virginia. Rector had completed his technical education aimed at engineering and now he was back from a tour of Europe to begin his career.

Grey and Otway Latham greeted their classmate with southern enthusiasm and proceeded to show him the town.

Among the wonders of Broadway was the Kinetoscope Parlor at 1155 Broadway where the dragon in electric lights, with a green eye and red tongue, was proclaiming the wonders of the new Edison wizardry, the living pictures in a peep show.

The three adventuring young Virginians turned in at the sign of the dragon and saw the little forty-foot pictures of Mme. Bertholdi tying herself in knots, Mlle. Capitaine revealing her agility on the trapeze, the cockfight, and all the rest of that primitive program.

"There, that's a business to get into," Grey Latham exclaimed to Rector as they emerged. "I'll tell you what—everybody's crazy about prize fights, and all we have to do is to get Edison to photograph a fight for this machine and we can take it out and make a fortune on it."

That was a moment of destiny for the motion picture. Amazing consequences and many of the controlling events of all subsequent screen history have their roots in that trifling moment that summer evening on Broadway in 1894. It has also filled the complex annals of the screen with a whole sequence of poignant life dramas.

The impulse crystallized into a plan and organization. After some preliminary inquiries at the Edison plant, Otway and Grey Latham, Samuel J. Tilden, Jr., and Enoch Rector formed the Kinetoscope Exhibition Company, for the special purpose of exploiting special peep show machines with prize fight pictures. It seems that it was on this restricted and special basis that the deal escaped the strictures of the prior Edison contract with Norman C. Raff of the International Novelty Company and the Kinetoscope Company.

Tilden and the two Lathams were busy with the affairs of their employments in the drug business. It was agreed that they should stay by their posts and the assured incomes therefrom, while Rector who was just casting about for a connection, should actively take up the project.

Rector's technical education now stood him in good stead. It was obvious that the Kinetoscope, limited as it was to the Kinetograph's output of about fifty feet of negative at a single loading, could not portray a round of a prize fight. Both the camera and the viewing machine had to be given a new scope in the recording of events in behalf of the Kinetoscope Exhibition Company's new project.

This technical fact is worthy of emphasis. It made the prize ring and pugilism the major influence in the technical evolution of the motion picture for the entire first decade of the art. Incidental effects and influences, equally important but less tangible, have followed through the years. The influence of the prize ring extended to and overlapped into a period of the increasing importance of the dramatic functions of the screen.

It is noteworthy, too, that it was the interest of the blithe Lathams which started the motion picture along the sporty primrose path. The outstanding fact is that they saw the motion picture as the means of re-creating the event of a prize fight, containing the emotional stimulus they most desired. This was the birth of production policy for the motion picture. It was, as time proved, too limited. The prize ring was a man's sport. In thirty years production policy has evolved to the point where all motion pictures are built about the event of supreme emotional stimulus to both sexes. But that idea was not entirely overlooked even in these early days, as we shall in due season observe.

In order to get the prize fight into the limitations of the motion picture, Rector, working at the Edison plant, tripled the scope of the Kinetoscope, getting a capacity of one hundred and fifty feet of film, and then planned a prize fight of abbreviated rounds.

One morning in July, 1894, the world's first prize fight pictures were staged at the Black Maria in West Orange. Michael Leonard, then known as "the Beau Brummel of the prize ring," met Jack Cushing, a likely contender for the lightweight title. They fought in a ten-foot ring. They went about ten of the snappy short rounds, of which the Kinetograph recorded six. At the finish Cushing was trapped by a feint and fell under a chop to the jaw. Nearly a thousand feet of film had been made. It was by far the longest motion picture that had yet been attempted.

External pressure and enterprise had already set out to take the motion picture industry out of the hands of Edison under whose auspices it had just been born. In less than six months he lost his exclusive control of the art, and in twenty-three years his name was to pass from the screen as a maker of pictures.

In August, 1894, the Latham-Rector-Tilden enterprise opened the parlor of the Kinetoscope Exhibition Company at 83 Nassau street in downtown New York. Six big special Kinetoscopes stood in a row in a store room. Each contained a round of the Leonard-Cushing fight. A sign was put in the window and a barker stood at the door proclaiming the wonders of "the living pictures of the great prize fight." New York was hungry to see. Throngs packed the place, and by the second day long lines of waiting patrons trailed back into the street. The police came to keep order. In the vernacular of the show business, they were "holding them out."

The Latham brothers were started on their way to a swift transient burst of prosperity. There were lively nights along Broadway. Pretty girls, dinners at the Hoffman House, and a considerable sprinkling of champagne.

With a hopeful, indulgent interest the father, Woodville Latham, looked on. He was anxious and wondering.

The Leonard-Cushing fight pictures which started out so

bravely began to lose their drawing power. A production problem had arisen for the first time in the new art. A change of program was needed. The decision was an obvious one, another prize fight, but a bigger and better one.

The Latham lads knew everybody on Broadway, including James Corbett, then in the glory of heavyweight stardom. Corbett was a bigger name than Leonard. They were looking for box office value.

The Kinetoscope Exhibition Company made an arrangement with Corbett to fight Pete Courtney of Trenton, New Jersey, before the camera. The contract specified that Corbett was not to be photographed for any other Kinetoscope concern. It was an exclusive star contract and the first in the world.

Meanwhile Enoch Rector, the production manager of the enterprise, laid down the specifications of the fight. They had taken their chances on what they could photograph of the very genuine fight between Leonard and Cushing. That was pure reporting. Now they wanted to be assured of results by a further pre-determining of the event to be re-created by the living pictures. It was therefore decided that the fight should go precisely six rounds of one minute each and that the sixth should be concluded by a handsome knockout delivered by the star, James Corbett. And so it was done. The picture neatly fitted the machines.

This pre-arranged prize fight was thus the ancestor of dramatic construction for the motion picture. Here was the first glimmering of creative motion picture effort, the first step toward having things happen for the camera rather than merely photographing events ordained by other forces.

The Lathams grew impatient of the slow trickle of spectators past the battery of peep show machines with the pictures of the Corbett-Courtenay fight. They wanted to be able to show the pictures on the wall to a whole room full of patrons at once.

The money would come faster that way. Like many another back along the line of the zoetrope experimenters of the century before, they thought of the magic lantern, that Magia Catoptrica of Athanasius Kircher of 1640 by now electrified and rechristened the Stereopticon. This was a technical task, and with this idea came the notion that their father, Professor Woodville Latham, would be able to perform it for them.

One day in September, 1894, Otway Latham induced his father to visit the Kinetoscope parlor in Nassau street.

"You see if we could project that picture on a sheet, like the stereopticon slides, there'd be a fortune in it. Can we do it?"

"You can project anything on a screen that you can see with the naked eye and which can be photographed," replied Woodville Latham. He was very positive in his answer. He was also very correct. Woodville Latham had only a casual academic knowledge of optics and photography. He was a chemist. Naturally neither he nor his sons knew anything of any of the prior efforts of the motion picture toward projection. The Edison experiments aimed at the screen were now some years in the discard, buried among the note books in the big laboratories in West Orange.

The Lathams and Rector set to work to take the motion picture out of Edison's little black peep show box and to put it on the screen. The making of the projected motion picture of the theatre screen, the entertainment of the millions of to-day, began then and there. The force of commercial ambition was taking up the burden of the problem of the living picture where Edison had laid it down. It was inevitable that the motion picture should be carried forward now to the screen. Edison had paused just before the shortest but most important step. He put out the little Kinetoscope to make money and sacrificed a golden empire.

The Lathams, to be sure, were not the only opportunists to

see a glimmering of greater things beyond the peep show Kinetoscope. Close upon them came other builders upon the Edison idea whose efforts were presently to make a battleground of the screen.

It appears to have been Otway Latham who took the aggressive hand in the matter of conducting the effort to put the kinetoscopic picture on the screen. Otway was impatient and impetuous, and his methods were those of simple propinquity. He went to the Edison plant again and made friends with the man he judged knew most about the motion picture—William Kennedy Laurie Dickson.

It was Otway who chose the location of the workshop laboratory where the Latham experiments were to be conducted. He found space in the Scott Building at 35 Frankfort street, a little old four story red brick structure of Civil War days, old when the Brooklyn Bridge towering above it was opened to traffic. The Latham laboratory was at the top of the last flight of stairs in a space twelve by fifteen feet.

Otway cast about for a mechanic to build their experimental projection machines and naturally sought one who might know something about what was known of the motion picture. He employed Eugene Lauste, a Frenchman who had worked on the Edison phonograph, and had from time to time done a bit in Room Five at West Orange. Lauste, if the court records of subsequent litigation are to be accepted, was not thoroughly in the good graces of everybody at the Edison plant. He appears to have been friendly with Dickson, with whom he has been associated at times long subsequent to their motion picture affairs.

Lauste went to work in the shop, along with Raphael Netter, a draughtsman employed to sketch out Professor Latham's ideas. Lauste literally lived with his work and slept on a cot in the corner of the little room. He expected a share in the fortune which seemed to loom ahead.

Otway Latham meanwhile was busy on reconnoitering errands in West Orange. He wanted to know all that could be learned there about this motion picture. He would let his slow, patient old father figure it out with midnight vigils over the drafting table if he could, but there might be a swifter method.

This blithe young Southerner made a less interested friendship with William E. Gilmore, then general manager of the Edison enterprises at West Orange. Gilmore, big of stature and with a belligerent personality, had just been called to West Orange from a post with the Edison General Electric Works at Schenectady, N. Y. He was due at West Orange on April 1, 1894. He reported promptly at his new desk at 8 o'clock on the morning of April 2.

"I wasn't going to start anything on April Fool Day," he explained.

It may be set down here that this is probably the first and last evidence of anything akin to superstition in all the brass-tacks career of William E. Gilmore.

Gilmore's first official act has not been recorded, but it is a safe assumption that he brought down a hard fist on a surprised desk and demanded action.

There was neither superstition nor sentiment in the new order of things at West Orange under Gilmore. He found that Edison, between his good nature and his concentration on scientific affairs, had allowed many to impose upon him. Meanwhile the Edison interests had been increasing in magnitude and complexity. There were problems of financing and administration. It is not that Edison might not have been able to cope with these problems, but rather that his stronger interests were elsewhere. Among other elements of the situation was a maze of patent litigations. It seems to have been painfully true that every important patented development from the Edison laboratories was sure to result in a flock of competing claims, seldom in good faith and not a few of them downright frauds conceived in criminal cleverness. The conspicuous successes of Edison made him an object of continuous attack.

"Damn the patents, give me the goods with your name on it and we will do business," was Gilmore's advice.

It is not testimonial to the court-made justice that the thousands upon thousands expended by Edison in defensive litigation probably never saved him a penny or gave him a nickel's worth of protection as measured by ultimate results.

The immediate crisis in Edison affairs which had brought Gilmore to the general managership was due to the erratic commercial course of the North American Phonograph Company. That concern, for merchandising reasons and competitions involving patent issues, had threatened to engulf the whole Edison institution in ruin. It was a situation which called for a stern dictator and rigid discipline. Gilmore was the iron man of the hour.

Gilmore started some house cleaning and some merchandising. He had campaign plans of his own to carry through. He was disposed to be friendly toward Otway Latham, on two counts. Latham was a customer, also he was an entertaining and cordial young man. He breathed the spirit of Broadway and the gaiety of the period. He was a contact for Gilmore, with this amusement world, in which it seemed probable that the Kinetoscope was likely to figure.

It was also to be noted that Otway Latham was being rather aggressively friendly toward Dickson.

Also, Gilmore began to disagree with Dickson at once.

JAMES J. CORBETT and PETER COURTENAY, when they squared off before the Edison camera at West Orange in the first fight picture to reach the screen.

FIRST QUEEN of the MOVIES, Carmencita, a music hall favorite, dancing for the Kinetoscope at West Orange in 1894.

CHAPTER NINE

DANCING BUTTERFLIES—INTRIGUE

THE friendship between the young Lathams and W. E. Gilmore had some rather direct effects on the whole course of the motion picture through its reaction on the production at the Edison studio under Gilmore's supervision.

The early Latham successes with the Leonard-Cushing and Corbett-Courtenay fight pictures led to the making of a number of minor bouts at the Black Maria for Raff & Gammon of the Kinetoscope Company, which is not to be confused with the Latham-Rector-Tilden Kinetoscope Exhibition Company. And yet further, and more interesting, the keen enthusiasm of Otway and Grey Latham for persons under the bright lights of Broadway led the Edison "Black Maria" studio to beckon into the films many of the gay butterflies of the stage who smiled on the handsome young Virginians.

Since the Lathams' Kinetoscope Exhibition Company had launched the prize fight pictures for the peep show with such success in their downtown parlor, Raff and Gammon of the Kinetoscope Company, with its uptown demonstration parlor on Broadway, sought to give competition with a real stellar fight.

Now, as we have noted, the Latham-Corbett deal was exclusive, and Corbett could not be pictured for Raff and Gammon and their customers.

Corbett, the handsome "Gentleman Jim" of the prize ring, was the first in the world to sign a motion picture star contract. It is remarkable that when Corbett recently wrote his autobiography, "The Roar of the Crowd," he had forgotten his early ring appearances before the camera, and cited the battle of his defeat, some years later, as the first to be photographed for the screen.

Bearing on this star contract situation of the first film year there is interest in the discovery among the old Kinetoscope Company records of a contract memorandum drawn up September, 1894, by which one Hugh Behan was employed at a contingent $3,000 a year to frame a fight between "such first-class fighters as Corbett, Jackson, Fitzsimmons, M'Auliffe, Griffo, Dixon or Maher, and a suitable opponent."

The old contract, still without the date filled in, bears the signatures of Behan and two attorneys, Frank Z. Maguire and Joseph D. Baucus, 44 Pine Street, New York, who were soon to share in the selling of the Kinetoscope with Raff and Gammon of the Kinetoscope Company. Evidently the contract was never signed by Norman Charles Raff for the Kinetoscope Company and International Novelty Company. The project produced no picture fights and was soon forgotten under the pressure of other more urgent affairs. The peep show days and companies were soon to pass.

There was, incidentally, an entirely mechanical reason for the persistent popularity of the prize fight as an early motion picture subject. The picture taking machine was not the facile portable instrument of to-day. It was a vast bulky device of about the dimensions of a large dog house. It was heavy. It had a rather fixed viewpoint. It could not be swung to cover panoramas, and it could not be tilted up and down to follow moving centers of interest. It had about the same pictorial availability as a knothole in a ballfield fence.

The ropes of the prize ring automatically limited the radius of action. It was simple to set the ponderous camera to cover the ring. The cameraman could then grind away, secure in the certainty that the picture was not getting away from him, unless indeed the combatants jumped the ropes and ran away.

For the same photographic reasons dance acts were especially available for the camera of the period of the Kinetograph, as Edison called his picture taking machine. Also, New York was as dance mad then as since. But in this period the performance was left to professionals on the stage, to be enjoyed vicariously from the comfort of music hall seats. The Columbian Exposition at Chicago had brought to our hospitable shores some of the best work of the justly famous Oriental movements perfected on the North African coast. Both more and less versions were being presented for years after at New York shows.

To Koster & Bial's Music Hall at Broadway and Thirty-fourth street, where the Macy store now stands, came Carmencita, a dancer after the Spanish manner, and a sensation of national scope in those days of 1895–6. A few squares away in Twenty-third street at the Eden Musee a damsel of lithesome grace known as Otero was presented in ardent rivalry. Self-appointed committees of the sportive gentry of old New York, in their long-tailed coats and silk hats, spent a deal of time comparing the merits of the dancers, and to this day it is impossible to get a real decision on their relative merits.

But this vast interest did result in one milestone for our history of the motion picture. Carmencita was drafted for the films. She went to West Orange and performed before the Kinetograph. The screen born verb *to vamp* was then uncoined, but the art itself was well established.

Annabelle Moore, another beauty of considerable music hall fame under the name of Annabelle-the-Dancer performed a little fifty-foot version of her act on the Edison stage. Annabelle appeared in the serpentine dance, wafting and manipulating endless yards of silken draperies. On the variety theatre stage this was one of the most popular numbers. The dancer was illuminated with changing shafts of colored light thrown by tint slides in a stereopticon. The Edison pictures were led into the first screen endeavors at color in imitation of the stage effect. Many of the prints of the Annabelle picture were tinted with slide colors by hand, a frame at a time, a most tedious process. This method of attaining screen color has continued for special purposes ever since. It has never attained, however, any particular importance in the screen art. It occurs only as a symptom of desire.

Annabelle was photographed for the peep show Kinetoscope, but within a few months both a revolution in the picture art and some exciting developments in her own career were destined to combine in making her the first celebrity of the motion pictures.

Otway Latham and Dickson talked motion picture a great deal in this period. Young Latham was afire with the possibilities of profit which seemed to be promised by showing pictures on a screen.

Dickson was not, it seems possible, entirely aware of what the Lathams were trying to do toward projection. But his conversations at least indicated to Otway Latham an enthusiastic anticipation that projection was possible and immensely desirable.

Dickson discussed some of his still continuing experiments. He told Otway of a plan he had to use a film and some Kinetoscope parts for an experiment in projection at Columbia University's laboratories.

"I could not get enough light through the 13-inch diameter shutter with a $\frac{1}{8}$-inch slot by the use of my Zeiss focus arc lamp and I mentioned this to my good friend, the Rev. C. H. Mann of Orange, N. J., who advised me to go and see his son, Professor Riborg Mann at Columbia College and bring a sample, and he would give me all the light I wanted," says Dickson in a letter of May 30, 1924, discussing this incident of thirty years ago which afterward figured in many a conflict with varying interpretations.

"Professor Latham and his sons were having supper at my house, 166 Cleveland street, Orange, and heard me say what I intended to do," continues Dickson. "I wasn't sure at the time if I should give way to the Prof's (Latham's) insistent request to be allowed to come—anyway he came—and Prof. Riborg Mann was awfully kind in running wires and screwing up the two little rollers for a short band to go over. A tin shutter was made and spun around the front of the film, and light was shoved on more and more—a small condenser held by me—the projecting lens in front of the high speed shutter—all simply to try and see what the loss of light was through an $\frac{1}{8}$-inch slot. Question, why—as I had carte blanche to experiment—was this Columbia College affair under such auspices and so openly conducted, so misconstrued afterward?"

Gossip of this Columbia experiment reached Gilmore and went on to Edison.

Meanwhile Norman C. Raff of the Kinetoscope Company was getting inquiries from customers who were anxious to get a machine that would project the pictures on the wall. The peep show parlor men were feeling the same pressure that impelled the Lathams. The motion picture was demanding to be liberated from the little black box.

Raff communicated this demand to Edison.

"No," replied the Wizard, "if we make this screen machine that you are asking for, it will spoil everything. We are making these peep show machines and selling a lot of them at a good profit. If we put out a screen machine there will be a use for maybe about ten of them in the whole United States. With that many screen machines you could show the pictures to everybody in the country—and then it would be done. Let's not kill the goose that lays the golden egg."

Raff argued longer, and Edison raised his estimate of the potential market of screen machines to perhaps fifty for the whole world.

The Kinetoscope Company was insistent. At last a concession was made. Edison would see about getting up a screen machine.

Now an odd thing happened. Dickson, who had conducted all of the motion picture experiments up to this time, was not consulted. Rather secretly, at least so far as Dickson was concerned, Charles H. Kayser, one of the several mechanics who had done some of the tinkering in Room Five, was set to work to evolve a projection machine. Instead of working in the Edison laboratory where he might have been discovered by Dickson, Kayser was sent over to the offices of the Kinetoscope Company in the Postal Telegraph building in New York. A large room on the mezzanine adjacent to the Kinetoscope general office was taken for his work. It is just possible that one of Edison's ideas was to put Kayser right under the noses of Raff and Gammon in his work, thus tending to satisfy their clamor for a projection machine.

Kayser struggled on and on, spraying flickering pictures on the ceiling wall and floor as his reconstructed peep show Kinetoscope tried to learn to throw at the screen.

Raff complained at the slow progress.

"I could go in there and make that thing work inside of a week, if I wanted to take the time to it myself," Edison replied. "Maybe he'll get it pretty soon." Edison was in no hurry.

Meanwhile Dickson learned with surprise through grapevine channels of the Kayser project over in New York, and thereafter saw to it that Kayser had no opportunity to learn of what had been worked out in Room Five or elsewhere in his experiments.

Now the Lathams began to urge Dickson to join them in the

building of a projection machine. Things were not going very promisingly in the little workshop at 35 Frankfort street.

If later testimony is correct, Dickson yielded a shade to the Latham importuning and broached to Edison the idea of joining them in a projection machine effort. Edison is quoted as replying that he could not consider such a step since he was under contract to the Kinetoscope Company for all of his motion picture devices.

Still the Lathams persisted and thrust upon Dickson an offer of a quarter interest in their project. Dickson hesitated and demurred. He was receiving a salary of thirty dollars a week from Edison, rather a fair figure in those days, and had prospect of a share in the Edison motion picture enterprises whatever they might prove to be.

Professor Latham in December of this year of '94, seeking to finance his affairs and put them into businesslike shape, decided to form a company. With a degree of modesty that has not always characterized the christening of motion picture corporations since, he translated the "L" of Latham into Greek and incorporated the Lambda Company. Perhaps too he relished the classic flavor of it.

The distinct character of the Lambda Company as apart from the Kinetoscope Exhibition Company, the earlier peep show enterprise, which included Rector and Tilden, must be borne in mind to avoid confusion over subsequent events. A new parting of the ways was almost in sight. Rector and Tilden were not in entire accord with the fancy which Grey and Otway had for the life of Broadway. Rector continued yet a while in the background of Latham affairs but he was planning a course of his own.

It was Professor Latham's intent that his Lambda stock should go to his sons, and to them he looked considerably for the execution of the business affairs of the undertaking.

Otway Latham, pursuant to offers of a quarter interest in the project to Dickson, turned over the stock certificates for safe-keeping in the hands of Edmond Congar Brown, a lawyer and friend of Dickson. Dickson, doubting and wondering, was not ready to accept it in his own hands.

The Latham experiments started, like every other subsequent attempt at projection, with films from the Edison Kinetoscope, the ready made camera record. The first efforts at 35 Frank-fort street were very much like Dickson's experiment with the powerful arc lamps at Columbia University, made with the con-tinuously running movement of the Kinetoscope. As Latham reached for a better effect he was influenced by the lantern slides of the stereopticon and decided that a large size picture would be desirable. The larger area would compensate in some degree for the great loss of light incurred in trying to pro-ject on the screen with the little Edison films in the continu-ously moving Kinetoscope mechanism.

To those technically unfamiliar with the motion picture it is necessary to point out that at this time the real vital principle of today's perfected projection was not even yet discovered, and that the Lathams' concept was still of a continuously running film in the projection machine. The step by step principle had been adopted for the camera by sheer force of photo-chemical necessity. The film had to be stopped to let the light soak in, but it was not as yet known that the same thing had to be done for the eye.

Latham was therefore trying to attain the visual effect by in-creasing the volume of light which passed through the picture to the screen. The final solution, which he was not to reach, was to be through an increase of duration, rather than of vol-ume.

Since he wanted a larger picture to let more light through to the screen, Latham had to abandon the use of Edison's little

Kinetoscope films and plan the building of a bigger camera, an amplified edition of Edison's Kinetograph.

At the same time Professor Latham inquired of the Eastman plant in Rochester for film stock of such a size as he required. He learned to his dismay that it would be necessary to buy a whole "table" of film—that is to say, one pouring of the Eastman film on the big one hundred-foot glass table of the Rochester factory. This entailed an alarming outlay for the Lambda Company.

Latham set out to have Lauste construct a camera which should use a strip of film approximately one and a half times the width of the Edison standard.

One of the puzzles of camera building for the Lathams was the matter of intermittently stopping the film, frame by frame, to allow the light to impress the image. They had learned enough to know that the continuous movement of the peep show Kinetoscope machine would not permit satisfactory recording of motion. Otway went ingratiatingly to Dickson. Dickson was trying to steer a middle course and avoid revealing too much of his work. And at the same time he felt a certain friendship toward the Lathams, more especially toward the father. Otway did come away from Dickson with at least the wisp of a hint that there was a very old movement used by Swiss watchmakers, known as the Geneva cross, which would give an intermittent motion from a continuously revolving shaft. This was hastily communicated to Lauste in the Frankfort street shop for the benefit of the new camera.

It was late in January of the year of '95 when the machine took more promising form, and a model was hurried into construction. Work went on night and day as the Lathams hung over Lauste's workbench.

Woodville Latham was breaking under the strain of his attention. He had weakened heart action, resulting from his ordeals in the Civil War and from his addiction to strong black coffee to aid him in his laboratory vigils. For days on end he was forced to keep to his bed at the Hotel Bartholdi.

Late in the night of February 26, Otway Latham, Dickson, now an occasional visitor in Frankfort street, and Lauste gathered about the work bench to look over the new camera. It was time to try it out. They threaded it with some of the precious wide gauge film from Eastman, and turned the machine on an electric lamp.

Otway Latham swung the lamp by its cord, while Dickson turned the crank.

With feverish haste they extinguished the lamps and put the film into the developing bath. There was a tense wait, and then the image began to come up in the developer. It had a clearly defined series of images of the swinging incandescent lamp. It was a demonstration that they could make a picture. The problem of getting it on the screen was yet before them. Thus far they had done only what Edison had done before them. But it was progress. They had what they thought would be a better film for projection.

After an uncomfortable, restive night, Woodville Latham awakened early the next morning. It was not yet daylight. He consulted his watch and found it was five o'clock. When he turned up the gas he caught a glimpse of a note that had been pushed under the door. Folded within it was a bit of film with the pictures of the electric light and a notation:

> To my friend, Woodville Latham:
> Compliments of W. K. L. Dickson.

The note itself read:

> Experiment most successful. We took a picture. Don't wake us up as we did not reach the room until 3 A. M.
>
> OTWAY.

There was vast encouragement in this for the patiently hopeful Professor Latham. When some days later his health permitted, he went down to the shop and looked over the machine.

Enoch Rector, with the problem of photographing prize fights and long rounds still in mind, labored with the new camera to increase its scope beyond that of the Kinetograph over at Edison's. When long films were put into the camera its intermittent movements often jerked and broke them. Something had to be done to take the strain off the supply reel. Rector evolved an extra feed sprocket which formed a loop of slack film from which the intermittent movement could take it without jerking the whole reel.

This tiny mechanical fact held a whole world of destinies in it. The little bow of slack film created in the Latham camera became known in subsequent film affairs as "the Latham Loop." The day was to come when millions of dollars were to be staked on that loop, after it had passed through a patent office career without parallel or precedent.

The immediately important aspect of the loop was its liberation of the camera. Equipped with this slack forming mechanism the camera could be loaded with any desired length of film. The first Edison Kinetograph, exposing about forty-five to fifty feet, could record a scene for only about fifteen seconds of time. This had been extended in the prize fight pictures slightly, but now the Latham camera with Rector's loop could be loaded with long films and operated for minutes on end.

There was about this time just a hint of friction with Dickson. Otway Latham remarked to his father that Dickson had developed a penchant for talking in French to Lauste. Otway did not understand French. The father then issued instructions that orders to the workman would come from his son and that English would be more popular about the place.

Meanwhile over at West Orange, William E. Gilmore, the

new Edison general manager, had been accumulating observation and information. He was not entirely pleased with what he had gathered.

It was April 2, 1895, just one year to the day after Gilmore's arrival, that a long impending explosion occurred.

There were three of them in the room, Gilmore, Edison, and Dickson.

"I was accused to the effect my relations with the Lathams were not honorable," is the way Dickson described the situation, relating the event on the witness stand many years later.

" 'I don't believe a damn word of it!' " Dickson quoted Edison's response.

Thereat Dickson, filled with a brief confidence, suggested that either he or Gilmore should leave the Edison establishment. There was, it seems, an awkward silence.

Then since Edison's "decision was not sufficiently whole hearted" as Dickson described it on the witness stand, he resigned on the spot.

Some days later Dickson returned to the Edison laboratories and removed his personal effects. It was an abrupt parting that was not without its elements of regret to Edison. Dickson had been with him many years.

Out of Dickson's departure and subsequent connections was to come the great war that for years filled the courts with bitter litigations and hampered the development of the motion picture art.

Turning ahead some five years in the drama of conflict between Edison and his laboratory assistant we come to the hour of 11 o'clock in the forenoon of January 29, 1900, with a weighty gathering of lawyers about the desk where Edison sat in the great study of his laboratory at West Orange.

John A. Shields, standing examiner for the United States Circuit Court of the Southern District of New York, is hearing evidence in the first of the big patent battles, Thomas A. Edison vs. American Mutoscope Company, et al., in Equity No. 6928. Richard N. Dyer, attorney for Edison, complainant, has his client sworn, and the court reporter notes: "Thomas Alva Edison, age 53, occupation inventor." Dyer proceeds with the examination, presently coming to this sequence:

Q—Who is the man who was principally engaged in this experimental work under your instruction?

A—Mr. Kennedy Laurie Dickson was the man who did all the photographing.

Q—Mr. W. K. L. Dickson.

A—Yes, sir—that is the man.

Q—Is Mr. Dickson still employed by you?

A—No sir!

Q—Have you heard where he is working?

A—Working I believe for the Biograph Company.

Q—For the defendant, American Mutoscope Company?

A—Yes sir.

Q—Did Mr. Dickson have charge of the notebooks relating to this subject?

A—Yes sir.

Q—Have you had search made for those note books since he left the laboratory?

A—Yes sir.

Q—Have you been able to find them?

A—Not a scrap!

Whereupon they called it a morning and adjourned for luncheon, which was still dinner in that early year of the motion pictures.

CHAPTER TEN

MAJOR LATHAM CHALLENGES

THE Latham shop in Frankfort street, now that it had a camera completed and perhaps also because William Kennedy Laurie Dickson was free of Edison obligations, soon attained a projection machine. The first model was completed presumably some time in March.

Professor Latham, true to the tradition of motion picture inventors, christened his projector in a decoction of Greek roots and called it the Pantoptikon.

This machine differed from the previous projection efforts of Dickson's experiments in Room Five at Edison's laboratory in only one detail, the size of the film. One frame of the Latham picture contained approximately twice the area of one frame of the Edison film. The Latham machine also provided for handling the films on large reels with a capacity for about a thousand feet, instead of on a spool-bank as in the Kinetoscope. This use of the reel, of course, meant that the film had to be removed from the machine and re-wound, whereas in the Kinetoscope the short pictures ran over the spool-bank in endless loops without the necessity of re-winding, repeating their course through the machine.

The Latham machine was still merely an enlarged Kinetoscope arranged to present a picture by transmitted light on the screen, instead of viewing through a lens set in a peep hole. It was in truth not much of a contribution to the art of the motion picture. It is of historical significance to-day only because it was an expression of the effort toward the screen, and because it did for peculiar reasons, to be later revealed, lead to a significance for the name of Latham out of proportion to the mechanical and scientific attainment of the Latham effort.

On the afternoon of Sunday, April 21, 1895, Woodville Latham gave an exhibition of his projection machine to reporters. He was ready to tell the world about it. The next morning the *New York Sun* carried a story about the showing. It was illustrated with an old fashioned chalk plate drawing, depicting something that was new to the world—motion pictures on a screen.

It was a somewhat partisan piece of reporting. The *Sun* was obviously influenced strongly by the name of Edison and the fame of the Kinetoscope. It interviewed Edison on Latham's machine, and devoted more space to his comment than to the somewhat new device. The *Sun* said:

MAGIC LANTERN KINETOSCOPE

Edison Says Latham's Device Is Old and
Promises to Beat It.

An exhibition of what Edison considers a kinetoscope so arranged as to throw the pictures, enlarged, upon a screen, was given yesterday afternoon at 35 Frankfort Street by Woodville Latham. He calls his arrangement the Pantopticon. The illustration gives a very good idea of what it looks like. The continuous film of photographic pictures with slots cut in the edges to catch the teeth of a sprocket that keeps it from slipping is reeled in front of the electric light of a sort of magic lantern, and so the pictures are thrown successively on the screen with sufficient rapidity to produce the well known kinetoscope or zoetrope effect of animated pictures.

The pictures shown yesterday portrayed the antics of some boys at play in a park. They wrestled, jumped, fought, and tumbled over one another. Near where the boys were romping a man sat reading a paper and smoking a pipe. Even the puffs of smoke could be plainly seen, as could also the man's movements when he took a handkerchief from his pocket. The whole picture on the screen yesterday was about the size of a standard window sash, but the size is a matter of expense and adjustment. Mr. Latham's camera will take forty pictures a second, and it can be set up anywhere, in the street or on the top of a house.

Mr. Latham says that he will try to obtain a patent on his apparatus, which thus enables the exhibitor to show kinetoscope effects to a large audience at one time.

A *Sun* reporter saw Mr. Edison last evening and described the Latham machine to him. Hearing the description, Mr. Edison said:

"That is the kinetoscope. This strip of film with the pictures which you have here is made exactly as the film I use. The holes in it are for the spokes of the sprocket, which I devised.

"The throwing of the pictures on a screen was the very first thing I did with the kinetoscope. I didn't think much of that, because the pictures were crude, and there seemed to me to be no commercial value in that feature of the machine.

"In two or three months, however, we will have the kinetoscope perfected, and then we will show you screen pictures. The figures will be life size, and the sound of the voice can be heard as the movements of the figure are seen.

"If Mr. Latham can produce life size pictures now, as we will do with the kinetophone, that's a different matter.

"When Latham says he can set up his kinetograph anywhere and take the pictures for his machine, he means that he has simply a portable kinetograph.

"We have had one of those for six months. The reasons that our pictures all had to be taken here at first was that our kinetograph was unwieldy.

"If they exhibit this machine, improve on what I have done, and call it a kinetoscope, that's all right. I will be glad of whatever improvements Mr. Latham may make.

"If they carry the machine around the country, calling it by some other name, that's a fraud, and I shall prosecute whoever does it. I've applied for patents long ago."

Edison's paragraph, "If Mr. Latham can produce life size pictures now, as we will do with the Kinetophone, that's a different matter," was the one vitally significant element of his interview. The Kinetoscope experiments made by Edison and Dickson, with the continuously running film and the narrow slotted shutter, had by the loss of light and consequent weakness of screen illumination held their picture down to a small scale. Edison knew that screen illumination was the crux of the problem, but he did not endeavor to go into that with the *Sun's* reporter. The only reason that Latham's picture was larger on the screen than Edison's was because the Latham film was larger. The results were probably equally faulty.

The next morning in his room at the Hotel Bartholdi, Woodville Latham turned to the paper to see what had resulted from his exhibition—the first screen publicity show in the world.

We can well imagine the scene with Major Latham hot with anger as he strode the floor with the paper clenched in his hand.

A generation before in the Latham family this would have been provocation for a challenge and an affair of pistols and coffee.

But presently he was Professor Latham again. He sat down to his desk and, with painstaking care and control, wrote such a letter as he deemed compatible with his dignity and the situation.

The first article in the *Sun* had won a double column space at the top of page 2. The next day on page 5, under a patent medicine advertisement, the *Sun* published Woodville Latham's letter:

LATHAM'S PANTOPTICON

The Inventor of It Denies That It Infringes Upon the Kinetoscope

To the Editor of the Sun—Sir: You take notice in this morning's issue of a device of mine for projection on a screen of photographs of moving objects, and if you had stopped at that I should now be in your debt. But along with your account of the apparatus you publish certain invidious utterances of Mr. Thomas A. Edison, which, if they went unchallenged, might reflect on me personally in the estimation of persons who do not know me or are acquainted with the facts, and I, therefore, very respectfully request that you will give similar publicity to a word of reply from me.

I am not acquainted with the interior structure of Mr. Edison's kinetoscope, and am unable, therefore, to tell whether there are points of similarity between his apparatus and mine or not. I have, however, seen the outside of his, and I do know that mine is not half as large, though it includes an appliance for projection, which his does not. Another obvious difference is that my machine can carry thousands of feet of film as well as shorter lengths, and can be used for making long exhibitions, while as I am creditably informed, his larger machine (first made, by the way, on the order of one of my sons) can carry no more than one hundred and fifty feet of film, and can afford an exhibition of only about one minute. These facts would seem to indicate a very material difference of make-up. However, I applied some weeks ago for letters patent on my apparatus, and it will not be a great while before the public will have better evidence that Mr. Edison's mere *ipse dixit* as to the priority of claim.

As to Mr. Edison's threat to "prosecute anybody that exhibits my machine under any other name than the one he chooses to call it by, it is something a great deal worse than puerile. I prefer not, at this time, to characterize it more pointedly. So far as his even qualified charge of "fraud" is concerned, I have only to say he would probably not have made it if he had reflected that the men to whom he is indebted for ideas touching his kinetoscope are quite as numerous, both in this country and abroad, as are those who, by any possibility, could appropriate his own.

If Mr. Edison can project pictures of moving objects on a screen, as he says he can, why does he not do it as publicly as I have done, and do it at once?

WOODVILLE LATHAM.

HOTEL BARTHOLDI,
April 22.

In this exchange of charges and challenges of thirty years ago is reflected the coloration of the embitterments that were to run down through the years of picture history.

It was natural, in view of the events of April 2, that Edison should look upon Woodville Latham as an interloper and an infringer. Just as it is obvious to-day that Latham was a man of rigid principles, of old fashioned rectitude, conducting himself in this complex situation in a manner that squared with his own conscience. Latham did not know all about his own shop. It is perhaps just as natural, too, that Latham should have misjudged Edison and belittled his attainment of the Kinetoscope.

It was a large misfortune to the motion picture. There was to be no peace from that day until the remote end of 1908, thirteen battle-wrung years ahead.

To give this period its proper place in the sense of time, it is of interest to note that the newspapers in this week of the motion picture's birth were spicy with the sensational disclosures of the Oscar Wilde case. Also that week Kaiser Wilhelm announced the opening of the Kiel Canal, and the United States accepted an invitation to send warships to the ceremonial.

Meanwhile the problem of screen projection was not so nearly solved as might be surmised at this point. The pictures which the Latham machine projected were highly imperfect and unsatisfactory. But the enterprise was not amply financed, and it was desirable to get it to earning an income as soon as possible. Hasty steps were taken to get the products of the Lambda company before the public as soon as possible.

The next move was the making of a picture. In view of the success that the Latham brothers had in showing their six round prize fight special in the peep show Kinetoscope in Nassau street, it was an easy consequence that they should decide upon another fight as their first production for the screen. This was just as inevitable as the imitative tendency of the motion picture industry of to-day, which follows every success with a score of make-overs, approximations and simulations on the same theme. Witness the Far North pictures that came in the wake of "The Spoilers," the endless imitations and appropriations of the punches of "The Birth of a Nation," the flood of copies of "The Miracle Man," and the flow of little shadows of "The Covered Wagon."

A bright sunny day soon after the first of May '95, Otway Latham in the role of director staged a fight between "Young Griffo" and "Battling (Charles) Barnett." The battleground was the roof of Madison Square Garden, where, high in the tower above, Stanford White the architect had his studio, the same world famous Garden redolent with historic glories and memories.

May 20, 1895, the Griffo-Barnett fight went on exhibition to the public at 153 Broadway. It ran its flickering way about four minutes of screen time.

The Latham picture activities now began to be a real challenge for public attention. Howard B. Hackett of the *New York World* wrote an enthusiastic forecast of the coming glories of the screen, and what he promised is something of an index of the cruder but more honest expressions of the public taste of thirty years ago.

"You will sit comfortably and see fighters hammering each other, circuses, suicides, hangings, electrocutions, shipwrecks, scenes on the exchanges, street scenes, horse races, football games—almost anything in fact in which there is action, as if you were on the spot during the actual event," Mr. Hackett promised for the motion picture theatre to be. "And you will not see marionettes. You will see actual people and things as they are. If they wink their other eye, as Miss Cissy Fitzgerald winks hers, or as Thomas C. Platt winks his, you will see the lid on its way down and up. If their hair rises in fright, grows gray in half an hour, you will see all the details of the change."

In the course of the article it was noted that the Lathams had planned to photograph the execution of one Buchanan, a murderer, at Sing Sing, but that the governor would not consent.

This article was rather widely clipped and reprinted in newspapers in various parts of the country. The *Chicago Inter-Ocean* of June 11, 1895, then one of the great papers of the nation, gave it large attention and big headlines, reading:

EDISON NOT IN IT!

Kenetoscope Outclassed
by Prof. Latham's
newest

Reproduces Continuity
of action accurately

Adapted for anything
from a change of
heart to a
prizefight

The story proceeded to proclaim that the peep show Kinetoscope, now rather widely known, had been vastly outdone with a machine that put the living pictures on a screen. The article and its pointed headlines found the way to the Edison laboratories in New Jersey and added considerable fervor to the Edison dislike of the name of Latham and all that pertained to it. Some years after, on the witness stand, Woodville Latham expressed annoyance at the attitude of the story published in his behalf and asserted it was not in any sense a quotation of him.

But some of the attachés of the Latham plant were not as guarded in their words as the old professor.

So the motion picture opened for the first of all first runs on Broadway. How far was that little four-minute picture-show on a magic lantern sheet in a storeroom from today's motion picture magnificences of upper Broadway, with its multi-million dollar screen theatres!

The opening May 20, 1895, ill-advised and imperfect as it was, was the first public showing of motion pictures on a screen in all the world. The pictures flickered and danced and glimmered. It was only a ghost of a show, but it was first.

Simultaneously with that opening the Lambda company started its commercial career by preparing to offer for sale state rights on the use of their projection machine. This method of territorial sale was following the precedent laid down by Norman C. Raff with the peep show Kinetoscope, which had been following the phonograph merchandising. The Lathams started building a number of machines and making a series of pictures to be shown on the new born screen.

A beginning had been made. But it was a beginning in the business of the screen rather than the art. The real founding of the motion picture as we know it to-day was well near a year in the future, with a tremendous complexity of events occupying the months between. The most extraordinary affairs were involved and the strangely negative reason for the survival of the name of Latham in screen history was yet to come.

THOMAS ARMAT of Washington, whose Vitascope began the commercial history of the motion picture on the screen in the United States and established the basic principles of film projection.

MAGIC-LANTERN KINETOSCOPE.

Edison Says Latham's Device Is Old and Promises to Beat It.

An exhibition of what Edison considers a kinetoscope so arranged as to throw the pictures, enlarged, upon a screen was given yesterday afternoon at 35 Frankfort street by Woodville Latham. He calls his arrangement the Pantoptikon. The illustration gives a very good idea of what it looks like. The continuous film of photographic pictures with slots cut in the edges to catch the teeth of a sprocket that keeps it from slipping is reeled in front of the electric light of a sort of magic lantern, and so the pictures are thrown successively on the screen with sufficient rapidity to produce the well-known kinetoscope or zoetrope effect of animated pictures.

The pictures shown yesterday portrayed the antics of some boys at play in a park. They wrestled, jumped, fought, and tumbled over one another. Near where the boys were romping a man sat reading a paper and smoking a pipe. Even the puffs of smoke could be plainly seen, as could also the man's movements when he took a handkerchief from his pocket. The whole picture on the screen yesterday was about the size of a standard window sash, but the size is a matter of expense and adjustment. Mr. Latham's camera will take forty pictures a second, and it can be set up anywhere, in the street or on the top of a house.

Mr. Latham says that he will try to obtain a patent on his apparatus, which thus enables the exhibitor to show kinetoscope effects to a large audience at one time.

A SUN reporter saw Mr. Edison last evening and described the Latham machine to him. Hearing the description, Mr. Edison said:

"That is the kinetoscope. This strip of film with the pictures, which you have here, is made exactly as the film I use. The holes in it are for the spokes of the sprocket, which I devised.

"The throwing of the pictures on a screen was the very first thing I did with the kinetoscope. I didn't think much of that, because the pictures were crude, and there seemed to me to be no commercial value in that feature of the machine.

"In two or three months, however, we will have the kinetophone perfected, and then we will show you screen pictures. The figures will be life size, and the sound of the voice can be heard as the movements of the figures are seen.

"If Mr. Latham can produce life-size pictures now, as we will do with the kinetophone, that's a different matter.

"When Latham says he can set up his kinetograph anywhere and take the pictures for his machine, he means that he has simply a portable kinetograph.

"We have had one of those for six months. The reason that our pictures all had to be taken here at first was that our kinetograph was unwieldy.

"If they exhibit this machine, improve on what I have done, and call it a kinetoscope, that's all right. I will be glad of whatever improvements Mr. Latham may make.

"If they carry the machine around the country, calling it by some other name, that's a fraud, and I shall prosecute whoever does it. I've applied for patents long ago."

ENLARGED KINETOSCOPE PICTURES THROWN ON A SCREEN.

THE FIRST SCREEN PUBLICITY story in the world — when the *New York Sun* told of Woodville Latham's demonstration of his Pantoptikon at 35 Frankfort street, April 21, 1895.

CHAPTER ELEVEN

ARMAT ATTAINS THE SCREEN

THE far flung seed of the Edison Kinetoscope by the late summer of 1894 carried the motion picture film well over the world, and by autumn many inventive minds had dallied with the notion of projecting the picture on the screen. The idea of the combination of the Kinetoscope and the magic lantern occurred independently to many persons.

The same early months of 1895 which saw the premature launching of the imperfect Latham projecting machine developed an international race to the screen, with experimenters at work in England, France, and the United States. None of these men was aware of the labors of the others. Each of them reached some sort of a solution of the problem, in some instances within a few days or weeks of one another.

The result of this unconscious race has been to confuse vastly the annals of the motion picture and to give opportunity to many patriotic expressions of partisanship unjustified by fact. In addition, complications affecting the experimental stage of screen research in the United States piled confusion upon confusion until now after three decades the truth has been so buried that the discovery of even glints of it generates a feeling of revelation. It is unfortunately true that few of the widely accepted understandings of the evolution of the screen are even approximately correct. We shall find the honors, such as they are, divided among many men of many nations. There is just a sufficient coloration of fact in the competing claims of screen priority to have made it possible for protagonists to build a tradition of priority for any of several chosen inventors.

Three important strands of development reached out from Edison's Room Five and his Kinetoscope, through Raff and Gammon's enterprise of exploitation.

A number of Kinetoscopes and various films and machine parts were sold, ostensibly for use in America, to two Greek persons, George Georgiades and George Trajedis. These machines, according to the daybook entries of Holland Brothers, eastern agents for Raff's first Kinetoscope Company, were delivered in August 1894 at 1 Columbus avenue, New York City. At the same address was one T. Mavro, of whom we hear no more, who received and signed for the Kinetoscopes, films and other equipment. Georgiades and Trajedis shortly took their machines and sailed for London, where, according to tradition, they had been candy merchants or green grocers. English film history began then.

Secondly, starting another strand, Lionel Werner, in behalf of Werner Brothers, purchased a battery of Kinetoscopes and exported them to France. In October, 1894, the Werners opened a Kinetoscope parlor in Paris at 20 Boulevard Poissonnière, inviting all and sundry to see the new marvel from the Wizard of Orange, U. S. A. And this was the beginning of the films in France.

The third and most significant extuberation of the Kinetoscope idea brings us to Washington, D. C., the unsung scene of most important phases of screen evolution.

One warm and steaming day of the Washington summer of '94, H. A. Tabb, a friend of Norman C. Raff and Frank R. Gammon, turned in at the office of T. C. Daniel and Thomas Armat, real estate, 1313 "F" Street. Tabb was an old friend of Armat, known from boyhood. He had always had his eye on Tom. Armat was an inventive chap, always up to making something. He had taken out a patent, too, something rather good in the way of a conduit for an electrical railway; and just then electric traction was the great innovation in transportation.

Tabb was full of enthusiasms about the great new Edison novelty, the Kinetoscope. Tabb had a deal on with Raff & Gammon to take a big Kinetoscope display to the coming Cotton States Exposition in Atlanta, to introduce the peep show with its vital living pictures to the South with a most pretentious presentation.

Tabb thought it would be a good turn, and maybe a stroke of business, to interest this young chap Armat in the Kinetoscope. Tabb thus became the agency of affairs much beyond his ken.

Tabb sat down and fanned himself with his straw hat while he unfolded the alluring story of the swift and magic profits of Kinetoscope exhibition. He was sure that Tom would take to the idea.

Young Armat deliberated and shook his head.

"No, I don't see much in a peep hole machine like that. But I'll tell you there would be a big field for a machine that would put the pictures on a screen like the stereopticon."

Armat was thinking again of the Anschütz Electrical Tachyscope that he had seen the year before at the World's Fair in Chicago, with its glass plate pictures and flashing Geissler tube illumination.

Tabb dissented. "Yes—it would be a big thing if you got it, but you'd probably have a hard time making one, if it can be done. You know Edison has been trying to make a projection machine, and it's a failure so far."

Tabb had heard about, and perhaps had seen, the efforts at projection that Charles H. Kayser was making at Raff & Gammon's office in the Postal Telegraph building in New York.

This was in the nature of a challenge to Armat. He started to prepare for some experimental work. It was more to his taste than the routine affairs of the real estate office.

In October, 1894, a few weeks after the Tabb conversation,

Armat enrolled in the Bliss School of Electricity in Washington. Professor Bliss had taken considerable interest in Armat's "Conduit Electric Railway" patent, No. 521,562 of issue June 19, 1894, on an application of March 28 of the year previous.

Soon after he entered the school Armat approached Bliss with an inquiry about the necessary resistance to be employed in circuit with an arc lamp. He explained to his instructor that he wanted to use the light in some experiments aimed at projecting motion pictures on a screen.

Bliss beamed with interest and remarked that there was another student in the school interested in something of the same problem. The next day he introduced Armat to this student, Charles Francis Jenkins.

This is the same C. Francis Jenkins who has more recently appeared so frequently in the popular science periodicals and on the radio pages of the daily press with promises of radio vision and broadcast transmission of motion pictures by wireless. Jenkins was also a young man, then employed as a stenographer and clerk in the Life Saving Division of the United States Treasury Department. He had been in contact with the Kinetoscope of the Raff & Gammon exhibit in the Columbia Phonograph Company parlors in Pennsylvania Avenue, Washington. These exhibitions were under the charge of E. F. Murphy, who, unforeseen years after, became laboratory chief for the Universal Film Manufacturing Company. Under the tutelage of Murphy and Bliss, Jenkins arrived at a modified type of Kinetoscope which was placed on exhibition at the Pure Food Show in Convention Hall in November of 1894. This machine does not appear to have been a very important departure from the Edison machine. It was apparently identical with it in most respects save that instead of a revolving shutter, to cut off the light in flashes as the film sped past the peep hole, it had revolving electric lights.

Jenkins also, at this time, had a tentative device called a rotary lens camera, built somewhat after the manner suggested or implied by a patent No. 61,973, which Louis Ducos du Hauron received in France, issued April 25, 1864, twenty-five years before there was any film to use in it. The Ducos camera idea was far more plausible than practical.

If this rotary camera had been capable of producing motion pictures in competition with the Edison Kinetograph or other subsequent kineto-cameras, it would have turned the tide in coming patent wars. The entire political history of the art of the motion picture would have been different. Also if this type of camera would work it would be of large value today.

The rotary lens camera notion is of great interest because of the ingeniousness of the Ducos concept. Ducos naturally thought of the flow of the living picture with its apparently continuous effect on the eye as a function to be performed by a continuously running vehicle. It was a logical but unscientific conclusion. It is obvious that Ducos, and many who came after him, had only a superficial understanding of the principles of vision. Ducos, therefore, dreamed on paper of a camera in which a photo-sensitive band—film was yet unborn—ran down a path of exposure on which a cluster of lenses, mounted on the rim of a revolving disc, successively cast images, traveling with the sensitive band. This type of camera has thus far never been made to operate successfully except by power of lead pencil and conversation.

Armat and Jenkins, at the Bliss school together, became friendly. Armat suggested that there was a possibility that something might be done toward projecting a picture on a screen, magic lantern fashion, by modification of Jenkins' revolving-light kinetoscopic machine. Armat had an idea of how this might be done.

Jenkins had already filed an application for a patent on his kinetoscopic machine under the name of the Phantoscope. The name was perhaps suggested by the old Fantoscope of Plateau at the University of Ghent, mentioned in an earlier chapter. Now that Armat suggested its use for projection of a picture on a screen, Jenkins amended his application for a patent to take in the projection idea. He also renewed a lapsed application for a patent on a rotary lens camera.

Armat was considerably impressed by the promises of this rotary lens machine. It seemed likely, and promised a source of film which could be independent of the patent-controlled Edison product.

Jenkins invited Armat to join with him in his photographic endeavors and drew up an agreement in writing. On March 25, 1894, Armat and Jenkins signed this document. Under the terms of this agreement, Armat agreed to build an experimental projection machine after the general design of Jenkins' adaptation of the Kinetoscope and to advance the money for this work. In return, Armat was to have, among other things, the right to make use of a certain number of Jenkins' rotary lens cameras, which Armat then believed commercially workable.

The next day they began the building of the machine which was expected to be a projecting Phantoscope; and on that day, March 26, a patent on Jenkins' application covering this machine was issued as No. 536,569. A short time later Jenkins received a patent on his rotary lens camera, No. 560,800.

While this contemplated Phantoscope projection machine was in construction Jenkins discussed it in the *Photographic Times*. This machine, like other approximately contemporary efforts, including the Lathams, aimed at projection from a continuously moving film, continuous because the movement in the Edison peep show Kinetoscope, the parent machine, was continuous.

This method of projection from a continuously running film not only entailed a tremendous loss of light, all but about one three-hundredth part of the lamp's output, but it also was extremely irregular and erratic on the screen. Perfect registration of the image on the screen would have required every frame of the film to register and synchronize with the previous one to within one twelve-thousandth part of a second, at the rate of projection then attempted, requiring about forty-eight images a second, which was beyond practical attainment. This first projecting Phantoscope with a continuously running film was inevitably a failure.

The Armat-Jenkins agreement had been fulfilled and might easily have ended there. Jenkins was discouraged, and Armat was baffled.

Armat decided to go ahead on ideas of his own, but invited Jenkins to continue with him. Armat advanced the money for further work. A considerable number of experiments followed in the next few months. From these experiments emerged a revolutionary idea and the basic principle upon which the whole technology of screen presentation of the motion picture depends. The research was formally at least a partnership and this new idea therefore was the joint property of Armat and Jenkins. There are many evidences which may be taken to substantially support Armat's later assertion that this new and important principle of projection was born in his mind. There was, however, at the time under consideration, no issue between the inventors. Now for the first time the correct and essential principle of motion picture projection was laid down.

Armat decided that the film must be presented, not as a continuously running stream of pictures, but step by step with an intermittent motion, and in such a manner *that each picture should be given a long period of rest and illumination on the screen, and a relatively brief period of movement from frame to frame.* The intermittent motion had already been evolved in the Edison camera for making pictures, but the relation of the period of rest to the period of movement for each of those tiny steps of the film, as applied to projection, remained for Armat to discover. By Armat's plan the film was to take precisely the same elapsed time getting through the machine, but it was to proceed by short jumps and long stops. He was going to give the little individual pictures, of each frame of film, time to soak into the eye.

It is of significance to realize that the movement or gait sought in this contemplated method of projection was identical with the movement of film through the Edison camera or Kinetograph in which the pictures were made. The essential difference between Armat's contemplated projector and the existing Edison camera lay in the fact that for photo-chemical reasons the period of illumination required to record an image on film negative was much shorter than the period of rest within which the exposures were made, whereas in projecting the film positive for the eye a maximum exposure to the screen, or complete use of the period of rest, was required. Meanwhile, it must be borne in mind, the movement and workings of the Edison camera in all probability were not known to Armat at that time.

In order to arrive at the intermittent motion desired for the film driving mechanism Armat decided upon a sort of specially constructed transmission, a "mutilated" gear. It was ordered made at the Boston Gear Works of Boston, Mass.

This intermittent gear arrived about the middle of August, 1895. Armat and Jenkins hastened to install it in the waiting mechanism. The hour of the great test was at hand. They threaded up the machine with an Edison Kinetoscope film, and started the motor. Their hearts were in their mouths. In a second their fingers were in their ears.

The thing worked. There was a living picture on the wall, probably the best motion picture that had ever appeared on a screen. But the noise was terrific. The picture, tearing madly, trying to reach a speed of forty-eight images a second, with the heavy three inch brass gear starting and stopping so often, lasted only a few seconds when the film ran out. They ran it over again and again. Very shortly the gear was battered out of shape by the intermittent stops.

Pound for pound this was the noisiest piece of machinery in the world. The art of the screen was born in boiler shop roar.

Obviously the principle was correct while the machine was very wrong. This was entirely unexpected.

Ever since that time the big Boston gear has been a paper weight on Armat's desk, where it may be seen today. It is a significant piece of machinery, worthy of place in a museum.

The problem had now resolved itself into the evolution of a method of giving the film the necessary motion without having to start and stop a relatively heavy machine part. Armat determined that the machine must move continuously while the film progressed intermittently. He would evade the obstacle of inertia.

An inspiration came to the rescue. Armat recalled a lens testing box, built the May before, when he and Jenkins were planning to use it for selecting lenses for the proposed rotary lens camera. It was built after the design of an identical device evolved by E. J. Marey and his associate, Georges Demeny, at Marey Institute, in France, when they set out to make successive pictures of objects in motion. It consisted of a sort of cam movement which would jerk a sensitized tape past a lens. As the eccentric or cam revolved, it wound the tape around it, getting thicker with each revolution and thus increasing the space between the successive exposures or pictures. This was no handicap to the purposes of Marey and Demeny, but it certainly was not capable of projecting a motion picture or anything that would pass for one.

Nevertheless, the old Demeny lens testing box can be found in the pages of motion picture history offered as a camera prior to the Edison Kinetograph. It has also been represented as a projecting machine. A description of this Demeny device was published in *The Photographic Times* of January, 1895, and there came to the attention of the Washington inventors.

The cam movement of this old testing box was precisely what Armat wanted to give the film of his projector the jerks of the intermittent movement required.

A temporary machine was thrown together from spare parts about the shop, and patterns were rushed through for a more substantial model to be cast in brass. This machine, first tested in August, 1895, worked as well as the noisy gear machine, and it had none of the old machine's faults. The busy cam slapped the film past the projection aperture with great accuracy and little noise. This was the beginning of what has come to be known throughout the industry as the "beater movement."

Armat made no claim to invention of the movement itself. It was under English patent No. 24,457, issued to Demeny in 1893, two years before.

The machine was ready for introduction now. Three of them were built, in August of 1895.

THOMAS ARMAT'S "beater" projector of 1895, the machine which established the essential principle, of a long period of rest and illumination in the intermittent film movement, on which all screen projection depends.

ROBERT W. PAUL of London, the British pioneer of the motion picture, and inventor of the Theatrograph.

CHAPTER TWELVE

PAUL AND "THE TIME MACHINE"

Now we shall trace for a distance the steps by which the American evolution of the art of the screen was being duplicated in parallel, and sometimes slightly prior, steps abroad.

Both in England and in Europe the work of the screen inventors began upon the foundation of the Edison Kinetoscope. There have been many efforts on the part of various patriotic writers of various nationalities to show other origins for the screen art overseas and to attribute priorities to those who really followed upon and amplified the work of Edison and Dickson, rather than anticipating them.

We have seen how much and how little was done at West Orange, U. S. A. But it was from that basic attainment of the Kinetoscope film that the magic screen of the whole world sprang.

How long the world might have waited for the motion picture film without the attentions of Edison and Dickson is a wide conjecture. But the film, the basic record of motion, having been attained, the world was soon to have the motion picture on the screen, through several agencies quite independent of each other.

When the two Greeks, Georgiades and Trajedis, arrived in London with their Kinetoscopes purchased in New York they opened an exhibition in a store in Old Broad street, E. C.

The instant success of the showing made them wish for more Kinetoscopes to extend their business. They evolved an enterprising line of action. Instead of importing more of the expensive Edison machines, at $300 each, F. O. B. New York, they would have duplicates made in England. They cast about seeking a machine maker.

Georgiades and Trajedis fancied a certain brand of Turkish in their cigarettes, which made them familiars in the cigarette establishment of John Melachrino, the same whose name may still be observed these many years later on a machine made product of similar character.

To their countryman, Melachrino, the Greeks confided their quest. The course of motion picture destiny had now become as thinly fanciful as the curling smoke of a cigarette. Melachrino in turn recalled an English customer for that same fragrant blending of the weed, one Henry Short. Now Short had gossiped over the counter of the skill of his old friend Robert W. Paul, maker of scientific instruments of precision. At Melachrino's the Greeks waited for Short and he took them to Paul with their mechanical problem.

Georgiades and Trajedis asked Paul to duplicate the Kinetoscope. He reflected and demurred, pointing out that it was undoubtedly patented by Edison and that it would be illegal to build it.

But when the Greeks persisted, Paul investigated the British patent records and found to his amazement that Edison had in fact not patented his machine in England. It will be recalled that Edison had some years before waved aside his attorney's suggestion of foreign patents.

This situation left Paul with a free hand. He forthwith filled the order of the Greeks and also proceeded to make some of the machines on his own account. These machines he placed on exhibition in Earl's Court, London, to a large and immediate profit.

The fame of Paul and the Kinetoscope spread, and a large demand arose in Great Britain and extended over to the Continent. Orders for the machines came from all directions. Edison had not only overlooked foreign patents, but the whole foreign market as well. When Paul and his assistants appeared at his shop in the mornings they found the stairways lined with waiting customers, some asleep on the steps after a night long vigil there in Hatton Garden holding their places to book orders for Kinetoscopes.

All of Paul's machines were necessarily dependent on the Edison studio in New Jersey for films. The only motion pictures in the world were being made at the "Black Maria." This foreign demand soon brought alarmed attention from Gilmore, Edison's general manager. Gilmore, striving to rehabilitate Edison finances, were clutching at every asset. He moved quickly to attempt a recovery of the overlooked foreign market. The supply of films for Paul was abruptly cut off. Frank Z. Maguire and Joseph D. Baucus, an attorney, went to London as Edison agents for the Kinetoscope.

But Paul, with a thriving business under way, was not to be thwarted now. He set about endeavors at a camera. He immediately recognized the necessity for an intermittent motion for the recording film, with a pause for each exposure. The first experimental idea, according to accounts, was adopted by Paul from a sketch for a machine to print still photographs from a roll of paper fed past the negative from a roll of stock, interrupted and clamped into contact for each successive print. This scheme was submitted by Birt Acres, in connection with his work for an English photographic supply manufacturer, and had no direct relation to the motion picture in its conception.

Responding to an inquiry aimed at establishing disputed facts and dates, Paul in a letter to the author July 23, 1924, said:

> I find that on March 29, 1895, I made an agreement with Birt Acres for him to take films for the Kinetoscope with a camera made by me. It has an intermittent movement of the film, effected by clamping and unclamping the film at the "gate" while under

tension provided by a spring jockey-roller. This gave unsteady pictures and within a few weeks (I think, days) was replaced by a sprocket, 7 pictures in circumference, actuated by a finger wheel and a 7-point star based on the idea of a Maltese cross.

In other words, Paul in his second camera arrived at a stop motion device very similar to that which the Edison-Dickson experiments had evolved in 1888 in West Orange. The date, March 29, 1895, established by Paul is significant in that he had just then arrived at the intermittent idea for the camera and was making films for the peep show Kinetoscopes. A great deal of complication and misunderstanding in motion picture affairs have grown out of claims of prior dates made in "Moving Pictures, *How They are Made and Worked*, by F. A. Talbot, an English writer on many diverse topics in the popular science manner. These enthusiastic patriotic claims of priority are, it must be understood, Talbot's, whose book is otherwise unbiased and highly informative. Paul, conservative and precise, does not indulge in undocumented memories.

The Paul camera differed markedly from the Edison Kinetograph in several important respects. The Kinetograph with its ponderous housing and battery and motor drive could only be moved with a horse-drawn wagon. The Paul machine was small and portable. Also Edison, striving for continuous effect on the eye and rather unaware of how easily the eye may be imposed upon in the matter of persistence of vision, used from forty-five to forty-eight exposures or images a second. Paul decided that twenty were ample to give the effect and just about half as costly in film consumption.

Among Paul's first Kinetoscope subjects were *Bootblack at Work in a London Street* and *A Rough Sea at Dover*. These pictures went out to his peep show customers.

Meanwhile Paul's observations at his prospering Earl's Court showing of the English version of the Kinetoscope and the pressure of a demand from his machine customers made it seem desirable to get a machine which should unite the Kinetoscope with the magic lantern to put the pictures on the wall for a whole room full of spectators at once. It was precisely the same pattern of experience which had set the Lathams to work and sent Norman C. Raff of the Kinetoscope Company to Edison demanding a projection machine.

It is of passing interest that one of Paul's Kinetoscope customers of the time was Charles Pathé of Paris, whose name is now familiar to the motion picture audiences of the world through the Pathé news reel and other screen products.

Paul's experiments in the course of the spring and summer of 1895 duplicated and paralleled in most respects those of the Lathams and of Jenkins and Armat in the United States. He, too, tried projection with the continuously running film of the Kinetoscope movement, and this was, of course, repeating the yet earlier efforts of the same sort made by Dickson for Edison. Some time before the autumn of 1895 Paul reached the notion of using an intermittent motion in the projector, permitting the picture to pause for the eye. Commenting on this in his letter, Paul remarks:

> *Early in 1895* I had not realized the necessity for intermittent movement of the film, but it is certain that I did so by October of that year; this of course refers to projection, and is the stranger as I had already made several cameras with intermittent motion.

Paul obtained the film for his experiments of 1895 from the Blair concern at Foots Cray, Kent. Blair was coating photographic emulsions on celluloid sheet stock imported from the United States.

Once set in the path of the pursuit of the intermittent motion, Paul soon applied his camera experience to the projector. The tale of his final triumph is a part of British film tradition. It was in the pale hour of three o'clock in the morning in the workshop in Hatton Garden. The machine was finally assembled, threaded with film, and started. When the picture flashed up on the screen Paul and his assistants set up a cheer.

This was a most unseemly occurrence in a London street at that hour of the morning. The outraged police rushed in, prepared to suppress the uprising, mutiny, insurrection or rebellion, whatever it might be, against the peace and dignity of the King of England and his law-abiding subjects.

Pleading extenuating circumstances the workers pointed to the strange machine and proceeded to demonstrate. Then the police joined in the cheering. Great Britain had discovered the empire of the screen, one large territory which the Lion has not benevolently assimilated.

Having arrived at the motion picture on the screen, Paul was still somewhat in doubt about what to do with it. He appears to have had some dimly prophetic vision of an evolving career for the new art of the picture.

That Paul saw it in the light of a scientific abstraction which might find concrete utility in the service of art is indicated by the counsel he sought.

Paul's attention was arrested by a conspicuous piece of fiction entitled *The Time Machine,* which appeared in 1894. There was a striking relation between the fancy of the story and the fact of the motion picture. The author of this story was H. G. Wells, a science teacher who had turned from the class room and lecture platform to fiction for his expression. His story *The Time Machine* was helping mightily to establish him as a writer. Remember this was thirty years ago. Wells had only fairly begun to write of his speculations and forecasts in the evolution of the doctrines and social opinion which today make him world famous.

In this story Paul saw an opportunity to use the special properties of the motion picture in a new and perhaps especially effective method of narration. He wrote to Wells, who went to confer with Paul at his laboratory at 44 Hatton Garden.

A reading of *The Time Machine,* even now, leaves one with a strong impression that the story was born of the direct suggestion of the behavior of a motion picture film. Wells, in a letter to the writer in 1924, said he was unable to remember details of the relation. But the evidence is such that if the story was not evolved directly from the experience of seeing the Kinetoscope, it was indeed an amazing coincidence.

The Time Machine is a fanciful tale of the adventures of a physicist who built a machine which could travel in time just as an airplane travels in space. The *Time Traveler* tells his story in the first person. In the third chapter of the Wells story he says:

> I drew a breath, set my teeth, gripped the starting lever with both my hands, and went off with a thud. The laboratory got hazy and went dark. Mrs. Wachett came in, and walked, apparently without seeing me, toward the garden door. I suppose it took her a minute or so to traverse the place, but to me she seemed to shoot across the room like a rocket.

In that paragraph one does not have to stretch his fancy to see what must be taken as the motion picture influence at the bottom of Wells' concept. The operation of the *Time Traveler* was very like the starting of the peep-show Kinetoscope, and the optical effect experienced by the fictional adventurer was identical with that experienced in viewing a speeding film.

But even more strongly is the motion picture character of the *Time Machine* idea evidenced in Wells' chapter thirteen, where the *Time Traveler,* nearing the end of his narrative, recites:

> I saw one little thing that seemed odd to me. I think I have told you that when I set out, before my velocity became very high,

Mrs. Wachett had walked across the room, traveling, it seemed to me, like a rocket. As I returned, I passed again across the minute when she traversed the laboratory. But now every motion appeared to be the direct inverse of her previous one. The door at the lower end opened and she glided quietly up the laboratory, back foremost, and disappeared behind the door by which she had previously entered.

This paragraph details precisely the effect of running a film backward with consequent exact reversal of the action. It is hard to believe that Wells did not take his notion directly from the peep show film. One of the earliest novelty effects sought in the Kinetoscope in the days when it was enjoying scientific attention was in exactly this sort of reversal of commonplace bits of action. It continues today a somewhat hackneyed bit of trick camera work. In the early days we saw runners backing up at high speed and backing locomotives swallowing their smoke in reverse gear. Nowadays we see Venuses in half-piece bathing suits spring from the pool and retrace the parabola of the dive to alight on the springboard. Such is the progress of art.

Returning to Wells, there is additional evidence of the motion picture root of the *Time Machine* idea in that he stresses the picture reversal effect in the phrase: "she glided quietly." Wells seems to have been thinking in terms of the picture exclusively. He for the moment ignored the fact that his *Time Traveler* in recrossing a moment of time should have experienced the sounds as well as the sights of that moment, both reversed. Mrs. Wachett might just as well also been heard backing up and closing the door. The thing had already been done in experimental reversals of the phonograph. It would seem pretty definite that the *Time Traveler* was all eyes and the story all motion picture.

Out of the author-scientist collaborations in Hatton Garden came a screen project to materialize the human wish to live in the Past, Present and Future all at once. It is all set forth in clear terms in a British patent application, No. 19984, drawn up by Paul under date of October 24, 1895, reading:

A NOVEL FORM OF EXHIBITION OR ENTERTAINMENT, MEANS FOR PRESENTING THE SAME

My invention consists of a novel form of exhibition whereby the spectators have presented to their view scenes which are supposed to occur in the future or past, while they are given the sensation of voyaging upon a machine through time, and means for presenting these scenes simultaneously and in conjunction with the production of the sensations by the mechanism described below, or its equivalent.

The mechanism I employ consists of a platform, or platforms, each of which contain a suitable number of spectators and which may be enclosed at the sides after the spectators have taken their places, leaving a convenient opening towards which the latter face, and which is directed towards a screen upon which the views are presented.

In order to create the impression of traveling, each platform may be suspended from cranks in shafts above the platform, which may be driven by an engine or other convenient source of power. These cranks may be so placed as to impart to the platform a gentle rocking motion, and may also be employed to cause the platform to travel bodily forward through a short space, when desired, or I may substitute for this portion of the mechanism similar shafts below the platforms, provided with cranks or cams, or worms keyed eccentrically on the shaft, or wheels gearing in racks attached to the underside of the platform or otherwise.

Simultaneously with the forward propulsion of the platform, I may arrange a current of air to be blown over it, either by fans attached to the sides of the platform, and intended to represent to the spectators the means of propulsion, or by a separate blower driven from the engine and arranged to throw a regulated blast over each of the platforms.

After the starting of the mechanism, and a suitable period having elapsed, representing, say, a certain number of centuries, during which the platforms may be in darkness, or in alternations of darkness and dim light, the mechanism may be slowed and a pause made at a given epoch, on which the scene upon the screen will come gradually into view of the spectators, increasing in size and distinctness from a small vista, until the figures, etc., may appear lifelike if desired.

In order to produce a realistic effect, I prefer to use for the projection of the scene upon the screen, a number of powerful lanterns, throwing the respective portions of the picture, which may be composed of,

(1) A hypothetical landscape, containing also the representations of the inanimate objects in the scene.

(2) A slide, or slides, which may be traversed horizontally or vertically and contain representations of objects such as a navigable balloon etc., which is required to traverse the scene.

(3) Slides or films, representing in successive instantaneous photographs, after the manner of the kinetoscope, the living persons or creatures in their natural motions. The films or slides are prepared with the aid of the kinetograph or special camera, from made up characters performing on a stage, with or without a suitable background blending with the main landscape.

The mechanism may be similar to that used in the kinetoscope, but I prefer to arrange the film to travel intermittently instead of continuously and to cut off the light only during the rapid displacement of the film as one picture succeeds another, as by this means less light is wasted than in the case when the light is cut off for the greater portion of the time, as in the ordinary kinetoscope mechanism.

(4) Changeable coloured, darkened, or perforated slides may be used to produce the effect on the scene of sunlight, darkness, moonlight, rain, etc.

In order to enable the scenes to be gradually enlarged to a definite amount, I may mount these lanterns on suitable carriages or trollies, upon rails provided with stops or marks, so as to approach to or recede from the screen a definite distance, and to enable a dissolving effect to be obtained, the lantern may be fitted with the usual mechanism. In order to increase the realistic effect I may arrange that after a certain number of scenes from a hypothetical future have been presented to the spectators, they may be allowed to step from the platforms, and be conducted through grounds or buildings arranged to represent exactly one of the epochs through which the spectator is supposed to be traveling.

After the last scene is presented I prefer to arrange that the spectators should be given the sensation of voyaging backwards from the last epoch to the present, or the present epoch may be supposed to have been accidentally passed, and a past scene represented on the machine coming to a standstill, after which the impression of traveling forward again to the present epoch may be given, and the re-arrival notified by the representation on the screen of the place at which the exhibition is held, or of some well-known building which by the movement forward of the lantern can be made to increase gradually in size as if approaching the spectator.

Robt. W. Paul

Paul, inspired by Wells' story, in this document of three decades ago exactly anticipated the photoplay, which was not to be born yet for many a year.

It was, viewed from the easy facility of the slowly evolved screen technique of to-day, a clumsy collection of mechanical expedients. He did not and could not know then that everything sought by way of revolving stages, combined stereopticons, projection machines, scenic settings, masked seating sections and platform rocking devices to simulate travel motion, would one day be done entirely on the screen. The photoplay of to-day moves backward and forward through Time with facile miracle from the Present into the Past and Future by the cut-back, flash-back and vision scenes. The Paul patent notion of sliding projection machines to enlarge or diminish the size of the picture is executed by the camera of to-day while the projector stands still in its theatre booth. Most amazingly, too, Paul and Wells in 1895 plainly had the idea of not only the cutback and close-up but also the fade-in and fade-out, the overlap-dissolving of scenes into each other and all of the supplemental tonal effects of sunshine, fog, rain, moonlight and the like, now common to the screen drama.

Many years of reading Wells' works have rather accustomed us to thinking of him as the forecaster of most of the scientific wonders which have become commonplaces of civilization, as for instance the airplane. But even that is no preparation for the surprising discovery in this long forgotten patent application that Wells and Paul forecast something infinitely more complex than any machine—no less than a whole art form.

The Wells-Paul feat of 1895 surpasses even that remarkable anticipation by which Savinien Cyrano de Bergerac completely described the phonograph, two centuries before its invention, in his *Histoire Comique des États et Empires de la Lune* published in 1656, the year after his death in Paris.

The anticipations of the phonograph by de Bergerac in the middle of the seventeenth century and of the screen drama in the end of the nineteenth are given still more interest when we realize that these two desires of sight and sound were fused in the one mind of Edison, and that through his single agency they were both materialized. The line between Art and Science is narrow indeed.

But the Wells-Paul idea, embodied in the patent application, contained gropings for a greater and new liberty for art. It sought to liberate the spectator from the instant of Now. The Now to which our consciousness is chained is but a mathematical point of no dimensions traveling ever forward, describing the line which extends behind us as the Past and ahead of us as the Future.

The same impulse of cosmic adventure which has colored Wells' writing feats of fancy in tales of other worlds and of hypothetical ages was at work here. He wanted free range to lead his audiences at will back and forth along the infinite hyper-dimensional line of Time. It was a plan to give the spectator possession, on equal terms, of *Was* and *To Be* along with *Is*. The motion picture was to cut away the hampering fog of the complex sequence of tenses of thought just as it was to cut back to reality through the misty attenuations of language.

This motion picture Time-machine idea was artistically at one with Ouspensky's mathematically mysterious philosophy and Einstein's philosophically mysterious mathematics. It was a promise of a more concrete application of their remote intellectual abstractions. The author and the philosopher alike often in their flights come beating against the walls of Space and Time. They are just expressions of the human wish to be liberated from the cage of the eternal Now.

Way back in the early '70's Nicolas Camille Flammarion, student of stars and dreamer of dreams, in France, wrote a scientific fantasy tale embodying related concepts, concerning the adventures of an interstellar race, masters of Time and Space. Flammarion's story was widely translated and circulated. In the United States, by coincidence, two editions were published in the '90's just before the birth of the motion picture. The peculiar possibilities of the motion picture's ability to petrify and preserve moments of fleeting time were here and there recognized even in the earliest days of the peep show. Witness the following fragment of an editorial from the *St. Louis Post Dispatch*:

KINETOSCOPE MARVELS

The kinetoscope, we are told, has recently been made to run backwards, and the effects of this way of running it are truly marvelous. In his remarkable romance, *Lumen*, the imaginative French astronomer, Flammarion, conceives of spiritual beings who, by traveling forward on a ray of light, see, with the keen vision of the spirit, all that ray of light carried from the beginning of creation. By reversing the process and traveling in the contrary direction, they witness the events of history reversed, so that men appear to be rising from the grave, growing young and finally disappearing in the process of birth.

It now seems that the kinetoscope is to make this wondrous vision possible to us. Already, by allowing it to turn backwards, the actions can be seen in reverse order. The effect is said to be almost miraculous. In the process of eating food is taken from the mouth and placed on the plate.

It has taken the motion picture more than a quarter of a century to grow from the Edison Kinetoscope into the photoplay's modern approximation of the *Time Machine* and the Paul-Wells concept of 1895!

Wells was the first writer, in other words the first professional re-creator of events, to come into contact with the motion picture. This circumstance led nearly to the attainment, at a single stroke, of the photoplay construction which has since come only by tedious evolution.

No writer or dramatist has since made so bold a gesture with reference to the screen as resulted from this tentative joining of Paul's invention and Wells' fancy. They were hampered by no precedent or built-up tradition of the screen industry, such as has affected the thought of every writer or dramatist of subsequent connection with the art. When, more than a decade later, the screen reached for the aid of the writing craft, it had established an audience and precedents of practice which did not permit the scenario writer to be a free agent of expression. The project of '95 conceived the motion picture as a tool and servant in the business of story telling, while the writers who came in after the lapse of years were to be the tools and servants of the then intrenched motion picture business.

The actual processes of the evolution which was to realize

some measure of this early vision did not well begin until some thirteen years later, in 1908, when D. W. Griffith began to assemble the mechanical and optical properties of the motion picture into a new dramatic technique peculiar to the screen.

The extraordinary machinery of the Past, Present and Future embodied in the Paul patent application was never built because there was no money available to carry out the daring idea. Paul dropped the project and did not proceed with the formalities necessary to the issuance of the patent. It was utterly forgotten until the researches of this history caused Paul to bring it to light to establish an incidental date. In the third specification of the proposed methods of the patent Paul defined the intermittent principle of the motion picture projection device included. The patent application therefore establishes the fact that it was some time prior to October 25, 1895, that he arrived at the idea of an intermittent motion in screen projection. Now by the date of the Acres agreement we have seen that in March of that year Paul's camera building, which preceded projection efforts, had just begun. The essential invention of the intermittent motion therefore fell between those dates, closely paralleling Armat's identical efforts in Washington.

When the Wells-Paul Past-Present-Future machine came to naught the whole Paul screen notion became dormant for a period awaiting the vitalizing influence to developments to come.

Some months later Paul, who was still inclined to view his machine as a scientific instrument, decided to show it to a scientific audience. On February 20, 1896, Paul's projector was demonstrated before an audience at Finsbury Technical College, and on February 28 it was shown in the library of the Royal Institution. These showings were accepted with due and grave appreciation. After two whole generations a British scientist had demonstrated an application of certain elements of that paper on *Persistence of Vision with Regard to Moving Ob-*

jects read by Dr. Peter Mark Rôget before the Royal Society. That was that, and the Royal Society proceeded with the regular order of business.

To the student of contemporary literature this near motion picture adventure of Wells is of interest in that it appears to have been a part of his experience when he was laying down the foundations of his writing career, which became an outgrowth of his work and considerations as a teacher of science. He broke from the class room for the greater liberty of the printed page. If he had given attention to the motion picture and its larger opportunity of mastery over Time by translations into the Present he might have set the screen's progress forward many a year.

The Past and the Future are at best mere fictions of Art. This is unconsciously understood by the more primitive minds uncontaminated with culture. The standard daily argot of the melting pot commonalty of the United States recognizes only one real tense, the present progressive. Witness the accurate recordings in the Americanese of Ring Lardner. Or collect your own samples in any subway crowd:

"I'm off with him now—we has a date last Sunday and he stands me up. Next time I sees him I says you cake eater you don't get away with that kinda stuff on me."

Purveying to the same audience, the sports writer gives his graphic narrative of the fight-by-rounds and the baseball-game-by-innings in the same progressive present.

The motion picture is a triumph over tenses. It is a Time machine in which we all ride with Lumen.

CHAPTER THIRTEEN

LUMIÈRE'S SIXTEEN-A-SECOND

THE Edison peep show Kinetoscope went into France at about the same time that it was taken into England. It was a most natural consequence that a parallel evolution was set in motion.

In the early autumn of 1894 one Lionel Werner, of Werner Brothers, opened a Kinetoscope parlor at 20 Boulevard Poissonière.

Louis Lumière, a maker of photographic materials, went to see this new photographic wonder.

Lumière saw the peep show pictures with a technician's eye and was immediately enamored of the notion of putting the picture on the screen.

In the private laboratory of their factory in Lyon, Louis Lumière and his brother Auguste went at the problem of projection. They began a line of experiments, traversing much of the same path of experience as their scattered contemporaries in the United States and England. Like the others, the Lumières started with the Edison Kinetoscope movement.

Europe could not supply the Lumières with film. They made their first experimental efforts with bands of paper. This enabled them to study the motions of their machines. This expedient of paper bands occurs elsewhere in picture annals, either as a method evolved by experimenters of an earlier date or as one fictitiously recalled by them seeking to build evidences of a priority over both Edison and the Lumières. The retroactive memory-fancies of some of the pioneers, both real and alleged, have filled the pages of screen history with pitfalls of error.

The Lumières would have been able to get very short bits of

—163—

celluloid from European or British sources, but only such make-shift material as Edison got from Carbutt in the pre-Eastman period.

This condition governing the film situation in Europe rather conclusively controverts the claims of some of the none too well accredited earlier British and Continental claimants of the middle Eighties to first motion picture honors.

The Lumières had the mechanical principles of their machine rather well in hand when they imported some blank celluloid film stock from the New York Celluloid Company, New York, U. S. A. This celluloid they coated with their own standard photographic emulsion at Lyon. For them the chemistry of motion picture photography offered no large problems. The Brothers Lumière were eminently fitted by scientific training and experience to do fundamental work. Their name is world known to-day for the Lumière Autochrome, the only widely available and commercially workable medium of natural color still photography.

The Lumières rather quickly decided that the continuous movement of the Kinetoscope would have to be supplanted by an intermittent motion for projection on the screen. While they were engaged on the building of a projector they also devised a camera to make the film pictures. They worked through the winter of 1894–5 and into the spring. They were not satisfied with the exposure speed of the Edison pictures, which required forty-eight frames of the film a second. They tried reducing the speed to ten images a second and found that too slow. Finally sixteen images a second became their adopted rate. The Lumière camera was evolved with a mechanism which gave an exposure of eight frames per turn of the crank, requiring two turns per second for normal operation.

This two turns of the crank per second was also the subject of some experiment aimed at discovering the speed which the

LOUIS and AUGUSTE LUMIÈRE, who
evolved the cinematographe from the
Edison Kinetoscope machine, photographed at Lyon, France in 1895.

SOLD BY ____________ DATE 12/10 1986

NAME ____________

ADDRESS ____________

REG. NO.	AMT. REC'D.	ACCT. FWD.

1	Film History	19	95
2	Were In the Money	4	95
3	Million & one Night	15	95
4			
5		40	85
6	Tax	2	66
7			
8		43	51
9			
10			
11			
12			
13			
14			
15			
16			

LARRY EDMUNDS BOOKSHOP
6658 Hollywood Blvd.
Hollywood, Calif. 90028
463-3273

1

5B400 REDIFORM THANK YOU

13 12
——
9087

Cop
——
4321

operator could most readily maintain with minimum variation. Unsteady cranking would have meant jumpy pictures. The Edison Kinetograph camera avoided fluctuation by using a battery driven electric motor, which made the machine expensive, complicated and immobile. The Lumière camera was cheap, small, simple and light. The Edison Kinetoscope made its first trips from the "Black Maria" on a one horse spring wagon. Louis Lumière carried his camera in one hand. This obscure little fact was to have considerable bearing on the first few years of screen business.

Some time in February of 1895 the Lumières had achieved both a camera and a projector, which they dubbed the Cinématographe. A French patent was issued to them February 13, 1895. This machine eventually carried its name around the world and gave us "Cinema" and "Kinema," by process of contraction.

On the garden walk alongside the residence of his brother, Louis Lumière photographed his brother Auguste, Mme. Lumière and their infant daughter at table having luncheon. This picture entitled *Le Repas de Bébé* had a world career ahead of it.

The Lumières were pleased with their machine, but in no hurry about presenting it to the public. The future of the motion picture was as little anticipated in Lyon as it was in West Orange. A little exhibition was given in the Lyon plant of the Lumières on March 22, 1895. The second exhibition of the machine was given on June 10 following, at the Congrès de l'Union Nationale des Sociétiés Photographiques de France, and two days later at the closing of the congress two films showing the members of the gathering taken the day before were shown.

The Lumière motion picture machine adhered rather closely to the gauge of the Edison machines and the dimensions of the Kinetoscope films. But since the large number of perforations in the Edison film seemed to make it rather fragile, and perhaps as well because they desired to be as original as possible, the Lumières gave each frame of the film one pair of sprocket holes instead of four pairs as in the Kinetoscope. The Lumière sprocket holes and the pins which engaged them were round, while those of the Edison machines were approximately rectangular, close to the form which continues as the world standard of to-day. In this first Lumière machine the movement of the film afforded a greater period of rest than of movement, but the shutter, a half circle, allowed the screen to be lighted only half of the time. This was, to be sure, a distinct advance over the brief illumination of the earliest Edison and Latham machines, but it produced a flickery picture. For a few months, before the broad career of the screen began, the Lumières had the best projection machine in the world. The intermittent motion of their film was produced by a cam movement, a type which tended to persist in European cinema apparatus.

After the showing of the photographic congress on June 12, 1895, the Cinématographe was retired for some months of development. Its real commercial exploitation was undertaken the next year. The Lumières have never been given to excited haste. December 28, 1895, they opened a small exhibition at 14 Boulevard de Capucines.

Now we have covered the progress of the motion picture to the screen, from peep show beginnings through four offices of invention: Latham in New York, the Lumières in Lyon, Armat in Washington, and Paul in London. There were yet others engaged in nearly parallel efforts which considerably affected the course of the screen, to be dealt with in the order in which they became factors.

For the sake of comparisons and to clarify somewhat the academic questions of priority, it is of interest that the original Lumière Cinématographe in March, 1895, was an intermittent projector in which the film had a greater period of rest than of movement, but equipped with a shutter which gave the screen exactly equal periods of illumination and darkness. In other words, the shutter did not permit the machine to operate at its full efficiency. A nice point is involved here.

The Latham Pantoptikon of April, 1895, was a considerably less effective machine because it adhered to the continuous movement of the Edison peep show Kinetoscope. The Lumière machine had a highly limited capacity of fifty feet of film. The Latham machine could handle so much as a thousand feet in one reel or roll, because its continuous movement, having no intermittent starts and stops, did not tend to break the film against the inertia of the supply reel.

Meanwhile the Armat machine coming into existence a few weeks later was, as has been described, designed to give the film an intermittent motion with a greater period of rest than movement and, most important, a shutter so cut away that it also gave the screen longer intervals of illumination than darkness. Armat's machine, in other words, gave the eye longer glimpses of the picture within the same period of rest.

These distressing complexities cannot be avoided if one is to see through the maze of litigations which came to control so much of motion picture development in the years that followed. There was no exchange of information such as the news now so often carries between inventors. So neither the Lumières, Latham, Paul nor Armat were aware of the others' work.

One naturally wonders what the Edison establishment was doing with the motion picture in this period while others were struggling toward the screen. We have noted the desultory effort which Edison made by assigning an assistant to work at the Raff & Gammon office in response to their demand for a projector. The only motion picture development of the time which Edison actually brought into manufacture was the Kinetophone, a combination of the phonograph and the peep show machine. With the phonograph ear tubes and the peep hole of the Kinetoscope the patron got sight and sound together. This was in execution of the original Edison idea, when he started his motion picture quest to supplement the phonograph. The phonographic programs of the Kinetophone were supplied by Edison records made to synchronize in a fair degree, by mechanical means, with the film movement.

The Kinetophone went on the market through the Kinetoscope Company, which through this same period was selling many ordinary phonographs to the peep show parlor men to supplement their show. The new combined phonograph and picture machines were now offered at $350 each, or a price of $150 above the now reduced price of the Kinetoscope. The literature of the Kinetoscope Company appeared to anticipate a vast impetus for the business on the basis of the new device. However, not more than fifty of them were made and probably not that many were sold. The talking pictures of 1895 had the brief life of a novelty, and in their short day, only a matter of weeks, ran down the same scale of diminishing interest which has characterized every subsequent advent of a talking-picture effort.

Readers passing this point enter at their own risk. Beware of the machinery! Having attained and demonstrated the motion picture on the screen, we can pause a moment in the rush of history to consider just what this picture is—if anything.

Ever since the first attainment of the projected film picture the simple statement of the principle of "persistence of vision" has been accepted generally as the complete explanation of the motion picture. That is too simple and easy to be true. After all, seeing a motion picture is something more and rather different from just piling one optical impression on top of another in the eye. True persistence of vision, or the holding of an image in the mind's eye until the next arrived to take its place, would result more likely in a jar between the successive phases of motion presented by the screen record. In rapid motions which are well portrayed on the screen this jar would be considerable.

Following the researches of the experimental psychologists we must admit that the eye can only see what is there to be seen, namely a series of still pictures. The mind does the rest. By simile we may say that the screen shows the eye a row of dots and that the visual imagination makes a continuous line of it. We often, elsewhere than the screen, think we see motion where none exists. There assuredly is no motion on the screen.

The successive still pictures of the object in motion appear merely to supply cues to an altogether mental process by which we build our impression of seeing it move. It would seem that there is something in our experience of seeing actual objects in actual motion which helps us see the movies move, always in a forward direction. An exception to this progressively forward impression occurs in the common screen phenomenon of the wagon wheels which turn backward as the vehicle goes forward. On the strict theory of the persistence of vision this would be impossible. It is possible only because the spokes are to the eye exactly alike and we can mistake a spoke behind in the progression of the wheel for the one which we saw ahead. In other words, our mind gets a miscue because of the failure of the eye to identify. If our eye were so faulty as to confuse two actors we might get even more exciting results, but they would be of the same category.

It is significant here that there is some evidence that we do not all see the motion picture exactly alike. It was a common experience, when motion pictures were less common, to undergo a process of acquiring the conventions of screen seeing. The screen unquestionably offers a much more complete optical illusion to those who have grown accustomed to reading it. It is to be noted that complaints of such technical faults as a lack of depth and of errors of perspective nearly all come from high and mighty operatic and stage critics who hold aloof from the screen and are really most inexperienced in screen seeing. They tend to quarrel with the optical cues.

Let us analytically consider one foot of motion picture film, occupying one second of screen time in the theatre and calculate just how little the eye can actually see. It will give us a clearer notion of what a will-o'-the-wisp this motion picture illusion is. In exposing the negative for that foot of film in the camera, sixteen separate and distinct individual pictures or snapshots of the subject are made. Under full illumination with the shutter aperture cut down, just as the amateur photographer speeds up the shutter in his kodak to reduce the light, these sixteen little snapshots may be exposed as briefly as one five-hundredth part of the second. This is a medium figure; exposures so brief as a five-thousandth part of a second are possible if the light is strong enough. Now with an exposure of one five-hundredth part of a second our camera's eye is open to take note of the happenings before it for only sixteen five-hundredths of the time our foot of film is traveling through the machine. This is a total of .032 of the total time. The camera makes note of what happens in sixteen instances of a five-hundredth of a second each. The camera is not recording what is happening approximately 97 per cent of the time. Yet when a positive print from that negative is presented in one second on the screen the spectator thinks that he sees what is going on continuously, all of the time. The spectator is only three per cent correct. It is not what we see but what we think we see that makes the picture. Pure persistence of vision does not explain that. Persistence of optical imagination is nearer the fact.

It is interesting to reflect that assuming the same rate of exposure, one five-hundredth part of a second per frame of the film, a whole battery of cameras, say fifty, could be set up side by side to picture the same event in the same time and make as many entirely different records of it. If each camera was timed to expose in succession after its neighbor down the row, there would result fifty negatives, no two of which would be technically and literally alike. A foot of film from each camera would contain its sixteen snapshots made in a different series of five-hundredth parts of the same second of time. All fifty negatives would be different, each from the other. Even more amazing, all of the total of eight hundred exposures included in the fifty one-foot negatives made in that second would be different. And yet when each of these fifty pictures were projected upon the screen they would all tell the minds of the audience the same story. No human eye could tell one picture from the other on the screen. The mind can put together eye-reported fragments amounting to 3 per cent and derive from that a sensation of seeing 100 per cent. The old saw about "putting two and two together" concerns a feat really trivial by comparison. We evidently believe a great deal more than we see. The eye reports facts but we see fancies.

The nature of the motion picture illusion is discovered to be further remarkable when we find that the projection machine presents the little snapshots, a frame at a time, for vastly longer moments on the screen than was used to record them in the camera. The camera works in jerky quickstep, with a quick wink of the lens in exposure and a long period of darkness, while the projection machine reverses this process with very swift movement between frames and a much longer pause behind the projection lens to let the picture register on the screen. The essential difference is that the chemical recording of the film is considerably swifter than the comprehension of the human function of seeing. The eye lens gets the message there just as fast as the camera lens does, but the silver salts of the negative behind the lens become aware of the picture long before the brain back of the human eye can perceive it.

Hence, on the screen we not only actually see only a tiny part of what happened in front of the camera, but we also see it for an entirely different set of periods of time. The camera's dots of time are converted into elongated dashes of time on the screen. But both the brief dotted instants of the camera and their translation into elongated moments by the projection machine's screen picture pass in the same total length of elapsed time.

While the camera's eye may be closed for as much as 97 per cent of the time, the projecting eye of the screen machine is in some models open for so much as 75 per cent of the time. So that in this instance we spend three-quarters of a second seeing what occurred about one thirty-second part of a second. In terms of a five reel picture running an hour and a quarter, or seventy-five minutes, we may actually look at action recorded in exposures totaling only two minutes and twenty-four seconds. And we think we are seeing all the time.

The comparison may be graphically illustrated thus:

1 second

Camera . . . .
Screen — — — — — — — — — — — — — — — — —

A somewhat extreme but entirely practical rate of camera exposure has been used for the purposes of this illustrative discussion. In actual practice camera exposures range from an ordinary minimum of around one-thirty-fourth of a second to a maximum of one-thousandth in all save the most extraordinary work.

The brevity of exposure in the camera, just so long as it is chemically sufficient to record the image, has not the remotest bearing on the visual effect on the screen. As the efficiency of photographic emulsions improves, the duration of exposure tends downward in an approach to zero. But while the camera may take its notes fast or slow, the eye will continue to read them on the screen at the rate at which they are presented.

No adequate conception of the facts of vision guided the early motion picture experimenters, as was evidenced by their efforts at projection from continuously moving films. But Thomas Armat, combining his theory with cut-and-try methods, found that the eye had to look upon the image much longer than was required for the camera to record it. This resulted, as we have seen, in the Armat machines which were the first to give the film periods of rest and illumination longer than the intervening periods of movement from frame to frame.

It was this reaching for a continuous effect on the eye which made Edison start with machines which recorded and presented the high rate of forty-eight images a second. He has denounced the modern reduction of rate to an approximate sixteen a second, as a commercial degradation of the screen product. It was not long, however, after the natal year of 1895 when the whole industry adopted the Lumière speed of sixteen-a-second, with a large consequent reduction in the consumption of costly raw materials.

Current motion picture practice is presumed to be based on the same standard rate, and ratios in the production of fast and slow motion pictures on the screen are calculated from that basis. There are sixteen exposures per foot of film.

The slow motion effect is produced by speeding up the camera so that the action occupying only a brief period of actual time is, because of the multiplicity of recorded images, spread over a long period of screen time. Considering the projection rate constant at sixteen-a-second, the method of producing slow motion pictures, may be graphed thus:

1 second

Camera................

Screen — — — — — — — — — — — — — — — —

By direct reversal of this set of rates the effect of extremely accelerated motion is produced by slowing the camera to space its recorded phases of motion so far apart that the action of a long period may be crowded into a short period on the screen. This method is the opposite of the generally held lay conception of the technique. It can be graphed thus:

1 second

Camera .   .   .   .

Screen — — — — — — —

In actual practice of the motion picture rates vary to a marked degree from the assumed standard. The public has grown experienced in screen seeing, while exhibitors are impatient to clear their houses rapidly for new audiences, or seek to crowd their programs with many subjects, tending to increase the projection rate.

This in turn has resulted in a time war between directors and exhibitors. Seeking to thwart the racing of the projectors in the theatres, directors have often tended to speed up the cameras in the studios, thus lengthening the pictures. The lack of a firm standardization of practice in this relation leaves the director considerably at the mercy of the projection machine in the matter of screen tempo, sometimes seriously affecting the dramatic effect.

The Society of Motion Picture Engineers in 1925 recommended standardization at sixty feet per minute in the camera and eighty feet per minute in the theatre projector. This rate is close to the average, and denotes the public desire to have its picture drama injected under greater pressure with an increasing dose, bigger than life and one and a third times as fast.

Theatre speeds of ninety to one hundred feet a minute are common.

The especially successful presentation technique of Samuel L. Rothafel, the world's most celebrated exhibitor and screen impresario, involves a close control of screen tempo. The projection room is as closely responsive as the orchestra.

It is of interest to observe that a tachometer test of the rate of exposure used by the head cameraman of the Douglas Fairbanks studios in 1923 indicated a rate of twelve exposures per second for normal action. This would give a decided acceleration on the theatre screen, adding to the agility of the agile Fairbanks. Both Fairbanks and Charles Chaplin as masters of screen tempo are given to manipulation of camera speeds.

The camera crank wrings the emotion of the audience.

CHAPTER FOURTEEN

ROMANCES OF THE LATHAMS

THE Lathams were aglow with anticipations when they started manufacturing projection machines and pictures for the market in the early summer of 1895. High hopes had been kindled by what they deemed to be their laboratory successes. They did not know that equivalent attainments in film projection were even then being attained and discarded by more patient contemporaries.

As we have seen, the Latham Pantoptikon, or Eidoloscope as the revised model was now coming to be known, was little more than an Edison Kinetoscope with an arc light behind it. But in that day of beginnings they did not know how much better the motion picture was going to be.

Major Woodville Latham saw the possibility of an achievement that might well crown a lifetime of devotion to scientific effort, and, perhaps equally important, might rebuild for his sons a fortune and an estate worthy of the family's traditions in Northcliff, Virginia, in the heart of the cavalier Old Dominion.

To the Major's sons, Grey and Otway, vigorous young gallants, fond of the taste of life, the motion picture on the screen seemed to promise wealth and all the things that youth fancies wealth can buy. They had prospered in a promising degree with the Edison Kinetoscope peep shows, and that success had given them a foretaste of what might be ahead. They found amusement successes came rapidly, when they came; and their experiences in showmanship consisted of just one successful venture—pictures of the Leonard-Cushing fight. On the basis of that precedent they had a large faith in the future. It seemed bright and certain then.

In this period of radiant hopes love first came to tilt with the destiny of the motion picture. And it will be interesting for a moment to recall the romances which at this time came swiftly into the lives of these two young film adventurers.

There came a certain romantic Irishman who somehow in a work-a-day world could hear the fairy pipers and follow the fantasy path that they tread so obscurely for the eyes of all save those born of grace. He was bound for the West and the excitement of seeking a new land of content somewhere in the Ozarks. He had a tract of the wildwood and a site by a mountain stream where the new home "Bonniebrook" was to be. He took all his children with him but one, a colleen bawn of seventeen. She was left in the care of a convent in New York, there to be safe from all that fathers would have fair colleens safe from.

Now this girl had an astonishing gift for drawing—astonishing to those who do not know. Of course to those who do it is exceedingly clear that the figures which flowed into being under the sure strokes of her pen were really just the Little People, the leprechauns and satyrs and sileni and fauns, all the sons and daughters of Pan, thus revealing themselves to mortal eyes. Sure and these bonnie folk live everywhere at once in all time and place and of youth forever. So it is no wonder at all, even within the forbidding brick walls of a convent, that a girl sufficiently Irish and fair in heart should find them trooping to her drawing block out of a well of India ink.

Of all this pagan truth we may well suspect that the good Sisters of the convent knew almost nothing. But they did know that in that hard and sinful outside world there were those who thought well of the works of their charming charge and gave them place of prominence in the pages of worldly magazines. In their gentle way they were proud that this recognition should come to one in their keeping.

But the mailman is an unfeeling mechanical agent. The girl with the gift wanted to see these editors who seemed so to like her pictures.

Now the Sisters know that colleens with a gift are not to be denied. It is the will of willful Pan himself, if fact be known, which it is not.

So it came that the girl of the golden curls and with the magic of the leprechauns in her tapering fingers went about the editors' offices of the matter of fact city, always escorted by a hooded nun, silent, watchful, persistent. Here was a cameo of vivid young life sharp etched against the old, old Shadow of the Cross.

The girl wanted to go about alone, without the silent shadow. She argued with a patient Mother Superior that it would be better so, that it was really unthinkably medieval to go picture selling to editors always accompanied by one in cowl.

It was reluctantly agreed that the girl might thereafter go alone and there were *paters* and *aves* for her protection, and mayhap candles burned to Saint Catharine, too.

Romance was waiting.

Grey Latham, handsome and debonair, knew editors, and in the office of one he often sat and chatted long.

Then one day came the girl. She delivered her drawings and was gone. Grey Latham's eyes were on her as she left.

"Who was that?"

The editor grinned and shook his head.

"You've got to tell me, and you've got to introduce me—when is she coming again?"

"My dear chap," replied the editor in his most editorial manner, "it can not be done." He told the story of the calls with a nun, and the protection of the sisterhood.

"Why, Latham, the Sisters would as soon have her meet the Devil himself as you!"

"No, no," Latham pleaded. "This is different—besides I think you need a highball—come on."

Grey Latham had a way of having his way.

Soon the girl artist went about the offices of the editors with an escort again, neither nun nor monk, but the devoutly attentive Grey Latham.

A few months later the girl and Grey Latham were married— without consulting nuns in hodden grey or parents in the Ozark wilds.

The girl was Rose O'Neill.

It was characteristic of the Lathams with their southern prides and chivalrous tradition that both Grey Latham and his father, the Major, deemed that it would be really impossible for a lady and the wife of a Latham to be professionally occupied, even in art. So by way of subterfuge Rose O'Neill's drawings now went to the editors signed "O'Neill Latham" in a most masculine manner.

There was a haunting, sirenical appeal in the drawings. They attracted the editors and sold. It was now assumed by the public that O'Neill Latham was a man, probably a very young and romantic man. Hundreds of letters from sentimental maidens, enclosing photographs and locks of hair, were sent to O'Neill Latham in care of magazine offices. They were duly forwarded, and Rose O'Neill learned about women from them.

Grey Latham, and sometimes his father, took the drawings about to the magazine offices, while Rose O'Neill Latham remained at home over her drawing board, more successfully protected then than she had been by the innocent nuns.

This marriage lasted five years and outlived the motion picture interests of the Lathams. Among the ardent purchasers of the drawings of "O'Neill Latham" was the editor of *Puck*, Harry Leon Wilson. After she ceased to be Mrs. Latham, Wilson became even more interested in drawings from the same hand, signed as in the beginning: Rose O'Neill.

Grey Latham followed the glimmering, glamoring lights of Broadway. Rose O'Neill followed her art and a new path of romance. She became Mrs. Harry Leon Wilson, for a time— but that is another story.

Down in Washington, D. C., at the home of the aged sisters of Major Latham, where the author called in 1921, a "Kewpie" doll, designed and autographed by Rose O'Neill, stood guard over the bookcase where the patent papers and relics of the Latham's lost motion picture hopes are treasured. It was this "Kewpie" doll which made Rose O'Neill famous all round the world. For the "Kewpie" was, you know, the youngest offspring of pagan Pan.

In this same day of early motion picture affairs, Otway Latham married Natalie Lockwood, a gifted young member of New York's smart society. Destiny awaited them with a dramatic adventure of tragic termination that one day, many years after their parts had been played, was to come again into motion picture history. But we must wait many chapters before completing their strange story.

Meanwhile Woodville Latham in New York was striving on with limited capital, making his first commercial machines and a program of pictures to be shown by them.

The showing of the Latham machine with the pictures of the Griffo-Barnett fight of 153 Broadway was moved over into a storeroom in Park Row. It was not drawing any great deal of attention after the first flurry of interest. The pictures were a failure as entertainment. They only sufficed to hint at screen possibilities.

Among those who paused to look in on the Griffo-Barnett fight pictures was Rich G. Hollaman, president of the Eden Musee, a remarkable sort of museum of oddities and amusement house in Twenty-third street near Sixth avenue. Hollaman had excellent reasons of showmanship for being interested in this promise of living pictures, and in time his interest was to make the Eden Musee of large influence in early motion picture affairs.

Since the ancestry of so many motion picture enterprises traces back to the Eden Musee, it is fitting here to take an excursion back into the history of that memorable institution and the kindred wax-works shows.

The story begins in the ominous latter days of the reign of Louis XVI of France, and pertains to the king's whim. One Christopher Curtius was then a surgeon of note in Berne, Switzerland. Incidental to his study of anatomy he modelled the human form and presently discovered he had a gift for doing faces. Prince de Conti, a cousin of the King of France, in his travels came upon the surgeon and urged him to abandon surgery for art and to move to Paris. With a prospect of royal patronage, Curtius went, taking along a niece, Marie Gresholtz, [1] a deft sculptress. The royal favor came and with it the attention of many celebrities, among them Benjamin Franklin, Voltaire, the Duc d'Orleans, and Marie Antoinette. Marie Gresholtz was sent to Versailles to be the companion of Madame Elizabeth, sister of Louis. The Swiss girl became in effect a member of the household. Sh modelled all the royal family in wax.

Had there been a motion picture in that day the royal camera man would have been exceedingly busy with the vanities of

[1] The Romance of Madame Tussand's by John Theodore Tussand, Odhams, Ltd., London.

Versailles. Sculpture in wax was the answer to the living picture Wish of the day. It was the nearest possible approach to the re-creation of events in terms of realism. The wax-work was the motion picture trying to be born.

Then came the Revolution and the Reign of Terror.

The revolutionists wanted a record of their work for the national museum. Models in wax were to be their news reels. Marie Gresholtz was forced into the dreadful service of modelling the guillotined heads of her friends. The tumbrils from the scaffold rumbled up to her door, bringing her the heads of Marie Antoinette, Louis, Danton, Robespierre and all that amazing list.

In 1795 the sculptress was married to François Tussaud and soon afterward moved to London, taking along the strange, tragic works in wax. There she opened the famous institution known as "Madame Tussaud's." She presided over the museum until she was ninety. The remarkable and long continued success of the gallery in London and similar shows in Paris, excited the emulative attention of Baron Sarter of Paris. He interested Count Kessler in Berlin and together they drew the Baron von Hoffman in New York into a project for a similar show here. Baron von Hoffman was allied with the banking house of Seligman & Wassermann. They started the Eden Musee in Twenty-third street. Theodore Hellman, son-in-law of Seligman, became its first president, subsequently succeeded by Rich G. Hollaman, an Englishman who came to New York to conduct a publishing business. With the coming of the kinetoscopic type of peep show in 1894–5, the Eden Musee began showing pictures and showed them continuously thereafter until the institution, bowing to the dominance of the screen art, sold its wax-works and closed in the winter of 1915.

Hollaman did not install the Edison peep show Kinetoscope, but chose a similar type of device, manufactured by the famous electrical concern of Siemens & Halske, in Germany. This machine ran until the world's supply of films was exhausted.

So it came that the Lathams' showing of "living pictures of the great prize fight" as announced by the barker at the door in Park Row promised opportunity to Hollaman. The pictures that could make events live over again, life size on a screen would, he felt, one day supplant the modelled groups of wax figures that told the stories of coronations, assassinations, executions and the like at the Eden Musee.

The flickering figures of the fighters were disappointing. But the idea was there, and the realization only a short distance away. Hollaman sought out Woodville Latham, who had removed from the Bartholdi Hotel to a most modest boarding house in the theatrical district above Twenty-third street. Major Latham outlined his hopes and his financial needs. He suggested that Hollaman might join in developing and perfecting the projector.

But Hollaman declined. In the faded eyes of the hopeful old professor of chemistry he could find no gleam of the thing that spells commercial success.

"But the Eden Musee will install the first perfected machine for throwing pictures on a screen," Hollaman offered by way of polite encouragement. He went his way, to await a better projector.

Despite the apathy of New York, Latham's Lambda Company went on with its project, making machines and pictures.

LeRoy Latham, a nephew, then about twenty years old, found himself in New York with nothing to do, owing to the closing of a lithographic plant in which he had been employed. An idea came to the lad that his Uncle Woodville's living pictures might contain an opportunity. He applied for the rights to the Eidoloscope for Chicago.

"The price for that territory is ten thousand dollars," the

uncle observed. They compromised on Virginia, their native state, at three thousand, half in cash and the remainder in installments from the earnings. This was the first state's sale in the film business.

The machines, the first set of Eidoloscopes, were to be ready for the customers late in June.

LeRoy Latham decided to open his show in Norfolk. Accompanied by a friend and associate from the lithographic studio, Henry C. Lindeman, he went to Norfolk and rented a store room, equipping it with a white screen and a hundred and fifty chairs rented from an undertaker, to await the coming of the machine and films from New York.

With Otway Latham as director-producer, the Lambda company engaged in the first motion picture making for the screen. The Edison Kinetoscope films were not available for the Latham machine, for a variety of reasons. In the first place, Edison would have violently objected; and in the second place, the Latham machine required a considerably larger film, approximately twice the Edison standard in dimensions.

Just at this juncture, the Latham picture interests encountered internal disarrangement that was soon to prove serious in its effect, and which by swift development was soon to effect vitally the whole subsequent history of the motion picture. W. K. L. Dickson, who, since his departure from the Edison service in April, had maintained a dallying relation with the Lathams, decided, in his own words, to "leave them high and dry."

Dickson had arrived at the notion that there was no important commercial future to the Lambda venture. So he abandoned it, along with the twenty thousand dollars worth of stock that had been put in the hands of his friend, Edmund Congar Brown.

Dickson was before long to become a very silent partner in a most notable picture venture.

In after years on the witness stand in a famous picture litigation, Dickson testified that his action grew out of his disapproval of the personal conduct of Grey and Otway Latham. He held that they were a trifle fast. There is indication Dickson never did like Broadway. He has been living in England and France nearly thirty years.

But Otway Latham went blithely ahead with his production schedule. When in August the first three projection machines were ready for delivery he had completed pictures for an exhibition that would last an entire twenty minutes on the screen. There were five "feature" subjects: the Griffo-Barnett fight, the Nicholas Sisters' act from Koster & Bials in their daring introduction of the "split dance," Duncan C. Ross and Ernest Roeber in a wrestling match, a picturization of a new song hit, *The Sidewalks of New York,* showing street gamins dancing to a hurdy-gurdy's plaintive refrain, and a scenic bit entitled *The Waves,* a picture of the surf at Alantic City.

The "studio" for these productions was the sunlit roof of Madison Square Garden. They were made with no equipment and the director did not carry a megaphone. Each picture consisted of one continuous scene. There was no semblance of scenario or plot. The principals went into action and stayed at it until the film ran out. The subjects were from fifty to a hundred and fifty feet long.

The first three sales of state's rights included the Virginia territory, Massachusetts, and Illinois. The Latham shows opened in Boston, Chicago, and Norfolk within a few weeks of each other.

LeRoy Latham, the young lithographer, was something of an artist but nothing of a showman. He experimented with his machine in the improvised theatre at Norfolk and decided that coming from the bright light of day outside into the pitch-black darkness of the interior might discomfort his patrons. In order to overcome this effect, he installed electric lights dipped in a purple paint. These lights gave a subdued and eerie glow to the interior. That was the rudimentary beginning of lighting effects in the motion picture theatre.

Not being a showman, LeRoy Latham forgot about advertising his opening. The day before the first showing he was standing in front of his theatre when a tattered negro boy approached and gave respectful attention to what seemed to be going on. At last, cap in hand, he approached deferentially.

"Boss, kin I take around d' handbills?"

"Black boy, I think you may have an idea," Latham responded. "Come with me to the printing office."

So Henry Southall, colored, became the motion picture's first advertising man. Henry therewith attached himself to LeRoy Latham, and became the doorman, usher, janitor, electrician, orchestra and valet to the management. Henry did handsomely on fifty cents a day, piecing it out, it was discovered later, by the use of the theatre in after hours for his own sterling presentation of the two Galloping Dominoes in the drama entitled *Come Seven!*

The opening in Norfolk that hot August of 1895 proved a decided success. There was just one complication. It was discovered that a license was required from the city authorities. But the only amusement license that seemed to apply was the circus license, rated at a hundred dollars a day. Obviously the picture show could not pay that. The city attorney and the exhibitor were both puzzled. Then LeRoy Latham came through with a regular Yankee idea. He advertised admission free, contributions of 25 cents each received from all satisfied patrons. This took the show technically out of the paid admission class, hence out from under the license ordinance.

Every one in Norfolk came to see the pictures at least three times, and the novel little show was violently prosperous for a while.

Delegations, skeptical about living pictures, called on the management for permission to stand behind the screen. They wanted to be sure there was no deceit. There was a strong suspicion that living actors were in some way casting their shadows through the canvas sheet.

Up in New York, meanwhile, Woodville Latham and his sons were having some difficulty with the finances of the Lambda company. Because of the success of his showing, LeRoy Latham had been remitting installments in payment for his Virginia territorial franchise with great enthusiasm. Daily wires came from Otway.

"Can we draw on you for a hundred?"

To motion picture men of to-day there is an amusing resemblance in this to the frequent situation between home offices and the film exchanges of a much more recent period. But the figures are bigger now.

At last the Norfolk show had to move because there were no new pictures to show. A month of the Nicholas Sisters and the surf at Atlantic City was all that Norfolk would pay for. Newport News was the next stop.

At Newport News a wandering adventurer, one Jack McConaughey, a boyhood acquaintance of LeRoy Latham, strolled in and offered his services as an expert.

"What you fellows want is a regular big top showman—that's me. I'm a circus clown, but I got so good the outfit got jealous—now I'm resting."

McConaughey joined. He suggested stretching the show by inserting an act. He proposed to pose as "living statuary." Tights were ordered by wire from New York, and an announcement was put in the newspapers. The tights did not arrive for the opening night. There was acute distress. In the last hour McConaughey got an inspiration.

"Send for some lampblack—I'll black up and pose as ebony statuary. That's a novelty—ought to be a hit."

And so it proved. The audience in the Newport News Opera House was thrilled. Henry Southall, master of effects, in the wings was peevish about it. Ebony statuary was no treat to Henry. McConaughey's closing number was entitled *The Fall of Man*. He sat immobile in the spotlight, holding aloft a gilded apple in a jet-fingered hand.

The Fall of Man, rang out the voice of the announcer. As the spotlight flashed on the posing artist, Henry kicked over the thunder machine and spilled the crash box backstage. The din shook the opera house. It sounded like the fall of the universe. The audience got its breath, and broke into a riot of applause.

Out a rear exit went Henry, with the ebony statuary in hot pursuit.

The run in Newport News was brief. The living picture show moved to Richmond, LeRoy Latham's home town where he had relatives and family traditions. By way of promotion it occurred to the young exhibitor that it might be well to give a special premiere presentation for the young daughters of the South in attendance at Richmond's most exclusive female seminary. In their dimities and organdies and muslins, accompanied by their prim preceptresses, the girls of the school marched en masse to the Richmond Opera House. The pictures of the waves at Atlantic City drew a rippling round of applause. *The Sidewalks of New York* went over nicely. But the Nicholas Sisters and their split dance did not seem to be so good. The temperature went off rapidly. The Richmond engagement was not an entire success.

LeRoy Latham returned to the north and lithography, putting

the Eidoloscope machine into a warehouse where it was to repose for many years.

Henry Southall's advertising job in the films was gone. He retired from the theatrical world to devote himself to golf—African golf. When twenty years later Henry began to see stories in the papers about the riches of the motion pictures he was sure his one time employer must be one of those New York film millionaires. Henry stowed away on a boat and came to New York, expecting to find his old boss and enter a basking service in some gilded mansion on Fifth Avenue.

Henry became a pathetic figure, ragged and wistful, going from theatre to theatre in New York.

"Please, does you know Mistah Latham?"

The very blonde lady presiding in the glass caged box-office and the uniformed doorman in his magnificence merely looked with dumb, haughty scorn at the forlorn Henry in quest of his master.

"Beat it, Shine,—whatyu trying to put over?"

Winter came on, and the quest wore Henry's purse thin. And his once supple fingers were perhaps no longer so able to work their bidding upon the permutations of the four squared toys of chance.

At last Henry gave it up. He walked down to the water-front and sought out the piers that berthed the boats from the Southland. He carried some one's luggage aboard a waiting vessel, and stayed there until it nosed into Newport News again. Down there things were better.

But it is writ that the faithful shall be rewarded.

One day in the busy year of 1920 LeRoy Latham, first in and first out of the business of exhibiting the motion picture, was aboard the Twentieth Century Limited returning to his New York office from a visit to Chicago. Latham had all but forgotten the motion pictures and his brief screen career of '95. It was put away and far behind him in his success in lithography. He was now the president of the Latham Lithograph Company with an imposing plant in Woodside, offices in New York overlooking Bryant Park, and with a country home on Long Island.

Late in the evening Latham strolled into the smoking compartment of his Pullman and came upon the porter devouring a fried chicken lunch.

"Don't eat yourself sick, George." Latham, like all the sons of the South, has a way with darkies.

"Never you mind, boss, this here chicken'll never make nobody sick—it wus cooked in Richmond, Virginny."

"So you're from Richmond, George!" Latham sat down and lighted a cigar. "Happen to know a colored man down there by the name of Henry Southall?"

The porter's eyes lighted up. "Does I know him, Boss? Yessuh, I does. I knows Henry mighty well."

"Well, well. So Henry's still alive and going."

"Yessuh he is, 'live and going considerable."

When LeRoy Latham reached his office in New York the next morning, he pushed aside the mail to wait and called a stenographer.

"Take a letter to Henry Southall—don't know the address; just make it Henry Southall, colored, Norfolk, Va. Maybe the postoffice can find him."

Four days later Henry, bowing and smiling, entered the office of the Latham Lithograph Company in the Æolian Building. He stood for a moment sizing up the place. He looked admiringly at the framed lithographs on the wall, and the furniture. He tapped the deep rug with an appreciative but ragged shoe.

"I just knowed Mistah Latham would be in a place like this."

Henry moved on into the president's private office to report. He has been the special messenger there ever since.

"If the boss and me'd a-stayed in that there fillum business we'd be billionaires right now," observes Henry. "But I'm satisfied."

At Christmas time Henry goes out to "de big house" of the Lathams at Plandome, to serve and to share the holiday largess. It is as in golden days of the old South. Even movie millions could make Henry no happier.

Shortly after LeRoy Latham's opening of the first public motion picture in all the world, in Virginia, his Uncle Woodville's machines went into service with a showing in Boston, and in Chicago. The Boston showing of the Eidoloscope is of interest only because it brought into motion picture contact two names which will figure in future pages of this history. They are Gilbert P. Hamilton, who operated the machine, and Lee Dougherty, who was connected with the dramatic production entitled *The Yankee Cruiser* which used the Eidoloscope's flickering pictures to fill the scene shifting periods between the acts. From the Chicago showing only one name, but an important one, survives—William Selig, who was merely a vastly interested member of the audience. The ensuing activities of Selig will figure in many phases of our story. One or two models of the Eidoloscope presently found their way to Europe. The showing of motion pictures on the screen had timidly begun. The films had just pushed over the border between the laboratory and the wide world of exploitation. Years of war-torn adventure and exploration were ahead.

CHAPTER FIFTEEN

THE LEGEND OF RICHMOND

THROUGH the same months of 1895 when the Lathams were making their first and somewhat ineffectual approach to the public with commercial offerings of the motion picture on the screen, Thomas Armat in Washington was preparing for the launching of the new "beater movement" projector evolved from his labors with C. Francis Jenkins.

This was the machine discussed in Chapter Eleven, born of many efforts and failures.

We have now come to the most important of all of the several independent efforts at motion picture projection, spawned of the parent peep show Edison Kinetoscope and its films. Through Armat we shall arrive presently at the final solution of the problem of the screen and the type of projection machine which, with minor refinements, serves the screens of the world today.

Yet for a medley of reasons, which can only become apparent through a survey of the whole world of projection inventions, Armat has been the least known of the inventors, through all the three decades of the screen. Every factor has conspired against fame for Armat, who may be styled the great unknown of motion picture history. Commercial expediency, personal modesty, the force of more conspicuous names and aggressive personalities, and the sheer luck of publicity—all these have tended to keep Armat obscure. And, in spite of that, his story is not a typical inventor's tragedy. He has won every material victory, as is of record, officially. In the terms of Fitzgerald's version of Omar, he "took the cash and let the credit go,"—in the days when there was little credit to be taken.

The needle of fact about film projection is buried in a technical haystack. No other subject of motion picture history has been so confused by contradictory presentations, both by the several competing inventors, the trade gossips and the writers on screen affairs. The researches back of this element of the history and this chapter have entailed a greater and longer effort than any other phase of the story.

Late in the summer of this 1895 Armat and Jenkins, still partners under a continuance of their original agreement, decided, or agreed, upon a commercial presentation of their new projecting machine at the Cotton States Exposition in Atlanta, Georgia. H. A. Tabb's original approach to Armat had directed his attention that way. The Cotton States show was the big event of the South, promising large crowds and presumably an excellent opportunity for the introduction of living pictures on the screen.

Since we are so given to thinking of invention as the special and peculiar gift of the Yankee, this Southern advent of the screen has some flavor of surprise, especially as we realize that Virginia contributed to early motion picture affairs more important names than any other state: Isaacs, Latham, Rector and Armat.

It was the middle of September, 1895 when the Armat-Jenkins motion picture show, in a little shedlike structure, opened to invite the visitors to the exposition to see life size living pictures on a screen.

Adjacent to the motion picture attraction stood "The Plantation," a cotton exhibit, and the Hagenbeck animal exhibition. There was a tinge of coincidence in that, for it was a picture of a Hagenbeck elephant, made in Germany by Anschütz for his Electrical Tachyscope exhibited at the Chicago World's Fair, from which Armat had first acquired his interest in the motion picture problem.

In Atlanta, some distance from the exposition grounds, Grey Latham was conducting an exhibition of the flickering Eidoloscope.

Armat's friend, Tabb, was at the exposition conducting a most elaborate display of the Edison peep show Kinetoscope, in connection with Norman C. Raff and Frank R. Gammon of the Kinetoscope Company in New York. The exhibit cost $8,000 and resulted in a heavy loss. The exposition crowds refused to be interested in a peep show.

The spectators at the exposition were also skeptical about this living picture screen promise on the placards about the Armat-Jenkins show. It did not seen probable. When a barker was put at the door, and it was announced that one might enter free and pay at the exit if satisfied, an audience was finally assembled. The moment the lights were turned off for the beginning of the show a panic ensued. The visitors had a notion that expositions were dangerous places where pickpockets might be expected on every side. This was, the movie audience thought, just a new dodge for trapping the unwary in the dark. Motion picture projection today succeeds admirably in a strong twilight, but in the beginning every projection room was made as dark as possible.

A few admissions were gathered but the prospect was discouraging. The promoters were trying to sell something that no one knew anything about.

The stellar picture of the program at the Cotton States show was *Annabelle-the-Dancer*, from the Edison Kinetoscope. All of the pictures were from the same source.

The *Annabelle* picture was in colors. Edison had hand colored versions of the picture, but the copy in the hands of the Washington inventors is said to have been hand-colored by the wife of a photographer. This picture was acquired through E. F. Murphy of the Kinetoscope peep-show at the Columbia Phonograph parlor in Washington, as evidenced by correspondence items still in existence. The Edison studio photographed *Annabelle* in the summer of '94 at West Orange.

The poor attendance at the Armat-Jenkins motion picture show made it evident that the enterprise was going to fail. It had borrowed $1,500 from Armat's brothers for the project, secured by the equivalent of a first mortgage, and now it looked as though an additional two thousand dollars would be lost.

C. Francis Jenkins announced that he was going home to Richmond, Indiana, to attend a brother's wedding. He borrowed one of the three projecting machines and some films to show his friends in Richmond. Jenkins departed and Armat expected that he would return in a few days.

Now Armat, who had been studying the projection machine under its first actual use in exhibition service, considered numerous deficiencies. Most important among them was the need for some means of mitigating the continual jerks on the film as it encountered the intermittent blows of the beater movement. The vibration tended to make the picture unsteady, and wear rapidly impaired the film.

Also, Armat was not yet satisfied with the method of giving the film that intermittent movement, the very heart of the projection machine.

Meanwhile to ease the strain on the films Armat worked out and applied a loop forming device above the feed tension and beater movement to bring down slack film from the supply roll of pictures. This let the intermittent movement jerk at four or five inches of loose, free film instead of putting the strain against the whole heavy roll of pictures.

This device was practically identical in character with the loop forming mechanism which Enoch Rector had applied to the

Latham camera a few months before. Armat studying projection with an intermittent movement had come up against the identical problem and reached an identical solution. Armat was the first to apply it to the projector, while Rector was first to put it into the camera.

This relatively small device was most important. It had a curious subsequent history in the United States Patent Office and emerged from the toils of controversy under the name of "the Latham Loop." It figured importantly in motion picture affairs for many years, and must be remembered for the understanding of many curious happenings which affected the destinies of corporations and their stars.

Meanwhile C. Francis Jenkins was in Richmond, Indiana, to attend his brother's wedding. On Tuesday evening, October 29, 1895, he gave an exhibition of motion pictures in his brother's jewelry store. The next day the *Richmond Telegram* published the following:

PHANTOSCOPE

A Wonderful Invention—Jenkins Jewelry Store the Scene of a Splendid Exhibition Last Night

C. Francis Jenkins was in the city last night with his "phantoscope," and delighted quite a number of his friends with an exhibition that was simply marvelous. The phantoscope is simply a reflex and condensing lens, between which revolves strips of film, on which are positive photographs that have been taken at the rate of 1600 a minute and is shown on a canvas screen at the same rate.

By means of this piece of mechanism any scene can be photographed in all its details and exhibited years after, just as it occurred. The photographs are 75–100 of an inch in size, and there are 800 on a strip. The strip passes before the lens at the rate of almost twenty miles an hour, giving a complete picture, with the changing expression of countenance and every movement of the figure just as in life.

The pictures presented upon the canvass last night at Jenkins' jewelry store were all life size, and those fortunate enough to see them were enraptured at the wonderful and beautiful effects seen. This is the invention of Mr. Jenkins, and he has a fortune in it.

It is scarcely necessary to point out that the newspaper's technical description was quite faulty as to essential facts. The article left out practically everything that one might want to know about the showing. The picture was, however, the classic favorite, *Annabelle-the-Dancer*.

The reporter for the Richmond paper also failed to record either the prior showing at Atlanta, the Washington origin of the device or Armat's participation in its evolution.

The article quoted is from a photograph of the item as printed in the issue of the *Richmond Telegram* of that date, a copy of which paper was transmitted to Thomas Armat by E. F. Murphy at the time. So far as can be discovered this copy of the paper, now in Armat's files, is the only one remaining in existence.

The Richmond showing in October, 1895, appears to have marked the beginning of a parting of the ways between Armat and Jenkins.

Early in November not long after Jenkins' departure, Armat left Atlanta, scene of their commercially unsuccessful show. He returned to Washington with the two remaining machines still in his possession. They had been, in the meantime, remodelled, embodying a number of Armat's improvements, including the loop forming mechanism. Armat set up one of the machines in the basement at the real estate office of Daniels & Armat at 1313 "F" street.

The picture project was in debt to itself and to Armat's brothers. It looked for the moment as though Thomas Armat had best turn back to real estate for a career. He had started in on the ground floor of the motion picture business and now it had landed in the cellar.

Armat was, however, still hopeful. Inventors are that way. The Atlanta verdict was not final with him. From time to time he slipped down to the basement to puzzle over the machine. On occasion he ran a picture for visitors who might possibly be interested in the development of this fantastic idea for throwing living shadows on the wall.

Jenkins returned to Washington from his Indiana vacation.

Not long after Armat, having read the Richmond paper, decided to call on Jenkins at his boarding house, 317 East Capitol street. On Jenkins' desk was a drawing of a projection machine. It caught Armat's eye. There was a discussion. They had it out and Jenkins announced that he had decided to go it alone, as the inventor of the projection machine.

This is borne out by the fact that the following day, November 25, 1895, Jenkins filed an application for a patent on the projection machine, as sole inventor. The most important claim of this application pertained to the principle of giving the film a longer period of rest and illumination than of movement. This was, obviously, identical with the previous joint application of Armat and Jenkins, based on their old noisy Boston gear machine and subsequent adoption of the Demeny "beater." Thus, in the parlance of the Patent Office covering such cases, Jenkins was "in interference" with Jenkins and Armat.

The filing of the Jenkins application as sole inventor inevitably meant a controversy and a hearing of the facts in the Patent Office before the examiners, for the determination of the true priority.

Now, before this interference came to a hearing and decision, Jenkins went forward elsewhere with his claims as sole inventor of the projection machine. On December 18, 1895, Jenkins appeared before Franklin Institute in Philadelphia. He read a paper which discussed the Projecting Phantoscope and he exhibited the machine.

John Carbutt, Wayne Junction, Philadelphia, maker of photographic plates and films under the trade name of Keystone, was a member of Franklin Institute and a friend of Jenkins. It was this same Carbutt, mentioned in an earlier chapter, who had supplied Edison with experimental bits of sensitized celluloid sheets in 1888. Carbutt was hopeful of becoming a more important manufacturer of photo materials, in competition with George Eastman of Rochester.

The situation was further involved. Carbutt was decidedly hostile to Armat, for commercial reasons. Armat had tried Carbutt's film. He was anxious to use it, since it was offered at a lower price than Eastman's. Armat had found the Carbutt film unsatisfactory and had tried to get a refund on a rejected consignment of it. Carbutt was resentful.

Meanwhile, with relations completely broken off with Jenkins, Armat in 1896 resorted to a writ of replevin to recover from Jenkins the projection machine loaned in October 1895 for the showing in Richmond, Indiana. This step was urged by Raff & Gammon. The author of this history holds the original correspondence from Norman C. Raff protesting to Armat at Jenkins' reported claims based on this machine. The replevin action was successful.

The issue between Armat and Jenkins, precipitated by Jenkins' independent filing of a patent application as sole inventor, went to hearing in the Patent Office Interference Case, No. 18,032, in November 1896. Armat was represented by Benjamin Butterworth, who was both before and afterwards commissioner of patents, and Julian C. Dowell. Jenkins' attorneys were Pollock & Mauro, also representing the American Graphophone company, with which Jenkins had a deal. Philip Mauro, famous in patent litigations, was in charge of the Jenkins case.

Jenkins was the chief witness in the endeavor to establish basis for his claim of priority of conception of the principle and device at issue in the interfering patent claims. The hearing involved many technicalities, exhibits and matters of dates, centering largely on an exhibit of drawings.

The conclusion of this case, Interference No. 18,032, was a victory for Armat's defense of the Armat-Jenkins joint application as opposed to Jenkins' application as sole inventor.

Jenkins signed a concession of priority for the Armat-Jenkins application and the patent sought was duly issued as No. 586,953 on July 20, 1897.

This was the end of the controversy so far as the Patent Office or legal record is concerned. The official status of the basic invention as pertaining to the projection machine—the principle of a long period of rest and illumination for the film, with a brief period of motion from frame to frame—stood at the end of that action as it stands today, officially recorded as the joint patent of Armat and Jenkins.

But the developments of unofficial screen history had only begun. The seed of the Franklin Institute address and demonstration by Jenkins, December 18, 1895, was now, regardless of the Patent Office, to put forth a sequel. In the Journal of Franklin Institute, file for 1898, page 79, appears an "abstract of proceedings of the stated meeting held December 1, 1897, discussing the Phantoscope and Jenkins, concluding:

> The award of the Elliott Cresson medal to the inventor is suggested, and is now under advisement. (Sub-committee; H. R. Heyl, chairman, John Carbutt, George A. Hoadley.)

It chances that Armat was at this time engaged in other litigations for the defense of his various machine patents. The contemplated action of Franklin Institute, because of the authoritative status of that organization, might prove prejudicial, Armat feared. He viewed it as a proposed reversal of the Patent Office.

Armat wrote in protest to Franklin Institute, offering to

appear and present evidence, the same evidence upon which he had won in the Patent Office. Henry Renno Heyl, chairman of the sub-committee of the Institute's sub-committee on Sciences and the Arts, received the protest in due routine and referred it to Carbutt. A considerable flow of inter-committee correspondence ensued, and, for complex and now unimportant reasons, became of legal record in one of the Latham litigations. A file of documents in this matter includes a letter from Carbutt in which he told Heyl that he considered Armat's protest "an impertinent interference." Armat was not heard in support of his protest.

The chairman of the main committee of Franklin Institute at this time wrote an unavailing letter, also yet of record, urging that Armat be heard. But the sub-committee and Carbutt prevailed. Eventually Armat received a letter from Franklin Institute, saying:

> . . . The subject matter, upon which the findings of the Committee in the case submitted by Mr. Jenkins, relates to his inventions made prior to his connection with you, as is indisputably shown by his applications for patents and exhibits antedating that time. . . .

A search for such applications for patents "antedating that time" has revealed to the author only two applications by Jenkins, to wit: the kinetoscopic peep show device with revolving lights, in which the application was modified to contemplate projection after the Armat-Jenkins agreement, and the contemplated revolving lens camera. In the event either of these could have been construed as an anticipation of the basic projection patent they might well have been cited against, and have prevailed against, Armat in Patent Office Interference case No. 18,032.

The Elliott Cresson medal was awarded to Jenkins, bearing on its obverse this inscription:

To
C. Francis Jenkins
for his
Phantoscope
1898

In 1898, after the medal award, a projection machine resembling the projectors used in Atlanta, appeared in the National Museum of the Smithsonian Institution at Washington. It bore a label reading:

Intermittent film projector
Invented by C. Francis Jenkins.

Meanwhile motion picture history was on its evolving way, as we shall observe in subsequent chapters, and the differences between the two Washington inventors, Armat and Jenkins, reposed as they were. Armat had the patent and Jenkins had the medal.

Incidentally the ownership of the Armat-Jenkins patent No. 586,953, passed to Armat and his brothers by way of settlement of the Atlanta showings' affairs and purchase from Jenkins for $2,500 for his interest.

Armat continued commercial efforts with his patent and meanwhile evolved a new method of giving the film an intermittent movement in the projector. Inspired by watching the pin-and-star-wheel movement of an odometer on his brother's bicycle, Armat hit on a sort of Geneva cross mechanism which he used to replace the old Demeny beater movement. This device born of the bicycle odometer will be found in the projection machines of today.

The years went by and Armat, in time, after many litigations with the picture makers, exhibitors and others, eventually received approximately a half million dollars in royalties on his projection patents. With his legal status assured, Armat paid little further heed to the old issues for many and many a year.

The question of invention and priorities involved might have slept on indefinitely into the centuries if chance had not intervened, bringing inquiring writers to stir among the memories and traditions for the story of motion picture origins. After a quarter of a century the old issues of the invention period, which had arisen and been settled as affairs of private concern in the days of their commercial importance, now were to become topics of public interest. It was significant of the arrival of the motion picture in a new status of maturity when it became a subject of historical research and discussion.

In view of the amazing complexities of the story it is well that inquiry began before the archives and evidences were too far scattered. After the very early work of Henry V. Hopwood in the '90's and the voluminous effort of Frederick A. Talbot about 1912, the next serious and pretentious endeavor to record something of motion picture history was made by Homer Croy, a magazine writer, humorist and novelist, author of "Boone Stop," "West of the Water Tower" and other works. Croy produced a volume entitled "How Motion Pictures are Made," a discussion of technique with several introductory chapters devoted to historical narrative, copyrighted and published by Harper & Brothers, New York, in 1918. Probably the most valuable new material presented in Croy's work was an account of the labors of Coleman Sellers, Sr., in Philadelphia in the '60's. Croy set forth the most complete and consistent narrative of motion picture origins that had been published. Now it chances that Croy summarized his findings in this intricate historical field with this paragraph:

To C. Francis Jenkins we owe the motion picture. Muybridge was the father of motion pictures, but his career was ended before they really were an established fact. Muybridge was the father but it was C. Francis Jenkins who brought up the child.

In the chapter leading up to this judgment, Croy gave an account narrating a showing of the pictures in the jewelry store of Jenkins' brother in Richmond, Indiana, with many details, and a brand new date of extreme interest, bearing on the priorities as between screen inventors. Croy wrote:

. . . The parting of that crowd marked the first time, June 6, 1894, that an assemblage had ever seen motion pictures as we know them today.

That evening the Richmond Telegram came out with the following head, announcing the event:

A GENIUS
C. Francis Jenkins
Formerly a Resident of this City

HIS NEW INVENTION, THE PHANTOSCOPE,
THE MOST WONDERFUL EVER INVENTED
BY A WAYNE COUNTY MAN

Croy did not reproduce or quote the article for which this is said to have been the headline. The article should have been most interesting.

However, Croy's book does give this account of the showing at the jewelry store:

. . . The arc began to splutter and out from the wall stepped a girl clad in garments more picturesque than protective and began to execute the intricacies of the Butterfly Dance. The dancer in question was Annabelle, a vaudeville favorite of the day who had been engaged by the young inventor for one special performance in the back yard of his Washington boarding house, with the audience consisting of himself and a camera. The lady's remuneration for interpreting the insect's terpsichorean movements had been five dollars, which seemed to cover adequately all the artistry displayed.

As the spluttering grew louder and the grinding more fervid, the girl began to reproduce on the wall the movements she had executed in the boarding house back yard, lifting her skirts by means of a stick in each hand and waving them in fancied lepidopteral imitation. . . .

Croy then proceeded to relate how Jenkins and Armat went to work in Washington, the next year, 1895, to make a projector, and told of problems they encountered.

Discussing the sale of Jenkins' interest in the Armat-Jenkins patent for $2,500, Croy wrote:

. . . . Small as this seems, this was the sum total that C. Francis Jenkins received for building up the foundation of the present motion picture industry. Later comers whose only claim to genius was that of being better able to drive a bargain were to clear that much in a week. . . .

Armat read the story with interest and addressed an inquiry to Croy raising some questions and received a reply stating that the story was substantiated by clippings in Jenkins' scrapbook and records.

Again the issue went into smouldering repose.

Croy's interesting book was much quoted and copied, sometimes perhaps pirated, by other writers, and his version and dates entered into the growing traditions of screen history. Edison, Lumière, Paul, and Latham fell into obscurity. Armat had always been there, so he just stayed obscure.

In 1921 the author of this history, then only a few months into the labors of "A Million and One Nights," reviewing the historical recordings of prior writers, came upon the Croy work, and many confusions of dates in various publications, which, viewed from technical angles, presented some problems. It seemed particularly difficult to understand why, if projection had been so successfully attained in Richmond, Indiana, June

6, 1894, that there should have been any such project as the Armat-Jenkins partnership endeavor of 1895 to solve that same problem of the screen. Why do it over again a year later?

An investigation in Richmond, Indiana, revealed only that the *Richmond Telegram* building had burned years before and with it presumably the files for 1894, the year of the priority showing alleged. The *Richmond Palladium*, successor to the *Telegram*, had no files of the period.

Now the quest turned to a long, tedious and seemingly hopeless search for *Annabelle-the-Dancer*, who might well be expected to remember such a novel experience as posing in her Butterfly Dance costume in a Washington backyard in 1894, for so unusual a device as a motion picture camera was then. A search of the rosters of thirty years of Broadway productions and of innumerable directories and newspaper files located *Annabelle-the-Dancer* at last, living happy ever afterward, now the wife of Dr. E. J. Buchan at 452 Briar Place, Chicago. Replying to inquiry, in a letter from Chicago dated August 6, 1924, Mrs. Buchan wrote:

> . . . It was a great pleasure to go to Mr. Edison's studio which was in the country and I remember well the wonderful dinners I had, so daintily served. They tried a number of experiments at the "Black Maria" with my "Butterfly," "Serpentine" and "Sun" dances. . . . About this Mr. Jenkins in Washington, I never danced for him. . . .

In Washington, in response to inquiry, Jenkins made available his scrapbook, containing various clippings and photographs from the early period of screen history. The scrapbook revealed no such story from the *Richmond Telegram* as had been anticipated by the author, and no reproduction of the headlines quoted as of June 6, 1894.

This Jenkins scrapbook did however include a series of pictures of a machine apparently identical with those used in the

Armat-Jenkins showing at Atlanta in 1895. The first of these pictures bore a written sub-caption reading:

First *successful* projecting Phantoscope
Full side view—built January 1895.

Thomas Armat was sought out in his laboratory, then in the Hutchins building in Washington. He referred inquiry to the records of the Patent Office, Interference No. 18,032, and related documents.

It developed, however, that Armat, presumably stirred by the increasing attention of publications to motion picture history, had started a review of the complexities of projection invention, when he addressed a letter to Dr. Charles D. Walcott, secretary of the Smithsonian Institution, challenging the National Museum's display of picture devices credited to Jenkins. Armat offered to submit evidence concerning the origin of the machine concerned, stating that he expected that Jenkins should have opportunity to controvert that evidence.

Under date of May 10, 1922, the following year, Armat submitted to Dr. Walcott a thirty-six-page brief covering the history of the controversy and citing the Patent Office records in Interference 18,032, among others. Jenkins submitted and later withdrew some papers.

In 1923 Armat was advised that the Jenkins projection machine exhibit concerned had been "temporarily withdrawn."

The author of this history then addressed an inquiry to Dr. Walcott. A reply was received under date of February 1, 1924, reading:

> The Jenkins Projecting machine said to have been used in Richmond, Indiana, June 6, 1894, has been removed from exhibition and returned to him.
>
> (Signed)   W. de C. Ravenel
> Administrative Assistant to the Secretary

The issue of priority was again thrown into a quasi public discussion with the publication of the *Transactions of the Society of Motion Picture Engineers*, Number Twenty-two, under date of September, 1925, covering the meeting of the organization at Schenectady, New York, May 18–21, 1925. At this session F. H. Richardson, technical editor of the *Moving Picture World*, oldest of the trade journals, presented a symposium of letters on historical affairs, including expressions from George Eastman, Thomas A. Edison, Thomas Armat and C. Francis Jenkins. Jenkins challenged Richardson's presentation, and in a sequel section of the *Transactions*, headed *Discussions*, made reassertions of priority with citations to testimony incidental to a patent infringement litigation, No. 5,167, U. S. Circuit Court, Southern District of New York, saying "There can be found the affidavit and testimony of the workman who made several of the machines for me, including the construction of the '1893–94 Phantoscope,' the construction of which was paid for by J. P. Freeman."

In this statement Jenkins did not describe the "Phantoscope" or state the character of the exhibitions to which he referred. Also no reference was made to the Richmond exhibition, the stories of which have stirred the interest on which the issues have been raised.

In the court records cited, an affidavit by one Emil Wellauer, employee of a Washington machine and model shop, can be found. Wellauer's testimony, however, does not establish the fact of a projection machine in 1893–94.

In conclusion of this somewhat intricate matter, it seems to the author that the evidence impartially considered must be taken to indicate that the projection machine presented by Armat and Jenkins at the Cotton states exposition in Atlanta in September 1895 was the first successful device for putting pictures on the screen in America.

It is equally apparent that this machine was produced under the joint efforts of Armat and Jenkins. It appears probable that if differences had not arisen between the inventors in 1895 the issues of priority as between them would not now exist.

The author must state in due frankness that an examination of all of the evidences, including many that it is not expedient to cite at length here, tend to support the view that it was Armat who conceived the effective principle of film movement in the projection machine—the principle which prevails in the projector of today.

One may not question the good faith of any of the parties at issue, either in this disputed matter, or in the many other controversial claims here and abroad pertaining to the motion picture. The evidence must be considered for what it is worth as evidence. In any event the issues are not material save as elements of history. After all, the final result of the motion picture on the screen was preordained from the day that Edison got his first sample of Eastman film—just as definitely as the invention of the gasoline engine was certain to give us the motor car and the airplane.

CHAPTER SIXTEEN

BIOGRAPH STARTS WITH A PUNCH

WHILE for the moment the main stream of motion picture development flowed in other directions, the part which William Kennedy Laurie Dickson played was not yet complete.

We have followed Dickson through the experimental difficulties of "Room Five" in the Edison service down to May, 1895, when he officiated at the picturing of the Griffo-Barnett fight on the roof of Madison Square Garden for the Lathams.

This Latham friendship and its affairs had cost Dickson his Edison connection and the associations in which he had enjoyed a share of the evolution of the motion picture.

Now, as will appear, Dickson had not given himself entirely to the Latham cause with his departure from Edison. This was indicated to a degree when Dickson's tentative quarter interest in the Lathams' Lambda Company was put into the temporary keeping of Edmond Congar Brown, a friend.

It must have become somewhat apparent to Dickson that after all the Lathams were dependent upon him and his, sometimes unwitting and unwilling, contributions of technical information, and upon the efforts of the other former Edison employees on their staff, including Eugene Lauste.

Also now that he was working with them even in a desultory, half-hearted sort of way, Dickson saw the young and ardent Latham brothers, Grey and Otway, at closer range. He felt that he could never agree with them, and their lightsome, casual Broadway ways.

Meanwhile another ramification of Dickson's motion picture ideas was developing under auspices considerably more congenial and carrying something of the color of the old Edison associations.

One of Dickson's old friends through his earlier Edison days was Henry Norton Marvin, abruptly signed H. N. Marvin on many a vital document of screen affairs in subsequent years. Marvin is a scientific person, a graduate of Syracuse and a one-time instructor in a high school at Tivoli, New York. How the motion picture industry came to overlook the opportunity to call him "Prof." Marvin is a mystery. Marvin became connected with Edison affairs for a time as the inventor of an electrically operated drill. In the Edison testing plant in New York City Marvin met Dickson, back in '87.

Some time in 1894 or early '95, about the time that Dickson was growing uncomfortable in his seat at the Edison Laboratories, if one is to judge by the evidence of subsequent dates, he wrote a letter to Marvin concerning the Kinetoscope and the possibility of some small simple device which could be made to show cheaply the final punch and knockout of a prize fight.

The old instinct of combat, expressed in the prize fights, was continuing to motivate motion picture evolution, a means to re-creation of an event of primitive thrills. Dickson had a new picture idea for showing a punch. The pictures have been hunting a punch ever since.

It seemed to be Dickson's idea that a little novelty of some sort could be made for popular sale. In line with this he evolved and suggested to Marvin a method of putting pictures on a book of cards, the pages of which would be flipped to present the successive pictures and an illusion of motion to the eye. To illustrate it, Dickson made up an experimental pack of cards and drew a series of crosses in varying positions on them. When the cards were thumbed the cross seemed to whirl and dance.

Marvin tinkered with the idea a bit and improved on Dickson's hand drawn pictorial effort of a whirling cross, by stamping the cards with a rubber stamp bearing a figure "1." It gave a better image.

Marvin was then, in 1895, associated with Herman Casler, a machinist from the Edison General Electric Company at Schenectady, in the Marvin & Casler Company of Canastota, New York, devoted to the making of machines of various types.

Marvin passed along the idea to Casler, who worked out the notion of making the pack of cards into a whole wheel of cards bearing pictures, to be turned by a crank and presenting a long sequence of action.

Dickson, Marvin, and Casler were all sure that this idea had a fortune in it. But it was going to need financing for the building of the machines required. The peep show Kinetoscope was prospering, and here there appeared to be a possibility of a device which would eliminate the costly batteries and films of the Edison invention.

Marvin chanced upon his friend, E. B. Koopman of the Magic Introduction Company, 841 Broadway, and engaged him in a street conversation on the project. Koopman was thrilled with interest. He had a flair for novelties. He was then engaged in the promotion and sale of his own patented pocket lighter and lamp, a pocket savings bank, and various other devices. Also he had been selling a toy kinetoscopic machine called the Viviscope, an improved Zoetrope into which various bands of printed pictures could be inserted. This had educated him to the motion picture idea.

Koopman watched Marvin flick the little book of cards with the spinning, dancing figure "1" on it, and then and there agreed to finance the project.

The K. M. C. D. Syndicate was formed, taking its name from the founders, Koopman, Marvin, Casler, Dickson.

Dickson had now come to his parting with the Lathams. He

left them, as he said, "high and dry." Also, he sold his interest in an electrical company and cast his fortunes with the K. M. C. D. Syndicate.

For their first experimental wheel of pictures on cards the experimenters took little pictures from a strip of Kinetoscope film. It worked rather well.

It occurred to Marvin that since this was an altogether divergent sort of a use for the Kinetoscope pictures, they might make an arrangement with Edison to supply them with subjects from his Kinetograph negatives. This was a rather venturesome piece of optimism. When Edison was approached with this opportunity to compete with himself, he replied with a resounding and vibrant "No!"

If Edison had said "yes" there would never have been any American Mutoscope & Biograph Company, and every subsequent fact of the industry would have been entirely different. Here began a chain of events leading down to today and Mary Pickford.

The K. M. C. D. Syndicate with a machine for showing pictures in a peep show now had no source of pictures. The experimenters of Canastota set out to reinvent the art of making motion pictures. They had as a guide Dickson's knowledge of some things that might be done, and also, of equal importance, what must not be done if they were to escape infringement on the Edison patents and the inevitable consequences to be dealt out by his active legal department.

They decided to build a machine which would take much larger pictures than the Edison camera with its little one inch film. The K. M. C. D. film finally decided upon was two and three-quarters of an inch wide, with each frame or image two inches high. This was nearly eight times the area of the Edison picture. A great deal of the intricacy of subsequent film affairs relates to this dry numerical fact. Since the K. M. C. D.

exposure rate was thirty images a second, as opposed to the commercial standard of sixteen presently adopted for the Edison gauge films, the film consumption was about fourteen times as great.

The reason for this large size picture was based on the fact that while the Kinetoscope picture was viewed by light cast through the film from the back, and magnified by the viewing lens, in the K. M. C. D. peep show machine the eye would see the card wheel pictures only by reflected light, as in looking at an ordinary photograph. A greater area was necessary to compensate for the loss of light.

Theoretically at least, the invention of the K. M. C. D. camera was left to Herman Casler. Too many ticklish legal points might have been involved if Dickson had been too closely connected with the work, in view of a possible contention of borrowing from his Edison experience.

In a few months Casler had a camera, using the great wide band of film. It is interesting to note wherein this camera evaded the specifications of the Edison motion picture patent. The Edison camera took a perforated film with holes along the edges to engage sprocket teeth in the driving train of the mechanism. The Casler camera used a plain unperforated film, which at the moment of exposure was punched with two registration holes, one on either side of the center of the image. The Edison pictures followed each other down the film in regular, precise order, equally spaced. Those words "equally spaced" were in the Edison patent. The Casler film made a great point of being studiedly irregular. The exposures were far from equally spaced. They staggered about the big wide film considerably, owing to slippage on the smooth rollers which carried the film forward, performing the same functions as the sprocket wheels of the Edison camera. The primary purpose of these

A CHRONOLOGY
OF FILM BEGINNINGS

BECAUSE OF CONFUSIONS AND CONTROVERSIES ABOUT PRIORITIES IN MOTION PICTURE INVENTION, ESPECIALLY WITH REFERENCE TO THE PROJECTION MACHINE, THE INITIAL DATES, AUTHENTICATED BY THE AUTHOR'S RESEARCHES, ARE SET DOWN HERE FOR THE MORE IMPORTANT INVENTORS.

EDISON

INVESTIGATION BEGINS AUTUMN OF 1887.

EASTMAN FILM STRIPS OBTAINED LATE IN AUGUST AND IN SEPTEMBER OF 1889.

EDISON PEEP SHOW KINETOSCOPE DEMONSTRATED BY WILLIAM KENNEDY LAURIE DICKSON AT WEST ORANGE, OCTOBER 6, 1889.

COMMERCIAL SHOWING OF PEEP SHOW KINETOSCOPE BEGINS AT 1155 BROADWAY, NEW YORK CITY, APRIL 14, 1894

THE SCREEN OFFSPRING OF THE EDISON PEEP SHOW KINETOSCOPE:

LATHAM, NEW YORK	LUMIERE, LYON, FRANCE	ARMAT, WASHINGTON	PAUL, LONDON
PRESS SHOWING OF PANTOPTIKON AT 35 FRANKFORT STREET, APRIL 21, 1895.	SHOP DEMONSTRATION OF CINÉMATOGRAPHE, MARCH 22, 1895.	SHOP TEST OF PROJECTOR LATER KNOWN AS VITASCOPE, JUNE 1895.	PROJECTOR IS DEVISED ABOUT OCTOBER 1895.
			DEMONSTRATED AT ROYAL INSTITUTION, FEBRUARY 28, 1896.
COMMERCIAL SHOW IN STORE ROOM AT 153 BROADWAY OPENS MAY 20, 1895.	COMMERCIAL SHOW IS OPENED IN BASEMENT AT GRAND CAFE IN PARIS, DECEMBER 28, 1895.	COMMERCIAL SHOW AT COTTON STATES EXPOSITION, ATLANTA, GA., SEPTEMBER 1895.	

BIOGRAPH'S FOREFATHERS, the first meeting of all the four members of the K. M. C. D. Syndicate, — left to right, H. N. Marvin, William Kennedy Laurie Dickson, Herman Casler and E. B. Koopman — when they posed on Casler's lawn at Canastota, New York, September 22, 1895.

Casler pictures was of course to supply card pictures for the wheels of the K. M. C. D. peep show machine, which they had decided to call the Mutoscope, adding one more gem to the nomenclature of the art. The two registration holes enabled their printing machine's selective claw movement to place the negatives exactly on the positives, regardless of the unequal spacing of the negatives.

The differences may be summed up in the statement that the K. M. C. D. film was as unlike the Edison film as ingenuity could make it.

Some time in 1895—the date is not clear but likely in September—the Casler camera was ready. The members of the K. M. C. D. Syndicate gathered and photographed a boxing match on Casler's lawn at Canastota. Boxing pictures had been the most successful among the subjects of the Kinetoscope, and boxing pictures had set the Lathams on the road to their brief effulgence.

The test demonstrated the success of the Casler Mutoscope camera. Koopman, the financier of the group, had invested well near all of his assets in the project. It had now reached the exploitation stage. He promoted the American Mutoscope Company. Among those whom he interested was the late Channing F. Meek, formerly connected with the Union Pacific Railroad and then engaged in the promotional affairs of the American Ball Nozzle Company. There were connections with the Empire Trust Company of New York City, which continued for many a day and contributed importantly to the creation of the business institutions of the screen.

In the promotion of the American Mutoscope Company, big business, the professional field of investment, and downtown New York had its first, and for many years only, contact with the motion picture. Among those who invested in the American Mutoscope stock was Abner McKinley, brother of William McKinley, and this, too, was presently to have something to do with motion picture destiny. Joseph Jefferson, the famous Joe Jefferson of the drama, also invested in this toy young cousin of the stage.

Jefferson posed for the Mutoscope camera at Buzzard's Bay, in a series of brief snatches of his celebrated rôle of *Rip Van Winkle.* The old Mutoscope catalogues list *Rip's Awakening, Rip's Toast,* and similar bits. Jefferson was the first stage star to pose for the motion picture camera. Here was indeed a famous player in a famous play.

When the winter of 1895 arrived the Mutoscope, the competitor of the Edison Kinetoscope, was ready for the market. A long career lay ahead of it. The Mutoscope has been continuously before the public for thirty years. Its superiority to the Kinetoscope swept it rapidly into a success which reached its zenith just before the nickelodeon age of the motion picture of ten years ago. Mutoscope parlors linger still in the poor quarters of many of the larger cities, still daily grinding out, at a penny a peek, the pictures made three decades ago.

But the peep show business, new as it was, was soon to become a mere backwater for the motion picture stream. The screen was near.

With its peep show problem solved in the Mutoscope, the K. M. C. D. Syndicate set itself at once at the invention of a machine for showing pictures from its great wide films on the screen. This was a labor of no vast mechanical obstacles, since between their camera and their printing machine for making the card pictures for the peep show they had all of the important components of an intermittent movement projector. The workshop at Canastota began to put together the device which bore the name of the American Biograph out to the world, when in due course the K. M. C. D. Syndicate inventors joined in the screen competitions of Lumière, Latham, Paul and Armat.

While the first Biograph projector was coming to completion, the Armat machine went out under most complex and interesting circumstances to challenge the world's attention for living pictures on the screen.

CHAPTER SEVENTEEN

A TRADE SECRET OF 1896

THOMAS ARMAT still had his improved projecting machine in the basement at the real estate office of Daniel & Armat in Washington. He was biding his time, yet hopeful.

Armat learned that C. H. Kayser's struggles with the Edison attempt at projection in the offices of Raff & Gammon in New York had not attained a success.

Meanwhile, rumors percolated that Raff & Gammon were growing impatient. The peep show Kinetoscope business was dragging and decreasing. The peep show parlor men were clamoring for a machine that would project the picture life size on the wall. The flickering Latham machine had served only to start talk and kindle hopes. The Kinetoscope customers looked to Edison, the Wizard of Orange, for a perfected machine.

Edison was still unmoved.

The situation of the time is to be gathered authentically from a letter written October 2, 1895, by Norman C. Raff to W. E. Gilmore, Edison's general manager at Orange, in the course of which Raff said:

> Mr. Gammon has repeated to me his conversation with you as to the Screen Machine and we feel confident you will do all you can to hasten the completion and perfection of the same and will put the matter into definite shape, so far as we are concerned, at the earliest practicable date. It has never been our intention to urge any undue haste, nor ask anything unreasonable, but in all our plans, we have been guided by what we consider to be for the best interests of both you and ourselves.

Nothing important had been done at the West Orange plant toward perfecting a projection machine and it seemed that nothing was going to be done. Gilmore, the general manager, was calling for merchandise, not inventions. Edison had done plenty of inventing. The business demanded goods to sell, and the motion picture was, after all, a small matter then.

The coming of the cheaper Mutoscope, brought out by the K. M. C. D. Syndicate, promised to wipe out the business of the cumbersome and costly Kinetoscope. Edison reduced the factory price of the Kinetoscope to $70, and insisted that the Kinetoscope Company should sell at $100. This failed to stop the ebb of the tide. In a letter to a stockholder in December of 1895, Norman C. Raff forecast an early liquidation of the Kinetoscope Company with a possibility of realizing perhaps so much as twelve thousand dollars on the assets.

With this condition of indifference in West Orange and of growing impatience in the office of Raff & Gammon in New York, a telegram to the Kinetoscope Company from Thomas Armat in Washington came most opportunely. Armat's wire promised perfected projection on the screen.

Raff & Gammon were interested but skeptical.

"We have heard of many screen machines," they answered, "but even Mr. Edison has not been able to perfect one."

"Will pay your expenses to Washington for a demonstration," Armat came back on the wire.

Frank R. Gammon on December 8, 1895, went to Washington to see the little machine in the basement of the Daniel & Armat real estate office. It was a makeshift affair, in view of the experimental additions which Armat had made, but it did throw the picture of Annabelle on the wall, clearly and steadily.

Raff & Gammon decided to take on the machine and find a maker for it, even if it meant a split with Edison to do it. But they hoped for a way out.

A complicated series of letters of negotiation with Armat followed with many redrafts of the proposed contract on which unseen destiny was writing the foundation of motion picture history.

The expectations of that day have a whimsical interest, as one turns the faded pages of the old correspondence. A letter to Armat written Christmas week of '95 says:

> We agree to make at least ten (10) machines after the contract has been signed, but we cannot agree to exhibit these ten machines at once in ten different cities. This would be a very unwise thing to do, and we would not in any circumstances bind ourselves in advance to such a proposition. . . . We must be careful to keep up the *novelty* of the machine as long as we can, and if it is exhibited all over the country at the very outset, the result would probably be injurious to our business, and the novelty of the machine would be largely reduced before we could interest the many parties we now have in view.

Meanwhile Raff & Gammon were finding the days filled with argument and differences with W. E. Gilmore at West Orange. He was vigorously sharp spoken and belligerent in the pursuit of Edison's interests at every turn. They were puzzled about this Armat deal. A month had passed since Gammon's visit to Washington, and that Armat contract would have to be signed soon, if at all. They decided to approach Edison through Gilmore and thereby try for a deal which would reconcile West Orange. Under date of January 13, 1896, in a letter to Gilmore, the Edison concern got its first authentic word of the solution of the projection problem. This is how they broke the news to the Wizard's establishment:

> We have discovered a *new screen machine;* have seen it in operation and *it is a success.* The inventor is a very intelligent gentleman of high standing and we find he has filed a very careful application for patent. The machine will, it is claimed, exhibit

a subject almost indefinitely, and our Mr. Gammon saw the machine operate for five or six minutes without any difficulty.

The party also has a machine for making films *and has successfully made them*. We ran into this by accident and it at once occurred to us that it would be best to secure an option of some kind on the machine, so that if, after consultation with you and Mr. Edison, it were deemed best to get control of this machine, we could do so. We got track of this machine by accident and at once traced it up and secured an option until *Wednesday evening of this week*. . . .

Again, we thought it would be a great deal better for us to control the machine than to have it *fall into the hands of parties unfriendly to you and to us*.

Now we can secure control of the machine, if you think best, and you can manufacture it and in fact make all of the supplies and other accessories, and probably secure as fully as great a profit out of it as from your present machine. Of course, this is on the presumption that this machine will prove as good a one as yours. Of course, we do not mean to say that it is; but we think it would be a good idea for you to see it, and then make comparison with your own machine so that if we think best to adopt that machine, and believe it is to our mutual advantage, we can do so.

There was a stormy session. But on January 15, Raff & Gammon wired Armat: "just perfected arrangements for manufacturing machines and films, exceedingly favorable for all, contract will be signed and forwarded tomorrow."

Armat launched into building a more presentable model of the machine to be used for the guidance of the Edison mechanics who were to put it into quantity production, and yet another model to be used by Raff & Gammon for demonstrations at their office.

There was a leak somewhere along the line. Rumors circulated that the Kinetoscope Company was in an unhappy state. W. K. L. Dickson, now busy with the competing Mutoscope Company, somewhat under cover, wrote from his home asking

Raff & Gammon about selling his Kinetoscope stock. He was advised to hold it for the liquidation of the concern, since it could bring no adequate price on the market.

The cheaper Mutoscope peep show machine of the K. M. C. D. Syndicate and the rumors of a new and successful projection machine were killing the parent Edison Kinetoscope before the career of the screen had begun.

Meanwhile, planning for a new business, Raff & Gammon cancelled their lease in the Postal Telegraph building in lower Broadway and took quarters at 43 West Twenty-eighth street, uptown, in a region which remained the world's motion picture center for the next twenty years.

After endless delays the demonstrating model of the machine was installed the week of March 9, 1896, at the new offices. A campaign of selling territorial rights aimed at the best of the Kinetoscope customers began. A. F. Reiser, became the first purchaser, taking the state of Pennsylvania. All machines were to be issued on lease at $300 a year each, and to remain the property of Raff & Gammon for purposes of control.

Many names then or subsequently widely known to the public appear in the flood of applications which flowed into the Raff & Gammon concern. One of the buyers of the yet unlaunched invention was Abraham White, the sensation of Wall street for his day. He wanted Rhode Island. A short time before White was poor and obscure. The United States government advertised the public sale of bonds in the sum of $100,000,000. White made application for a million and a half dollars worth of them, investing precisely forty-four cents in a letter, postage and registry fees. His subscription was allotted by Secretary Carlisle, but the conditions required gold paid down in the U. S. Treasury before delivery of the bonds. White took his notification of allotment boldly to Russell Sage, then New York's most conspicuously rich man, introduced himself and borrowed the million and a half on a note secured by the bonds, if, when and as issued. "The Street" gasped, caught its breath and laughed. White took a profit of $100,000 on his forty-four cents, and announced himself as a banker and broker at No. 16 Broad street. This adventurer of the marts was fittingly one of the first to take a flyer in the motion pictures.

The rumor of the new machine reached far overseas, and in the very week of the signing of the Armat contract a letter came bringing inquiry from Sir Thomas S. Bazley, Bart., Ratherop Castle, Fairford, Gloucestershire, England. He received an offer of British rights on the machine for £5,000, which ended the negotiations.

Among the advance inquiries about a screen machine, found in the Kinetoscope Company's files, is a letter from John P. Harris of Pittsburgh, Pa., written February 27, 1896. Ten years later and many chapters ahead this name will re-occur in this history with most interesting significance in connection with the rise of the screen theatre. Our year of 1896 contained no vision of that remote development.

Meanwhile Raff & Gammon, at the instance of Armat, waged a campaign with the Edison concern to get the Eastman company to coat special clear film for the projection machine. The old peep show film had a ground glass finish on the back to give it a background when viewed under the Kinetoscope lens. But the projection machine needed the clearest possible film to pass light to the screen. This brought on a new set of technical complications, threatening a new delay for the screen.

While promotion work was going on, Raff & Gammon struggling for a name for the new machine submitted a long list of suggestions to Armat. He elected "Vitascope," a new noun in the terrific nomenclature of the motion picture.

If Armat had held any curiosity about Raff & Gammon's deal with the Edison establishment to manufacture the Vitascope, it was set at rest by their letter of March 5, 1896, in which they unfolded a merchandising plot, thus:

. . . We assume that you, like ourselves, have gone into this thing with a view to making all the money possible, and judging from our acquaintance with you, we feel sure that no undue consideration of pride or other feelings which might influence the practical results will be entertained by you. The point we now refer to specifically is this: Kinetoscope and phonograph men and others have been watching and waiting for a year for the announcement of the perfection of the Edison machine which projects Kinetoscope views upon a screen or canvas. No matter how good a machine should be invented by another, and no matter how satisfactory or superior the results might be, yet we find the greatest majority of the parties who are interested and who desire to invest in such have been waiting for the Edison machine and would never be satisfied with anything else, but will hold off until they find what Edison can accomplish. We find that many of these parties have been approached in the last few months to invest in similar machines, but they hesitated to do so, evidently believing that Edison would in due time perfect and put out a machine which would cast the others in the shade.

This being the case, you will readily reach the same conclusion that we have—that in order to secure the largest profit in the shortest time it is necessary that we attach Mr. Edison's name in some prominent capacity to this new machine. While Mr. Edison has no desire to pose as inventor of this machine, yet we think we can arrange with him for the use of his name and the name of his manufactory to such an extent as may be necessary to the best results. We should not of course misrepresent the facts to any inquirer, but we think we can use Mr. Edison's name in such a manner as to keep within the actual truth and yet get the benefit of his prestige. The machine might be made with a place upon which we could inscribe the words "Armat Design" or something of that kind, and you understand that after we have disposed of our territory and the business is fully established, and we have reaped the respective rewards, we will then make it our business to attach your name to the machine as inventor, and we are confident that you will eventually receive the credit which is due you for your invention. We regard this as simply a matter of business and we trust that you will view it strictly in the same light.

Armat agreed. It was to be a long time before he was to "eventually receive the credit which is due."

CHAPTER EIGHTEEN

FIRST NIGHT ON BROADWAY

CONTRACTS had been signed for the launching of the Vitascope, Edison had agreed to lend his valued name, and his shops were building ten of the machines by the end of March, 1896. But Edison had not seen it yet! He was that enthusiastic about the screen.

Raff & Gammon urged Gilmore to persuade Edison to attend a demonstration and he went to bed with a cold.

On April 1, Armat arrived from Washington to operate the machine and look over the Edison shop work.

On the evening of April 3 there was a demonstration of the Vitascope for Edison and the press at the Edison plant in West Orange. Edison saw the pictures with the reporters.

This line of publicity activity was not at all of the Edison pattern. It resulted from the aggressiveness of Norman C. Raff, anxious to merchandise the Vitascope as a novelty and more especially anxious to be sure that it was to be known as the latest of the marvels produced by the wizardly Edison. Thomas Armat and his brother, J. Hunter Armat, who was to remain at the West Orange plant in supervision of the making of Vitascopes, were discreetly in the background at the press showing.

Neither Edison nor Armat were especially fond of the arrangement, but it was accepted by them at the dictation of Raff as a matter of commercial expediency. It was ultimately to be proved of no especial value to any of them.

Just how completely the Vitascope was launched as an Edison enterprise may be gathered from the contemporary newspaper attentions. In its issue of April 4, 1896, the New York Herald proclaimed:

MR. EDISON'S LATEST

A Favored Few Treated to an Exhibition of the Inventor's Most Recent Production.

CALLS IT THE VITASCOPE

Spectators Witness a Skirt Dance and a Derby Race with Life Size Figures.

THE KINETOSCOPE PERFECTED.

What Will Be Possible When the Machine is Connected with an Improved Phonograph

A new invention by Thomas A. Edison was shown to a few favored persons last night. The new machine is really a grown up kinetoscope, and it is a success.

Mr. Edison calls his latest invention the Vitascope, which he says means a machine showing life, and that is exactly what the new apparatus does.

The vitascope, which has been in process of perfection at the Llewellyn laboratory for the last seven or eight months, under Mr. Edison's direction, is the ideal he had in mind, he says, when he began work on the kinetoscope machine, with which he has never been satisfied.

The vitascope is an improvement of the kinetoscope, by which moving life size figures of men, women and animals are thrown upon a screen by means of bright lights and powerful lenses. The trial of the new machine was made last night in a cold corner of the big foundry at the works, and Mr. Edison, with Richard N. Dyer, William J. Gilmour, manager of the phonograph works; Raff & Gammon, of New York, and a few invited guests huddled around a red hot stove and gazed at and admired the marvellous figures thrown upon the big white screen at one end of the room.

What the Visitors Saw

The first picture shown was a colored panorama of a serpentine dance by Anabelle, who went out to West Orange to pose one day last summer. The film roll on which the photographs were attached was arranged over a half dozen spools and pulleys, and the machine was set in motion.

Even the inventor himself was surprised at the result, although with his usual critical eye he discovered flaws in the film which he declared must be disposed of before the vitascope would come up to his ideal.

Anabelle danced for five minutes, and then a panorama of the latest English Derby was thrown upon the screen.

The feature of the new machine which astonished all who saw last night's views was the almost entire absence of vibration in the pictures as they appeared on the screen, and which had been the hardest obstacle to surmount in perfecting the apparatus.

The *New York Journal's* account of the same date had a shade more color:

For the first time since Edison has been working on his new invention, the Vitascope, persons other than his trusted employees and assistants were allowed last night to see the workings of the wonderful machine. For two hours dancing girls and groups of figures, all of life size, seemed to exist as realities on the big white screen. . . .

No one was more pleased at the success of his work than the great inventor himself. Wrapped in a big overcoat which hung to his heels and rose to his hat brim, he walked about the cold room chuckling and joking with the men who had done so much to make his work what it is. . . .

. . . the inventor clapped his hands and turning to one of his assistants said:

"That is good enough to warrant our establishing a bald-head row, and we will do it, too."

The English Derby picture mentioned in the *New York Herald's* account of the press showing had been forwarded to Edison from Maguire & Baucus, the London agents of the Kinetoscope. The Derby picture had been photographed over there by Robert W. Paul as part of his independent supply of films for his own replica of the peep-show Kinetoscope.

Just how Edison really felt about this Armat machine is nicely indicated by his testimony in a later litigation. On the witness stand in 1898 Edison said:

> Raff & Gammon got hold of this man named Armat and they wanted us to build the machine. The machine was brought over and we saw it was our machine except that it had a different movement for feeding the film along intermittently. Messrs. Raff & Gammon wanted us to build that machine and they wanted to use my name and as the movement seemed to be a good one and could be built very quickly and cheaply, I gave them permission to use the name for the reason that all there was in the machine that we did not have was simply his movement. And the machines were made and built by us and called the Edison Vitascope and the whole thing was mine except that one movement of Mr. Armat's.
>
> We don't use that Armat movement any more but use our original Geneva stop movement.

In view of the fact that there is no important element of invention in a projection machine save the device that moves the film along intermittently it would seem that Edison was a trifle conservative about giving credit to Armat.

However, this was testimony given in the heat of a lawsuit, not a statement made for publication. To-day Edison is more inclined to rest his claim on the Kinetoscope.

In a letter to Armat in May, 1922, discussing some misrepresentations of alleged screen history, Edison remarked incidentally:

You will probably notice that in interviews given by me I have stated that I had a projection machine, but that when you came on the scene I saw you had a very much better one than mine, and that I dropped my experiments and built yours, which was the first practical projection machine.

There is a certain finality in that letter of Edison's, written after the years have buried the biases of legal sparring for commercial advantages, that may well be the answer to many of the clamorous claims of priority for other inventors.

At the time when the Armat machine was new there was one tiny but amazing fact which doubtless chafed Edison. For years he had had standing in his laboratory a machine which lacked only about two minutes' work to make it a projection machine the equivalent of Armat's. The Edison camera, or Kinetograph, would have been a most excellent projection machine if only he had removed the shutter to allow the full flood of light to reach the screen. Edison's camera had an intermittent movement which held the film still nine times as long as it took to move it from frame to frame, but the camera shutter used only a fraction of this nine-to-one period. That shutter stood between Edison and the basic patent and principle of projection. Here is another of those obscure little technical facts which underlie the beginnings of the big and conspicuous affairs of the screen world. If Edison had been just a shade more interested in the screen he would long before have had that little shutter off and solved the problem first.

The technically minded reader may recall that Dickson tried that camera as a projector, as related in an early chapter, but Dickson did not then know that it would work better without the shutter. That made all the difference in the world.

Armat, the inventor of the Vitascope, was conspicuously absent from the press notices, as befitted the policy of the deal.

The story of the wonders of the Edison Vitascope went swiftly over the world and drew the usual obeisances and admirations on the editorial pages of the newspapers.

The *Brooklyn Eagle* offered promising comment:

> . . . Of course, now it is only an enlarged kinetoscope, the adaptation of a toy to the requirements of actual life, but that is just what was done with the telephone. Once that was a curious toy, now with it you can talk with a man in Chicago and recognize the tones of his voice. It will not be safe to decry the possibilities of the new living panorama. Edison is a mighty ingenious fellow —and electricity in its application to the arts is *in its infancy*.

For just thirty years since it has been the custom of editorial writers, critics, cultural uplifters and the like to refer to the motion pictures as being "in their infancy." It gives a glow of archæological satisfaction to discover the origin of this hackneyed bit of cant in Brooklyn.

The press showing that cold night in West Orange was by way of tuning up the newspapers for the coming presentation at a theatre, and to give the launching all of the wizardly stamp of Edison. It was sound merchandising.

The advertising of Koster & Bials' Music Hall, Thirty-fourth street, Herald Square, for the week commencing Monday evening, April 20, 1896, announced the coming of "Thomas A. Edison's latest marvel, the Vitascope." The music hall was on the site now occupied by the Macy department store.

Thomas Armat came up from Washington to supervise the installation of the Vitascope on the balcony of the music hall.

The opening was delayed because of the time required for the installation of the machinery. The sensation was sprung on the night of April 23. Armat was in the projection booth at the machines while the crowd, thrilled with the dancing of Annabelle, life size on the screen, acclaimed Edison. Edison in a box at the show did not respond in person.

The pictures were thrown upon a twenty-foot screen, set in an overwhelming gilded frame. The program included pictures of a bit of the finale number of Hoyt's *The Milk White Flag,* a dash of prize fight, several dancing girls who displayed their versatility to the camera, and one of Robert W. Paul's pictures, the surf at Dover, in England. The Dover picture was accepted by the audience as something from down the New Jersey coast.

The Vitascope used at Koster & Bials' was equipped with a spool bank and endless loops of film, so that subjects might be repeated indefinitely without rewinding the pictures. The machine was capable of handling film on reels, but the idea of subjects that should occupy the length of a modern reel of a thousand feet was remote indeed from the picture makers of '96.

The audience was deeply puzzled at this magic of the screen. When the waves at Dover came rolling in to crash in jets of spume and spray there was a flurry of panic in the front seats.

In public attention on Broadway that week, honors were about equally divided between the new wonder of the screen and Albert Chevalier, the famous singer of coster songs, who was then appearing at Koster & Bials' in the glory of his first engagement, introducing to the eager American ear *My Old Dutch, The Nipper's Lullaby* and *Our Court Ball.*

Koster & Bials' audiences were as full of silk hats as an undertakers' convention. The amusement world was agog with speculation about the invention.

Charles Frohman, the rising star of theatrical magnates, was in that first night audience. He gave the *New York Times* an interview.

"That settles scenery," said Frohman. "Painted trees that do not move, waves that get up a few feet and stay there, everything in scenery we simulate on our stages will have to go.

Koster & Bials' Music Hall,

34th Street, west of Broadway,

Koster, Bial & Co., Proprietors.

Albert Bial, Manager.

New York, March 24th 1896.

Messrs Raff & Gammon
   The Kinetoscope Company
    253 Broadway

Dear Sirs

  In reply to your favor of 23rd inst. we beg to say that we are ready to put up your Machine and give the performance suggested by you, and will call on you and arrange further details —

    Yours truly

    Koster Bial's Co

    A. Bial.

THIS IS THE LETTER which started the screen career of the motion picture on Broadway, at the famous Koster & Bials' Music Hall, where the Vitascope had its premiere a month later.

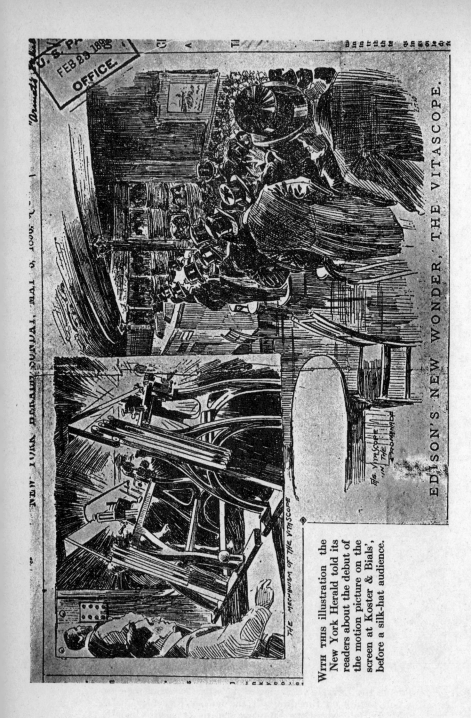

EDISON'S NEW WONDER, THE VITASCOPE.

THE MECHANISM OF THE VITASCOPE.

THE VITASCOPE IN THE PROSCENIUM.

WITH THIS illustration the New York Herald told its readers about the debut of the motion picture on the screen at Koster & Bials', before a silk-hat audience.

NEW YORK HERALD SUNDAY, MAY 3, 1896.

Now that art can make us believe that we see actual living nature the dead things of the stage must go.

"And think what can be done with this invention! For instance, Chevalier comes on the screen. The audience would get all the pantomime of his coster songs. The singing, words fitted to gestures and movements, could be done from the wings or behind the curtain. And so we could have on the stage at any time any artist, dead or alive, who ever faced Mr. Edison's invention.

"That in itself is great enough, but the possibilities of the Vitascope as the successor of painted scenery are illimitable."

Charles Frohman died before the screen had attained its greater triumphs of the modern period, but his prophecies have been translated into terms of practice. In a large sense the living shadows of the Vitascope have supplanted what he called the "dead things of the stage." Even the name that he left, Charles Frohman, Inc., to-day is the incidental property of Famous Players-Lasky, a motion picture corporation.

That showing of the Vitascope on the night of April 23, 1896, at Koster & Bials' Music Hall was the true introduction of the motion picture to Broadway. Herald Square, the scene of that premiere, was the heart of that gilded thoroughfare then. In thirty years the *Herald* has become a memory and ten blocks up Broadway, Times Square rules as the capital of the amusement world, while on above in the northward path of Manhattan's march is the Capitol, the world's greatest theatre, with a weekly turnover of more money that the first years of the whole motion picture industry saw.

To place this entry of the motion picture screen in a sense of time, note that the Greater New York consolidation bill, creating the city of to-day, had just been passed by the state legislature, and that this was the last year of the administration of Grover

Cleveland, Democrat, statesman and fisherman of honored memory.

The same Monday newspapers which reviewed the offerings of the Vitascope at Koster & Bials' carried a story of a Sunday sermon by the Reverend D. Asa Blackburn, pastor of the Church of the Strangers, on the theme of "You can not serve God and skylark on a bicycle." That was indeed a dim long ago. The bicycle as the outstanding diversion of the public before the movie era was then the orthodox subject of attack by the church. The fundamental sin of the bicycle was in its involvement of the use of legs, the existence of which was not admitted by any proper female person. Worse yet, the bicycle led to bloomers, just as inevitably as, the Maine Puritans say, "oysters lead to dancing." The Reverend Mr. Blackburn lost the great opportunity to have been the first to denounce the movies, which daily reveal more and better legs than the entire world's output of bicycles from the reign of Queen Victoria to date.

CHAPTER NINETEEN

THE INVASION OF LONDON

AFTER the first flourish of the Koster & Bials' Music Hall presentation the states' rights sales of the Vitascope came rapidly for a time. Prices ranged from $1500 for lesser territories to $5000 for the state of New York.

Rumors were coming from overseas that in France and England other projection machines were about to be offered. Raff & Gammon urged Armat to apply for all the foreign patents obtainable, especially in England, France, and Germany. When Armat received his patent papers back from Italy he discovered that Rome had claimed him for its very own, changing his name, on all the patents isued, to Thomas Armata.

For the benefit of inquirers remote from Broadway Raff & Gammon issued the world's first place of avowed motion picture advertising literature in announcement of the Vitascope. It was most elaborate and ornate for its time. The booklet was printed in black and red, all shot up with sensational typographical effects and bound in purple crêpe-finished stock bearing on the cover the simple legend: A MARVEL.

This booklet related a varnished version of the history of the device:

. . . Since then, Mr. Edison's experts have been putting his ideas and suggestions to practical test and execution and, in addition, some of the original ideas and inventive skill of Mr. Thomas Armat (the rising inventor of Washington, D. C.) have been embodied in the "Vitascope," the final result being that to-day it can almost be said that the *impossible* has been *accomplished* and a machine has been constructed *which transforms dead pictures into living moving realities.*

—235—

THE VITASCOPE shows human beings instinct with vitality and with every detail of changing expression and movement, every feature of costume and accessory, every surrounding object, figure and scene standing out from the canvas, startlingly distinct, an exact representation or reproduction of nature—in fact, we might almost say, nature outdone. . . .

"Nature outdone" was a large promise—on which the motion picture has in thirty years all too often made good.

One paragraph, showing the effort necessary to convey the full purport of the new machine, reads:

It will be readily seen that a large audience can thus be accommodated between the machine and the canvas upon which the subjects are projected.

This passage was made emphatic by the use of a silhouetted picture of a pointing Devil. This was presumably merely an accidental pick up from the print shop miscellany known in typographical parlance as the hellbox. But it is a nice coincidence that this first booklet concerning the screen should have involved even this casual use of the same star with which Athanasius Kircher introduced his Magia Catoptrica in Rome centuries before, and which Plateau of Ghent used in his primitive picture wheel of the Phenakistoscope under the title of *Le Diable Soufflant*. Evidently one can not keep the Devil away from the movies.

This booklet was hurried to press to be a part of the ammunition for an early invasion of the foreign field. In their dealings at Koster & Bials' office, Raff & Gammon had incidentally interested Paul Cinquevalli. He anticipated that he could sell the Vitascope for large sums abroad. A tentative price of $25,-000 each was set for England and France. Cinquevalli sailed for London, even before a demonstrating model was available.

Cinquevalli's name, which comes for only this fleeting glimpse

How KOSTER AND BIAL'S program for the week of
April 20, 1896, announced the Broadway opening
of the motion picture, projected on the screen by
the Vitascope, as the eighth and closing number
on the variety bill.

CARMENCITA, FIRST "VAMP" of the motion picture, a music
hall favorite of the Naughty-Nineties, in the most daring
pose that the press agent for Koster & Bials' could imagine,
then.

as one of the early figures in the pageant of the screen, is one of gloried memory among the great of the amusement world. One gets a glint of that in a paragraph from a screed on the writing of novels in which Arnold Bennett, some years ago, was moved to say "I have in turn been convinced that Chartres Cathedral, certain Greek sculpture, Mozart's *Don Juan*, and the juggling of Paul Cinquevalli, was the finest thing in the world."

Cinquevalli should interest us, too, because he was one of an amazing succession of magicians, prestidigitators and necromancers to be attracted to the miracle-art of the motion picture. There was a subtle something which for many years after this made the magicians seek the screen with the eager optimism of the alchemist reaching for the philosopher's stone. Also, the public's admiring appraisal of Edison as a wizard is well near identical with that same public's awed appreciation of the feats of Hermann-the-Great and Houdini. The famous Cinquevalli was only the first of many genii of the stage to be fired with motion picture expectations.

When Cinquevalli arrived in London he discovered that the motion picture had in Europe simultaneously passed through stages of evolution closely similar to those of the United States. The foreign machines had sprung from the same seed, the Edison peep show Kinetoscope. The competition of the Vitascope had been born with it.

Over in France the Lumière Cinématographe had introduced the screen art with its first showing for the public at an admission price on December 28, 1895. This exhibition was held on the ground floor of the Grand Café in the Boulevard des Capucines. The program included the first four little pictures made by the Lumières:

Le Repas de Bebe—showing Auguste Lumière, Madame Lumière and their infant daughter at luncheon.

Sortie de L'Usine Lumière—the employees leaving the Lumière photographic manufacturing plant in Lyon.

Arrivé d'un train en Gare—an express train entering the station at Lyon.

L'Arroseur Arrose—concerning a lad's pranks with a hose in the Lumière garden.

These four pictures became as much a part of classic tradition in screen history as the Edison pictures of Fred Ott's sneeze and the Butterfly Dance by the celebrated Annabelle.

From the Grand Café the Lumière Cinématographe went to theatres in Paris and to showings in halls and cafés in the principal capitals of Europe.

With a clever notion for box office values, the Lumières made local scenes and incorporated them in the programs. This was a direct following of a precedent laid down in the early exploitation of the phonograph, when traveling showmen carried blank cylinders to record the efforts of local elocutionists for local consumption. This expedient applied to the motion picture helped in giving the Lumière project a stronghold on the European market, rather successfully held for some years against all comers.

At the same time picture affairs were astir in London. The Lumière Cinématographe was given a press showing at the Empire on February 7, 1896, and a private showing was given to the Duke of Connaught on March 11.

Neck and neck with Lumière came Robert W. Paul, the London instrument maker, with his picture projector, demonstrated February 28 at the Royal Institution. Paul had been highly congratulated by the gathering of scientists. They looked upon his projector as merely a most interesting optical attainment. Its large potential relation to the affairs of the world outside of the laboratory was beyond anticipation by any man in that gathering.

But there was a woman there.

Lady Harris, wife of Sir Augustus Harris, the famous British theatrical magnate, then operating the Olympia in London, was in the audience. She gave the pictures a keen, discerning attention. She reported on them to her husband that night at home.

The next morning Robert W. Paul was surprised by an invitation to breakfast with Sir Augustus Harris.

Sir Augustus appears to have been very canny about it. He talked at length about the Lumière invention of which, it seems, he had heard, by way of Paris rather than from the British showing of the Cinématographe. Then, having paved the path with this suggestion of competition, he asked Paul for a proposition for the showing of his picture machine at the Olympia.

Paul hesitated. He had some deep doubts about the value of pictures on a screen for public entertainment.

"I suppose it will not draw for more than a month, but what do you say to a sharing basis, 50 per cent, on the receipts," Harris suggested.

Paul agreed and the machine, now christened the "Theatrograph," went on at the Olympia with such a pronounced success that the manager of the Alhambra, a vaudeville house, engaged Paul to install another machine for a fortnight's run. That run was ultimately extended to four years.

William Friese Greene, who, it will be remembered, followed Renaud's Praxinoscope, excited to action by the success of Paul at the Alhambra, began an injunction suit claiming priority of invention. Greene failed against Paul as he did repeatedly in subsequent similar efforts to support his claims in England.

The showmen of Great Britain went picture mad and beset Paul with orders.

The Paul workshop in this period brought to the screen industry the name of Cecil Hepworth, whose subsequent picture enterprises continued into the modern period. Hepworth, only a short time before, on his twentieth birthday, received a turning lathe for working metals. It was a present from his father, a lecturer on scientific subjects. Young Hepworth was interested in picture projection through service at the stereopticon for his father's lectures. His first effort with his new lathe was the construction of an arc lamp. It seemed suitable for projection purposes, and the young machinist took his lamp to Paul seeking an order. The Hepworth handfeed lamp, which enabled the operator to trim his light and center the arc behind the film, well suited Paul's purposes. The new arc went into the Theatrograph.

So it came that Cinquevalli found London enjoying the motion picture as presented by Paul at the Olympia and Lumière at the Empire when he arrived in London to sell the Vitascope, armed only with a trunkful of purple bound booklets.

Charles H. Webster, dispatched by Raff & Gammon, arrived in London from New York with a model of the Vitascope on April 30, 1896. Cinquevalli was at the station to meet him when the ship train arrived.

Webster's letter written the next day to Raff & Gammon is the best record of that historic period in British picture presentation:

I did not set up the "V" Thursday as Mr. C. wished me to see the Cinèmatograph, which is showing at the Empire, and I must say I was surprised to see such good results, although I did not tell Mr. C. what I thought of them. They have been at the Empire for two months and exhibit afternoons on a 50% basis, and evenings they get 10£. Mr. C. tells me it runs close to $600.00 a week and it makes the hit of the show. In operation it is noiseless, being operated by hand power, and takes but about 2 sq. ft. The wait between pictures is between 15 and 20 seconds. They use the transparent screen and are located about 20 ft. from it (being on the stage). The light is about ½ as bright as ours, and the picture a trifle smaller. Quite a few of them were full of defects and blurs etc., but the audience do not notice such things. Their minds are concentrated on the nature of the subjects, which by the way were of a local nature and all true to life, such as:

Landing passengers from a steamer

Two babies pulling each other's hair

Boys bathing at the seashore

Boys sailing boats on a pond

Scene in Trafalgar Square at noon

Arrival and departure of a train

Laborers tipping a brick wall over

Man watering a garden (This was very funny. Boy steps on the hose and the man looks in the nozzle when the boy steps off, water squirts in his face) This caught the house by storm.

Boatman rowing a boat

Two acrobats

Scene in a Public Park.

Making ten subjects in all. You see they are all local and cost a mere nothing in comparison to ours. They have no colors, prize fights or dancers, yet are received with cheers nightly for the past two months. They take a new subject almost daily and change but one or two subjects each week. There are two or more machines in London, making three in all, but the one at the Empire is the best of all.

P. S.—Have just found out the other machines are sold for $200.00 and that quite a number have been sold in France.

The "two other" machines to which Webster referred were the Robert W. Paul "Theatrographs," by now showing at the Olympia through the enterprise of Sir Augustus Harris, and at the Alhambra music hall.

The London showing of the Lumière Cinématographe was under the personal charge of "Professor" Felicien Treuwé, a French magician and showman of large fame. Treuwé is a figure of outstanding interest in the picture of the period.

When M. Treuwé walked abroad he went attired in a frock
coat and a high hat, bearing himself with a clerical manner of
deep dignity. As he strolled the boulevards and dallied about
the cafés of Paris, those who did not know him sometimes
smiled and whispered behind their hands. "There goes a
reverend abbé, incognito at his pleasures."

Treuwé had most surely a very priestly mien, recalling on
reflection the richly ecclesiastical make-up of our own Belasco.
But Treuwé had come by his less by deliberate design. His
father had mistakenly chosen the priesthood as a career for his
young Felicien, sending him away into the training of the Jesu-
its. Felicien was an apt pupil, always very apt to spring some
new and magic pagan devilment for the consternation of the
good fathers. Treuwé steadily improved in the technique of
illusion to the detriment of his Latin. He abandoned prospect
of the cloth for the boards. He was to be a priest of the proscenium presenting prayerless miracles.

Now there is something delightfully reminiscent of that other
and earlier Jesuit, Athanasius Kircher and his shadow-throwing
Magia Catoptrica in Rome, in the major attainment of Treuwé's
career. Like Kircher he put on a shadow show, but unlike
Kircher he did not star the Devil. Treuwé's shadow magic portrayed bits of happier sagas of love, adventure and romance.
Presumably the Treuwé shows were, so far as he was aware, entirely original with him, but they must inevitably remind us of
the very old shadow dramas of the Orient.

Treuwé's method was a capable approximation of the motion
picture. He placed a canvas screen before the audience and
at considerable distance backstage an open calcium light. With
his fingers and ingenious little silhouettes worn thimble fashion
he cast life size moving shadow figures on the canvas. He presented bits of pageants and playlets. A sentimental episode
entitled *The Serenade* was his masterpiece. A maiden came to

the casement window of the castle while her shadow lover strummed a lute below—*Romeo* and *Juliet* no doubt. Treuwé's shadow casts included knights and monks and kings and jesters, the whole race of hieroglyphic types standard in all the narrative arts.

Naturally enough Treuwé found an absorbing interest in the Cinématographe, and its able mechanical attainment of effects in tune with his own deft fingered art of the shadow.

But propinquity was a greater factor in making him a screen show pioneer. Priest and alchemist are likely to be found often together. Treuwé was a friend of the Lumières and a familiar about their establishment in Lyon of long standing. He was a crony of Antoine Lumière, father of Louis and Auguste, the makers of the Cinématographe. Treuwé and the elder Lumière sat in the garden at their cards and good *vin rouge* while Louis and Auguste were at their labors in their laboratory. One of the first of the experimental pictures made with the working model of the Cinématographe showed Antoine Lumière and "Professor" Treuwé at the little table in the garden. And one has to be a very good friend indeed to play at cards with a magician.

Treuwé was therefore in at the birth of the Cinématographe, and it was but natural that he, as the famous showman, should have been given the honor of its introduction to the world capital of London. Between Treuwé's shadow shows and his close association with the beginnings of the screen many have become confused, and in the writings of Americans and Englishmen in particular one often finds him credited with having invented the projection machine.

The point which Webster made in his letter about the local subjects shown on the Lumière machine was most important, as a factor of its success. The Cinématographe was available for all three operations of motion picture making. It was at once a camera, a printer and a projector. The Cinématographe plus two water buckets for developing tanks and a ruby light was in fact a portable motion picture plant complete. With it the itinerant showman could expose films by day, project films in the evening, and spend the dark hours of night developing and printing the day's exposures. If he got through before breakfast the rest of his time was a total loss. A Lumière showman had the steadiest job in the world.

The Lumière method of including scenes of familiar local personages, events and locations was exceedingly important in conveying a conviction that motion pictures were real reproductions of real things. To us in this picture-familiar age it is difficult to appreciate the naïve viewpoint of the first audiences. It was not that local events were of major interest to those screen audiences, but that they constituted the evidence that the other marvels were genuine, therefore more marvelous. With the masses, art as art never gets anywhere. They must believe.

Meanwhile, the Edison camera, nearly as heavy as a parlor grand piano, was still anchored to the "Black Maria" studio in West Orange. It could only picture that portion of the world which could be brought within those tar paper walls.

Lumière was sweeping all the European capitals as well as London. George Kemp, another foreign courier of the Vitascope, arrived in Budapest to find the Cinématographe in possession there and in Vienna.

The Lumières had, at the beginning, broken away from the limitations of electric power and illumination which naturally for a long time bound every machine which issued from Edison's works at Orange. Edison was an electrician first of all, and whatever he wanted to run was to be run by electricity if possible. The Lumières, however, evolved a lamp, fueled with ether to supply illumination, and cranked the intermittent motion of the Cinématographe by hand. This machine could take the motion picture into the many regions where electricity was yet to be introduced.

The Lumière picture in the original Cinématographe was in fact hardly as satisfactory as the Vitascope's screen product, despite Europe's enthusiasm. The Vitascope being a shutterless machine, as has been pointed out, passed much more light to the screen and operated with less flicker than the Lumière device which held the screen dark just half of the time, with a half circle shutter.

But in a world which had thus far no standard of comparison the Lumière machine was able to make a vital impress on the new industry.

The influence of Webster's report on the Lumière show was almost immediately apparent in the new subjects made by the Edison Kinetograph in New York. Within a few weeks Raff & Gammon were offering pictures of Herald Square, the closest equivalent of Lumière's Trafalgar Square, a picture of the Black Diamond Express to compete with Lumière's *Arrivé d'un Train en Gare*, and finally a parade of the New York mounted police in their best approximation of the Lumière film of a French cavalry charge. Then, as now, every screen success was copied with an absurd, unimaginative literalism.

CHAPTER TWENTY

FIRST PSALM OF THE CINEMA

THE Vitascope had given New York the miracle of the screen only one week when it burgeoned, burst, bloomed, floriated, foamed, frothed and flourished into Literature. Exactly that.

William Kennedy Laurie Dickson, late of the Edison staff, erupted as the author of the first work on the motion picture. It was a pamphlet, succinctly entitled: *HISTORY of the PHOTOGRAPHIC and SCIENTIFIC EXPERIMENTS and DEVELOPMENTS leading up to the PERFECTION of the VITASCOPE.*

Dickson, before his break with Gilmore and Edison at West Orange, had taken his pen in hand to write a few lines on the original Kinetoscope late in 1894. In this work he had anticipated projection, and now Armat had attained it. The pamphlet in 1896 suddenly acquired a new title, a new cover and a frontispiece in a leap to catch step with the new Vitascope.

Dickson sounded high "C." His ecstasy of appreciation for the motion picture may one day be equalled, never surpassed. It was written in the Super-Victorian that can be achieved only by a really impassioned Englishman.

A certain editorial technique made it entirely clear that Dickson was not intending to let any part of his light be obscured by the Edison bushel. The booklet offered one large picture of Edison, and three lesser but reiteratively arranged pictures of Dickson, some of them triple exposures. The full velocity of the rhapsody is only beginning to develop when the reader arrives at a description of the "Black Maria" studio:

—246—

As we peer into the illusive depths we seem transported into one of those cheerful banqueting halls of old where the feudal chief made merry with human terrors, draping the walls with portentous black, and thoughtfully providing a set of coffins for the accommodation of his guests. And what is this mysterious cell at the other extremity, sharply outlined against the dazzling radiance of the middle ground and steeped in an angry crimson hue? Are these inquisitorial dungeons, and is that lurid glare the advence guard of the awful Question? Is that gentle persuasive in process of administration, and do these half-guessed recesses conceal the hellish paraphernalia of rack and screw, glowing iron and crushing stone? Has the doom of ages overtaken our wizard at last, and is he expatiating with twisted limb and scorching flesh, the treasures of his unlawful kingdom?

It would be a suspicious reader who would at this point detect the faint tinkle of a padded hammer ringing against the fame of the Wizard of Menlo Park. It was the fashion of the day for photographers to demonstrate their skill with strange pictorial conceits. Here, in perfect psychological harmony with the horror motif, Dickson garnishes the text with an illustration reproducing a photograph of his own head served on a platter. Thus in fancy he shared the fate of that other great advanceagent and prophet, St. John-the-Baptist. Now on with his lay:

Ah, me that the prosaic truth must be told. No dungeons are these, thrilling with awful possibilities, but simply a building for the better taking of kinetographic subjects. . . .

No department of the wizard's domains is more fraught with perennial interest than this theatre; none are more interwoven with the laughter, the pathos, the genius and the dexterities of life. No earthly stage has ever gathered within its precincts a more incongruous crew of actors since the days when gods and men and animals were on terms of social intimacy: when Orpheus poured his melting lays into the ears of the brute creation, and gentle Anthony of Padua lured the suffering beasts to the mouth of his desert cave. . . .

When Dickson got around to the business of forecasting the future of the films he really opened up and expressed himself freely. This portion should be read aloud, in the open air. With some talk about photographing an organ grinder's monkey and the return of Professor Garner, monkey-linguist and naturalist, from Africa, Dickson continues:

He proposes a second trip shortly, and will bring the wide resources of the kinetograph to bear upon additional phases of animal life, so that our aristocratic sybarites may enjoy the thrilling dramas of jungle and forest, without imperilling that "repose which is the essential attitude of good breeding," or embrowning the delicate cuticle on their patrician countenances. When music, oratory and histrionics have lost their power to charm, they may ensconce themselves in the yielding recesses of ruby or violet thrones, with the scent of hot house flowers around and the memory of a Lucullus feast titillating the cultured palate. From that luxurious stronghold they may contemplate the awful rush of maddened brutes, the tawny flash of the savage eyes, the lightning play of the vigorous muscles, may hear the shock of the reverberating earth, the roar of the great cats, the grinding of fangs, the tearing of iron claws, the scream of the dying elephant, the sardonic laugh of the merciless hyena—robber and violator of the dead—the whirr of mighty pinions, as the vultures descend to their ghastly feast, all the "travailing and groaning" of burdened creation. The sunlight will tremble through the leafy arcades and cast its fantastic shadows on the opulent growth: will extract, through its own unapproachable alchemy, each superb *nuance* on tree and flower and creeper; will vivify the tawny beauty of tiger and lion, and give to the lustrous plumage of the bird an added glory; will burnish the scale of the Ophidian and encase the flashing Coleoptera in mail of metal and gem. . . .

To the final development of the kinetographic stage, than which no more powerful factor for good exists, no limitations can possibly be affixed. The shadowy histrionics of the near future will yield nothing in realistic force and beauty to their material sisters. The rich strain of a Seidl or Damrosch orchestra, issuing from a concealed phonograph, will herald the impending drama, and attune the hearts of the expectant throng. The curtain will rise, exposing some one of the innumerable phases of pictorial art, some soft English pastoral or cosy interior of a mansion, some fastness in the Alps or Himalayas, some tempestuous ocean scene, quickened with the turbulent anguish of the unresisting sea, some exquisite landscape, steeped in the jeweled lights of sunset or the rosy sheen of morn. The actors will enter singly and in groups, in the graceful interweaving of social life, the swirl of the dance or the changeful kaleidoscope of popular tumult. . . . All these effects of sight and sound will be embraced in the kinetoscopic drama, and yet of that living breathing throng, not one will be encased in a material frame. A company of ghosts, playing to spectral music. So may the luminous larvæ of the Elysian fields have rehearsed earth's well beloved scenes to the exiled senses of Pluto's Queen.

Now let Griffith, DeMille, Rothafel and Riesenfeld laugh that off if they can. In those conservative words in 1896 Dickson forecast the super-features, the orchestral accompaniment, and the plush loge seats, choice of two colors. In fact, Dickson did not, in the fever of his *grandioso-crescendo,* overshoot the mark as far most seers do. Even his "luminous larvæ," are now found in abundance on the Elysian fields of the screen, but denoted in these less elegant days as "lens lice." But let us proceed to his bigger and better promises.

This line of thought may be indefinitely pursued with application to any given phase of outdoor or indoor life. . . . Not only our own resources but those of the entire world will be at our command, nay, we may even anticipate the time when sociable relations will be established between ourselves and the planetary system, and when the latest doings in Mars, Saturn and Venus will be recorded by enterprising kinetographic reporters.

Why Dickson so limited himself to the solar system is not entirely clear. Astronomy in the intervening decades has really much extended the limits of the potential market. His closing ode is recommended as suitable for recitation at cornerstone layings, theatre dedications and reading in the school and churches.

What is the future of the kinetograph? Ask rather, from what conceivable phase of the future can it be debarred. . . . It is the crown and flower of nineteenth century magic, the crystallization of Eons of groping enchantments. In its wholesome, sunny and accessible laws are possibilities undreamt of by the occult lore of the East: the conservative wisdom of Egypt, the jealous erudition of Babylon, the guarded mysteries of Delphic and Eleusinian shrines. It is the earnest of the coming age, when the great potentialities of life shall no longer be in the keeping of cloister and college or money bag, but shall overflow to the nethermost portions of the earth at the command of the humblest heir of the divine intelligence.

There in a word you have it—the art of the motion picture— summarized, by the first man to crank a camera, in the flower of his success of thirty years ago. Will Hays himself could say no more, today.

CHAPTER TWENTY-ONE

A DANCE FROM CAIRO AND A KISS

THE first viewpoint of the motion picture industry as exemplified by the early career of the Vitascope was that it was a machinery business.

Edison was an inventor of machines.

It was entirely inadvertent of Edison that he had invented a machine which had cut back through the ages and delivered to the world a new ability to use its oldest language, the re-created event of the picture. It is excusable that he should have failed to see that the pictures were vastly more important than the machine.

It was a part of this same viewpoint and the desire to sell more machines which had made him oppose the coming of the screen machine which could show pictures to a whole audience at once. He had sold some hundreds of peep show Kinetoscopes, and he thought that fifty projection machines would be ample to cover the world with screen pictures.

This attitude, held generally about the Edison works, became at once a factor of large influence in the first two years of motion picture production. The future of the motion picture was so great that it could not possibly have been foreseen. We are always so far from the past that we have no perspective on the future.

Even before the peep show had begun to yield to the Vitascope screen, Raff & Gammon had found that the handful of pictures supplied were not going to satisfy the trade.

Demands for a change of program began to come, and it was necessary for the Kinetoscope company to make arrangements to take in used pictures on exchange for new subjects. The selling price of the Kinetoscope subjects started at a flat ten dollars each. They were exchanged for new ones for a fee of two dollars.

Something beyond the inventor's ken had happened. He had built a machine which would make pictures move, and he was done. The public, however, had looked in wonder at the pictures that moved, and now wanted to see yet others move. It was the wee dim beginning of the public insistence that the new-old picture language be made to say nothing.

Here was a situation which cried for a screen story teller. The motion picture had to wait and wane nearly to extinction before the story teller came and gave it something to say.

Raff & Gammon were brought up against this condition by their Vitascope customers. On July 8, 1896, E. F. Albee, general manager of the B. F. Keith Amusement Enterprises, wrote from Boston:

> I am obliged to have some new films for next week, or make next week the last one of the Vitascope, for the interest in the old ones is so strongly on the decrease that it will not be profitable for me to run it any longer, unless I have something new. I hope you will see the importance of this and act accordingly.

Edison and Gilmore, his general manager, were slow to react to Raff & Gammon demands, and from the beginning it was the selling agents of the motion picture who carried the editorial load of production. Among the quaint accounts of the Kinetoscope Company one finds entry of an item of one dollar expense incurred by one Alfred O. Tate in attending the show at Tony Pastor's variety theatre in Fourteenth Street "looking for subjects."

The Edison-Gilmore apathy toward new pictures is reminiscent of the backwoods Maine postmaster who protested to an inspector that it was no use sending off the mail bags until they were full. They did not see any use for new pictures until every one in the world had seen the old ones.

Also, as a part of this condition, the first star and studio troubles began out at the Black Maria in West Orange. In the course of a letter pleading for co-operation Frank R. Gammon under date of March 25, 1896, wrote to Gilmore:

> I was out there yesterday with a party to be taken for the Kinetoscope, but had great difficulty in persuading them to go into the theatre in their thin silk costumes, as it was just like going out into an open field in midwinter. We had to keep them there at least an hour, and if some of them do not take cold and die, I shall be agreeably surprised. Upon inquiry I was informed that the part of the roof which raises was stuck, so that it could not be lowered. If it could have been closed, and a fire in the stove during rehearsal, and then opened when ready to take the scene, no complaint would have been made. Two or three subjects which we have endeavored to secure have absolutely refused to go out there, as they have learned from others the true condition of the place. I am now glad that we did not succeed in inducing Loie Fuller to go out there, for as soon as she understood that she had to go into that cold place, I am sure she would have become indignant, and returned to New York without being taken. You will probably call this a kicking letter, but it is not my intention to find fault, and am only endeavoring to impress you with the needs requisite for the success of the business, and to enable us to secure the large volume which we have right in our grasp, if we can only secure your co-operation and attention to details.

Subsequent correspondence and records reveal a thirty year old secret of the screen. LaLoie Fuller never was cajoled into the well refrigerated "Black Maria." Her sister, also a dancer, went out and put on the act for the screen record which went around the world under the famous name of the great LaLoie. This is beyond doubt the first instance of the use of a screen double, long since a commonplace of studio practice. Critics of '96 gushed over the excellence and realism of the Vitascope's reproduction of LaLoie's inimitable grace on the screen, but they never saw it.

The sums paid to these early performers of the screen ranged from ten to fifty dollars, plus their expenses to West Orange and return. When the Vitascope press notices began to blossom, lesser variety stars began to push in with offers of their service for the mere benefit of screen publicity. Then prices went down.

This supply and demand condition of the motion picture talent market of '96 is highly reminiscent of the recent and recurrent debates over the question of payment for contributions to radiocast performances.

The very morning that the newspapers carried the news of the Vitascope opening at Koster & Bials' Music Hall, one Albert C. Waltz, "introducing a marvellous and sensational act of pedal cycling, contortion trick and acrobatic skating act" at the Casino in Fall River, Mass., wrote to Edison offering his services under the title of "the world's renowned champion ice and roller skater of the world."

Mr. Waltz's next jump was Rochester, N. Y., where he found a letter from Raff & Gammon awaiting him with this form reply:

Replying to your favor to Mr. Thomas Edison, which is referred to us by him, we have no doubt but that your "Act" would be interesting and successful in the Kinetoscope or Vitascope, but on account of the widespread and valuable advertising which subjects receive through the exhibition and advertising of our films, we do not have to purchase their services, as we have more volunteers that we are able to avail ourselves of. We should be pleased to take your "Act" without charge, but under the circumstances you will readily see that we could not pay for the same.

A catalogue search indicates that Mr. Waltz did not avail himself of this sterling opportunity.

But Raff & Gammon were none the less looking for stellar material on "the big time," as revealed by the following letter addressed to the impresario of present Broadway fame for "glorifying the American girl":

Mr. F. Ziegfeld, Jr.   April 29, 1896
Netherland Hotel
New York City

Your telegram to Mr. Edison with reference to the Vitascope has been referred to us, as we have control of the machine, and are attending to all of the business in connection with it.

We would be glad to have you call at our offices at 43 W. 28th Street when we will explain to you our plan of handling the Vitascope, and will be pleased to negotiate with you for the right to exhibit in any country of the world.

We would also like to ask whether it would be agreeable to Mr. Sandow to go out to Mr. Edison's Laboratory at Orange and be taken again for the Vitascope. He was good enough to go there two years since and permit us to take photographs of him in his "act" for exhibition on the Kinetoscope. The original negative is worn out, and we would like to secure a new one for exhibition on the Vitascope. We believe it would result in a big advertisemen for Mr. Sandow, and we will endeavor to reproduce him in one of his "acts" life sized, and it would probably be exhibited throughout the world.

If Mr. Sandow is willing to go out, we would be glad to extend the courtesies of our firm to him, and one of our firm would also accompany him at such time as it may be convenient for him to go.

Hoping to hear from you soon, we remain

Very truly yours
RAFF & GAMMON.

The canny Ziegfeld did not deliver his stage Hercules to the camera, so the motion picture career of Eugene Sandow, greatest of the strong men, began and ended in the peep show.

The motion picture was beginning to be just dimly awake to its possibilities in those ancient days, but the basic idea of the pictures had been evolved, as indicated by a paragraph from the following letter of May 6, 1896, to W. D. Stansifer of Butte, Montana, a Kinetoscope peep show exhibitor who was looking for something arranged to the taste of the copper town:

> We are confident that the Dolorita *"Passion Dance"* would be as exciting as you desire. In fact, we will not show it in *our* parlor. You speak of the class of trade which wants something of this character. We think this will certainly answer your purposes. A man in Buffalo has one of those films and informs us that he frequently has forty or fifty men waiting in line to see it. We do not send out films for inspection.

So in peep show days motion picture censorship began from the inside, where the industry has tried to keep it ever since.

Dolorita's dance consisted of an Americanized version of the "Ouled Nail" girls' dance from North Africa, done in charming synchronism to the tom-tom and flute, imported with such decided success in *The Streets of Cairo* on the Midway of the Chicago World's Fair of '93. This picture held the box office record of the slot machines of the Kinetoscope parlor on the Boardwalk at Atlantic City.

Then one day an uplifter, giving the Boardwalk a careful sociological examination, observed the line at the "Dolorita" machine. He waited his turn and had a long and nourishing look at the "passion dance."

Two days later H. R. Kiefaber, owning the Kinetoscope parlor on the Boardwalk, wrote Frank R. Gammon:

> "The authorities request us not to show the Houchi Kouchi, so please cancel order for new Dolorita, also order for Amy Muller, colored. The emulsion on the Rope Dance is coming off in large pieces."

In view of the difficulties encountered in attempting production at the Black Maria in West Orange, L. Edson Raff, stepson of Norman C. Raff, decided to meet the situation by the entirely daring and thoroughly original expedient of establishing a motion picture studio right in New York City, handy to Broadway, where celebrities might readily be brought before the camera.

A studio platform was erected on the roof over the Twenty-eighth street office of Raff & Gammon. Edison agreed to supply a camera and camera man and to do the technical and finishing work at West Orange, making the negatives for Raff & Gammon and supplying them with prints on order.

The peep show motion picture business had entailed a total investment of $1,118.67 in the making of subjects. With the coming of the screen costs were climbing in direct ratio as the screen had to have something to command patronage. Production costs have been climbing for the same reason ever since.

In this period of Raff & Gammon affairs two names of long survival in screen annals became connected with the concern: Percy L. Waters, destined to important posts in the once great General Film Company and the more recent Triangle Film Corporation, and James H. White, subsequently long identified with Edison enterprises.

The roof studio in Twenty-eighth street made a bit of slapstick comedy with a burlesque barber shop scene, a bar-room travesty with a pretty maid serving a policeman in uniform, and a Chinese opium den in action. The boys seem to have had the movie idea from the start.

Up on Broadway May Irwin and John C. Rice were the celebrities of the current stage hit entitled *The Widow Jones,* a parlor ancestor of the bedroom farce. *The Widow Jones* had its high moment in a prolonged kiss between the principals. It was one of those persisting, adhesive osculations, doubtless made more delightful by the sweeping model of the hero's moustache, a hirsute ornamentation of the type which reached its zenith among British cavalry officers in India and among the Texas Rangers. It was also a high vacuum kiss, attended at its conclusions by sounds reminiscent of a steer pulling a foot out of the gumbo at the edge of a water hole. It was, in brief—and in length—the world's greatest kiss, as of that date, 1896 A. D.

Obviously nothing whatsoever could have been a more fitting subject for the Vitascope. Here was a jewelled dramatic moment which this motion picture could peretuate and disseminate for the delectation of the multitudes in the hinterland.

Under the title of *The May Irwin-John C. Rice Kiss* this emotional item was photographed on the roof in a total of fifty throbbing feet of film.

It was perhaps the world's first educational motion picture. the kiss had come to the screen and the future of the art was from that day assured. Every development of the motion picture since may be summed up as a dramatic artifice for preliminary action leading up to the presentation of the same identical pictured climax, the "close-up, fade-out clinch." See any screen any day for specimens of this hardy perennial.

The *Kiss* as it came to be known in the film trade was a charming close-up, nearly as close as they shoot the same action today. It was a roaring hit. Critics everywhere announced this glory of the Vitascope as worth the price of admission for the entire show on any bill. It overshadowed the press notices for Black Patti and Albert Chevalier.

And just as the metaphorical apple, undoubtedly a green one, of Eden was followed by gripes of conscience, the discovery of the screen kiss brought on the symptomatic cramps of censorship to come.

When the Vitascope reached Chicago with this precious film, it came to the chance attention of Herbert S. Stone, publisher of *The Chap Book*, a periodical for the cognoscenti, the intelligensia and the literati. It was of consequence a magazine of small circulation, large liberty and pungent words. This history is indebted to Randolph Bartlett, screen writer and editor, who, prowling through the literary debris of Powner's book shop in Chicago, came upon a file of *The Chap Book*. In its issue of June 15, 1896, Stone raised his fowling piece and let go with both barrels in the following words:

> One's acerbities of temper are not pleasant things to emphasize, and geniality and indulgence are tempting. But the ever recurring outrages to decency and good taste which I see in books and on the stage force me constantly into the rôle of *Jack-the-Giant-Killer;* in common phrase "I have my hammer out most of the time."
>
> Now I want to smash the *Vitascope.* The name of the thing is in itself a horror. Its manifestations are worse. The *Vitascope,* be it known, is a sort of magic lantern which reproduces movement. Whole scenes are enacted on the screen. LaLoie dances, elevated trains come and go, and the thing is mechanically ingenious, and a pretty toy for that great child, the public. Its managers are not satisfied with this, however, and they bravely set out to eclipse in vulgarity all previous theatrical attempts.
>
> In a recent play called *The Widow Jones* you may remember a famous kiss which Miss May Irwin bestowed on a certain John C. Rice, and *vice versa.* Neither participant is physically attractive, and the spectacle of their prolonged pasturing on each other's lips was hard to bear. When only life size it was pronounced beastly. But that was nothing to the present sight. Magnified to Gargantuan proportions and repeated three times over it is absolutely disgusting. All delicacy or remnant of charm seems gone from Miss Irwin, and the performance comes near being indecent in its emphasized vulgarity.
>
> Such things call for police interference. Our cities from time to time have spasms of morality, when they arrest people for displaying lithographs of ballet-girls; yet they permit, night after night, a performance which is infinitely more degrading. The immorality of living pictures and bronze statues is nothing to this. The Irwin kiss is no more than a lyric of the Stock Yards. While

we tolerate such things, what avails all the talk of American Puritanism and of the filthiness of imported English and French stage shows?

The "living pictures" to which Stone referred were the then common stage tableaux. Many newspaper references of the time will be found to contain comparisons between the motion pictures and the "living pictures." The "living picture" was born of the pre-motion-picture days as poses or reconstructed moments of history and legend, as, for instance, *Napoleon at Waterloo*, *Cleopatra and Antony*, and *Pygmalion and Galatea*. The frequency of the presentation of *Pygmalion and Galatea* must not be taken to indicate that our theatre-going public of the '90's was passionately devoted to classic allusion. It merely points to their ardent admiration of the well-fitting costume of French chalk and calcium worn by *Galatea*. The living picture tableaux re-created a frozen moment of the event, while the newcomer, the motion picture, now brought on the visual impression of the whole event in the process of delicious eventuation.

This *Kiss* picture won wide attention for the Vitascope and became a fertile text for that persistent race of people who make a career of writing letters to the newspapers.

Miss Gladys Rice, a singer of current Broadway fame for her appearance on Rothafel programs at various screen theatres, is a daughter of John C. Rice, who appeared so immediately opposite May Irwin in that famous *Kiss* picture of '96.

The *Kiss* continued to flourish until the negative was worn to tatters. A screen examination of the sole surviving print today reveals it as a mere quaint commonplace, by present standards. Its daring of 1896 is lost in its archaic humor of 1926.

The picture being in high demand was the subject of much feverish communication from Vitascope exhibitors. One pleasantly ambiguous telegram from the old Vitascope company files reads:

Saratoga, N. Y.

Raff & Gammon
43 W. 28th Street, N. Y.

Alternating current don't penetrate heavy films.   Can you send thin kiss?

ANNETTE REYNOLDS

The reply to that message was dictated in great formality and signed with the company's impersonal rubber stamp.   Raff & Gammon were taking no chances with kisses, thick or thin.

CHAPTER TWENTY-TWO

VAUDEVILLE ADOPTS THE FILMS

Within two months of the introductory showing of the Vitascope at Koster & Bials' Music Hall in New York, the precedents to govern the next ten years of presentation of the motion picture to the public were laid down.

It is whimsically true that these precedents came not with the exploitation of the American made Vitascope but rather with its French rival, the Lumière Cinématographe.

To pick up the thread of this development we must turn back in theatrical history to some two years before. Probably the best introduction to the man involved is a bit of an incident which the late Robert Grau, the last of a famed line of impresarios, often related with zestful memory. Grau was sitting with Tony Pastor in his little bird-cage of a theatre in Fourteenth Street. They had been watching a variety bill. It was rated a strong bill, with Maggie Cline, Filson & Errol, Barry & Bannon, and a handful of others equally famous then. But the attendance was light, and the audience was most indifferent.

"Bob," observed Pastor, turning to Grau, "the old time variety show is dead. It's going to be 'refined vaudeville' now. That fellow Fynes up the street at Keith's Union Square is putting us all to sleep. He's going to raise Cain with the variety business all over this country if something doesn't stop him."

This invading disturber of the show world was J. Austin Fynes, who had now been some twelve years on Broadway. He had come from the night editor's desk of the *Boston Herald* to

—262—

THE KISS, May Irwin and John C. Rice, re-enacting for the Edison Kinetograph the high climax of their play *The Widow Jones* playing Broadway that season of 1896 — This picture gave the screen censorship movement its start.

J. Stuart Blackton's motion picture career began that day in 1896 when the *New York Evening World* sent him to Orange to interview Edison and make this sketch. It led to the organization of Vitagraph fame and fortune for "Jimmy" Blackton.

Zoopraxographical Hall at the Chicago World's Fair in 1893, where the glass plate motion pictures evolved by the methods of Isaacs and Meissonier were exploited by Eadweard Muybridge. This may be called the first screen theatre, but it never showed a film.

join the staff of the *Clipper,* a dramatic weekly. Incidentally he became the dramatic critic of the *Evening Sun,* to be succeeded in that post by Charles Dillingham, afterwards a dramatic producer.

Fynes, filled with notions about the sins of the old variety theatre, found his chance when B. F. Keith, the Boston "continuous variety" showman, entered the New York field.

The new-born picture was part of Fynes' opportunity. But the Latham Eidoloscope was unsatisfactory, and the Vitascope was, for New York showings, in the hands of Koster & Bials' Music Hall, uptown competitors.

But Keith's foreign agent, on whom his theatres largely depended for novelty acts, reported on the success in France of the Lumière Cinématographe. It appealed to Fynes as probably offering more that would be now interesting in competition with Koster & Bials' than any American picture service. Keith's agent made an exclusive deal for New York, and the Cinématographe was dispatched to New York.

The deal got gossiped up and down Broadway. Rich G. Hollaman of the Eden Musee, alertly attuned to opportunities for purveying picture-made emotions to his public, was interested. He had had some slight dickerings with Raff & Gammon over the Vitascope and had not been able to get his terms. At any rate, Hollaman seemed to have the habit of looking to Europe for things. The Musee idea was born over there. Now he went post haste to Fynes, and argued him into allowing the Lumière pictures to be booked to the Eden Musee, on the contention that that unique institution of thrills in wax work was a museum not a theatre. So it came that on the night of June 29, 1896, both Keith's Union Square theatre and the Eden Musee in Twenty-third street presented the same program of motion pictures on the screen. The advance notice in the *New York Times* of Sunday, June 28, 1896, reads:

One of the English equivalents of the vitascope, called the Lumière Cinématographe, will be placed on exhibition at Keith's Union Square tomorrow night. It is much better than its name, as was proved at a private view yesterday. It is said to be the first stereopticon kinetoscope exhibited. Its pictures are clear and interesting. One represents the arrival of mail trains in the railway station, another the bathing pier at Nice at the height of the season.

Somewhat as Tony Pastor indicated, all eyes were on Fynes, the newcomer in the New York amusement field.

Fynes was setting a pace. His adoption of the motion picture as a standard portion of his program was a cue to all the vaudeville houses in the country. It was the enterprise of Raff & Gammon which put the picture into the vaudeville show for its début, but it was the competitive move of Fynes which gave it the stamp of acceptance in the world of showmanship.

The motion picture soon became a staple number on the vaudeville program. It filled a turn, soon at a lower price than any ordinary act.

From this beginning, the vaudeville screen continued to be the principal avenue to the public for almost exactly a decade. Its vaudeville career was both a blessing and a curse upon the screen. It served to keep the film alive and slowly evolving by supplying it with this narrow activity. While keeping the picture alive, vaudeville enslaved it and cheapened it until the time came that the films were known merely as "chasers," marking the end of the show and clearing the house for the next performance.

Until the screen grew into a medium of expression with something to say of its own, a turn in vaudeville was the biggest job it could hold. It could be an interesting mirror of topical events or novelties for fifteen minutes. Then it was done.

If H. G. Wells, Alexander Black, or any of the trained tellers of tales had followed up their first flitting contact with the motion picture its history would have been tremendously affected. More than likely we should have had *The Birth of a Nation* in terms of its evolutionary equivalent by 1904 instead of 1914.

The singers of the sagas were many a year becoming aware of the new instrument. They had waited so many ages for the coming of the motion picture that they were no longer looking for it, and it was unrecognized when it came.

Now for years the motion picture art was to be left to the hands of inventors, machinists, and petty exploiters. We shall see some of these men, a limited few, grow up with the screen and become variously skilled in its use as a medium of expression. But more largely we shall find the motion picture outgrowing its sucessive dynasties of masters, leaving discarded personalities behind.

While the Cinématographe was building vaudeville precedent for the screen in New York, the Vitascope was being booked into the Keith house in Boston and through concessionaries into the Orpheum Circuit houses of the middle west.

The secret compact for the selling of the Vitascope under the name of Edison came near to leaking to the public when the *Post* of Hartford, Conn., sent a reporter to get an advance story on the coming of the marvel to that city. The *Hartford Post* of May 25, 1895, relates:

> For several days a bright young fellow has been stopping at the United States hotel, registered as Christopher Armat. He is one of three brothers, who with Edison are the only men in the world who thoroughly understand the vitascope. He is in demand all over the country and as soon as he can teach an electrician how to run the machine he will move on to the next city. . . .

In Boston the newspapers' dramatic writers found the Vitascope inspiration for forecasts interesting to review now after the lapse of three decades.

The *Boston Herald* remarked:

> May not small towns see city shows by the Vitascope? May not actresses, who realize how fleeting youth is, preserve themselves in their prime? Indeed to what use may not the Vitascope be put? Lectures of travelers may now be illustrated actively, and take a new lease of life. Victims of seasickness can see life more in the Orient. But all this is in the future.

But the *Herald* hedged a bit in its forecasts. After referring to the importation of a set of phonograph records of the entire performance of *The Sporting Duchess*, the writer added:

> . . . Of course there is not the slightest chance that any universal use of that sort will be made of the invention (Vitascope) yet there is here a chance that great actors can leave their work behind them. Fancy, if this invention had been made before Edwin Booth died, his business, at least for *Hamlet*, might have been preserved. . . .

The *Boston Traveler's* column entitled *Stage Whispers* was more enthusiastic:

> Who knows how the new invention and those that are to follow may revolutionize the amusement world. Perhaps our great-grandchildren may know nothing except as historic memories of stage performances as we have them today. Who knows that each country will not have its stage "foundries," so to speak, for each of the various forms of dramatic and musical act? Here finely drilled companies could give performances to be perpetuated by the Vitascope and the phonograph or their successors. Duplicates of the records could be sent by flying machines broadcast over the world and London's new play or latest sensational dance could be enjoyed in every quarter of the globe within a few days of the initial presentation.

The Boston showing attracted a notable attendance of scientists and society folk to Keith's, and gave the reviewers a thrill at the sight of such a profound representation of Harvard, Commonwealth Avenue, and the Back Bay.

The newspaper forecasts of the coming relation of the motion picture to the stage were, as we shall see, remote indeed. It was to be many a year until the screen came into recognition as a medium of expression beyond a mere recording of the wonders of other older media.

The screen art received a testimonial of recognition as an important newcomer to the theatre when Weber and Fields presented the *Flickerscope* at the Alhambra theatre in New York. This act depended for its humor on a parodying of the faults of the projector. A pair of dancing girls appeared in a burlesque of the performances of Annabelle, performed before a white sheet. They were illuminated by spot lights so manipulated as to give a grotesque exaggeration of the pulsations of the screen picture.

In this day of the primary stage of presentation no relation between the screen picture and the printed word had been discovered. The little fifty foot subjects did not even carry a designating title on the screen. An announcer, invariably in frock coat, stood beside the screen to make appropriate remarks and identify the subjects as they flickered into view. Presently the announcements came to be made along with other vaudeville acts by a lettered card on an illuminated stand at one side of the proscenium.

The announcer evolved into a lecturer as films grew longer in the ensuing years. In a short time films acquired main-titles, labels of convenience, but it was a full ten years before it was found that title inserts could make the picture a broader medium of story telling. It took another ten years to discover that editorial and dramatic intelligence could fuse the picture and the printed word into the hybrid screen art which to-day we call the photoplay.

As one follows the evolution of the screen art the increasing importance of the relation of the word becomes apparent. Only the primitive pictures required no titles. Pictures remained primitive until they got titles.

It may be balm to the no-title purists among screen critics to consider that the union of picture and word produces only a seeming bastardy anyway, since we have covered already the tedious path which shows the words to be an attenuated shorthand for pictures. The photoplay is a rejoining of the currents of the same flood, divided up yonder near the headwaters, when communication grew impatient of picture making.

Today many a screen title is as long as an entire motion picture subject of 1896. The fifty foot pictures of that day could not have afforded footage for words, but in their utter simplicity they had no more use for words than a cave man had for a Christian name.

CHAPTER TWENTY-THREE

RECRUITING THE PIONEERS

W ITH its commercial career opened, the motion picture began to acquire a personnel, the men to whom fate was entrusting the pioneering of a new and mighty institution—the first great proletarian art.

Like the gathering in a caravanserai they came from near and far, from office and mart and factory, from the prairie and mining camp and the farm. Mostly a take-a-chance lot, these first picture men ventured small stakes and a large daring.

Miracles for sale never fail to draw a crowd. Raff & Gammon were selling the wizardry of Edison in their merchandising of the Armat Vitascope. The magic of that name Thomas Alva Edison was strongest then. The technical age which Edison did so much to bring into existence has given us whole constellations of genius to share his firmament now. In 1896 there were for the public no such names as Wright, Ford, Steinmetz, Zeppelin, Holland and all that innumerable array of the machine-made great. Edison was a lone star then.

The buying of Vitascope territorial rights in the spring and summer of '96 enlisted many of the names which afterward became institutional in motion picture history.

Among the earliest customers came the late William T. Rock, long since famed in film affairs as "Pop" Rock, then operating a billiard hall in Harlem and dabbling a bit in peep show machines. Rock bought the Vitascope for the state of Louisiana on June 16, 1896, as attested by his contract in the archives of the Vitascope Company. The consideration was $1,500, and the contract ran to January 9, 1901, a date which was far too sanguine of the Vitascope's commercial destiny. Rock's partner and co-signatory on the contract was Walter J. Wainwright, a tight wire walker and carnival showman known professionally as "Wainretta." Rock and Wainwright bought Louisiana because of their attraction to the money making possibilities fringing the Mardi Gras fête in New Orleans.

The firm of Rock & Wainwright stocked up with films and headed south. They opened in New Orleans June 28, 1896, and operated there for three months.

In New Orleans Rock picked up a friend, a persistent admirer and follower, one Sigmund Lubin. Lubin was an immigrant somewhat newly from Europe, struggling to establish himself in this wonderful America. He was for the time an itinerant vender of spectacles, including smoked glasses with which he implored the Mardi Gras visitors to prepare to observe an impending eclipse of the sun. The pompous "Pop" Rock, with his massive gold watch chain across his vest and his diamond handshake and richly genial manner, was to the hopeful Lubin a very personification of that American success and prosperity which he desired to overtake. Lubin pursued Rock for a clue to his method. Lubin watched the Vitascope with profound interest. This was something to get into. Lubin eventually did, ten million dollars' worth in the next twenty years.

The Rock venture in New Orleans was successful in getting a neat crop of newspaper attention for the introduction of the marvelous motion pictures. The May Irwin-John C. Rice kiss subject was particularly fruitful. It broke into print in the following manner:

New Orleans, July 28, 1896, Editor Daily Item:—

I see it is suggested to exhibit the Edison Vitascope now at West End, at Audubon Park. This would undoubtedly prove a popular move for the traction company.

But permit me to suggest that the too suggestive kissing scene be dropped. This may capture the fancy of the lascivious, but it is actually repulsive to the clean of mind. I am sure that the young ladies who resort to the park, and all careful parents, must prefer not to have this scene produced any more.

"F."

Henry Dufilho, the dignified editor of the *Item*, deemed this occasion to take his pen in hand for comment, published with the letter, saying:

Children show their friendship for each other by kissing, play-mates do likewise. Lovers indicate their affection by such acts; husbands and wives commit the same offense, morning, and evening, on the departure and return of the former. Fathers and mothers kiss their little ones any number of times a day. Kissing has been a custom time out of mind. That it should now be pronounced indecent is to open the eyes of the world to a flaw in something that they had ever held to be without blemish—EDITOR.

After playing the season in New Orleans, Rock took his Vitascope on the road for a time, touring the state. Somewhere along the line "Wainretta," the tight wire walker, seems to have faded out of the firm of Rock & Wainright and his name does not again appear in the history of the new born art of the motion picture.

Several developments in the new business, mostly difficulties, were reflected in the correspondence between Rock and the agents of the Vitascope. Here is an indicative letter:

New Orleans, Nov. 25, 1896.

Raff & Gammon
Gents:—

Your letter of November 20th to hand and would say I will except some of your 2nd hand films of yours in exchange for the 6 I send you I do allow that 3 of them were bad, but only sent them for you to see how bad the stock was in them expecting you would make some allowance on them to us. I expressed

you from New Iberia back a very poor film a new one you sent
me of the Steamship *St. Louis* and asked you to send me Cissy
Fitzgerald not colored in place of it I have not received it yet
will you please send it if you have not done so allready Now
about the proposition you make about opening all of the territory
I sent you a letter about it and have received no answer to it as
yet please let me know how many sighners you have and what
prospects there are of getting them all and I may join in
I will sighn immediately if I can go into Texas and Miss or Ala
Immediately   There are lots of machines down here

The Phantoscope is here in New Orleans in Canal st with a Man
on the door crying out come in and see Edison's Vitascope and
also have large sighns up with Edison's name and pictures   Cannot something be done about this to stop it.   When we paid you
our money it was for Edisons name and nothing else exclusive for
the state of Louisiana now please answer this letter as soon as
possible

        & oblige
          Yours truly
            Wm. T. Rock

Thus in brief we discover that film stock was still unperfected
and causing trouble, that editorial content of the pictures was
becoming important, and that competition was already arising.
The Phantoscope to which Rock referred was a recrudescence of
the Jenkins' claims expressed in a competitive machine.   The
Phantoscope appeared sporadically in several regions, notably
Chicago and Philadelphia, where Sigmund Lubin set himself
up in the optical and film business equipped with Jenkins-made
equipment.

In Chicago the Phantoscope was booked to a vaudeville theater.   Its appearance there alarmed the Raff & Gammon agent
into action.   *The Chicago Inter-Ocean* related:

> The Edison Vitascope Company and the Chicago Talking
> Machine Company had a bout before Judge Seaman in Federal
> Court yesterday afternoon.   The vitascope people claimed the

talking machine people were operating a "phantoscope" in showing pictures on a screen, and advertising it as the vitascope. Judge Seaman examined the advertisements complained of and directed the entering of an order restraining the talking machine company from displaying the name vitascope in such a manner as to mislead people to think it was the vitascope which was being exhibited.

The Chicago Evening Journal the next day editorialized with considerable fervor, saying:

> The tiresome Phantoscope has been tossed off the Great Northern roof, to the great relief of everybody. It was a mortifying failure for a management unused to failures, and a terrific bore to the audience. It jolted its successful way through two nights and having ruined the whole vaudeville program was forcibly ejected. The man who was trying to make it work said it was invented by the same "party" responsible for the Vitascope. The "party" ought to have called it a day when he finished the latter machine, which is really interesting and brings creditable results. The bringing of the Phantascope was primarily an attempt to make a noise with other people's thunder, and it was a case of just retribution when it fell by the wayside.

But after all perhaps the Phantoscope was not quite as bad as all that. The Vitascope Company in New York presently received a letter on the ornate stationery of the "Hopkins Circuit of Continuous Theatres" reading:

> GENTLEMEN:
> The Phantoscope which appeared a couple of times on the Great Northern Roof Garden in this city made a big "frost," and is dead here for sometime to come. I had a great deal to do with the failure of the machine, as one of our electricians was engaged to run it—so you understand the rest of it. I then worked the papers strong in regard to the failure. Kindly send me a "Kiss" scene immediately as the one we have is worn out.
> Very truly
> JOHN D. HOPKINS

The motion picture business was beginning to develop competitive methods and ethical foundations of great sincerity. There was more of this to come—thirty years of it thus far.

The Vitascope continued to enjoy newspaper attention. In this period an English lad known to Park Row as Jimmy Blackton was working on space rates as a free lance reporter for the *New York World*. He was a bit of an artist and supplied both text and illustration. The half-tone process was still so slow and tedious that the daily papers continued to use line drawings reproduced by the old chalk-plate process for the illustration of the more immediate news. Jimmy was one of the rough and ready artists of the chalk plate school.

Jimmy Blackton was most ingenious. Since he was paid in direct ratio to the amount of white paper his efforts covered he became very capable at making the subject matter proper for a one column drawing spread itself over two or three columns. His most reliable source of revenue was a sort of stock story about the poor family ejected from a tenement by a heartless landlord. With a change of names, dates, and locations, and a new drawing this story with a sob in it was good for a column most any time. Jimmy did it often. He liked the theme because he had done it so often that it had become easy. It was sure-fire copy, and by depicting all of the furniture of the homeless scattered on the walk up and down the block, he could make the illustration quite large.

This young man was, by newspaper assignment, put into contact with the motion picture, with an ensuing chain of events which now for three decades after continue in development. The city editor of the *World* evidently wanted something less doleful out of Jimmy and sent him to West Orange to interview Edison on his new marvel, the Vitascope.

Jimmy had another bag of tricks. He was an entertainer as well as a journalist. He had a chalk-talk act which he presented at club entertainments and the like, usually appearing on the same bill with his friends, Albert E. Smith, the spirit cabinet performer, and Ronald Reader, a prestidigitator.

When Blackton reached Edison he followed the true pattern of the actor and proceeded to do all his "business." The Wizard of Orange took an instant liking to the aggressive youngster. He laid aside the labors of the laboratory and sat laughing and "haw-hawing" as Blackton's deft pencil limned the features of Grover Cleveland, the genial statesman then in the White House, David B. Hill, and Major William McKinley, who had his name on the new high tariff. When Blackton squared back in his best artistic manner and swiftly drew the features of Edison himself, the Wizard was completely won over.

Edison took Blackton by the arm and led him into the sanctuary of the Black Maria where the Kinetograph was making a film for the Vitascope. Blackton posed for the camera and did his chalk-talk business all over again. Under the title of *Blackton, the Evening World Cartoonist*, the picture went out to the world of the new born screen.

Blackton talked over the marvels of the Vitascope and the geniality of Edison's reception with his friend Smith. They determined to buy one at once.

Blackton went back to Orange and interviewed Edison. Instead of a Vitascope he got a deeply inside tip.

"The Vitascope is only leased, not sold," Edison explained, "but before long we will have a new machine out, the 'Edison Projecting Kinetoscope,' and if you want one I will see that your name is put down among the first applicants."

Raff & Gammon and Thomas Armat had yet no inkling of the coming of competition from within. Edison was not resting content as the maker of Armat's machine, even though it was presented under the brand of the wizard. Here were the makings of conflict aplenty.

Blackton and Smith postponed their purchase awaiting the coming Edison screen machine.

The future held a large destiny for Smith and Blackton and a coming fusion with the interests of "Pop" Rock, now remote in Louisiana. These tiny beginnings in 1896 gave rise to the institution that the present motion picture public knows as Vitagraph.

In Buffalo the Raff & Gammon agency found a customer for the Vitascope in Mitchell H. Mark, the proprietor of Edsonia Hall. Mark was in the business of selling the wizardry of Edison as agent for phonographs, kinetoscopes, X-ray machines and sundry supplies. Now the establishment became known as Edsonia and Vitascope Hall, where it proclaimed the new wonders to the public in Ellicott Square. Mark installed a Vitascope and gave daily exhibitions. This was one of the earliest permanently located and exclusively motion picture exhibitions, a distant forebear of the now famous Mark Strand theatre in New York.

Richard Paine and Robert Balsley of Connellsville, Pa., bought a Vitascope territory and started one of the machines on a wandering westward career which terminated not long after in California. Each of the eighty-and-odd Armat Vitascopes made by Edison to Raff & Gammon's order became a shuttle weaving a strand of destiny as the fabric of the screen was forming.

The Vitascope was acting as an agency superimposed on the earlier pioneerings of the peep show Kinetoscope and frequently merging the two. A picturesque example is afforded in the career of Thomas L. Tally, who has for many years been an important factor in motion picture affairs.

Tally emerges into the dawn of the motion picture history on a bald faced pinto, riding out of the purple sage of the Llano Estacado into Waco, Texas, one dusty, thirsty day in 1896.

He was a two fisted, hard riding, hoss wrangler or cowpuncher, or whatsomever—anything but a sheep herder. He was tired of the range and those elaborately extensive open spaces so highly spoken of by our Wild West writers in their New York apartments.

Tally rode up and down the main street of Waco looking for pleasure and excitement. A sign announcing Winnie Brothers' "Kinetoscope Parlor—Living Pictures" greeted the range rider's eager gaze. He dropped the bridle reins over the pinto's head, slapped the alkali dust out of his chaps and with spurs a-jingle entered to examine this matter.

Tally observed the graces of Carmencita and Annabelle in the peep show machine and lingered to observe also the considerable line of customers. He decided to linger further and get into the business. The orders from Winnie Brothers to the Kinetoscope Company and Raff & Gammon in New York began to bear the signature of T. L. Tally.

The range rider was started on the road to a million or so and the founding of the First National Exhibitors' Circuit some twenty years ahead.

In August of that same 1896 a sign at 311 South Spring Street, Los Angeles, announced that T. L. Tally had opened there a "Phonograph and Vitascope Parlor" where one might hear the latest song hits from New York and see living pictures. Motion pictures were served in three varieties. The peep show Kinetoscope pictures, the American Mutoscope, the Casler peep show machine, and on the screen as presented by the Vitascope. Tally had chanced to come into possession of the Paine & Balsley Vitascope which had been doing duty at the Los Angeles Orpheum. The machine lingered to start a long strand of events.

Mr. Tally found that his patrons down in Spring Street were wary about going into a darkened room to see pictures on the screen. To meet this condition he fitted up a partition with holes in it, facing the projection room screen, so that patrons might peer in at the screen while standing in the comfortable security of the well lighted phonograph parlor. A real sport could put the phonograph tubes to his ears and look at the pictures at the same time. Three peep holes were at chair level for seated spectators, and four somewhat higher for standees— standing room only after three admissions, total capacity seven. The price per peep hole was fifteen cents.

The Tally showing was typical of the motion picture business of the West in that period. The screen was feeling its way into public acquaintance.

The fame of the Vitascope was reaching into the far places. All the world was beginning to feel a stirring interest in the new art. The Edison files of the period contained many evidences, among them this earnest letter:

T. A. Edison, Esq.   Metropolitan Hotel
Orange Grove   Wellington
New York   New Zealand

DEAR SIR:

Some time ago what is called "the cinémategraph" was exhibited in London by two brothers named Lumière. I fancy it is (if described correctly by the papers here) a copy of your Kinetoscope. I would be obliged if you could send me prices and particulars, if you have any particulars on hand on this new invention. Your name is as well known here as that of God Almighty himself and that is why I am sending for reliable information to yourself.

Yours truly
G. P. HAUSMAN

Another letter out of the same file is tinged with the flavor of long ago:

Edison Mfg. Co.
Orange, N. J.

Rochester, N. Y.
June 20, 1896.

GENTLEMEN:

We have received a letter from Eug. Pirou, 5 Boul'd St. Germain, Paris, asking us to inform him where he can obtain one of the Edison Vitascopes for *living photographs*. Please communicate direct the necessary information, and oblige,

Yours truly,
EASTMAN KODAK COMPANY
by GEO. EASTMAN

In the years ahead these same "living photographs" were going to bring to Eastman a greater fortune than to any of the other screen made millionaires.

On June 10, 1896, the Vitascope Company made its first foreign sale, when Luis Manuel Mendez of Maracaibo bought the motion picture rights for Venezuela and Colombia, South America, paying $750.

With the competition of infringers, imitators, foreign invaders, and all manner of legal complications, the course of the Vitascope Company was becoming difficult. An atmosphere of peevishness was arising among its customers. The following letter, written by one of the major customers, the buyer of the rights for Illinois, Massachusetts, New Jersey and Maryland, reflects the situation:

EDISON'S NATIONAL VITASCOPE
AND ADVERTISING COMPANY
Philadelphia, Pa.
July 2, 1896

Vitascope Company
43 West 28th Street
New York, N. Y.

GENTLEMEN:—

After leaving you yesterday, I went to see the French machine and it made me tired so I left for home. It is no use considering the idea of operating foreign countries with that kind of a competitor. There must be somebody getting up their new scenes with some business and ability. You never saw living pictures until you see this machine.

I hope you—Mr. Raff and Mr. Gammon—will get Mr. Gilmore and go see that machine without a moment's delay. You will agree with me that I say if your people do not get more important views than you have in the past, you had better get ready to store the Vitascope machines, for inside of two months, no one will want to look at the views that have been exhibited. It is ridiculous; the few films I brought from your place yesterday. There are not two good scenes in the whole lot.

I wrote Mr. Gilmore today. You folks certainly will have to get a hurry up on your business or I would not give much for the chances on the Vitascope.

Yours respectfully
P. W. Kiefaber, Manager.

The facile and portable Lumière camera, operated by hand, was telling against the ponderous Edison Kinetograph, anchored to the studios, the "Black Maria" at Orange and a roof-top near Broadway. The Edison picture makers were trying to bring bits of the world to their cameras. The Lumières were taking the camera out to see the world. Their advantage was in the content of their pictures, not in any superior ability of their projection machine.

The demand began to be expressed in terms of subject matter. No longer was it sufficient to show pictures which merely moved. Now they must do something interesting.

CHAPTER TWENTY-FOUR

WHEN CORBETT FOUGHT "RUBY ROBERT"

WHILE the Vitascope and the Lumière Cinématographe were working out the major theme of motion picture destiny, the Latham project continued a wavering struggle for existence.

The gay carelessness of Otway and Grey Latham, who made merry with their first flush of success, produced frictions within the concern with Enoch J. Rector and Samuel J. Tilden, Jr., who were more seriously attending to the very immediate technical and commercial problems of the new business.

This situation acquired tension until it broke. Rector and Tilden parted company with the Lathams to go their own way. The Latham interests in the screen project went into a newly formed concern, the Eidoloscope Company.

Rector and Tilden retained, in their portion of the assets of the old Lambda concern, the exclusive fight picture contract with James C. Corbett, which had been negotiated in connection with the Corbett-Courtenay fight for the Lathams' special Kinetoscopes.

In the autumn of 1895 the world's championship in its periodic cycles became an issue again, with the challenges by freckled Bob Fitzsimmons.

After the usual preliminaries a fight between Fitzsimmons and Corbett was to be staged in Texas. All arrangements were made. Rector, who had maintained diplomatic relations at the Edison establishment despite the Dickson episode and the competitive character of the Latham project, arranged to have four Edison cameras, the great ponderous storage battery machines, planted at ringside.

Dan Stuart, the fight promoter, got into difficulties with the authorities and a tangle of legal complications. The fight was called off. Corbett, considerably annoyed, returned to New York and handed over his championship belt to Peter Maher.

Stuart, still hopeful, sought to arrange a combat between Maher and Fitzsimmons in El Paso. Agitation against the fight arose again, and the governor forbade the contest on Texas soil.

Rector, with $15,000 of motion picture investment at stake, began to get active. He suggested to Stuart that the fight might be held at some convenient place across the border of Mexico.

Secretly Rector went up and down the Rio Grande reconnoitering. At Langtry he found the river narrow and the banks suitable for some hasty bridge work.

Stuart and Rector conferred and set a date for the fight, February 21, 1896. Arrangements were made for a special train, and tickets were sold for the fight, with the scene of the combat a secret.

Rector laid aside motion picture considerations for the moment and became a structural engineer. He had to bridge the rolling Rio Grande river, secretly, and do it in one night. The sovereign state of Texas and the border officials of the United States and Mexico had to be evaded. The films had now become the text of international intrigue.

In Langtry where Rector concentrated his workmen and laid his plans for the coming nocturnal engineering dash into Mexico, new troubles arose in the person of the august Roy Bean, the self-constituted boss of the region.

Over the front of Roy Bean's saloon was a sign:

"LIKKER AND LAW WEST OF THE PECOS"

Bean carried a pair of six-guns, with the tips of the holsters tied down for a quick draw. He dispensed whiskey and justice with a kick in it. In the words of Louis, King of France, Bean's slogan was, "The State, that's me!" He decided who might come and who might go. It was all done with extreme practicality and grim humor.

Bean made a demonstration calculated to impress Rector and Dan Stuart. While the fight preparations were in progress, some of Bean's henchmen came upon a dead Chinaman near the river bank.

Bean convened court at once in the name of the "Law West of the Pecos." He commanded that the Chinaman's body be brought into his official presence and searched. The pockets yielded $22 in silver and a toy pistol.

"It is the judgment of this court," proclaimed Bean, "that the deceased, defendant in this action, is fined $22 for carrying concealed weapons—give me the money."

Bean raised a number of expensive legal points about the building of the bridge on the night of February 20.

Rector pleaded and argued.

"I think that a big man like you ought to be in a country where there are more people. You haven't got a chance to show your real genius out here among the cattle rustlers and greasers —come to New York with me and I'll see you are started right in this picture business."

Bean felt better under the glow of flattery. He poured himself a handsome portion of Belle of Maryland, right from the wood.

"You'd show those New Yorkers something, I'll bet," Rector went on admiringly.

Bean gargled his drink, shifted his gun belt, and beat himself on the chest.

"You bet—now let's get that gang to work on the bridge."

At five o'clock in the morning, across the river in Mexico, the arena was done and the ropes up. The bridge over the river was complete and approved by Judge Bean, now fast asleep after his supervisory labors.

A breath of wind arose in the south with a fresh smell of moisture. The country had parched, rainless for eighteen burning months. Now rain came.

All the day of the fight dark skies and a slow drizzle covered the scene. Photography was impossible, but a train load of fight fans demanded action. The fighters went into the ring while Rector and his camera stood helplessly by.

Fitzsimmons sparred with Maher for two flashing moments, then knocked him through the ropes, and out. One spectator, who had journeyed all the way from New York to see the fight, missed it while sitting in a ringside seat. He had just tilted a flask skyward for a drink when the fight occurred.

Judge Bean woke up and did a large business at his dispensary over the river. He had forgotten quite that matter of seeking a new jurisdiction in New York, and bade Rector a curt farewell. Thus history records the screen's first great loss of genius. Roy Bean and his six-guns would have been an invaluable factor in the motion picture industry of New York.

Seeking to salvage the expedition, Rector took his retinue and photographed a bull fight at Juarez. This picture went through the peep show machines owned by Rector and Tilden. It did not reach the screen.

The pictorial fiasco of Langtry in Roy Bean's country ended the relations of Rector and Tilden with the Edison establishment. Rector, annoyed at the limitations of the Edison camera, desired a more facile instrument. In a little shop in Pearl street, New York, he went at his labors. He built a small, light camera which could be operated by hand, somewhat after the manner of the Latham equipment, but using the Edison standard film. From a lofty window in the Flatiron building, he photographed the Sound Money parade of the McKinley campaign, and put the picture on at Hammerstein's Olympia theatre. Rector's next subject was a run of the Newark fire department and scenes of fire fighting, soon to become a hackneyed, staple motion picture stereotype.

While the picture was running at a Newark theatre, a detective in the audience recognized a familiar face in the crowds on the screen. He followed the picture intently, and presently on the fringe of the fire scenes saw his man pick the pockets of a bewhiskered countryman.

The detective got a sample of the film and went into the street after the pickpocket. Dan-the-Dipper went to prison, the first victim of motion picture evidence.

Again the prize fight fans were clamoring for Corbett to resume and defend the world's championship title which had been knocked out of the ring by Fitzsimmons in Mexico.

Rector's exclusive picture contract with Corbett still stood. Dan Stuart, who aspired to be the Tex Rickard of his day, shopped about for a place to hold the fight. Public opposition and politics barred him everywhere. In desperate last resort Stuart went to Nevada and camped, lobbying for a bill through the legislature to permit the fight.

Nevada with the smallest population among the states obviously could have less public and less public opinion. Stuart succeeded, at considerable expense.

Meanwhile Rector was improving his cameras to give them more facility of movement and a higher photographic speed. He struggled for capacity against another possible rainy day. Also revising the original Edison camera specifications as he went, he reduced the number of exposures from forty-eight per second to twenty-four. This was going to mean a tremendously important economy in film. The Lumière machines, it will be recalled, were meanwhile at the minimum of sixteen exposures per second, the theoretical standard of to-day.

By the terms of his agreement Rector was to pay Corbett and his manager, William A. Brady, today known as a theatrical magnate, twenty-five per cent of the proceeds of the pictures. Over at the old Bartholdi Hotel, where the Lathams had lived, Rector made an agreement with Fitzsimmons and his manager, Martin Julian, to hand them $13,000 when the fighters entered the ring. Fitzsimmons learned of the Corbett percentage deal and screamed that he had been tricked. The whole deal was thrown into the air.

Fitzsimmons went away to Carson City, Nevada, with Stuart and Rector in pursuit. When peace was made Tilden, Rector and Stuart financed the fight, while the fighters and their managers took twenty-five per cent each of the picture profits and Rector and Tilden divided the remaining fifty per cent with Stuart.

On the seventeenth of March, 1897, Corbett and Fitzsimmons went into the ring at Carson City.

Rector was at the ringside with three cameras and forty-eight thousand feet of film, the largest single lot of negative that had gone out on location. The prize fight which had been so much an influence in liberating the motion picture from the peep show was now stretching it lengthwise. There was yet no known purpose in such camera capacity other than to photograph a fight.

The fight went its vicious and bloody length, with Mrs. Fitzsimmons cheering her husband to victory.

When the battle was over, Rector had exposed 11,000 feet of film. This was the world's record in photographing a single event.

Rector and Tilden were not yet sure of an avenue to the market for their picture. There was considerable discussion with Raff & Gammon of the Vitascope Company.

Under the new name of the Veriscope Company, Rector and

THE CORBETT-FITZSIMMONS FIGHT, March 17, 1897 at Carson City, Nevada, as recorded by Enoch J. Rector's Veriscope, a motion picture machine especially made for the event, carrying a film two and three-sixteenths inches wide. Rector painted the copyright notice on the ring platform. These scenes, never before published, are from fragments of the film in the possession of Jean A. Le Roy of New York, a motion picture pioneer and exhibitor in 1895.

"THE EMPIRE STATE EXPRESS," the thrilling train picture with which Biograph opened its first night program at Hammerstein's on Broadway in the autumn of 1896.

WILLIAM KENNEDY LAURIE DICKSON, laboratory assistant to Thomas Edison in his work on the Kinetograph and Kinetoscope. Here Dickson is pictured as he was in 1886, the year before Edison's motion picture work began. Dickson, in his later connection with Biograph, photographed the "Empire State Express," shown above.

Tilden determined to present the picture in New York and market it territorially themselves.

The Rector projector, known as the Veriscope, was installed at the Academy of Music in Fourteenth street, where the picture ran through the early summer. This was the first film invasion of the famous old Academy, dedicated to the ancient arts, and redolent with the memories of Pietro Brigloni, Ole Bull, and the names of Max Strakosch and Maurice Grau. For many years the Academy of Music has been a motion picture theatre, a sort of withered crone, flamboyant with garish electric garlands in the tragic gaiety of a desperate old age. The queen, deposed, is a rag picker now.

From the Academy the Corbett-Fitzsimmons fight and the Veriscope went in July to the Park theatre in Brooklyn. The *Brooklyn Eagle* of July 4, 1897, indulged in a column of editorial excitement beginning:

> The man who would have predicted, at one time in our history, that an event of a prior month would be reproduced before the eyes of a multitude in pictures that moved like life, and that lightning would move them and light them, would have been avoided as a lunatic or hanged as a wizard.

The pictures were meanwhile appearing all over the United States, presented by buyers of territorial rights from Rector and Tilden.

The Veriscope Company with its fight pictures was the first to encounter two of the evils which later beset the picture industry with devastating piracy.

In Pennsylvania, which is to-day among the greatest strongholds of motion picture censorship, politicians snatched at the agitation of the Women's Christian Temperance Union as pretext for a special legislative bill to prohibit the showing of the fight films. Word presently arrived at the Veriscope office that the bill would be permitted to die in committee if a certain exhibitor in Philadelphia were to get the picture on his own most reasonable terms. There were rumblings in New York state, but Samuel J. Tilden, Jr., of the Veriscope Company, carried some coloration of the political power of the Tilden name. The family seat being at Columbia, N. Y., adjacent to Albany, also created a circle of effective influence.

In Philadelphia, Sigmund Lubin stepped forth with an amazing project, advertising films of:

THE GREAT CORBETT-FITZSIMMONS FIGHT
(in counterpart)

Lubin had employed two freight handlers from the Pennsylvania terminal to re-enact the combat as a prompter read the fight by rounds from the newspaper account of the championship battle. This was art,—the re-creation of an event—and the "fight by rounds" column was a scenario, but Lubin did not know it. Lubin's picture did enough business to make it profitable and there was then no legal recourse against it.

The camera was still merely a reporter. It took what happened and passed it on. The conception of having things happen specifically for the camera in terms of the great film spectacles of to-day was beyond the scope of the picture makers' imaginations then. The only thing which the fight picture suggested was more fight pictures.

Enoch Rector had an inkling of the greater possibilities, and wasted many a day talking dramatic pictures. Most of his friends and associates were staid men of business, engineers, bankers and the like. They assured him he was a crank and discouraged experimentation. Rector continued for a long time in the business, drawing toward the technical side of motion picture operation.

One marked effect of the Corbett-Fitzsimmons picture as the outstanding screen production of its day was to bring the odium of pugilism upon the screen all across Puritan America. Until that picture appeared the social status of the screen had been uncertain. It now became definitely low-brow, an entertainment of the great unwashed commonalty. This likewise made it a mark for uplifters, moralists, reformers and legislators in a degree which would never have obtained if the screen had by specialization reached higher social strata.

CHAPTER TWENTY-FIVE

THE LATHAM STAR DECLINES

DESTINY worked a swift sequence of disasters for the Latham organization after the withdrawal of Enoch J. Rector and Samuel Tilden, Jr. Major Latham's hopes were thrown back upon his sons, Otway and Grey. But most of the technical skill and what of stability there had been in the Latham group went from it to the Rector Veriscope concern.

In casting about to fortify his interests Major Latham approached F. A. Anthony of E. & H. T. Anthony & Company, a progenitor of the photographic supply company now known as Ansco. The Anthonys were engaged in the making of still cameras, plates and papers. Many of the ponderous old portrait cameras in the professional studios of today still bear the name plate of E. & H. T. Anthony.

The Anthonys listened and took an interest in the Latham enterprise. It seemed to Major Latham a timely aid, then,— which it was. However, subsequent events and competitive conditions to arise in the photographic industry were to make it impossible for the Latham projects to prosper under these auspices.

At about this juncture the Latham's Lambda Company faded out, and its successor, the Eidoloscope Company, was formed. The Latham projector was born under the name of the Pantoptikon, but when, following upon the discoveries of Armat, it acquired an intermittent movement and lost its shutter, it became the Eidoloscope. The Anthonys advanced the capital for the building of a dozen new Latham projectors, which were to go out under yet another name, the Biopticon. In security Major

Latham assigned to the Anthony company a control of his patent claims.

Major Latham, having acquired this new backing, felt renewed assurance, entirely unwarranted in view of the complications ahead in his path.

The imposing fight picture plans of Enoch J. Rector, as their new competitor, inspired the newly rehabilitated concern to send Otway Latham to Mexico in an equally pretentious effort. He was to photograph a bullfight, and to make pictures, if possible, of the rites of the Flagellantes in annual presentation of a half-savage version of the Passion Play.

Foreign expeditions for the making of motion pictures became commonplace enough later, but this was the first one, and a sensational departure. It involved the expenditure of several thousand dollars, at a time when the peak of production in the motion picture art was represented by the fifty-foot Edison pictures made in the Black Maria studio, or about the streets of New York.

The arrival of Otway Latham in the City of Mexico was an event of some local acclaim. The Mexicans were fired with interest. They had heard of the art of the motion picture through Paris and the Lumière Cinématographe. Paris was the world capital for Mexicans. This was in the days of Diaz, the dictator. There were fêtes and bull fights and garden parties, bright with the zest of Latins at play. Otway Latham made many friends and social contracts. He liked Mexico City. It had action and color. He did not have time to trouble about the Flagellantes. He completed his bullfight pictures and turned back to the States, reluctantly.

The bullfight pictures were shipped by express, destination New York. At the border, despite caution labels, the custom officials in their photographic ignorance opened some of the cases and exposed parts of the undeveloped negatives to the light.

About half of the film was ruined. Official blundering on many an international boundary has repeated that disaster since.

Such of the film as escaped fogging at the hands of the customs was developed and printed for the Eidoloscope in New York. It was put on show in a balcony projection room at the old St. James Hotel in Fifth avenue. The bullfight pictures were a wonder of the moment and drew considerable crowds. The films were, by today's standards, exceedingly faulty. The Latham camera lacked the panoramic tilting and turning devices which enable the modern operator to follow a moving center of interest. Therefore the bull in the Latham pictures often ran off the screen. The Latham shop lacked the technique of film cutting, so the blanks showing only the dust of the arena had to stay in the picture. In their establishment even the existence of film cement, by which films may be spliced after cutting, was unknown. The pictures had to go on the screen just as they came from the camera.

Meanwhile it was found that the new Latham machine to be sold as the Biopticon was faulty. The machines which had been so expensively manufactured for the market were put aside without being offered. Further difficulties ensued, too, upon instructions issued to the operators of Latham projectors to remove the shutters from their machines to permit a greater efficiency of illumination. This was interpreted as an infringement of the Armat invention, which was the first to take cognizance of the importance of giving the film a period of rest and illumination greater than the time of movement from frame to frame. Also, the Latham projectors, in competition with the Armat Vitascope, had been equipped with a loop forming mechanism in the film feed—the famous "Latham loop." The fact was that, with reference to the camera, this loop was the invention of Enoch J. Rector, while yet a member of the Latham organization. But the use of a loop for use in a projection machine had been independently invented and applied by Armat. The loop is an absolute essential to a machine with a jerky, intermittent motion. When Rector applied it to the camera the Latham group was still working on a projector with a continuous movement. Armat's intermittent projector raised the same problem as Latham's camera, and it was solved with the identical loop device. Therefore in terms of patent law the loop was Latham's for cameras and Armat's for projectors.

All of the technical issues, some of which were to determine the whole course of screen history, were thrown into the controversy known in United States Patent Office records as "Interference No. 18,461." This was a triangular struggle between Woodville Latham, Herman Casler of the K. M. C. D.-Mutoscope-Biograph group, and Thomas Armat. It was a hard fought and long combat of technicalities, resulting in ultimate victory for Armat.

Major Latham continued on after this defeat, supported by the Anthony backing. He met with a transient and peculiar success of no final importance. By a special hearing before an examiner in the Patent Office, in ex-parte proceedings, Major Latham won a patent, issued in 1902, on the strength of a contention of improvement of the Armat machine by the elimination of a tension device at the film gate of the projector. It was in truth no invention, in that the most casual actual demonstration would have proven the tension necessary—just as it is on every projector in use today.

This was the last wisp of a victory for Major Latham. Even that might have soon been upset by an appeal to the courts had not a new series of events intervened.

In July, 1901, and some distance ahead of the main current of our history, E. & H. T. Anthony & Company took over the Goodwin Camera & Film Company, which held the patent claims of the Rev. Hannibal Goodwin, inventor of the process of making celluloid film for photographic purposes.

The Anthony concern had invested some ten thousand dollars in the Latham patents, in legal fees and like expenses. Now the company was confronted with another large investment in the erection of a plant to make film, and another long legal war. The concern became the Anthony & Scoville Company. In December, 1902, a suit was brought in the name of the Goodwin concern against the Eastman Kodak Company for infringement of the Goodwin patents.

Thereafter for many years the Anthony & Scoville interests were put to their utmost to maintain their litigations against the powerful Eastman concern, trying the while to continue general commercial operations against the desperate commercial warfare waged by George Eastman. There remained neither energy nor capital with which to pursue any possibilities which may have reposed in the Latham patents. The Latham inventions went to rest as a mere bundle of costly papers filed away in a vault, a frozen asset. Likely it is only thus that the Latham patents survived, in suspended animation, to reappear afterward in screen affairs. If the issue impending had been fought then they would doubtless have brought down destructive decisions in court.

The motion picture star of the Lathams so far declined by the spring of 1898 that even they held no further hope. Grey Latham took a despairing fling at the stock market. The market declined. There were margins to cover at once. Grey appealed to his father. Major Latham's only asset in the world was the patent in the hands of the Anthony company. He applied to the Anthonys for a loan and got one thousand dollars, secured by the Major's remaining interest in the patent. It was agreed that if the loan were not paid when due at the end of the year the patent should become solely the property of the Anthony concern.

The thousand dollars were wiped out in one morning's vibrations of the ticker. The year went past. Grey Latham then sought the Anthonys and was granted an extension of time on the loan in behalf of his father. Twice again the time was extended, but at last the Anthonys were forced to foreclose and take the patent. It was really of small consequence or none in the fortunes of Major Latham.

F. A. Anthony wrote the Major a letter notifying him of the foreclosure, but generously promising that when affairs were in such shape that the projectors could be manufactured and sold royalties would be paid to him as the inventor. It was a promise beyond the terms of the agreement. But that day was never to come. The foreclosure of the loan closed out the last interest of the Lathams in the motion picture. The progress of the screen went on through other agencies and other hands. More competent workers, better technicians and more efficient business men had already taken over the motion picture.

The process of decline, as rapid as their rise into a flashing prosperity with the peep show Kinetoscope, had been begun. It colored alike the lives of Major Latham and his two sons. Grey Latham was even now, early in '98, nearing the end of his romance with Rose O'Neill. He turned to brokerage and real estate for a living.

Otway Latham, who had wooed and won Natalye Dole Lockwood, an artist and a dashing member of New York's smart society, sought commercial pursuits and travelled much in quest of a new golden opportunity. Natalye Lockwood was a painter of considerable attainment and large promise. She first appeared in the pages of the newspapers and magazines when she was considered by the art committee of the Union League

Club of Brooklyn to paint Herbert W. Bowen, United States minister to Venezuela. That tropical republic was in those days a large diplomatic fact, as much in the public prints then as the nervous little states of the Balkan and Mediterranean regions now. While visiting in Venezuela, the girl artist painted President Castro and figured conspicuously in the merry social life of Caracas. It was rumored about that she was engaged to Don Jose Gil Delgado, the acting chargé d'affaires of Spain at Caracas, affectionately known to his intimates as "Don Pepe."

In New York Natalye Lockwood painted the reigning social queens, among them Mrs. John Jacob Astor, Mrs. Philip Lydig and Mrs. Stuyvesant Fish.

While Otway Latham was trying to find a new career for himself after the collapse of his motion picture hopes, he and his bride revisited Mexico City. During their sojourn there tragedy overturned their romance. There were quarrels and tears. They parted there, and Natalye Lockwood packed her trunks and fled to New York. She took a studio in Forty-second street and devoted herself to her art.

She established residence in Providence, Rhode Island, for the purpose of obtaining a divorce outside the publicity glare of New York, and then changing plans again finally took a New York decree against Otway Latham. He presently married Mercedes Allen, an actress. Natalye Lockwood went on with her art, and later moved to Paris.

Natalye Lockwood Latham thought she had put something out of her life forever. Her unhappy love and its distractions had been left behind, dead and buried in the City of Mexico. But this was not to be the end. Something of that love lingered and specter-like was one day to re-enter the drama.

Major Woodville Latham, weary with the weight of years and many disappointments faced the future with less hope than his light hearted sons. The old man cast about uncertainly and

apprehensively, seeking a new field. At the end of his Civil
War service, in the lost cause of the South, he had been a great
chemist and engineer. The tremendous progress of the technical world in the years between, while he had been cloistered
in colleges or futilely pursuing fortune in real estate and the
motion pictures, had left him far behind. Edison and the
electrical age had come to make a new scientific world. The
tragic fact was that Major Latham was hopelessly out of date.
He could not now resume his teaching and he was unfit for employment in any technical capacity.

After a fruitless quest for a professional connection, Woodville Latham moved away from the Madison Square district and
the scenes of his shortlived dream of affluence. He took quarters in a rooming house far uptown and never looked on Broadway again. The years through which the screen began to rise
in power, with its shower of gold for luckier men saw the old
Major forgotten and unknown, going from house to house as a
book agent. He rang doorbells and waited on doorsteps trying
to sell *The Children's Hour* and giftbooks laden with smug
platitudes. A scattering of relatives and friends bought the
books. But very often haughty maids or annoyed housewives
slammed the door in his face with exclamations of scorn, leaving the old man to fold up his sample case and move on to try
again.

He had been Woodville Latham of Virginia, sir! A Major
of artillery for the Confederate States of America, a professor
of chemistry at the Universities of West Virginia and Mississippi, a consulting engineer of renown. Now merely Old
Man Latham, book agent.

The taste of the years was bitter. Old Man Latham grew
dour and silent and irritable. He was given to sleepless nights,
long eye-tired hours of reading and endless cups of black coffee.
The habits of the study and the laboratory survived their

significance and pursued him as a curse. The landlady complained of his long use of the lights in his little hall room. It was past her understanding why a man who sold books all day should want to read books all night. She, of course, could not understand that the books he tried to sell were not the books he read.

Here for a long time we must leave Major Latham, book agent in Harlem. We shall come to him again for his brief but dramatic last hour in the world of the motion picture—an hour which it is a mercy that he could not foresee.

CHAPTER TWENTY-SIX

CHICAGO—SPOOR AND SELIG

W E have seen the budding beginnings of the screen in three world capitals, New York, Paris and London, rising from the Edison peep show Kinetoscope, scattered like thistle seed in the path of the wind. Evolutionary forms appear where the soil is fertile and life abundant.

The same forces which decided that the motion picture was to be brought into being in the great New York industrial zone spreading out over the meadows of New Jersey gave it a chapter of development in Chicago, third of the cities of the world.

Less than an hour's ride north from the Loop of Chicago, up at Waukegan, a lake shore village and manufacturing district, another inventor, Edwin Hill Amet, was at work in the winter of 1895 on the problem of projection of Kinetoscope pictures. Precise dates on Amet's labors are not available, but he was sufficiently close in point of time to the efforts of the eastern inventors to become involved for a moment in the first Patent Office disputes. Amet's inventive labors were not destined to contribute to the mechanical progress of the art but they did set in motion a chain of events of far reaching effect in the commercial destiny of the screen.

Amet found himself in his motion picture labors in the traditional and typical position of the inventor. He needed money to go ahead. He had just completed the invention of an automatic platform scale which for one cent delivered to the patron a ticket with her weight printed on it. Now, in his workshop in the rear of the Chicago Scale Works, down by the rail-

—299—

road tracks in Waukegan, he turned to the problem of the pictures on the screen.

Reflecting on what he deemed to be the possibilities of the device, Amet decided to consult a theatrical authority. Theatrical authorities even today are ordinarily rather scarce in Waukegan. On this particular eventful evening a road show was playing a one night stand at the Waukegan Opera House. The house was ringing with the voice of the hero as he triumphed over the dark deep villain just before the last curtain, when Amet tapped at the window of the box office.

A man at the ticket stand was counting the night's receipts. Amet introduced himself. The showman took his hand and gave his name, George K. Spoor.

With the dignity and calm reserve which characterizes all good poker players and most Scotchmen, Spoor listened to the inventor's story with a profound but outwardly casual attention. He had heard of moving pictures, but he had not seen them move. He was willing to admit that if they could be made to move, in sight of an audience, they might have a box office value. Yes, he would look at a machine. He even admitted that if it looked promising he would just possibly invest a trifle.

Spoor let Amet do most of the talking. He did not mention that at the moment his capital consisted of the twenty-eight dollars and eighty-five cents profit on the night's show, and that his regular business was the operation of the newsstand and lunchroom at the Northwestern Station in Chicago. That night he was a showman and a magnate.

The two of them, inventor and magnate, talking in terms calculated to impress each other, walked across lots from the opera house to Amet's workshop. There they surveyed the array of gears and mechanical miscellany which Amet said was a projection machine in the making.

Spoor and Amet talked for an hour. Reluctantly, and with faint heart under his firm voice, Spoor ventured to ask the important question of the evening: "How much capital will you need to finish this?"

Spoor was set for a shock. He expected a demand for a thousand or two.

Amet stood by thoughtfully. He did not want to make a mistake in front of this big theatrical magnate from Chicago. He did some elaborate figuring.

"Well—it will take about sixty-five dollars to finish it—and I could use twenty-five right away."

Spoor swallowed hard.

"I guess that can be arranged." He spoke with all of the quiet conservatism of J. P. Morgan buying a railroad or of John D. Rockefeller bestowing a souvenir dime.

Spoor counted out the bills, carefully and slowly, each face side up in the manner of a man who has respect for money.

"You can draw on me for the rest of the sixty-five along as you need it."

All the way back to Chicago that night Spoor wondered just what kind of a fool he had been to take such a flyer in the flimsy idea of putting Kinetoscope pictures on the wall.

But that was the night when Spoor caught the turn of the tide to fortune. Out of that slender start grew the once powerful Essanay concern which for its day enjoyed worldwide fame and piled up a fortune of between seven and ten millions for Spoor.

The Amet machine was completed early in 1896, and was offered to the western market in Chicago under the name of the Magniscope. It was christened by George Kleine, then a dealer in lantern slides, stereopticons, and related optical goods in Chicago, who became an agent for the Amet machine. Kleine was making his first tentative contacts with the motion picture. He was beginning one of the most remarkable careers of the industry, devoted with an amazing singleness of purpose to picture merchandising, the only continuously active success of the business with an individual history of thirty years.

Amet quickly became involved in a Patent Office interference with Armat and Latham. His claims were abandoned without a struggle, presumably because of an inability to prove a priority in conception or reduction to practice.

George K. Spoor, the magnate of the one-night stand in Waukegan engaged in the exhibition of pictures with the Magniscope and, being remote from the main seat of picture activity in the East, escaped the attention of the busy patent lawyers.

Simultaneously, or at least in close sequence, another equally important Chicago factor in the history of the screen was germinating. It is the story of a roundabout path.

Drifting southeast from California into Texas went William N. Selig, a young showman. He was a versatile, inventive person with considerable photographic skill and experience. In the town of Dallas he came upon a Kinetoscope parlor where the Edison films were displayed in a peep show, just such an establishment as the Lathams had conducted in downtown New York. Selig spent several days investigating the machine and its films. He, like the rest, got a magic lantern idea and a notion of pictures on a screen.

This Selig was something of a plunger in his methodical, sure way. Showmanship in the open West had given him that. And since his name and works run in a continuous thread through all the subsequent motion picture history down to today and now, it is significant to turn back the pages even a little earlier than that day in 1895. From his home in Chicago, some years before, Selig went into the West in quest of his health, lingering a while in Colorado and then journeying on to California. He became manager of a health resort known as Chicago Park. Renewed energy came and he went on the road with a bit of entertainment. It consisted mostly of tricks of parlor magic, deftly done, including the old master performance of extracting the Belgian hare from the tall silk hat. That rabbit might be said to have been the progenitor of the famous Selig Zoo, but that is a decade and a half ahead in our chronology.

Mr. Selig was rewarded so handsomely for his successful manipulation of the docile rabbit and the trick hat that he developed his show business into a full-fledged minstrel attraction. It was a genuine fast black show, and it had the flavor of genius about it. In a little upstate town in California, Selig paused on the street one day to observe a lonely, forlornly idle darky. He was a yellow boy. He yawned a deep, wide open watermelon expanse of mouth and settled himself to let the sunshine soak in. He saw Selig looking at him and smiled. The smile was approximately one foot on its major axis. Selig admired it greatly.

"Boy—want a job?"

"Whut at, boss?" The yellow boy was casually interested.

"In a minstrel show—just stand up and open your mouth, that's your act."

"I most suttinly kin, boss—when does we start?"

That was the beginning of the career of Bert Williams, a genius whose death a few years ago was a matter of world news and regret. When Williams joined the Selig show that day he found in the cast the man who was later for years to share his fame as the other half of Williams & Walker. Walker was surly. Williams was all smiles.

This was, incidentally, Bert Williams' first appearance on any stage. Being light of hue, fifteen-sixteenths white in ancestry, he was ordered into burnt cork make-up. Stage fright overtook Williams in the first ensemble number, and the sweat of distress poured down his face. His make-up ran in streaks of alarming perpendicular zebra effect. When the end man fired his funny question at Williams, the novice's eyes opened in terror and beads stood out on his forehead. He couldn't remember his lines. In dismay his mouth flew open. The house roared.

"If Ah says anything those folks'll laugh at me." Williams backed out into the wings. His hit was made, in spite of him. With the little Selig wagon show in the nineties he laid the foundation of the fame that took him into every great world capital, and which quite incidentally one day, years after, gave him a transient motion picture success of sensational brevity.

William Selig had the bankroll of his minstrel show profits in his pockets when he discovered the Kinetoscope in Dallas and saw the greater promise of the picture that could be put on the screen.

Selig went back to Chicago and rented a workshop on the second floor of a most humble building in the midst of the hectic night life of Chicago's tenderloin. It was the now historic 43 Peck Court, and probably the only reputable tradition of that red-lighted byway.

Selig had taken cheap quarters to stand a long siege. He had, like all the rest of the projection machine inventors, samples of Edison Kinetoscope film for experimental purposes. He set to tinkering with a scheme to wed it to the stereopticon. It was once again the same quest in which we have followed the labors of Latham and Armat and Lumière and Paul.

Meanwhile, by way of potboiling for current income Selig began a commercial photographic business, making carbon prints for the portrait studios and large scale photographic enlargements of landscapes for the railways.

While Selig was puzzling over the projection problems, the Latham and Lumière machines appeared in Chicago at the Schiller theatre. Selig saw the shows and secured samples of the films.

Now a curious incident intruded.

A most mysterious person, a man of some fifty-five or sixty years of age, speaking broken English with a heavy French accent, appeared at the shop of the Union Model Works in Chicago with a strange request. He had one small part of some sort of a machine in his hand. He wanted this duplicated. He offered no explanations, gave no name, and maintained an atmosphere of deep secrecy.

The work was assigned to the shop's most expert mechanic, one Andrew Schustek. Schustek examined the machine part, made a working drawing of it, and duplicated it.

Thereafter, day by day, the mysterious Frenchman called, taking away a part and leaving another to have it duplicated.

Each time Schustek made a working drawing of the part. Meanwhile the model maker learned that the Frenchman was in some way connected with the showing of the Lumière projection machine at the Schiller theatre.

As Schustek studied over the drawings he arrived at the conclusion that the machine which was being duplicated bit by bit was a Lumière Cinématographe, designed for the dual purpose of taking and projecting pictures.

Finally the last of the parts was made and delivered. The old Frenchman paid his bill, for three hundred and fifty hours of the machinist's time at sixty cents an hour, in cash, and departed, without even leaving a name on the books.

Now Selig's experiments in projection machines had outgrown the capacities of his crowded shop in Peck Court. By sheer coincidence he, too, turned to the Union Model Works for assistance. His orders were also given to Andrew Schustek for execution.

On Schustek's workbench Selig caught a glimpse of the working drawings of the Lumière machine, which had been built there on the same bench, bit by bit.

Selig and Schustek talked it over. Selig ordered another duplicate of the French machine.

Schustek now threw his whole attention to the motion picture machine. He and Selig opened an experimental shop at Irving Park boulevard and Western Avenue, then a remote part of Chicago. From the French machine the one famous Selig Standard Camera, and the projector known as the Selig Polyscope, were evolved.

Selig, probably with an eye to sidestepping possible patent litigation, sold his manufacturing equipment to Schustek and became his customer, ordering cameras and machines in quantity.

Under the name of the Selig Polyscope Company, he began a small business in making and showing pictures in and about Chicago, at vaudeville houses and various places of entertainment. Thomas Persons was the first camera man on the Selig staff.

The early Selig pictures were made about the streets of Chicago and in back yards when it was desirable to escape the curious passersby. One of the classic first Selig productions was *The Tramp and the Dog*, a back yard comedy. It was nearly a hundred and fifty feet long. In this startling drama a tramp knocks at the back door for a hand-out and is chased off the premises and over the fence by the vigilant bulldog. An unforeseen happening added vastly to the success of this picture. As the tramp clambered over the fence the dog attached himself with great tenacity to the seat of the tramp's ragged pants. There was a brief struggle in which the genuinely frightened actor tumbled down the outside of the fence as the dog dropped back victorious with a large mouthful of pants in full view up stage, center.

The bulldog scene was a tremendous hit, just as it would be today. Here was the discovery for the screen of the basic humor of pants. Pants have always been a joke, despite all efforts to dignify them as trousers. Motion picture comedy without pants would be unthinkable.

Selig, too, was on the road to fortune. The coming years were laden with adventure and attainment for the Chicago trio, Spoor, Kleine and Selig, yet unknown to each other and one day to be partners in an amazing prosperity.

We have come at last to the end of the array of inventors of motion picture projection. Seven times in seven places, each independent of the others, we have seen the projection problem solved, liberating the picture from the peep show Kinetoscope. Here was evidence enough of the evolutionary force behind the new art. The history of invention holds no parallel for the multiple invention of motion picture projection. It was inevitable, as inescapable as gravitation.

CHAPTER TWENTY-SEVEN

THE LAWLESS FILM FRONTIER

FRONTIERS have ever been lawless lands. The pirates and blackbirders, the cattle rustlers and road agents, the faro dealers and claim jumpers are all inevitable and serving pioneers. They differ from the more glorified trail blazers and empire builders only by the slightest divergences in matter of sheer convention. As the shadows lengthen they merge; and, looking backward indeed, what trivial differences may we honestly see between Captain Kidd hanged for a felon and the honored Sir Francis Drake? Who can fairly choose between Alexander the Great and Attila the Awful? All good men in their day and well remembered.

Frontiers are not exclusively borders in geography. There are also frontiers in Time. The early years of the motion picture constituted such a frontier. The progressing outposts of the screen have often been established by enterprising gentry operating in splendid swashbuckling disregard of established codes in other business. In the newly discovered world of the screen there was no law.

As the autumn of 1896 approached, the motion picture business was growing in what appeared to be rank and piratical disorder. Raff & Gammon, who had started with the industry presumably under their sole control, straight from the fountain head of Edison to the market, were beset with irregular and destructive competition. Coming from the orderly world of banking, they had taken every reasonable precaution to protect and conduct their business in the regular commercial pattern—

all to no avail.   Ethics seldom transplant; they must be raised from seed, in each new field.

In this, the first year of its existence, the motion picture matriculated in the bitter, desperate school of experience, and began paying the tuition of folly.

The art of the screen was not to be controlled and disciplined in 1896.   It was a ruthless period in which a new set of commercial conventions had to be evolved and established.   The contributions of many men and minds had to be made, and in the sum total of picture evolution it mattered little or not at all whether these contributions of development were made within the established lines and laws of older businesses, or over the bandit border among the interlopers and infringers.

Raff & Gammon had sold territorial rights to their Vitascope customers with at least an implication of exclusive rights and protection.   Now motion picture machines of all sorts began to appear, boldly or surreptitiously.   The projection machine and the camera were being re-invented, copied, fabricated and re-adapted in defiance of presumable but unestablished rights. A few scattering legal actions stopped some few of the infringers for a moment, but with no permanent effect.   Raff & Gammon grew discouraged with the effort to suppress the invaders.   A crop of them appeared every morning, fresh as asparagus.

Most discouraging of all, rumors began to seep into the market that Thomas Edison was himself about to bring out a machine to supplant the Vitascope, which was still in the public mind believed to be his.

The report said that Edison's new machine, which was to be known as the Edison Projecting Kinetoscope, to differentiate it from his first machine, the peep show Kinetoscope, and Armat's Vitascope, was to be sold on the open market.

This rumor wrecked the morale of the Vitascope business.

The state's rights buyers of the Vitascope jumped their boundaries and went pell mell after business, wherever and whenever they thought they could find it. And on their heels ran the infringers with their make-shift, copied, and pirated machines. The gold rush had begun—the Devil take the hindmost.

Trouble and the motion picture business became synonyms. There was safety and assurance nowhere for any one engaged in the affairs of the screen—but there was always ahead the vision of vast profits. No one appears to have had foresight, which is not remarkable, since foresight never exists except in the reminiscences and autobiographical writings of fortunate men. Instead of conscious individual vision there was the broad atmospheric pressure of the age long human wish which the screen could serve. No motion picture man saw beyond the end of his nose, which obviously has always given a great advantage to those with big noses.

Shreds and shards of the little disasters of which the whole hash of screen affairs of the day was made may be found by the searcher of contemporary records. The Brooklyn section of the *New York Tribune* for September 3, 1896, contains this specimen:

Eidoloscope Attachment

After a long chase and many fruitless efforts to serve papers on Wade Hampton de Fontaine in a suit brought against him for work performed and materials furnished, the plaintiffs, tired at last, and on their application Justice Van Wyck of the Supreme Court yesterday issued an order of attachment against Fontaine on affidavits which state he is likely to depart for parts unknown. The defendant is or was the proprietor of the eidoloscope exhibition at Coney Island, and the bill of the plaintiffs is for erection of the building in which the show is given.

The process servers finally got action at de Fontaine's impressive office at 114 Fifth Avenue, but the Eidoloscope business, at Coney Island and elsewhere, was an empty shell, no longer worth attachment.

The last significant stroke of business for the Vitascope came with the booking of the machine with films and operator as an act in Proctor's Pleasure Palace and Proctor's Theatre in Twenty-third street, New York, beginning the week of September 13, 1896. The Proctor theatres have continued as customers of the motion picture now for thirty years.

In November of '96 the break between Edison and Raff & Gammon occurred. Eighty Armat Vitascopes had been made and delivered. The Edison Projecting Kinetoscope was announced.

The motion picture had slipped out of the headlines of the metropolitan press after its first flush of novelty. The films were already a commonplace in the vaudeville houses of the larger cities. Turning to the files of the *New York Times* for November 8, 1896, we find a typically casual notice, precisely like the press notices of the vaudeville houses of today:

> Eben Plympton will appear at Keith's Union Square theatre tomorrow night in Bronson Howard's "Old Love Letters," supported by Agnes Proctor. The Cinématograph will begin its twenty-first week with the exhibition of several new views and the variety bill will be up to its usual standard.

It will be noted that the simplification of motion picture nomenclature had begun with the dropping of the final "e" on Cinématographe. It was on its way to become cinema.

The Edison Projecting Kinetoscope was proclaimed by letterheads and minor advertisements as "an improvement over the Vitascope." The Armat Vitascope, manufactured in the Edison plant for Raff & Gammon, had been put out under territorial restrictions. The purchasers of Vitascope rights bought states and regions for exploitation. The new Edison Projecting Kinetoscope, with all the weight of Edison's name behind it, broke the restrictions, weak as they were proving to be, wide open. The Edison machine could be bought by anybody for use anywhere, any time.

This move was in line with the policy and early advice offered by W. E. Gilmore when he became Edison's general manager: "Damn the patents, give me the goods."

Past performance of the Edison organization had given Gilmore provocation. Amazing as it may seem Edison had not then and has never since profited as the inventor of the incandescent lamp or most of his other important inventions. Edison spent more trying to protect his patent on the electric lamp than the invention was worth to him. The only profits which he has made on the great contribution of the incandescent electric light has been as a manufacturer, on a working parity with other licensees making the same lamps.

It was natural enough that it should now in the autumn of '96 appear that Edison's only chance to make money on the motion picture was as a manufacturer of picture machines, to be sold to all comers like any other machine.

This immediately made a breach between Raff & Gammon and Edison, and created a tension between Raff & Gammon and Armat, whom they expected to defend the Vitascope against Edison's invasion of the projection field.

Here was the beginning of the strife which made the motion picture a battle ground for the next twenty years. There was an ultimate victory far ahead for Armat, whose fight became one of the incidental campaigns of the general conflict.

Somewhat away from the main stream and never to become really a part of the screen institution, the late Lyman Howe, whose name is known to thousands in the trans-Appalachian country, began an independent motion picture career. Howe's home and headquarters were at Wilkes-Barre in Pennsylvania.

As early as 1884 he began to be a showman, exhibiting a miniature coal mine and breaker at Glen Onoko, near Mauch Chunk. When Edison's phonograph appeared Howe saw special opportunity in it. The phonograph at that time was offered with listening tubes. The patron put a nickel in the machine, inserted the tubes in his ears, and took the consequences. Howe supplanted the ear tubes with a tin horn so that a whole audience could listen.

The application of the tin horn, which Edison had of course also previously considered, was a procedure prior to but identical with the application of the magic lantern to the Kinetoscope peep show.

Howe's letterhead of '96 carried a proclaiming top line, saying: PHONOGRAPH CONCERTS—No ear tubes used, an audience of 3,000 people entertained at one time.

On this same letterhead under date of March 13, 1896, Howe had written to Edison asking the price for the rights on the Vitascope to Pennsylvania. The letter went to Raff & Gammon, who had a previous bid which they had to accept. Howe was offered New York state, exclusive of Kings county. He was disappointed and outraged. He wrote that the whole proceeding gave him "a feeling of pain." He seemed to think that as a member of the Edison family he was being treated as a cold outsider. Howe abandoned the Vitascope idea and set about having a machine built for him. He achieved this, after many trials, before the announcement of the new Edison projector, and took to the road again with his Animatoscope and films. The common projectors of the period ran the films through the mechanism of the supply reel and dropped them into a basket. Howe applied a take-up mechanism to wind up the film. Very probably his machine was the first to use this device, which was however repeatedly re-invented in various parts of the world.

In part, because of the friendly attitude of Edison and, more largely, because Howe operated in the hinterland between the conspicuous centers of New York and Chicago he escaped involvement in the heavy warfare of patent litigation. Howe's patrons were the church societies and Chautauqua type audiences. His shows withstood the degradation of the nickelodeon age and played consistently to fifty cent admissions when the rest of the screen offered only a shoddy nickel's worth. His business continued on the same policy under the administration of S. M. Walkinshaw, who joined one of Howe's traveling shows as a musical director in 1898.

While these developments were taking place in New York a new factor of destiny was unostentatiously arising in Chicago. George Kleine of the Kleine Optical Company, who had begun his motion picture career with a tentative agency for the Amet Magniscope now found that machine variously so enmeshed in controversy as to be unavailable. Kleine went to West Orange and saw the new Edison Projecting Kinetoscope, which he ordered at wholesale in one-twelfth dozen lots.

This transaction brought Kleine into the Edison sequence of motion picture affairs, to become, as we shall eventually see, one of the most capable strategists in the big war of the movie kings to come. We shall encounter Kleine occasionally ahead in these pages, and much more often we shall discover his works with the man himself retiring into a remote background.

Kleine is today one of Edison's warmest friends—this in sequel to a desperate commercial and legal conflict with the Edison establishment in years which this history has yet to cover.

Across the Atlantic, Lumière was sweeping the European world with the Cinématographe. The Lumière camera-showmen with their portable outfits, starting in the summer of '95, began long tours which in the next handful of years showed the films in every city and many a hamlet from the Baltic to the Golden

Horn. F. Doublier, now a motion picture laboratory technician in Fort Lee, New Jersey, took the Cinématographe through Holland and all the Russias down into Turkey. Similarly equipped expeditions, each with an advance agent, ventured into the Orient, Oceania and South and North America.

Posters everywhere announced the coming of the Cinématographe and the making of local pictures. Throngs gathered at the appointed places to see the marvel of motion pictures being made, and to be in the pictures. The capacity of the Lumière Cinématographe as a camera was about thirteen meters at one loading, or forty-five seconds of exposure. To insure the patronage of large numbers the operators often cranked an empty camera before the crowds for hours on end.

The standard admission price of the Lumière shows was two francs. In class conscious Russia patronage demanded a gradation. Front seats within ten feet of the screen were priced at one rouble. The one rouble patrons usually however yielded to the eye strain and moved back into the fifteen kopeck back seats.

Doublier, who continued on his grand tour for some four years, attained a signal stroke of showmanship in southern Russia. When he arrived with the Cinématographe in Kiev, he found the large Jewish population tremendously interested in the revelations of the famous Dreyfus military affair in France. Sorting through his stock of films Doublier selected bits of a military parade with a tall, impressive French captain at the head of a column. This captain he labelled Dreyfus. Further inquiry located a picture of a French government building which would pass in Russia for the scene of Captain Dreyfus' trial. A long range picture of some warships at Bordeaux became in Doublier's ready fancy a picture of Dreyfus being taken away to exile and prison. For a month this synthetic sensation played to a capacity business in Kiev and thence through the whole country about. This profitable fiction would have been deemed most unseemly by the dignified Lumières, had they known of it, back at their laboratories in Lyon.

Each of the far ranging couriers of the Lumière expeditions was given a share in his receipts and a special bonus in addition which was his reward for safeguarding the internal secrets of the Cinématographe. It was the iron rule that never by night or day was the machine to be permitted to be out of the sight and reach of the Lumière representative. No person was to be permitted to inspect it. The little box went with the operator through all his work and pastime, from the theatre to the wine garden. If he became, as often happened, an honored guest of local notables the Cinématographe went to the banquet, too, and stood under the table between his knees. It was his companion by day and his pillow at night.

But even that precaution did not suffice to keep the Lumière's secret. All through Europe experimenters began to come forth with similar machines, variously adapted from or copied after the Cinématographe. Some of them might perhaps have laid fair claim to having been independent without being actually original. The very character of the film itself, basically established for the art of projection by the prior Edison Kinetoscope, tended to predetermine the character of all the devices made to handle it.

It is more than a probability that the work credited to one Max Skladanowski, an early experimenter in Berlin, is properly to be classified as a part of the wave of inventive and simulative interest which followed in the wake of the first Lumière showings in the European capitals.

Skladanowski's name first emerged from an opaque obscurity for a tiny flurry of attention in the summer of 1924, when he was discovered, if we are generous in the use of the word, by the Fox News, a bi-weekly screen topical. The Fox news reel and related publicity material issued to the press sought to attain sensation by announcing the discovery of the first motion picture machine in the world, a device on which Skladanowski was said to have begun work in 1870 and completed in 1888. This was accompanied by presentation in the newsreel of various pictures said to have been made by Skladanowski in 1890, including notably Prince Otto von Bismarck.

Pursuit of facts behind this announcement came to an impasse when Hans Tintner, press agent of the Berlin office of the Fox concern, averred that he was entirely unable to remember where he had found Skladanowski or in what manner he had arrived at the dates given. Examination of pictures of the Skladanowski machine show that it was evolved after celluloid film became available and its mechanism is distinctly reminiscent of other machines of the kind built in 1896–7. Since Bismarck died in 1898, the machine falls between those dates and has no element of priority, and no major importance beyond the purposes of the Sunday supplement scientists.

It is of significance that Maximilian Harden, who so intimately enjoyed the confidences of Bismarck's later days, expressed the opinion in correspondence with the author, that no such picture of Bismarck was made, pointing out that after his death the Iron Chancellor was capably impersonated by an actor on the German stage.

In France three new machines, under as many names, appeared in a matter of months after the Cinémotographe show began in the little basement room on the Boulevard des Capucines.

George Melies, magician and prestidigitator extraordinary, whose name was identified with the Theatre Robert Houdin, built an experimental projection machine and camera, using a film considerably wider in gauge than the Cinématographe, which was of approximately the Edison standard. Melies soon abandoned the wide film idea and accepted the Edison size. Charles Pathé who had begun with a peep show, of Edison type Kinetoscopes and films from Robert W. Paul in London, built a camera with a cam and claw movement reminiscent of the Lumière intermittent mechanism.

Then shortly Leon Gaumont, whose name in the film world was for many years second in magnitude only to Pathé's, came forth with a camera and launched into the widening field. Gaumont's camera was perhaps a slightly more definite divergence from the Lumière principle. Gaumont had been connected with Jules Carpentier, the constructing mechanical engineer who manufactured the Cinématographe for the Lumières in Lyon, on designs made by Charles Moisson, engineer. France was very closely paralleling the mechanical motion picture history of the United States.

Joseph D. Baucus and Frank Z. Maguire, who had gone to Europe with the Edison peep show Kinetoscope, by reason of the rapid evolution of the business now found themselves dealers in pictures rather than machines. Their foreign market was below expectations because of foreign manufacture outside the possible restraint of Edison patents. But to compensate for this, they saw the opportunity to send back to the United States a selection of foreign films. As was noted in the discussion of the Vitascope opening at Koster & Bials' Music Hall, some of Paul's English pictures were the first to be imported. But the wide geographical scope of the Lumière operations made the French pictures even more attractive. In a circular issued in August of 1896 on the letterhead of Maguire & Baucus, Ltd., Dashwood House, London, and 44 Pine street, New York, they announced their first wholesale importation, saying:

> We have made arrangements to handle a number of foreign films. These are now enroute and will probably reach us within the next ten days. They are of standard width, about 52 feet long

and are suitable for use on either Kinetoscopes or Projecting Machines.

The scenes on these strips will undoubtedly prove very interesting to people in all parts of the country, especially to those who have never been abroad. The acquisition of such subjects must enhance the earning power of any exhibit, and we can recommend them to all progressive exhibitors.

The following is a *partial* list of subjects. *Price per film* $25.

SCENE FROM CORONATION OF THE CZAR OF RUSSIA, taken at Moscow, the Czar passes within about twenty feet of the camera and is plainly recognizable to any one familiar with his portraits.

RUSSIAN SAILORS, Scene on board a Man of War.

THE GONDOLAS, Showing a scene on the Grand Canal in Venice, showing St. Mark's Square.

MARKET SCENE, Showing the Market Place in Vienna, Austria.

BOATS ON THE SEINE, at Paris, Showing steamers, pleasure barges, etc., passing, bridge in background with carriages passing.

PLACE DE LA CONCORDE, A scene on one of the famous Parisian boulevards, showing carriages, pedestrians, etc.

RUE DE HAVRE, A street scene in the business section of Paris.

TRAIN SCENE, Taken at one of the Paris Railway Stations.

THE FIRE ENGINE, Shows engine leaving house for a fire, Paris.

We take pleasure in quoting discount (to dealers) on lots of five 20 per cent., on lots of ten or over 30 per cent., and hand you herewith sample picture for inspection and comparison. Our terms are spot cash.

MAGUIRE & BAUCUS, Ltd.

Apparently all or most of these subjects were made by Lumière or with a Cinématographe. Since the Lumière film was of very nearly the same gauge as the Edison pictures it was only necessary to supplant the Lumière two hole perforation system with a continuous row of holes to fit Edison sprockets to make the pictures suitable to American machines.

But the business of film importation was destined to an exceedingly brief prosperity. A charming discovery was made in American laboratories. It was found possible to make a film negative from any original positive print by the exceedingly simple process of putting the print through the film printer with a piece of raw stock in the usual manner. From the resulting negative any number of copies, identical with the original print, could be made. The great art of duplicating films, soon to be described in trade vernacular as "duping," was born. Films were not copyrighted, and at that time probably not even admissible to copyright. The motion picture had no recognized editorial values. Physical possession constituted title to the picture. Those were primitive days.

"Duping" became a universal practice, in the United States at least. The process produced, to be sure, a print inferior to those from original negatives, but when "duping" began there were no standards of comparison. When the day came, some years ahead, that such a comparison was made, one of the most significant fights of the film world resulted. It will be well to remember the beginning of the film "dupe." Purists have called them "contratype prints" in the literature of the law. No such purists of diction exist in the film world.

Practically every foreign picture made in the first ten years was "duped" and widely sold by all of the film makers in the United States. The American market was good for just enough prints to make the dupes. Frequently samples were duped and returned for credit. The earliest Lumière pictures all went through the duping mills. Their subject *L'Arroseur Arrose— The Adventures of the Boy and the Garden Hose*—first of the slapsticks of the screen, was duped with especial enthusiasm.

The picture duping process represents no early iniquity peculiar to the motion picture. The art and industry of literature and book making, in these same free and untrammelled United States, only a few decades before enjoyed a similarly liberal view concerning writings and works from abroad. Parallel practises are a part of the early history of every art which has any measure of industrial application. It has recently been observable in the radio. For a combination of geographical and political reasons, Philadelphia has from the beginning been the headquarters for the highest attainment of the film duper's art. It began there when the process was not specifically illegal, and continues even to-day for the supplying of outlaw prints shipped to the remote parts of the globe.

Philadelphia's master film duper is wealthy and so well bulwarked politically that prosecutions have proven impractical and he has seldom been annoyed by indictments.

Between the aggressiveness of the English and French motion picture projection inventors we have seen the foreign expedition of Paul Cinquevalli to introduce the Vitascope fail. Charles H. Webster, who went to London in behalf of Raff & Gammon to install the Vitascope for demonstration, returned in the late summer of 1896 discouraged with that project.

Having seen all the rest of the world plunging into the making of competing projection machines, Webster determined to take a fling at it, too. He and Edward Kuhn of Orange, a former Edison employe, whose wife had handcolored the famous Annabelle dance pictures, organized the International Film Company and set forth in New York to make and sell films and a machine to be known as the International Projectorscope. This was one of many machines which began to appear in the season of 1896–7. Edison's battery of lawyers began to look about and take notes. Down in Washington Thomas Armat went to consult his attorneys. There was stormy weather ahead.

CHAPTER TWENTY-EIGHT

Every succeeding week of the fall of 1896 added to the complexity of the motion picture situation, and added to the diverse factors to figure in the struggles to come. The progress of development increased in velocity week by week. The state of the screen was like a boom town on the prairie. A jumble of ideas and a tangle of experimental forms, technical and commercial, sprang up in all the crudity and haste of an oil field metropolis.

The motion picture was an open game. Anybody might become important overnight. Every man who came in contact with the screen might claim it for his own.

For some months we have lost sight of William Kennedy Laurie Dickson, who after parting company with Edison and then again with the Lathams went to the K. M. C. D. Syndicate, taking with him all his expert knowledge gained as laboratory assistant to Edison in bringing forth the Kinetoscope. We have detailed the invention of the peep show Mutoscope, accredited, legally at least, to Herman Casler of Canastota. It was a definite part of the purposes and policy of the Mutoscope group to keep Dickson out of the limelight of attention. It would have been inviting trouble and patent suits to make him conspicuous. But the troubles and the suits were bound to come.

Because of this policy of quiet and secretive operation, with a workshop in upstate New York at Canastota, it is difficult to arrive at an exact date when the first successful demonstration of the K. M. C. D. Syndicate's projection machine was made.

Even the testimonies in the long litigations which followed do not make it clear.

And this K. M. C. D. projector is important because it was the device on which the most glorious tradition of the motion picture art was founded, the Biograph Company.

We have seen already that the K. M. C. D. group set out merely to make a better peep show than Edison and found the motion picture bursting forth to the screen under their hands while they were at work. As we trip down the years we shall see this same remote primitive effort as the direct beginning of the strand which has woven into screen annals the names of D. W. Griffith, Mack Sennett, Mary Pickford, Blanche Sweet, the Gishes, the Barrymores and all that marvelous galaxy of stars and idols past and present.

The K. M. C. D. machine bearing the enterprising patriotic name of "The American Biograph" made its initial appearance before the world on the night of Wednesday, October 12, 1896, at Hammerstein's Olympia Music Hall. It is still a theatre, now known at Loew's New York. The amusement page of the *New York Tribune* of the next morning related:

A MOVING PICTURE OF McKINLEY

ENTHUSIASM AT OLYMPIA—ATTRACTIONS
AT THE VARIOUS OTHER MUSIC HALLS.

Anybody who thinks that the enthusiasm of the modern music-hall audience is all for European singers of questionable propriety should have been at the Olympia Music Hall last night. The audience went fairly frantic over pictures thrown on a screen. Several machines for the throwing of moving pictures have been shown here, but the new biograph, for all its horrible name, is the best of all of them. The biggest part of the enthusiasm began when a view of a McKinley and Hobart parade in Canton was shown. The cheering was incessant as long as the line was passing across the screen, and it grew much greater when the title of

—323—

the next picture appeared: "Major McKinley at Home." Major McKinley was seen to come down the steps of his house with his secretary. The secretary handed him a paper which he opened and read. Then he took off his hat and advanced to meet a visiting delegation.

The biograph showed some other interesting pictures, notably one of the *Empire State Express* rounding a curve, which was one of the best if not the very best moving picture that has yet been exhibited here. The Music Hall performance of last night was altogether an interesting one. Sampson, the strong man, reappeared and showed that he had acquired a good deal of nickel-plated apparatus since he was last seen on Broadway. The programme was filled out by Vanola, the equilibrist; A. O. Duncan, Dutch Daly, Amann, the Poluski Brothers, Papinta, Miss Kitty Mitchell, Wood and Shephard, Moa and Goodrich, and the flying ballet. Seven boxes were occupied by members of the National Republican Committee and their friends, who came to see Major McKinley walk across his lawn.

The reviewer failed to record that the McKinley film closed with a handsome view of the Stars and Stripes, waving vigorously.

A great deal of history is to be extracted from this newspaper item. It appears, perhaps unfortunately, to have been written by a press agent for the theatre. The initial dig about "European singers of questionable propriety" was very simply directed at the major competition, Koster & Bials' Music Hall, where the Barrison Sisters were giving the gallery what it wanted in song and dance. The Barrison number was so good that the newspapers extended its message by descriptive editorials guised as rebukes. Besides this, Koster & Bials' had introduced the Vitascope, with which the American Biograph expected to compete.

This was the first presentation of *The Empire State Express* picture, which is to be remembered as a classic primitive of the screen art. The Empire State Express was the New York Central's crack train running between New York and Buffalo. It was as famous then as the Twentieth Century of later years. It was photographed for Biograph by Dickson. This was the first picture to capitalize the great American adoration of big engines and the romance of the rails, the lure of which in pre-motor days turned out every little town on Sunday "to see the train come in." *The Empire State Express* film delivered the power-and-speed thrill to the theatre for the first time.

Strong men stood up and shouted and frail women screamed with delicious terror as the great locomotive on the screen came comet-like into a rushing close-up amid the uproar of the orchestra.

The Biograph enjoyed a long run at Hammerstein's. Checking week after week the notices of its appearances, the archeologist's soul is filled with joy to discover that motion picture memories are enriched by an association of the Biograph with "the peerless Cherry Sisters" who came to the Olympia to appear on the same bill the week of November 15. The *New York Tribune* in a critical evaluation says of the Sisters Cherry: "Robed in the choicest confections of Cedar Rapids' modistes, in Iowa, Illinois and Kansas they have often tickled an audience to death."

There was distinct recognition of dramatic and news value, which are identical, in Biograph's presentation of the picture of William McKinley, this night in the midst of the campaign of '96. But that is not the whole story of the McKinley picture. When E. B. Koopman of the K. M. C. D. Syndicate went out to get money for the project he went downtown where money is. The "Gold Standard" against Bryan's "Free Silver" was pre-eminently the cause of "downtown" New York. It was the battle of Wall Street, sage and experienced of barter, against the dream hopes of a commonalty which was willing to believe that their Uncle Samuel could spit on a chip, call it money, and make everybody rich. William J. Bryan, the Nebraskan, was making a career out of the hopes of the economically ignorant.

The Republican answer to Bryan's dream vending was another bit of showmanship embodied in the "Full Dinner Pail" slogan, aimed with considerable accuracy at the spot where the belt buckle should have been in that age of suspenders—plus an effective monopoly of the screen for presentation of McKinley, the gold standard candidate.

What with Abner McKinley's stock participation in the American Mutoscope & Biograph Company and its other "downtown affiliations and the relations between the family of Norman C. Raff, of Raff & Gammon, bankers of Canton, Ohio, and McKinley's neighbors, the Bryan cause had not the remotest screen chance.

The correspondence files of the Raff & Gammon Vitascope office of this same October, 1896, yield a letter from Robert Fischer, a bicycle repairman of Great Falls, Montana, then engaged in introducing the Vitascope to Denver, in which he pleaded:

> If it is possible, send me a film of W. J. Bryan before November 3rd. It would not be *safe* for me to show *McKinley's* here until after election.

Fischer had delivered a correct opinion on the election, but also he knew the temper of the silver producing state of Colorado. It was, however, not possible to fill his order for a picture of Bryan.

The motion picture screen was, thus we observe, born Republican, which it has remained ever since in striking consistency.

Through the remaining weeks of the campaign of '96 the picture of *William McKinley at Home* continued on the screen at

Hammerstein's Olympia to the considerable profit of the management. The Republican National Committee became in effect a press agent for the house and one of its best customers. Every visiting politician was sent to see the picture. There is no evidence that the screen with its scant circulation of that day exerted an appreciable influence on the election, but whatever it had it delivered to the G. O. P.

The screen enterprise of the American Biograph differed markedly from other film projects both in the technical aspects of the machine and the plan of commercial operation. Both of these differences must be understood in some detail because of their very large subsequent importance on motion picture affairs.

The Vitascope was being sold on the state's rights plan. The Edison Projecting Kinetoscope was coming on the open market as a mere piece of machinery, available to any purchaser, regardless of territory or intended use. A half dozen infringing machines, too important to name, were also on the open market. But the Biograph determined neither to sell nor lease its machines. It aimed especially at the vaudeville theatre market, supplying the machine, films and operator to be booked as an act. Biograph intended to sell nothing but the shadow on the screen.

In point of technical quality the Biograph picture which flashed out on the screen that night of October 12, 1896, was the best the art had attained. The quality of the screen image was vastly improved because the big Biograph picture required only one-eighth as much magnification as the Edison, Lumière and Paul films.

The great size of the Biograph film was a factor in determining the selling policy and subsequent happenings. Using eight times as much film and silver salts for each frame or image as the Edison standard pictures, the Biograph product was so expensive that it could not hope to compete except in big theatres where cost was low in relation to earning power.

Further, the mechanical peculiarities of the Biograph projector tended to limit its distribution. The mechanism which handled the film was driven by friction rollers and cams which evaded the patent specifications covering the positive sprocket wheel drive of Edison's machines. The resulting action allowed the film to creep or lag slightly and thereby required the application of a governing device constantly under the hand of a skilled operator. The American Biograph could not be made fool proof. Anybody with skill enough to run a meat chopper could grind the films through an Edison or Armat type projector. This again influenced history, out of all apparent proportion to the dry fact.

Biograph immediately became a large purchaser of Eastman film. It used thirty-six of its giant frames of film per second. It therefore consumed nearly twenty times as much raw stock as the equivalent modern picture.

The advent of the American Biograph is an event of highest historical importance. Here was born the competitive force which was to make the motion picture a great industry, and remarkably, too, to contribute more importantly than any other single influence toward making it an art.

In the years ahead the great issues of the industry were to be fought out between Biograph and Edison. Progress and precedents of large import came from their conflicts.

The Biograph set up a metropolitan studio on the roof of the Hackett-Carhart building, and proceeded to the making of pictures for the dual use of the Mutoscope peep show machines and the American Biograph. The Biograph, like the other picture machines, went into the vaudeville houses for its principal service. The greater scope of interest and abilities of the four components of the K. M. C. D. Syndicate, Koopman, Marvin,

Casler and Dickson, was reflected in a range of ingenious subjects.

One of Biograph's notable early pictures was a step by step stop motion picture of the wrecking of the old Star Theatre building in Broadway. A camera was brought to bear on the building as demolition started. One frame of the film was exposed by an automatic electrical timing device every thirty minutes for weeks thereafter until the site was cleared. The result on the screen at normal projection speed showed the building melting down in a few minutes.

This was apparently the first use of the technique by which we now are shown the oversped processes of the opening of the rose, the hatching of chicks, and many comic exaggerations of motion.

Following up its success with McKinley, Biograph went camera gunning for notables at large. Theodore Roosevelt, police commissioner of New York, wasp-waisted in a frock coat, was one of the early subjects.

Koopman, who had ventured his all in the first financing of the Mutoscope project, hastened abroad to promote the interests of the new business. He put the Biograph to work in London with a repetition of the New York success, and established Biograph concerns in all the leading capitals of Europe, including, it is charming to record, the Nederlandsche Biographe en Mutoscope Maatschappij, 19 Utrechtschestratt, Amsterdam.

W. K. L. Dickson rather early in Biograph affairs left New York, returning to his native England, where he resided until his recent removal to France. Eugene Lauste, the mechanician who began his motion picture work in Edison's Room Five under Dickson, following him to the Latham enterprise, followed, too, to Biograph. Lauste also went abroad and was for a time in Biograph's service in France. It may have been the mere incidental purposes of business which took these men abroad, and again it may have been excellent policy to remove their irritating presence from the sight of Edison. Lauste eventually returned to New Jersey where the quest of this history found him, in the town of Bloomfield.

William Bitzer, known to all the screen world later as "Billy Bitzer, Griffith's cameraman," entered the service of the American Mutoscope & Biograph Company in this first season as an electrician. All of the early motion picture machinery produced either by Edison or Biograph was electrically equipped. This fact and the prevailing notion of Edison as an electrical wizard have tended to give the layman an impression that in some obscure way the motion picture is a bit of electrical magic. Electricity is scarcely any more vital to the motion picture than it is to the washing machine. The camera had to be weaned from the storage battery before it could go anywhere.

Closely following the advent of the Biograph machine, the Edison plant was ready to deliver the first lot of the new Edison Projecting Kinetoscopes. Edison had kept his promise to J. Stuart Blackton, that day when the young cartoonist interviewed the "Wizard of Orange." Blackton and his partner, Albert E. Smith, received Edison projector No. 13.

In November of 1896 Blackton and Smith began giving exhibitions with their machine. They listed a program which included: *Sea Waves at Coney Island, Blackton, the Evening World Cartoonist, The Bad Boy and the Garden Hose, Shooting the Chutes* and *Fire Engines Responding to an Alarm.*

Smith and Blackton prospered in their little way with their Projecting Kinetoscope, but they felt the spur of creative impulse. Buying pictures ready made from Edison was not enough. Blackton as an artist and cartoonist was a maker of pictures at heart. Smith's works of magic and spirit cabinet marvels were founded, as with all performances of the kind, on special contrivances and a considerable mechanical ingenuity.

Given this situation and opportunity something was sure to result. It did.

Smith contrived a housing for the intermittent mechanism of the Edison projecting machine, and lo, it was a camera!

There was a deal of tinkering to be done, but Smith made the thing work at last. Together the young entertainers made some trial strips of pictures in the streets, recording interesting bits of action. Then they were overtaken with a most revolutionary idea. They decided to make a synthetic event, to have something happen especially for the camera, a bit of a story. This project was close to the photoplay idea.

Now to be comfortably safe from street crowd interference and to get ample light for their versatile projection machine which doubled as a camera, Smith and Blackton chose the roof of the Morse Building at 140 Nassau street above the little ten by twelve office of their business, for a studio.

The story was conceived to fit the existing facilities. The scenario is in the title, *The Burglar on the Roof*, produced in the autumn of 1897.

Smith as the technical expert operated the camera, which rather forced the stellar rôle of the burglar on his partner, Jimmy Blackton.

Blackton was supported in the title rôle by a cast which included Mrs. Olsen, the janitress of the Morse Building, Ernest Oakes, the Blackton-Smith office boy, Ronald A. Reader, and any miscellaneous persons who could be induced to invest lunch hour time. The massive production when completed occupied forty-five linear feet of film, or about as much as the credit titles which tell who painted the sets and cranked the camera on a modern multiple reel super-drama.

Smith and Blackton now felt that they had put a considerable inventive hand into the motion picture business. They had to have a name of their own for the results. "Vitascope" was an established name, but it was hardly to be appropriated with impunity. They decided on "Vitagraph." And that was the origin of a name which conspicuously survived in the motion picture industry, until 1925.

So in Vitagraph's Latin and Biograph's Greek the screen labelled itself "life writer" in two languages, both dead. This was, the reader will doubtless be pleased to learn, the last of nearly a century of borrowings and fabrications from classic terminology. Since the day of Vitagraph's birth motion picture word coinages have been mostly indigenous, contemporary, ready, and usually rough, Americanisms. The day of Dædaleums, Phenakistoscopes, Stroboscopes and Zoopraxographology was over when the motion picture escaped from the bewhiskered savants of the laboratories. After long struggles the processes of the photo-synthesis of the optical evidences of the phenomena attendant upon the transmogrification of objects in space have been boiled down to merely "the movies." We have passed all the high hurdles.

The motion picture has been invented, christened, and sent out to go to work.

CHAPTER TWENTY-NINE

BARNUM'S GRANDSON ENTERTAINS

THE art of the screen was a full eight months old when it experienced the spicy tang of its first sensation,—a choice affair of beauty, wine, and song, and dance, emblazoned with famous names.

It was the Seeley dinner of distinguished memory, a classic of gay and naughty days in the New York of yesterday.

The sensation, with its names high and low and its splashes of dramatic color, was so much greater than the film art of the day that the tradition, in popular acceptance, has lost all reference to the motion picture's participation in its striking sequences.

The facts as they appear in the ample records present a glimpse of the glories of the '90's calculated to inspire mingled mirth and envy, rather than to transmit a shock today.

It appears that Herbert Barnum Seeley, a blithe young man about town, had inherited the interesting sum of $444,444.40 by the bequest of his grandfather, the late Phineas T. Barnum, better known as P. T. Barnum, America's first super-salesman. A glance at the figures taken from contemporary accounts would indicate that 4 cents were missing, but that minor statistical detail can be passed at this late date. It also appears that Herbert Barnum Seeley felt impelled to give a stag dinner to his brother, Clinton Burton Seeley, as the date of that young man's approaching wedding to a New York society belle grew near. It was to be the young man's farewell to bachelorhood. It was,—and never, since Tosti wrote his, has there ever been a more famous farewell.

If the diligent student will give his attention to a row of calf-bound dinner books in the present offices of Louis Sherry, Inc., he will find one dated 1896, and near the end of it a page written in a fine copperplate script suggesting the hand of an old French clerk on which there is the following notation:

NAME—Mr. H. Seeley   22 persons
DATE—December 19, 1896   TIME—9.00 P.M.
MENU
Huitres
Potage Marmite
Les Hors d'Oeuvres
Terrapin
Champignons Sauté a la Russe
Selle de Mouton a l'Anglaise
Legumes Japanaise   Pommes Château
Ris de Veau a la Grammon
Soufflé a la Yorkshire aux Moeilles
Paté en Croute
Artichauts Hollandaise
Sorbet in Glasses
Grouse Roti
Salade Celeri
Glacé Surprise
Gateaux   Bonbons
Fromage   Fruit   Café
Piano on floor—Large chairs, Stage, Crash on floor, round table with center cut out and plants on floor, electric light.
Chablis, Cliquot-Brut, Sherry and Pommard Cocktails (Manhattan & Martini) Flowers

By order of LOUIS SHERRY

For these thirty years the Seeley dinner has been a whispered reference in gossip of the sinful Babylonian grandeurs of those wicked days. Remember it was years before the coming of the cabaret, years and years before the invention of the night club. It belonged to the era when all virtue was grey and all joy was pink, in the American code. Also, wealth conveyed a presumption of vice.

The menu with its wine list is sufficient in itself to indicate the dinner as an affair for gentry of substance and taste, and to place the function too poignantly in the remote, glamored past of the old New York.

However, we have not come to a mere prattle of drinks and delicatessen, but to larger affairs of great import in the world of art.

Phipps & Alpuente, theatrical agents, were employed to supply divertissements befitting this Roman occasion. The symptoms appeared to call for dancers and dancing.

Now the most famous of all dancers at the moment was Annabelle-the-Dancer, star of the gorgeous, shimmering, silken serpentine of music hall delight, star of the Edison pictures graced by her name,—and the toast of Broadway.

Also Annabelle was seventeen and beautiful.

Bear in mind that Annabelle was not famous because she was in the motion pictures. She was in the motion pictures because she was famous.

But the circulation of the hundreds of films of Annabelle, in her Butterfly dance, through the peep show Kinetoscopes and again, with the coming of projection, on the screen, had carried her Broadway fame out to the nation and even overseas.

It will be well not to jump at conclusions about Annabelle and her relation to the Seeley dinner. It seems that a number of persons did, with unpleasant consequences, including injustice to her. The Seeley saga of some thirty years is generally wrong.

Contemporary accounts relate that a representative of the theatrical booking agents employed to decorate the dinner with acts asked Annabelle to appear, specifying details of the desired performance.

Annabelle did not appear.

The dinner went on in the small and private ballroom at Sherry's, Fifth Avenue and Thirty-seventh street, beginning at the scheduled hour of nine o'clock, with drawn shades, and proceeding merrily from *huitres* to *café* and from *Martinis* to *Pommard* in hospitable abundance.

Among the guests on this memorable occasion the newspapers of the day listed Stanford White, Horatio Harper, Marmaduke Tilden, Wilson Marshall and others of names equally distinguished in New York's world of art, science, society and letters.

While they had failed to book the première danseuse, the program was so bounteously, and perhaps so delightfully, filled that she was hardly to have been missed.

The feast of Belshazzar, before that memorable subtitle warning flashed on the wall, could not have been merrier.

It was mellow midnight of the Saturday before Christmas in the year of 1896. There was Cliquot-Brut and Pommard. There was music. There were girls, and there was dancing. There was laughter and on occasion well timed patters of applause. Everything was good—and getting better, fast.

Where the windows of Sherry's faced the streets they were blank and dark behind the heavy shades. There was no gleam of warm brilliance within straying out into Fifth Avenue, now still and deserted save for the cruising horse-cabs expectantly angling for belated fares.

Down the street came a rigidly erect, stiff gaited man in blue.

He walked briskly, with eyes fixed ahead on Sherry's and sniffing from afar. Behind him, right flank rear, followed two policeman with their night sticks.

The man ahead, as any one might have known by the mutton-chop whiskers, was Captain Chapman of the Tenderloin police station. Later, famous as Inspector Chapman, he was always to be found either there or on the first page of the newspapers.

At Sherry's the patrolmen caught up with the officer in command. At a whispered word they deployed and took up positions. Chapman tried the door. It was locked. He did not rap, but stood waiting. Faint, muted music from within reached his ears.

In time the door opened slightly as a menial appeared to whistle for a hansom. Chapman pushed through, called to his men, sprang inside and up the steps toward the ball room. His uncertain but hurried steps found him, with his men at his heels, in the dressing room occupied by the entertainers.

All was excitement.

Screams, squeals, curses and flashing draperies!

Guests from the dining table poured into the dressing room with an angry buzz of voices, strident with the fervor of Pommard.

Little Egypt, with all her beads a-glisten, quivered in excited rage, and a borrowed make-up towel. A great deal of dressing was done in the dressing room in a brief period, if accounts be correct.

"Outrageous, outrageous! Officer, what does this mean?"

The distinguished guests gasped, caught their breath and flamed in ire.

Policemen in Sherry's!

The world had not known such a horror since the Commune.

There were words upon words.

"Shame, shame," Chapman snorted as the dancing girls scattered. He strode out.

Monday an incensed prominent citizenry made complaint against Captain Chapman at the office of Theodore Roosevelt, police commissioner. It was charged that Chapman had without cause or purpose invaded the privacy of a dinner attended by a group of gentlemen whose very names were an earnest of its absolute and unassailable propriety.

It leaked to the newspapers. Everybody was interviewed.

The *New York Daily Tribune* appeared Tuesday morning, December 22, 1896, with a highly unbiased account under the headline "The Invasion of Sherry's." This article did, however, quote Chapman with great clarity of terms:

> William S. Moore of No. 207 West 40th Street came to me and said his daughter had been asked to dance at the performance at Sherry's, and to drop her skirts and appear nude before the guests at the dinner after the dance.

The *Tribune* took occasion to remark that the Barrison Sisters' act on the public stage was also admitted to be a strong number, presumably for the purpose of indicating that the Seeley dinner was not so bad.

From here on the plot begins to jell definitely. William S. Moore was the step or foster-father of Annabelle-the-Dancer. He was also a vaudeville and theatrical booking agent in competition with Phipps & Alpuente.

A great deal of conversation and some hearings were had. Moore told of Annabelle insulted and in tears. Captain Chapman stayed on the force to flourish for years of spectacular service along The Great White Way.

Incidental to the excitements of the case the newspapers found and interviewed E. P. Whitford, father of Annabelle, a Postal telegraph operator in Chicago.

Annabelle was considerably annoyed at the limelight and attention of the press, which however worked no harm to her theatrical fame. She now became an outstanding personage whose every move was an item of queenly importance. As the girl who did not dance at the Seeley dinner she became better known than any of the girls who did.

When Annabelle's pet guinea pig died, the wake was worth a column of newspaper space.

When Annabelle was arrested for speeding on her bicycle on upper Broadway March 21, 1897, she was a Page 1 feature. It is worth chronicling that she was accused of doing fifteen miles an hour right in the middle of the street. She was excused.

But the significant reaction was in the affairs of the films.

Raff & Gammon had a considerable stock of her *Butterfly Dance* pictures. The price had been ten dollars each. After the Seeley dinner they closed out the lot at one dollar a foot, or forty dollars the copy. And the Edison laboratories got a rush order for more.

Annabelle had become the highest priced film feature in the world.

It does not seem to have occurred to any one to make a new and longer picture of Annabelle to meet the new demand. The motion picture did not even slightly suspect its own possibilities then. A similar event of today might easily result in a six reel feature and a long term contract.

Annabelle went on to further fame on the stage. In 1899 she appeared with Olga Nethersole in *Sappho* and at Miss Nethersole's instance changed her name from Moore to Whitford. For some years Miss Whitford appeared in Ziegfeld's *Follies*, ending at last in 1912 with a valedictory appearance in Chicago and a farewell dinner at Al Hausman's marble walled emporium in Monroe street. There were *Follies'* beauties for place cards along the bar spread as a banquet table, with sculptured marble fauns at either end. That week Annabelle was married, to leave the stage for a home by the lake shore in Chicago's smart North Side. Never since 1895 has she been photographed for the films.

Unlike the careers of so many later alumni of the *Follies*,

Annabelle's romance has proved happy and enduring. This is perhaps a testimonial to the well poised discretion which enabled her to move through the hectic excitements of the girl-show stage untouched and leave behind in the record only a reproof for speeding on a bicycle.

Tradition is always subject to the hazy faults of the public mind, however, and in the years between there has been a deal of word of mouth telling and some newspaper writing which erroneously indicate that Annabelle was among those present at the Seeley dinner. More than twenty years ago she found it necessary to write a New York publisher, saying:

> You are aware of the facts of the case and they are that I was never present and that the publicity of the affair was caused by my step-father, Mr. Moore. At that time I was hardly old enough to know the proper thing to do.

Herbert Barnum Seeley's career was at flood tide in 1896. He scattered the heritage from his grandfather to the winds of whim—baccarat at Basle, roulette at Monte Carlo, races at Longchamps. In 1905 the host of the famous dinner at Sherry's stood behind a wicket and sold tickets at the New York Hippodrome. A few years later he died in a village in Maine. His dinner had been worth pages; his obituary took a stick and a half of type.

This was the screen's first contact with sensation. It was not enough to teach the picture makers the nature and market value of fame and beauty. They might have known then that nothing is worth photographing for the screen but a pretty girl. This would have saved many years.

THE FIRST FAMOUS GIRL of the screen, Annabelle Whitford
Moore, known as *Annabelle-the-Dancer*, who did the *Butterfly Dance* for Edison's Kinetograph, and afterward came to
fame when her refusal to dance at the Seeley dinner caused
a raid on Louis Sherry's famous restaurant.

H. R. H. Prince of Wales' first screen appearance — from a
fragment of American Mutoscope & Biograph Company
film, made by Joseph Mason about 1901.

CHAPTER THIRTY

"EDISON, JR.," ON THE SPANISH MAIN

THE men of destiny of the motion picture were mostly unknown even to themselves in 1896. Many of them entered as casuals of adventure, embarked upon something which might prove to be either a puddle or an ocean.

Edwin S. Porter, able seaman and electrician, came ashore in the spring of 1896 with his discharge papers from the U. S. Navy and a notion that somewhere he would find opportunity in the unfolding technical era.

Porter packed his salt water togs in his ditty bag, donned "cits" and looked about New York. The horseless carriage seemed to promise development and excitement, and he came near to trying out as a motor mechanic. But from the home town, Connellsville, Pa., he had some word about this marvelous thing, the Vitascope. Paine and Balsley, fellow townsmen of the Porters, had invested in the machine with enthusiastic anticipations.

So it came that Porter presented himself to Raff & Gammon, the Vitascope agents. Since the young sailor admitted a certain familiarity with electrical devices he was greeted as an expert and put to work, operating the projectors at Vitascope exhibitions around New York.

As the summer wore on Porter observed the rising strife of competition and infringement. He, with the rest of the Raff & Gammon men, began to look about with an eye to the next move. It was evident to them that the Vitascope interests would be unable to prevail in their effort at monopoly. The

—341—

motion picture was going to be either a free field or a free-for-all field at least.

While he was in this incipient state of mind Porter struck up an acquaintance with one Harry Daniels, a specialist in ventriloquism, catch-as-catch-can showmanship, and the retail merchandising of patent medicines. Daniels had recently done well with electric belts and Indian Miracle Oil down in the Carribean sea countries. He was so favorably impressed with the region that he suggested to Porter that it would be profitable to invade the Spanish Main with the new magic of the living pictures.

As partners, Porter and Daniels bought a Projectorscope from Kuhn and Webster's newly organized International Film Company and set sail for the ports of the ancient galleons.

The first showing was in Jamaica. There Daniels and Porter picked up an interpreter for the Spanish regions. The interpreter was a negro who had gone into the West Indies with "Black Patti," the singer. He had found Costa Rica his idea of a country and San José his ideal of a capital, and so elected to remain to impress the dark population with his imported metropolitan airs and accents. The interpreter urged playing San José, capital of his adopted country.

The motion picture attraction was greeted with impressive officialdom and gold lace at San José. The Government Theatre was leased for a term of eight weeks. This fact alone amazed the Costa Rican capital. The best travelling show that the island republic had ever seen had managed only a week of business there.

The palm lined avenues were billed for the coming show, "personally conducted by Mr. Thomas A. Edison, Jr." The Mr. Edison, Jr., was Edwin S. Porter's nom de plume of showmanship adopted for use in foreign parts only.

The projection booth was installed, and curtained, behind the gilded presidential box. The opening night brought a packed house. The Costa Ricans were out in ornate strength. Every smart dandy of San José carried a cane.

When the first picture went on the screen there was an impressively deep silence. It continued for tense minutes after the picture ended and the curtain went dark.

"It's a frost," Porter whispered to Daniels, as they made ready for the next picture.

Just then the storm broke loose. Costa Rican applause consists of battering down the opera house with the canes.

The rapping of the canes crashed like musketry at close range and roared up in volume to the tune of artillery.

Then came a hush and cries rang out.

"Edisan, Meester Edisan, Edisan."

San José just would have its curtain calls answered.

"Edisan, Edisan!"

Porter, boiling in the bath cabinet projection room in the reeking tropic night, was stripped to the waist as he worked at the machine.

He started another picture.

Again the rapping of the canes and the calls, "Edisan, Edisan!"

Quickly Porter shut down the machine and, snatching a curtain for a towel, hastened into his clothes. He dashed out of the theatre around to the stage entrance and shortly stepped out before the curtain, bowing with damp dignity.

He bowed through the thunderous applause and hurried back to the booth to run the next picture, undressing again with one hand as he cranked the Projectorscope with the other.

When the show was over His Excellency, Señor Rafael Iglesas, the president of the great Republic of Costa Rica, and his staff visited the projection booth, where "Thomas A. Edison, Jr.," was surprised in the act of putting on his shirt again.

By august invitation a special showing of the projectorscope was given by "Mr. Thomas A. Edison, Jr." at the presidential palace the following day. By way of appreciation he was presented with a handsomely printed official pass on the state railways of Costa Rica by the president.

But back at the National Theatre the gendarmes waited. "Thomas A. Edison, Jr.'s" name was written large in a most imposing warrant. He was arrested and marched off to court, amazed and wondering.

Through the dark interpreter it was finally learned that the charge was violation of one of Costa Rica's most sacred statutes.

It was ordained and provided in the code that immediately prior to the opening of any opera, drama, musical entertainment, show or other diversion given in the National Theatre of the Republic of Costa Rica, three aerial bombs should be fired in rapid succession from the battery of mortars in the plaza before the theatre.

This the aforesaid "Thomas A. Edison, Jr.," had utterly and negligently failed to do, knowing naturally nothing about the laws in such case made and provided. He was thereupon fined by the court in the total sum of fifty Costa Rican dollars, the same being $21.55 in New York exchange.

The second evening of the show was made pleasant to Porter by a coffee planter millionaire who approached "Mr. Edison, Jr.," right after seeing Annabelle do the *Butterfly Dance* in the pictures. The coffee planter desired to go back stage at once. He handed "Mr. Edisan" a ten dollar American note. Porter accepted it and applied it to the fine account.

At the close of the show the planter-johnny, crestfallen and annoyed extremely, expressed the conviction that the performance was a mere illusion. The wings and star dressing rooms were sadly vacant. The whole show was in a tin can. This was a great dramatic discovery that the planter and a good many others did not recognize at the time.

In the spring of 1897 Edwin S. Porter concluded his career as "Thomas A. Edison, Jr." in the West Indies and returned to New York to see what might be stirring by way of new opportunities in the picture industry with which he had cast his lot.

As he had expected, Porter found something that was truly new. Kuhn & Webster, from whom he had bought his Projectorscope and West Indian rights, were engaged in making the first advertising films. Porter was employed to handle the projection of these pictures on a screen billboard facing Broadway at Thirty-fourth street, Herald Square. The pictures were made for a Scotchman who conceived the idea and owned the venture. Although his name has been lost to memory, the merit of his advertising lingers in the recollection that his first account was the bonny, brave Haig & Haig highland whiskey. Other groceries of the day advertised on the screen were Pabst's Milwaukee beer and Maillard's chocolate.

From nightfall until midnight Porter ground off the advertising films from a little coop on the top of the Pepper Building. The advertising was interlarded with short bits of current subjects and the brief topical snatches of the day. The machine was behind the screen, a large translucent fabric sheet.

The pictures stopped the Broadway crowds. Throngs formed at vantage points up and down the street. The car tracks were blocked and the sidewalks filled to impassability. Pickpockets fattened on the crowds.

The exhibitors of motion pictures in the adjacent amusement houses were also displeased with this public broadcasting of their medium of profit. Somebody said a word at the Tenderloin police station.

A few nights went by and then Porter, looking out from his

projection coop, in the midst of a showing, saw Inspector Chapman, the hero of the Seeley dinner raid, in all the glory of his side whiskers, coming stealthily over the roof, accompanied by a uniformed squad.

Porter was arrested on a charge of blocking traffic and marched to court. That was the end of the venture, the first showing of advertising films.

Porter and Daniels then trooped off with their Projectorscope, attaching themselves to the then celebrated Wormwood's Dog and Monkey Show, on a tour of Nova Scotia and Quebec. They obtained from Lumière the first prints of the films of Queen Victoria's Jubilee celebration available for import to America, as a special attraction for Canadian showings.

On his return to the United States, Porter, by now well launched in the main current of showmanship, came in contact with William L. Beadnell, who handled the advertising and promotional affairs of the Eden Musee for Rich G. Hollaman. Motion pictures had become an important part of the Eden Musee shows, and, owing to the aggressive interest of Hollaman, the institution was becoming something of a center of motion picture activity.

This is not to be accepted as merely coincidental happening. The Eden Musee with its wax-work reproductions of persons of fame and events of saga quality was most definitely, even if not entirely consciously, seeking to adopt, for its original and continuing purpose, the new method for re-creating the event—the films. The Eden Musee was not seeking radical novelty and innovation in entertainment, if we view the matter in strictest analysis. More accurately, it was seeking the greater efficiency of the new mechanism for purveying identically the same thrills and the same emotions to the same audience. The mobile, living pictures appealed as the inevitable successors to the wax images and narrative paintings. The screen had come to the

Musee to add the fourth dimension of time to its pictorial re-creations.

The Eden Musee institutionalized the purposes and materials of art in their most primitive form presented for the most primitive audiences. It represented the purest flowering in the late nineteenth century of the prehistoric forms of expression—cave sculpture. It was inevitable, through the early years before the motion picture had attained an institution of its own, that the Eden Musee should become pre-eminently the most important motion picture show-house in the world, and the most consistent patron of the screen art.

While elsewhere motion pictures were flitting from hall to hall in fitful lyceum stage appearances, and occupying the place of a turn in vaudeville programs, the Eden Musee, beginning in that first year of 1896, provided a permanent showing and an exclusiveness of attention and policy accorded the films nowhere else in the world. Operation under that policy continued for nineteen years, or until the growing screen claimed for its own all of the public served by the neolithic art of the old Musee sculptures.

Hence there is no surprise in finding Rich G. Hollaman, as the executive head of the Musee, experimentally dealing with the new medium of the old sagas. Hollaman was not content to be merely a consumer of the film wares offered. As the screen's most ardent exponent and the most consistent purveyor of the films to the public, he was first to feel the pressure of demand for better film expression. Forces of which he was for the time an instrument now arose to extend their influence down through all the motion picture history to come.

One of the first of the expressions of this fecund interest was an effort at better projection machine under the patronage of Hollaman. Frank Cannock, a mechanic trained in the Singer sewing machine plant in Scotland, set to work on it. Cannock was a very personification of Scotchness and exactness. His notion of the requirements of machine fitting placed the thousandth part of an inch as the limit of latitude and on important parts a ten thousandth was his customary requirement. This unrelenting pursuit of perfection was in time the undoing of Cannock, but for his day he served the screen well. The foundation which his work established has given the industry its standard projection machine.

Beadnell and Porter became interested in and connected with this machine project under the auspices of the Eden Musee. Porter presently entered into the service of the Musee as operator of the motion picture equipment.

A tiny, obsolete, but still competent, projection machine which saw service in the old Eden Musee now stands in the private laboratory where Porter, after many years of screen adventures, long presided as the executive head of the Precision machine company manufacturing the Simplex projector of modern theatre equipments.

The film supply of the Eden Musee in this early period was as comprehensive as the world supply would permit. Hollaman indulged in large purchases and importations. In addition to all the available American films the Eden Musee purchased the output of Melies and Lumière in France, Robert W. Paul in London, and even the intermittent, tentative products of Charles Pathé in Paris.

It was inevitable under this policy, made necessary if the program were to be kept up to standard with frequent changes, that there should be an accumulation of picture films physically still in working condition but no longer useful in that theatre.

Here was the first obtrusion of the primary problem of motion picture distribution, and the first evidence of the opportunity upon which the film distributing system of the industry of to-day has been erected, after years of travail.

The immediate results in 1897 were more interesting than important.

William T. Rock, whom we have seen operating in New Orleans as one of the purchasers of the Vitascope, was a resourceful and observant person. In his comings and goings in New York he noted this accumulation of the films by the Eden Musee.

Rock sought out Porter, custodian of the Musee's films, and paid him a great deal of attention. There was a great lavishness of dinners at M. Mouquin's restaurant, with an abundance of game and wine of vintages which made that establishment famous.

Rock was in consequence enabled to borrow a great deal of film. It would perhaps have been quite as much a bargain to have bought second hand films outright from Raff & Gammon or their competitors, but that simple operation did not so appeal to the bargaining instincts of "Pop" Rock. We are therefore at least approximately warranted in recording that the first film exchange operations were established on a barter and bottle basis, as simple, primitive and effective as the Puritan method of buying furs with West India rum.

Meanwhile, Porter is a person to be borne in mind. He appears often and importantly in the development of the screen.

The screen was furtively seeking its avenue to the public. The showing in the vaudeville theatres, Porter's side show venture with the Wormwood Dog and Monkey Show, the street showing of advertising pictures, and the Eden Musee's daily picture show were all faltering efforts toward the institution of the motion picture theatre as we know it today.

In the summer of 1897 something very closely approaching the motion picture theatre appeared. From Scandinavia came Alexander F. Victor, a traveling magician, billed as "The Great Victor." Like Melies in France, Victor saw in the motion picture the suggestion of new possibilities of magic. He set a machinist to work on a camera with which he hoped to achieve new screen wonders. By way of gaining more familiarity with the new medium he determined to experiment with a show to be devoted exclusively to motion pictures.

Victor found a merchant in Newark, New Jersey, with a store room standing idle while awaiting equipment and stock. There Victor opened his picture show with an Edison Projecting Kinetoscope and a miscellany of films, including *The Black Diamond Express,* which was Edison's reply to the challenging popularity of Biograph's *Empire State Express.* The little theatre boasted two hundred seats and charged an admission of twenty-five cents. Victor found it necessary to strengthen the program by booking Bowman's Military Band. There was the embryo of the big theatre orchestra idea of film presentation to-day.

This first store-show was short-lived. Patronage began to wane for lack of new films of sufficient interest. The productive ability of the motion picture had not yet reached ability to support a theatre. Before the season ended the merchant claimed his leasehold and the little film show gave way to the first of the chain of Hilton clothing shops.

Alexander Victor took to the road with his pictures and his magic. A few years later a fire halted his showmanship, and Victor turned to the application of his mechanical skill to invention, adding importantly to the beginnings of the present flood of electrical appliances. One of the first and perhaps the very first of electric washing machines was invented by Victor. More recently he has turned again to motion picture devices. The magician has become strictly utilitarian.

As the motion picture went down into its second year, 1897, its reduction to commercial practice tended to bring about betterments and refinements in its equipment, most notably the projectors. One of the major faults of the early shows was the tendency of the film to slip "out of frame." This is a projection accident that still occasionally occurs in the poorer theatres, due now to carelessness rather than the equipment. In the beginning the uneven shrinkage of film stock and maladjustments of the machines often so marred the projection that it was necessary to shut down the exhibition for several minutes and reset the mechanism. The audience resented this, inevitably, and the development of the business was seriously hampered.

Albert E. Smith, partner of J. Stuart Blackton in the American Vitagraph project, meditated at length on the problem involved. Smith was the technical genius of the partnership, bringing to the screen all of the skill of his spirit cabinet miracles, dependent mostly on clever mechanics. Smith was returning to New York from a western exhibition in which he had especially troubled with "miss-frames" when an idea for a movable framing aperture which could be adjusted while the machine was still in operation occurred to him. In the shop on Nassau street he built and applied the invention. The resulting advantage to the Vitagraph was tremendous. It was enough to give Blackton and Smith a large advantage for the months in which they enjoyed the exclusive use of their method, and might, without too much of a stretch of fact, be credited as a deciding factor in the career of the famous Vitagraph.

In due season the framing device appeared on the other projectors, without immediate compensation to Smith. He was to profit from it importantly in the end, but that is many a chapter ahead.

In less than three years, riding on a train that same return journey to New York, Smith once again had a revolutionary inspiration. He was now puzzling over the flickering quality of motion pictures, their major remaining screen fault.

As Smith regarded the New Jersey meadow landscape through

the train window he noted the similarity of the screen flicker to that produced by the sweeping past of the telegraph poles. And again as the train flashed through a station he compared the slow flicker of the poles with the dancing but almost imperceptible flicker on the line of vision as he looked through the picket fence separating the tracks. This gave him the notion of dividing up the flicker of the motion picture by adding blades to the then single bladed shutter. He tried this out and found that by multiplying the flicker in fact he eliminated it in effect. The resulting betterment of projection was extraordinary.

So the movie shutter is related to the Pennsylvania railroad's picket fence at Manhattan transfer.

CHAPTER THIRTY-ONE

THE CHARITY BAZAAR FIRE

PUBLIC and official opinion holds a most positive opinion that motion picture film is a deadly explosive. The reputation of nitro-glycerin is trivial beside it.

Like all public dogma the strength of the conviction far exceeds the warrant of the facts. Motion picture film is in truth about as explosive and about as dangerous, pound for pound, as yellow pine shavings from a carpenter's work bench.

This widely held fear of the films, reflected in legislation, ordinances and restrictions the world over, took its beginning from the first and greatest film fire. The disaster was so terrible and spectacular that the memory of its horrors has blotted out recollection of its motion picture origin, never generally understood.

It was the Charity Bazaar fire in Paris, in the second year of the screen art.

Many a thread of history and destiny is interwoven into the story. Fate has never set a more dramatic stage for catastrophe.

The Charity Bazaar was the annual benefit function of the *Société Charité Maternelle* founded by Marie Antoinette. That fair lady of royal France was confused enough in her economics to ask "Why don't they eat cake?" but sex sympathy made her a benefactress of the poor mothers of Paris.

Probably it was the royalist origin of the Charity Bazaar which continued its existence down through the nineteenth century as a political and social relic, quite as much as an affair of charity. To be a patroness of the Charity Bazaar was to be touched with a faint glow of the glories of the Kings Louis, and it was to align one's self with the most shining of who was who.

The Charity Bazaar of 1897 was held, as had been the custom some years, in a temporary structure in Rue Jean Goujon just off the Champs Elysees, and just across the street from the imposing stables of the Baron Rothschild.

The afternoon of May 4 found the bazaar thronged with the French nobility. Debarred from politics and national affairs by Republican France, the dispossessed heirs of the monarchy were busy at society play.

The building was gay with banners and buntings. Grand dames in all the somber glory of the great lost cause were there to see and be seen, the while renewing their faith and communing in social rite with Marie Antoinette.

At four o'clock, just when the throng was at its thickest, a surge of flame shot through the building. The flimsy tar paper and light wood caught like a drift of leaves.

A chorus of piercing cries rose with the crackle of the fire. There were a few moments of panic and struggling flight from the narrow exits. Then came a hush more terrible than the cries as the voices died and the roar of the flames increased.

By five o'clock the site was a heap of ashes and horrors.

Royalist Paris began to count its dead.

The final tally was close to one hundred and eighty, of whom a hundred and thirty were nobles and notables of France.

The list of dead read like pages from the Almanach de Gotha, with the names of the Duchesse d'Alençon, sister of the Empress of Austria, Baronne Elisabeth Caruel de Saint Martin, Comtesse d'Hunolstein, Marquise de Bouthillier Chavigny, the Baronne St. Didier, Mlle. Casseron de Villenoisy, and on and on until it seemed that every great house in Europe had paid toll.

And hardly had the tidings spread over the world when word

came from Sicily of the death there of Henri Eugène Philippe Louis d'Orleans, Duc d'Aumale, the leader of the royalist hope, stricken in his exile by the news of the death of his niece, the Duchesse d'Alençon.

Paris went into profound mourning.

On the posters of the Opera, the Opera Comique, the Comedie Française and the Odeon appeared bands of white and the word *Relâche*.

At Notre Dame a great and solemn service was held for the Catholic dead.

The voice of old royalist France spoke through Père Olivier in his sermon at the cathedral, when he spoke of the victims of the fire as those "who fell as a sacrificial holocaust and in expiation of the sins of French free-thinkers."

Père Olivier did not recall, as he might have, to the benefit of the mourners there, that the Rue Jean Goujon, scene of the fire, was named to perpetuate the memory of that Jean Goujon, the artist, who was counted among the dead after the auto-da-fé à la pole-axe of St. Bartholomew's Eve.

A week later, in due deliberation, official France began to inquire into the fire, and the first inklings of the motion picture's part in the disaster appeared.

A report of a session of the Municipal Council of Paris on May 10, 1897, recites:

> M. Lepine made an interesting declaration as to the question of responsibility in the cause of the fire. He gave it as his opinion that had the building containing the cinématograph been detached from the bazaar the disaster would not have occurred. M. Lepine regretted that the nature of the cinématograph was so little known and urged that it be submitted to police regulation.

On the morning of May 13 the police commissaries of Paris received orders to send to the Prefecture of Police a list of all the motion picture machines and shows in their various districts. The Prefect of Police was in turn under "invitation by the Minister of the Interior to take measures to prevent the risks of fire in Paris theatres and music halls."

There was a strong conviction that the fire had been first seen in the region of the bazaar's motion picture show.

On the evening of May 15, M. Bellac, a cinema operator in charge of the machine at the bazaar, appeared and made a statement. He was reported by the Paris police as saying that he had found the cinematograph lamp was burning low and tried to fill it with ether. He struck a match that he might see more clearly. The vapors of the ether ignited and spread to the hangings around the apparatus, and the fire was under way.

"M. Bellac and his assistant have been allowed their liberty, provisionally," *Le Temps* reported. "The inquiry into the disaster is now closed."

If we are to credit the statements given out, it is obvious that it was not at all a film fire, but a result of the careless handling of the lamp fuel, which might as well have happened with a stereopticon show or any other use of similar illumination. But the films got the blame, and they have it yet.

Before the month was out the tradition of film peril was under way. A dispatch that went to all the newspapers in the world read:

PARIS, May 24—The dangers of the lighting of the kinematograph were again shown this afternoon. A fire broke out in a small exhibition in the Boulevard Poissonière. Fortunately only twenty persons were present. They rushed out panic stricken, as also did the operator, and nobody was hurt.

The immediate effects of the disaster upon the motion picture became apparent to all of Europe. Prejudical feeling arose to impair seriously the status of the screen in the mind of the upper classes and their followers.

The mood of the day is indicated in a letter written by an American observer in June, 1897, in which he remarked:

> It has become a sort of fashion here at present to go about in mourning garb, to avoid being seen in public assemblies and to adopt the ways of those who mourn some victim of the great fire. Pretty nearly everyone in Paris is in black, and everybody you meet was just on the point of going to the bazaar when the fire broke out. I know a young woman, a foreigner, who had gone into strictest mourning because on the eve of the disaster she was a saleswoman at one of the stalls.

It became equally unfashionable to patronize the films, and it was the height of proper emotion to shudder at so much as the mention of them.

The fire received its last considerable line of publicity when the Comtesse de Castellane, née Gould (Anna), gave a million francs for a permanent structure for the Charity Bazaar. Students of European amity might also enjoy contemporary French newspaper comment on a gift of ten thousand francs by Kaiser Wilhelm.

America got from all this Parisian excitement mainly an impression that motion pictures were extremely dangerous. Here was laid down the foundation of public opinion which has given the United States some drastic protective legislation. It is highly illegal to carry a roll of motion picture film in baggage on railways and steamships. It is entirely lawful however to carry a whole trunkful of film for hand-cameras, in rolls or packs. The composition is identical, but in strips one inch wide it acquires the curse of the cinema.

CHAPTER THIRTY-TWO

MARSHALL FIELD AND A BOOK AGENT

Up to this point our history of the motion picture has been mostly the inventors' story. Now after slightly more than a year of commercial venturings, in 1897, the influence of business men, administrators and exploiters begins to appear as an increasingly important factor. This swift following of phase upon phase has been a characteristic of the dizzy progress of the screen.

Among the first important exploiters of the motion pictures came Charles Urban, whose name became of international prominence in film affairs, and at times the symbol of considerable power.

Turning back a few years prior to the screen period under consideration, we discover this Urban, young, dignified, silk-hatted and frock-coated, evasively parleying for an interview with Marshall Field, the merchant, at his Chicago establishment.

"Your name and business?" The man in the reception room was crisp, automatic and chill. A great many called and few were chosen, at that portal.

In the days of the fullblown pride of Marshall Field as a merchant prince it was harder to see him than the Grand Lama of Lhassa as of the same date.

Urban was aware and unawed.

A man in a high hat is either gifted with sublime assurance or profound misgivings. In the '90's a high hat meant assurance.

As the reception clerk stood radiating refrigeration Urban reached for a chastely impressive card case, with the large deliberation of an important man of affairs.

"My card, for Mr. Field."

"And your business?" The clerk was insistent.

Urban looked at the interrogator with a mild, bored air.

"My business?—perhaps you might call it business—it will be discussed only with Mr. Field. It is important, urgent and strictly private."

The clerk was a shade impressed. He disappeared in the direction of Field's office.

A detective disguised, as detectives always are, in blue serge cut in reminiscence of a uniform, walked by with that obvious casualness which outshines a nickel plated police star.

Urban looked utterly through, past and beyond the plain-clothes operative. Such persons were much less than invisible to him.

The caller also noted, while not apparently noting anything, that all those who were in turn admitted to the Field offices were required to leave behind all walking sticks, parcels and the like.

The merchant prince was uneasy on his throne. His wealth and repute for wealth made him a mark for cranks. He feared dynamiters, blackmailers, cut-throats and gunmen. And this was Chicago, mind you. The weather and police records of half a century show that every day is a bomby day in Chicago.

Urban shifted a neat parcel from his lap to a concealed position under his coat where he could hold it with the pressure of his left arm.

The parcel was in the nature of a bomb for Marshall Field.

"Important, urgent and strictly private."

Those three words and a silk hat won. Marshall Field did have quite a number of affairs that were possible of classification under those headings and he decided to spend at least two costly minutes on the chance the three words were true.

Urban went past the gauntlet of secretaries, with the leisurely, assured step of one above and beyond haste. He was ushered into the presence. Field rose in welcome, out of sheer habit. Usually all but the welcome ones were filtered out before they got that far.

"Ah—Mr.—Mr. Urban?" Field read from the card, noting with a casual thumb that it was an engraved card.

Urban deposited his two gallon hat carefully on a corner of Field's desk, seated himself with graceful comfort, and produced his parcel, depositing a volume before the puzzled Marshall Field.

"I am here," Urban setforth, smiling and suave, "to give you the first opportunity in this great city of Chicago to acquire this handsome, full morocco bound de luxe edition of 'The Stage and Its Stars,' the only complete work of its kind and a remarkable value for only $125."

Field drew up in surprise.

Cornered by a book agent!

The like of that had not happened to the august Marshall Field in all the years of his kingdom. It was therefore, not an annoyance but sheer adventure. A smile chased across his face.

"Tell me," Field demanded, "how did you get into my office with that book?"

"Oh, I just brought it along," Urban replied feigning a wide innocence. "You see I could hardly hope to interest so shrewd a buyer as Marshall Field without showing the goods. I brought it because I had to—you see as soon as I have your order Mr. Otto Young over at the Fair store has agreed to subscribe for a set."

"Otto Young, eh!" Field was grinning now. He glanced idly at the volume. Here was a chance to play a practical joke on his department store competitor. That was worth a hundred and a quarter to Marshall Field any day. Urban got a check.

The rambling young Urban tired of the road and the excitements of book agenting. He went into a partnership in a stationery and bookshop in Detroit. There presently he met R. L. Thomae who had recently left the service of Raff & Gammon and the Kinetoscope Company, to take care of the affairs of the Michigan Electric Company. The Michigan concern was being absorbed by the North American Phonograph Company.

Thomae's friendship led Urban into a venture in selling phonographs. The phonograph campaign in the Michigan territory was following Edison's original idea of utility—merchandising the machine for the recording of business dictation. The notion appealed mightily to Urban who in his enthusiasm crossed the river into Canada and sold a large order of dictation machines to Hiram Walker, distiller of a straw colored whiskey of great vigor.

This and other important sales attracted the favorable attention of the home office of the phonograph interests back East, and the fame of Urban spread.

Some of the local results were more immediately interesting. The girls who typed in Hiram Walker's establishment were alarmed. They complained of "electricity in the ears" and lamented that the machines were doing their work and would soon cost them their jobs as stenographers. The best part of a stenographer's work has always been walking into the office of the boss and sitting opposite in the middle of the picture. When dictation comes from a machine at the end of an ear tube the typewriter becomes employment rather than a stepping stone to opportunity.

The girls plotted direct action.

It was that slick salesman in the silk hat, Charles Urban, who was to blame for the new peril. The girls told their beaux.

A committee of young gallants of Walkerville tried to waylay Urban with a purpose of convincing him of the unwisdom of his enterprise.

Urban sidestepped the committee and its bricks.

As a matter of strategy, Urban argued Walker into raising the salary of a few of the typists using the phonographic dictation machines, announcing it as a reward for increased efficiency. That hushed the objectors.

With the standing of his phonograph sales behind him and profits going into the bank, Urban grew more ambitious. The Michigan Electric Company brought on the Edison peep show Kinetoscope. This caught Urban's eye. Then he heard about the wonderful Vitascope and the Lumière Cinématographe in New York and went excitedly down to the metropolis to see them. Returning to Detroit he struck up a deal with the Michigan Electric Company and merged his phonograph business with theirs. The electric company at this time acquired the agency for the new Edison Projecting Kinetoscope. It will be recalled that this machine as presented in a previous chapter was a motor driven device, using an electric arc for illumination and carrying its film in fifty foot lengths in a complicated spool bank, like the old peep show Kinetoscope.

Urban jumped in with his customary enthusiasm to sell the projectors and films. After a few city sales he was blocked. Few Michigan towns had any electrical facilities whatever. The machine could not venture out beyond the arc light zone.

Salesmanship again came to the rescue. Urban hurried down to New York. He had a number of ideas for betterment of the machine. First he wanted one that could be turned by hand, and which could use an ordinary source of light, as for example the calcium or limelight that stereopticon lecturers carried. Also fifty foot films, with the interruption of rethreading the spool bank, seemed a needless annoyance. He rigged up a reel made with two pie tins and an old thread spool. He spliced films with fish glue. By this method he could run a thousand feet of film at a time, just as the Lathams had done the year before.

In New York Urban looked up Walter Isaacs, an acquaintance of phonograph days, and arranged with him to make in his New York shop a number of the new hand-driven projectors, to be known as the Urban Bioscope.

Back in Detroit Urban cut loose from the Michigan Electric Company and turned to selling the Bioscope. This machine was in all probability the first of its type, which soon became widely distributed. The Bioscopes went as fast as they could be delivered. This machine offered the possibility of taking the new motion picture out into the small towns and lumber camps. Dozens of lecturers went out equipped with Bioscopes and a stock of Edison films, which Urban continued to handle.

The successful salesmanship of Urban and his rapid orders for film led Maguire & Baucus to call him into New York and offer him the management of their London office.

When Urban inspected conditions in London he found that competition was using anti-American propaganda against his concern. He decided to change the address and become British, for trade purposes at least. The business blossomed out anew under the very English name of the Warwick Trading Company, in Warwick Court, High Holborn. The Warwick concern prospered. In time Urban acquired the business and developed a large export and import trade.

Urban was early confronted by the British demand for British film subjects, while the American product preponderated in his stock. Urban met the situation by bringing out the Warwick camera, designed at his order, to produce British pictures. This camera later figured importantly in the American film patent wars.

Urban's first British picture was made at the British naval

base at Portsmouth. He had heard enough of *Rule Britannia* to know the box office value. His edited picture was 1,200 feet long, a sensational production for 1898.

Urban went gunning against all competitors for business and cast an envious eye on the Biograph company's contract at £200 a week at the Palace theatre. He succeeded in demonstrating that the little narrow gauge Edison standard film would project as good a picture as the wide Biograph product and won the business. There at the Palace Urban presented the first consistent line of scientific pictures, under the title of *The Unseen World*. They were microphotographic studies made by Martin Duncan. One memorable subject entitled *Stilton Cheese* caused a sensation in London, which takes its cheese seriously. The picture showed the lives, loves and wars of the cheese mite. A delegation of cheese makers called on the Palace management and Urban with a demand that they destroy the film.

Protests about the pictures were nearly as common then as now. In 1902 Urban presented pictures of the coronation of King Edward VII. The exterior scenes were genuine. The actual coronation in Westminster Abbey was from a motion picture reconstruction of the event staged in Paris by George Melies. The thing was done in an imposing way, with the most pretentious set that had yet been constructed for the purposes of the films. Everything was excellent but the one little detail of the crown. It was too small for the actor who sat in the rôle of Edward VII. In the course of the ceremonies the crown skidded a trifle and created an impression that his Royal Highness was slightly jingled. There were violent denunciations of the picture and it seemed discreet not to persist in the showings.

Cecil Hepworth, whose first connection with the pictures had

CHARLES URBAN, American-British pioneer, whose patronage and promotion first gave the screen natural color in Kinemacolor productions.

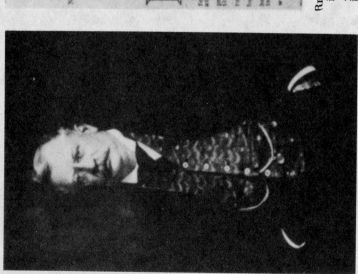

RICH G. HOLLAMAN, president of *The Eden Musee*, the first important amusement institution to become a patron of the motion picture — and producer of the first *Passion Play* film — advertisement of the Hollaman-Eaves Passion Play, appearing in the *New York Herald*, Sunday, February 6th, 1898.

been in supplying arc lamps for Paul's Theatrograph, entered the service of the Warwick concern and there evolved the first film developing machine, the ancestor of the modern devices which have eliminated hand processing in the great film laboratories of today.

CHAPTER THIRTY-THREE

THE SAGA OF CALVARY

In quest of new thrills to purvey, the motion picture stepped from combat to religion in the autumn of 1897.

The first pretentious effort of the camera was the battle of Carson City, a picture built on the glory of fight and the defeat of James Corbett.

The next to come, a few months later, was the film presentation of the saga of Calvary and the crucifixion of Christ.

This was the screen's first step toward conscious art.

The Corbett-Fitzsimmons fight was the simple recording of an event. The making of the film version of the *Passion Play* was to have been merely that, too, and by force of circumstance evolved into a more creative endeavor, the first construction of a dramatic event especially for the camera.

The step fits the evolutionary pattern of growth. In the swift passing of the months the motion picture was experiencing all the phases of development by which, down the ages, the cave-wall drawings of pre-historic man grew into language and drama, even into the letters and words upon this page.

Beginning with Edison's camera in the studio at West Orange the motion picture started to record forty foot flashes of bears, dancing girls and sundry feats of prowess by Sandow, Buffalo Bill, Indians and Mexican knife fighters. This was the Magdalenian age of the films, and the cavernous darkness of the "Black Maria" may stand for the Cro-Magnon cave of Dordogne.

With the Corbett-Courtenay fight picture, made first for the Kinetoscope and shortly thereafter projected by Latham's

Pantoptikon, the fœtal films emerged from the peep show to their first wavering steps on the public screen. And with the Corbett-Fitzsimmons fight, presented by Rector's Veriscope, the motion picture reached a scope and pretension like unto the sculptured boasts of war and chase on the ancient temple friezes from Nineveh to Luxor.

And now, with the *Passion Play*, the motion picture, in the third year of the film and the second year of the screen, was to catch step with the art of medievalism and its major saga. This was inevitable. It always happens so in art; the new medium strives until it can tell the big story. Our history of this autumn of '97 is concerned merely with how the new minstrel learned the old song.

The steps of this progression began when W. B. Hurd, American representative of the Lumière film interests, returned to New York from an excursion abroad. Hurd came announcing that he had acquired the right to photograph for the screen a folk presentation of the *Passion Play* at the village of Horitz in Bohemia. It was an annual re-enactment of the tradition-hallowed decennial performance at Oberammergau.

Because the Eden Musee had become the most conspicuous center of motion picture exhibition in the United States, Hurd first approached Rich G. Hollaman with an offer of the *Passion Play* project. The price was $10,000 and it was estimated that a like sum would be required for making the picture.

Hurd was right. Hollaman was a customer. The idea of a *Passion Play* picture fitted with extreme patness into the policy of the Eden Musee with its merchandising of the *mysterioso*, shudders and knicknacks of emotional stimuli, death masks of Napoleon, executions of wax criminals by wax elephants, an automaton chess player and a program of song and sometimes dance.

"Yes," said Hollaman, just departing on a trip,"I'll be back in ten days and close with you."

When Hollaman returned the rights had been sold to Marc Klaw and Abraham Erlanger, the theatrical producers. Here came the first endeavor of the established art-industry of the stage to reach out for the new medium of the films.

There were hot words from Hollaman when he returned.

The K. & E. expedition sailed for Horitz with "Doc" Freeman in charge, made its pictures and returned. With managerial caution the pictures were taken out of town for a try-out. The City of Brotherly Love seemed to be suitable. When the pictures went on the screen for their Philadelphia first night Rich G. Hollaman was in the audience, accompanied by Frank Russell, an actor of some note in that day. Russell was a familiar about the costume establishment of Albert G. Eaves, and Eaves and Hollaman were friends. Russell was along this night for a purpose. Something new was brewing.

Hollaman observed without overwhelming disappointment that the Horitz expedition had not been entirely successful in making a convincing picture. He was thinking of a remote affair of dramatic history, now suddenly endowed with a new importance.

Seventeen years before, Salmi Morse, a great patriarchal figure of a man, with haughty carriage and a long white beard, dramatist from San Francisco, came to establish himself on the Rialto of New York. The ambition of his eventful and adventurous life had been the production of the *Passion Play*, staged as an awe inspiring spectacle.

For years, between potboilers and odd jobs, Morse had tinkered with his script, polishing it to his ideal of perfection. Now he had come to New York, in the fullness of his years, to see it produced.

This Morse was a strange mixture, by turns an ascetic locked in his cubicle of a hall room study, and then again a bon vivant and raconteur of the merry resorts of Broadway.

Morse in his hope turned to the foremost theatrical figure of the day, Henry E. Abbey, who was remarkable in the commercial world of the theatre for his artistic ambition. His long Broadway career was marked by pinnacles of success and some deep valleys of depression. It was Abbey who presented to America the greatest artists of his generation, Bernhardt, Patti, Albani, Nordica and others well near as illustrious. Abbey was also the sincere pioneer of the Metropolitan opera.

The *Passion Play* idea presented by Morse found willing attention from Abbey. The artist-manager threw himself and his resources into the project. An old church in Twenty-third street, midway of the block west of Sixth avenue, was taken under lease and converted into a theatre. Adjacent property on the other side of the square was acquired to give the stage the extraordinary depth of a whole half block. Abbey drew Albert G. Eaves, the founder of the famous costume house, into the project. Forty thousand dollars were invested.

Salmi Morse, now on the verge of success and fame, forswore the delights of Broadway again and lived in endless vigil at the theatre. Several full dress rehearsals were given with all the brilliance of the regalia and settings. Down the amazing vistas of the great stage the invited audiences saw the old Jerusalem, the garden of Gethsemane, the scene of the Cross, all on a vast and realistic scale. Herds of camels, sheep and donkeys figured in the historic reproductions. The staging was on a scale that had never before been attempted in New York.

The play was ready and the premiere announced at the height of the season of 1880–1, when at the instance of offended religious interests the mayor of New York forbade the opening.

The world had crashed for Salmi Morse. The theatre was closed and soon Abbey gave up the lease. It was the beginning of the end of his great career. Morse abandoned hope. He went back to play-tinkering and potboiling. He was often in want.

A few melancholy years passed. Then one winter morning the police took the body of Morse out of the North River uptown.

Abbey went on through his tangle of troubles, losing ground with successive defeats, and died at last October 17, 1896, a year before the period of this chapter.

The costumes of the *Passion Play* went back to Eaves and storage to wait the new turn of fate. Along with them went the Salmi Morse manuscript of the *Passion Play*. It went into a chest along with the robes for the cast. There they stayed for sixteen years.

Hollaman, filled with ire and a desire to outdo this Klaw & Erlanger effort at Horitz, now recalled the old Morse-Abbey production.

Salmi Morse's ill-fated script was brought to light, to become the first motion picture scenario. Hollaman induced Albert G. Eaves to join in a project to produce the *Passion Play* in New York, to be a synthetic equivalent to the imported film.

The roof of the Grand Central Palace, the building in Lexington Avenue now occupied by offices of the New York Central lines, was leased for studio purposes. The agent for the structure was annoyed later when he found the freight elevator laden with camels going aloft to the new Holy Land on the roof.

The cast of the production included Frank Russell, as the *Christus*, Frank Gaylor playing *Judas Iscariot*, and Fred Strong in the role of *Pontius Pilate*.

Through an advertisement Hollaman employed William C. Paley, an Englishman who had built a camera and thus far escaped an Edison injunction.

L. J. Vincent, the venerable stage director of Niblo's Garden Theatre, was employed as director.

In December the making of the picture started on the Grand Central Palace roof. The film stock was purchased from Lumière in France, with the fear that an order placed with Eastman here would come to the attention of Edison. With their biblical costumes over heavy flannels the actors started to work in the bleak New York winter winds. There were mornings when the snow had to be swept out of the Garden of Gethsemane. Because of promotional plans, all operations were conducted with the utmost secrecy.

One of the major difficulties encountered arose from the fact that the director, the aged and authoritative Vincent, believed that he was making a series of lantern slides for stereopticon presentation. All efforts to explain to him that the camera recorded motion continuously failed entirely. It was Vincent's practice to put the company into rehearsal and when a striking moment arrived to dash out before the camera and scream "Hold it."

There were internal reasons why Vincent could not be dismissed. Frank Russell and the camera man connived to make the picture by subterfuge. Each day after a round of futile operations under Vincent's direction Paley would cast an eye skyward and announce that the light had failed. When Vincent left for the day the company reassembled and proceeded with the picture.

The *Passion Play*, New York version, was completed early in January, 1898, in a total of twenty-one hundred feet, the most daring and, in a practical sense, the only effort toward dramatic construction that the motion picture had made.

Advertisements were placed in the New York papers announcing its first public presentation at the Eden Musee, January 30, 1898, with performances at three o'clock in the afternoon and at nine at night.

When the advertisements appeared there came a call from

Marc Klaw to Rich Hollaman. Hollaman visited the Klaw offices.

"You can't put that picture on at the Eden Musee. We own the exclusive rights," Hollaman was informed.

"Exclusive rights to the *Passion Play?*" Hollaman snorted in derision. "Who did you get them from, the original cast?"

The picture went on at the Eden Musee and Hollaman filled the first night audience with friends, showmen and the convivial spirits of Broadway. Since the art of subtitles for pictures had not yet been born it was necessary to accompany the film with the spoken word. Frank Oakes Rose was the lecturer of the *Passion Play* presentation. Musical numbers were given in the two intermissions between the three reels to add to the effect.

The *Passion Play* appears to have been a surprise, not to say shock to that first night audience.

"I knew I had them when I saw the tears in the eyes of those Broadway sports," Hollaman commented.

Frank Russell who had played *Christ* in the picture was prohibited from entering or appearing in the vicinity of the Eden Musee lest he be recognized by some keen-eyed member of the picture audience. This would have damaged the Oberammergau atmosphere considerably.

But Russell climbed a fire escape in the dark and attended his own first night incognito.

The newspaper notices were filled with high praise. The pictorial presentation of the *Passion Play* met no such opposition as the Abbey-Morse stage production had received. This was due perhaps in part to the fact that the impression was that it had been made at Oberammergau, where the ritualistic *Passion Play* had acquired the authority and sanctity of tradition.

The newspaper attentions were favorable for at least a week. Then something happened. It is not to be implied that the able house of Klaw & Erlanger had anything to do with it, but in some fashion a word leaked out to the *New York Herald* that there was a story to be had. A squad of reporters went about asking questions. Then the news broke out. The *Herald* of February 1, 1898, said:

> There was a large audience at the Eden Musee yesterday to witness what has been generally understood to be a cinématograph reproduction of scenes from the Oberammergau *Passion Play*. The spectators apparently were much interested in the pictures, and at the close generously applauded them.
>
> All the preliminary announcements of this exhibition have tended to convey the impression that this is a genuine reproduction of the celebrated *Passion Play* at Oberammergau. Of course the cinématograph has been invented since the last performance at Oberammergau. But a gentleman at the Eden Musee on last Friday, when a private exhibition of the scenes was given for the press, took the trouble to explain to a *Herald* reporter that the peasants who were accustomed to appear in the *Passion Play* at Oberammergau had been induced to go through a special performance, at which the cinématograph scenes had been taken.
>
> As the lecturer at the Eden Musee dwells upon the Bavarian performance spectators are further impressed with the idea that the pictures are directly from Oberammergau, and that the scenes are genuine reproductions of the *Passion Play*. That the public has generally been led to form this impression is evidenced by letters of inquiry regarding the matter received by the *Herald*.
>
> WHERE THE "PASSION PLAY" OCCURRED
>
> The truth is, however, that the cinématograph pictures at the Eden Musee were taken not at Oberammergau, but right here in New York on the roof of the Grand Central Palace early last December.
>
> This may lead to the supposition that the cinématograph *Passion Play* to be given at Daly's Theater during Lent is something of the same sort. The Daily exhibition, however, is genuine and the cinématograph pictures to be shown there were actually taken

at Horitz, a small town in Austria, where for many years the peasants have given performance to the *Passion Play* at stated intervals.

Mr. W. W. Freeman, who has prepared the views, says he visited Horitz last summer and persuaded the peasants to give a special performance for him and it was at that performance he secured his cinématograph pictures. To vouch for this he not only
has the contract he made with the peasants by which they agreed
to go through the performance, but also a letter from the bishop
of the diocese.

This publicity attack had no important effect on the success
of the Hollaman-Eaves *Passion Play*. Its pictorial superiority
overcame any question of authenticity with the public. Hollaman, being approached by other showmen in non-competitive
regions decided to add to the profits by selling prints of the
picture. The *Passion Play* in its twenty-one hundred feet went
on the open market at $580 a copy.

Now Hollaman and Eaves made further productions, all embodying great moral lessons, on temperance and kindred subjects. They also issued a two reel production entitled *The
Opera Martha*, accompanied by allegedly synchronized phonograph records, price $280. For reasons set forth in the next
chapter, Hollaman's films were delivered by the Edison
laboratories in West Orange.

William T. Rock was among the first customers for the *Passion Play*. He saw it as a drawing card for his Louisiana
shows.

Now that showmanship had borrowed a great dramatic
property of the church, religion came in turn to borrow of
showmanship in terms of the new art of the films.

Colonel Henry H. Hadley was a spectacular evangelist of the
day. He had first been a corporation lawyer, a New York newspaper man and latterly a reformer with a punch concerned most

with the iniquities of hard liquor. He had a message for the masses.

Colonel Hadley saw the *Passion Play* picture at the Eden Musee and decided that it contained elements of value to the pulpit. He obtained a print for the purposes of his meetings. He preached a vigorous brand of damnation and salvation with a vast fervor.

"These pictures," observed Colonel Hadley, "are going to be a great force. It is the age of pictures. See the billboards and the magazines and the newspapers; more and more pictures all the time. These moving pictures are going to be the best teachers and the best preachers in the history of the world. Mark my words, there are two things coming; prohibition and motion pictures. We must make the people think above the belt."

Colonel Hadley's first effort to bring the picture to aid the cause of religion met a churchly rebuff. He tried to put on the *Passion Play* pictures as an accessory to his preaching at Ocean Grove, New Jersey, the summer religious colony. The opinion of the community was against it. They classed all motion pictures with girls in tights and the *May Irwin Kiss.*

"Very well," said Colonel Hadley, moving his pictures over to an abandoned merry-go-round tent across the bridge from Ocean Grove at Asbury Park. "Now the virtuous citizens of Ocean Grove can come over to see the *Passion Play* without having their own precincts defiled by the moving pictures. They are new, therefore immoral."

The Ocean Grove people did cross the bridge and the picture-sermons achieved an important success. Thousands saw moving pictures in the merry-go-round gospel tent.

Colonel Hadley included a musical program with the pictures, breaking his accompanying lecture into parts. Samuel Hopkins Hadley, the evangelist's young son, a gifted tenor, sang. The musical numbers included *Ave Maria, O, Holy Night* and

The Palms. The boy tenor's voice brought him to the attention of a musical comedy producer and the *Passion Play* engagement with his evangelist father led directly to the stage.

In his second season in 1899 with the *Passion Play* pictures Colonel Hadley opened at Young's Pier in Atlantic City. The piers of that resort had a somewhat unsavory character then, and the proprietor shrewdly figured that the religious atmosphere lent by the presence of the evangelist would bring more respectability.

The following summer Colonel Hadley went on the road with the *Passion Play* pictures, taking them and his message into many small communities which had never before heard of the screen. His was undoubtedly the first use of the motion picture for propaganda.

Colonel Hadley had long since passed to his reward. His son, the boy tenor of 1888, by coincidences of his dramatic career, was drawn into pictures as a scenario editor in 1911 and is now known to Broadway as "Hopp Hadley." He is engaged in the promotion of pictures and his evangelistic days are unknown to Times Square.

The influence of the *Passion Play* and its precedents was most important. Crude as it was with its twenty and odd scenes, without titles and but a slender dramatic thread, it was a departure, even though slight, from the entirely parasitic line of production which had preceded it. A production taking up more than two reels of action had been staged for the camera. It is true that this beginning was in fact largely a recreated event, a makeshift for the rights to picture the play at Horitz, but it had enough of originality in it to open a new line of progress.

Many prints of the picture were sold when Hollaman released it to the open market. Copies went abroad and covered the world of the motion picture. The success of the Hollaman-Eaves production resulted in many similar attempts.

Sigmund Lubin in Philadelphia, who had distinguished himself by staging an imitation of the Corbett-Fitzsimmons fight with freight handlers in the fighters' rôle, came sweeping along in the march of progress and produced another version of the *Passion Play,* in close simulation of the Hollaman-Eaves picture.

Rough and ready production characterized the Lubin establishment in that primitive time. The stage was placed in a backyard in Philadelphia. A cast of nondescript actors from New York was employed. They did not take their work with any deep seriousness. "Pop" Lubin's days were full of grief. Much of his slender capital was tied up in the venture and he was desperately serious.

Midway of the picture *Judas Iscariot* betrayed the anxious producer and went on what can be described only as "a bender," while *Simon Peter* absented himself to shoot "craps" in an adjacent barn. Graphic tales are told of the troubles of "Pop" Lubin laboring to keep his twelve apostles before the camera.

Eventually the Lubin *Passion Play* was completed. It sold with some success despite some minor flaws of direction and technical detail. The picture contained elements of interest that were not in the script. Back of the stage was a dwelling. As the painted backgrounds flapped in the wind this house was occasionally revealed. Frank Tichenor, who in after years came to figure in the motion picture business, was startled to see on the screen the Philadelphia girl to whom he was paying attentions, revealed leaning out of the window to watch the actors, in the midst of one of the *Passion Play's* most impressive scenes.

"Pop" Lubin was broad minded enough to overlook such inadvertences, and if he had known that he had an anachronism in the picture he would have charged more for it.

The year of 1897 saw an ingenious effort to find a place for the motion picture in the technique of the stage by its inclusion in a drama.

The play was *The Good Mister Best,*" written by John J. McNally, the George M. Cohan of the '90's. The major interest of the piece revolved about a bit of business by which the master of the household could press a button and see revealed on the wall what was taking place in any room of the establishment. He saw plenty. The revelation on the wall was a motion picture. The film work was done by J. Stuart Blackton and Albert E. Smith with their American Vitagraph. The cast of the play included Julius P. Witmark, then an actor and singer, with his conspicuously successful career as a music publisher all ahead of him.

Witmark sang a number entitled *Sadie* that opening night of *The Good Mister Best* August 23, 1897, at the Garrick in New York, with so many encores that the *New York Times* felt called upon to remark upon the large number of his friends in the audience. The play ran a month in New York. The motion picture was not to be made an incidental property of the stage.

COLONEL HENRY HADLEY, New York attorney, journalist and evangelist, who with the *Passion Play* picture of '97 was the first to seek the screen as an aid to the pulpit.

THE VITAGRAPH TRIUMVIRATE of pioneer fame — William ("Pop") Rock, J. Stuart Blackton, and Albert E. Smith, pictured in the days of the Patents Company's glory.

CHAPTER THIRTY-FOUR

AND THEN THE FIGHT STARTED

THE morning of the seventh day of December in the year of 1897, a law clerk walked casually into the offices of the clerk of the United States Circuit Court for the Southern District of New York, and tossed down a document bound in the usual propriety and formality of a legal blue jacket.

Another clerkly person on the other side of the filing desk adjusted his glasses and inspected the document, beginning with the inscription and checking through the formidable routine of signatures, seals and attests on the last page.

This matter was discovered to be the institution of an action entitled:

THOMAS A. EDISON
    vs.
CHARLES H. WEBSTER, individually and as a member of the INTERNATIONAL FILM COMPANY; and EDWARD KUHN, individually and as a member of the INTERNATIONAL FILM COMPANY.

Thereupon the filing clerk dipped a fine nibbed Spencerian pen in blue ink and wrote the title down in a big book of ruled lines, adding the identifying notation, "In Equity, No. 6,796, Dyer & Dyer, attys for plntf."

War was declared in the land of the motion picture.

Great events have little ways—two clerks across a desk in a shabby court office, brass cuspidors, blue coated bailiffs, hatchet faced process servers, the acrid incense of Pittsburgh stogies overshot with the spice of Cremos and General Arthurs, over it all that air of dusty doomfulness which takes possession of every room dedicated to the law business of the United States of America.

This was the beginning on that seventh day of December three decades ago. Twenty years of strife, legal and illegal, were ahead. The new art of the screen was born to battle, destined to grow up in ruthless, relentless strife.

The age old jungle competition for the determination of the fit and the unfit, the lucky and the unlucky, had begun again to repeat the interminable pattern of all things in creation. All that was new was the film.

Ever since that December of 1897, nearly thirty years ago, the leaderships of the motion picture have been involved in offensive or defensive actions in the courts.

This was the fateful day when Thomas Edison began to think just slightly more of the prospects of the motion picture. He was urged and advised in this new attitude mostly by W. E. Gilmore, his new general manager, busy salvaging Edison assets from the wrack and tangle of phonograph business troubles.

Edison had expected little of the motion picture,—so little that he had allowed it to slip from his control. The peep show Kinetoscope had been put out as a catch-penny novelty, largely because Thomas Lombard had insisted. Now, behold, the screen had come, and with it hints of promise and profit.

Edison and his attorneys, Dyer & Dyer, were in hurried pursuit of the escaped maverick art, invoking the law to return it to the home corral.

The case at law was a petition for a permanent injunction to prevent Webster and Kuhn from continuing their business with the Projectorscope on the allegation that it infringed Edison's United States Patent No. 589,168.

It is just possible that Edwin S. Porter's daring in taking one of these machines on a West Indian expedition under the pseudonym of "Thomas Edison, Jr.," may have had a shade of influence toward the selection of Kuhn & Webster for the opening attack. More likely, however, it was the clearness of the case to be made against them that made their concern the first objective of the offensive. Anyway, it was just a beginning.

This same day a similar action was instituted against Maguire & Baucus, naming personally Joseph D. Baucus, president, Frank Z. Maguire, vice president, and William M. Payton, secretary. This concern, as we have noted, entered the business as Edison's agents for the introduction of the peep show Kinetoscope in England and Europe. Now it was bringing European films back to the United States to compete with the output of the Black Maria at West Orange.

In the next few weeks Dyer & Dyer opened up a bombardment of suits, intended to sweep the American field clean. On January 10, 1898, in the United States Court for Eastern District of Pennsylvania, Edison sued to enjoin Sigmund Lubin who had begun business in Philadelphia with equipment purchased from C. Francis Jenkins, and in the Northern District of Illinois brought action against Edward H. Amet of Waukegan, maker of the Magniscope. On February 8 the papers were served on the Eden Musee American Company in Twenty-third street, New York, home of the wax works with the death mask of Marie Antoinette and the Chamber of Horrors. Rich G. Hollaman, the Musee's president, was remembered with a personal subpœna in addition.

The Eden Musee was using what Edison considered outlaw films and projecting machines. Further, that secretly produced *Passion Play* picture was now perfectly well known to have been made in New York, obviously with a camera that did not bear the authority of Edison.

Edison had sold no cameras and intended to sell none.

The picture was running at the Musee and the *New York*

Herald's exposé story had been printed a week before. The case against the Musee appeared to be definite.

In the face of this Hollaman was pondering on the problem of putting prints of his *Passion Play* on the market. This court fight promised to tie up his project. At this juncture Frank Z. Maguire of Maguire & Baucus appeared with words of advice.

"If you turn your negative over to Edison and buy your films from him, it might be different," Maguire suggested.

Hollaman sent the *Passion Play* negative to West Orange and lived happy ever afterward. The service of the subpœna in the Edison suit was the last entry ever made in that docket.

Edison was out after everybody in sight, now. On February 16 he sued Marc Klaw and Abraham Erlanger, theatrical magnates, for their audaciousness in sending "Doc" Freeman to Horitz to bring back a picture of the *Passion Play*. A month later Augustin C. Daly was discovered to have film ambitions and had his name inscribed on the court docket downtown under that fatal patent No. 589,168. The next week, on March 22, it was considered time to stop the activities of Walter S. Isaacs of New York, phonograph mechanic, who had made Urban's portable Bioscope and was now making machines for anybody.

This was just a fair start. Now that they had their tools whetted, Dyer & Dyer set out for the bigger timber. On May 13 they started the most momentous line of litigation in all the litigious history of the screen, the case entitled:

THOMAS A. EDISON

vs.

AMERICAN MUTOSCOPE COMPANY
and BENJAMIN F. KEITH.

This also was instituted in the United States Court in New York, an action in equity, No. 6928, seeking to enjoin the Mutoscope concern from an alleged infringement of the Edison camera patent. Benjamin F. Keith, the Boston vaudeville magnate, was made a party to the suit because his theatres in New York, Boston and elsewhere were the principal customers of the American Mutoscope's new projection machine service, the American Biograph.

Superficially this case at the time looked like all the rest. Actually however it was much more important. Remember that William Kennedy Laurie Dickson, Edison's laboratory assistant in the pre-screen days, had gone over to the K. M. C. D. Syndicate which had given birth to the Mutoscope peep show and the Biograph screen machine. Bear in mind too that this American Mutoscope Company was at this time, May 1898, the only motion picture enterprise in the world which was directly connected with the great institution of organized capital and big business. This was an incidental but vital result of the financing in which Koopman had interested downtown New York.

The American Mutoscope was therefore better fortified both in the technology of the motion picture and in the craft of big-business-at-law than any other motion picture enterprise in the world against which Edison could press his claims. This defendant was an intrenched corporation.

The inevitable result was one of the longest and most desperate patent fights in the history of American industry. We shall find that this lawsuit begun May 13, 1898, has exerted a determining influence on most subsequent motion picture history. It was the whimsical destiny of this action that Edison was to fail ultimately in his effort to suppress Biograph, and in failing to win a vast success.

The next day the subpœnas were served and an appearance for the American Mutoscope Company was entered by its attorneys, John T. Eason and the firm of Kerr, Curtis & Page. Lawyers were now beginning to appear in battalions.

While the lawyers struggled with motions and arguments H.

N. Marvin of the American Mutoscope & Biograph company sought a commercial solution which came near to changing the whole course of motion picture history. He recognized that the only hope of prosperity in the films was a peace, and that there could be no peace without Edison. By secret and private negotiation with Edison, Marvin on April 12, 1900, secured an option to buy the entire Edison motion picture interests for a half a million dollars. It would have meant control of the industry for the life of the patents. Marvin paid down $2,500 on his option and arranged a bank loan for the coming payments.

With melodramatic fatality a few months later, on the day when the first payment, a sum of $300,000, was due, the bank failed. So the court war had to go on. The psychology of the situation in the Edison establishment had changed, and there could be no peace.

July 12, 1898, while the air was full of motions and legal gestures in the many previously instituted cases another suit was brought against J. Stuart Blackton and Albert E. Smith, and their assorted firm names including Commercial Advertising Bureau and the American Vitagraph Company. This was also due to occupy the courts many years. Relations between Edison and his erstwhile friend Jimmy Blackton, the *New York Evening World* cartoonist, were now slightly cooler.

Something of the intensity of the legal struggles is indicated in the testimony of Albert E. Smith on the witness stand in a government suit sixteen years later, when he said, concerning an injunction against Vitagraph: "I know I was so worried, and it worried my wife, and we had a little baby at the time and it killed that baby."

At one juncture in the fight with Edison, Blackton and Smith were forced to withdraw and for the time turned their business over to the conduct of Walter B. Arthur. Meanwhile Sigmund Lubin in Philadelphia, under pressure of similar attack, abandoned his business and fled to Europe, returning later when the skies cleared a trifle.

One of the truces of the Edison-Vitagraph battle was reached by an agreement by which the Edison plant took Vitagraph's negatives and sold the prints on a royalty basis.

The Edison legal battery wound up the year of 1898 with a suit against Eberhard Schneider of New York, filed December 21. Schneider was important as the maker of much of the best of the motion picture apparatus used by the invading newcomers. His name, long since lost in the march of affairs, was for some years one of the most important in the field by dint of sheer technical proficiency.

For the next two years this rapid fire of Edison patent suits continued. Meanwhile Thomas Armat in Washington and the American Mutoscope & Biograph interests in New York, both in the possession of strong patent claims, were potential aggressors waiting a shift of the tide to start back fires and enfilades from other angles of the complex situation.

Armat became, for the time, quiescent. The outlook for him then was discouraging. Raff & Gammon, disappointed in their split with Edison and upset by the invasions of numerous other imported and homemade infringements on the Armat Vitascope, expressed dismay and annoyance to Armat in letters of protest. Complication was added to complication when the Columbia Phonograph Company was found to have a much disputed claim to C. Francis Jenkins' technical partnership share in the first Armat projection machine patent.

In 1900 Armat began to assert his claims, and filed a series of suits against the makers and users of machines, including the Biograph company, Edison and sundry others. Also, he made license agreements with a scattering of exhibitors using projection machines embodying his patented principles. Among the Armat licensees were E. Burton Holmes, the travel lecturer then on his upward way to fame, and Bob Fitzsimmons, the pugilist, appearing with his show entitled *The Honest Blacksmith*.

Marvin of Biograph made a crafty move to strengthen the position of his concern by accepting an injunction under the Armat patent suit and making a nominal license agreement with the Washington inventor.

"The strength of this business will be in its patent control," Marvin argued. "We could fight and break your patents, but we all want the patents to stand up." The policy expressed was to win in the end, years ahead.

The increasing activity of Colonel William N. Selig in Chicago marked him for attention and an injunction suit by Edison. The Selig establishment was hardly prepared to cope with the expensively equipped and manned law department of Edison. The situation became desperately serious, and it appeared grimly certain that the little shop at 43 Peck Court would have to be shut down. Help came, at the eleventh hour.

About 1900, Selig made a series of motion pictures showing the operations of the Armour packing plant in Chicago. The work had especially interested Philip D. Armour, the founder and head of the concern. He made many trips down to obscure Peck Court to see his plant on the screen.

In February, 1906, just when it seemed that Selig could stand out against the Edison forces no longer, Upton Sinclair's now historic *The Jungle*, heavily press agented by Isaac Marcosson, came off the presses of Doubleday Page & Company in the East. The sensational revelations of *The Jungle* with reference to the packing industry shook the country. The packers were suddenly on the defensive.

Philip D. Armour recalled the motion pictures made by Selig. These pictures would be, he decided, excellent propaganda against the charges of *The Jungle*. The plant had been on dress parade when the pictures were made and Packingtown looked its best on the screen.

There was a hurry call for Selig and the films.

"I am afraid I can not do anything for you—you see the Edison company is about to put me out of business in this patent fight," Selig explained.

It was not the way of Philip Armour to let details like that stand in his way. The large, expensive and exceedingly crafty legal machine of the packers was thrown in as eleventh hour re-inforcements to the defense of Selig.

Colonel Selig was vibrating between oblivion and success through all those days. His response to emotional pressure came to be readily observable to the members of his busy staff. When the Colonel achieved any important step of progress, from a good order to a legal victory, he was accustomed to signalize his joy by indulging in a long exhaustive session in the barber chair, running in the entire gamut of delights—shave, hair cut, massage, shampoo, singe and a dash of tonic.

In February, 1906, he had one of the best hair cuts of his life.

The Jungle saved the Selig motion picture enterprise through the crisis and preserved to the world of the films an institution destined to play a large rôle in screen development.

The history of motion picture patent litigation in the United States includes no less than 202 major actions, with a list of approximately three hundred replevins and the like. England had a dozen or more considerable litigations and France a handful.

The records in this half a thousand litigations contain the pre-ponderance of the history of the art and industry of the motion picture. The stenographic reports of many of the trials run into the thousands of printed pages. This same legal record intensively examined over a period of several years, is the basic authority for this history of the screen. The confutation of false claims to glory and the rectification of erring traditions which occupy so many of these pages, have been empowered largely by the testimony given years ago by the men concerned themselves.

CHAPTER THIRTY-FIVE

BLACKTON, SMITH AND ROCK

THERE was a fever in the air in the days of '97 in the United States. Forces hardly recognized were stirring the national consciousness. The next immediate few years held a deal of destiny. The isolated nation was stirring in its cocoon of content about to emerge as a world power, recognized by its overseas neighbors, always mentioned in the newspapers of then as "the powers."

The newspapers were filled with tales of braggadocio and gallantry and color. The United States was enjoying its war with Spain.

The motion picture caught step with the martial tune of the nation and went marching on.

First to snatch at the patriotic opportunity were J. Stuart Blackton and Albert E. Smith with their little studio atop the Morse building in New York. They rushed up to the roof that April 21, while the wires were still singing of the declaration of war, and made *Tearing Down the Spanish Flag*.

Tearing Down the Spanish Flag was a tremendous success.

Cheers rocked the vaudeville houses and hats were tossed into the orchestra pits when the hand of righteous destiny reached out to tear down the Spanish banner. It was Blackton's hand.

Hundreds of copies of the subject were sold by Smith and Blackton. And from obscure sources dozens of imitations of it sprang up to meet the market demand.

In the larger centers of Chicago and New York the motion picture was undergoing evolutionary growth with the birth of a topical or news bearing function in connection with the war.

—389—

Biograph, Blackton and Smith, Edison, and Lubin in the East and Selig and Amet in the West were making the most of the war, with pictures of troops marching away, transports loading and the like. A few cameramen, among them William Paley, photographer of the *Passion Play*, got to Cuba and made pictures of the landing of the troops. But the new fangled and cumbersome motion picture camera was not accorded the remarkable liberty which marked the movement of the war correspondents. The motion picture camera did not get to the front.

A few of the old timers of those expeditions survive, telling tales of photographic desperation and film making amid the shock of clashing battle lines and bursting shrapnel. But all these tales end with, "And then a big shell came along and blew up my camera and I never got back with any of the film."

Out at Waukegan, Edward H. Amet went most pretentiously into making of war pictures, centering his efforts on the sinking of the Admiral Cervera's fleet at Santiago. In miniature he constructed the Bay of Santiago in a tub, with all the ships participating in the action, working them up with a great fineness of detail and equipping them with guns, all to fit exactly with the pictures and descriptions in the periodicals. The models were proportioned to the lens angle to create perspective with great accuracy. Electrically controlled devices supplied waves, and push buttons controlled the guns and ship movements.

By Amet's device the whole naval battle of Santiago could be fought on a keyboard. He had one assistant, William H. Howard, who stood at the switches while Amet turned the camera.

"Number One, Billy!" Then the black smoke rolled from the funnels of the ships under forced draught.

"Number two." Another button and the ships were under way with a curling bow wave at the cutwaters.

"Number three." Every ship went into action with shells bursting about, splattering on the armor. A destroyer charged the U. S. S. Iowa and a twelve inch rifle lowered and fired point blank. The destroyer lurched under the impact, settled by the stern and sank with a mound of waves rising as the bow went out of sight. So the battle raged.

Amet's pictures went out as having been made with a telescopic lens on a camera aboard a dispatch boat at six miles distance from the action. There was never a denial and the pictures met many a critical eye.

Amet took his pictures to the U. S. Naval Training Station at Lake Bluff, Ill., and showed them to a body of officers after the war.

There was only one doubting Thomas, an officer who had been aboard the old dynamite ship U. S. S. Vesuvius, an odd experimental craft armed with three great air guns which tossed high explosive bombs a half dozen miles.

This dynamite gunner watched the terrific upheaval caused by one of these bombs.

"I don't see how you could have got that picture—we only operated at night."

"Easy," replied Amet, with one hand on his magniscope projector and the other covering a grin. "You see we used moonlight film."

Later a print of that able film fake went to Madrid, purchased for the solemn military archives of Spain.

Shortly after his Santiago pictures went out Amet sold out completely to Williams, Brown and Earle of Philadelphia and went into electrical work. Spoor acquired an Amet camera and films to continue his growing exhibition business among the vaudeville theaters of the west.

The exhibition business of the provinces attracted to itself a large number of the itinerant adventurers of the time, carnival men, medicine show men and the like. In cramped illiterate hands they wrote to the mail order house of Montgomery Ward, ordering machines and lectures and films. This department was administered by Richard Nehls, who later became a figure in the film industry. Mostly tall gaunt persons they were, given to wearing frock coats and Prince Alberts slightly green at the back and shoulders, slightly greasy in the lapels. They chewed fine cut, natural leaf and plug, and spat with the keen accuracy engendered of long range work from the outer rim of the groups that gathered about the cannon ball stoves of the country hotels.

These knights errant turned with facile ease from the oratory of merchandising rattlesnake oil and the elixirs of eternal youth, from the manipulation of the three walnut shells and the fickle pea, from the sideshow exhortations in behalf of Madame La Fatima, Jo-Jo, the Dog Faced Boy, and all the allurements of tented mystery, to the new art of the moving picture.

The lectures came on printed sheets packed in the boxes with the slides and films. Anybody could be a lecturer, and anybody was.

A complete outfit could be had for about three hundred dollars, and soon there was second hand equipment for less.

Films were bought outright by the exhibitors and passed from hand to hand as they grew stale.

The old films ran through rattletrap machines suffering from the lack of expert attention and thus contributed considerably to the early bad repute of the motion picture in many regions.

But a catastrophe was to bring a new flavor of verity into the pictures. On March 17, 1899, the Windsor Hotel in New York burned and forty-five persons lost their lives. Blackton and Smith covered the fire with their camera, getting short bits of film showing the burning ruins. Probably for the first time the motion picture camera pictured news in the process of happening.

About this time Blackton and Smith were notified by the Proctor theater management that their films and service would be no longer required, as better terms had been offered by William T. Rock. "Pop" Rock, who had bought the Vitascope rights to Louisiana territory from Raff & Gammon, had returned to New York. The Vitascope franchise and territorial restrictions had been set at naught by the territory jumpers and the invasions of new machines. Every Vitascope exhibitor was now a free lance with the whole world to roam in.

"Pop" Rock and Blackton and Smith met at Rock's billiard hall in 125th street in New York's Harlem. In the high chairs overlooking the tables they talked it over.

"How much of an outfit have you boys got?" Rock asked at last.

"Three machines and a hundred and fifty subjects," Blackton responded, opening a bag which contained the entire American Vitagraph library.

Rock opened the door of a safe and displayed a large array of films. "And I've got two projection machines," he added. "Suppose we get together."

"Let's," responded Blackton and Smith. So there in the billiard chairs in the smoky Harlem hall the Vitagraph company was born. There was no written agreement and for years their business went on as a simple tri-part partnership, which in effect continued for nearly thirty years down to the sale of the concern in 1925 to Warner Brothers Pictures, Inc.

CHAPTER THIRTY-SIX

MELIES MAGIC AND THE PIRATES

AFTER the flurry of patriotic and topical interest in the pictures of the Spanish-American war the motion picture industry fell into decline in the United States. The screen had nothing to say. The novelty of pictures that moved was gone. Authorship was lacking. The potentialities of the screen art were as pigment on the palette with no artist to transfer them to canvas.

Then magic came to the rescue.

George Melies, who had been an understudy of the celebrated Robert Houdin in Paris, began a rapid rise as a producer of pictures of mystery and tricks of magic.

The Melies pictures viewed with the sophistication of today would scarcely hold the attention of a screen audience. But they were sensations of their day. A world market opened for them and they became the instruments of a new technique. In his efforts to mystify and startle his audiences Melies evolved the fade-out, the overlap dissolve, the double exposure and like expedients which have become commonplaces of camera practise since.

One of the early Melies subjects presented a simple row of chairs which performed antics on the screen. Nothing more complicated than moving the chair a bit at a time between exposures was involved. But this trivial trick had to be discovered.

Melies pictures grew in pretentiousness, and with their slight beginnings brought fantasy and constructive imagination to the screen. For the first time ideas for the use of the camera as an instrument of expression, rather than of mere recording, were being born.

—394—

The titles of some of the old Melies pictures are indicative: *A Trip to the Moon*, *Cinderella* and *The Kingdom of the Fairies*. The business of Melies was magic and he had no thought for realism, otherwise he might have become the father of the modern photoplay.

The Kingdom of the Fairies was a particularly pretentious effort. It was exploited with a large impressive herald for audience distribution like pictures of today. More remarkable still, it was accompanied by a special musical score at its premier presentations in New York, London and Paris in September, 1902.

In the general and accepted piracy of those days most of the American film makers made "dupe" copies of the Melies subjects and sold them as their own. George Melies became so disturbed by this flattering recognition of his art that he dispatched a brother, Gaston Melies, to New York to safeguard his interests. Gaston opened an office at 204 East 38th street and issued a catalogue of Melies' "Star Films," probably the first trade mark and brand name in the business. This catalogue presented a foreword, saying:

CAUTION

GEORGE MELIES, proprietor and manager of the Theatre Robert Houdin, Paris, is the originator of the class of cinématographic films which are made from artificially arranged scenes, the creation of which has given new life to the trade at a time when it was dying out. He conceived the idea of portraying magical and mystical views, and his creations have been imitated without success ever since.

A great number of French, English and American manufacturers of films who are searching for novelties, but lack the ingenuity to produce them, have found it easier and more economical to advertise their poor copies as their own original conceptions. This accounts for the simultaneous appearance in several issues of a well known New York paper of advertisements of the celebrated *Trip to the Moon* by four or five different concerns, each pretending to be its creator. All these pretensions are false. The *Trip to the Moon* as well as *Gulliver's Travels, The Astronomer's Dream, Cinderella, Red Riding Hood, Blue Beard, Joan of Arc, Christmas Dream* etc., are the personal creations of Mr. George Melies, who himself conceived the ideas, painted the accessories and acted on the stage.

In opening a factory and offices in New York we are prepared and determined energetically to pursue all counterfeiters and pirates. We will not speak twice; we will act!

GASTON MELIES
General Manager

It is to be noted that M. Melies made studied and emphatic use of the term *artificially arranged* scenes. This alone signified the departure and progress in technique. This was just one tiny step beyond the advance represented by the staging of the Hollaman-Eaves version of the *Passion Play*. That was the literal re-creation of an event, but now Melies was conceiving events to be created for the camera.

There was a wide indirect influence from the success of the Melies pictures. The coloration of their exaggerated action and far-fetched improbabilities extended to all picture making. Imitative influences tended to make every player before the camera grimace and gesticulate like an excited Frenchman in a fantastic rôle. The motion picture makers worked so hard for effect that they lost sight of conviction. The most serious efforts of the time when viewed on the screen now seem grotesque.

While the screen stood marking time in commercial progress it continued to add to its technique, slowly gathering up the abilities which were to make it a real medium of expression.

The prevailing paucity of pictorial ideas now led the Biograph company to make the signal departure of employing a director. Up to this time the creative phase of film making had not received attention. First it had been the incidental function of the inventor, then it passed to the cameraman. Now with the employment of a stage director, known to memory as Old Man McCutcheon, Biograph yielded to the necessity for creative work and editorial direction of the camera.

The motion picture also had yet to discover for itself the basic appeals of art. A glint of the slowly accumulating experience comes from the recollections of a member of the first board of directors of Biograph. A staid and prim downtown financier member of the board had been uttering protest at some of the peep show pictures appearing in the company's Mutoscopes.

"It's what the public wants," was the defense.

Records from an arcade in Fourteenth street were brought forth, reading like this: *U. S. Battleship at Sea*, $0.25; *Joseph Jefferson* in *Rip's Sleep*, $0.43; *Ballet Dancer* $1.05; *Girl Climbing Apple Tree*, $3.65. The objecting director looked thoughtfully at the ceiling.

"Then," he said, "I think we had better have some more of the Girl-Climbing-Apple-Tree kind."

The production policy of the motion picture was ordained forever in that decision. The dominant note had been struck.

Anything that smacked of novelty, fame or near-fame was material for the Mutoscope. The old cardwheel pictures, purveying entertainment to the slot-machine audiences of the proletariat, became a record of the variegated flow of contemporary celebrity, much as the news reels are today. The Mutoscope continued in active functioning for a full decade. One of the later masterpieces of the peep show machine embedded the last and greatest of the Bowery Boys, George Washington ("Chuck") Connors, in the imperishable amber of the cinema saga. It was a sunny day in 1906 when "Chuck" Connors, in person, appeared on the roof-top studio of the American Biograph & Mutoscope Company with a pictorial inspiration.

"Chuck" was delivered to the attentions of Roy L. McCardell, who was dividing his editorial ministrations between the peep show pictures and the newspapers of Park Row.

Connors was accompanied by a round-faced yellow boy, one Sam Yip, formerly of Canton, resident of Mott street, a candidate for fame as a professional boxer under "Chuck's" auspices.

"It like dis," explained Chuck. "I makes a mess of de monk, and then youse puts a sign over the peep show: 'Drop a Penny and See Chuck Connors K. O. Sam Yip, Champ Lightweight of China.'"

There was not a gleam of understanding in the sepia placidity of Sam Yip's face while Chuck negotiated his star contract—"a sawbuck for Chuck and a fiver for the monk," gross charge $25.

Connors and Sam Yip, attired for the ring, took their places before the Mutoscope camera on the roof.

Chuck was clowning the fight and strutting his stuff while he roughed the China boy. Sam Yip was cool under the drubbing. Then suddenly his left connected with Chuck's inferior maxilla and disconnected him from the contemporary world for five whole minutes.

With cold water and brandy the picture makers beckoned Chuck back to this side of the Great Divide and he withdrew for conference with Sam Yip.

"De noive of d' monk!" exclaimed Connors returning to the camera. "He's holdin' out now for half de gate for doing it over right and taking the K. O. from me. I ain't tight, but it's a sin to give a Chink money like that."

Matters were arranged and the picture re-made. It may still be seen in Mutoscope machines in the backwash coves of the amusement world where relics of the old Bowery arcades still bid for pennies.

The status of general production of pictures for the peep

show days can be measured by a review of a Biograph catalogue, current in the '90's.

134—*The Pretty Stenographer; or Caught in the Act*—New York studio—26 feet—An elderly but gay broker is seated at his desk dictating to his pretty typewriter. He stops in the progress of his letter and bestows a kiss on the not unwilling girl. As he does his wife enters. She is enraged. Taking her husband by the ear she compels him to get on his knees. The pretty typewriter bursts into tears.

209—*The Bad Boy and Poor Grandpa*—New York studio— Grandpa is peacefully reading his newspaper and the bad little boy creeps up behind and sets it on fire.

539—*How Bridget Served the Salad Undressed*—New York studio —22 feet—This is an old and always popular story told by motion photograph. Bridget of course mistakes the order and brings in the salad in a state of dishabille hardly allowable in polite society.

1863—Anna Held—59 feet—A stunning picture of the well known actress in the drinking scene which made such a hit in *Papa's Wife*.

2161—Eva Tanguay—48 feet—New York—the eccentric comedienne from the New York Theatre in the popular and amusing *Sambo Dance* from *The Chaperones*.

It was clearly time for new ideas and a director. But no immediate and revolutionary development was at hand.

A chance discovery of this time gave us the effect with which the fluffy golden blonde heroine always enters the picture with an aureola of glorifying light gleaming through her hair. Like most of the progressions of the art it came from a situation of adversity.

Edwin S. Porter, back from his wanderings as *Thomas Edison, Jr.* and carnival showmanship, sought employment with the Edison establishment and was assigned to the operation of a camera. He was sent to cover the races of Shamrock I for the America's cup—and the fame of Sir Thomas Lipton's tea.

Some twenty or more press photographers were aboard the referee's boat and Porter was handicapped in their jockeying for points of vantage because of his ponderous motion picture camera. The press photographers resented Porter and his big machine. They combined against him. Porter took refuge with his machine against the stern rail so that no one could stand in front of his lens.

At a thrilling moment the racing yachts under full sail swept down between the referee's boat and the sun. Porter ground away at his camera. A laugh rose from the watching news-photographers.

"Say dummy, don't you know that you can't photograph against the sun?" Porter, surmised in dismay that they were right, but to bluff it through he kept on with his picture making in at least outward defiance.

Back at West Orange the films were rushed through the laboratory and that night prints of the day's race went on the screen on Broadway. The backlighted yachting pictures were revelations of photographic beauty. They were filled with the gossamer shadow traceries of the sail fabrics and the jewelled highlights of the rippling water. It was a new effect.

The motion picture was teaching its ancestor, the still camera, how to make pictures.

CHAPTER THIRTY-SEVEN

ALASKA, WAR AND TAMMANY

THE excitements of the Spanish-American war had subsided when the mad rush for Alaskan gold fields began. Many men who had been shaken free of the routines of life by the war swept on into the new thrill of gold hunting.

The first gold strike in Alaska had been made back in '96, but communiciation and social infection was slower then than now. The motion picture, the great visual medium of news, was, as we have seen, just coming into being.

But along into Alaska, close on the trail of the miners, went the motion picture camera in 1899. And it was on no mere shadowy errand of amusement that the motion picture was sent. The first pictures of the golden wilderness of the north were for plain commercial purposes. It was in the fall of 1898 that Tom Crahan, a broadhatted westerner from Montana and points northerly, appeared as a customer at the Edison establishment. In behalf of the Northwest Transportation Company, with a line of boats between Puget Sound and Alaska, he wanted motion pictures of the country made for promotional purposes. Most especially they were to be shown at the Paris Exposition in 1900.

Crahan contracted to take eight thousand feet of motion pictures of Alaska at a price of five dollars a foot for the negative. Pictures of the ports and trails and tent towns of the gold hunters were made by Robert Bonine of the Edison staff, and brought back to West Orange for development.

Harry and Herbert Miles, Cincinnati photographers and adventurers, had by 1900 enough of the Caribbean and Cuba

and they, too, caught the Alaskan fever. They hurried away
to the northwest.

The Miles Brothers, equipped with motion picture and still
camera, went up the coast to Alaska. A vast interest was
aroused in "Nome City" when their big painted sign went up:

Miles Brothers
PHOTYGRAFTERS & MUG ARTISTS
Cabinets $27 a Dozen
Cash, Dust or Nuggets

The photographers did a tremendous business. The price
was modest in the extreme in a country where oranges cost two
dollars each and imported raspberries from the States could be
had at twenty-five cents each.

Miles Brothers made motion pictures of the affairs at Nome
and sent them to New York to Biograph for distribution.

There were many notables-to-be on the beach at Nome that
year of the rainbow quest. Rex Beach and Jack London were
there, mining more ore of literature than gold. And in the
crowd that gathered to watch a parade in honor of the birth of
Nome's first white baby there was a very quiet young man standing at London's elbow of whom, in time, we shall have much to
tell in this history of the motion picture. He was Jesse Lasky,
the adventuring young son of Isaac Lasky, a merchant of San
José. Young Lasky had grown impatient of the languors of
Hawaii where as a cornet player he had the distinction
of being the only white man in the Royal Hawaiian band at
Honolulu.

In Alaska, Lasky was one of the many who found gold but
not enough. Leaving the diggings he went to Dutch Harbor
and, with a rented rowboat, ferried passengers from ships at
anchor. Then with a hundred dollar push cart he went into
the baggage business at twenty dollars a load. Presently, be-

tween freighting and panning gold, he found he had enough to book passage home. Ten years of experimenting with destiny had to pass before Lasky was to join the industry of the "life motion pictures" that Miles Brothers were introducing in Nome. The next season the Miles Brothers opened at the Opera House in Juneau on Friday, July 26, 1901, with a "family show" of motion pictures and a handful of dance acts. When one gave a show in Alaska deemed fit for the whole family he had to advertise it.

The program of that show reads:

THE GREAT AMERICAN BIOGRAPH

Showing Life Motion Pictures of the Scenes and Incidents that have engaged the Attention of the entire World, selected from 10,000 feet of film, which includes: President McKinley's Triumphal Western Tour; The Galveston Disaster; Beaumont, Texas, Oil Fields; Paris and Pan American Expositions; Chinese, Philippine and Boer Wars; Carrie Nation, the Kansas Saloon Smasher.

First night in Juneau took admissions at seventy-five cents, but when the show moved into the gold camps the price was two dollars a seat. It was fourteen years before Broadway saw motion pictures at that price.

Back in New York important developments were coming. The motion picture was on the verge of a rebirth.

The synthetic process of making news pictures as begun by Blackton and Smith in their destruction of Cervera's fleet and by Amet with the same subject and his "Execution of Six Boxers" was growing bolder. The Edison company was naively out to reproduce the Boer-British war, which was occupying a large and sympathetic attention in the United States. James H. White, of the Kinetoscope department, was the general in charge of military operations. The war was conducted with several handsome stovepipe cannons mounted on carriage wheels

—403—

and two armies of Bowery drifters arrayed in costumes from the Eaves establishment.

The Edison picture forces might have fought the Boer-British war indefinitely if it had not been abruptly terminated by a one-man strike. Charles Geoly, general utility and office boy for Eaves, grew unhappy because the Bowery armies left the uniforms inhabited by cooties. He packed up the war and sent it back to New York to be fumigated. When the armies appeared they had nothing to wear for the next battle. The war was over, for Edison.

In a very similar fashion Vitagraph conducted a war of its own across the veldt of Long Island. In this year of 1900 Vitagraph blossomed out from a verbal partnership into a corporation capitalized at $6,000, still owned, however, entirely by Blackton, Smith and Rock. The concern signalized this step by moving its offices, always a popular pastime with motion picture concerns. Established in the Morton Building at 116 Nassau street, they erected a stage on the roof and entered more seriously into fabricated production.

Picture making on the roof was considerably complicated by the clouds of exhaust steam from the engine room in the basement. In a shifting wind the stage was often entirely obscured. Caught in a gust of steam, the director would cry, "Hold." Whereat the cast on stage would freeze motionless in the posture of the moment. When the steam passed the camera started again.

Now the motion picture was to make its début in politics. Percy Waters of Maryland, who had been in the service of Raff & Gammon in the first year of the pictures, returned to New York in 1901. Waters was no longer connected with motion pictures, but as he saw the rising preparations for the memorable Tammany campaign of that year his mind turned to screen

propaganda.   Waters was a Republican.   He had an idea that
street showings of pictures could be used to draw crowds to listen to the orators against Tammany.

Waters went to Republican headquarters and found them
distinctly formal and formidable.   They did not want to hear
about motion pictures there.   After trying three days to get an
appointment with the campaign manager he was not able to get
past the first secretary.

The patience of Waters was exhausted.   He was peevish.
He stepped through two swinging doors in Fourteenth street to
get something to pour on his overheated disposition.   He was
just feeling enough better to talk when a Tammany acquaintance
came along.

"You're playing with the wrong crowd, Percy, come along
with me and see the chief."

So presently Percy Waters and his friend were closeted with
Richard Croker in Tammany Hall.   Croker listened attentively.
It was the most critical fight of his career.   Croker wanted every
available aid.   When the plan had been unfolded, Croker sent
for Thomas Smith, secretary of Tammany Hall.

The contract they made that September morning took Waters'
breath.   Tammany wanted a hundred projection machines and
operators to cover as many speakers' stands.

After he had gone out into the street again, Waters took stock
of the situation, with minglings of excitement and alarm.   There
were not a hundred available projection machines in all the
United States.   There were not even half a hundred and there
were no operators to man them.

Night and day in shifts the Edison plant turned out projecting
machines for Waters' Tammany contract.   Meanwhile Waters
scoured the town for motion picture operators.   As his need
grew more desperate Waters took in training any man he could

pick up anywhere. Much to the annoyance of Edison he impressed into service the elevator men at the Edison office building in Fifth Avenue.

When the campaign started, fortunately for Waters, Tammany had been able to get locations for only eighty machines. The shows went on, drawing big crowds to the range of the spellbinders.

There were some careless operators in that emergency crew. One of them, in charge of a machine placed over a saloon down in Twenty-first street in the East side, dropped a cigar into his bag of films. The awning in front of the saloon burned. A report of this accident came to Waters. In a rumbling hack he galloped down into the gas house district.

A husky chap in his shirt sleeves strode out.

"Here's trouble," thought Waters, planning a speech of conciliation.

"I'm the picture man," he started.

The shirt-sleeved proprietor raised his hand and smiled.

"It's all right, boy, I'm Charlie Murphy."

And what had been done in the cause of Tammany was all right with Charlie Murphy, who was to come in his turn to be Tammany's chief.

This was a bitter political war in which the motion picture had come to play its part for the first time. William Travers Jerome, then Justice of the Court of Special Sessions, preached flaming indictments of the abuses and evils of the city. And despite the aid of the films, Tammany lost. Richard Croker abdicated the Wigwam and sailed away to his castle in Ireland to spend the rest of his days away from the scenes of his power.

With the campaign over Waters had on hand the biggest single stock of motion picture projection machines in the world. His Kinetograph Company had them as a profit of the campaign since the contract had paid for them. For the first time the standard price of $125 for an Edison projector was cut.

Waters offered his second hand machines for about $85 each. They sold rapidly, and spreading over the country became an important agency in the spread of the industry. A new attitude toward the films was developing, too, out of the experiences of the vaudeville theatre managers in 1900 when the actors, under the leadership of George Fuller Golden, organized the White Rats and struck against the newly formed managerial combine. The motion picture saved the day for a considerable number of theatres which would not have been able to open otherwise. The theatrical world was beginning to see possibilities in the screen.

CHAPTER THIRTY-EIGHT

BRIGHT LIGHTS AND DARK DEEDS

ONCE again comes the prize fight to lead the motion picture on to progress.

We have seen how Enoch J. Rector's effort to record the Fitzsimmons-Maher fight at Langtry, Texas, extended the capacity of the camera to cover long periods of action. Now a match between Jim Jeffries and Tom Sharkey, the sailor, was to be the agency by which the motion picture was to become independent of the light of the sun.

The Jeffries-Sharkey fight was under the managerial auspices of William A. Brady, of Brady & O'Rourke, the same William A. Brady ever since known to Broadway fame in a theatrical career growing out of his early days of fight exploitation.

Brady approached the American Mutoscope & Biograph company with a daring proposal that motion pictures be made of the fight, which was to be held the night of November 3, 1899, at the arena of the Coney Island Athletic club.

All previous efforts at making motion pictures under lights had failed. No sufficient illumination had been produced. Biograph took the contract and engaged in mighty preparations. Brady was prevailed upon to reduce slightly the size of the fight ring to restrict the area to be lighted. Biograph's technicans, among them William Bitzer, years afterward famous as Griffith's cameraman, went to work on the lighting problem. Approximately four hundred arc lamps were suspended over the ring. They were massed as closely as they could be hung. Biograph hoped that all the light possible would prove to be at least enough.

While these preparations were in progress a counter plot in the film war was forming. James H. White of the Edison motion picture department had a jealous eye on the project.

Albert E. Smith of the Vitagraph concern was amazed to receive a call from White of the Edison opposition. It was a whispered session.

It appears that some mysterious adventurer wanted to finance an exploit in pictorial buccaneering. He had approached the Edison establishment, which had refused to enter into the project. Now it was proposed, for due consideration and interest, that Smith should invade the arena, properly surrounded by twenty guards, and working under the cover of the general excitement, make the picture by grace of Biograph's lights. White was to be the master of ceremonies, and general of the expedition.

The night of November 3, Smith with his camera equipment, met White at Cohen's roadhouse in Coney Island, to be introduced to the adventuring angel of the project. This personage proved to be the celebrated Joe Howard, writer of popular songs. But unfortunately, and most embarrassingly, it was revealed, plans had gone slightly awry and Howard found it inconvenient, not to say impossible, to supply the tickets for the admission of the party of four, made up of himself, Smith, Charles French, a camera assistant, and White. The important matter of the promised twenty strong arm guards to protect the camera was ignored and forgotten.

It was no time for turning back, in Smith's opinion. He and French produced the price of four ten dollar seats.

A mob of eleven thousand fight fans pressed upon the entrances of the fight arena. The conspirators, with the camera apparatus divided between them and concealed under coats, pushed in with the crowd, found their seats and prepared for action.

Inside Howard discovered "Manny" Friend, a sporting figure of the day. And with Friend was the famous "Snapper" Garrison, the jockey whose startling track performances have become immortalized in the term "a Garrison finish." Garrison and Friend were added to the party in seats in front of the camera.

Howard borrowed a hundred dollars from Friend and bet it on Jeffries with Garrison.

Biograph's regiment of arc lamps flamed up and the fight started on its bloody course of twenty-five rounds.

The Biograph crew was absorbed in the labor of photography and lamps at ringside, while Smith twenty rows back in the audience ground away with the pirating camera.

The ceiling of throbbing electric arcs broiled the fighters in the ring. The heat accumulated round by round. Between rounds the seconds held umbrellas over the corners while attendants fanned and ministered to the fighters.

The electrical connections overhead, loaded to the limit with current, grew so hot that they threatened to burn out. Biograph workmen raided the refrigerator of an adjacent saloon and applied ice to the sizzling plugging boxes and switches. The melting ice sent a steady trickle of hot rain down upon the ring, adding moist misery to the gory fight.

Meanwhile William A. Brady discovered the pirate camera working in the twentieth row. A flying detachment of Pinkertons was sent to oust Smith and his camera. It was time for the promised and non-existent strong arm guard. But luck smiled on Smith. The spectators about, mad with the frenzy of the ring battle, fought off the Pinkertons and the invading camera was unmolested.

At the end of the fight Smith entrusted the precious negative to the agile and speedy "Snapper" Garrison, who promised to take it to their appointed rendezvous at Cohen's roadhouse.

THE FIRST "STILL" — one of a series of photographs made at Edison's little New York studio in the Chelsea district about 1901, to illustrate a German newspaper correspondent's feature story about the "new American art." The production appears to have been a comedy.

WILLIAM A. BRADY, Broadway theatrical producer, erstwhile
promoter of motion pictures, as he appeared in the brave
days of the '90's, a member of the firm of Brady & O'Rourke,
impresarios of the prize ring.

In stealth and haste the conspirators hurried away, separating in the milling crowds at the exits. In a room on the second floor of the roadhouse they met again, and to Smith's vast relief there was "Snapper" Garrison with the negative.

Howard with his winnings repaid his hundred dollars to Friend and bought champagne. He overlooked the little matter of the advance of forty dollars for the tickets from Smith and French. White trickled in and shared the wine.

Garrison slipped out buoyant with the uplift of the champagne.

Smith and French, feeling elated and secure, were packing up their apparatus and the treasured film of the night's affair, when the roar of an angry throng, one of those backstage sounds of menace, rose from the bar-room below. The voice of Brady rose above the rest.

"Snapper" Garrison had told.

Smith tiptoed to the stairway. His heart froze. Jim Jeffries and his cohort of trainers were swarming up the steps shouting for reprisal and vengeance.

Smith fled down the hallway and called a warning into the room where his party still dallied with the wine.

As Jeffries and Brady with their gang entered the hall, the fleeing picture pirates in rapid succession swung out from a window on a rope fire-escape and dropped down into the darkness.

Jeffries led the pursuit and followed. Smith clutching his film cases under his arm ran as he never ran before. He felt the hand of the mighty Jeffries reaching for him in the mad chase through Coney Island. Smith turned a corner, breathless, and stopped in a sheltering nook. Jeffries, under way like a wild range bull, stormed past.

Smith made his way to the Vitagraph plant in Nassau street. There he worked through the night developing the pictures. At last he saw them safe and perfect on the drying drums.

The first motion pictures made under lights had succeeded, for Biograph and Vitagraph together.

Smith leaned back in a chair to regard the fruit of his exciting labors, and dozed off to sleep. Some one tiptoed into the room.

The heavy hand of "Pop" Rock awakened him hours after in the broad light of day.

"Where's the films?" Rock bellowed.

Smith rubbed his eyes and looked at the drums. They were bare. The pirated pictures had been pirated again!

The missing negative found its way to the Edison picture plant and prints were made, while Vitagraph, hampered by its status under the patent litigation and charged with infringement, fought to regain the negative.

Meanwhile elaborate preparations were made for presentation of the picture. A packed audience filled the theatre. But as the picture started Brady leaped up across the orchestra from the audience and made a fiery speech of denunciation. Stage hands rushed in and there was a general mêlée with the police in at the finish. It broke up the show. Later Brady won an injunction against the showing, leaving the field to the authorized Biograph pictures.

Meanwhile, with typical Vitagraph luck, Smith's clamor at the Edison establishment won a peace offering of one print of the twice-pirated picture. This hard won film was booked by Vitagraph to Riley & Wood, vaudeville producers, for twenty weeks at $200 a week.

The Biograph picture, which consumed some seven miles of the ponderous wide negative, was long in process and when it reached the market failed of a sensation. It was offered to the trade in the terrific length of 5,575 feet.

The only lasting significance of the affair was in the furtherance of the powers of the camera with the introduction of photography by artificial lights. Today four or five modern motion picture arcs would serve as well as the four hundred Biograph used over the ring that night.

This was destined to be the last service of the prize ring to the motion picture. All the fight pictures which have followed in these twenty-odd years have exerted a detrimental influence on the social status of the screen.

CHAPTER THIRTY-NINE
THE "STORY PICTURE" IS BORN

'Twas the dark hour just before the dawn in the motion picture history in the early twentieth century. The film was again on the wane.

Men who were before long to become masters of millions won in the new art, were then running tent shows, furriers stores, haberdasheries, peep shows, pants pressing shops and loan offices.

The public was weary of pictures of prize fights, snatches of acrobatics, freaks and tricks on the screen. The picture had nothing new to say. What with the depressing effect of the patent wars, inhibiting initiative that might have come to freer minds, and the falling off of patronage it appeared probable the films would disappear even from the screen of the vaudeville houses where they were used to mark the end of the show and clear the house.

There had been tiny, trivial efforts to use the screen to tell a story, exemplified by Cecil Hepworth's *Rescued by Rover*, the adventures of a little girl and a dog, photographed in London, and *The Burglar on the Roof* made by Blackton and Smith of Vitagraph. They were mere episodes.

Now in the Edison studios, where the art of the film was born, and also where it was best bulwarked against the distractions of the fight for existence, came the emergence of the narrative idea.

James H. White was in charge of Edison's "Kinetograph Department" and Edwin S. Porter, becoming a cameraman, was the chief fabricator of picture material. Between them evolved a five hundred foot subject entitled *The Life of an American Fireman.*

This picture was built up from the germinal thrill of the first fifty-foot subjects showing a fire department run. White cast himself for the lead in this picture. When W. E. Gilmore, general manager for Edison, screened the picture he ordered retakes to eliminate White, on the ground that it was subversive of corporation policy for an executive to be an actor. He did not state it in exactly those words.

The Life of an American Fireman portrayed the routine duties of a fire chief. The audience was taken the rounds of the firehouse and inspection with the chief. Then cutting in with an inspirational beginning of a new technique, came a scene showing a simple cottage, with a baby asleep in a crib, by a window with curtains fluttering close to the burning gas jet turned low. The curtains flicked into the flame and the fire crept up the window and licked along the window casings. The mother awakened in the smoke-filled room. Then the picture cut back to the fire house where the alarm tapped out a signal.

The firemen leaped to action, sliding down the brass poles from their dormitory into the engine house. The horses were hooked up in a flash, and with smoke and sparks flying the outfit thundered down the street.

Then the long arm of old John R. Coincidence, the perennial first aid to scenario writers ever since, reached out and got into the first motion picture drama. It was the fire chief's house.

The picture cut back to the baby's crib again, back to the frenzied mother in the swirling smoke. Then again to the rushing fire engine.

Mark this: it was the grand staple situation of dire peril, with relief on the way, the formula that has made Griffith famous, or that Griffith has made famous, as you choose to view it. It was and is yet the greatest screen situation, of unfailing power. It may be the innocent man on the gallows with the pardon on the way; it may be the pursuing vengeance of the K. K. K.; it may be the maid in desperate conflict with the villain as the hero speeds towards the scene; but the bleached abstract barebones of the situation are the same.

In this ancient drama, *The Life of an American Fireman*, the chief arrived at last and leaping down rushed into the fire, emerging with his wife and child in his arms. Saved at last. The breathless race was over and the happy ending came in the closing close-up.

All this was crudely done measured in the light of our day. It was a gripping masterpiece then. It swept the motion picture industry.

Now Porter of Edison made a casual subject of no great screen importance that was to prove a stepping stone to an important extension of the story film idea. In the advertising department of the Delaware, Lackawanna & Western railroad was Wendell P. Colton, a young man with a highly successful advertising idea —the famous "Phoebe Snow," a mythical girl in white who rode on *The Road of Anthracite* without soiling her gowns, all to the rocking horse rhythm of accompanying jingles. Marie Murray, a photographer's model, was cast for a motion picture rendition of the Phoebe Snow rôle by Porter. The picture was made on the Lackawanna and Porter got on friendly terms with the officials of the railway. This was soon to prove valuable.

Not long thereafter Porter was talking of possible actors for some bit of a playlet with Billy Martinetti, acrobat, scene painter and handy man.

"I know a fellow that used to be in *The Great Train Robbery* on the road," suggested Martinetti.

Porter got a flash of an idea from the title. *The Great Train Robbery* was a stage production and was of no relation to

Edwin S. Porter, the cameraman-director of "The Great
Train Robbery," with an early model of the Edengraph,
a projector invented under the auspices of the Eden Musee.

THE FIRST MAE MURRAY — she was the model for the famous
Phoebe Snow, all in white who rode on *The Road of Anthracite* —
which led up to "The Great Train Robbery," first of the "story
pictures" — and below is George Barnes, actor from Huber's Museum, the desperado of the closing close-up of that dime novel
classic of 1903.

the motion picture that resulted from this casual mention.

Porter went to work on the idea, writing a memorandum of the scenes of a simple story of a train hold-up, a pursuit, a dance hall episode, and an escape. This was a step a little farther into the creative realm than *The Life of an American Fireman* had been.

In the fall of 1903 Porter started *The Great Train Robbery*. He looked about for a cast. At this time the benches of Union Square, the rendezvous for variety actors and unappreciated Hamlets, were the hunting ground for Biograph, Edison and Vitagraph in quest of performers. But this picture was a shade more exacting. It was necessary to have stunt actors. Frank Hanaway, an actor with experience in the U. S. cavalry, was induced to work in the picture because he could fall off a galloping horse without killing himself. George Barnes, a performer at Huber's Museum, a Fourteenth street variety house, was selected for the rôle of the robber.

At this juncture a vaudeville performer, with a sketch of his own to put on, appeared at the Edison studio casting about for a possible engagement. He was Max Aronson, who by the theatrical transmutation of names, had by this time become Max Anderson. It was not long after that he became G. M. Anderson by another stage in the process—the same who became world famous as Broncho Billy, which is another story.

"Can you ride, Anderson?"

"I was born on a horse and raised in Missouri," Anderson snapped back, in just that dashing western way. He had come on from St. Louis.

"Good," Porter decided. "You're a train robber in this picture."

Then Porter prevailed on the Lackawanna to loan him a special train. The train scenes were made near Paterson in New Jersey. As one of the thrills, the fireman, doubled by a dummy, was tossed from the train as it neared the high bridge on the Passaic river. The dummy fell on a trolley track below in front of a speeding car.

The emergency brakes screeched, and the car came to a violent stop, filled with fainting and screaming passengers. A riot followed when the unintended victims of the scene discovered the deception.

The riding scenes were made in the wilds of Essex County Park in New Jersey. Porter with his cast started from a livery stable in West Orange to ride to location. When the company arrived Max Anderson was missing. It was too late and too expensive to trouble about a missing star then. Porter doubled the part and went ahead. Essex Park resounded with rough riding and loud shooting.

In the evening when the horses were returned to the stable, Porter made inquiry about the missing Anderson.

"Lost a man somewhere along the line—did you see anything of him?"

"Oh, that guy—yep, the hoss throwed him about a block down the street and he led him back and took the next train back to New York."

So the legend runs of the first horse exploit of Broncho Billy. Anderson returned to appear in the train scenes only.

Marie Murray, the Phoebe Snow model, appeared in the dance hall scenes.

The Great Train Robbery vibrated with inserts and cutbacks in true photoplay fashion, and closed with a punch, consisting of a close-up of George Barnes as a robber pointing a revolver into the eye of the audience.

The picture was, for its day, the sort that the picture makers now would advertise to the public as "an epoch making achievement of the art of the motion picture" and to the exhibitors as "a box office knockout."

The Great Train Robbery went on its first runs at Huber's Museum, at the Eden Musee and at Hammerstein's. With the picture as their principal property, numerous exhibitors started with temporary store shows and traveling picture outfits. There was a new invasion of the back country with this thriller.

Porter swiftly followed this initial success with *The Great Bank Robbery* of like calibre.

The motion picture was now abreast of the dime novel.

Here was the first long step since the Hollaman-Eaves version of the *Passion Play* in 1897–8. *The Great Bank Robbery* was staged in a New Jersey village where one of the merchants, deciding it was real, opened fire on the company with lead, adding to the realism considerably.

Sigmund Lubin in Philadelphia hurried a competitive production to the market with an advertisement in *Billboard* of October 15, 1904:

BOLD BANK ROBBERY
The Greatest Production in 30 Motion Tableaux

Length 600 feet   Price $66

Send for Illustrated Catalogue, which contains 30 half-tones and full description. Lubin's 1905 Exposition Model Cineograph and Stereopticon combined, together with Electric Lamp, Adjustable Theostat and Calcium Light..........................$75.00

Two Cineograph Films (100 feet each), 200 ft. films at $11.00 per 100 feet............................... 22.00

Two Monarch records, playing the music for the above Cineophone Films, $1 each.......................... 2.00

Total....................................$99.00

With this outfit complete for $99.00 we will give FREE OF CHARGE Victor Talking Machine Complete, including horn and sounding box. This Victor Outfit is the latest improved model and could not be purchased at retail for less than $37.50.

S. LUBIN   23 South Eighth Street
                                          Philadelphia, Pa.

"Pop" Lubin's advertisement shows how a motion picture exhibitor could begin his career on ninety-nine dollars. It points to the primitive conditions of the time when calcium lights had to be carried for communities that had no electric service. And there, too, was one of the several early day synchronizations of film and phonograph with the "cineophone" pictures and the little Victor talking machine.

In tracing the development of the screen drama it is significant to note the use in this advertisement of the term tableaux for scenes. The very words used then show the reluctance with which the screen story idea developed.

Vitagraph was following a course of screen development parallel to the evolution that we have seen sharply outlined in the efforts at the Edison studio. About contemporary with *The Life of an American Fireman* was Vitagraph's tabloid version of *A Gentleman of France* with Kyrle Bellew. It was something between the embryo of a screen play and a mere photographic reproduction of an excerpt from the stage play, in which Bellew was appearing under the auspices of Theodore Liebler & Company. This film was really an excuse for the topical function of picturing the famous sword combat on the stairs, the high point of the play. But it was in such indirect and incidental paths that drama was beginning to creep into the motion picture.

The next milestone in the development of the screen as exemplified by Vitagraph, was a most pretentious effort in one whole reel, a thousand feet of film, *Raffles the Amateur Cracksman*, made in 1905 in the little studio among the steam clouds atop the Morse building. This was also a Liebler stage play. Vitagraph paid for the motion picture rights by an agreement to give Liebler & Company credit on the main title. Stage plays cost the screen more now. In 1920, D. W. Griffith paid $175,-000 for *Way Down East*.

SIGMUND LUBIN of Philadelphia, the humorist of the Patents
Company, and the founder of the Lubin theatres, which under
Stanley Mastbaum became the first important booking com-
bine, now known as the Stanley Company.

J. Stuart Blackton, with the first Mrs. Blackton and their son "Buster," pictured when the motor car was young, at the old Brighton Baths, near Coney Island.

Raffles in a thousand feet was produced about a year later than *The Great Train Robbery* in its eight hundred feet.

It is an interesting coincidence that both of these pictures, so significant as indices of the development, should each have brought to the films names destined to fame in the years to come—G. M. Anderson in *The Great Train Robbery*, and Jimmy Sherry, now J. Barney Sherry, in the title rôle of *Raffles*. Sherry is still a star appearing in current productions. He was probably the only figure on the screen of 1925 whose career before the camera extended back so early as 1905.

By this time G. M. Anderson had entered the service of Vitagraph and was a collaborator with Blackton and Smith in the making of *Raffles* and a number of pictures which followed.

Porter wrote the scenario for *The Great Train Robbery*. Vitagraph took a ready made stage play. The issue between the original script and the borrowing from the media of the stage and printed page began we see, at the very birth of the photoplay.

Tracing the development of photoplay technique we find Porter following *The Great Train Robbery* with *Kleptomaniacs*, a picture play of about equal length. It presented the parallel stories of a rich woman caught shoplifting, and considerately treated as a victim of kleptomania, and of a poor woman arrested on the same charge and ruthlessly rushed to jail. The two stories ran through the film neck and neck. Both in treatment and theme there is something about it that suggests an early conception of the treatment that Griffith used in *Intolerance*.

Biograph swung into the new trend toward the story picture following up the success of *The Great Train Robbery*. McCutcheon, the director, evolved a story around an advertisement in the "personal" column of the *New York Herald*. This column was celebrated and notorious and popularly considered immoral in many of its aspects. It eventually involved the *Herald* in a deal of trouble. The plot of the Biograph picture concerned itself with the adventures of a beau-gallant who advertised his willingness to meet a pretty girl at Grant's Tomb on Riverside Drive. The picture derived its action largely from an ensuing chase involving citizens, policemen, workmen and a general wild miscellany.

This mammoth production ran a full reel in length. It was released August 8, 1904, and may be considered a landmark as being first to present the chase idea in full bloom. The chase, dramatic action in its simplest form, remains the most valuable element of slapstick comedy today.

Lubin, as was inevitable, joined in this great institution of a new school of action art by a masterful imitation of *Personal* entitled *Meet Me at the Fountain.*

Lubin was willing to follow the flaming torch of progress anywhere, but it was the lament of his later days that in twenty years of production he never surpassed the success of his triumph of 1897, entitled *Horse Eating Hay.*

Biograph, developing the story picture idea, produced *The Moonshiners* with its climax in the first big screen fight, a conflict enacted by Wallace McCutcheon and Harold Vosburg. This was the archaic, primiparous film translation of the combat emotion from the simple record of the prize ring into terms of drama.

Biograph archives of the period reveal that the present Prince of Wales was photographed for the screen for the first time by the British Mutoscope & Biograph company in 1901. A peep show machine with this picture was installed on H. M. S. Ophir when the present King of England went on his cruise around the world, and a special showing was given for King Edward and Queen Alexandra at St. James's Palace. Joseph Mason was the cameraman of the occasion, and with him was William Kelley, who had come on from New Jersey to London to fresco peep show parlors. Ten years later Kelley appeared in motion picture affairs as the inventor of the Prizma color process.

In Chicago, William N. Selig, busily making and showing pictures, competitively responded to the story picture inspiration of *The Great Train Robbery* by the making of a one reel subject entitled *Trapped by Bloodhounds, or, A Lynching at Cripple Creek.*

It is regrettable that the cast of this first Selig dramatic effort is unknown. The Selig establishment was still at this date at 43 Peck Court, a little alley in downtown Chicago. At the saloon on the corner the cast was picked up and hired for a Sunday's picture work in the wild suburban district of Rogers Park. The wages consisted of lunch and one barrel of beer.

Viewed as a drama, *Trapped by Bloodhounds; or, A Lynching in Cripple Creek* lacked something of the finish of later screen work from the Selig studios. The opening scene depicted the murder of a lone woman, neatly choked to death by a marauding tramp. Thereafter the picture, for some hundreds of feet, consisted of a pursuit by men and dogs, said to be bloodhounds. The dogs did not want to go along and they were dragged through the woods and the picture by the posse. The great dramatic climax was the handsome hanging scene at the finish. It would have been rather realistic if the actor had not twisted on the rope and displayed the improvised harness which supported him.

In spite of those minor imperfections the picture was an important success, the first Selig drama. Some hundreds of prints were sold to the trade.

The photodrama idea was born, but it was advancing none too rapidly. Evidence is submitted in the primitive record character of an outstanding success of 1905, described in the catalogue of Paley & Steiner of New York, producers of Crescent Films, thus:

The Flatiron Building on a Windy Day

—This side splitting scene was taken January 25, 1905, when the wind was blowing a gale, and gives one a general idea of what women experience on a windy day around this noted corner. The great velocity of the wind can be plainly seen by the manner in which the pedestrians are clutching at their hats and skirts and grasping at anything for support. It is at this corner where one can get a good idea of the prevailing types in hosiery and lingerie. *This is the finest picture that has ever been taken at this corner, and we can safely recommend it as something exceptionally fine.*

In those distant days ankles were a treat and knees were an orgy. While we are smiling at the crude obviousness and low status of the movies of 1905, let us turn to the *New York Times Magazine* of December 13, 1925 in which we discover a page cartoon entitled: "Number Ten, Tony Sarg's New York—A Study of Action at the Flatiron Building." Sarg's cartoon is obviously addressed to the cultured customers of that publication. The optical center of his linear composition is occupied by precisely the material which attracted the discerning eye of William C. Paley, the cameraman of twenty years before.

After all art culture is merely a matter of media, traditions, technique and decor. The stories are basic, identical, eternal. The apogee tends to the hypogee.

As long as the wind blows around the Flatiron it will be a good story.

CHAPTER FORTY

THE SCREEN THEATRE ARRIVES

ALL the way down through screen history the art of the motion picture and the industry of the motion picture have run a relay of alternate steps of progress. Each advance in the art has brought a resulting advance in the business. It was therefore inevitable that the period of the birth of the story picture should be marked by important commercial departures and developments.

The morning of April 16, 1902, a reader of the theater advertising column on page one of the *Los Angeles Times* would have discovered a modest announcement:

ELECTRIC THEATER, 262 S. Main, opp. 3rd St.
New Place of Amusement
Up to date high class moving picture entertainment, especially for ladies and children. See the *Capture of the Biddle Bros., New York, in a Blizzard,* and many other interesting and exciting scenes. An hour's amusement and genuine fun for
10 CENTS ADMISSION
Evenings: 7:30 to 10:30

This was the way that Thomas L. Tally informed Los Angeles that the motion picture was making its début as an independent entertainer. He saw that its destiny was not locked up in the peep show machines in his phonograph parlor.

The advertisement of the next day indicates that the business of the opening night was so encouraging that Mr. Tally had decided to open his house in the afternoon with "matinees for children, five cents admission."

By April 27, Tally had discovered an improvement in nomenclature calculated to make the public understand better what it was all about. He called the Electric Theatre's program "A vaudeville of motion pictures lasting one hour." The bill had also been improved by adding pictures of Prince Henry of Prussia who was then visiting the United States. This show continued through May, and on June 1 there was a complete change of program to make room for *A Great Bullfight, fought before President Diaz and his entire Cabinet in the City of Mexico, Feb. 2, 1902.* Melies' *Trip to the Moon, Gulliver's Travels, The Kingdom of the Fairies,* and similar subjects appeared on the Electric's screen.

When Edison's *The Great Train Robbery* arrived, Tally was so filled with enthusiasm at its success that he sold his theatre and took the road, showing the exciting one reel super feature of 1903 all over the West. He later returned to Los Angeles and resumed the operation of motion picture theatres. He has been an exhibitor continuously for more than twenty years.

Closely contemporary with Tally were David Grauman of San Francisco, father of Sid Grauman, who now exhibits pictures in Los Angeles, and Anthony Lubelski of Oakland. Also Fred Lincoln in Seattle and Charles Peckham in Spokane conducted motion picture shows in the same period. They appear on the old accounts of George Kleine's Chicago concern with standing orders for films as early as 1901.

Early in 1903 Harry Warner and his brothers, now engaged in the motion picture on a large and international scale, opened a ninety-nine seat store show called the Cascade Theatre in their home town of Newcastle, Pa. The chairs were hired by the day from the town undertaker and on days when there was a funeral the audiences at the theatre had to take their amusement standing up.

All of the first theatres alike had to purchase their films outright from the makers in the East or their agents, concerns like

THOMAS L. TALLY's phonograph and picture parlor in Los Angeles, 1897–8 — At the left Edison peep-show Kinetoscopes, in the center Mutoscopes, at the extreme rear, center, are the eyeholes through which patrons, timid at the darkness of the projection room, could view a picture thrown on a screen, eartube phonograph customers at the right.

CHIEF GEORGE C. HALE of the Kansas City, Missouri, fire
department, whose invention of the Hale's Tours show device in 1903 made a film exhibitor of Carl Laemmle and
opened careers for many another famous name of today.

the Kleine Optical Company of Chicago, or Richard Nehls' film department at Montgomery Ward's. The standard price for motion pictures then was ten or eleven cents a foot, making a reel cost approximately a hundred dollars. This was a heavy burden of expense upon such modest enterprises as the first screen theaters. The film exhausted its entertainment value in any community long before it was worn out. The remaining value in it was a dead asset on the hands of the theatre man. A change in the system of distribution had to come before any considerable growth of the industry was possible.

Harry J. Miles, who had returned from his adventures with the motion picture camera in Alaska, was struck with an idea. The idea had more gold in it than was ever taken out of Alaska. There was Grauman buying a reel a week for a hundred dollars to show it in San Francisco and there was Lubelski doing the same thing in Oakland across the bay. It was the summer of 1902. Herbert Miles, Harry's brother and partner on the Alaskan expedition, had gone to New York to sell their films to Biograph and had connected with that concern as an independent sales agent.

"If you will send me some films," Harry J. wrote to Herbert Miles, "I can rent a reel to Grauman for a week for $50 and then get another $50 from Lubelski. After that whatever we get is profit."

So the motion picture exchange was born.

This first exchange was the parlor floor of the boarding house where Harry Miles was stopping, at 116 Turk street in San Francisco.

It seemed an interesting but unimportant venture then. But it was the most important development in the motion picture since the invention of the projection machine.

From that point onward distribution developed until it became the controlling element of the film institution.

The first tentative efforts at film exchange operation began with Raff & Gammon's plan of 1895 for the return of old subjects from the Kinetoscope on a trade-in basis. It was developed slightly by Percy Waters and Edson Raff, stepson of Norman C. Raff in 1897–8, but the real rise of the film exchange had to wait for the emergence of the screen theatre, a permanently located exhibition, with a demand for change of program.

The motion picture was not yet, in 1902, done with novelties and by-paths. The development was not yet lined out in a clean cut, well defined direction. The industry was still gathering to itself in these meanderings the men who were to rise with it from timid beginnings to positions of world importance in the motion pictures of today.

The early picture makers were so given to picturing the fire engine on its spectacular dashes through city streets that there seems fitness in the fact that a fireman came to discover a new screen opportunity and give a new impetus to the business of showing films.

In 1900, George C. Hale, chief of the Kansas City, Mo., fire department and inventor of most of the modern fire fighting apparatus, took an expert fire team to London to a world conclave of fire fighters held at the Crystal Palace. Automatic devices and the extraordinary discipline of his crew enabled Hale to take all of the prizes and made him the sensation of London for the day.

Hale's fire fighters were so fast that they were out of their cots, hitched and out of the exposition firehouse before the timers of the show had set their stop watches going. They had done in seconds what the best European fire departments did in minutes.

This made a showman of Chief Hale. At the Crystal Palace, he learned something about thrills and how to get the crowd out on the edge of the seat.   He got an inkling of the profits of successful entertainment.

When the St. Louis exposition opened in 1903 one of the novel attractions was *Hale's Tours and Scenes of the World*.   It was an odd sort of sideshow arrangement, a kind of theatre.   A replica of a railway coach, with a man in conductor's uniform as ticket taker, standing on the rear end, greeted the patron.   Inside, the seats also simulated the arrangement of a railway car. When the show started there was a clang of bells and the car apparently began to move.   At the distant end in front of the audience a motion picture panorama of speeding scenery started.   The car swayed on its rockers and wheels spun. There was a moderately successful illusion of travel.

This Hale device was a flowering of the H. G. Wells "Time Machine" idea which Robert W. Paul had contemplated in London nearly ten years before.

In the next two years *Hale's Tours* were sold all over the United States from Coney Island, New York, to Dutch Jake's place in Spokane.   Chief Hale and his partner, Judge Fred Gifford, Kansas City's police magistrate, made a profit of approximately half a million dollars on the project.

Hale's Tours gave the inspiration of a new interest to the exhibition of pictures and brought an array of new showmen into the business.   The time was near at hand when these novitiate exhibitors were to graduate into greater opportunity.   The motion picture theatre experiments typified by Tally's "Electric" in Los Angeles were about to result in a nation-wide sensation of development.

In the autumn of 1905 Harry Davis and John P. Harris of Pittsburgh, variously engaged in stage theatre and real estate projects, found themselves with a vacant store room in Smithfield street, between Diamond Alley and Fifth avenue.   It is merely incidental that we mention now that the Keystone jewelry store, a couple of doors away, was presided over by one Lewis J. Selznick. Some chapters ahead we shall come to the name of Selznick again.

Harris pondered on the problem of the unrented storeroom and struck upon a notion to experiment with motion pictures. An old projector was produced from a warehouse, and odds and ends of discarded and surplus fittings from the Grand Opera House were installed.

The day before Thanksgiving that November of 1905 the theatre opened. It had less than two hundred seats. The opening program was *The Great Train Robbery*, the photoplay sensation of 1903. The first day's receipts were $22.50. The next day they jumped to $76. The business grew amazingly and swiftly reached the full capacity of the little theatre. Within two weeks the show was starting at eight o'clock in the morning and running continuously until midnight. The vacant store room was now producing a profit of nearly a thousand dollars a week. The project was under the management and operation of Harry Cohen, years afterward one of the organisers of Metro Pictures Corporation.

News of the success of the project in Pittsburgh swept through the amusement world like the tidings of a gold strike. A wave of "store shows" and "nickelodeons" swept over the land. With a trivial investment in a projection machine and a few chairs any one could become a showman and prosper. Within a year there were nearly a hundred "nickelodeons" in Pittsburgh, and the fever was invading New York, Chicago, St. Louis, Cincinnati and most of the major centers.

Now that the motion picture had attained the photoplay it had become an independent art, seeking its own channel of service to the public. It was a natural consequence that this art, expressed in the simple, primitive and universal language of the pictures, should find its first burst of large development in the populous centers filled with polyglot populations. Pittsburgh, in the heart of the coal and iron country, with its vast numbers of poorly assimilated imported laborers, contained a wide array of differing linguistic groups. To these aliens the American theatre and American arts in general were either unintelligible or without appeal. Amusement was expensive and labor was cheap. The motion picture offered no linguistic barriers. A story on the screen was a story alike to Pole, Slovak, Russian, Magyar or Italian. And it was cheap, the price of a glass of beer. So it came that the motion picture theatre rose in the foreign labor centers of the great cities first and spread thence back into the hinterland.

The store show wave swept into the picture industry many of the men, who, in the developments of the next decade, were to become the most important agencies of film destiny. The stories of two of these men are typical and of special interest.

In 1903, Adolph Zukor, a capable and modestly successful furrier in Chicago, decided that he would go down to New York and see what could be done about the plight of a friend to whom he had loaned three thousand dollars to go into the penny arcade business. The penny arcade located at Sixth Avenue and Fourteenth street did not seem to be prospering. Now $3,000 was something, not the whole of Zukor's fortune at that time it is true, but it was a considerable fraction thereof.

The effort to salvage the loan put Adolph Zukor into the penny arcade peep show and phonograph business, got him into association with Marcus Loew, who was similarly interested, led to the acquisition of William A. Brady's *Hale's Tours* shows, and converted the arcades into motion picture store shows. By 1906 Zukor was a full fledged theatre proprietor, with the Comedy Theatre presenting the best motion pictures he could find to the amusement seeking crowds of New York's Fourteenth street.

Zukor had started out to rescue a bad loan and had found a new career. Famous Players-Lasky Corporation, the world's biggest motion picture concern resulted.

Up in Milwaukee another matter of a loan was even more indirectly working to bring another significant personality to the motion picture. John R. Freuler was a real estate dealer in 1905. He was principally concerned at the time with finding buyers for a shooting preserve club project in which, incidentally, he was associated with Rex Beach.

Some years before Freuler had loaned an acquaintance fifty dollars. The borrower was everlastingly grateful and usually without money. He called occasionally at Freuler's office to make a payment of a dollar or so. These calls about the fifty dollar loan probably took up about a thousand dollars' worth of Freuler's time. One day in 1905 this borrower appeared with another dollar and some great excitement.

"I got a big chance for you; you've got the money to put it over, Ruddy."

"Yes, go on." Freuler was looking out the window.

"A friend of mine has just come in off the road with a traveling picture show—those moving pictures you know. His outfit is worth four hundred and fifty dollars and if you'll put in that much cash against it he and you can start a regular theatre. There's a lot of money in it."

Freuler's acquaintance with motion pictures consisted of one visit to a *Hale's Tours* show. He did not think much of the films. Up in Milwaukee they were not considered respectable in the circles in which the Freuler family moved.

But enthusiasm won and John R. Freuler became a partner in the picture show business with a red headed ex-policeman, with a portable projector and two reels of film. They opened the Comique Theatre, with a phonograph at the door and a white front in Kinnikinnick Avenue, Milwaukee. It was a secret with Freuler. The family knew nothing about it.

Freuler owned a two cylinder motor car of the type of those days, and an evening drive was a part of the daily program. Mrs. Freuler did not find out for a long time why her husband took such a long way home and drove down the miserable pavements of Kinnikinnick avenue. He wanted to get a sidelong glimpse at that little Comique Theatre. It was beginning to interest him.

By the hundreds the store shows were springing up and the demand for films was increasing. The little picture plants in New York and Chicago were working at top speed. The film makers were wondering how long the "picture craze" would last.

CHAPTER FORTY-ONE

ROOSEVELT AND DOCKSTADER

JUST as the era of the photoplay and the screen theater was born, the blundering young art of the motion picture went out and fell headlong into an international sensation.

A trivial incident of picture making, involving an amazing set of coincidences and misunderstandings, precipitated a national political crisis and set the daily press from Park Row to Golden Gate agog with violent headlines and extra editions. A motion picture suddenly became the subject of a violent and outraged anxiety for President Roosevelt, a topic of secret midnight emergency sessions of the Cabinet in Washington, and a desperate quest by the operatives of the Department of Justice.

It was all a mistake.

In time the sensation died, but the inward facts of the affair have remained for years a secret.

It was the summer of 1904 while *The Great Train Robbery* was making its sensational introduction of the story telling function of the screen, when Lew Dockstader, minstrel and monologue artist, came to New York to furbish up his act for the approaching season. He had a fatal inspiration to use the motion picture.

Dockstader's act in this period consisted principally of a sort of geographical monologue. Seated in a basket supported by a stage balloon, he appeared surveying a shifting landscape projected on the screen below him by a stereopticon. As the scenes changed Mr. Dockstader in blackface make-up offered a running fire of comment on places and personages, somewhat in the character of the current utterances of Will Rogers, the philosopher of the *Follies*.

Dockstader hunted out Edwin S. Porter, the maker of *The*

Great Train Robbery, at the Edison studio at 41 West Twenty-first street, on his arrival in New York.

"I want you to make me some film to use in my act," Dockstader explained. "I want a couple of views down in Washington. I will appear in them."

So Porter packed a camera and went to Washington, along with Dockstader, Harry Ellis, a singer in the Dockstader act, and Jean Havez, Dockstader's press representative and author of many of his lines. It is interesting to note parenthetically that Havez is now a member of the craft of "gag men" who contribute funny ideas to film comedies.

When the party arrived at the Hotel Raleigh in Washington Dockstader unfolded his plan, deliciously naïve.

"You know Roosevelt and I are good friends," he explained to Porter. "Now I want to make a scene in front of the White House. It shows me where I have fallen from my balloon right in front of the steps. Roosevelt comes out and picks me up and dusts me off and sets me on my feet and we walk off together."

"Wait, wait a minute—say that again!" Porter was protesting. "You may know Roosevelt and he may know you, but the President of the United States isn't doing that kind of thing just now."

"Leave it to me—I can get him to do it," Dockstader insisted.

But the day went by and Dockstader's courage waned. Maybe this Edison man was right.

"How are we going to get away with it—what do you think?"

"I think," the camera man suggested, "that we'd better make up your Mr. Ellis here to look like Roosevelt and fake the incident down in front of the Capitol building. People know it better than they do the White House, anyway. There's a good light early in the morning now and we can do it before anybody is about and get away." So it was planned.

Ellis made up with vast care, dressed in characteristic Roosevelt clothes. A Victoria, similar to that in which Roosevelt was accustomed to ride about Washington, was hired to be on the spot right after sunrise.

The Capitol's white columns were just fairly illumined in the sun of the next morning when a watchman was surprised to see President Roosevelt come down the long vista of stone steps and pick up a black man who had dropped from nowhere. The watchman was still watching in wonderment when he saw Roosevelt and his darky friend get into the Victoria and drive away.

A man with a strange box on a tripod was apparently surveying the proceedings.

The Victoria stopped around the corner out of the picture. Porter shouldered his camera to join Dockstader, when the Capitol watchman came up smiling.

"What is Teddy up to now?"

The watchman was sure he had seen Roosevelt.

"Just a little private stunt," Porter replied and hurried away. When the picture party reached the hotel Dockstader suggested breakfast.

"No," said Porter looking at his watch. "About the time that watchman tells somebody about seeing Roosevelt down at the Capitol at six in the morning the excitement around here will start. And when it starts we are going to be on our way. There's a train back to New York in an hour and we are going to make it."

When the Dockstader party arived in New York shortly after noon that day they heard the newsboys crying an extra.

"Picture Plot against T. R. Extra! Extra! Read all about it!"

The strange happenings of the early morning on the Capitol grounds had leaked to the newspapers and the wires across the continent were sizzling with the news.

It chanced that only a few weeks before campaign material

had been made by the enemies of Roosevelt out of an engagement of the President to lunch with Booker T. Washington. There had been considerable discussion of it, aimed to arouse the animosities of a race prejudice against Roosevelt.

Now a black-faced man had been photographed in front of the Capitol with another man made up like the President. They had been pictured going arm in arm to a carriage and driving away together. The deductions of the political experts, the President and the newspaper men were inevitable. The picture had been made to ruin Roosevelt in the South. It was unquestionably a dastardly Democrat trick.

Later editions came along with further details ferreted out by the sleuths of the secret service and the Washington newspaper men. The actor in blackface had been found to be Lew Dockstader. It was found that Dockstader's party registered originally at the Hotel Raleigh, had in the night moved to the St. James to be close to the Capitol where the heinous photographic deed was done at sunrise. The stealth was apparent. The circumstantial evidence was conclusive.

Roosevelt sent a hurry call to the cabinet. The strange enemy exploit was discussed in a late session at the White House. The experts of the attorney general's office were consulted. They searched the law for a ground of action. There was no legislation or statute that contemplated such a situation.

The council of earnest politicians and patriots shuddered over the effect of that picture in the Solid South. No word of contradiction would avail. There was a popular impression that the camera couldn't lie. What was to be done? The strategists were distraught.

There came a decision to bluff it through. The subsequent action suggests that it was formulated by the determined T. R. himself.

The following morning when Porter appeared at his office at

the Edison studio in New York, he found Dockstader sitting there waiting. Alongside was a stern, dignified person of official bearing.

"I'm pinched," Dockstader announced. "This man's from the secret service. I've got to give him that negative we made in Washington or go back with him—let's have it."

"Sure," Porter replied, sparring for time. "I'm sorry, but I sent it over to the laboratory at West Orange to be developed and it will take a while to get it back here. I'll send for it right away."

Then at a hint from Porter, his brother, E. M. Porter, went into the projection room adjacent and began running motion pictures. Porter invited the secret service man to watch the pictures, thus maneuvering to get Dockstader alone.

"I've got that negative in the back room here, but I can give this fellow a roll of unexposed film just as well. He'll fog it anyway and they won't be able to tell the difference between it and the real negative."

"Don't do it—give him the real negative—I don't want trouble. This is getting serious," Dockstader wiped a beaded brow.

"Very well," Porter replied, and went out of the room.

Presently he handed the secret service man a little tin can. "There it is."

The man with the star under his lapel jerked the can open and pulled out the creamy roll of films. It fell in ribbons about him.

"There ain't any picture on this! Don't try to put something over on me, now."

"There was a picture on it until you opened it and exposed it to the light," Porter explained. "You've spoiled it now. That is undeveloped negative."

"Guess the president won't mind my spoilin' it." The secret

service man pocketed the film and bade Dockstader and Porter good day.

One evening shortly after that, down in Washington, there was another meeting of the cabinet at the White House. Theodore Roosevelt and his confrères repaired to a sheltered place on the lawn and there was a lurid brief bonfire as they watched the film burn.

Meanwhile Porter had the original negative developed and carefully put away in New York. Dockstader was unaware of that until months after. He dared not use it in his act. Porter kept it.

More than a year later Roosevelt and Dockstader met at a luncheon table.

"Why did you ever try to put that Booker T. Washington stunt over on me?" Roosevelt asked the famous minstrel.

"You had me all wrong," Dockstader replied. "I was made up for my stage part. That film was for my own show."

"If I'd known that I would have let you get away with it," Roosevelt replied. "But it's one on you—you see we couldn't find any law or legal method of getting at the thing anyway."

"But you didn't get the film—it's up in New York now," Dockstader retorted. "You burned a blank."

But Fate had its way. The historic roll of film was stored in a chest of Porter's archives in his office at the Famous Players studios when they burned some ten years later. They might just as well have given the film to Roosevelt.

CHAPTER FORTY-TWO

WHEN ACTORS SCORNED THE SCREEN

THE rise of the motion picture theatres, beginning in 1905, created a demand for story pictures which reacted with revolutionary effect on the art of the films. The mere ability to crank a camera and develop films was no longer sufficient. Now the motion picture had to reach out for players and stories and directors. A whole creative craftsmanship had to be evolved, and all this tedious but hurried evolution had to take place in an industry torn with desperate legal wars.

But in this turmoil of creation and strife were the forces destined to produce a new and glamorous race—the stars.

The roof-tops and makeshift establishments of the picture makers were outgrown. The motion picture reborn with the advent of the photoplay had to re-establish and re-equip, with men, machinery and ideas.

The American Mutoscope & Biograph Company abandoned its crude plant atop the Hackett-Carhart building and took over the old brownstone at 11 East Fourteenth street in New York. In its days of early glory it had been a residence of great magnificence. Now with the coming of the motion picture it was to be the gateway to fame for a galaxy including Griffith, Pickford, Sennett, the Gishes, Sweet and many another.

Biograph was following up its experience with the making of the Jeffries-Sharkey fight under lights, and at 11 East Fourteenth street, deliberately turned its back on the sun for a plant equipped with mercury vapor lamps. It was the year of 1906.

Edison's picture staff abandoned its downtown location in Twenty-first street and took up operations in a pretentious new studio in the Bronx where it stands today, accumulating cobwebs and the dust of silence, stages piled high with the props and accoutrements of the forgotten dramas which brought to fame the names of the old Edison stock company, Mary Fuller, Mabel Trunnelle, Herbert Prior, Charles Ogle and the rest.

The Bronx location, adjacent to Bronx Park, was chosen by Porter, for reasons significant enough in their day and themselves a measure of the status of the industry then. The site in Decatur street was just a five minute walk from the end of the Third Avenue elevated line. It was far enough from Broadway that abashed actors need not fear they would be discovered in the artistic felony of working in pictures. It was close to the outdoor locations of the park. It was a five cent car ride to most any desired location elsewhere.

J. Searle Dawley, then engaged in presenting skits between the acts of the Spooner Stock Company in Brooklyn, was employed to supply story ideas for the Edison studio.

Through Dawley and his dramatic connections a number of well remembered names came into the motion pictures. Maurice Costello, of the Spooner Stock Company, came from the haughty dignity of the "legitimate" to play a part in Edison pictures, back there in those beginnings so obscure that even the subjects have been forgotten. Many others followed, among them Ben Wilson, Jack Adolphi and Sydney Booth. Porter brought in William Sorrelle, who had played on the stage with Richard Mansfield, Laura Sawyer, Charles Forrest and others whose names have faded from memory.

The first member of the Edison Stock company to be employed on a regular salary was Sorrelle. He had been getting five dollars a day when he worked. There was excitement about the place when it was learned that he had been "put on steady" at thirty dollars a week.

It was among the duties of Dawley to hunt out actors for the rôles of the simple little dramas of the Edison shop. His favorite hunting ground was the vicinity of Thirty-ninth street and Broadway, where actors out of work, "resting," as they called it, in the euphemistic argot of the stage, stood about hoping to be chosen by some manager.

The motion picture had no respectability then, and actors were scornful. The casting director on the hunt had to seek out the hungry ones and tactfully suggest work in "the pictures."

Actors who met on the motion picture stages of Edison, Vitagraph and Biograph in those days kept their film shame a secret.

The Edison studio, too, went on drawing on the stage for material. William Ranous, a famous "heavy" of stock company fame, went to the Edison studios to play the Irish landlord in *Kathleen Mavourneen*. Shortly, Ranous went over to Flatbush to work in Vitagraph pictures and soon utilized his stage craft to become a director.

Meanwhile Vitagraph, the Blackton-Rock-Smith combination, was undergoing a similar evolution. The studio on a roof in downtown New York was outgrown and they ventured to acquire land in Flatbush.

Late in 1906 the Vitagraph's picture makers were working on a location near Sheepshead Bay. There was a crowd of spectators gathered behind the camera to see the curious performance of shooting a picture. In that group was Florence Turner, the daughter of an actor family living in the vicinity. Miss Turner made the acquaintance of the pictures there and fell into a conversation that presently led her into a job at the new Vitagraph studios in Flatbush, the first of those who made up the Vitagraph stock company. A bit more pretentiously organized than some of the other concerns of the time, Vitagraph had a method of holding its players by giving them jobs, "doubling in brass." Miss Turner drew eighteen dollars a week as the mistress of the wardrobe. That was a minimum guarantee, in effect. If she acted in pictures, then she received a total of five dollars a day, and might, when production conditions were especially fortunate, earn a total of thirty dollars a week, just like Sorrelle over at Edison's.

It was accepted practice then to impress the actors into service as carpenters, scene painters and the like.

But when Maurice Costello went over to Vitagraph from Edison a precedent was established.

"I am an actor and I will act—but I will not build sets and paint scenery."

Costello drew up majestically and won on his dignity.

G. M. Anderson, leaving Vitagraph, went to Chicago and joined forces with Colonel Selig, on the strength of *The Great Train Robbery*. He was the bearer of the flaming torch of the drama to the outposts of the motion picture. In a few months the impetus of Anderson's enthusiasm carried Selig production well into the field of the dramatic picture.

Anderson, still bent on a project of his own with "story pictures" as the new golden opportunity, looked up George K. Spoor, the proprietor of the Kinodrome Circuit, showing motion pictures in the Orpheum vaudeville theaters of the West and headquartering in Chicago.

Spoor was now the proprietor of the National Film Renting Company at 62 North Clark street in Chicago, an exchange through which he extracted earning power from films that he had run through his vaudeville circuit showings. The exchange was growing up to become quite as important as the Kinodrome business and there was a scarcity of pictures for the clamoring store show men. Anderson arrived at the opportune time.

Spoor and Anderson organized the Essanay Film Manufacturing Company in February of 1907 and started making pictures, with the famous Indian head borrowed from the copper cent piece as their trade mark. The stamp of *The Great Train Rob-*

bery with its Wild West atmosphere was on the project. Anderson went to Golden, Colorado, for locations in the spring of 1908 going thence to Niles, California, and, for three hundred and seventy six weeks thereafter, produced a one reel *Broncho Billy* cowboy adventure story. Being the first actor-author-producer to become an owner of a motion picture enterprise, he was first to get his name on the screen, and probably was the most successful in keeping it there. Three hundred and seventy-six weekly pictures establishes a record never approached elsewhere. Pursuit of the "story picture" idea carried West by Anderson set Essanay and Selig on the road to millions.

Francis Boggs of stage experience, the star of the melodramatic success, *Why Girls Leave Home,* went into the Selig organization to take the place that Anderson left and carry on the "story picture" idea. He continued with the Selig organization for years. He met his death in tragic motion picture fashion at last, when a Japanese extra man employed at the California studio ran amuck and shot Boggs to death on the lot, incidentally wounding Colonel Selig at the same time.

Over in Paris at the establishment of the Pathé Freres there was a very blond and hard-headed sales manager bent on the conquest of new fields for his concern. This was Jacques A. Berst, a Frenchman of Strassbourg ancestry, who had begun his Pathé connection as the editor and author of a novelty trade journal financed by Emile Pathé, a tobacconist brother of the better known Charles Pathé.

Following on the producing precedents of Melies of Paris, the Pathés were rapidly rising to an important place in the world market for film. Because all the Latin peoples of the world came to Paris to shop Pathé films in even that remote day had well near covered the globe, figuring in every market except the United States.

Since many of the orders came from Parisian buying agents

for foreign clients, Berst saw to it that every shipment contained a card craftily wound into the film, bearing the Pathé address and calculated to bring in direct orders thereafter, eliminating the middlemen.

A dull day came in the rounds of Sigismund Poppert, Pathé's salesman in Germany and England. Berst suggested a trip to look over America, where, thanks to the skill of the film "dupers," few Pathé pictures were bought but many were sold. The store show audiences were developing a taste for Max Linder, the funny French actor.

Poppert's reports of what he found by way of a new market brought Berst over within a few months.

The Frenchman looked New York over with a solemn interest and because he had heard more of Madison Square than of anything else in America, he selected an office there and prepared to take a hand in the game. The Pathé red rooster was getting ready to scratch in the sprouting American film garden.

CHAPTER FORTY-THREE

CARL LAEMMLE TAKES A CHANCE

In Chicago the Cochrane brothers, Bob, Phil and Witt, were in 1905 conducting an advertising agency. One of their major accounts was the promotion service of a large clothing manufacturing and wholesaling concern. A side line of less importance was a ready-made advertising service for small retail clothing concerns. This consisted principally of display ads, written, set up and supplied with a blank space for the insertion of the name and address of the local clothing store.

This was the era when the advertising business was coming into its modern development. It was filled with rewritten platitudes and amateur literature of psychology, presenting to the less critical consumer a fine substantial atmosphere of scientific discovery.

Among the many customers of this pre-digested advertising service of the Cochranes was the Stern Clothing Company's store at Oshkosh, Wisconsin. The manager was Carl Laemmle, who had married a niece of Samuel Stern, the owner of the business.

This Laemmle made himself conspicuous in the mail of the Cochrane agency in Chicago. Laemmle not only used the Cochrane's ready made ads; he took them seriously and studied them, amending them for his special purposes. He continually wrote in comment and inquiry. He wanted a lot of advice. This was rather outside the purpose of the ad service and Robert Cochrane, who dictated the replies to the mail order clients of the agency, was by turns annoyed at the troublesome customer at Oshkosh, and pleased at his aggressive interest. He gave

Laemmle's letters faithful attention and a good deal of service that was not in the regular line of business.

This disinterested labor on the part of Robert Cochrane was before long to be rewarded beyond his largest dream of affluence.

Laemmle took these letters to heart. The man in Chicago whom he had never seen was a real friend. Also to the little clothing salesman in Oshkosh this Chicago person was an imposing figure in the business world, a master of the science of merchandising. This small acquaintance grew. Laemmle had some personal problems that he ventured to confide to Cochrane, seeking advice. One day in the winter of 1905 when Cochrane sat down to his desk and went at the morning mail, there was a larger letter than usual from Oshkosh.

"Wonder what's on his mind now?" Cochrane paused in his dictation and scanned the pages. In substance Laemmle said this:

"I am sore and tired of this job. I'm just a figurehead manager here. The store is full of relatives and they won't pay any attention to what I say and they go over my head to Mr. Stern when I try to make them do anything. I am thirty-nine years old now and I've got $2,500. I want to get into business for myself if I can. What do you think?"

Bob Cochrane cleared his throat, hitched his chair a little closer the desk and as the stenographer sat with pencil poised, started a reply. That letter read today reminds one atmospherically of Coué, Doctor Munyon, Herbert Kaufman and Elbert Hubbard.

"Don't be a salary slave!" it opened.

"If you are going to be anything in this world you must start before you are forty, before your period of initiative has ended.

"Do it now!

"Today is the day. Delay, procrastination, uncertainty—these are the negative sins of the business man.

"Action—etc., etc."

When Laemmle got the letter up there in the Oshkosh clothing store he opened it with expectancy. The writing of it had not been much in Cochrane's life, but it was a great deal to Laemmle. Laemmle was seeking an answer to the biggest problem of his life. He read the letter several times that day. He took it home with him and read it to his wife. There had to be a family decision. It was a grave, important day.

Two weeks later a secretary entered Robert Cochrane's office and announced, "There's a Mr. Laemmle from Oshkosh wants to see you."

The client had followed the doctor's advice with a completeness that was overwhelming. Laemmle, a solid, smallish chap with an imported German accent, came in.

"I have resigned and I am ready to start over. What shall I do?"

Inwardly Cochrane made a resolve to be more careful in writing advice to out of town clients thereafter. His copy was evidently too powerful.

Meanwhile here was Carl Laemmle in Chicago, aged 39, capital $2,500, waiting to be shown the route of delivery from salary slavery, waiting to start something "before forty." Here was a man of determination and dogged adherence to his convictions, continuously evidenced since his first day on his first job in America. Employed as a farm hand in Iowa, Laemmle was sent out to feed the hogs. Laemmle was heir to ages of taboo against pork, dead or alive. He quit and set out jobless to try again.

There was considerable conferring now. Cochrane was in touch with the wholesale clothing business. Laemmle had experience in the clothing trade. Simply enough, the first quest led in that direction. The Cochrane agency put out some feelers to find a small clothing store into which Laemmle might put his money and services. There was some delay in getting promising responses. Meanwhile Laemmle was looking Chicago over and getting some ideas for himself.

One day the man from Oshkosh was walking down State Street wondering what was to be done next when he observed a line of people standing before some sort of a show place. Closer inspection revealed that this was one of those new *Hale's Tours* devices, a railway coach theatre in which scenery went sweeping by on a motion picture screen. The admission was ten cents and the dimes seemed to trickle in all day.

Laemmle watched a while, then sought his friend Cochrane up at the advertising agency.

"I've found a good business—faster than selling clothes."

"Steady, now—don't be in a hurry," Cochrane interrupted. "You want to look into this thing carefully. You can't afford to make any mistakes with a thing like that."

Cochrane was highly dubious about the amusement business in general and this novelty of the motion picture especially. He liked this earnest little chap from Oshkosh and wanted to see him started right. There was a certain sense of responsibility about that very convincing letter he had written.

"Now, Mr. Laemmle, you'd better get all the facts about this business so we can make some sort of an analysis of it on a real business-like basis. Go count the number of customers, find out how much the place costs to operate, help, films, light and all that kind of thing."

Laemmle went diligently about those very errands. This man Cochrane was a scientific business man and Laemmle knew it. This was the way to do it, because Cochrane said so.

Cochrane had a stretch when Laemmle went out. This would keep the man from Oshkosh busy for a day or so—meanwhile something interesting might turn up by way of a clothing store opportunity, and that would be the end of it.

For two days the little man from Oshkosh stood down in State street, moving just enough to keep from being conspicuous, while he counted the attendance that went in to see the *Hale's Tours* pictures. When he got through he had an accurate notion of what kind of people went to see the pictures, what hours of the day they found the time to do it in, and how many of them there were per hour and per day.

This simple and scientific method is of interest to the student of business. In exactly this same manner today the locations of the United Cigar stores and the Woolworth establishments are chosen.

With judicious questions in various places Laemmle discovered what it cost to go into the business and how films were bought and rented from exchanges. He made a rapid intensive study of his tediously acquired facts. Then he went back to Cochrane's office. He had listened a lot to Cochrane. It was Laemmle's turn to talk.

Laemmle had facts and figures, whole columns and rows of them.

He talked hard and fast to Cochrane. Probably there was a notion in his shrewd head that if he was able to sell the idea to Cochrane it would be a rather good indication that he was right.

There is no suspense to this story. The world knows that Carl Laemmle went into the motion picture business, still sticking appreciatively to Bob Cochrane and his advice.

Laemmle effectively sold the motion picture idea to Cochrane that afternoon. That conversation made it the big day in the business lives of both of them.

Laemmle looked about for a location, one that was not too expensive and one on the sort of a street where the traffic carried plenty of the kind of people he saw going into the *Hale's Tours* show in State street.

February 24, 1906, at 909 Milwaukee Avenue, in Chicago's

west side, Carl Laemmle opened the ticket office of his theatre and made ready to receive the first nickel.

This may sound like the end of the excitement, with plain sailing ahead. But it was the slightest beginning. Laemmle had just set up his tent on the edge of the battle-ground, as he was soon to discover.

But ever since that date twenty years ago, Carl Laemmle and Bob Cochrane have stood together in the motion picture turmoil —and prospered.

Within six months Laemmle had a film exchange in operation and was extending his theatre business with more store shows. He was on his way. He had decided that he was through with the clothing business for a long time.

While this was going on in Chicago a very similar development was occurring eighty miles north in Milwaukee, where John R. Freuler was finding his Comique theatre in Kinnikinnic Avenue an interesting investment. The theatre seemed to do well, but the payroll kept close pace with the gross receipts. Freuler's partner had an endless supply of relatives to employ, it seemed. So with some reluctance at sparing the time from his real estate operations Freuler bought out his partner and started to run the theatre himself.

An interesting, convincing salesman with a suitcase full of films called at the Freuler real estate office.

"I'm H. E. Aitken, Chicago Film Exchange," he introduced himself. He sold an order of films for the Comique.

Freuler found some of the details of the business puzzling. He paid about thirty dollars a week rental for a reel with yards and yards of film pictures on it. Apparently the reel was just as good when he returned it as when he got it. He decided the business of renting reels must be profitable.

Presently as their acquaintance blossomed Aitken suggested that if Freuler would go on his surety to the Chicago Film

Exchange he would be able to carry a larger stock and it would be a pleasant favor.

"I don't see any profit to me in that, if I do," Freuler remarked. "But if this business is so good, why can't we go into it? I'd rather do that than go on your bond."

It was delightfully simple.

On July 23, 1906, Aitken and Freuler opened the Western Film Exchange of Milwaukee, offering films for rental to the theaters of the region.

Thus in Milwaukee the seed that grew into more than twenty transiently famous film corporations was sown. Out of that meeting of Aitken and Freuler came a series of sequels to figure in screen development, among them the once important Mutual Film Corporation with the winged clock trade mark that announced "Mutual Movies Make Time Fly," and the briefly dominant Triangle Film Corporation which made dollars fly.

Blind Chance, the casting director of the drama of the motion picture industry, made the next choice reaching down into the woollen goods district of downtown New York, in the heart of the cloak and suit zone. Sol Brill, the proprietor of a cloth sponging business, learned from an uncle employed in Brooklyn that there was a penny arcade and picture show for sale over at 700 Broadway in the City of Churches and perambulators. It looked like a coming business.

Brill sought his friend William Fox, also a cloth sponger, and together they acquired the arcade and five cent screen show upstairs. The investment was about a thousand dollars. This was late in 1906.

Within six months Brill withdrew and later became an independent exhibitor. "I didn't like the business and the kind of people we had to deal with," he says.

Fox stayed. He was due to conduct a spectacular war, all of his own, against the rising patent kings in the next few years.

MAURICE COSTELLO, among the earliest of real stars of the
screen, who set a precedent for actors at Vitagraph by
being the first player to refuse to help the stage carpenters.

DAVID WARK GRIFFITH, from a photograph of
the period when he was at Biograph, evolving
the new technique of the motion picture and
laying a foundation for fame.

CHAPTER FORTY-FOUR

ENTER D. W. GRIFFITH WITH MSS.

THE name of Edison led many seekers of screen opportunity
to ride up to the end of the Third Avenue "L" to the glass studio
in the Bronx. Of the many who went at that early day to find
a place in the new art of the pictures, few names remain, but
there is one outstanding survival of those beginnings—a rambling actor by the name of D. W. Griffith, sometimes billed on
the stage as Lawrence Griffith.

Young Mr. Griffith arrived in New York late in the season
of 1907, at the end of a long road tour with Nance O'Neil.
For a while, as Broadway says, he was "resting." He was looking about for some way to terminate the resting period. He
was all rested up and tired of it.

Griffith tended a bit to authorship. In yet earlier days he
had been a book agent and later a newspaper reporter in Louisville. He sometimes did a bit of verse. Now the motion picture suggested possibilities. The film concerns were beginning,
he heard, to buy "suggestions."

So D. W. Griffith, with the scenario for a screen version of
La Tosca in his pocket, rode up to the Bronx to see the Edison
people about it.

La Tosca, with its many scenes as Griffith had it arranged in
his script, seemed a trifle too pretentious for the Edison establishment to attempt. Griffith suggested that he could act as well
as write.

"Well, I am looking for a man for a part," the director, E.
S. Porter, admitted slowly, as he sized up Griffith. "But it is

a sort of a woodsman-mountaineer part and I don't think you are husky enough for it."

"I could pad up for it a bit, don't you know," Griffith argued.

Rather reluctantly Porter agreed to use Griffith in the part.

The picture was entitled, *The Eagle's Nest*. It was a one-reel story of the baby that was carried off into the Alps by a great eagle and rescued by the daring mountaineer, who climbed the crag and engaged the bird in battle on his lofty perch.

The long shots of the picture were made on the Palisades of the Hudson, while the close-ups were photographed in the Edison studio. The cliff and eagle's nest were constructed and painted by Richard Murphy, who began his scenic career as a paint boy for the Spooner stock company and developed into one of the screen's most effective technical experts.

The dramatic high point of the picture was the battle on the crag between the hardy mountaineer, played by D. W. Griffith, and the eagle, played by a stuffed bird from a taxidermist's shop. The eagle was supplied with hinged wings, manipulated by invisible black threads. The bird put up quite a battle for the baby but Griffith managed to triumph in the end.

Griffith got his five dollars a day for a couple of days' work in the picture and went his way, to offer his scenario ideas and his services as an actor elsewhere. But his screen career had begun; years ahead of him Fate was waiting with the unborn *Birth of a Nation*.

At the Biograph studio Griffith met McCutcheon, the director in charge.

The scenarios would be considered, and also there was a possibility that Griffith might work in some of the pictures.

Soon Griffith was working frequently in Biograph's pictures, and Arthur Marvin, a cameraman, observed that this quiet young actor seemed to have ideas that set him just a shade apart from the miscellaneous dramatic flotsam of the studio's shifting casts.

Close to this time another young man with a handful of destiny took a ride up the Third Avenue "L" to the Edison studio in the Bronx. He was Michael Sinnott, a Canadian, known, but very slightly known, as Mack Sennett, a bit of a chorus man, spear bearer, and light comedian with a pleasant voice and a naturally whimsical manner. He got a part in one of those early and forgotten Edison dramas, played a few days and came downtown again. He, too, joined Biograph.

Biograph was steadily striving to improve its pictures. Biographs were openly called "rotten" on the market. The quality had fallen low, while attention was centered on the legal wars. Now the studio began to be important again. Marvin decided that better direction and better stories were necessary.

The scene changes to midnight on Park Row. Down in Dennett's restaurant Stanner Taylor, a rambling free lance newspaper man, was at his supper in one of those arm chair affairs. Taylor had strolled over from the *Tribune* office where he used a typewriter after hours. He was meditating on the high lights of his recent adventure in musical comedy and the abrupt closing of *The Gibson Girl* in San Antonio. This had sent him back to newspapering and New York.

A stranger came into the restaurant where Taylor sat alone. There were many empty seats about but the stranger chose one next to Taylor.

"You're Taylor, ain't you?"

"Yes, what of it?"

"Well—Dick Spillane over at the *Sun* told me about you— I'm looking for somebody to write things for moving pictures."

Taylor listened to the story of Biograph and its requirements. Then he went home and dashed off a couple of picture ideas in tabloid form, three hundred words each. It was one of those easy performances which the scenario schools try to make the aspiring reader of advertisements think is so readily profitable today. These picture ideas Taylor—Stanner E. V. Taylor—submitted to Biograph. They resulted in a call at Marvin's office and a check for $30.

Now space rates on the newspapers were about eight dollars a column, much the same as they are now. Six hundred words for thirty dollars opened Taylor's eyes. He talked to Marvin about more ideas.

Outside the door down in the studio there was a heated argument going on, to which Marvin and Taylor might have listened with some amusement.

It seems that David W. Griffith, actor, had spoiled a pair of shoes in the course of making a picture the day before. He was demanding settlement in the sum of five dollars.

"No," McCutcheon, the director, roared. "Those shoes never were worth five dollars—what the hell would an actor be doing with a five dollar pair of shoes anyway?"

When Taylor emerged from Marvin's office he had an arrangement to write scenarios in quantity for Biograph and to get a guaranty of $25 a week, whether they used as many as two a week or not.

Biograph was rapidly getting ready to make two reels a week.

It was early in June when H. N. Marvin called in his brother Arthur.

"We've got to put on another director to help out McCutcheon. One a week is all he can make. Who can we get?"

"There's an actor out there, that fellow Griffith," observed the cameraman. "He seems to have a lot of sense and some good ideas."

Marvin recalled Griffith. This new actor had worked in a number of pictures. There was the release called 'Ostler Joe, a bit of a comedy in which Griffith played with Eddie Dillon, the comedy lead.

"I'll give him a try—send Griffith in," Marvin decided.

Griffith appeared. He stood speculatively looking out the window into Fourteenth Street, deep in reflection, as Marvin unfolded the proposal that he try directing pictures.

"I want you to take this 'suggestion,'" said Marvin, picking up a script by Taylor, "and make a picture out of it. See what you can do with it."

Griffith shook his head.

"No—I'd rather not."

"Why—it is better work, advancement and better pay and more future than just acting."

"Yes," Griffith responded, "but you see I've got responsibilities and all that, and I am working regularly for McCutcheon now. If I try directing he will not like it and if I fall down he won't give me any more parts."

Marvin smiled at the earnest young man.

"I never go over the heads of my people—you know that," Marvin offered reassuringly. "But in this case I will make you a promise that the result of this experiment will not be permitted to impair your position with Biograph."

Griffith with some perturbation set about hunting a cast for his first picture, entitled *The Adventures of Dolly*.

Griffith went exploring up Broadway. On the stairs of a booking agency he passed a type that suited him exactly. He dashed into the agency.

"Was that man that just went out of here an actor?"

"Guess so," the attendant replied.

Griffith turned about and ran full tilt back to the street and on the trail of the actor. When he overtook him he was out of breath.

The object of pursuit paused and grinned at the panting pursuer.

"Are—are—are you an actor?" Griffith gasped.

The actor drew himself up to his full height with all of the dignity of the best traditions of the old stock tragedian. He thrust his hand into the lapel of his coat and bowed.

"Upon that point, sir, there are two highly diverse opinions—I am Arthur Johnson."

"I want you for a picture," Griffith suggested.

"Well—it has come to this," Johnson proclaimed in mock tragedy.

"But it is not seemly that we should stand thus talking of paltry employment in the open street—let us to yonder tavern."

Johnson was cast for the picture. Others that Griffith chose were Charles Inslee who had worked a bit in Biographs, and Linda Arvidson, an actress occasionally employed there.

It was a perfectly concealed secret that Linda Arvidson was Mrs. D. W. Griffith.

The Adventures of Dolly, the story of a child kidnapped by gypsies, was completed in due time. It was a simple one-reeler with few studio interiors and with locations in New Jersey.

Griffith began his march forward that day.

Viewed in the perspective of time *The Adventures of Dolly* would seem rude indeed, but it was a burst of new genius in '08. It told a plausible story in a natural, logical manner.

Arthur Johnson, the leading man in that first Griffith picture began therewith the career which made him the first matinee idol of the screen. Johnson had a long dramatic career back of him, beginning when he ran away from his father's home, the Episcopal rectory at Davenport, Iowa, to join the William Owen Dramatic Company.

Some years later Johnson, after various film engagements, became the dominant star of the Lubin organization in Philadelphia. Success took him down the Primrose Path to the finish of all "jolly good fellows." He died in 1916.

The beginning for Griffith proved the beginning of the end for Johnson.

CHAPTER FORTY-FIVE

KALEM AND THE FIRST "BEN HUR"

THE rising prosperity of the film industry's growing market among the nickelodeon theatres now in the days of '07 inspired the organization of a new concern, known as Kalem. It was a synthetic name based on the initials K-L-M, representing George Kleine, Chicago exchangeman, Samuel Long and Frank Marion, both of experience with Biograph.

Kalem was financed with delightful simplicity. Long owned four hundred dollars worth of partitions in a loft building where the plant was to be located. Marion contributed six hundred dollars working capital and George Kleine guaranteed the account of the company for the purchase of a Warwick camera from Charles Urban in London.

Kalem began with the production of a comedy on location near Marion's home at Sound Beach, Connecticut.

Kalem among others had a chance at D. W. Griffith's scenario of *La Tosca* that day that he went to Biograph. But Kalem's spectacular early success was to be developed under other hands.

While Griffith was laying the foundation of his career at Biograph, Sidney Olcott began high pressure production at the Kalem studios in Twenty-first street.

Sidney Olcott's connection with the motion pictures began with the peep show Mutoscope pictures at Biograph about a year before. Olcott was playing with Marion Leonard and Joe Santley in *Billy the Kid,* a road show, when he first heard the call of the motion pictures. It was a very faint call—at three dollars a day. Down at the Biograph studio the production of the little cardboard wheels for the peep show end of the

—459—

business, the Mutoscope machines for the arcades, was under the charge of Frank Marion, who promptly employed Olcott.

Olcott's first part for the Biograph-Mutoscope camera was the lead in a one minute farce entitled *Wanted, a Dog.*

In response to a want ad for dog extras, sixty pups of high and low degree were delivered that day at 11 East Fourteenth street. Among them was an undershot, underslung, low minded and high biting brindle bulldog. He whipped the bunch before the picture started. In a bit of actor whimsy, Olcott, thinking lightly of his new job anyway, made himself up to resemble the features of the bulldog as much as possible. He went on in the make-up and thereupon made the hit with Marion that took him along to Kalem, when it was organized a few months later.

So Sidney Olcott broke into the kingdom of the film drama made up as a bull pup and supported by a cast of sixty alley hounds.

Over at the Kalem studios many an actor destined to large parts in the latter affairs of the motion picture was first introduced to the camera under the auspices of Marion and Olcott. Trivial happenings in the days of the beginnings were to control the careers of many of those who became famous with the rise of the photoplay.

Early in his work at Kalem, Sid Olcott discovered the picturesque badlands of the Palisades of New Jersey and elected Coytesville as the center of a new Wild West of the pictures. The first western pictures of the screen, a type of production that became the staple thriller for many years, were made within gunshot of the Hudson river—this long before the real West was filmed.

Among the members of the road company playing *Billy the Kid* was one Robert Vignola, a capable person of Italian extraction. While casting one of his synthetic Wild West dramas Olcott recalled that Vignola was the owner of a costume that might pass for Mexican. Vignola was drafted for the picture at once, and rode to his first location on the Fort Lee ferry along with the flannel shirted actors of Kalem, carrying lunch boxes.

The effete requirements of motion picture technique had not yet been evolved. In that day everyone on the set lent a hand to everything that was to be done. Olcott, in addition to directing, helped build, erect and shift the sets at the studio. While engaged in making this long forgotten "western" Olcott looked up one day, breathless and exhausted with heavy lifting. His eye lighted on big Bob Vignola.

"Give us a hand, Bob."

Vignola proved to be both kinds of a "heavy." He hove with a will.

"Say," Olcott decided, "you're too strong for just an actor— you're promoted to assistant director, starting now. Grab the other end of this flat and let's go."

That was the fall of 1907. In 1922 that same Vignola, who strong-armed his way into the motion pictures, directed Marion Davies in the million dollar production of *When Knighthood Was in Flower*.

At about this same time another name now widely known to the fame of the screen was drawn in on an equally attenuated gossamer thread of chance. Olcott had a picture with a society scene. He had to have a "nifty looking man in a morning suit." He looked about for days trying to find a player with such an item in his wardrobe. A few had evening dress and dinner jackets—but the morning suit, that was a step beyond. Probably few actors ever got up in the morning, anyway. It seemed hopeless and Olcott was about to rewrite the scenario when he encountered George Melford, striding down Broadway in all the elegance of a profoundly correct formal day attire fresh from the tailor shop.

"You're it—come across the river."

Melford precipitated a studio fuss by taking a fifteen cent drink on Olcott at lunch that day.

In December, 1907, Kalem boldly stepped out with a most daring and spectacular project, *Ben Hur* in one whole reel. It was planned as an inexpensive production. Miss Gene Gauntier prepared the "working synopsis," as they called it then, from the book, and the settings were ready made at the Pain's Fireworks show at Manhattan Beach. The advertising, consisting of a herald or leaflet, issued in January, 1908, announced:

BEN HUR

Produced under the direction of Frank Oakes Rose and Sidney Olcott.

In sixteen magnificent scenes with illustrated titles.

Positively the most superb moving picture spectacle ever made in America.

There was just one minor oversight in connection with the picture. Kalem failed to acquire the motion picture rights to *Ben Hur*—largely for the rather simple reason that motion picture rights were unknown. It was not at all certain that there was any such thing. And in all instances of the kind the motion picture industry always generously gave itself the benefit of the doubt.

The Kalem film version of *Ben Hur* went out to attract considerable attention.

Then one day a process server from the offices of David Gerber, attorney, dropped down to 131 West 24th street and proceeded to serve Frank Marion, secretary-treasurer of Kalem, with the papers in an action brought in the United States Court of the Southern District of New York by Harper & Brothers, publishers of *Ben Hur*, Marc Klaw and Abraham Erlanger, producers of the spectacle drama *Ben Hur*, and Henry Wallace, as administrator of the estate of Susan E. Wallace, deceased, heir of Lew Wallace of Crawfordsville, Indiana, author of the novel *Ben Hur*. In other words, Kalem was sued with great completeness and vigor.

This suit was the first issue of the kind. It was the precedent making action that was to establish the legal character of the motion picture as a medium of dramatic and literary expression.

The suit was strongly defended by Kalem and fought through to the United States Supreme Court. Kalem made an effort to show that the production on the screen was "merely a series of photographs" and also set up the plea that after all the picture was just a good advertisement for the book and the stage play.

A final decision against Kalem was handed down in 1911. Kalem settled for $25,000. That, plus the expenses of the litigation, made *Ben Hur* the most costly one reel scenario in the entire history of the business. Length considered, the price has never been equalled—but of course it took the United States Supreme Court to collect it.

Ben Hur was neither the first nor the last story to be thus boldly "adopted" into the motion pictures. But the purloinings of the screen from the field of literature and drama thereafter were disguised with new titles and some reconstruction.

Late in 1925 Metro-Goldwyn-Mayer completed the production of a highly pretentious film version of *Ben Hur* after three years of costly labors from Rome to Hollywood. It is alleged that several millions were spent in production, in anticipation of making it the screen's most grandiose gesture. Ramon Navarro, one of the school of Latin-lover types swept in on the Valentino wave, appeared in the title rôle, under the direction of Fred Niblo. A quarter of a million dollars was spent in staging the chariot race scene in California. It is said to present a run for the money. The picture was announced for its première at the

Cohan theatre in New York Christmas eve, 1925, just eighteen years after Kalem's one reel effort.

The career of the Kalem concern was the most perfect exemplification of the placer mining gold rush method of its era in the films. Kalem was launched without investment and swiftly rose to profits of more than $5,000 a week in 1908, continuing on a rising scale through the golden days of the Patents Company and the General Film Company. Its pictures were made with a minimum expenditure and at high speed for the nickelodeon audiences in the days when the manufacturer received his price per foot regardless of content or quality. Kalem was a soundly conducted exploiter of a transient opportunity. When picture evolution raised standards and entailed both expense, labor and risk for the producer Kalem quit, pocketed its profits and retired.

Kalem's two most important contributions to the personnel of the motion picture were Sidney Olcott and Marshall Neilan. Neilan's connection began at the West Coast studio driving a car. He attached himself to the staff of Pat Hardigan and became an assistant to the director. When Hardigan resigned by wire, a second messenger boy went tripping into the office of Frank Marion in New York with a message from Neilan announcing he was taking over the job.

Marion strode into the office of William Wright, his general manager.

"Who is this fellow Neilan?"

"Oh, he's a handy lad out there," answered Wright. "Why?"

"Well, he's taken charge of the studio. I like his nerve—let him keep it."

Ruth Roland became a star under Neilan's direction at Kalem.

ARTHUR JOHNSON, who went from the stage to play in Griffith's first picture at Biograph, and became the first screen player with the fame and following of a matinee idol.

GEORGE KLEINE, the diplomat and peace-maker in the secret negotiations that ended the Biograph-Edison war and made the motion picture an industry.

CHAPTER FORTY-SIX

JEREMIAH J. KENNEDY, HARDBOILED

Every studio was a guarded stronghold in 1907. Pictures were made behind locked and guarded doors. There were secret ways about everything.

All the makers of pictures were hiding their methods, mostly with the fear of being discovered in their infringements and in part because they had inventions and formulæ of their own to guard.

The business of the motion picture was in a state of feudal war. The art of the motion picture got only such scant attention as could be spared from battle.

Al McCoy, of the Edison secret service, was the bogy man of the movies then. He haunted the paths of competing, infringing picture makers for evidence. Where McCoy went on his prying errands, lawyers and processes servers followed.

Enforcement of his control of the camera patents was Edison's hope for regaining his original possession of the motion picture which he had brought into being.

But the coming of the story picture, the photoplay, and the consequent rise of the screen theatre, made the profits of the business so alluring that law and patents and the ethical customs of business were as futile as Prohibition. Peace had to come before progress. And the final peace had to be a compromise.

October 24, 1907, Judge Christian Kohlsaat, in United States Court in Chicago, rendered a decision holding that the cameras used by William N. Selig infringed on the Edison patents. Here was a decisive blow. A shudder went through the studios.

—465—

J. Stuart Blackton of Vitagraph, which had also felt the heavy hand of the Edison legal department in the years of battle, was in Chicago when the Selig decision came. Blackton sought counsel with George Kleine, then the principal dealer in motion pictures in the West. Kleine, among all the film men, was the most interested in an end of the destructive patent wars. He dealt in the products of practically all of the studios, both in the United States and abroad.

There was a luncheon at Rector's in Chicago, with Kleine presiding and Blackton, with George K. Spoor of Essanay and Colonel Selig about the table.

"I'll go to Edison and see what we can do toward making peace," Kleine promised. His luncheon guests were dubious. They had enjoyed some ten years of war with Edison.

A month later Kleine went to the Edison establishment at West Orange in New Jersey and held a conference with W: E. Gilmore, the general manager. Then he crossed the river to Manhattan and sent out invitations to a very quiet little dinner at the Republican club, in Fortieth street facing Bryant park.

Gilmore attended that dinner and the fellow infringers sat all about, marvelling at his cheery cordiality. They had been used to fire and brimstone. Out of the talk around the table came an understanding that an agreement could be made upon a plan by which all of the picture makers could be licensed under the Edison patents in consideration of royalty payments.

Soon thereafter at a dinner held at the Hotel Astor the Edison Licensees group was formed, including Kalem, Vitagraph, Lubin, Selig, Essanay, Melies and Pathé.

This session, incidenally, stamped the Astor with a certain official status in the film world, continuing down to today. It was a reiteration of the old, old rite of breaking bread and sharing the salt together at the making of peace. Every important controversy of the endless strife of the motion picture has been settled over the coffee.

But Biograph refused to dine.

Biograph was offered a peace and a license from Edison on the same terms with the rest. Biograph refused and demanded recognition on an equality with Edison. Biograph contended that it held patents as necessary to the art as Edison's. After ten years of war, Biograph was just beginning to fight.

Meanwhile Frank L. Dyer, representing Edison, went to Chicago to address the assembled motion picture exchangemen and announce the alleged dawn of a new day, under the Edison license.

The rise of the nickelodeon consumption of film had created a market condition which seems strange in retrospect. The nickelodeon program consisted of a number of reels, from three to five, often changed daily. This resulted in a tremendous consumption of subjects, since the subjects were normally just one reel long. The clamorous demand was for film, film, film —regardless of quality or content. The only requirement was that it be new. The basis of value was age. First run film just out of the can from the factory was worth on its first day from ten to twenty times as much in rentals as it was on the thirtieth day. After thirty days it was all of one class, disdainfully designated in the trade as "commercial."

This made release dates arbitrarily fixed by the producer of large importance. Competing exchanges strove to get as much as one day's advantage in the shipment of film. Release dates were normally violated with great vigor. The practice of the trade was full of price cutting and every conceivable dishonesty and chicanery.

Now Dyer announced the central control of film making under the Edison license system would hold everybody to the rules.

The exchangemen listened with great attentiveness and left the session to resume their throat cutting.

If the Edison Licensees group had been a complete pool of the industry it could have enforced its orders.

But Biograph was on the outside, supplying film of its own manufacture and importing it. The exchangemen could not be put out of business without a coalition with Biograph.

Also a forceful factor had come into the situation. The Empire Trust Company being disturbed about long overdue interest payments on a loan of $200,000 to Biograph, sent one Jeremiah J. Kennedy up to 11 East 14th street to see about it. It was the anticipation that it would be necessary to wind up the concern's affairs and liquidate. Kennedy was to be the undertaker.

Now this Kennedy was a kind of man utterly new to the motion picture. He was a born boss. Down at 52 Broadway his name was, and still is, on the door in neat gold letters with a subscription announcing him as a consulting engineer.

When Kennedy began he was a rodman with a surveying gang on the Norfolk & Western railway. He was Jerry Kennedy then. He came from Philadelphia and the odds are excellent that he was not of Quaker stock. He made his way up in the technical world and held his own out on the raw edge of things in the life of construction camps and the places where muckers and hard rock men moil and toil. The young engineer learned to talk to a gang foreman in language that could be understood, and he could punctuate with either fist.

Kennedy worked his way upward in the engineering world of big works until finally the trail emerged in the realm of big money and business. And like many another engineer he became quite as much an executive of business as of the technical concerns of engineering. He became more and more a commander of men and a student of the migratory habits of the eagle embossed on the obverse of the American dollar. He had made money, about all the money he wanted. He had done plenty of hard work. He had been the housecleaner and reorganizer of several large enterprises including one of the Gould railroads.

Now, despite the fact that Kennedy had no interest in pictures, his banker friends wanted him to do something up at Biograph.

When Kennedy got through with his first look around at Biograph he decided to be a doctor instead of an undertaker, and that the whole field of the motion picture was to be the patient.

This Kennedy was outwardly blunt, pungent, swift and positive. In the subsequent years of his domination Kennedy often appeared as much a person of magic intuitions in the films as John W. Gates seemed in the barbwire and steel business. The fact was however that Kennedy, precisely like Gates, made his spectacular decisions and swift splashes of ruddy action, only after an army of espionage agents had reported and assistants had graphed and analyzed and sifted the facts.

To the surprised showmen, cameramen and adventurers of the film trade Kennedy became a miracle man, because they could not know or understand that machinery of draftsmen, statisticians and map makers he organized at 52 Broadway to supply the tiny memoranda that came to his desk.

In all this Kennedy was in his way a dramatist of high degree, the kind of a dramatist that can make a three card draw look better than a pat hand. A glint of his eye for detail appeared in one of his first orders, when the name of the Biograph film processing plant in Hoboken was changed from "factory" to "laboratory." "Because," Kennedy observed, "we can get a better class of people to work in a laboratory. It sounds like

something and a film plant ought to be a laboratory, anyway."
The term still obtains as the standard designation for film fac-
tories.

The ground work of Biograph's coming fight had already been
capably laid by H. N. Marvin, calm but crafty. Now a number
of events affecting the personnel of the industry were to clear
the path. Differences arose between Thomas A. Edison and W.
E. Gilmore, his belligerent and effective general manager. Gilmore left to take up the affairs of the Essex Press, a printing
concern, and Frank L. Dyer, who had been Edison's personal
attorney, took his place in the Edison organization. When Gilmore went he took with him most of the personal feeling against
William Kennedy Laurie Dickson, whose departure had carried
that animosity to Biograph.

Now also changes came in the affairs of the Anthony & Scoville company, which had these years been holding the Latham
patent among its frozen, inert assets. Old Major Latham had
long since been reported dead. Thomas W. Stephens of Montclair, New Jersey, became the head of the concern under the
new name of Ansco. Stephens sought a buyer for the Latham
patent, which appeared of no use to Ansco, engaged only in the
making of photographic materials.

On the golf links of Montclair, Stephens offered the patent
to Frank L. Dyer. The price was $10,000. Dyer did not hold
the Latham patent in that high esteem. Probably he was technically correct and strategically wrong. Presently it was offered
to Biograph and sold through Marvin for $2,500, February 5,
1908. Biograph was arming for the big drive.

Late in March Marvin, with all due stealth to avoid the shad-
owing Edison agents, took a night train to Washington and there
at the Hotel Willard held long argumentative conference with
Thomas Armat, who had an array of projection machine patents.

When Marvin returned Biograph had possession of the stock certificates of Armat's company, on an option to buy them for $3,000,000 and an agreement that Armat should have half as much as Biograph out of any profits of the movement on foot. The three million was a bluff, aimed at keeping other bidders discouraged. The stock went into a safe deposit box at the Empire Trust company, there to play its share in the big game.

Events began to move faster now.

Kleine of Chicago, who had been an influential factor in the transient and partial peace of the Edison Licensees, was in the background now working toward a bigger peace that would take in Biograph.

Out of this came a luncheon on July 11, 1908, at the Claremont up on Riverside Drive, away from the noise and strife of downtown New York. Dyer, Marvin and Kennedy talked it over. Biograph offered a guaranty that if their patents and Edison's were pooled, Edison's share of the profits would be $150,000 a year.

It seemed improbable and Dyer declined.

In the Edison camp there appeared to be an opinion, too, that Biograph was quite as much an infringer of the Edison patents as all the rest.

Kennedy determined on a daring move. Secrecy was for the first time thrown aside. Edison's experts were invited into the Biograph plant and a picture, with Griffith directing, was made with the peculiar Biograph camera. They handed it to the Edison observers to develop in their own plant.

Winter came and the negotiations were still pending. The year was slipping away and Biograph's financial condition was not improving. Something drastic had to be done. Marvin and Kennedy sat together in the downtown office at 52 Broadway.

"If anybody came along and offered five dollars for our chances I'd take the five," Marvin remarked.

Kennedy was of the same mind. He took a fresh grip on his cigar and walked the floor.

The telephone rang and Kennedy snatched it up. He listened a moment. There was an Edison lawyer on the line.

"Say!" Kennedy exploded, 'if that agreement does not go through, just the way it is, without the change of one word in it, Biograph is going to bust this business wide open. We will put our cameras on the market and license everybody. If we can't get together and control this business we will make a first class wreck of it—and we'll have it now."

Kennedy had played the last card.

The next day was the seventeenth of December. That afternoon there came a call to a meeting at the Hotel Brevoort in lower Fifth Avenue, for the following day. It was settled.

In the afternoon, December 18, the great peace was signed.

The Edison and Biograph officials, George Kleine, and all of those whom Edison had licensed, Vitagraph, Lubin, Selig, Essanay, Pathé, Kalem, and Melies were represented. They pooled their patents and claims to special rights. The Motion Picture Patents Company was born. This was the beginning of the most powerful concern in all the history of the motion picture. The decade of war was over.

The next day the event was signalized by a peace dinner at the Edison laboratories in East Orange, N. J., served in the great library that adjoins the Edison workshops and laboratories. This dinner was attended by all of the participants in the big peace.

CHAPTER FORTY-SEVEN

AND NOW COMES CENSORSHIP

Rivers have made nations and mountains have bulwarked the affairs of empire. Now certain less majestic matters of geography enter into the destiny of the motion picture with censorship arising from a dot on the map and extending cloud-like over all the world of the screen.

Let us regard for a moment the intersection of Madison and Dearborn streets in the heart of the Chicago loop, in 1907. On the southeast corner rose the *Chicago Tribune* building. Across Dearborn street was Stillson's Café, bar attached. In the adjacent block west in Madison street several all night nickelodeons, with glaring arc lamps and raucous ballyhoo phonographs, stood like carbuncles on the landscape.

When the highball hour approached, and the editorial staff of the *Tribune* went over the way for its midnight milk, all the roaring Loop was still, save for the buried rumble of the press room below and that screaming phonograph falsetto from the nickelodeons.

Late in March 1907, less than two years after the emergence of the nickelodeon, an editorial appeared in the *Tribune* entitled "The Five Cent Theatre." The subjoined text was a neat job of damning the nickelodeon up hill and down dale.

> . . . without a redeeming feature to warrant their existence . . . minstering to the lowest passions of childhood . . . proper to suppress them at once . . . should be a law absolutely forbidding entrance of boy or girl under eighteen . . . influence is wholly vicious. . . . There is no voice raised to defend the majority of five cent theatres, because they can not be defended. They are hopelessly bad.

The nickelodeon was partly "in wrong," because it had the bad judgment to erupt in the presence of the *World's Greatest Newspaper*. This was, historically, ages before the *Chicago Tribune* thought of *The Illustrated Daily News* of New York.

That phrase about "no voice raised" was premature. George Kleine, of the Kleine Optical Company, consumer of a third of the Edison film output and importer of foreign cinema wares, probably then the world's largest dealer in pictures, officing up in Randolph street, took up his pen and wrote liberally, to the *Tribune*, and to the trade press calling for a rallying of the defenders.

The censorship pot was on to boil—forever, apparently.

Chicago at that date had 116 nickelodeons, eighteen ten cent vaudeville houses, and nineteen penny arcades, showing motion pictures, screen and peep show. Kleine estimated a daily attendance of a hundred thousand for the screen in Chicago.

There was, as usual, something to be said on both sides. The swiftly rising foes of the films broke into print. A judge set the reformers agog with a letter to the papers, saying "these theatres cause, indirectly or directly, more juvenile crime coming into my court than all other causes combined." A list of the pictures shown at Chicago nickelodeons April 13, 1907, was printed, including:

Cupid's Barometer	*The Unwritten Law*
Old Man's Darling	*The Bigamist*
Modern Brigandage	*Course of True Love*
A Seaside Flirtation	*College Boy's First Love*
Child Robbers	*The Female Highwayman*
Beware, My Husband Comes	*Gaieties of Divorce*
Paris Slums	*Raffles, American Cracksman*

Kleine replied and cited the films of *Cinderella, Quaint Holland, Wonders of Canada* and the *Passion Play*, remarking on their use in schools and churches. He averred that sensational pictures on the whole were as good as the stage melodrama in tone.

One deduced that if the adolescent picture patron were set on the high road to hell by the *Gaieties of Divorce* he would in turn be brought back on snowshoes by the *Wonders of Canada*.

The exchanges of remarks raged through the papers in April and on May 2, Jane Addams of Hull House presented a resolution at the City Club advising regulation rather than suppression of the picture theatres. In June Miss Addams sought to lead the way by converting Hull House Theatre in Halsted street into a nickelodeon, with an electric sign and a barker at the door. The handpicked subjects presented there drew an audience of thirty-seven, perhaps because of the adjacent competition of *The Defrauding Banker* and *The Adventures of the American Cowboy*.

The excitement spread to New York almost instantly, and simultaneously. The Children's Society started a fight against the penny arcades and nickelodeons. In May they caused the arraignment of John Hauser, proprietor of a theatre at 416 First avenue, giving testimony that his house was packed with youngsters from four to fifteen years old, enjoying his peerless film presentation of *The Great Thaw Trial*.

This picture constituted the screen début of Evelyn Nesbitt Thaw. Its graphic sequences included a marriage ceremony, a drugging scene, and an effort to portray the abrupt demise of Stanford White on the roof at Madison Square Garden.

Now Harry K. Thaw, the Pittsburgh sociologist, joined the reform element in its attack on the films. Being otherwise detained at the moment, Thaw dispatched his attorney Dan Reilly to the Yorkville Court, where Hauser was arraigned, to convey opinions on the film production.

Thaw thus enters the pages of screen history as the first great authoritative critic of the films. His exceptions to the picture were dramatic and technical.

"Mr. Thaw desires to point out to the court that the picture of his wife is not good and that the pictures do not show the marriage ceremony as it occurred. This also applies to the tragedy of the roof garden."

Providence, Rhode Island, hastened to join in with a local aethetic movement of its own directed against the film drama of *Murphy's Wake.*

The picture starred the deceased *Murphy,* with candles about the bier, and his friends gathered for the keening. When the attention of the mourners was diverted, from time to time the deceased helped himself from the surrounding bottles.

Members of the Clan Murphy of Pawtuckett sent word to Mayor McCarthy of Providence that they were coming over to suppress the picture in person. The Lyric theatre ran the film anyway, and a pleasant time was had by all.

Mayor George B. McClellan of New York received a report on the arcades and nickle shows from Police Commissioner Bingham, June 8, 1907, recommending that they be wiped out by cancellation of their licenses. The People's Institute of New York began a study of motion pictures and the theatres in which they were shown. Their report stated that "these places were not to be condemned in toto; that they were needed to meet the demands of the majority and that attention must be given them in a constructive way."

Out in Chicago the city council passed an ordinance of censorship, November 4, 1907, entrusting the issuance of picture permits to the chief of police, effective November 19, that year. This was the first direct censorship legislation addressed to the motion picture, so far as the writer has discovered. It was only a beginning.

In New York, the very day of the dinner of jubilation over

the peace of the patents war, December 19, 1908, real trouble began. That day Mayor McClellan gave abrupt notice that, on December 23, he would hold a hearing to inquire into the advisability of allowing the motion picture shows to operate on Sundays and to go into the general question of the physical safety of the screen theatres.

No very astute investigator would have been needed to trace back to some of the influences which brought about this action. The theatre of the speaking stage, now after three years of the motion picture houses, was feeling competition. The roadshow business was dying rapidly, and in that day a Broadway run was merely an introduction to the roadshow market of the stage. Now it is an introduction to the films. That is precisely what the stage magnates desired to prevent.

The spirit of the investigation, held by Mayor McClellan, was rather clearly evidenced when at the hearing that followed Charles Sprague Smith, head of the People's Institute, ventured the suggestion that there were in New York "things more rotten than the motion picture that need attention" and thereby drew down on himself a violent reproach from the mayor.

The hearing started in the crowded aldermanic chamber at two o'clock in the afternoon and it raged for five hours. The reformers were out in force and full of words.

Following the session Mayor George B. McClellan went to his country home near Princeton in New Jersey. He left behind him an order revoking the licenses of all five cent motion picture theatres in Greater New York and instructing the police department to see that they were closed at midnight December 24, Christmas eve.

It was 4:55 P. M., December 24, when a newspaper reporter at the City Hall learned of the order and telephoned to Gustavus A. Rogers, an attorney, for an interview. That was the first notice to the industry of the Mayor's action.

The news wires carried the story across the United States, proclaiming the shame of the motion picture. Christmas morning the world read that New York's mayor had clamped the lid of the law down on the city's motion picture theatres as unclean and immoral places of amusement.

A wail of deep grief and pain rose from the five hundred motion picture exhibitors affected by the order. A call went out for a mass meeting, held Christmas Day at the Murray Hill Lyceum, Third avenue and Thirty-fourth street. Israel was smitten and there was no balm in Gilead.

William Fox, who had risen from his penny arcade beginnings to a dominant position as an exhibitor, was chosen chairman of the meeting.

It was a noisy, stormy, vociferous session, flaming with indignation and humorously tragic.

"We elected Bill Fox chairman because he could holler the loudest," one of the film men present recalled.

The session began in the forenoon and lasted far into Christmas night. An organization was formed for defensive purposes, with William Fox and Marcus Loew among the officers.

William Steiner, now in the exchange business following his producing ventures with the firm of Paley & Steiner, who made the Flatiron building classic noted in an earlier chapter, was one of the leaders in the meeting. A conference held on the platform agreed that each exhibitor should be assessed twenty-five dollars as a membership fee, to be used in court fights against the mayor's order.

"Lock the doors, before you ask for the money," Steiner whispered to Fox. "These guys will beat it if you don't."

When the announcement of the assessment for the defense fund came from the stage the crush at the doors was terrible and futile. Each exhibitor wanted to let his fellows finance the fight for his benefit.

When order was restored the membership and payment of fees was recorded. A large number of payments were in checks that came back a few days later marked "N. S. F."

A legal campaign was instituted at once by the law firm of Rogers & Rogers. Gustavus A. Rogers was interested with William Fox in the Dewey theater in Fourteenth street, which they held under lease from "Big Tim" Sullivan of Tammany Hall. The motion picture situation was not without its political developments in the course of the years indicated. Saul Rogers, also a member of the law firm, is now general counsel and an officer of the Fox Film Corporation.

For some seventy-two hours Gustavus Rogers labored continuously in the courts or in the preparation of processes. He obtained four injunctions against the execution of the Mayor's order, one before Judge Blackmar and three before William J. Gaynor, justice of the Supreme Court, Kings County. Rogers swore he would not go to bed until every picture show was open. Then he got twenty-four hours' sleep.

The situation brought a great deal of attention to the whole subject of stage entertainments and a new enforcement of the Sunday laws. Vaudeville programs were hurriedly revised to give them an uplifting educational character. The only pictures that could legally be run on Sunday were those "illustrating a lecture of an instructive or educational value." The picture shows suddenly created a demand for lecturers. The lectures were charmingly educational.

At Hammerstein's Victoria the lecturer stood in the orchestra and watched the screen. When a train appeared he spoke up brightly. "These are railroad tracks." "More railroad tracks." "We are now passing a mountain." The lecture was the best act on the bill. It got a great hand.

Then and there the word "educational" as applied to motion pictures acquired a bitter taste in the mouth of the motion picture exhibitor. Bowery and Fourteenth street audiences went to the motion pictures to see the villain hurled over the cliff and they hissed at close-ups of bumble-bees buzzing in the clover and the evolution of the rose. From that day onward the worst that could be said of a picture to damn it in the eyes of the motion picture exhibitor was to call it "educational." It is still an unfortunate word in the business. It has the flavor of medicine in the exhibitor mind. But out of the misfortunes of Christmas week of 1908 the motion picture found a real set of friends.

In the course of the arguments for tolerance the motion picture men expressed a willingness to have the pictures submitted to a board of judges or censors before their exhibition to the public. They were guided by the example of the city of Chicago where the year before the police department had begun previewing pictures. The New York picture men were not eager for a censorship, but they were willing to accept any temporary refuge and expedient to avoid closing their houses.

Charles Sprague Smith, who had founded the People's Institute and had inaugurated the community center movement in America, came forward to extend his cooperation and good will. With him was associated John Collier, secretary of the Institute, an idealist who saw what the motion picture might be.

It was of significance that when the motion picture had not yet evolved standards of art or morals or conduct for itself, these genuinely disinterested friends were ready to save it from itself and its own follies. They recognized more of the future of the screen than most of the picture makers themselves.

It should be recorded here that neither Charles Sprague Smith nor his associates were exponents of censorship. The ensuing steps were to be guided rather by expediency than theory, however.

"Censorship" became a necessary word, because to satisfy

JEREMIAH J. KENNEDY, Biograph's war chief in the great Edison patent conflict and organizer of the powerful Motion Picture Patents Company — first czar of the industry.

The Cartoon War of the Independents and the Trust.
Above — a pictorial thrust from Carl Laemmle's trade
press attacks on the Patents Company's two-dollar-a-week
fee for licensed projectors. Below — The *Film Index*,
organ of the Patents Company, lampoons the Independent
producers and exchangemen.

MOVING THE "JUNKMAN" ALONG

the public and official mind of the day the naughty, naughty motion picture had to be spanked on the wrist.

The motion picture craved a "censor" then just as baseball besmirched with scandal wanted a Judge Landis so it could turn to the world and say, "Now we've got somebody to make us be good."

Early in 1909, a few weeks after the Christmas week disaster, the People's Institute, in cooperation with the newly formed Motion Picture Patents Company and its members, formed the National Board of Censorship of Motion Pictures.

The formation of the National Board of Censorship was warmly welcomed by Kennedy of the Patents Company, on two counts: first, the broad general welfare of the industry; second, a certain added vantage to Patents Company control of the art by taking under his wing, so far as might be, the body that gave the product the stamp of respectability.

There was no intent on the part of the People's Institute to play a part in the interior politics of the motion picture industry, but through the sheer awkwardness and hesitancy of the scattering independent picture makers who came to contest the Patents Company there remained a certain atmospheric advantage in that direction. The "independents" did not know how to approach the board.

The name of the newly formed organization was most unfortunate, even if expeditious. It gave impetus to the censorship movement in many directions. In 1915 the name was changed to the National Board of Review, which continues in cooperation between the motion picture industry and its public, with Wilton A. Barrett, the executive secretary in active charge.

Many cities followed the example of Chicago in enacting censorship ordinances. In 1912 New York tried it and encountered a veto from Mayor Gaynor. State censorships began as early as 1911 when Pennsylvania enacted a law which has provided the world with one of the most entertaining of censorship boards. Kansas enacted a censorship law in March, 1913, and Ohio followed in April. The state of Maryland, home of terrapin and H. L. Mencken, created a censorship board in 1916. New York State achieved censorship in 1921.

Continuously since the days of the first prize fight film legislation, discussed in another chapter, there has been an agitation for a federal censorship in the United States.

The most conspicuous banner of leadership was carried by the Reverend Wilbur Fisk Crafts, superintendent of the International Reform Bureau, until his death in December, 1922, since which the Reverend William Sheafe Chase, of Christ Church, 317 Bedford avenue, Brooklyn, has dominated the movement. Canon Chase has, however, been active from the beginnings in 1907–8, and much of his superior finesse controlled the efforts of the less polished Reverend Mr. Crafts.

The Reverend Mr. Crafts was violently aggressive, always sincere and sometimes misinformed in his extravagant enthusiasms. His life was filled with restless movements, a continual reaching for action. He was born in Fryeburg, Maine, January 12, 1850, and at the age of seventeen had become a Methodist minister. By 1880 he moved from Methodism to Congregationalism, which held him only three years when he joined the Presbyterian church, in which, by the way, Will Hays is an elder.

In 1895 Crafts founded the International Reform Bureau. He travelled, wrote and pamphleteered extensively. He gave up a comfortable charge to move to Washington and live in the most meager circumstances to be a lobbyist of the Lord and work for legislative enactment of his views of morality. He crusaded against opium, alcohol, sex and celluloid.

In 1915 hearings by a congressional committee were held in

Washington taking statements ranging over the whole field of motion picture activities, financial and moral. The chief result was a group photograph of film men on the steps of the Capitol.

Intermittently since national censorship bills have been introduced at the various congresses, all of them strangely enough, introduced by representatives of states in the southern areas of illiteracy and Daytonism.

The Reverend Mr. Crafts in 1920 sought to proclaim a jehad, handily summarized in the following dispatch which went to the newspapers:

> Washington, Dec. 10—The lobby of the International Reform bureau, Dr. Wilbur Crafts presiding, voted tonight to rescue the motion pictures from the hands of the Devil and 500 un-Christian Jews. As the first step in removing the menace of the movies, Dr. Crafts told the reformers that he would appeal to the Catholic Church and that he would crash into Congress backed by the Christian Churches and reform organizations, which was the only way to defeat the $40,000,000 slush fund the movie men had come to Washington with.

This dispatch betrays several of Dr. Craft's major errors. In the first place he should have known that taking the movies away from the Devil would be a mere chore as compared with taking them away from the able gentlemen who have them. He should also have realized that if the movie men of 1920 had surrounded $40,000,000 they would have gone to Albany and incorporated a new company, not to Washington to spend it.

Canon Chase is the author of a compendium of about all that has been said against the films, revised and kept up to date by editions and inserts, under the title of *Catechism on Motion Pictures in Inter-State Commerce*, published by the New York Civic League.

That ably edited volume continues the jehad movement with

citation of the familiar document known as *The Protocols of the Wise Men of Zion* and reference to the Dearborn Publishing Company's reprints of the articles which so popularized Henry Ford on Broadway a few years ago. Also the better movie scandals are competently presented, with names, dates and newspaper references.

When, following his lecture on *The Mistakes of Moses*, Colonel Robert G. Ingersoll was twitted with ignoring some of the things that might have been said in the favor of the great leader, the lecturer replied: "Ah, yes, but I am not attorney for Moses." Canon Chase is not attorney for either Moses or the movies.

The chief expression of the censorship movement, crystallized after three annual conferences in Washington, is embodied in the Federal Motion Picture Council in America, Inc., the Reverend Charles Scanlon of Pittsburgh, president; Canon Chase, general secretary.

Censorship laws and agitations have probably exerted less influence upon the pictures than their own automatic improvement. The major effect of censorship is local trouble for film exchangemen. A slight influence is to be noted in the evolution of new screen hieroglyphics, typified by the technique of Monta Bell in a scene where he denoted the pedestrian members of the oldest profession by a close-up of a girl dusting foot ease powder into a shoe.

The efforts toward influencing motion picture production on the part of club, church, civic and other organizations are endless. They are in the main indicative of a minority demand for a sort of picture not generally available, and in part these movements point to the fact that quite a number of persons are looking for a cause. In 1924 the Women's Christian Temperance Union joined in the movement.

The General Federation of Women's Clubs has been considering the films, pro and con for many argumentative years, with various internal movements for and against censorship.

In the early years of the motion picture's struggles against the censorship movement Vitagraph sent Rose Tapley, one time a screen player, touring the country to make pleasant talks about the triumphs of the screen art. Elizabeth Dessez, now connected with Pathé pictures, was engaged by George Kleine in an effort to relate the film business to the non-theatrical demand in church, club and school movements.

The literature of motion picture censorship is extensively incoherent. The most illuminating published expression is *The Morals of the Movie* by Ellis Paxon Oberholtzer, formerly of the Pennsylvania board. It contains, for the benefit of the consumer of printed words, a faithful presentation of some of the choicer items of screen obstetrics and tasty bits which came under the Philadelphia axe during his eventful administration. There is the lilt of a motion picture subtitle in the heroic dedication of this volume: "To Katherine A. Niver, my comrade in arms in the thin red line."

CHAPTER FORTY-EIGHT

THE TRUST WAR BEGINS

THEN the members of the Film Service Association filed into their assembly room at the Imperial Hotel in New York for the opening of their convention in January, 1909, they found an announcement from the newly formed Patents Company laid in each chair.

The Film Service Association was made up of the exchangemen who bought films from the makers and rented them out to the theaters. This new combination of the film makers in the Patents Company meant some kind of a new deal.

It was a tense and vital moment. These exchangemen were now on the high road to millions. Haberdashers, cloth spongers, bookmakers, cowpunchers, loan sharks and carnival followers were taking their first glimpse of a real prosperity and more money than they had expected to see in all the world. Things might have been a bit complicated and speculative under the old catch-as-catch-can régime but they were prospering anyway. Now came a new order. They feared it.

For the first few minutes of the convention there was only the rustling of papers as the exchange men read the portentous document from the Patents Company, and reading was a tediously slow art with many of them.

Observers for the Patents Company were judiciously spread about to gather the comment that might arise.

Frank L. Dyer of the Edison Company addressed the gathering and explained in more detail the plans of the Patents Company, placing emphasis on the vast benefits that would accrue from the elimination of litigation over patents, and saying much less about the iron handed control that the new concern would exercise over the business in general and the exchanges in particular. Stenographic records of the session do not seem to have included any parentheses enclosing (laughter) or (applause).

In brief the Patents Company proposed to license exchanges to deal in the film to be made by the licensed studios, which film was to be rented only to theatres using licensed projection machines. Various rules and fees were provided, including a charge of two dollars a week for each projection machine. No unlicensed film could be handled and no licensed film could be served to any but licensed theatres. It was all a neat package from studio to exchange to theatre. Everybody had to have a license except the patron and he paid at the box office.

The Film Service Association solemnly acknowledged the arrangement. Meanwhile there were whispered conferences about the Imperial and in secluded corners of the busy bars of Broadway.

The majority were sure that the Patents Company had the best of the situation and they would have to accept its terms. If William Swanson, a Chicago exchangeman, and Carl Laemmle had been so minded this story would have been considerably different.

Swanson had become a considerable factor in film distribution in the West. He made his first contact with the motion pictures in the remote season of 1897–8, when he was presenting a "lunette show" with a carnival company. The lunette show used a black tent and deeply darkened interior, in which a girl attired in white went through mysterious eerie movements, apparently defying gravitation, but in reality riding the end of a long lever arm concealed in the dark.

When Swanson joined Percy Mundy's carnival company in Wisconsin he found that organization already supplied with a lunette show, so he attached himself to Edwin S. Porter's moving picture tent and learned the film game. Meanwhile, he occupied otherwise idle time instructing the yokelry of the carnival route in the eccentricities of dice and the laws of chance.

Swanson was a person of facility and dexterity. On this day of the Patents ultimatum, he was on the warpath. It was near midnight when George Kleine, George K. Spoor and Colonel W. N. Selig, the Chicago triumvirate of the Patents group, strolled into Jack's restaurant in Sixth avenue for a snack of supper.

At a table not far away sat Swanson and a group of secretly dissenting exchangemen. Swanson sauntered over to a table occupied by the three Chicago producers. Swanson's manner was ultra carefree and jovial, but the conversation at the Chicago table lulled. There seemed to be a notion that Swanson came with long ears.

Spoor, Selig and Kleine arose to go. Swanson arose with them and followed them, despite their "good night," over to the Republican club in Fortieth street.

Swanson persistently insisted on conversation and entertainment. He would not be shaken off. There were orders for drinks now and then, with George Kleine taking Apollinaris. It was three o'clock in the morning when they gently put Swanson to bed down the hall. They were reasonably satisfied he would have nothing but a headache to remember in the morning.

It was half past three when Swanson arose and tiptoed away. He had made up his mind about what to expect from the Patents Company. By noon he had collected a list of twenty-eight exchangemen pledged to oppose the combine's terms and licenses.

An insurrection was in the making.

But meantime, with the exchangemen outwardly accepting the terms of the patents combine, a maze of plots and counterplots arose among them. The thread of the story begins in June of 1908, the year before, and is spun out of the irrelevant fact that it was then that Governor Hughes of New York signed the bill which forbade race track gambling in New York.

The law against race track gambling was a triumph for the agitation and campaign by Canon William Sheafe Chase of Christ Church, Brooklyn, who appears in censorship annals. Meanwhile this race track bill, by curious circumstance, became Canon Chase's largest impress upon the screen. The other end of the thread will bring us eventually to Charles Chaplin, the Triangle Film Corporation, and many another screen landmark, with sundry knots and kinks on the way.

The race track law resulted in a flurry of raids on the bookmakers. Out at Sheepshead Bay, Adam Kessel was one of the many repeatedly arrested and stripped of betting rolls.

This annoyed Kessel extremely. After it happened a number of times he decided to quit the business. He had prospered and he had been generous with his money. Now, in the words of the cartoonist, "Them days was gone forever."

"It's all off for Addy, I'm through," Kessel told Charles Bauman, a sheet writer in his organization.

Kessel went home to think it over. Some weeks later it occurred to him that in the gala time of easy money he had loaned twenty-five hundred dollars to a friend, one Charles Streimer. Now was a good time to collect.

Down at 106 Fulton street Kessel found Streimer. "Say, Charlie, where's my twenty-five hundred bones?"

Streimer pointed up to a shelf on which reposed a dozen flat tin cans, a foot in diameter and about two inches thick.

Kessel pulled down one of the cans and opened it, taking out a reel of film. It fell from his unaccustomed fingers and heaped up in a tangle about him.

"What's these *wheels?*"

"Moving pictures."

"What do you do with them?"

"I rent them to theatres—get ten dollars a day for the good ones, sometimes."

"And then they bring 'em back to you and give you ten dollars?" Kessel was incredulous.

"Yes—that's the game."

"Much obliged, this is my business," Kessel announced. He sat down at the desk and took charge. Streimer went into his employ and a few days later they started out with a horse and buggy and a willow basket full of film canvassing the theatres for customers.

Kessel's exchange became, in due course a member of the Film Service Association, pledged to eliminate "duping," price cutting and all manner of abuses in the trade. But the price cutting went on, and presently Kessel discovered that the virtuous exchanges of the association were often operating secret sub-exchanges which carried on the old nefarious practices. He was losing customers to them.

Kessel decided to acquire a sub-exchange. He sought out his erstwhile friend and associate of bookmaking days, Charles O. Bauman. He found Bauman operating a racing tip service and doing well selling "selections for today" and "best bets" to the racing fans.

"Charlie, this is the bunk—these moving pictures are the new graft, come on in."

Bauman was skeptical, but Kessel set a box of films in a side room of Baumann's establishment and sent a man in to take care of the new business. Bauman & Kessel were in the film business now. The sub-exchange prospered so mightily that their competitor friends in the Film Service Association retaliated by a move which cut off their supply of licensed film, which now under the combine meant all of the film available in the United States.

Here was another big moment in screen history. Bauman and Kessel insisted on having pictures, so they set out to make them.

Over in Brooklyn they found Fred Balshofer in possession of a motion picture camera, unlicensed and outlawed by the Patents company, to be sure. They employed Balshofer and set out to produce. On the side streets of Brooklyn they made a picture, building the story as they went along. The principal members of the cast were Adam Kessel and Charles Bauman. The picture was not as bad as they had expected it to be. It was eight hundred feet long and cost almost $200. The producers titled it *Disinherited Son's Loyalty* and tried it in their film service. It appeared to be acceptable to their customers.

This effort so encouraged the conspirator-producers that they borrowed a wolfskin rug from a taxidermist and made a more sensational drama of wild life entitled *Davy Crockett in Hearts United*. Kessel in the rôle of Crockett shot the wolfskin rug with tremendous effect at the climax. This picture undoubtedly marks the beginning of wild animals in screen drama. This, too, was a box office success.

At Mouquin's restaurant in Seventh avenue, Kessel, Bauman, Balshofer and Louis Burston, attorney, met to talk things over. They decided to form a corporation to make pictures. It was all settled but the name.

When Kessel got outfumbled for the dinner check and found that he was the host, he produced a new ten dollar bill. The bill bore the figure of a charging bison.

"There's the trademark," Kessel announced. "What Uncle Sam puts on his money is good enough for us."

The new concern was christened "Bison Life Motion Pictures." It went into production with Charles Inslee, acquired from Biograph as the dramatic expert. Bison's first effort was *A True Indian's Heart* made in the wilds of Coytesville, N. J., with Charles French in the leading rôle.

While it was the original plan of Bauman and Kessel to make the picture for their own exchanges, they offered them experimentally on the open market. They all sold, rapidly. Even the first feeble effort, costing two hundred dollars made a profit of fifteen hundred dollars.

"Never mind the expense, we'll spend as high as $350 a picture," they instructed Inslee.

Independent production had begun and several new wars were brewing.

The opening uprising against "the trust" began on March 20, 1909, when William Swanson announced on behalf of his exchanges that he had gone "independent." April 12, Carl Laemmle burst forth with a similar announcement and followed it the next week with boldfaced type in the trade journals asserting "I am as Happy as a Sunflower." On May 1 he began baiting the Patents Company with an advertisement headed "Good Morrow—Have you Paid $2 license to pick your teeth?" With cartoon and broad innuendo Laemmle's advertising, written and directed by his friend Robert Cochrane, campaigned against "the trust."

The independent exchanges rapidly created a market for independently made pictures. So again a host of new infringers was to arise. Now came the Actophone Company among the earliest of the new line of invaders. It started with a studio at Eleventh avenue and Fifty-third street in New York's famous "Hell's Kitchen" zone.

Al McCoy, the Edison agent, was put on the trail again. The first thing discovered was that William Rising, trained in the making of pictures in the Edison studios by Edwin S. Porter, was the Actophone director. Actophone was slated for marked legal attention.

Behind the Actophone Company's beginnings was a typically adventurous sequence of events. Back in 1903 Mark M. Dintenfass of Philadelphia, salesman of salt herring, fell out with his father and quit the parental fish business. Two years later found him the proprietor of "Fairyland," Philadelphia's second screen theatre, an impressive establishment of one hundred and thirty seats. He had forgotten the salt herring, but they were still to be a factor in his experience and a bigger factor in screen affairs of years yet to come.

Dintenfass, seeking novelties, installed the Cameraphone, a talking picture made by Bert Whitman in New York. It was a synchronized film and phonograph record device, presenting such numbers as Eva Tanguay in her famously abandoned song "I Don't Care," Blanche Ring in her current hit, a dash of "The Merry Widow" and the like.

The Cameraphone, like all similar talking picture efforts, ran a short life and failed. Dintenfass found himself in possession of the remains of the company, including a camera. He changed the name to Actophone and declared himself a producer.

The Actophone studio was always locked and all who entered passed peephole examination by the watchman. In added precaution the camera, an imported Pathé, was enclosed in a sheet iron turret, within which worked Harry Ferrini, an expert hired away from Edison's studio. Not even the actors were permitted to see the camera.

But the camera went out on location one day. A casual street loafer stood awkwardly by and asked Ferrini foolish questions while he manipulated the machine. Then the loafer slouched away. His name was Al McCoy—of Edison. The injunction suits began at once.

The stubborn Dintenfass was called to court three times and twice cited for contempt of injunction orders. On his last day of grace, facing a handsome prospect of jail, he made peace by a promise to abandon the making of pictures.

But a few weeks of repentance healed his fears and presently Dintenfass was again making pictures in a tiny shack hidden in the deep woods that crown the Palisades of New Jersey near Coytesville.

Soon the detectives of the Patents Company were on the trail again, suspicious but not certain. Dintenfass was filled with alarm. If he were found this time there would be no chance of clemency.

But he would not quit the motion pictures. Money was there to be had, easy money. An inspiration came to him. The one safe place for him to work would be in one of the Patents Company's own studios. They would never find him there. Over at Philadelphia on a roof in Arch street Sigmund Lubin had a studio no longer in use. Lubin, in his new prosperity with the Patents company, had outgrown the little roof top.

Dintenfass slipped away to Philadelphia and rented the studio from Lubin. It was just a little personal deal, one that Lubin did not feel obligated to report to the Patents Company. On the Arch street roof Dintenfass proceeded with his picture making undisturbed.

"Pop" Lubin was eminently practical in his point of view in this curious transaction. Perhaps too he had a certain sympathy with the plight of Dintenfass. Lubin had himself been considerably pursued by Edison agents in the days before the Patents Company peace.

In that safe hiding place Dintenfass pursued his film activities undisturbed, his whereabouts for that period remaining a mystery. Later when the war between the Independents and the Patents group had really joined issue in a big test case, Dintenfass, no longer in personal peril, emerged to play an erratic and spectatular part in film history. His most conspicuous project of the modern period was the production of a picturization of Ambassador James W. Gerard's *My Four Years in Germany*, in conjunction with Warner Brothers.

"Pop" Lubin's sub-rosa share in this phase of the rise of the Independents recalls an incident of the same period in which is illustrated something of his humor, and which as well indicates how much the motion picture through successive stages had tended to inherit its ancient outlawries. One of the early official acts of the Patents Company was a piece of internal discipline, involving Lubin.

The charge was gravely made that one of the licensed Melies pictures had been "duped" or copied in the Lubin plant. A meeting was held at the company offices at 80 Fifth Avenue.

Lubin listened in silence.

"The fine will be one thousand dollars."

This stirred "Pop" to protest.

"I didn't dupe it," Lubin exclaimed. "Besides I didn't make any money on it and I won't pay any fine."

Another immediate outgrowth of the demand for independent film in the fight against the Patents Company was the formation of the International Film & Projecting Company, an importing concern, by J. J. Murdock, now known to the amusement world in connection with the Keith vaudeville interests, and Hector J. Streyckmans of the *Show World*, a Chicago trade journal. Murdock went abroad and acquired for America the films of all of the foreign makers not allied with the American patents combine. The foreign film served and prospered for a time, in a stop-gap sort of way. But the American audiences were not satisfied and their demand gave new encouragement to the early independent producers, Actophone, Rex, Yankee and others.

By midsummer of 1909, Carl Laemmle, with his big system

of exchanges demanding film, decided to go into production. In the fall Tom Cochrane, one of the members of the advertising agency which put Laemmle into the film business in Chicago, was sent on to New York to make pictures. He rented space in the Actophone studio and employed William Ranous of Vitagraph as the first director of the concern, the Independent Motion Picture Company, soon abbreviated for trademark purposes, to the since famous "Imp." The first production was *Hiawatha* with Gladys Hulette, who later became a star of renown on the screen.

Now also the independent forces gained in strength of personnel by the acquisition of Edwin S. Porter, the Edison director and producer of *The Great Train Robbery.*

Porter left the Edison organization when Horace Plimpton, a carpet dealer and New Jersey friend of Frank L. Dyer, was placed in charge of the Edison picture activities. Porter started picture making, working like the rest at the Actophone studio in Hell's Kitchen. Shortly, in partnership with Swanson, he formed the Rex concern and evolved for it a trademark with a rim of stars—the same stars which the public sees today on the famous trade mark of Paramount. Lois Weber and Phillips Smalley appeared in the first Rex pictures.

At Mount Vernon, New York, P. A. Powers, a dealer and jobber in talking machines, who had made his contact with the motion picture as an Edison invention along with the phonograph, opened the studio of the Powers Picture Plays, with Joseph Golden as his director, Ludwig Erb the cameraman and technical expert, and Irving Cummings the leading man and head of the casts. The Powers company introduced several famous names among them Mildred Holland of stage fame in *The Power Behind the Throne.*

On January 27, 1912, Juliet Shelby, now known as Mary

Miles Minter, made her first screen appearance in *The Nurse,* a one reel production from the Powers studios. Juliet was then playing with Dustin and William Farnum in *The Littlest Rebel,* at the Liberty theater.

This P. A. Powers was about to become a dominant figure in the wars of the Independents which followed. He was and continues today one of the most aggressive, belligerently active men of the industry. All this was predicated from the beginning. Way back in his boyhood up at Buffalo, Pat Powers, with his husky Irish shoulders, labored over the anvil in a forging shop and hammered out an idea for himself. He was receiving three dollars a day. There was no more in sight no matter how hard he worked. Therefore forthwith he organized a labor union to get his wages increased. That was Powers' way. He can always see a way. The same spirit and daring made him glad to take a chance with the Independents against the Patents Company machine that claimed the screen for its exclusive own.

The efforts of the Motion Picture Patents Company to monopolize the technology of the motion picture right at the source, resulted in many bizarre efforts at the making of a camera which would not infringe the Edison patent. Most of these efforts were dismal failures.

Now after these many years the careers of the phonograph and the motion picture crossed again. Joseph Bianchi, recording expert for the Columbia Phonograph Company, evolved a camera which performed the amazing feat of recording a motion picture on a continuously moving film. He used an optical system which made the image forming rays follow the moving film. This camera in consequence avoided infringement on the Edison intermittent movement and the Latham loop.

Through Paul Cromelin, one of Columbia's vice presidents,

a new system of licenses, paralleling in pattern the Patents Company scheme, was made available to the Independents, who made it a brave display in their advertising.

Because of the delicate adjustments necessary in the Bianchi camera it did not prove satisfactory in practice and the Independents used it and the "Columbia License" as camouflage for operations with infringing cameras.

The era of the Columbia license system brought in the establishment of the once famous Thanhouser concern. Most of the picture makers blundered into the business. Edwin Thanhouser, a dramatic producer with a stock company in Milwaukee, came to New York for the deliberate purpose of entering the motion picture business. In an old skating rink, converted into a studio, Thanhouser began operations in New Rochelle in March of 1910, aligned with the Independents under the Columbia license.

But the very word "license" was malodorous in the nostrils of the Independents. It stood for everything that was in their way. It was back of all their troubles. It was the fighting word of 1909–10. An elegant sample of the literature of the time was issued by Joseph R. Miles, an Independent exchange man. It was a pamphlet which quoted the Patents Company's printed statements about its license system. In the quoted passages, however, Miles revised the orthography to make it appear "LICEnsed manufactures, LICEnsed exchanges, LICEnsed projection machines," etc. Over it all he printed a title, "A LOUSY STATEMENT from the PATENTS COMPANY."

MARY MILES MINTER — she was Juliet Shelby then — when she made her first motion picture appearance under the belligerent banner of P. A. Powers. The picture was "The Nurse."

MARY PICKFORD, pictured in 1916 when the fate
of half a dozen motion picture corporations
hung in the balance as the producers battled
to get her name on a contract.

CHAPTER FORTY-NINE

INTRODUCING MARY PICKFORD

AㅤLITTLE miss in a gray jacket, with curls down her back and an earnest, wistful face, stepped off a street car at Fifth avenue and went walking slowly along Fourteenth street looking up at the house numbers.

This was in early May in 1909, seventeen years ago by the calendars, but a century ago in the affairs of the motion picture.

The little girl was on her way to see if by chance there might be a place for her in Biograph pictures. She jingled a couple of stray pennies in her pocket, to remind her that her last nickel had gone for carfare and, if she did not get the job that she hoped for, there would be a long walk back to the boarding house way uptown in Thirty-seventh street.

No one gave special notice to this rather unimportant little person of sixteen, except perhaps the passing glance of approval that youth and a pretty face always get in New York. She was just one of the crowd that is always passing in the busy forenoon in Fourteenth street. But if it were announced today that this same little girl would walk along that same path in that same street the police reserves would have to be called to keep back the crowds and business would stop as proprietors, clerks and customers rushed to the doorways. The girl was Mary Pickford, the Cinderella queen-to-be of the motion picture.

In just six years more the amazing day was to come when the little girl with the curl could smile into the face of an anxious motion picture magnate and say, in all seriousness: "No—I really can not afford to work for only ten thousand a week."

that last five cent piece invested in a car ride to Fourteenth street was the beginning of a remarkable journey.

But back of that day in 1909 Mary Pickford had a life experience on the other side of the picture, worthy of recording here by way of contrast and for those who see her successes of today through the eyes of envy.

At sixteen Mary had been at work for eleven hard years. She was already old with experience of the stern realities of this workaday world. She was born into the most humble circumstances of life and lived close to the shadow of want.

Miss Pickford was Gladys Smith, an infant of four when her father died in Toronto, leaving his widow nothing, except a family of three, with Gladys the oldest.

That morning when one of the neighbors came and took Gladys away for the day the little girl knew that in the darkened "best room" her father lay dead, with candles burning about the crucifix that stood at his head. She knew, too, that things were going to be harder now for her mother. In a vague childish way she wanted to help.

There were many other tragedies after that.

The slender capital of the family was invested in a little candy shop that shared half of a fish store. The candy counter did a small business, selling gum drops at a penny each to the passing school children, but it sufficed for the time.

Then came the ill fated day when Baby Jack was left alone in the store with the family's pet dog. Jack found that the dog liked candy and fed him the entire stock of the establishment. The dog died, Jack was spanked, and—the candy store was bankrupt.

Gladys's mother went out to look for work. The little girl was old enough to go along with her mother when she went to interview the manager of the Valentine Stock Company of Toronto, and it was ambitious little Gladys herself who suggested that she might have the baby part in the production under rehearsal. The amused director tried her, found that Gladys could act and promptly engaged her for the part.

From that day on Gladys Smith was on the stage. The next season she played in *The Little Red School House*, and not long thereafter appeared in the cast of that sterling melodrama entitled *The Fatal Wedding*. Many other melodramas followed. Then came an engagement for the whole Smith family, mother, Lottie and Jack, with Chauncey Olcott, in *Edmund Burke*. Jack, by the way, was cast as a little girl in a frilly dress, to the extreme unhappiness of the young man. In the course of this engagement the mother decided to put away the popular but unromantic name of Smith for the purposes of the stage and took for the family name Pickford, the name of her paternal grandmother. "Gladys Pickford" did not ring right to her ears and so Gladys was changed to "Mary," the most glorious name in Ireland.

Mary shared with her mother the burdens and responsibilities of the family as best she could and developed an initiative of her own. She strove mightily in her way, trooping with the road-shows and living the often precarious life of the wandering player. She was of those itinerant folk of the roadshow melodramas, who call Broadway home, but seldom see it except in those unhappy idle days when they were "resting" while "at liberty." Mary was on her way up in the world if she could find that way. She learned to read and write on the road and between scenes backstage, under the tutorship of the "female heavy" of a melodrama company. Meanwhile Mary listened and learned of the world about her. She heard a very great deal of the chesty gossip of melo actors discussing "when I was with Belasco," and came to learn that on this wonderful Broadway Belasco was master. This established, she made her decision. She would play with Belasco.

One day when the company was called for rehearsal for a change of bill over in a little New Jersey opera house Miss Pickford was missing. Over in New York Mary was storming the stage door of Belasco's theatre, demanding audience with him.

"But he won't see nobody at all, he's rehearsing the company, right now." The guardian of the stage door thought that ought to be enough and final.

"I don't care if he is—I cut a rehearsal over in Jersey to come and he's going to see me." Mary Pickford charged past the astonished doorman in a gust of mingled rage and determination. He followed, on tiptoe, prayerfully hoping that this slip would not bring down on him the wrath of Belasco and the loss of his job. The doorman was just in time to see Mary dash into the center of the stage, where a company was rehearsing *The Warrens of Virginia*.

Belasco was in a bad humor over the play. It was going all awry, mostly because of an unsatisfactory child part.

The abrupt appearance of little Mary, projecting herself into the middle of his troubles, struck Belasco with the full force of its drama. He stopped, waved his company to silence and smiled down on his caller. She was breathless and awed, but she had yet the courage of her sensational entrance.

Ten minutes later Miss Mary Pickford was rehearsing in *The Warrens of Virginia* under the eyes of the great Belasco. She had come to Broadway and won. For three seasons, until she had outgrown her part, Mary played in this production.

With the courage of this conquest behind her it is easy to see how it came that Mary was willing to toss her last nickel for carfare on a long chance that she might get into the pictures with Biograph. That was her way. She decided what to do and forthwith did it.

When Mary came that June morning to Number 11 East Fourteenth street and turned up the steps to the Biograph studio, she was faced with even less promise than the day she applied at Belasco's stage door.

The reception room at Biograph was presided over by a secretary whose disposition had been written off as a total loss years before. Her slender impatience had been worn away by the abundant annoyances of the motion picture business. Her words were sharp and few. Mary tiptoed up.

"I want to see Mr. Griffith."

"Mr. Griffith is busy, he will not see anybody——"

Then the secretary looked up and into the wistful smile of Mary.

Griffith, with his mind bent on his work in the studio above, was passing at the moment. He stopped abruptly when he heard an amazing change of tone come into the voice of the woman behind the desk, still addressing the caller—

"—but he might take time to see you, my dear."

Griffith wheeled about. Who could this be that the reception room clerk would address so tenderly? What miracle had been wrought? Then Griffith saw Mary. Together they went up the big staircase to the studio.

The Lonely Villa was in the making. It was a typical Griffith drama of the day, a Biograph feature, to be one whole reel in length, twice as long as the skits and comedies that made up the staple film output of the trade.

Marion Leonard was the leading woman in *The Lonely Villa*. Robbers were trying to break into the villa, while the wife, with her children clutching at her skirts in terror, frantically tried to telephone for help. Her message of dire distress was but half told to her husband miles away.

Mary Pickford was put in to play the part of one of the children, imperilled while the robbers battered at the door.

That afternoon at quitting time Mary got a handsome blue

ticket which enabled her to draw five dollars at the cashier's window, in payment for her first day's work in motion pictures. Her last nickel had been returned to her a hundredfold—and, although she did not suspect it, she had entered upon a career that was in time to make her the most famous woman in the world and endow her with a wealth beyond her most ambitious fancy.

Griffith had a bit of difficulty with his complicated drama of *The Lonely Villa*. The robbers were expected to batter away at the door of the villa, while the rescuing husband with reinforcements was on the way, arriving at last in the well known nick o' time, winning against all obstacles, including motor trouble in a horseless carriage.

The work of the robbers at the door was just a shade unconvincing. Griffith was not satisfied and decided on a retake, which was considered rather a wasteful procedure in the motion picture practice of the day.

While the remaking of these scenes was in progress a stranger found his way as far as the studio door. It was James Kirkwood, just off the road from playing in *The Great Divide* with Henry Miller, and, by the bye, with Henry Walthall, a fellow member of the company. Kirkwood had wandered into Biograph, looking for his friend Harry Salter, an actor who had become an assistant to Griffith.

Salter introduced Kirkwood to Griffith.

Griffith sized up Kirkwood at a glance.

"Here, put on a beard and get into this scene as one of the robbers." Kirkwood had heard of these motion picture things, but he had the standard and orthodox actor's suspicious contempt for them. "No, no! I can't do that."

"Yes, you can, and you'll fit the part fine."

Griffith and Salter would have their way.

—504—

Mary Pickford's first real part, playing opposite David
Miles, in "The Violin Maker of Cremona," a one-reel
drama released by Biograph July 7, 1909.

"The Lonely Villa," a Griffith one-reel melodrama produced at Biograph in 1909, with Marion Leonard, at the
telephone, and Mary Pickford at her right.

MABEL NORMAND, with John Bunny, at left, and Jimmy Morrison, in one of her first screen appearances, "Troubles and Secretary," at Vitagraph — after that came Biograph, Keystone, Sennett and fame.

"If I wear a beard nobody will know me anyway—here goes," Kirkwood decided. He went on.

Kirkwood joined the mob of robbers smashing in the villa door. He remained with Biograph the rest of the year, and presently Henry Walthall, who had been with him in *The Great Divide*, came down to join the company.

The Lonely Villa, aside from its historic service as the vehicle of the introduction to the screen of Mary Pickford and James Kirkwood, is worthy of remembrance because of the durability of the plot. It has lived in Griffith's memory ever since, and in 1922 it came to flower as a pretentious feature drama, somewhat modernized and revamped, under the title of *One Exciting Night*. The basic elements of the two stories are well near identical.

Mary's appearance in that small part in *The Lonely Villa* was enough to show Griffith something of the screen value of her winsome face. She was cast for the part of *Giannina* in *The Violin Maker of Cremona*. The hero rôle was played by David Miles, an actor from the stage who had been added to Biograph stock by Griffith.

The Violin Maker of Cremona was released by Biograph June 7, 1909, in 936 feet, subject No. 3575, as may be seen in the old catalogues of the period.

There was joy in the Pickford family at Mary's success and the prospect of steady employment through the summer.

Even in 1909 the peep show machines, which readers of earlier chapters will recall as the foundation of Biograph's beginnings, were still widely in service in penny arcades, and at odd moments between more pretentious subjects the Biograph studio turned out the little one-minute dramas and farces for the Mutoscopes. Lottie and Jack Pickford made their first appearances before the motion picture camera for these Mutoscope subjects, through arrangements made by Mary, who let no opportunity for the family pass untried.

Griffith delegated the direction of these Mutoscope pictures as much as possible to budding directorial material in his company. Many of these reels were directed by Eddie Dillon and Harry Salter. And the little card wheel pictures of the peep shows contained casts with now famous names that no feature drama of the screen has ever brought together. Mary Pickford played bits, too, in those days, one reel dramas, split reel comedies and peep show pictures, all the grist of Biograph's mill.

This same season of '09 added other names of subsequent renown to the growing roster of picture players. Over at the busy Vitagraph plant in Flatbush a photographer suggested to J. Stuart Blackton, that he knew "the prettiest girl in New York."

"She is posing for style pictures for the Butterick people. They use them in *The Delineator*," the photographer confided.

"Bring her over."

And that was Mabel Normand's introduction to the motion picture stage. She was not an exciting success at Vitagraph, however, and before long came back to Manhattan to join the Biograph stock company and make the acquaintance of Mack Sennett, the young man who wanted to make comedies with policemen in them.

An almost identical agency brought Alice Joyce, also a photographer's model, employed by Davis & Sanford, to the service of Kalem. Kalem was making "westerns" in the authentic badlands of New Jersey at Coytesville.

"Can you ride? It would be worth ten dollars a day if you could," the director suggested.

"I couldn't do it if mother didn't need the money," Miss Joyce responded. She was a practical sort. She began her working life at thirteen as a telephone operator.

Over in Philadelphia the Lubin studio acquired Harry Myers and Rosemary Theby, as additions to the roster of stars-to-be.

Down in Florida the Kalem company, moving south to escape the New York winter, pioneered the motion picture history of Jacksonville, which continued for some years to overshadow Los Angeles as the winter studio capital. Kalem was still running strongly to outdoor action dramas, inspired by the low cost and high profits of the Coytesville wild west subjects.

In the making of one of these pictures Sid Olcott encountered John P. McGowan, an adventuring person of parts who had seen service as a dispatch rider in the Boer-British war. McGowan became a picture actor because he could shoot a rabbit on the run from the back of a galloping horse—a highly essential piece of business in the making of Kalem's *Seth's Temptation*.

And, while Kalem was experimenting with the sunshine of Florida, J. Searle Dawley of the Edison company, enthused with the eloquences of J. Parker Reed, a free lance who had offered countless scenarios with a West Indian setting, took a company to Cuba, seeking winter sunshine.

The motion picture world was widening its horizons. It had outgrown the little rooftop studios of Manhattan, and now was fairly started toward making in reality "all the world a stage."

CHAPTER FIFTY

GRIFFITH EVOLVES SCREEN SYNTAX

WHILE the bosses and merchandisers of pictures were engaged in their wars of the patents and intrigues of business, evolving the business pattern of the industry, down at 11 East Fourteenth street in New York D. W. Griffith was leading the motion picture art forward to a new and more effective technique.

The prosperity of Biograph under the Motion Picture Patents Company peace was maintaining a safe haven in which the art could flourish and be elaborated.

Griffith's Biograph pictures now came to command the homage of the whole industry. They were studied by his competitors in the studios, licensed and unlicensed alike. And "Biograph Day" was a drawing card announcement at the little nickel show picture houses.

Griffith began to work out a syntax of screen narration. He started to use the close-up for accents, and fade-outs for punctuation. With cutbacks and manipulations of sequence, he worked for new intensities of suspense. The motion picture spent the years up to 1908 learning its letters. Now, with Griffith, it was studying screen grammar and pictorial rhetoric.

Historically considered one of the most important pictures of the year was *The Little Teacher*, in which the title rôle fell to Mary Pickford. This picture was Mary's first real hit. It established her possibilities rather clearly in the mind of Griffith. He began, probably unconsciously, to build a screen repute for her by designating her in the subtitles of Biograph's subjects as "Mary." It was no clear intent, because Biograph steadfastly refused to give any screen credits at anytime anywhere.

Griffith's Biograph family gathered at lunch about a rough table in the basement of the old mansion at 11 East Fourteenth street to eat sandwiches rustled from an adjacent saloon lunch counter by Bobby Harron, custodian of properties, general utility person and errand-boy-at-large.

A considerable part of the art of the motion picture was evolved in the lunch table discussion between the actors, cameramen and Griffith, the experimenting director. The talk was pictures, pictures, everlastingly pictures. Everything was new then and many, many things had yet to be tried.

Griffith's pictures were conspicuous for the way in which he brought the action up close to the camera, frequently cutting off the actor's feet at the bottom of the pictures. This was considered by many of the critics as a terrible piece of barbarity. Some of the more conservative producers felt that it was waste of good money to hire an actor and then not photograph all of him in the picture.

The very simplest elements of motion picture story telling and the evolution of the use of the camera as an instrument of expression rather than of mere record all had to be tediously worked out. And some of the old fetishes of early day motion picture superstition still survive. As late as 1922, Cecil Hepworth, one of the leading English producers, informed the writer that he held it a serious mistake to have any character appear on the screen without entering the scene full length, feet and all.

In these early experimental days Mack Sennett was an untiring student of picture technique, following every step that Griffith took. When no better provocation offered he carried the camera to be among those present.

When the supply of scenarios to his liking failed Griffith called for suggestions from the company.

"Fifteen dollars for the best split reel comedy idea!" was a welcome announcement.

With pencils and paper, twisting their tongues and scratching their heads like schoolboys laboring over slates, the Biograph actors could be found in all corners of the studio trying to erupt with screen ideas.

Just one thing was inevitable in these sessions—Mack Sennett would come forward with a policeman scenario. It is not on record that Sennett ever sold one to Griffith, but he persisted with a patience that made Sennett's policeman comedy scenario the best standing joke of the studio.

All who remember the Keystone cops that eventually came forth under Sennett's direction some years later will admit that Mack made good his threat. It would seem probable that the extreme violence of Sennett's Keystone cop comedy resulted from his early repressions and discouragements at Biograph.

Mary Pickford was a more successful contributor of scenarios. She was the author of a surprising number of the early Griffith Biograph pictures. Among Mary's scenarios were several which will perhaps linger in the memory of some of the old followers of the screen, including *The Awakening*, featuring Arthur Johnson, *Getting Even*, with James Kirkwood, *Caught in the Act*, *Lena and the Geese*, *The Alien*, *Granny*, in which Lottie Pickford played, *Fate's Decree* and *The Girl of Yesterday*.

The rich eventfulness of Mary Pickford's experience in road show melodrama gave her a fund of that special sort of material which Griffith desired.

In this wonderful school of the motion picture Mary grew up with the art of picture making itself, learning it as fast as it evolved, and herself contributing to its evolution.

The world prefers to think of Miss Pickford as the pretty little girl with the curl, pursuing a dramatic pictorial destiny through a pollyanna world of just-so arrangements. But in point of truth she is as diligent a student of her business as any

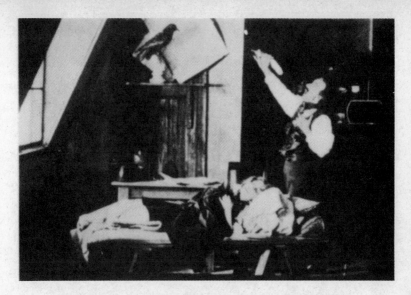

"THE RAVEN," a production of Biograph's "golden age," with
Herbert Yost in the leading rôle — He concealed his identity
from the shame of the cinema under the name of Barry
O'Moore, then.

"THE ITALIAN BARBER," a Biograph comedy presenting
Mary Pickford, Mack Sennett, Joe Graybill and Marion Sunshine, long before Sennett was discovered to be a director
as well as a comedian.

"THE WAY OF A MAN," an old Biograph classic, with Mary Pickford, Florence Lawrence, and Arthur Johnson, the first famously romantic leading man of the screen.

"A CORNER IN WHEAT," presented by Biograph December 13, 1909, with Jeanie McPherson, in the plumed hat, Henry Walthall and Frank Powell, the director who later brought Bara to film fame.

office-prisoned executive, dour with the weight of his responsibilities.

Among the best known players introduced to the screen in this period was Edwin August Philip von der Butz, who came with some stage repute and an experience that began with the rôle of *Little Lord Fauntleroy* at the age of eight. To the motion picture he was known as Edwin August. He played for a few weeks with the Edison stock company and then went to Biograph, where he appeared in many a famous production, along with Mary Pickford, Kirkwood, Walthall and the rest.

The conservative minded chiefs of the Patents Company group were distinctly opposed to publicity for players. They had observed the salaries that theatrical managers had to pay for stars who caught the public's favor, and they did not want a parallel experience for the motion picture.

But across the Atlantic the public wanted stars and personalities. The foreign selling agents of American film met the demand by inventing names for the favorite players, playing a bit upon patriotic preferences in their fabrications. The foreign screen names for Edwin August afford an excellent example. In England he was billed in the pictures as Montague Lawrence, in Australia as Wilkes Williams, in Ireland as John Wilkes, in Germany as Karl von Bussing, and in the Orient as David Courtlandt.

Florence Lawrence was in that day the stellar light of Biograph casts. She began her screen career with her husband, Harry Salter, at Vitagraph and joined Biograph with the rise of Griffith to directorship.

Miss Lawrence's screen appearances were so successful that the whole of the motion picture world came to know her as *The Biograph Girl*. It was an automatic, anonymous stardom —and presently to prove a factor in the Independent fight.

Marion Leonard, an actress from the melodrama stage, in this brave year of 1909 set the high mark for screen salaries when she demanded an entire hundred dollars a week from Biograph, and compromised for seventy-five.

In the course of this summer Florence LaBadie, an artist's model, following in the footsteps of Mabel Normand, the fashion plate model, came to Biograph to play a bit and began the career which made her one of the great stars of the screen a few years later.

The demand for screen stories was growing with the industry and rumors of easy money "writing for the pictures" went through the gossip channels of the actor tribes, reaching picture patrons as well. The beginning of the scenario writing craze was in sight. And through this the motion picture added some notable figures to its personnel.

The technique of scenario writing began to evolve parallel to Griffith's development of pictorial narration. Frank Woods was among the first and most famous of the scenario writers to come under this influence. It all resulted from a chain of circumstance, beginning with the panic of '07, when Woods was on the staff of *The Dramatic Mirror*. The road shows suffered in that time of financial stringency and the *Mirror's* advertising fell away to a whisper. Just at this juncture a heated difference arose between Minnie Maddern Fiske, the actress, and her producers, Klaw & Erlanger. The K. & E. advertising support was withdrawn from the *Mirror*, which was controlled by the Fiskes. As an emergency measure the *Mirror* sought advertising from the despised motion picture and Woods became the editor of a movie column to give support to the advertising solicitors. A few weeks of screen observation brought Woods in contact with Lee Dougherty, who was Biograph's editorial department, and resulted in the sale of three "suggestions" for pictures, at $15 each.

One of Woods' "suggestions" was a plot lifted from *Enoch Arden,* and entitled *After Many Years.* Griffith made it into a picture, with cutbacks and close-ups. Here contact was established between Griffith and the man who some years later was to bring him the script of *The Birth of a Nation.*

The whole *Dramatic Mirror* office went scenario mad, when Woods' success with "suggestions" became known. George Terwilliger, another member of the *Mirror* staff, also began a scenario writing career that led to directorship.

Out in San Diego Anita Loos, a sixteen year old high school girl, thought she had an idea for a picture and wrote an outline entitled, *The New York Hat.* She addressed it to "Manager Biograph Studio, New York" and dropped it in the mail.

Little Miss Loos of course had considerable knowledge of dramatic technique. Her father was R. Beers Loos, a newspaper man and the proprietor of a traveling repertoire show devoted to blood curdling melodramas. He belonged to that California school of the stage known as "The Coast Defenders" because of their travels up and down the Pacific shores west of the mountains. It was in its way a famous dramatic region, too, out of which came such names as Laurette Taylor, Marjorie Rambeau, Blanche Bates, Frances Starr, and David Belasco.

Anita Loos was not permitted to play in her father's wild and woolly dramas, but she had had a share of stage experience playing the part of a little boy with Nance O'Neil in *The Jewess* some three years and again appearing in that ancient classic, *East Lynne.*

At San Diego the R. Beers Loos company had so improved its status that Miss Anita was permitted to take a part. She attended school days and worked on stage at nights.

She had almost forgotten *The New York Hat* when a check for $15 came through from Biograph in New York, along with a request for more scenarios.

Between scenes down in her dressing room in the San Diego theater Miss Loos worked on her picture ideas, making notes for scenarios, on scraps of old lithographs, with the ardent ruby red lipstick from her makeup box.

In New York *The New York Hat* had come to the attention of Griffith, who found in it a part that interested him. It fit the possibilities of a young actor he had met a few days before at luncheon, Lionel Barrymore.

Young Barrymore had just returned from a sojourn in Paris, where he had for a season been studying painting. Now he was ready to work.

So Barrymore and Mary Pickford appeared in *The New York Hat*, Anita Loos' first scenario.

The motion picture was beginning to show evidences of an evolutionary tendency toward a much more complex form and a fuller development as a medium of expression. The relation of the printed word in screen titles to the ensuing action was yet undeveloped and the titling of '09 and '10 was crude in the extreme.

In many establishments, notably the Imp, big rolls of stock titles which could be used in most any drama were kept on hand, ready printed. The stock title list included all such vital expressions as, "The next day," "Ten years elapse," "Happy ever afterward," "Forgiven," "Wedding bells," and "One hour later." The titles were hauled down by the yard and inserted where needed, by Jack Cohn, Imp's film editor.

The student of motion picture technique will find it of interest that the average motion picture of 1909–10 contained only eighty feet of titles per reel of a thousand feet. The same screen footage today requires ordinarily close to two hundred and fifty feet of titles. The screen story of today cannot all be told by the camera.

But the dramatic picture in 1909 had not yet come into the

practically absolute dominance of the theatre screen which obtains today. Topical subjects, camera records of actualities, still made up a pronounced percentage of the total output of motion pictures.

One of the topical screen sensations of the fall of '09 was the Great Northern's pictures of the arrival of Doctor Frederick Cook at Copenhagen in Denmark, after his then entirely accredited discovery of the alleged North Pole. The Great Northern, as it was known in America, was the leading Scandinavian concern, better known in earlier days as the Nordisk. The Great Northern was represented in New York by Ingvald C. Oes, who figured in many of the movements of the Independents with whom the Great Northern was aligned.

The topical tendency which made so much of Doctor Cook on the screen was also exemplified in such pictures as Mark M. Dintenfass' first production under his "Champion" brand, a picture purporting to cover the ride of Louis and Temple Abernathy, sons of Catch'em-Alive-Jack Abernathy, of Oklahoma, who came by pony from Oklahoma to New York, released in July, 1910. It was all made in New Jersey.

In story and topicals alike the one-reel picture had, by this time, become fairly well established, but there was abundance of "split reels," which included a number of short comedies and sometimes scenic bits. Biograph, of the licensed manufacturers, issued many split reel comedies held in special esteem.

The first significant breaking over to multiple reels came from the European studios, notably with the *Fall of Troy,* and other like subjects equally unsuitable for American consumption. The motion picture theatre was not yet prepared to believe that the public would be interested in any subject that occupied more than one reel, or fifteen minutes of screen time.

Europe's efforts to make the screen the vehicle of the classics were largely wasted on the American market. The motion picture theatre men and their audiences wanted Indians and action. When P. P. Craft went out to roadshow a foreign production, entitled *Homer's Odyssey*, a considerable precentage of his patrons demanded to know if Mr. Homer was travelling with the show to make personal appearances.

A conspicuous effort at a realization of star values was made with a three-reel version of *Camille*, with Sarah Bernhardt in the title rôle. The picture was loudly proclaimed in advertising by the agents of the amateurish French concern which made it, but it failed utterly of theatre attention. A curious sensation comes to the searcher into dusty files after Bernhardt's death to find her quoted in those decade-old advertisements with the line: "I rely upon these films to make me immortal."

Neither the great names of the stage nor of literature could make an impression on the motion picture mind of the time. The exhibitors, with their little nickelodeon shows and their audiences as well, were not of those who patronized the art of the stage or any form of literature, except, perhaps, the daily newspapers. This world of the illiterati had to create its own stars, manufactured of its own fame with no share in and no relation to the renown and fame of careers and creations in the older arts.

Little Mary of Biograph, as they knew Mary Pickford, and *Broncho Billy* of Essanay, were better known to this world of the motion picture than the late Mr. Homer, of ancient Greece, or Sarah Bernhardt, of modern France.

In the fall of '09 J. Stuart Blackton, at Vitagraph, produced *The Life of Moses* in five reels. But it was released a reel at a time, one reel a week for five weeks, beginning in January, 1910. No theatre thought of trying to present a full five reel show. They did not consider Moses a big enough drawing card.

Vitagraph followed this pretentious effort with a three reel version of *Uncle Tom's Cabin*, also released a reel at a time, in July of the same year.

What appears to have been the beginning of the feature movement, interestingly enough, is to be accredited to Pittsburgh, Pa., in 1909, where five years before John P. Harris and Harry Davis of the Grand Opera House had started the motion picture theatre movement in the East, liberating the film art from the constrictions of vaudeville programs. In this 1909, P. P. Craft, a showman of experience, with Colonel Cody, went into the film business with Harris and Davis.

Craft thought he saw opportunity for motion picture entertainment on a grander scale. He was full of the show instinct and an appreciation of the public's liking for things done in a spectacular way. He arranged to put out a screen road show to be called "Harry Davis Motion Pictures—Direct from the Grand Opera House, Pittsburgh!" The plan was fine, but pictures of a quality to support a road show charging fifty cents admissions in legitimate theatres were not to be had.

Craft's next step was to plan production. If he could not buy the pictures he wanted he would proceed to make them. He was inspired of the notion that *The Life of Buffalo Bill* would make a drawing title. He pursued the *Buffalo Bill* show and overtook it on the lot at Williamsport, Pa. Craft dickered for a contract and got it, paying Major Lillie, Colonel Cody's manager, a thousand dollars in paper bills across the ticket wagon counting table.

In New York, Craft found P. A. Powers sufficiently alert to outside opportunities, amid the turmoil of the battles of the industry, to be interested. Powers and Craft became partners in the project. Paul Panzer, who had made his screen début with Vitagraph, was employed as director. They proceeded to shoot large quantities of film. When the shooting was all over and the dust settled in the editing room it was found that the only usable film was that portion of Colonel Cody's story devoted to the Wild West show. The picture was assembled in three reels and offered for state's rights sale.

Hyman Winik bought the first state, California, and opened with the picture in San Francisco. The picture was a pronounced success. Craft and Powers divided a net profit of fifty thousand dollars, which in that period was a sensational figure for a single picture.

This first feature was, of course, an Independent, or unlicensed, production. It caused many exhibitors to become Independents, sometimes against their will, as the Patents Company cancelled the licenses of all theatres playing unlicensed films. It is significant that the feature picture began with the Independents.

A tendency toward a sharper division between the creative dramatic pictures and the recorded topicals of the screen now developed with the rise of the first avowed news reels. The idea was imported, along with the establishment of an American studio by the French Pathé interests, identified with the Patents combine group.

In April, 1910, the American Pathé studio started in a remodelled cash register factory at Bound Brook, New Jersey. Among its first players were Paul Panzer and Octavia Handworth, who had been trained in the Vitagraph studios, Pearl White, a vaudeville performer with a dash of experience with the Powers Picture Play company, and Crane Wilbur. Louis Gasnier was sent from the French studios to be the first director.

As an incidental activity of this American enterprise, J. A. Berst, the manager, established the *Pathé Weekly*, with H. C. Hoagland as its first editor. The news reel idea had first crystallized into defined form in France, somewhat earlier, with the establishment of the *Pathé Journal*, a little theatre devoted exclusively to the showing of news pictures.

CHAPTER FIFTY-ONE

T. R. GETS NATURE-FAKED, AGAIN

WHEN in the autumn of 1908 the news percolated out that Theodore Roosevelt was planning an African hunt as his grand flourish of a vacation after leaving the White House, Colonel William N. Selig sped to Washington with a notion.

The idea was to take young Kermit Roosevelt to the Selig Polyscope Company's studios in Chicago and train him in the use of the motion picture camera for the purpose of recording the adventures of the expedition.

"Bully!" exclaimed Theodore the Mighty. "Bully—see me on this again." He slapped Selig on the back and sent him away smiling.

Colonel Selig built big plans on the anticipation. The week before Christmas he went to Washington again and talked to Roosevelt about the plan. The President was now not so positive, but he promised that if a Selig camera did not accompany the expedition there would be no other. Both of them apparently overlooked the fact that the arrangements of the expedition were in the hands of the Smithsonian Institution. When, in May 1909, the Roosevelt party sailed for Africa an English cameraman employed by the Smithsonian officials went along.

Colonel Selig heard the tidings and made appropriate remarks. That was no way for one good Republican to treat another. He sat down at the Union Café with himself and hatched a plot.

One end of the Selig studio out in Irving Park boulevard began to resemble one of those pictures of an African jungle that used to decorate the school geographies.

—519—

Up in Milwaukee Colonel Selig discovered a bargain sale on lions. For four hundred dollars he acquired a second hand lion, only slightly damaged by moths, from the owner of an unprofitable zoo. The lion was venerable but not senile.

Selig now had Africa complete, except for the black porters of the safari party. These he readily obtained from Chicago's own black belt. They were fittingly provided with raffia costumes.

By fortunate coincidence a vaudeville actor, whose name is either lost to history or mislaid, then appeared in Chicago with an impersonation of Roosevelt, including teeth. The actor was employed and cast for the rôle of Roosevelt in Africa. Otis Turner directed.

Incidental scenes for atmosphere were made, including camp fires and the like. Then an iron cage was erected to house a corner of the jungle and they brought on the aged lion, ill-humored at being awakened from his siesta.

The actor playing Roosevelt was unfamiliar with firearms, so his property weapon was loaded with smoke bearing blanks, while a crack marksman with an army rifle and smokeless ammunition was concealed out of camera range for the real shooting.

Every one was rehearsed except the lion. He seemed to be feeling worse every minute.

At the appointed signal the lion was released into the jungle set while the blacks arose beating tom-toms. The actor fired his futile blanks bravely with sublime trust in the hidden marksman.

The marksman missed and the lion, stung by the paper wads from the blank cartridge of the stage rifle, became positively annoyed. As the lion advanced the concealed expert fired again and nicked the beast in the jaw. The lion now determined that the situation was definitely unfriendly and prepared to clarify the scenery. The actor flew to the top of the cage and clung, while the blacks of the safari bolted through a handy emergency gate, disappearing in the tall grass of the adjacent Drainage Canal. Some of them, so far as is known, are going yet.

The lion had the stage. He lifted his voice and got it up quite a distance. The actor clinging to the top of the enclosure was suffering so acutely that there was a great uncertainty as to which should be shot first.

Tom Persons, at the camera, re-set for a close-up and they shot the lion, this time with complete success.

After first aid treatment, and an extensive change of costume, the actor posed over the carcass of the lion as the conquering Roosevelt.

The picture was prepared for the market and stored. Colonel Selig was watching the papers. When at last the cables brought word that Roosevelt had slain a lion the Selig picture went forth entitled: *Hunting Big Game in Africa*. Selig carefully refrained from using Roosevelt's name. He trusted the public for that.

Among the theatres the African picture was accepted as genuine. It was a thrill, a scoop and a hit. Selig sent many prints of the picture abroad and profited extensively.

When Colonel Roosevelt arrived in Berlin, on his post-African tour for the purpose of telling Europe and the world where it got off, he gnashed his dentistry at the discovery that what purported to be his distinguished self in Africa was appearing on the kinema screens of Berlin.

Came the day when once again the Colonels Selig and Roosevelt met, at the Republican club in New York.

"What the etcetera and soforth, did you mean by that lion fake, Selig?" Roosevelt was fed up. He remembered that Dockstader episode of his first term.

"If you'd taken an American cameraman I wouldn't have

—521—

done it," Selig responded, reaching for the button, doubtless to order a glass of milk for Roosevelt.

Whereat Roosevelt smiled, close-up and wide.

But the Roosevelt expedition exerted screen influence in two dirctions. It inspired Selig to the acquisition of a zoo for the making of animal pictures on a large scale, starting a vogue which continued to the end of the nickelodeon era, and it made hunting in Africa a fashionable pastime for wealthy Americans, resulting in several important expeditionary pictures.

WHEN THEODORE ROOSEVELT forgot his promise to take a Selig camera on his African hunt, Colonel Selig nature-faked a screen version in his Chicago studio.

FLORENCE LAWRENCE, "The Biograph Girl," the actress that
Laemmle took for "Imp," in his first daring raid on the
Patents Company's stellar talent.

CHAPTER FIFTY-TWO

IMP KIDNAPS TRUST STAR

Now, out of the war of the Independents against the Trust, came the first glimmerings of the star system. Just as new planets are presumed to be created out of cosmic clashes, the new race of screen stars took its origin from the impact of commercial strivings.

Carl Laemmle, in prospering dominance among the Independents, observed with a jealous eye the superiority and success of the licensed Biograph product.

"The Biograph Girl," Florence Lawrence, was the outstanding visible and obvious figure of that product. She was in fact a star, although the motion picture world did not know it.

Soon after the formation of Laemmle's Independent Motion Picture Company, the famous "Imp," Miss Lawrence vanished from the Biograph studios.

A story reached the newspapers from out in St. Louis that she had been mysteriously slain.

Then on April 2, 1910, a due and proper sequel to any such story dated April first, Miss Lawrence appeared under Laemmle auspices, whole and sound and in person on the stage to let the world know that "The Biograph Girl" was now "an Imp."

Laemmle had hit at the Biograph and the "Trust" to make a spectacular play before the customers of his exchanges. And, along with Miss Lawrence, he acquired the services of Harry Salter, her husband and director.

This move was the beginning of the star system.

From this time onward stars became increasingly important in the affairs of the screen—as the pawns in the hands of the producer-distributors engaged in the game of the film business.

Nearly ten years had to elapse before the pawns themselves learned to play the game alone—with the formation of United Artists which is another story to be told in a later chapter.

This St. Louis exploit, also engineered as a piece of Cochrane strategy, may also be pointed out as the first "publicity stunt" in behalf of a motion picture star. This was the beginning of a system of exploitation now developed to extravagant proportions with armies of "exploiteers," and a condition where to-day's first page murder may tomorrow develop to be merely the announcement of a new picture.

Close upon this time King Baggott was invited to the Imp studio to become the leading man playing opposite Miss Lawrence. Baggott was brave with the laurels of success in St. Louis stock companies and he had an engagement with Marguerite Clark in *The Wishing Ring*. He smiled and waved the absurd film aside. Twelve weeks later *The Wishing Ring*, out on the road, closed and Baggott came back to New York and went to Imp for a screen career which far overshadowed his stage fame.

The aggressiveness of Laemmle served to keep him much in the mind of the Motion Picture Patents Company, which kept up an unabated legal pursuit, vigorously seeking to shut down his Imp studio and all the rest of the Independent plants.

But J. J. Kennedy of Biograph, the most strenuous executive of the Patents Company, had other war plans in the making. He operated with an intelligence system that would have done credit to Bismarck. By ingenious and obscure channels he kept advised of every movement among the Independents. He had daily, almost hourly, reports on their affairs. He was informed by his espionage machine of everything. He knew most of their secrets. He was informed of even what they ate and drank and who they drank it with and what they said. He had figures on their business, what they spent for film and where they got it, and to whom they sold and rented film and for how much. His offices at 52 Broadway were rapidly expanding to cover a floor. There was the base and headquarters for the big war.

The Patents Company had started by offering licenses to the exchangemen to sell licensed film to licensed theatres. The exchangemen were making a great deal of money and from the Patents Company's point of view also a great deal of trouble.

The Patents Company set out to enforce its rulings on licenses. Raiding squads seized license film which was found in the hands of unlicensed independent exchanges. When licensed pictures appeared at unlicensed theatres the prints were seized and investigation started to find on whose responsibility the picture had escaped. Kennedy's secret service seemed to reach everywhere. Raids came fast in all parts of the country.

Durant Church, a collegian fresh from the football gridiron, was employed as the head of a raid-and-replevin squad to enforce the Patents Company's discipline on the film trade. His father, by the bye, was Melville Church who had been connected with the United States patent office in the early period of motion picture affairs, and who presently, after entering private practice, took over the legal affairs of the Motion Picture Patents Company.

License violations were breaking out all over the country. The next move in Kennedy's mind was to take the exchanges away from these troublesome fellows, eliminate a vast deal of waste and turn the profits of the exchange system into the pockets of the Patents Company group.

Doubtless another contemplated step was to take the theatres too, giving the Patents Company control from the making of the film clear down to the box-office—but that step never came, in the life of the Patents Company.

Kennedy found opposition for his idea within his own group.

The licensed film makers feared that any move to open their own exchange system would alienate their customers. They were thriving. They wanted to let well enough alone. But Kennedy had his way of prevailing. His mind was made up.

February 10, 1910, the motion picture world was excited to learn that the General Film Company of New Jersey had been incorporated at Trenton with a capitalization of two million five hundred thousand dollars!

The motion picture is quite casual about millions now, but a two and a half million dollar corporation in 1910 was a stupendous thriller.

The dry and formal incorporation announcement from Trenton gave little nourishment to the speculations of the motion picture men. The names were all strange and meaningless, being dummy incorporators carefully chosen by Kennedy. The new concern was to engage in the distribution of motion pictures. That was all. Here was the menace of a new trust!

The exchange men talked, violently, vigorously and freely.

The agents of Fighting Jeremiah Kennedy listened and reported. When it was all over he had the pulse of the situation counted and an accurate estimate of what it would cost to buy the exchanges the "Trust" desired.

Meanwhile, or rather simultaneously, just to keep the morale of the situation up, the Patents Company instituted a new action against the Imp, charging infringement specifically of the Latham loop patent.

The talk of some impending move of the "Trust" grew stronger. It was the subject of nightly debates at secret meetings of the Independents held at the Kessel & Bauman Empire Film exchange in Fourteenth street. Something would have to be done to present a united front against the foe.

Out of these conferences, the Motion Picture Distributing & Sales Company was formed, to ship the product of the Independents, collect the money for it—and, most important of all, deduct a percentage to go into a fund for the common defense in the legal wars of the Independents against the Motion Picture Patents Company. Carl Laemmle was chosen president of the Sales Company.

Internal dissensions began to arise in the Sales Company at once. A split of the Independents impended even as they combined.

Nothing more was heard of the General Film Company of New Jersey. It had been but a shot fired to flush the game and stir up telltale talk and action.

But on April 10, the Patents Company executives and licensed film makers gathered in a hotel room at Portland, Maine. There they concluded the legal details of incorporating the General Film Company of Maine, capitalized at two millions.

The incorporators quietly returned to New York and, unlike the New Jersey concern, nothing was heard from the General of Maine for some weeks. On May 27, 1910, the *Film Index*, organ of the "Trust," announced the General Film Company and its purchase of the exchanges belonging to George Kleine in various cities, and the Lubin exchange in Philadelphia. Of course, it will be recognized at once that both Lubin and Kleine were closely identified with the Patents Company. Since 1908 Kleine had been advocating the General Film Company idea.

An interesting and little known fact is that General Film, the maker of so many millions, did not represent any investment whatever, unless one counts the fifteen thousand which Kennedy loaned the company at its incorporation, just by way of having something in the center of the table.

The General launched into a campaign of buying desirable exchanges. It was out to swallow the business.

There was a little black book in J. J. Kennedy's pocket which contained the essence of all the statistical facts about all of the motion picture exchanges. It was all in code and the memoranda were meaningless without a certain sheet that stayed locked up in Kennedy's safe at 52 Broadway.

Kennedy set forth to buy out the motion picture business with its own money. The exchanges were purchased at a price based on the amount of film they had bought from the licensed manufacturers, and the price was paid in a small allotment of stock and twenty quarterly installments of cash, reaching over a period of five years.

If the exchangemen did not care to sell to General Film— well there was the Patents Company ready to cancel licenses for any violation of its complex rules. And no license meant no film.

The net result was that between April, 1910, and January 1, 1912, the General Film Company bought the fifty-seven principal exchanges of America for $2,243,089 in cash and notes, and preferred stock with a face value of $794,000.

Kennedy in behalf of the Patents Company combine built up the first foundation of statistical data for the guidance of the business. Fred Hawley, with experience in Wall street accountancy, was brought in to carry on the elaborate task of keeping record of the rapidly multiplying theatres from which license fees were to be collected.

The records of October 31, 1910, show that the United States had a total of 9,480 picture theatres, a growth of only five years. The trust served 5,281 of these, leaving 4,199 to the Independents. Twenty months later, July 12, 1912, the number of theatres had grown to 12,869. The Promised Land was growing richer.

The Trust got every licensed exchange save one. The fifty-eighth and last on the list it did not get, and thereon hangs history. This last was the Greater New York Film Rental Company, owned by William Fox. There were reasons why Fox was last. He was strongly intrenched. He had large theatre holdings all over the city of New York, and he had allied with him various persons of financial and political power, among them Tim Sullivan, an astute citizen often depicted by the cartoonists as strolling Fourteenth street with a large striped Bengal tiger on a leash, in the vicinity of a temple known as Tammany Hall.

In the autumn of 1911 there were dickerings with Fox, who did not want to sell. His license was cancelled, then on a tentative promise to sell it was reinstated. Then, while the deal pended, Gustavus A. Rogers, attorney for Fox, launched an injunction suit and line of legal action which compelled the delivery of licensed film to the Fox exchanges. The fight went eventually into the Federal courts. Meanwhile Rogers, busy in Washington, incited, fomented and poulticed an attack on the Motion Picture Patents Company as an unlawful conspiracy in restraint of trade. Rogers conferred with Attorney General George W. Wickersham, and wrote letters to President Wilson. When the Patents Company won an apparent victory in the Federal courts, Rogers won an apparent victory in the Federal courts, Rogers stirred up a counter-fire of trust prosecution.

Meanwhile detectives for Fox and Rogers shadowed Kennedy, while detectives for the Patents Company and Kennedy shadowed Fox and Rogers.

The resulting government dissolution suit against the Patents Company went to hearing January 15, 1913, around an oval table in Parlor B of the Hotel McAlpin in New York. Edward Hacker, special examiner, presided. H. N. Marvin of Biograph, and William Pelzer, of Edison counsel, were the first witnesses.

It dragged its complex way through the years, with a final decision against the trust, which was punished solely by an order to "discontinue unlawful acts." The decision, as in most film litigations, was too late to have any effect because the growth of the screen had swept on past the ground the fight started over.

But while the court fight pended, there were battles that had little to do with the law. Some of them erupted in mysterious night raids at the Greater New York exchange. There was strong-arm work to be done.

A significant bit of Fox strategic policy came with the acquisition of Winfield Sheehan, now vice president and general manager of the concern, who went to the film organization from his post as secretary to Rhinelander Waldo, then police commissioner of the city of New York. If Fox needed a militia, Winnie Sheehan knew where there were recruits.

While the Fox fight was gathering force, the very anti-trust rumblings which it set up reacted in a peculiarly indirect manner to the benefit of the Independents. The legal hazards of patent infringement presented only one phase of the Independent's problem. The Patents Company held control of the output of the Eastman Kodak Company's motion picture raw stock. It was the basic raw material of the art.

True enough there were several brands of film made abroad, but so far inferior to Eastman's that their use was one of the large handicaps of independent picture making.

The result was an underground traffic in Eastman stock. Shipments ordered from Rochester for export were waylaid at steamship docks from Vancouver to New York, the cases opened and looted. Film was stolen, pirated and smuggled with all of the ingenuity now evident in the devious ways of the rum runners. But the amount thus obtained by the Independents was inconsiderable and costly.

The film stock made by the Lumières in France, sold by Jules E. Brulatour, dealer in photographic supplies, was the chief source of lawful supply to the Independents.

Early in 1911, after many approaches, Brulatour convinced

George Eastman that the Independents offered a market for a million feet of film a week. Eastman agreed to take the matter up with the Patents Company, to see what they might allow under their exclusive contract.

Now with the trust situation as it was, any further sitting on the lid would have been politically and legally dangerous in several respects. The lid went off and the sale of Eastman stock to the Independents began March 1, 1911. After which Brulatour amassed a fortune as the Eastman agent to the film trade.

The effect was to give a large impetus to the Independents' product. They were now able to attain a photographic quality equal to that of the licensed studios.

Three years later the long fought litigation against Eastman in behalf of the claims of the Reverend Hannibal Goodwin, film inventor, ended with a victory for the Ansco concern and Goodwin's heirs. A settlement was made on March 28, 1914, for the reported cash sum of $3,000,000.

It may be noted in passing that the fortune of George Eastman, maker of film stock, estimated at upwards of a hundred millions, is many fold greater than that of any producer of motion pictures.

CHAPTER FIFTY-THREE

THE DISCOVERY OF CALIFORNIA

WHEN the murky days of the autumn of 1909 settled down on the studios of New York and Chicago the picture makers went hunting sunshine.

The thousands of nickelodeon theatres with their daily changes of program were consuming films at a rising rate and the output of the industry could scarcely keep pace with them.

Despite Biograph's early use of electric lighted stages the motion picture still largely depended on daylight. Soon after the birth of the motion picture theatre, tentative exploring expeditions to sunnier regions began, including Florida, Cuba and California.

One day late in 1907 the first motion picture invaders detrained in Los Angeles. The party consisted of Francis Boggs, director for Selig, and Thomas Persons, who was cameraman, property man, business manager, assistant director and whatever else conditions required.

The immediate business of Boggs and Persons was the completion of a one reel version of *The Count of Monte Cristo*. The interior scenes had been made in the Chicago studio. Now, ignoring the little technical matter of an entire change of cast, the rest of the picture was to be made in California.

Persons searched about Los Angeles to find some one sufficiently abandoned to accept work in motion pictures. He at last discovered a hungry hypnotist, starving on his earnings in a dime museum. The hypnotist had never heard of the movies but he was in condition to accept anything. He was cast for the rôle of the *Count of Monte Cristo*.

The big punch of the picture was to portray *Monte* rising

from the sea. Persons made up his hypnotist with a white wig and proceeded to the seashore to shoot the scene.

A great wave broke over *Monte Cristo* just as he got the signal to rise. The hero failed to emerge. He went down carrying the title rôle with him. That was not in the script.

"Hey!" Persons shouted to Boggs, "I put up a ten dollar deposit on that wig."

The director and the cameraman stood gasping at each other, stunned with horror at the thought. The wig was drifting out toward Honolulu.

Boggs and Persons both leaped into the sea to save the wig. While they were out there they saved the actor, too. It was very little extra trouble, anyway.

January 30, 1908, Selig released *The Count of Monte Cristo* in one thousand feet, a full reel, the first big California feature. Meanwhile, Persons and Boggs set up a studio on a roof top in Main street in downtown Los Angeles. California production had begun.

The pressure of the Patents Company's attack on the Independents was a contributing factor to the development of motion picture geography in this period. Independent picture making activities in and about New York were beset by difficulties. Cameras vanished from under the noses of the guards. Mysterious chemical accidents happened in the laboratories, resulting in the loss of costly negatives. The fight was not confined to the courts.

A climax came with one of the New York Motion Picture's operations in the making of a big scene at Whitestone Landing, on Long Island. This impressive spectacle called for a total of twenty extra people, a vast army for that time. Just as the critical drama moment in the scene came, a riot broke out among the extras. Rocks and clubs and fists flew. It was a fight apparently over nothing. Nine of the extras fought together as a clan. When the dust of battle settled, they were found to be professional gunmen and gangsters. Some mysterious agency had sent them out to make a riot instead of a picture. Five of the actors went to the hospital out of that engagement.

What with the weather and such mishaps, Bauman and Kessel decided to transfer the operations of the N. Y. M. P. into the safe distance and sunshine of California. Fred Balshofer and a stock company, including J. Barney Sherry, Ethel Graham, Fred Gephart and Mona Darkfeather, were sent West to found a new studio. The first N. Y. M. P. plant was a defunct grocery store on the outskirts of Los Angeles.

Among the licensed film makers in the East, Griffith of Biograph led the way to California. In early January of 1910 the Griffith company went on a California excursion. The company included Henry Walthall, Mary Pickford, Owen Moore, Jack Pickford and Tony O'Sullivan.

In Los Angeles, Griffith rented a loft in which to store properties for his pictures, and engaged a vacant lot at Twelfth and Georgia streets for a studio. Tent dressing rooms were ranged around the edges.

In the course of this first California season, Griffith found something of a lack of the large array of available extra people that the pictures were able to draw upon in New York among the unemployed of Broadway. Casting about for actors, he sent word to the Oliver Morosco stock company that Biograph could offer day-time employment to extras.

This bit of casual broadcasting of opportunity was the agency that brought to the screen the now famous name of Marsh. In the current Morosco production, Marguerite Marsh, oldest daughter of a family of five, was appearing in a song number, *My Gal Irene*, with Charles Ruggles. Marguerite was helping her mother, Mrs. Mae Marsh, a widow with the growing cares of the family. All of the rest of the children were in school.

She was a plucky and resourceful person. She had suffered the loss of her home in the disaster that San Francisco mentions only as "The Fire," and now she was in Los Angeles, running a hotel. Marguerite reported on the Biograph lot and was cast for a part in *The Mender of Nets*, a story written for the screen by Edwin August. This was in the season of '09. The next winter, when Biograph again migrated to California sunshine, Marguerite again played in the pictures. Her little sister Mae, chafin , with the irksomeness of school books, was vastly enamored of the wonders of her big sister's exploits on stage and screen.

Mae confided to her mother that she had decided that she would be either a great actress or a queen. For a while it looked as if queening would be it. On holidays away from school, Mae upset the household by organizing the children of the neighborhood into a royal court, which bowed and made obeisance at her imperious command.

But, after all, there did not seem to be any very good opening in the queen business in Los Angeles. Mae decided to look into the actress situation. She played hooky from school and ran away to the location where the Biograph was at work, where she surprised and annoyed sister Marguerite considerably by her truancy.

Mae stood about in open-mouthed wonder for a while, watching the mysterious camera, before Marguerite discovered her presence.

"You go back to school this minute—I'll tell mother."

Mae made a face and scampered away. This acting thing did not look so very exciting—maybe it would be more fun to catch butterflies.

The little runaway was engaged in turning over rocks looking for interesting bugs, when she caught the eye of Dorothy Bernard, of the Biograph stock company. Miss Bernard called to Griffith.

"See that cute kid—she looks a lot like Billie Burke."

Mae was oblivious to impending destiny. She was absorbed in the wiggles and kicks of a particularly large and entrancing beetle she had found in the grass. She looked up with her bewitching Irish smile.

"She does, at that," Griffith replied. "Call her over."

Mae's first bit was in a Spanish picture, and then came the now classic *Sands of Dee* and *Man's Genesis*. *Man's Genesis* was a one-reel drama of the cave man age. It is interesting as an early expression of the experimental curiosity about human affairs and social organization which so frequently is the thematic undercurrent of Griffith dramas.

These California excursions of Biograph and seasonal trips of the various other concerns were without any consciousness of establishing a new seat of industry. All of their California plans and arrangements were temporary and transient. The motion picture was not yet ready to make an investment in California and its sunshine. Back of the studio operations and the art of picture-making, the business of the motion picture, officed in New York, was sitting in suspended judgment. It was not at all certain in the mind of any man in the motion picture business that it was a permanent institution. Newspapers, inspired considerably by jealous theatrical magnates, talked casually of the motion picture craze as one of the passing whims of the public.

Carl Laemmle's Independent Motion Picture Company, the "Imp," was struggling under patent prosecutions and injunction orders with a maze of plans for escape. One of these had an incidental result in the founding of an entirely unrelated business.

Watterson R. Rothacker, the Chicago representative of *Billboard*, an amusement journal, in the opportune year of 1910 was struck with the possibilities of a business devoted to the making of motion pictures for industrial and advertising purposes. He looked about for backing and discussed his project with Carl Laemmle and Robert Cochrane, of the Independent Motion Picture Company.

Cochrane and Laemmle were not interested in advertising pictures, but they saw a handsome legal loophole in sight. They agreed to finance Rothacker's project if he would name it "Industrial Moving Picture Company"—thus giving it those same valuable, trademarked initials, I M P. In the event the Independent Company was shut down by the courts, the producing activities could, at an instant's notice, be shifted over to the Industrial Company and the trademark would be saved along with the product—at least until a new injunction should issue.

The trend of the court war shifted over night and it chanced that the "Imp" did not take occasion to avail itself of its newly organized corporate initials. Some two years later when the legal crisis had passed Rothacker, who had meanwhile built a flourishing business in industrial pictures, purchased the Laemmle interest and the concern took its present name, the Rothacker Film Manufacturing Company. From the beginning, as early as Haig & Haig's movie billboard in 1897, there had been efforts at motion pictures for purely business purposes, but Rothacker was first to build such a business. His first release was *Farming with Dynamite*, a one-reeler intended to show that nitro-glycerin is mightier than the plow.

In its squirmings against the Patents Company's injunctions the "Imp" first weighed plans to produce in California and at last determined to escape the jurisdiction of the United States courts entirely, by flight to Cuba.

The critical situation leading to this move was an aftermath of a second raid on the Biograph studios. The acquisition of Florence Lawrence, known as "the Biograph Girl," had proven most profitable. Now an emissary was sent downtown to see if "Little Mary," a rising screen favorite, could be lured away from Griffith. She was, of course, Miss Mary Pickford. The name of Pickford was unknown to the screen, but the girl herself, so often designated as *Mary* in Griffith's sub-titles, was known as "Little Mary" to all the motion picture world.

"Little Mary" was employed to work in "Imp" pictures at the amazing figure of $175 a week. Owen Moore, with whom Miss Pickford had played at Biograph, went along to "Imp." They were assigned to the stock company working under Thomas H. Ince, a newly appointed director.

Ince chanced into the pictures in the fall of 1910, when he arrived in New York at the end of a road show engagement, broke and "resting," as they say on Broadway. A street meeting with Joseph Smiley of the "Imp" stock led Ince to a day's work as a "heavy" at the Laemmle studio. Ince thereby earned his first five dollars in the films. In less than fifteen years the movies were to give him about a million.

Ince was born of a stage family and grew up in the life. As a youngster he appeared in many of the plays which took the road from New York, most notable among them perhaps being James A. Herne's production of *Shore Acres*. There was an interlude in his stage career one summer when Thomas H. Ince was a bus boy, carrying the dishes at Pitman Hall, a White Mountain resort. He took the ups and downs as they came, probably never dreaming of the ups that were to come. In the cast of *Hearts Courageous* at the Broadway theatre in New York, Ince met William S. Hart and struck up a friendship that was filled with potentialities of the future for both of them.

One of Ince's smiling reminiscences was of the gloomy Christmas Day of 1905 when he, Hart and Frank Stammer, also an actor, found themselves cheerless and broke, at the Barrington hotel in New York. Just when the day seemed the most dismal, Stammer received a present of a roasted turkey,

Mae Marsh and Bobby Harron, in "Man's Genesis," made
by Griffith in 1912 — the golden age of Biograph. Miss
Marsh was just sixteen then.

THE OLD IMP COMPANY, pictured in the roaring days of the Independent war in the season of 1910–11.

1 Mary Pickford
2 Owen Moore
3 King Baggot
4 Thomas Ince
5 Jack Pickford
6 Isabel Rae
7 Lottie Pickford
8 Joe Smiley
9 William Shay
10 Mrs. David Miles
11 Joe MacDonald
12 Hayward Mack
13 Mrs. Joe MacDonald
14 John Harvey
15 George Loane Tucker
16 David Miles
17 Mrs. Pickford
18 Robert Daley
19 Tony Gaudio

accompanied by fitting decorations. In the years ahead it was on the cards that Ince and Hart were to share a good deal of "turkey."

While Ince was working on his first picture at "Imp," Mrs. Ince, known to the stage as Alice Kershaw, found an engagement playing in Biograph pictures under the direction of Frank Powell. The director suggested that she might bring her husband to the studio. So Thomas Ince made his one and only Biograph appearance in a comedy, entitled *His New Lid,* the Biograph release of November 24, 1910.

But when Ince next encountered Smiley he was invited back to "Imp."

"You made a hit," Smiley informed him. "Go see Tom Cochrane—he likes your work."

By this time the shrewd young man Mr. Ince had made a discovery for himself. He was rather short and unheroic of proportions. He decided that he was not of the architecture of which stars of the screen would be made. He therefore decided that he would be a director.

Ince argued with Cochrane that, if he returned to "Imp," he should be given the first opening as a director. This was reluctantly agreed.

Then came the day when, overhearing a telephone conversation, Ince discovered that a director had quit. He marched up to Cochrane.

"That makes me a director," Ince announced.

Cochrane hesitated. Presumably he had not intended this development at all, but Ince was cocky and insistent.

"Yes, sure." A smile spread over Cochrane's face. He had to see it through. "You start now."

The actors of the "Imp" company had seemingly less enthusiasm for Ince as a director than Cochrane. The cast gave the new director the cold shoulder. Ince was annoyed with the amateurish high school girl scenarios available and resurrected a bit of verse, entitled *Little Nell's Tobacco*, for his first production. Hayward Mack, later a director, played the lead.

When the picture was completed, Carl Laemmle, accompanied by Mr. and Mrs. Ince, went down to Fourteenth street to see it in the "Imp" projection room. Throughout the screening of the picture Ince plied Laemmle with rapid conversation and expounded vigorously on the super-merit of the picture. It seems to have been a masterpiece that needed a good deal of boosting. Then, as it finished on the screen, Ince seized Laemmle by the arm and rushed him out of the room before any adverse comments from the rest of the audience could be overheard.

In this fashion Ince made himself a director.

The first Mary Pickford production at "Imp," directed by Ince, was a love story entitled *Their First Misunderstanding*, with Owen Moore playing opposite "Little Mary." It was boldly advertised with a line *"Little Mary is an Imp Now!"* This was a challenge to Biograph and the Patents Company, bringing such a sharp response from the legal batteries that the "Imp" prepared to flee.

C. A. Willatowski, a laboratory expert known to the industry then and since as "Doc" Willat, was sent to Cuba to make advance arrangements, while Ince gathered his company and made ready for sailing.

The vessel which carried this fugitive film company had hardly cleared Ambrose channel out of New York when Mrs. Charlotte Pickford, mother of Mary, presented herself to Ince and the captain, demanding in great excitement that they put about and return to port. She had discovered, not entirely to her pleasure, that Little Mary and Owen Moore had been secretly married shortly before the sailing.

Peace was restored with difficulty and, in due season, the party was landed in Cuba—followed by the sleuths of the Motion Picture Patents Company and J. J. Kennedy's intelligence service.

Doc Willat had leased a forbidding stone structure as quarters and studio for the company. There was that about the place which seemed chilling and inhospitable to the actors. They were vastly reassured, however, when it was explained that this was nothing less than the "Palacio del Carneado of Vedado." Joseph Smiley and King Baggot, however, did some inquiring on their own account and found that, in spite of its sumptuous name, the Palacio was in fact an abandoned jail. They moved.

The company had been at work but a few days when everyone became mysteriously and desperately ill.

The situation was doubly critical. "Imp" in New York was dependent for its very existence on the uninterrupted output of the company in Cuba.

Ince, recovering, first made a searching investigation. He found that Charlie Weston, the property man, with an eye to business and personal profits, had taken to Cuba with him a very large wholesale tin of cold cream. Weston calculated that there would be no drugstores in Cuba and that he would make a fortune out of selling his cold cream to the actors for the nightly removal of their make-up. So far so good. But he stored his drum of cold cream in the kitchen ice box. The Cuban cook decided it was just a fancy perfumed American lard and proceeded accordingly.

In Havana, Ince met J. Parker Read, who had been adventuring about Cuba as a salesman. He employed Read as an interpreter for his dealings with the Cubans. Read became a producer in various associations with Ince extending over many years.

CHAPTER FIFTY-FOUR
A COWBOY, AN UNDERTAKER, ET AL.

Here is an array of easy lessons in success, a study in dramatic entrances and how some of the great of the screen took their first steps on the path to fame.

The choicest of these is a tradition of the Biograph days of 1909, unverified but circumstantial enough to be true. It appears, as the story goes, that there happened to be a certain street car conductor on the cross-town line which passed 11 East Fourteenth street, the Biograph number, who observed with special interest the comings and goings of the picture people.

Now this conductor was not a mere routine street car man, but a romantic adventurer taking things as they came and facing life with a whimsically curious interest. The job on the cars was merely one of the turns of the dice of destiny. There was always something different just ahead.

Even the job on the street cars had come along that way in the miscellaneous sequence of happen-so. Before that he had been a dispenser of foaming steins in a German garden uptown, and doing rather well. Then, one busy night, just as he rounded a turn from the tap room into the garden, a fellow waiter gave him a playful nudge and his high held tray, balanced on one hand, went slam at the feet of the headwaiter, a wreck of beer and glassware. He resigned on the spot, thereupon abandoning the retail end of the brewery business to take up the study of the transportation business, also retail.

Now there was gossip up and down Fourteenth street about the easy money that people got for working in motion pictures.

There might be opportunity for a willing hand and a quick head in that old brownstone at Number 11.

Presently, abandoning his uniform for natty tweeds, the adventuring young man presented himself at the Biograph studios and intimated that he would confer the favor of an interview upon the management. His bearing was dignified and distinguished, and his accent foreign, "M. Henry Lehrman of Paris."

The management learned to its entire excitement and delight that the caller was a celebrated motion picture expert, recently connected with the Pathé establishments in France and that he would consider an American connection. M. Henry Lehrman was welcomed to Biograph's staff. He seemed to have a leaning toward comedy and was cast for it.

Presently a faint tinge of suspicion arose that perhaps M. Lehrman was not, after all, a French motion picture expert. The story was whispered about and soon a nickname was born on it. He was "Pathé" Lehrman thenceforward. For some years thereafter and in the cast of many a production the name stuck and appeared on the screen.

Probably France could not have made a more genuine contribution, anyway. In the opinion of not a few of his contemporaries, Lehrman added importantly to the development of screen comedy technique and, as an assistant to Mack Sennett, helped to evolve the style of screen extravaganza which, in after years, made Keystone and Sennett famous. Life is a "Keystone" to this adventuring Monsieur Lehrman. His humorous quips and quirks were an early part of the evolution of the now well-recognized craft of the picture specialist known as the "gag-man."

In the early summer of 1910, Colonel Selig sent a camera crew into Oklahoma to make pictures of frontier life, a topical subject. A whole constellation of star cowboys was rounded up to perform for the camera their feats of skill and daring.

While the cowpunchers circled and wheeled and galloped and jumped their bucking mounts by the camera, a United States marshal, with a bright silver star on his beaded buckskin vest, sat lazily with one leg over the saddle horn, watching the proceedings with an interested eye. From time to time he nimbly rolled a cigarette in a bit of corn husk, Mexican fashion. His air of indifference would have indicated that he thought very little of the cowboys' performance, but he was interested in the clicking camera.

This United States marshal was Tom Mix, a person who might be interested but seldom thrilled. He had rather run the gamut of the thrills of the West and the well known "great outdoors of God's country where men are men." Tom was born into that stuff. His father was Captain Mix, of the hellroaring Seventh United States Cavalry, a veteran wounded at the battle of Wounded Knee.

And Tom himself in his turn had had more than a smell of powder. A youngster, with the experience of the Southwest behind him, he went to Cuba as a scout in the Spanish-American war, thence to the Philippines and on to the fighting in China at the battle of Tien-Tsin. Then, back from foreign adventures and scarred with the wounds of conflict, he went into the Texas Rangers. Up in the valley of the Pecos in New Mexico, it was Tom Mix who rounded up the bandit Shont brothers and collected a rifle nick in his shin bone along with the prisoners. The prisoners were brought back, dead and alive respectively, fifty-fifty. Now, settled down with a rich ranch in the Cherokee Nation, Mix had nothing to do but be United States marshal and ponder on the passing of the good old days of general excitement in the big West.

This day had brought him the sight of something new under the sun—the motion picture camera. He felt impelled to participate.

"Is this a private round-up—or can I get in?"

"If you've got any speed, help yourself to the excitement," replied the cameraman. "I reckon there's room."

Mix slipped back into the stirrups and shot his pony out into the field. There was action aplenty. Then, just by way of topping it off, he roped and bulldogged a steer in a close-up in the matter of sixteen seconds.

In July, Selig released *Ranch Life in the Great Southwest,* and Tom Mix was started on his way to fame and the career of a motion picture cowboy. Today he rambles the boulevards of Hollywood in a long-nosed sport car with Spanish saddle leather and Mexican silver trimmings, combining the decorative tradition of the range with the luxuries of the storybook life of the screen star. In 1925 his salary with the Fox Film Corporation was quoted at $17,000 a week.

While the big Southwest was making a contribution of the picturesquely talented Mix, the backwoods of wildest Maine sent out another young man with a taste for the adventures of the open places to wander into New York and a screen career. Larry Trimble was an eerie youth, rich with the lore of the forests about his native village of Robbinston and the ways of the wild things that lived there. He was a writer of adventure tales. He came to New York to get closer to his market and, mayhap, to study the editors as he had studied the lynx and the minx up in Maine.

New York was full of wonders to this exploring young person, alert, red-headed and vigorous. He found copy everywhere. In quest of a story about the rising art of the motion picture, he went over to Flatbush to visit the Vitagraph studios and was entranced with the marvels and excitements of the busy establishment, where he found Moses, Napoleon and Lincoln lunching together between scenes. Trimble went to write a story for a magazine and stayed to take a desk in the scenario department.

He took the trifling beginner's salary of fifteen dollars a week to be close to this gold mine of new material.

Then came the day when Florence Turner and her director came to an impasse with a Pomeranian dog that could not act to their liking. Trimble was looking on.

"I've got a dog at home that can do better than that mutt," Trimble suggested.

"Bring on your dog," the director replied.

So the next day Trimble appeared with Jean, a collie destined to a large share in screen fame in Vitagraph dramas.

Trimble, it seemed, knew a great deal about dogs. He averred he could talk the language of dogs and make them understand. He put Jean through her part with Florence Turner with such marked success that the collie was put on the payroll for twenty-five dollars a week and worked in a long series of pictures. Some men might have been annoyed to have their dog offered a higher salary, but not Trimble. He appreciates dogs.

Along with the success of Jean, there was soon a fuller recognition for her master. Florence Turner suggested to Commodore Blackton that Trimble might be as successful directing actors as he was with dogs. So Trimble shortly became a Vitagraph director. Twelve years later, Trimble brought Strongheart, most famous of movie dogs, to the screen.

This same season saw the screen advent of the late John Bunny. Bunny found himself with nothing to do this summer of '10, following the close of an engagement with Annie Russell in *A Midsummer Night's Dream*, in which he had the rôle of *Bottom*. Back of that was a typically varied actor life story and experience.

Bunny was a native born New Yorker. He grew up in Brooklyn and, after public school, found a job in a market where he sold shoestrings and potatoes. This was tedious and unromantic. He ran away with a minstrel show and became a rambling player. He appeared with Sol Smith Russell, famous to an earlier generation, and added to his laurels in the rôle of *Hi Holler* in *Way Down East.*

From Shakespearean rôles to the motion picture was perhaps something of a drop, but Bunny in his way was a philosopher. He ambled over to Flatbush and joined the waiting throng of volunteer extras in the Vitagraph yard.

It was early on a heated summer morning. Fat John Bunny was hot and uncomfortable. He took off his hat and wiped a beaded brow. Just at this juncture Commodore Blackton and Albert E. Smith, Vitagraph executives, were looking out of an office window that overlooked the yard. Together and at the same instant they spied Bunny.

"What a face!"

In that instant Bunny's fortune was made.

One of Bunny's earliest screen appearances was in *The New Stenographer,* with Flora Finch playing opposite. The story was written and directed by Commodore Blackton. It was a hit, and lives today as a screen tradition.

Bunny was among the earliest players really starred. Since he appeared in comedies written around him and his vast girth, it was a logical step to include his name in the titles, giving him an early entry into screen publicity. In 1912, Bunny grew alarmed at his weight and dieted off forty pounds. It was almost fatal to his work. His popularity went off with his tonnage. Bunny went back to three meals a day and fattened the box office reports.

This same year that saw the beginning of the famous Bunny's screen career, brought in Norma Talmadge.

The Talmadge sisters three, Norma, Constance, and Natalie, lived over Ocean avenue way in Brooklyn. While Norma was yet a school girl, her first pictorial experience came when an admiring photographer induced her to pose for song slides. The rise of the motion picture theatre had given impetus to the industry of making the stereopticon accompaniment for the illustration of the song numbers which decorated the intermissions of the picture programs in the nickelodeon theatres. There was a large demand for pretty girls to pose for the still cameras that made the slides. A notable number of the day was Irving Berlin's "Stop, Stop, Stop!" a song hit which went out to the nickel shows with Miss Talmadge on the slide pictures. This had no direct connection with her subsequent screen career, save to turn her attention cameraward.

One of the diversions of the Talmadge sisters was playing "make-believe movies" in their home. One of these playtime parlor performances was observed by a chance caller, who volunteered the opinion that Norma might really prove capable in motion pictures. This caller supplied a letter of introduction to a casting director at Vitagraph.

It was an exciting day for Norma when she made ready for her invasion of Vitagraph. Accompanied by her mother, she fared forth and pushed into the throng that crowded Vitagraph's yard. In that busy medley of people and affairs she was a long time presenting her letter to the casting director. He looked Norma up and down.

"Walk around out there in front of me."

Miss Talmadge was mayhap a little self-conscious at this critical moment. She perhaps wondered, the way girls do, if he could guess that the brave gown was a made-over dress of her mother's.

"I guess you'll do."

Norma Talmadge's name and characteristics went down in the book and she was to be called when needed. Meanwhile, she was invited to take a look about the studio.

Florence Turner, her particular screen favorite, was working on the first set encountered. With a happy cry, Norma dashed into the scene to embrace Miss Turner and pour out her admiration.

The director, angered at the interruption, shooed Miss Talmadge off the set and started a re-take. The first scene in which Miss Talmadge appeared never went on the screen.

One of her earliest appearances was a trifling comedy drama of one reel entitled *The Household Pest* and built around the then less hackneyed humor of a "camera fiend." Throughout the entire picture Norma's face did not appear. She was always to be discovered on the scene with her head under a focusing cloth.

Maurice Costello, the dean and veteran of the Vitagraph stock company, pleaded Norma's cause the day it was decided she would never be an actress.

Perhaps because he wanted to humor "Cos," or maybe because he felt the force of the argument, Van Dyke Brooke, the director, cast her for a part opposite Costello in *The First Violin*, an ambitious two reel subject.

Not long thereafter Norma Talmadge appeared in Vitagraph's *Tale of Two Cities*, riding the tumbril to the guillotine with Maurice Costello in the rôle of *Sidney Carton*, under the direction of J. Stuart Blackton. This picture because of its forceful character is most often but erroneously recalled as Miss Talmadge's first screen appearance.

With the success of this picture Miss Talmadge's period of probation came to an end. Costello was vindicated and it was admitted that after all she was an actress.

Those were days of the glory of Vitagraph, the period of its greatest prosperity when, at the zenith, it had twenty-nine directors working and an army of hundreds of actors and employees. Salaries and production costs were low and the money was coming rapidly. Smith, Blackton and Rock were prospering mightily after the lean years of their wars with Edison. At Christmas time there was holiday largess of bonuses and, in old Number 4 studio, the Vitagraph chiefs stood at a long table passing out turkeys as the employees marched by.

On this wave of prosperity J. Stuart Blackton took to the sea with an amazing series of costly speed boats and became the Commodore of the Atlantic Yacht club, acquiring the title that he has carried ever since in the motion picture world.

This speed boat diversion brought into Blackton's service Wallace Van Nostrand, a motor and racing expert, who tinkered the Commodore's boats and engineered his marine exploits. Van Nostrand followed the Commodore ashore and also joined the Vitagraph family, becoming known on the screen as Wally Van.

Vitagraph now acquired Hugh McGowen, a fat and funny person. McGowen, despite his cheerful predisposition to slapstick, was, according to his contemporaries at Vitagraph, an undertaker in Ocean avenue when he followed the crowd of extras into Vitagraph yard, curiously seeking to see what all the excitement was about. Nothing seemed to be taking place, so McGowen rested his bulk on a bench and dropped off to sleep.

Now this was the most outstanding studio trait of the distinguished John Bunny. It followed by the logic so peculiar to the motion picture mind that another fat man, who was equally sleepy, might very well be also funny. They poked McGowen into wakefulness and put him to work. He broke into motion pictures in his sleep—probably the only instance of its kind in the history of the industry. To the followers of the screen the merry undertaker became known as Hughey Mack.

Out in Chicago Essanay began increasing its stock company and acquired J. Warren Kerrigan, who then rejoiced in the title of *The Gibson Man*, presumably because he was at least as handsome as the Gibson Girl of Charles Dana Gibson's creating.

It was early in 1910 when Kerrigan made his first screen appearance in Essanay's *A Voice from the Fireplace*. Kerrigan's fatal beauty, by the way, had led him to pose for New York illustrators, and he had some share of stage repute from his appearances in the Shubert productions of *Brown of Harvard* and *The Road to Yesterday*.

. . . .

The motion picture was now uncomfortable with an uncertain nomenclature. The parlance of the day had run through a series of experimental terms and words of horrific design, starting with Cinématograph and Kinetoscope in the early vaudeville days of the screen, to nickelodeon, nickelette, theatorium and nickelshow in the early days of the screen theater. All these names were awkward misfits. All England and Europe had rather settled to *Cinema* in some form of spelling, except Germany, which, with characteristic Teutonic explicitness, arrived at *Wandelbilder*—wandering pictures—*Lichtbild* and *Lichtspiel*—light play. There was no acceptable suggestion for America there.

The motion picture industry in the United States was making a serious effort to kill the rise of the word "movie." "Movie" began to get circulation in newspaper comic strips in 1909. Within a year it was well on its way to nation wide usage.

The Essanay company with an eye on advertising opportunity, offered a handsome prize of twenty-five dollars for a new name for the motion picture.

The contest concluded with the announcement on October 12, 1910, that Edgar Strakosch, a musician and exhibitor in Sacramento, California, had been awarded the prize for coining the name "Photoplay."

This did not settle the matter, however. The advertisements of the time are filled with the verbal blacksmithing of the film makers in an effort to arrive at a significant term. Vitagraph was proud for a long time of its phrase, "Vitagraph Life Portrayals," while Bauman and Kessel toyed indefinitely with the phrase, "Life Motion Pictures."

While the motion picture was still trying to name itself, in Chicago a legal decision of vast but forgotten significance came to add to the dignity of the new art. On March 9, 1909, Tony Piazza and Tony Graziona entered the theatre of one Susanna Lange, at Wentworth avenue and Sixty-ninth street, on Chicago's West Side, and were promptly thrown out. Through James LaMantia, they brought suit under the civil rights act, and the defense was set up against them that they were heavily scented with garlic. In June, Judge Heap handed down his momentous decision, saying: "The odor of garlic may, at times, be an obstacle permitting the refusal of a person's entrance at a public entertainment, and I find for the defense." It is to be regretted that appeals did not carry this case to a confirmation in the United States Supreme Court so that a national precedent might have been established.

CHAPTER FIFTY-FIVE

THE LATHAMS' LAST DAY

NEARLY a decade and a half had passed since the name of the Lathams had figured in the affairs of the motion picture, when in 1910 the forgotten efforts of the old Confederate Major suddenly become important again.

Woodville Latham's death had been evidenced in court in the course of the patent wars and to most of the litigants he was a misty figure of tradition.

Now it developed that proof pertaining to the conception of the device known as the "Latham Loop" must be had in behalf of the Patents Company which was pressing its infringement suit against Carl Laemmle, leader of the Independents, and head of that annoying "Imp."

Parker W. Page, attorney for the Patents Company, began a search of the archives, Patent Office records and legal files. The papers most sought were missing. Records and relics, now important pieces of evidence, had been burned by a janitor for the Ansco company in Binghamton, N. Y. after the sale of the Latham patents to Biograph.

The only hope for equivalent evidence was in other possibly surviving papers and perchance the memories of some of Latham's relatives if they could be found. Investigators were set to work. Reports came back to the office of Page, Kerr & Cooper, attorneys, burdened with tales of tragedy in the Latham family. All of the Lathams were found to be dead. Otway, the younger son of the Major, had been stricken with appendicitis and died in hospital a few years before the search began. Grey Latham hardly a month later, was found dead on the pavement in Ninth street near Broadway in New York. He had a wound in his head and his pockets had been looted, presumably by the Apaches of the gas house district.

And from Paris, where Natalye Dole Lockwood Latham had taken refuge from the unhappy ending of her romance with Otway Latham, came yet another chapter of disaster. After divorcing Latham, Natalye Lockwood had devoted herself with marked intensity to her painting and she was on the threshold of such a success in Paris as she had enjoyed as "the feminine Whistler" and painter of society portraits in New York.

But there were sad days in the studio at 21 Rue Viete. The Marquis de Bernis came now and then to sit for a portrait that was long in the painting. His last sitting was on the afternoon of March 6, 1907. When the Marquis had gone Natalye Lockwood arrayed herself in a ball gown, slipped on her wedding ring and carefully arranged her hair in the way that Otway had liked best.

The excitable old French caretaker downstairs thought that he had heard a shot. He ran in his clattering sabots after a gendarme.

Natalye Lockwood Latham was dead. There was the end of the heartache which started with the parting in Mexico City that blighting day years before.

Considerably disconcerted, the lawyers for the Patents Company abandoned the quest of the Lathams on the clues centering in New York. One morning in April a junior member of the staff of Page, Kerr & Cooper, arrived in Washington to begin a quest for possible acquaintances of the family. In a city directory the young lawyer came upon the names of the Misses Ella G. and Sallie Evelyn Latham. He called on the telephone and asked if they were in anywise related to Major Woodville Latham.

"Yes, we are his sisters," came the reply on the phone.

The investigator waited for nothing more. He put in a call for his New York office. S. S. Durham of the legal staff hastened to Washington and called at the Latham sisters' apartment.

"There is some important litigation involved, and it would be a great favor if you would tell us all you know about Major Latham's motion picture inventions," the lawyer began.

"Of course we would be glad to tell you anything," Miss Sallie Latham replied. "But why do you not talk to our brother and let him tell you himself?"

The lawyer was first startled, then puzzled. Could it be, he wondered, thinking rapidly, that these aged spinsters were, by some curious fantasy of hope, denying their brother's death?

"But—but—he has been dead for many years." The attorney tried to be gentle.

"No, sir, you are surely mistaken—he is living." The prim Miss Latham was unperturbed and positive.

"Where, please?"

"In New York, at 227 West 116th street, sir."

So up there in 116th street they found Major Woodville Latham. He had, through all the years of the legal fights and searches, been living less than a half an hour's distance from the center of conflict.

Since 1897, thirteen years, Major Latham had been dead so far as the world of the motion picture was concerned. Now even his despairing efforts as a book agent trudging the streets of Harlem were near to an end. He was ill, broken, beaten, but proud still, a chivalrous relic of the Southern gentility. He was trying to make a fight of it yet. When bright sunny days came he struggled out with his worn samples.

When Parker W. Page, the attorney, called, Major Latham had taken to his bed in a final surrender. He was not going to try to sell books any more. He was going to try to live on the little allowance that his aged sisters could send him from Washington. One of them had a position in the Smithsonian Institution, the last of the family within the strongholds of science.

One can imagine the emotions of the old Major on this bitter day, ferreted out in his poverty, by men battling over the empire of the screen. Industry was taking a profit in millions out of the claim that he had located, staked and lost. Newcomers were fighting over the pot of gold they had found at the end of an old man's rainbow. And they wanted to ask him about it! They wanted to know just how and why and when he had dreamed out that rainbow.

Page, the attorney, was patient. He explained how the Latham patents had passed from the Anthony-Scoville Company to the Ansco Company and from the Ansco to the American Mutoscope & Biograph company and from the Biograph Company until now they reposed at last with the Motion Picture Patents Company, to be the proudest part of the legal foundation of that great combine. True enough the Major's personal title in that patent property had passed, but none-the-less this was a fight to prove his fundamental rights, to vindicate what he had done.

There was keen hidden tragedy here. As one who has followed in careful detail the facts of the patent fight leading up to the formation of the Patents Company can discover, the survival of the Latham patents was due first to the apathy and preoccupation of the Ansco interests and second to film politics. This did not matter legally, now. The only patents upon which the Latham patents could be invalidated, the Armat inventions, were also in the strongbox of the Patents Company.

The Major rose out of his indifference as he scented a battle of vindication. There was a spark, small but bright, in the old man's heart yet.

"Yes," he would, "by the Almighty, sir," take the witness stand and tell them.

A physician came to minister to the Major. There was a nurse, and new comforts and some long careful conferences with the lawyers.

On April 25, 1911, a little more than a week after the discovery of the Major, he walked feeble but erect into a surprised court room, and held up his trembling right hand before the clerk.

For days Major Latham detailed his story of the first efforts at motion picture projection, the rise of his friendship with William Kennedy Laurie Dickson, the employment of mechanics, the struggles of the workshop in Frankfort street, the exchange of challenges with Edison, the first screen shows and the decline of the project under a swelling tide of adversities.

When Page concluded the aged witness was subjected to the raking fire of cross-examination by the lawyers for the Independents. He stood his ground and faced the tedious ordeal with fortitude befitting his tradition. His testimony is to be found in the records of the case of the Motion Picture Patents Company vs. The Independent Motion Picture Company et al., in the United States Court for the Southern District of New York.

In a strict legal sense the Motion Picture Patents Company, having properly acquired the Latham patents by purchase, had no obligation to the old inventor. But even corporations have their sensibilities and emotions.

There was a carefully phrased suggestion, avoiding all appearance of charity, to Major Latham that the Patents Company in consideration of his service would be pleased to give him a continuing fee, a sort of retainer as an expert—more plainly, of course, a living. He was asked what his requirements in that connection might be, pending such time as perhaps an ultimate court triumph for his patent might permit a substantial royalty.

Major Latham flushed and hesitated.

"I think, sir, that I should be able to do nicely on—say fifteen dollars a week."

This was repeated to Jeremiah J. Kennedy, the gruff iron boss of the Patents Company. Kennedy choked back an exclamation.

"We'll give him twice that," Kennedy ordered.

Then he stopped abruptly. That was not the sort of thing that corporations are supposed to do. It was not business.

"Send the old gentleman thirty dollars every week—out of petty cash. We don't want that on the books."

So Woodville Latham received thirty dollars a week thereafter. But the old Major's health and spirit declined rapidly. The sessions in court had given him a glimpse of the golden land of the motion picture which he had glimpsed so long before and never enjoyed.

Thanksgiving Day, 1911, Major Latham died. The Patents Company gave him a funeral—the last voucher on the petty cash report "account W. Latham."

A winter's day in 1921 the writer went on a lone pilgrimage to Rock Creek Cemetery, near Washington, D. C., seeking the grave of the tragedy haunted old pioneer of the screen.

The quiet cemetery office was empty. Out across the snowy distance a gnarled old grave digger was at work.

"I am looking for a grave," the visitor began, addressing the old man in the deepening pit.

"There's a lot of them here," he replied, bending at his spade with indifference.

"But it's a special one—Major Woodville Latham's—an old timer."

The grave digger clambered out and dropped his tools.

"Yep, he's here—way over yonder—buried ten year ago— cremated—didn't need no permit" the grave digger volunteered leading the way.

Going straight across a half a mile of cemetery thick with headstones he led directly to the granite shaft bearing the name of Latham. It seemed a marvelous feat of memory in that populous city of the dead.

"Do you know where they all are, like this?"

"All them that fought for the South, I do," the old grave digger responded. "He was a major in th' war."

The case of the Patents Company against the "Imp" ended at last, years too late to have a bearing on the future of the films, with a decision for the defense from the United States Supreme Court in 1915. After twenty years of war the "Latham Loop" patent failed of its purpose. Yet every motion picture machine in the world today uses that loop.

And so passed the name of Latham from the history of the motion picture.

The case against the Independent Motion Picture Company, in which Woodville Latham became so important a witness, brought in another personality of more interest than importance, William Friese Greene, of London.

As has been indicated, Greene was a persistent claimant to past honors as the original inventor of the motion picture.

Because in their efforts to discredit the Motion Picture Patents Company, the Independents had made much of the claims of Greene to a priority over the American inventors, he became on this wave of propaganda a personage of promised importance in the fight. P. A. Powers of the Independent forces, planned to spring a surprise upon the Patents Company. He communicated with Greene and arranged for him to come most quietly to New York, prepared to take the witness stand and explode the entire American patent situation.

All went nicely. Greene came to New York, and was stowed away at a hotel with considerable secrecy. Then the lawyers for the Independents went into secret session with the imported star witness.

Greene expanded and expounded at length on his claims and talked glowingly of his invention of the motion picture camera.

But there was just that little technical matter of proof, a documentary presentation of facts about these imported British patents of which he spoke.

Alas and alack! Greene was much annoyed—for, said he, he had forgotten and left all of his patent papers in London.

So, just as quietly, just as secretly, Greene was bundled off to London, before the Patents Company could discover him.

After the Kinemacolor litigation which followed this episode, William Friese Greene disappeared from the motion picture affairs of England. In 1915 he was discovered in want and the concerns of Film Row in London raised a fund of about seven hundred dollars to supply his immediate wants. The British picture men were beginning patriotically to desire an original "inventor-of-the-films" all their own.

But tragedy followed fast on the footsteps of Greene. On the night of May 5, 1921, he was invited to a dinner in London given by the film trade. As "the father of the industry,"

Greene was called upon to make a speech. He rose and once again he told his story—at the end of it fell dead across his chair.

Due largely to fictions that are built about the name of Greene, there are many in the motion picture industry today who feel convinced that the art was born in England.

CHAPTER FIFTY-SIX

ADVENTURES OF KINEMACOLOR

THE striving for natural color in motion pictures began with the beginnings of the picture itself. The course of color history in the films has been as romantically adventurous as the story of the screen.

Now in 1909 the dreams of the inventors came to flower with the first color picture on the screen.

Many had fancifully played with the idea of screen color, including William Friese Greene of London, whose dallying contact with the motion picture idea has been noted in earlier chapters. But among the first significant laboratory efforts were those of Edward R. Turner, an English chemist.

Turner, beginning as a student of processes for making still pictures in color, had been at work on the motion picture color problem several years when in 1901 he enlisted the aid of Charles Urban, as the most aggressive factor in the British film trade. Turner held a British patent, No. 6202, issued March 22, 1889, on a color film process. But it was in effect only an invention on paper, not reduced to practice.

Turner's first backer was F. Marshall Lee, a breeder of fast horses for the British turf. Lee's participation in this early effort in screen color has a flavor of coincidence when one recalls that it was another horseman, Leland Stanford of California, who financed the Isaacs-Muybridge researches in the '70's.

Urban acquired Lee's interest in Turner's work in behalf of the Warwick Trading Company, the picture concern which had developed out of his invasion of Britain in behalf of

Maguire & Baucus, the Edison agents. Six months later, after £500 had been spent without tangible results, the company wearied of the quest and Urban took up the burden.

Turner was laboring with an effort to combine the three primary colors on the screen by projection, in an optical equivalent of the three color printing process. In time he succeeded just sufficiently to give hope. Perfection demanded three perfectly matched lenses, which the optical workers declared impossible.

Turner set to work to seek a new approach to the problem.

One day in 1902, as Urban sat at his desk nearby, there came a crash from the workshop where Turner was striving with his perplexities.

Urban ran into the room and found Turner dead on the floor.

Turner's notes, models and formulæ were scattered about in confusion. No one else knew the meaning of half of them. The most of what Turner had attained died with him.

Urban cast about for another researcher to continue the effort and retained G. Albert Smith, a photographer and scientific experimenter. Turner's materials were removed to Smith's workshop at Brighton.

Years slipped by, with Urban journeying down to Brighton at week-ends.

At last Urban and Smith decided that the three color process was hopeless. They were in despair. Then, in its usual eleventh hour manner, Fate intervened, this time in their behalf.

Urban was in Paris on one of his monthly excursions to look into the affairs of his Urban-Eclipse studio there, when, with that color problem uppermost in his mind, a street vender of novelty postcards arrested his attention.

These cards, it must be blushingly admitted, were Parisian. They were in two transparent parts, one red, the other green. Either, viewed alone, presented a commonplace view of scenery. When super-imposed and held to the light they presented not scenery but obscenery.

Urban invested a franc in these cards, hurriedly and furtively concealing them in his inside coat pocket. He strolled on down the boulevard, trusting that he had not been observed in this seeming frivolity, and wondering if here in these silly cards might not be something related to the secret that puzzled the week-end conferences at Brighton.

With these cards as the beginning Urban and Smith tried a new attack on the color problem. Instead of continuing the three primary color process, as Urban puts it, "we jumped over the fence of theory," and sought the same result with two colors. They had been working with red, blue and yellow. Now they divided the yellow between the red and the blue, thus getting two colors to play with, a red-orange, and a blue-green.

This, if it worked, would immensely simplify the process and all of its related devices. Five tedious years had now elapsed. The solution seemed close at hand.

A Sunday in July 1906, came and all was ready for the first test of the two color principle. Camera and projector were waiting. It was a beautifully sunshiny day in G. Albert Smith's garden at Brighton. He dressed his little boy and girl in gay clothes with a variety of colors. The little girl was in white with a pink sash, the boy in sailor blue and carrying the British Union Jack. They were posed on the green grass, with the red brick of the house as a background.

The camera was loaded with a fifty foot length of prepared color-sensitive film and in thirty seconds an exposure had been effected.

Urban and Smith went together in the little darkroom in a corner of the red brick house and put their precious film into the developer.

Two feverish hours followed, while Smith and Urban dried their color negative and made, developed and dried a positive print for the projection test.

Then, with shades drawn to darken the experimental projection room, they put the test picture into the machine.

The projection machine was equipped with the same red and green filters as the camera, the color lesson learned from the absurd French picture cards. It was the hope that the picture just made, projected through these filters, would combine the colored light light rays and endow the effect on the screen with the tints of nature.

The test film flashed through its fifty feet in half as many seconds. There on the screen for that half minute, was the little girl in white with a pink sash and the little boy with his sailor blue suit. And the grass was green and the bricks of the house were red.

For the first time in the world a motion picture in natural colors was projected on the screen.

The little picture was hardly half through the machine when Urban leaped up and yelled.

"We've got it—we've got it!"

The newborn process was christened "Kinemacolor."

Urban withdrew from other film interests and set about exploitation of the invention. May Day of 1908 the first public demonstration of Kinemacolor was given at the opening of Urbanora House in Wardour street, London. Urbanora House, by the way, began the movement of the film trade from Warwick Court, known as "Flicker Alley" to the modern "Film Row" of Wardour street.

Kinemacolor was presented for scientific consideration at an exhibition on December 9, 1908, before the Royal Society of Arts. Then the new color pictures, following in the footsteps of the first films, went on the screen for the public at the Palace theatre, under the auspices of Alfred Butt, subsequently Sir Alfred. The commercial career of color began there with a matinee on February 26, 1909.

Now a new company was formed, Urban acquired Smith's interest in the patent, and a world-wide career for Kinemacolor ensued, with engagements in Berlin, Paris and all the capitals of Europe.

But the United States was the golden land of picture opportunity and Urban looked to America with a special interest.

In New York, with the film industry in the throes of the war of the Independents and the Patents Company, Urban showed his Kinemacolor pictures at Madison Square Garden December 11, 1909. The ten chiefs of the Patents Company attended the showing. They were outwardly filled with enthusiasm. A tentative deal was made to buy the American rights for $250,000. It was to be closed the next morning.

There was a handshake all around. Among the Patents Company magnates was "Pop" Rock of Vitagraph. He remembered with some sincere appreciation the event of years before when Urban's plea to Maguire and Baucus, Edison agents, had saved the little Rock picture show, storm-stranded in the South. Rock edged up to Urban and spoke behind his hand.

"Charlie—let me slip you something straight. These fellows are just kidding you. I sat there along with the rest of them and promised to put up my twenty-five thousand, but they'll never ask me for it. They don't want Kinemacolor here and they won't go through with it. It's scared them. You'll never get away with it—you watch."

Urban was disturbed but not convinced.

The next day he turned up for the appointment to close the deal and waited two hours. No one appeared. Word came that the Patents company crowd was in an important conference over the projected making of some prize fight pictures. They would see Urban later. Repeated efforts through the day resulted in an appointment for dinner with the executive committee, at the Republican club, that fated spot where so much of the secret history of the motion picture has been enacted.

Seated at dinner, Urban tactfully as may be, opened the subject.

"Let's not talk shop at dinner," they reproved him. "After dinner we'll get at it and clean the thing up." This from the captain of an industry which does all of its work over the lunch table.

After dinner Urban again tried to open the subject of Kinemacolor.

"Now we want to relax a little, first. We don't like to talk business right after dinner. We'll just have a few hands of poker first."

Up in a private room in the club the august gathering seated itself for the consideration of what may happen with five cards, joker wild. The night wore on, with Urban more interested in his Kinemacolor contract than the cards.

"Just a couple of rounds more, and we'll go into that."

One in the morning came and the game broke up. Urban was conspicuous among the contributors of the evening's diversion in the sum of perhaps five hundred dollars.

"Now about the Kinemacolor contract," he remarked cheerfully.

"Oh, not now—we are all tired out now."

Urban went away to his hotel, so annoyed that on second thought he decided to return to London at once and let the deal go hang.

The next afternoon he sailed.

The facts were apparent. The motion picture chieftains of the United States did not want any ventures in color. They were making easy millions in black and white pictures. This color process was to them strange, complicated and speculative. The status quo suited them immensely. Why disturb it? They were making money, why be concerned about making pictures?

Urban's ship was hardly clear of Ambrose channel when a stranger and an unknown in the motion picture world dashed into New York in a heated quest of the proprietor of Kinemacolor.

This man was Gilbert Henry Aymar, a real estate dealer of Allentown, Pa., who had attended the Madison Square Garden show merely because someone had given him a pass. Aymar was now afire with a desire to exploit Kinemacolor.

Aymar and a friend James Klein Bowen, a wealthy wholesaler of groceries in Allentown, sailed for London where they overtook Urban and acquired Kinemacolor rights for the United States.

The Kinemacolor Company of Allentown, Pa., quickly encountered difficulties and was reorganized through a New York financial house, with J. J. Murdock, the vaudeville magnate, as president.

Ambitious production activities were instituted with a flourish. Studios were established at Whitestone Landing on Long Island, and at Los Angeles yet other studios were put in operation.

David Miles, to be remembered as an early member of the Biograph stock company, became the director in chief. It was about this time that David W. Griffith and his wife, Linda Arvidson Griffith, parted company, Mrs. Griffith went to Kinemacolor as the leading woman for the West Coast studios. In the East, at Whitestone Landing, William Haddock was the principal director.

Many pretentious stories were put into production, among them Thomas Dixon's *The Clansman*, which, a few years later under Griffith's auspices, was destined to mark a great milestone of the screen as *The Birth of a Nation*. Kinemacolor produced *The Clansman* in the vicinity of New Orleans with the members of a traveling stock company in the cast. Legal complications concerning the right to the use of the story for the screen arose and the picture never saw the light of a theatre.

Lillian Russell, who, in 1912, was still the reigning queen of stage beauty, went to Kinemacolor to appear in *La Tosca* this season.

The first theatre showings of Kinemacolor pictures were, naturally enough, of pictures purchased from the British concern. Kinemacolor pictures were of necessity "Independent," being so thoroughly outside the pale of Patents Company sanction. Projection machines unaccountably got out of order. Films broke and burned. Operators made mistakes and so maladjusted their machines that the red and green images of the color picture were reversed with bizarre but trying optical effects on the screen. Licensed exhibitors who ventured to show Kinemacolor pictures found their licenses cancelled by the Motion Picture Patents company, which brooked no use of Independent film. Kinemacolor went through a career of costly failure in the United States in a period when it was making millions in a world success elsewhere.

The most pretentious effort of Kinemacolor was the picturing of the Royal Visit to India and the famous Durbar at Delhi, which Urban photographed under sanction of the British crown.

Rumors of hostile plots on the part of the black and white film competitors of Kinemacolor floated about. It was whispered that something would happen so that Kinemacolor would never reach London with its negatives. Whereupon a guard of British troops was stationed about the Kinemacolor tents, where

Urban and Joseph du Frane, his chief of the camera staff, developed and guarded the precious films. A pit was excavated under Urban's tent and there the negatives were buried in sand. The tent floor rug was spread over the spot and over it Urban's bed stood. He slept with his treasure.

Back in London Urban made elaborate and pretentious arrangements for the presentation of the Durbar picture. A vast stage set reproducing the Taj Mahal was built at the Scala theatre. Special musical scores were written for the pictures. The orchestra was augmented to forty-eight pieces.

Urban was laughed at a bit by his competitors with their black and white films, which had reached London in advance of Kinemacolor and had run their life in a few weeks. But he had plunged on Kinemacolor and went on to see it through. The opening at the Scala was a brilliant success and five road shows went out to play the back country. In fifteen months the Durbar pictures grossed three-quarters of a million dollars.

Urban was on the high tide of success.

Royal favor beamed. Arrangements were made for a royal visit to the Scala to see the Durbar presentation. The date set was May 11, 1912.

The word was quietly passed to Mr. Urban that it would be well for him to acquire court robes, since knighthood awaited him.

May 10 came and all was prepared for the presentation. Then, abruptly, Urban was stricken desperately ill in his office and went away to a hospital, on the verge of death. It was a tragedy reminiscent of the unfortunate death of Turner, the first of the color inventors, in Urban's office years before.

The night that the royal party was seeing the Durbar in Kinemacolor Urban was coming out from under the ether.

The party at the Scala included King George V, Queen Mary,

Queen Alexandra, the Dowager Empress of Russia and some thirty other royal personages.

Kinemacolor scored a triumph and an unkind fate cost Urban a knighthood.

The success of Kinemacolor inevitably attracted attack. A suit on the patent was brought by William Friese Greene, the perennial British claimant to film honors, Urban won the fight through the lower courts and lost at last on an appeal to the House of Lords, on the pin-point technicality that the patentee had failed to specify the colors used in the process with sufficient accuracy.

This decision was of no profit to Friese Greene. It threw the Kinemacolor process open to the world. The Kinemacolor method became in consequence the basis of practically all subsequent color processes.

The commercial career of Kinemacolor abroad was interrupted by the World War in 1914. Meanwhile in the United States inventors were at work evolving new applications of its principles.

Kinemacolor depended upon filters in a special projection machine to color the light rays reaching the screen. The newer and subsequent processes have embodied the color in the film. The first of these to command screen attention was the Prizma process, evolved by William Kelley, who appeared first in the early affairs of the Biograph company. In 1912 experimental work began and in 1918, after nearly three quarters of a million dollars had gone into the process, Prizma began its showings with scenic subjects. In 1921, J. Stuart Blackton used Prizma color for a full length feature drama, *The Glorious Adventure,* produced in England with Lady Diana Manners in the leading rôle.

Prizma for financial reasons went into a decline, and in the same period the Technicolor process, arriving at somewhat similar results by secret but not entirely unrelated methods, rose to conspicuous position among color enterprises. Also William Kelley engaged in production with Kelleycolor, an ingenious method of applying color to prints made on standard film stock.

As this chapter is closed the color processes appear to be definitely in the process of being made an integral part of the art of the motion picture, as exemplified by the color prologue of *The Ten Commandments,* and color sections in various dramas. Douglas Fairbanks after several years of tentative experimentation, in 1925 engaged in the producion of an all color picture, *The Black Pirate,* making a special effort to subdue hues and tones to escape the bold garishness which has characterized most color film products.

Nearly ten years were required after the attainment of the screen before the photoplay was evolved. About an equal time has been required since the attainment of screen color to make it a part of the photoplay.

Meanwhile the quality of ordinary "black and white" screen photography is showing marked improvement through the gradual adoption of panchromatic negative, a film stock sensitized to record color values in truer relations of tone. It is estimated that ten percent of dramatic photography is now done with panchromatic film.

Extraordinary possibilities yet to be explored are offered in a special film stock, sensitive to infra-red, evolved by Dr. Kenneth Mees of the research staff of the Eastman Kodak Company. This enables a photographic record made with light entirely below the visual range of the human eye. In a landscape scene a picture made by the full light of day becomes a fantastic thing of black skies and ghostly trees, suggesting an unearthly moonlight.

Urban's Kinemacolor Camera at the Durbar, at Delhi in India, as the Royal Procession approached, making the screen's first and greatest triumph in natural color photography.

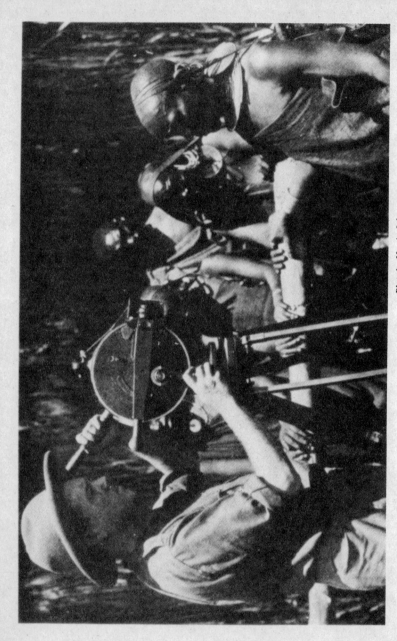

MARTIN JOHNSON, who began adventuring as a member of the crew of Jack London's "Snark" in 1908 and became a camera-hunter in the strange far-away lands of the South Seas, Borneo and Africa. Pictured here somewhere north of Niarobi in British East Africa.

CHAPTER FIFTY-SEVEN

TOM INCE RAISES A MOUSTACHE

JEREMIAH J. KENNEDY of 52 Broadway, the boss of the Patents Company, with his black Doomsday book in his pocket, held the Independents in terror by his spy system. Someway, always an unknown mysterious way, this Kennedy found out things, everything.

When Kennedy was well underway checking off the exchanges listed for purchase in that little black book, in the summer of 1910, a group of western exchangemen decided on a council of war. It was to be deeply secret. This time it would be held far from the listening walls of New York, remote and safe in St. Louis.

The coded summons to that meeting gathered in an array of names since conspicuous in film annals, including: Richard Rowland and James B. Clarke of Pittsburgh, Robert Lieber of Indianapolis, Emanuel Mandelbaum of Cleveland and John R. Freuler and H. E. Aitken of Milwaukee and elsewhere.

Then at the eleventh hour the meeting place was abruptly changed from St. Louis to Indianapolis, just to make the secret safer.

The meeting came to order in a parlor at the Claypool hotel in Indianapolis and it was voted that those present would stand out against a sale to the trust.

Then there was a rap on the door.

A bellboy, with a telegram on a tray, entered.

The message was opened and read:

Wish you boys success at your meeting—you have nothing to fear —regards.

J. J. KENNEDY

The next day Kennedy added to the consternation of the situation by purchasing the Pittsburgh Calcium Light Company exchanges from Rowland and Clarke for a quarter of a million dollars.

Richard Rowland was glad to cash his motion picture winnings. He had gone into the business by a route of accident and seeming misfortune. Rowland's father was engaged in the stage lighting business in the calcium light period. He died while young Richard was in school and threw the responsibilities of the family and a business which he did not relish on the youth. As Edison's electrical devices began to sweep the calciums off the stages of the theatre, Rowland turned to the business of manufacturing oxygen for medical purposes, a development from the chemical side of the calcium light business. Then Edison electricity hit Rowland again with the coming of the electrolytic process of oxygen manufacture. But among Rowland's customers remained country showmen beyond the electrical zones still using calcium lights, and they demanded film. Rowland came to New York and bought pictures. By this step the Pittsburgh Calcium Light Company began to evolve into a film concern. Now the Edison film business, as represented by the Trust, was buying Rowland out at great price, which seemed fair enough. But Rowland was not destined to stay out of the film business long.

John R. Freuler left that Indianapolis meeting to return to Milwaukee with a determination to turn Independent. He had read the signs—including Kennedy's telegram.

A few weeks thereafter a most unobtrusive concern entitled the O'Malley & Smith Advertising Company was incorporated in Illinois. There was nothing in that which could mean anything to the spies of J. J. Kennedy's espionage machine. Whoever Mr. O'Malley and Mr. Smith may have been, the real incorporators were John R. Freuler and his new associate in business, Samuel S. Hutchinson, formerly a Chicago druggist and now a film distributor interested in the Hutchinson & Hite exchange in Chicago.

Gilbert P. Hamilton, quietly acquired from the licensed studios of the Essanay company, went with due stealth to the sandy shores of Lake Michigan, at Benton Harbor, and made a one reel picture, entitled *Romantic Redskins*. Evidently O'Malley & Smith wanted to see if it could be done. It could.

O'Malley and Smith having served, passed on. The trade journals of October 5, 1910, carried the proud announcement of The American Film Manufacturing Company, and boldly listed twenty experts of motion picture making, each designated as "formerly of Essanay."

The Essanay staff had been cleaned out over night.

Among those listed were Allan Dwan, today one of the screen's foremost directors, J. Warren Kerrigan, in after years a famous star, and Charles Ziebarth, a technical expert now high in the service of Bell & Howell, makers of motion picture machinery.

George K. Spoor of Essanay retaliated with an injunction against further raids on his staff.

Diplomatic relations between the exchanges in which Hutchinson and Freuler were interested and the Patents Company terminated promptly.

The producing staff of the American went into the southwest to make "westerns" and started there the "Flying A" trademark for years famous in the screen trade. The "Flying A" learned to fly, eluding the heated pursuit of the Patents Company.

Marshall Neilan, working with the camera on location at La Mesa, California, found himself under the rifle fire of a sniper concealed in the cover of a mesquite thicket. Cameras were scarce and costly then. One properly placed bullet might have delayed the productions of the "Flying A" for months.

In New York Charles O. Bauman and Adam Kessel, assured by the prosperity of their first producing project, now in this autumn of 1910 formed a new company to make film drama and named it Reliance.

The incorporation papers for Reliance had scarcely been filed when word drifted down Fourteenth street that Arthur Johnson, then Biograph's best known player, was at outs with D. W. Griffith. It appears that Johnson was perpetually late arriving at the studio and that at times when he arrived he did not precisely resemble the young minister type for which he was usually cast.

There were some sharp words and Johnson left to console himself at an adjacent bar.

C. O. Bauman edged alongside offering soft words and hard liquor. Johnson went to work for Reliance. With him Reliance acquired, also from Biograph, Henry Walthall, James Kirkwood, Gertrude Robinson and Marion Leonard.

The title of the first Reliance release, starring Arthur Johnson, was entitled *The Grey of the Dawn*. It may have been reminiscence or prophesy, for Johnson.

Despite the raids on its stock company, Biograph remained the dominant producer of pictures of quality under Griffith. This season brought recognition to Mack Sennett who was assigned to the direction of *Comrades* for Biograph.

Now the plot thickens considerably. H. E. Aitken, who will be recalled as associated with John R. Freuler in the exchange business, stepped forth with a new independent producing concern rejoicing under the name of Majestic.

Carl Laemmle, owner of the Imp concern, in an unguarded moment, went off to Europe to take the waters at Carlsbad.

Shortly thereafter the Majestic announced the acquisition of Tom Cochrane, late of Imp, as general manager. Also Mary Pickford, the pride of Imp, went to Majestic for the startling salary of $275 a week. Cochrane took his pick of the Imp company and acquired George Loane Tucker, Herbert Prior, Mabel Trunnelle, Anita Hendrie and David Miles.

Laemmle came back from Carlsbad at once. There was another war brewing.

November 26, 1911, Majestic offered its first Pickford, entitled *The Courting of Mary*. Miss Pickford and Owen Moore soon left Majestic to return to Biograph.

Now Bauman and Kessel, increasing in daring and prosperity, let it be known they were ready to employ the most able director obtainable, at a high salary.

This report reached young Thomas H. Ince, who was progressing merrily but not conspicuously as a director for Laemmle's Imp company. Ince gave a demonstration of Yankee strategy. He regarded a very young face in his shaving mirror and decided that it would be well to have a bit of a moustache to conduce to a scenic effect inferring more age and experience. When the moustache had reached the required pictorial proportions, Ince borrowed a large and impressive ring set with a four carat Kimberley monolith and went to call on Adam Kessel.

As they sat talking across the corner of Kessel's desk, Ince held his chin propped in his hand in a thoughtful deliberate pose, which, quite incidentally of course, exposed to Kessel's dazzled view the scintillations of the big diamond.

The diamond ring, by the bye, was and probably still is the property of "Doc" Willat, who was then Imp's technical chief.

Kessel blinked at the diamond and listened respectfully to Ince's impressive remarks. Kessel quite forgot that this same Ince was something of an actor as well as a director of pictures. In fact Kessel was so impressed that he did not even tap the motion picture's grapevine telegraph to find out what Ince's salary might be at Imp. Instead he took another look at the diamond and murmured something about possibilities for advancement and a startling salary of a hundred dollars a week. That was just forty more than Ince was getting at Imp.

But Ince stroked his new moustache with tender consideration and yawned. He was not outwardly moved. He pretended not to have heard Kessel's offer. A man with a diamond that big could hardly afford to listen to a mere hundred a week.

"Oh, I'll see you again some day," Ince replied and sauntered out.

This was most convincing. Kessel sent for Ince after a few days had passed.

"How about $150 a week?"

Ince deliberated two or maybe three seconds before he could trust his trembling voice to say "Yes" without too much color of anxiety.

Ince, accompanied by Mrs. Ince, Ethel Grandin, Ray Small-wood and Charles Weston of the Imp company, went to Los Angeles to make pictures for the N. Y. M. P. at the old Edendale studio.

Kessel and Bauman were ready to plunge. Charles O. Bauman went to the west coast to see the new director launched in his work. Ince's first N. Y. M. P. effort was a one reeler en-titled *The New Cook*. Tradition says it was a hit. En route to a mountain location near Santa Monica canyon, Ince discovered that Miller Brothers' 101 Ranch show was wintering in the vicinity. He remarked with a director's yearning that it would be a grand thing to have that show to play with in the pictures.

Bauman seemed to like the notion. He did some negotiating and then wired Adam Kessel:

"Can get 101 Ranch show for the winter at $2,100 a week, what do you think?"

Kessel thought it over and answered in good race track fashion: "Take a chance."

The reader accustomed to the billion dollar publicity barrage laid down by the press agents of the screen of today can scarcely realize what a speculation this two thousand dollar a week project was in that day. It was without parallel or precedent. It was an epochal beginning. The art of the motion picture was about to enter upon its astonishing career of spectacle building.

Bauman signed the 101 Ranch show for the season.

No one could have been more amazed, delighted and perplexed than one Thomas H. Ince. He had grown accustomed to the ordinary problems and methods of the director of the day. But this matter of operating a Wild West show in conjunction with a motion picture company, was something else again.

That first morning when Ince saw the Miller Brothers 101 Ranch show strung out on the road, an imposing caravan which seemed to reach clear into infinity, he bethought himself of the cost—twenty-one hundred dollars a week!

"This," he remarked abruptly to his cameraman, "had better be pretty good."

Up to this juncture Ince had no scenario for the utilization of the big Wild West show. However, he started shooting scenes and the story was born then and there, under fire. It became a two reel picture entitled *Across the Plains*. The covered wagon had become a screen property.

This expensive departure in production brought a new and costly higher standard. It was certain to have important reactions, working as always, through the business machinery of the motion picture. Events were shaping up a new alignment, soon.

Carl Laemmle on his return from Carlsbad, full of the bitter aperient waters and the tension of the film situation, was minded to deal with that bold Harry E. Aitken, who had dared to raid the "Imp" company for "Little Mary" Pickford. Laemmle, dominant in the Sales company through which all of the Independent film wares were marketed, decided that Aitken's Majestic brand pictures would have to pay a higher percentage to the Sales company than the founders group.

Aitken slapped back with a complaint in Washington that the Sales company was a "combination in restraint of trade," and proceeded to form the Film Supply Company of America, to be a new alliance of Independents.

But concurrently yet another development was underway to remake the film map. One snowy day in December 1911, John R. Freuler sat in a room at the Hotel La Salle in Chicago and toyed with a list of names on the back of a laundry slip. He had in mind a project to combine some independent exchanges into a pattern like the General Film Company.

This came to flower under the joint ministrations of Aitken and Freuler with the formation of the Mutual Film Corporation in March 1912. The Mutual's address became 60 Wall street. That told the story. It was launched as a promotion. Aitken interested Crawford Livingston, an investment banker, who in turn, interested Kuhn, Loeb & Company. The modern period of Wall street picture financing began. Mutual acquired some seven hundred stockholders.

The Mutual took from the Sales company various sources of films, including the Thanhouser concern of New Rochelle and the American company, successor to the great O'Malley & Smith Advertising Company.

Laemmle and his associates countered with the formation of the Universal Film Manufacturing Company, announced June 8, 1912, with Laemmle as president and Charles O. Bauman one of the aggressive organizers.

The Independents were now in two camps, Mutual and Universal, with some straggling minor concerns on the fringe. It was all simple and arranged now. Except—Freuler and Aitken were not agreeing in Mutual and Laemmle and the Kessel and Bauman combination did not agree.

The Kessel and Bauman vs. Laemmle fight broke at Universal's second meeting. Kessel beckoned Bauman aside.

"They're out to trim us for a couple of Dutchmen. Let's beat it."

Now the Kessel and Bauman product was decidedly important to Universal's program. It included those Ince pictures from the West and the Reliance pictures from the New York studios.

The law suits started promptly.

And the fight did not wait on the slow processes of the courts. The Universal set out to take possession of the Kessel and Bauman studios of the New York Motion Picture company, both east and west.

Accompanied by some robust assistants, Mark Dintenfass was dispatched to the N. Y. M. P. studios at 251 West Nineteenth street to take possession of the property. A stenographer engaged the expedition in conversation while a warning was telephoned to Kessel and Bauman.

Kessel went into action, recruiting his forces as he went. He arrived at the studio with a taxicab load of strong arm men and a pitched battle ensued. The police records of June 28, 1912, relate a riot and the arrest of two men, said to have been employed by Universal. Neither of them otherwise figures in screen history. But from that day on a battalion of gunmen and sluggers was employed to protect the premises.

P. A. Powers was not satisfied that Dintenfass had exercised sufficient force and strategy, so he organized a night attack of his own. The shooting and slugging was free and promiscuous. The raid would have been more successful if some of the mercenaries of the attacking army had not discovered that they belonged to the same gang as the defenders.

The state of siege brought many precautionary moves. Adam Kessel contributed to the gaiety and content of the besieged establishment by cooking "hot dogs" for all hands about the studio.

William Swanson was sent West to take possession of the Kessel and Bauman studios in California. Thomas Ince, advised by wire of impending difficulties, found himself invested with the responsibilities of a general as well as director in charge. An old Civil War cannon was mounted to command the studio enclosure, loaded to the muzzle with scrap iron, and guards with sawed off shotguns stood at the gates. Ince grew a corn on his hip carrying the largest obtainable size of Colt's frontier model forty-five revolver. A clash of arms was avoided or the canyon of Santa Monica would have been running deep with gore.

When the war was all over after a confusion of moves, legal and illegal, Kessel and Bauman parted with $17,000 and the brand name of 101 Bison, and were permitted to withdraw from Universal.

The product of the New York Motion Picture studios now went to the Mutual Film Corporation and, through subsequent developments, brought many now famous names into the motion picture.

Mutual was in the first flush of success when, in the late summer of 1912, this same industrious team of Kessel and Bauman, while at lunch at August Luchow's justly celebrated restaurant in Fourteenth street, spied Mack Sennett of Biograph at an adjacent table. They drew him into conversation and suggested that he ought to be making comedies on his own account. There was, they intimated, an opportunity for a bright young man to go into business for himself.

Out of that idea came Keystone Comedies, the pictures which carried Sennett's name to fame.   The Keystone trade-mark was adopted from the Pennsylvania railroad, with no royalties.

The first Keystone comedy was entitled *Cohen at Coney Island,* released September 23, 1912.   Along with Sennett, Keystone acquired Mabel Normand, Ford Sterling and Fred Mace.

CHAPTER FIFTY-EIGHT

HERRING, DIAMONDS AND SELZNICK

THE peace which followed the settlement of the Kessel and Bauman controversy in the Universal must have lasted almost a day.

The Universal's dominant figures were Carl Laemmle, William Swanson, Mark M. Dintenfass and David Horsley, a new Independent producer—and P. A. Powers. And, Robert Cochrane, sitting back of Laemmle, was writing the official utterances.

It appeared that Laemmle decided to control Universal, and that Pat Powers also decided to control Universal.

Dintenfass and Horsley occupied most uncomfortable positions on the fence, while Swanson dashed from side to side as the vantages of battle changed.

The top of the fence became exceedingly uncomfortable and Mark Dintenfass wandered, down, off and out. His stock was for sale. Since there was considerable question in those hurly-burly days as to whether that stock was ever to be worth anything, there were no bids from either side. Powers seemed to Dintenfass the logical customer, but Powers professed an attitude of high scorn. He was moved to break the profound pride and dignity of Dintenfass, if possible, by studied indignities.

Dintenfass became highly disturbed. The ructions in Universal were doing him and his Champion brand pictures no good. Any move any day might bring ruin.

Business called Dintenfass to Chicago. He boarded the Broadway Limited and settled for the long ride west. Across the aisle of the Pullman he presently discovered that the young woman opposite was more interesting than the diversion of counting the telegraph poles. Before long they were in conversation and he was showing her the flamboyant heralds advertising Champion films, with the imposing name of Mark M. Dintenfass, president.

"And where are you going?" he asked by way of conversation.

"Pittsburgh."

A flash of recollection came to Dintenfass. He lived again for a moment those carefree days when he went to Pittsburgh selling salt herring for his father's Philadelphia fish house. And there was that blithe and witty chap that he met at the fish shop where the two pretty girls presided at the counter. They had a good time together, the four of them. He remembered it all now. That fellow had a job in a jewelry store in Smithfield street, and kept a bachelor apartment—what was his name? Then it came to him.

"You know," Dintenfass remarked to the young woman alongside, "I'd get off at Pittsburgh myself, if I could find a fellow I used to know there—wonder what became of him—Louie Selznick."

The young woman sat up abruptly.

"Who did you say?"

"Louie Selznick—L. J. Selznick—why, do you know him?"

"Sure—he's my brother-in-law. I've just been to New York to visit them."

"Well, now, isn't it a small world," etc., etc.

At this especially fateful period, Lewis J. Selznick was conducting with most indifferent success a jewelry store in Sixth Avenue, near Fourteenth street, in New York. The business was falling off. In fact, it was so anæmic that Selznick decided to turn his defeat into a victory by holding an auction, the conventional and often profitable last resort of ailing jewelry stores. The auction left Selznick with nothing pressing to do and a whole waiting world to do it in. History shows that this is a time when things happen.

Dintenfass presently returned from Chicago. He called Selznick on the telephone.

"I'll bet you don't know who this is—Louie."

"Ach—I smell salt herring," Selznick responded.

"Wonderful, wonderful!" Dintenfass exclaimed. "What a head for remembering you have got."

They got together for a talk about the old days, the jewelry shop and the salt herring and all—*schoen gemuthlich.*

And then came the film business into their discussions, along with it Dintenfass' troubles and his efforts to negotiate with P. A. Powers.

"He pretends everything must be so secret that he can't talk to me anywhere in the office," Dintenfass complained. "He says, wait for me out in the washroom—and then he tries to keep me waiting for hours."

Selznick, with a profound sense of humor, scented both amusement and opportunity. Now that he had auctioned himself out of the jewelry trade there might be something to do here.

"What kind of a fellow is this Powers?"

In response came a detailed description of the august, vigorous and domineering personality of the battling Mr. Powers. It was indicated that he was, among other things, a bit inclined to nifty garb and an appearance befitting a magnate of the new art on Broadway.

"Nifty dresser—eh?" remarked Selznick. "I will see him for you and see what we can do, maybe."

"How will you see him? If you tell him you come from me he will say 'meet me in the washroom.'"

Selznick waved his hand.

"Never mind, I will see him easy enough—you wait."

Not long after this conference, Lewis J. Selznick, formerly jeweler in Sixth Avenue, presented himself at the office of P. A. Powers. No, he would not state his business. He would speak only to Mr. Powers in person and privately, and it was about a matter in which Mr. Powers was profoundly interested. This eventually got Selznick private audience in the Powers sanctum.

Mysteriously and persuasively Selznick smiled himself into a seat at the corner of Powers' desk. He reached into a vest pocket and produced a little parcel in thin white paper and unfolded it with a deft manner of profound consideration.

Powers looked on curiously.

After another pause to make the move dramatically correct as a bit of salesmanship Selznick lifted the paper and poured a glittering stream into his palm and then spread a handful of unmounted diamonds on the edge of the desk.

Selznick's manner toward the diamonds was almost reverential. It was as though he had unveiled all of the treasures of Zion.

This, of course, was only a manner. In the philosophy of Lewis J. Selznick are two gems of polished thought:

(A) "Jewelry is for suckers."

(B) "There is always a demand for jewelry."

But that is beside the point. This day Selznick was ostensibly selling diamonds of great value at, oh, the merest song of a price. As he had calculated, Powers was interested, and enough appreciative of a bargain to feel friendly. He bought.

Selznick brought his chair a bit closer.

"Why don't you buy my friend Dintenfass's stock in this Universal company? He only wants seventy-five thousand."

Powers grinned—so that was it.

"I don't want his stock—if I did I'd get it."

"Yes, but you do want it—it would give you control—that's what makes it worth the price."

Powers would not deal.

Lewis J. Selznick has often been baffled, but so far not ever conclusively beaten for long.

He still had a pocket full of diamonds and a perfectly workable idea. He made certain inquiries pertaining to the tastes of Carl Laemmle. He was minded to sell some more stones.

With the little white paper of stones, Selznick went to call on Laemmle. They got along famously, dickering back and forth over the sparkling blue-whites.

"Now this fellow Dintenfass, maybe you think his stock isn't worth much, but it would give you control of the company."

This time it worked. Laemmle bought the stock and Dintenfass was happy, for the moment anyway. Laemmle was now the biggest stockholder in Universal, but he said nothing about that for the time.

Selznick still had plenty of diamonds, but his visits to the Mecca Building had given him motion picture ambitions. He shrewdly sized up the men he saw about in the offices and lobby. He knew nothing about motion pictures, but he knew a great deal about men.

The diamond broker from Pittsburgh had, besides a taste for salt herring, a bottomless thirst for action, excitement, power and, maybe, down at the end of the list somewhere, also money. He decided to declare himself into the motion picture. It seemed to be standing there waiting for him to cut himself a piece of cake.

A little more conversation resulted in Selznick ingratiating himself into a somewhat undefined job and a desk in the office of the Universal. It was the hazy general understanding that he was to be useful to the corporation in general and to the Laemmle interests in particular.

Sitting on the inside, Selznick found the film business even more interesting and full of opportunity than he had suspected. No one knew just what Selznick was there for, and he was in an equally open minded state. There may have been doubt, but surely no uncertainty.

Universal was so thoroughly split into factions and split so widely that none of them knew what the other was doing with any accuracy. All strangers were assumed to belong to the other faction until identified. Meanwhile they were treated with such consideration or inconsideration as might be deemed safest in a tremulous even if not delicate situation. This situation of weakness and incipient chaos was Selznick's opportunity.

One of Selznick's first discoveries was that the corporation did not have a general manager. This was an oversight to be remedied. He appointed himself at once. He took no one into his confidence in the matter except the stenographer who got out his letter of announcement. This was not as daring as it may seem, since in this period motion picture men were not accustomed to reading their mail.

Free lancing about the office at 1600 Broadway, Selznick rapidly took on things to do. He put himself in charge of all purchases and expenditures. He had a whole bag of tricks, familiar enough in the business game of wits, but new to the motion picture.

The internal amusement and delight which the adventuring jeweler and diamond salesman enjoyed may well be imagined. No musical comedy extravaganza ever embodied a more whimsical plot. As we have seen in many chapters, there were endless ways to get into the motion picture industry. This is, however, the first instance of forcible entry by simple declaration. The blond stranger from Pittsburgh, adrift on the sea of circumstance without a paddle, floated in on a log that landed him on the beach of the Isle of Easy Money in the Broadway Archipelago. Shaking off the brine he strode up the coral strand and, seeking out the chieftains, dazzled their eyes with shining beads and helped himself to coconuts. With one hand he began to order the natives about as he held the attention of the chiefs with feats of prestidigitation with the other. The theme of this chapter ought to be carried along with an orchestra. The typewriter lacks the tonal range to record the fantasies of fact.

The inward truth of the situation never escaped the dexterous and able Selznick. The richest of his rewards have ever been the thrills and laughs of the game. Regardless of the figures that may ultimately add up his total of successes and failures, the only true measure of history will be as of Selznick-the-Jester. He came to Broadway with a tiny paper of glittering stones and stayed to emblazon his name in the electric lights and play battledore and shuttlecock with the affairs of a whole industry.

But back to Universal and 1912. Very presently P. A. Powers discovered that Laemmle had acquired a certain new force. There was a stiffening of the hand. Powers decided maybe that Dintenfass stock might be worth having. Dintenfass, riding high on his wounded dignity, was not to be approached. Powers called up Selznick.

"What's the matter with your friend Dintenfass? He won't speak to me."

"Oh," exclaimed Selznick with an affectation of surprise. "I will see if I can't make an appointment with him for you—in the washroom." Powers made other plans. He is a bit of a jester, too.

A vigorous dispute between Powers and Laemmle soon broke into the open. Powers contended that his exchanges were not getting the benefit of the same low prices from Universal that Laemmle's enjoyed. He wanted a rebate. He got refusal.

Selznick was rejoicing in his self-made job of general manager one morning in this period when the manager of one of the Universal studios in New York called up in great excitement.

"Pat Powers is up here with a gang of trucks moving the props away, and we're right in the middle of a picture. What shall I do?"

Selznick grinned. "Call the police and then report again to me in a half hour."

At the end of the half hour the studio manager was on the phone again.

"Did the police come? How are you getting along?"

"Yes, the police came," the voice on the wire replied. "And they are getting along fine. They are helping Pat Powers load the trucks."

So ran the comedy of the Universal war from day to day.

But the time came when Selznick's expanding powers in his self-appointed post undid him—and liberated him for further adventures. One afternoon a secretary from Laemmle's office went to Selznick's desk and laid a letter before him, glancing up at the clock as he did it.

"Mr. Laemmle went to Chicago on the Century—he told me to give this to you two hours after the train left."

Selznick opened the letter, but he could read it without looking at it. It was "accepting your resignation."

Selznick reached for his hat. He was on his way out into the world of opportunity to play the new game he had learned.

The Powers-Laemmle war meanwhile progressed merrily. When in doubt, Powers attacks. At about this juncture he caused a receivership action to be brought against the Universal. Nothing especially resulted but more fighting.

The annual meeting of 1913 found this situation at high climax. The meeting opened in a highly dignified manner at the company's offices at 1600 Broadway. There was, however, an electrical tension in the air and a good many private policemen were in the hall. The Laemmle stronghold was well manned.

The reading of the minutes was barely under discussion, however, when Powers and his occasional partner, William Swanson, ventilated the situation by neatly tossing the books and the great seal of the corporation out of the window into the upper air of Broadway.

This may have been connected with the presence of certain persons waiting below. Anyway it was a valiant move with every promise of success.

But, some way, Fate so often intervenes in the affairs of melodrama. The nick of time is always being nicked.

The lone horseman galloping across the horizon in this thriller chances to have been William Oldenow of the Consolidated Film Company, of Atlanta and elsewhere southerly. Oldenow had just arrived from the South and was making his way with hastening steps to the office of his friend Carl Laemmle.

We left the books and the seal going out the third floor window of the Mecca building. When they came down it was at the feet of Oldenow. If his train had arrived one one-hundredth of a second earlier he would have been precisely under the books and the great seal as they arrived at the sidewalk level. As it was, the visitor stumbled over the crashing heap and then picked it up. A glance at the books told him volumes. They obviously belonged to Laemmle's office.

A crowd surged about Oldenow and the police rushed in. They took the visitor and his catch up to the offices of the

Universal. A court action ensued and the books were tied up for a long period.

Paul Gulick, who holds the motion picture industry's record for continuous survival amid the high mortalities of press agentry, joined Universal that stormy week and became its war correspondent.

In one of the many alignments on the checkerboard, Horsley's stock became of vital importance. Laemmle held an option on it, so did Powers. One afternoon, in this merry year of 1913, Robert Cochrane and Carl Laemmle raced about the banks of New York to get $179,000 in cash to take up the stock. Horsley demanded spot cash. After a quest of hours, the taxicab was laden with small bills. The entire sum was in denominations of ones, fives and tens—mostly ones. The motor car raced across the Hudson river to Horsley's New Jersey establishment. He had prevailed on a bank to stay open to receive the money, and insisted that it be counted three times, personally inspecting each bill. At four o'clock in the morning the tired bank clerks for the third time verified the total, marked the bundles and tossed them in the safe. But Powers contended with some measure of success that the stock could not be delivered to Laemmle because of his option. Laemmle contended the Powers option expired at noon, Powers said midnight.

When the fighting was all over and endless changes and maneuvers, Universal was practically divided between Laemmle and Powers, the latter holding some forty-odd percent of the stock. In May 1920, he sold to the Laemmle-Cochrane interests and the reports of the price ran from one to two millions.

CHAPTER FIFTY-NINE

ADOLPH ZUKOR AND SARAH BERNHARDT

I⊤ was the year of 1912. To place it in the perspective of time, remember it was the year of the Titantic disaster, the discovery of the South Pole, the election of Woodrow Wilson and the Rosenthal murder in New York. Motorists still wore linen dusters. Skirts were ankle length. There was a new war in the Balkans. It was the year of the tango eruption, and the year of *Alexander's Ragtime Band* and *Call Me Up Some Rainy Afternoon*. It was about the end of the Middle Ages in screen history.

One afternoon in March of this 1912, an obscure little man of no special importance presented himself at the office of the Motion Picture Patents Company. He sent in his name— Adolph Zukor.

Zukor was meek and patient. It was fortunate that he was patient. They let him wait three hours.

Zukor was the custodian of what he suspected of being a great project.

Twenty two years before, Zukor, a lone emigrant lad from a hamlet in Hungary, landed at Castle Garden and found a job uptown sweeping a fur store. In 1903 he left a fur business in Chicago to return to New York to see if he could salvage $3,000 loaned to a relative who had sunk it in a penny arcade of peep show pictures and phonographs. He progressed in the show business with arcades, *Hale's Tours* shows and nickelodeons, arriving at last in the post of treasurer of the Marcus Loew Enterprises, a mixture of screen and vaudeville theatres.

But Zukor was not happy there. He did not seem to be held

in very high esteem, and the office staff nicknamed him "Creepy" just because he was quiet.

Zukor was looking for something, and now perhaps he had found it.

This idea had come a long way round about. Over in Paris Louis Mercanton had made a four reel picture entitled *Queen Elizabeth* with Sarah Bernhardt in the title rôle, and Lou Tellegen in the part of Essex. Now it chanced that this picture, when it reached London, attracted the attention of Frank Brockliss, agent for American producers. Brockliss wrote his enthusiasms to Joseph Engel in New York. Engel was connected with Edwin S. Porter and William Swanson in making Rex pictures for Universal. Engel in turn told his friend Frank Meyer, manager of the Western Film Exchange in New York, and Meyer talked to Al Kaufman, manager of the Comedy theatre in Fourteenth street, and incidentally brother-in-law of Zukor, the proprietor.

The oft-relayed enthusiasm of Brockliss fell on fertile soil. The idea had found its man. Zukor was interested.

Zukor, Engel and Porter formed the Engadine Corporation and bought the American rights to *Queen Elizabeth* for $18,000. Then Zukor went on his errand to the Patents Company to get it licensed. There was opposition, but H. N. Marvin and J. J. Kennedy of the Biograph prevailed and this meek but daring outsider got a license. It was revolutionary procedure. The internal fact was that Marvin and Kennedy were trying to spur the laggard film makers of the Trust to more pretentious screen production.

The gradually unfolding idea was pushing itself along. Edwin S. Porter, now interested in the Engadine project, was, it is to be remembered, the exponent of the "story picture" beginning with his famous one reeler *The Great Train Robbery* made nine years earlier. Porter was a picture maker. It was a natural and direct consequence that in the new alignment with Zukor and the idea embodied in the Bernhardt picture there should result a project to produce.

Hence it came that a new concern was formed and named Famous Players Film Company. The Sarah Bernhardt picture had evolved into a policy of famous players in famous plays.

The idea as it grew began to surround itself with more men. Adolph Zukor's attorney was Elek J. Ludvigh, who also handled legal affairs for the Marcus Loew Enterprises. Ludvigh had connections with and access to the Frohmans. Daniel Frohman came into the Famous Players, bringing with him the authority of the greatest name in the world of the dramatic stage.

Charles Frohman could not have been less interested or more annoyed if his elder brother had announced that he was going to open a hot dog stand at Coney Island. From his august position in the drama Charles Frohman saw the motion picture as a trivial passing madness of the masses. But Daniel Frohman brought to the service of the screen in the next few years many a great play and great name which helped to build up the institution of the motion picture, and in time his brother Charles' enthusiasm was enlisted, too. It is a bit of irony, but a kindly irony, that the institution of Charles Frohman, Inc., which today continues the production of plays and keeps the Charles Frohman tradition alive on Broadway, has become the property of the once scorned Famous Players. The humble motion picture, humble no longer, has become the master.

"Daniel Frohman presents" was the big line over the announcement of Sarah Bernhardt in *Queen Elizabeth* when the picture went on at the Lyceum Theatre for a promotional showing July 12, 1912.

How to get *Queen Elizabeth* to the market was now the problem. It was decided to road-show the picture, meaning that its owners would engage in retailing it to the public.

The road showing of *Queen Elizabeth* was not proving a success. If the new idea was to succeed it had to be sold. Here was a situation which called for a man. It found him.

The announcement advertisements of the Sarah Bernhardt picture caught the eye of Alexander Lichtman, a film salesman with a deal of experience and enthusiasm.

This Al Lichtman had covered a curious path to the motion picture. He began as a water boy, carrying trays of glasses to the audiences of Tony Pastor's theatre in Fourteenth street, New York. Then he became an actor. Only two years before the coming of the *Queen Elizabeth* picture he had been a soldier in the U. S. Army, serving as the immaculately military young man pacing the sidewalk in front of the recruiting station in Douglas street, Omaha. On a furlough in Chicago, he saw an employment bulletin on the boards at the old Revere House in North Clark street, a caravansarie conducted for rambling showmen, and that led him to a job selling pictures and on back to New York.

When Lichtman read the Famous Players' announcement he pulled himself up to his desk and wrote an elaborately long letter addressed to Adolph Zukor, whom he did not know, setting forth his enthusiasms and qualifications. He wanted to sell those famous players in famous plays. Then he read the letter and tore it up, put on his hat and went down to the Famous Players' office in the *Times* building to call on Zukor.

The *Queen Elizabeth* road shows came in and Lichtman went out to sell the picture to the state's rights buyers. The picture sold for a total of approximately $80,000, which made it handsomely profitable.

Meanwhile Famous Players began the production of pictures

on its own account.   Daniel Frohman lured James O'Neill from the stage into the production of *The Count of Monte Cristo*.   E. S. Porter directed the picture in the Crystal studios in New York. This production was hardly completed when the Selig studios in Chicago released a three-reel version of the same story through the General Film Company.   This was a serious blow at the young Famous Players concern, with its slender assets largely tied up in its first production.   The picture had to go on the shelf to await a later turn at the market when the Selig version should have been forgotten by the exhibitors.   Famous Players turned to the production of *The Prisoner of Zenda* with James K. Hackett, which appears in the records of today as its first picture.

The better, bigger picture was ready now, awaiting on its development for the evolution and growth of a system of distribution.   It will presently be seen how the product exerted a force which brought into existence a new machinery for putting the picture into the theatres.   The state's rights buyers who started with *Queen Elizabeth* and *The Prisoner of Zenda* were almost automatically selected to become factors in a new confederation of interests, rising in power until it dominated the industry.

Some of the comment of the day concerning this idea of long pictures was an illuminating exposure of some timid minds. Many of the wise ones were sure that eye strain from four or five reels, uninterrupted by song slides, would drive audiences from the theatres.   Others were sure that it would be impossible to hold the interest of any considerable proportion of the motion picture public through a subject which occupied an hour of screen time.

From the established camps of the orthodox motion picture producers, licensed and unlicensed alike, arose condemnatory pronouncements against the big picture idea.   For the next ensuing three years "the feature craze" was the stereotyped phrase in the mouths of the old-line film makers and distributors.

They were unconditionally opposed to the idea. These long pictures promised to cost money. They cost something even more serious—creative thought.

Here the film business was just beginning to get going well on the quantity production program idea and along came this fellow Zukor trying to knock things into a cocked hat with his stage stars and stage plays and high-sounding words and those everlastingly long pictures! Pictures were good enough. Why couldn't they have peace and settle down and just make money?

The opposition among the Patents Company's picture makers prevented issuance of further licenses to Zukor, and he automatically became an Independent, with most of the Independents against him. The formalities of an injunction suit ensued, but to no consequence. The art of the motion picture could not be bound by court control. The laws of growth are stronger than the laws of property.

Closely contemporary with the formation of Famous Players, another pretentious feature venture blossomed forth in the Helen Gardner Pictures Corporation, destined to a short and uneventful life. Miss Gardner was a teacher of pantomime when she went to Vitagraph early in 1911. She played minor parts for a time and first came to real attention in the rôle of *Becky Sharp* in *Vanity Fair,* one of Vitagraph's successes of the day. Inspired by the urge toward bigger pictures, Charles Gaskill, a scenario writer, and Miss Gardner formed their independent company and established a studio at Tappan-on-Hudson. Eugene Mullin, then a member of the Vitagraph scenario staff, went along as a member of the organization. Mullin was then well near a veteran in the young art of the scenario, with three whole years of experience behind him. He was a youngster of a ticket agent in an office on the Long Island railroad in 1909 when he became inspired of a notion that Sir Walter Scott's *Lady of the Lake* should be done in motion pictures, and forthwith sent a scenario to Vitagraph. Vitagraph accepted the idea and sent for the aspiring Mullin. *The Lady of the Lake* was made with Edith Storey in the rôle of *Ellen*. It ran to the amazing length of four reels, released one at a time on the General program.

Among the effective influences toward opening to the way for more pretentious pictures must be counted the Rainey African hunt, which went to the screen in nine reels in the season of 1912–3. The making of these pictures was an incident of an expedition by Paul J. Rainey of Philadelphia, coal dealer and sportsman. The films were exploited by a special subsidiary concern formed by the Universal group, because the existing machinery of film programs could not cope with such a pretentious attraction. The Rainey hunt pictures helped importantly to prove that the scope of the screen was not limited to the trivial one and two reel films which dominated the market offered by the nickelodeon theatres.

The Rainey hunt paved the way to the screen for such notable adventure subjects as Martin Johnson's *Captured by Cannibals*, and *Hunting African Animals*, Dr. Leonard O. Sugden's Prizma color pictures of Alaska and the White Horse Rapids, Robert J. Flaherty's *Nanook of the North*, conceived as propaganda for Revillon Frères, Ira Jay Ingraham's *Around the World with the Speejacks*, a record of the marine rambles of A. Y. Gowen, a Cleveland cement magnate, and Merian C. Cooper's *Grass*, the tale of a Persian migration.

Dr. Sugden, who died not long since in Alaska after a career of world wandering, was a figure of romance in the Yukon and on the Trail of '98. Robert Service's ballad *The Cremation of Sam McGee* records an episode of Sugden's service as a surgeon of the Royal Northwest Mounted Police.

Martin Johnson has been an important contributor of adventure pictures for more than a decade. His first contact with showmanship was a bellboy carrying ice-water to John Ringling at the old Saratoga hotel in Chicago. When Jack London started to sail the *Snark* around the world Martin Johnson shipped as cook. On a beach in the South Seas Johnson became acquainted with the films through a camera carried by a Pathé expedition from Paris, which had missed connection with the 'round the world cruise of the U. S. Navy in '08. Johnson lectured over the Orpheum circuit on South Seas subjects on his return. He struck up an acquaintance with Martin Beck, leading to a connection with the *Orpheum Travel Weekly*, a one reel film release edited by Johnson.

Some years later Johnson sailed again for the South Seas to make cannibal pictures. This cruise came near to an ending down the Alimentary Canal, at the invitation of Chief Nagipate of Malekula. Despite that they became friends, although not as intimately associated as the chief first intended.

When Johnson returned to Malekula in 1919 he carried a projection machine and a set of the cannibal pictures to show Nagipate. Johnson also edited a special prologue film for this royal showing, consisting of scenes of himself and Mrs. Johnson in a motor car on Fifth avenue, supplemented with pictures of the Armistice Day crowds.

This extraordinary production was projected on a tent fly in the Malekula jungle, while Johnson lectured to the squatting savages. He explained how the cheering throngs turned out to see him off on his journey and to send the greetings of America to the great Nagipate.

The cannibals sat stolidly through the picture and, being

accustomed to pay for their services, charged Johnson a case of trade tobacco for looking at the film. The showing was, however, a valuable contribution to the world peace movement. Chief Nagipate confidentially informed Johnson that he was surprised to see how many white people there were in the world and announced that he would abandon a long cherished plan to eat them all.

SARAH BERNHARDT in "Queen Elizabeth," produced by Louis Mercanton, the motion picture which gave Adolph Zukor his "famous players in famous plays" idea and laid the foundation of his spectacular success.

FRANCIS X. BUSHMAN, an idol of the screen in the days of his
fame with Essanay, in his return to the screen, after years of
eclipse, in the rôle of Messalla in "Ben Hur," Metro-
Goldwyn-Mayer production of 1925.

CHAPTER SIXTY

THE GISHES, "PINK" AND "BLUE"

THE years from 1912 to 1915 found the screen engaged in strivings for escape from its one-reel bondage. The length, approximately a thousand feet of film, was a heritage of the early period when the vaudeville theatre was the motion picture's chief avenue to the public.

As a component of the vaudeville program the pictures were booked as a "turn" and, in almost automatic response, the film projector evolved a mechanical capacity to fill the average time of a vaudeville act approximately twelve minutes.

Through the years when the motion picture was acquiring its technique of story telling this arbitrary length imposed no limitations. But meanwhile it became so woven into the commercial fabric of the art that nothing less than a commercial revolution could break it. The orthodox, established motion picture world was one-reel minded. The business of the motion picture had to be disrupted to let the art of the motion picture grow.

The intrusion of Adolph Zukor with his "famous players in famous play" idea expressed in five-reel pictures was to prove the most significant of moves in the coming revolution of the pictures. Very shortly Mary Pickford was to become, most unexpectedly, a vital force in the movement of events.

Mary, whom we have seen purloined from Biograph by "Imp," and carried off from "Imp" to Aitken's Majestic studios, now in 1912, went flitting back to Griffith and Biograph again.

Miss Pickford's return to Biograph was to prove but a brief sojourn, from which she was soon to move on to play her greater part in screen evolution. Meanwhile in that season at Biograph, she became the chance agency which added the Gish sisters to the celebrated roster of those who shared the glories of the Griffith era at Biograph.

The dramatic careers of Lillian and Dorothy Gish began some years earlier. The two little girls and their mother had been left to make their own way in the world. They were living in a New York boarding house where there were on occasion players from the road shows of the stage.

One of these boarding house acquaintances, Dolores Lorne, was promised a part in a road company if she could find a child to play with her. Miss Lorne prevailed on the reluctant Mrs. Gish to let her take Dorothy. So little Miss Dorothy Gish made her first appearance before the public at the age of four as *Little Willie* in *East Lynne*.

After that came a whole series of melodramas and soon Lillian followed Dorothy to the stage. Some of their appearances were in the melodramatic classics entitled, *The Little Red School House*, *The Convict's Stripes* and *Her First False Step*.

Somewhere in this round of road shows the Gishes met Gladys Smith, a child actress of the melos in those days before her stage re-christening as Mary Pickford. They were friends, and in the dull idle days of summer when the road shows "rested" in New York, their mothers met, shared apartments and their sewing.

After a time the Gish sisters were sent away to school, Dorothy to Baltimore and Lillian to Massillon, Ohio.

When, in June, 1912, Lillian and her mother came east to meet Dorothy at Baltimore, they celebrated with a visit to a "ten cent show," which was of course quite the best of picture theatres of the day. It was "Biograph day."

When the picture opened the Gishes were all agog with a thrill of discovery. The film conspicuously presented their little friend Gladys Smith in the leading rôle. They made note of the fact that the picture was made by a concern called Biograph in New York.

Not many days later, Dorothy and Lillian presented themselves at the Biograph reception room in the old brownstone mansion at 11 East Fourteenth street and told the girl at the switchboard they wanted to see Gladys Smith.

"There's no one here by that name," the girl at the board responded.

"Yes, there is, we saw her in one of your pictures—it was *Lena and the Geese*," the Gish sisters insisted.

"I guess I know who you mean." The telephone girl inserted a plug and called for "Miss Pickford" on the studio floor above.

Mary came down and there was a chatterfest of busy little girls in the hall. As they stood talking, a serious, sober-faced man came down the big stairs and walked past with a glance at the trio of youngsters.

"That's Mr. Griffith," Mary whispered, awesomely. "He's the director."

They were still talking when Christy Cabanne, then an assistant to Griffith, approached and inquired if Miss Pickford's friends would like to help out in the making of a scene for the picture then in work.

This was an adventure. They certainly would.

Up in the studio under the green-blue glare of the lamps, Lillian and Dorothy sat in the front row of an audience scene. They had made their start on the screen as extras.

Griffith took an interest in the Gish sisters, and their first engagement led to another. Soon they were getting real parts and, presently, their first important picture rôles in *The Unseen Enemy*.

The busy Griffith had some difficulty in telling the sisters apart, so it was arranged that they should wear distinguishing colors.   Dorothy became "Pink Ribbon" and Lillian was "Blue Ribbon."

The next few years were to bring them so far into the limelight of film fame that millions could tell them apart without a ribbon.

This period also brought to the screen a number of the names that were to figure conspicuously in the new and dawning era just ahead.   Wallace Reid was making his first screen appearance in Vitagraph's *Leather Stocking Tales,* directed by Larry Trimble.   When not otherwise engaged Wallie played the violin for studio atmosphere.   Wallace Reid, who came into nation-wide fame in a few years, was the son of Hal Reid, a writer and producer of melodrama, then attached to the Vitagraph scenario staff.   In 1912, James Young and Clara Kimball, soon to be his bride, came from a Salt Lake City stock company to appear in Vitagraph pictures.   Clara Kimball Young's first part was in the rôle of *Anne Boleyn* in a Hal Reid story, entitled *Cardinal Wolsey.*   This was a one-reel picture, also directed by Larry Trimble.

Essanay in Chicago acquired Frank X. Bushman, erstwhile sculptor's model, actor and handsome man in general, the winner of a contest conducted in *The Ladies' World.*   Then Beverly Bayne, a Minneapolis girl on a visit to a Chicago friend, was seeing the sights of Chicago, including the Essanay studio in Argyle street, when the roving eye of Harry McRae Webster, a director, picked her out of a crowd of spectators and started her on the road to starland.

Zukor's importation of the four-reel *Queen Elizabeth* and the increasing aggression of the "feature" picture idea might well have been expected to set up important reactions.

When D. W. Griffith again left with his Biograph players on his annual hegira to California for the winter of 1912–13 he too had a pretentious feature picture idea simmering. Meanwhile he lost Mary Pickford once more, when she abandoned her motion picture career to return to David Belasco. At the call of the impressario, Mary went into the cast of *A Good Little Devil*, faithful to her promise, made years before, that she would return if he ever should need her.

Early in 1913 the feature picture movement received a new impetus from abroad by the unprecedented success of *Quo Vadis*, in eight reels, a spectacle produced by Cines in Italy. This daring picture was imported by George Kleine, one of the leaders of the Motion Picture Patents company group. But the film was beyond the scope of the Trust's General Film Company and its nickelodeon customers. Kleine resorted to presentation of *Quo Vadis* in the large legitimate theatres, opening April 21, 1913 at the Astor theatre in New York. *Quo Vadis* startled the amusement world by playing a run of twenty-two weeks on Broadway with a top admission price of one dollar. It achieved a similar success in most of the larger cities. The profits were tremendous.

Quo Vadis immediately became a direct influence upon production, both in the United States and abroad. Its ancient setting, its coloration of religious interest and its spectacular phases were to be found reflected, imitated and approximated in many subsequent efforts of the picture makers.

The magnates of the stage began to consider the screen more seriously. They wanted a share in the new bonanza. Rumor began to leak up and down Broadway that Klaw & Erlanger, then masters of the speaking stage, were planning something in pictures. The Shuberts were mentioned. Leibler & Company began to get chummy with Vitagraph.

Out in California Griffith plunged into the making of his most ambitious picture, *Judith of Bethulia*, a four part spectacle of ancient and religious atmosphere. It was estimated that the picture would cost $18,000, and it was completed for $36,000, an alarming figure for Biograph.

Blanche Sweet played the title rôle in *Judith of Bethulia.* This picture marked the beginning of a new phase in Griffith's career. The theme and treatment decidedly keynoted the Griffith idea. The picture, despite the fact that for various reasons it did not attain a marked commercial success, was an important contribution to the screen art.

With this picture and his season's work on the coast completed, Griffith returned to New York and the Biograph studio in One Hundred and Seventy-fifth street. There he found a number of things not entirely to his liking.

The low murmuring rumors of a Klaw & Erlanger invasion of the motion pictures on a grand scale and with bold, pretentious plans were now verified by fact. The Protective Amusement Company had been formed and an arrangement had been made for the Biograph to photograph its pictures, to be produced from the selected successes of the K. & E. stage productions. These pictures were to be imposing five-reelers for presentation in summer showings at legitimate theaters and such of the motion picture theatres as might be induced to pay for this mighty and *de luxe* film service. Klaw & Erlanger had broken into the motion picture business, under the manufacturing wing of Biograph, ablest of the producers and, politically, the strongest concern of the industry. It was on the slate that K. & E. were to make the great productions of the day and do it in Biograph's plant. This naturally did not appeal intensely to the ambitious Mr. Griffith.

The time approached for the renewal of Griffith's annual contract with Biograph. He called on J. J. Kennedy and suggested that he be given stock in the company. This met with no enthusiasm and the response that Biograph had no stock available for issue. Griffith then asked for an arrangement to pay him ten per cent of Biograph's profits.

"The time has come," Kennedy answered, "for the production of big fifty thousand dollar pictures. You are the man to make them. But Biograph is not ready to go into that line of production. If you stay with Biograph it will be to make the same kind of short pictures that you have in the past. You will not do that. You've got the hundred thousand dollar idea in the back of your head."

While these negotiations were in progress, the gossip of Griffith's discontent got about. Adolph Zukor was enthusiastically interested in Griffith's work. Famous Players needed more talent.

There was grave alarm in the office of the Famous Players when Zukor announced that he had offered Griffith a salary of fifty thousand dollars a year to direct for the company.

Daniel Frohman was now certain his associate had lost his reason. The Famous Players concern did not have fifty thousand dollars in sight. The company was not worth that much.

To the re-amazement and relief of Zukor's associates, this Griffith person had the colossal nerve to reject the offer.

Twelve years later, in 1925, Famous Players employed Griffith at the rate of $156,000 a year.

Meanwhile, the Klaw & Erlanger productions went ahead. Among the notables introduced to the motion picture by Pat Casey, the manager of the Protective Amusement Company project, was Bert Williams, the negro comedian. In a remotely early chapter this history told of the discovery of Bert Williams in California by Colonel Selig's minstrel show in the days before the motion picture. Williams was now an international celebrity. He made two comedies under the K. & E. Biograph auspices. One of these required a graveyard location. Williams discovered a satisfactory graveyard on Staten Island, where a thrifty sexton locked the gates and held off a funeral while the scenes were photographed. Another Williams comedy, *Darktown Jubilee,* started out to be a profound hit, when a wave of race antagonism arose and terminated his screen career. At a Brooklyn presentation of this picture a race riot resulted in the death of two men.

The ambitious Klaw & Erlanger film project was foredoomed. There were many reasons. A large number of the motion picture exhibitors had never heard of the august concern of K. & E. Many of those who had were showmen with old grudges against the stage magnates of Broadway. Also there was a feeling in the office of Klaw & Erlanger that any theatre ought to be willing to pay a minimum of fifty dollars a day for a K. & E. picture play. This was in a period when the better theatres were just beginning to dare to charge ten cents admission. Fifty dollar a day film rentals were few and scattered.

Eventually the five-reel K. & E. plays were cut from five reels to three and offered along with little two and three reel "features" of the General Film Company, sold for what they might bring in the run of the trade.

This was but one of the first of stage efforts at an invasion of the screen. Experience was to prove that the motion picture was another and independent art.

The shadow company in the little tin can had already begun to take the place of the road show and the stock company. Only a few years ahead, the show in the tin can was to claim a share in the lights of Broadway and overshadow the glories of the stage on its own Great White Way.

The Warner brothers, led by Harry Warner, who had risen from store-show beginning through the exchange business, were making a venturesome independent effort at pioneering in the new era with Warners' Features, in New York.

Otis B. Thayer, an adventuring director, freelancing with an

eye to sales through Warners, happened into Denver, Colorado.
Thayer had a technique of utilizing local raw materials, no matter how raw. In Chicago he had made *The Landing of Columbus* for Selig, using the old caravel models, relics of the Columbian Exposition, and Lake Michigan. Prospecting in Denver,
Thayer found Judge Ben Lindsey in the full flower of his juvenile court publicity. Also George Creel, erstwhile Kansas City
Star reporter, jokesmith of *Judge,* then a Denver editorial writer
and publicist, was conspicuously trying to float a new civic morality on the thin air of that mountain-fevered metropolis.

Thayer suborned a scenario by Creel, entitled *Saved by the
Juvenile Court* and shanghaied Judge Lindsey into a heroic
rôle before the camera. Since the plot seemed to lack movement Thayer sprigged it with Wild West material from the adjacent Cheyenne rodeo. This helped make the picture move
and opened screen careers for Bud Chase, an equestrian authority from the Rosebud reservation re-mount station, and Joe
Ryan, a Cheyennese corral athlete, now a serial star.

The studio was under the management of Arthur S. Kirkpatrick who thus descended into the films from a background of
engineering with the United States Steel Corporation. Kirkpatrick is now sales head of the Educational Films Corporation.
When payday arrived without material manifestations Kirkpatrick took the three untitled reels of the masterpiece and went
on the road to get revenge and recompense from the public.

The horses bucked better than Lindsey, so when Kirkpatrick
arrived to open his show in Pendleton, Oregon, for Round-up
Week, the title had changed from *Saved by the Juvenile Court*
to *Ride 'em Cowboy.* It was a very elastic production. Later
when George Creel, police commissioner, dimmed the red light
of his city, the Lindsey-Cowboy film was retitled *Denver's Underworld.*

In such majesty the epic art of the screen swept on to triumph.

CHAPTER SIXTY-ONE

THE SCREEN DISCOVERS SEX

A ND still we linger in the days of 1913, while yet the motion picture was feeling its way and trying to find its own proper place in the world of expression.

One memorable title, significant of many aspects of motion picture evolution, survives in memory conspicuously among the scores of experimental efforts of the period. It is the lurid *Traffic in Souls*. The history of the project illuminates that age of the motion picture art with special clarity.

This was the day, now a decade past, when the social movement that has given the present era its startling sex frankness, was just evolving from laboratory considerations of the practical sociologists of pulpit, politics, press and stage, into a recognized universal interest. The motion picture, then in the beginnings of the feature era, had just attained the scope to share in the movement.

It all began, it seems, back in the '90's when Dr. Parkhurst went into the Tenderloin of New York and came forth with the revelations of the vice world which resulted presently in the famous Lexow investigation, and for twenty years a long sequel of similar revealing movements in many centers, notably in Chicago and New York, with activities rising from the aggressive interest of Hull House settlement, resulting also in the sensational but somewhat suppressed inquiries of the Chicago Vice Commission and the Committee of Fifteen.

It became apparent to the usually unconscious public that there was a national and international traffic in "white slaves," well organized and capably managed. In time this ran the

—612—

CLARA KIMBALL YOUNG and JOHN BUNNY, in a playtime pose one summer's day long ago, when the Vitagraph players went to "Pop" Rock's country place for an outing.

GEORGE LOANE TUCKER, director of "Traffic in Souls," for
Universal, the production with which the screen discovered
the tremendous box office value of sex.

customary gamut of expression, starting with newspaper headlines, and thence successively into Sunday supplements, periodical fiction, novels, and latterly plays of the stage. Here are
some reminiscent titles: *The House of Bondage, The Lure,
Damaged Goods.*

The actor-directors of motion pictures of the time were but
newly from the stage and the drama of the stage still occupied
their most serious attention. The larger destiny of the motion
picture was still uncertain.

Among these actor-directors was the late George Loane
Tucker, later famous as the maker of *The Miracle Man,* the
picture which made Betty Compson, Thomas Meighan
and Lon Chaney stars. But in 1913 Tucker was merely one
of the several industrious young men engaged in grinding out
one-reel routine pictures for the "Imp" release on the Universal
program.

Tucker saw everything on Broadway, including *The Lure* and
The Battle, both of which were so highly colored that they
brought police intervention. He was afire with inspiration.
He would make a great revealing motion picture, a police picture
dealing with the white slave traffic. At the studio-laboratory
he bubbled his idea to Jack Cohn, the film cutter and editor of
Imp releases.

It was a part of the scheming economy of the Imp administration to try to induce its directors to photograph what they
thought were one-reel pictures and then to pad them into two-
reel releases in the cutting room. If the directors had realized
fully that they were engaged on such pretentious projects as
two-reel pictures their prices and the cost of production would
have gone up. A great deal of the practical diplomacy of this
technique fell upon Cohn. In execution of the policy he became
interested in talking picture story ideas to the directors to decoy
them into exposing enough film footage to permit the applica-

—613—

tion of the amplification process in the cutting room. This had made him a literary confidant of Tucker.

Now Fate had laid exactly the proper background for Tucker's white slave picture idea. Jack Cohn's father had been a police outfitter, with an establishment not far from the old Tenderloin station. In his pre-picture days Master Jackie Cohn was a raid fan, who answered all of the exciting calls for the reserves along with the officers. Jack knew the subject. He of course infected by Tucker's enthusiasm.

With the assurance born of this interest, Tucker went to Carl Laemmle, the president of Universal, to get authority to put the picture into production. Laemmle and the chieftains of the motion picture in general in that day were concerned with concentration on the business of controlling the industry and not at all interested in the pictures themselves.

Laemmle was of short patience with young men who wanted to bother him with such details—especially since Tucker admitted that he wanted to spend $5,000 on his picture. That was enough money to make a dozen Imp program pictures.

George Loane Tucker found himself and his little white slave idea talking to themselves in the hall at 1600 Broadway with the door shut behind them.

Tucker went back to the studio to report defeat. A conspiracy was born. Five of the enthusiasts plotted to make the picture even without the approval of the big boss, and then, if in last resort he could not be won by a screen demonstration, to pay the costs themselves. The five conspirators agreed to stand good for a thousand dollars each. They were Tucker, Herbert Brenon, King Baggot, Jack Cohn and Bob Daly.

Luck played into their hands. Julius Stern, the Imp studio manager, was called away to Europe to settle a dispute between Baggot and Brenon, who had been sent to England to make *Ivanhoe*. Stern was connected with Laemmle by family ties and he was the watchdog of the administration at the studio. In his absence, Mark M. Dintenfass, owner of the Champion brand pictures on the Universal program, was brought across the river from New Jersey to take charge of the Imp studio. Now, as has been indicated in early chapters, Dintenfass was up to his ears in the internal wars of Universal and the battles at 1600 Broadway.

While Dintenfass was busy concentrating his attention on the affairs of the Powers-Laemmle war, the boys at the studio were merrily engaged in photographing *Traffic in Souls,* a scene at a time in odd moments when opportunity permitted, keeping up meanwhile the continuous grind of one and two-reel pictures. *Traffic in Souls* was cast by Jack Cohn and directed by Tucker.

In four weeks the picture was photographed. It was ten reels long, without titles. By this time Dintenfass had begun to spare more attention to the studio, resulting among other things in altercations with Tucker, who quit and went to the London Film Company in England.

Meanwhile Universal was unaware of the existence of the ten-reel negative. Tucker sailed with a final admonition shouted at Cohn at the steamer dock not to cut the picture below seven reels in length.

Cohn was left alone with the ten reels of negative and Laemmle to face. He hid the negative in the bottom drawer of his safe and worked on it secretly at night with the door locked. In a month he had it in six reels, including titles.

The day had arrived for the showdown. Cohn swallowed the lump in his throat, loaded the film into a taxicab and headed for 1600 Broadway.

The home office viewing committee was called together and filed into the projection room to look at "Tucker's Folly." But the home office was all agog with the latest shower of bricks in the Powers-Laemmle fight. Carl Laemmle and one of his lieutenants sat through the picture in angry whispered discourse about their new line of action.

Cohn left downhearted. It looked as though he would be liable for his share of the guaranty of the five underwriting plotters of the project. Late that night he reached the desperation of a decision. He had to put this thing through. In the middle of the night he went to Laemmle's residence and aroused him.

"I've come about *Traffic in Souls*. You talked all through the picture and you didn't see it. Nobody can look at a picture and talk business all the time. Won't you come down now and really see it?"

The film fared better on its next showing. It was admitted to be a picture. But there was a big question as to what might be done with it. The Universal program was made up of one and two-reel subjects. This was a six-reeler. No motion picture theatre of the day considered such a monstrosity. The few long pictures that had been shown before, such as the *Fall of Troy, Quo Vadis? Queen Elizabeth* and the like had gone into legitimate theatres and town opera houses. The situation was further complicated by the internal politics of Universal. The opponents of Laemmle were charging him with having squandered the company's money on a fool director's fool idea. Investigation proved that *Traffic in Souls* had cost $5,700.

It became the text of a violent meeting of the board of directors.

"All right, I'll take the picture off the company's hands and pay $10,000 for it," Laemmle shouted.

Then came a lull, a whispering in conference. Dire suspicion arose in the opposition.

"If you'll put up ten thousand it must be worth a million," taunted the opposition, crying a bid of $25,000. This resulted in the picture remaining the property of the Universal.

Reaching for a channel of distribution, a representative of the Shubert theatre system was called in to see the production. The Shuberts bought a third interest in the picture for $33,000 and took on its exploitation.

Universal now had a profit of $27,300 on an investment of $5,700, and retained a two-thirds interest in the production.

Traffic in Souls opened at Joe Weber's theatre on Monday afternoon, November 24, 1913. The announcing advertisement read:

TRAFFIC IN SOULS.—The sensational motion picture dramatization based on the Rockefeller White Slavery Report and on the investigation of the Vice Trust by District Attorney Whitman —A $200,000 spectacle in 700 scenes with 800 players, showing the traps cunningly laid for young girls by vice agents— Don't miss the most thrilling scene ever staged, the smashing of the Vice Trust.

The picture played to thirty thousand spectators in the first week. There were four showings daily and five on Sunday. The admission price was a flat 25 cents all over the house. In a short time the picture was playing a total of twenty-eight theatres in Greater New York. Its gross receipts totaled approximately $450,000.

The cast included Jane Gail, Matt Moore, Ethel Grandin, William Welsh, Howard Crampton, William Turner, Arthur Hunter and Laura Huntley.

George Loane Tucker, meanwhile, was in England with the London Film Company. He never saw *Traffic in Souls* in its completed form on the screen, although its astonishing success contributed considerably to his career. By the time he returned to the United States it was off the screen, and never to the day of his death some years later did opportunity present itself for him to see it.

A wave of ensuing white slave pictures swept the screen.

The Inside of White Slave Traffic, produced by a series of concerns built around the promotional activities of Samuel H. London, a former government investigator, was presented at the Park Theatre in Columbus Circle, New York, December 8, 1913. It became the focus of considerable police action and various kinds of litigation which helped to establish precedents for the motion picture.

This picture carried the advertised endorsement of Mrs. O. H. P. Belmont, Mrs. Carrie Chapman Catt, Mrs. Inez Milholland Boissevain, and Frederick H. Robinson, president of the Sociological Fund, *Medical Review of Reviews.*

Here was the beginning of the testimonial and endorsement method of motion picture exploitation, an application to the screen of the method that has never failed in the patent medicine field.

The stage presentation of *Damaged Goods* by Brieux, technically the best of the plays on the vice curse theme, opened at the Grand Theatre in New York, December 21, 1913, with Richard Bennett in the leading rôle. This play became the vehicle of the last important motion picture of this type, issued in the autumn of 1915. Richard Bennett appeared also in the screen version of *Damaged Goods.* Made at a cost of about $40,000 for the negative and the promotional opening at a Broadway theatre, including a lecture by Dr. Carleton Simon on civilization by syphilization, it brought in a gross of $600,000.

But sex fashions change. As a fruit of the Parkhurst movement and the fading of the bagnios and brothels, a red light in New York came to denote merely a fire exit. Cultural interest swept on from vice to birth control by the same gradation, for purposes of both parlor and screen. This flowered in the films with an uplifting drama of abortion entitled *Where Are My Children?* clinical, clutching and climactic. It was produced by Lois Weber with Tyrone Power playing the lead. Miss

Weber had been an actress and a pianist before she joined the screen. She followed this triumphant idyll of interrupted gestation with *Hypocrites,* a profitable drama which realized upon an absolute bare possibility.

Picture production kept pace with the current sex technology and *Where Are My Children?* issued by Universal, found a sequel in Mutual's *Motherhood* starring Marguerita Fischer and directed by Harry Pollard, which supplanted the surgical motif with contraceptives and attained the essential moral climax with the orthodox scenic cinema hell and many smoke pots. The educational message of *Motherhood* was greatly enhanced by a New York exhibitor who changed the title to *The Doctor and Your Wife!*

When the sex text, by process of an overlap dissolve in public thought, passed to psychoanalysis and the new assertiveness of youth, bobbed hair and the flappers, the film art in its untiring service of progress moved along to such titles as *Flaming Youth, We Moderns,* etc. Screen sex, day by day, in every way gets prettier and prettier.

The status of the motion picture during the nascent days of film sexing is indicated by a suit filed in 1914 by Arthur Hammerstein against David Belasco, demanding damages on the ground that a theatre's repute had been serious injured by a sub-lease for a film showing, specifically *Traffic in Souls.* Hammerstein won in the first court and lost on appeal.

CHAPTER SIXTY-TWO

LASKY RENTS A BARN

THE difference between the typical nickelodeon of a decade and a half ago and the modern motion picture theatre is approximately the difference between a hot dog stand and the Ritz-Carlton.

Adolph Zukor, with his famous players in famous plays idea, found himself swiftly entangled in the problems of the evolutionary revolution he had helped to launch with his long pictures. New machinery of distribution from the studio to the box office had to be created if the feature picture idea was to survive.

When Al Lichtman came in off the road from the selling of *Queen Elizabeth* and *The Prisoner of Zenda*, he brought with him a clamor for more pictures to save the business. The state's rights buyers had paid well, but they were losing money despite the success of the pictures. The market needed a continuous supply of such pictures to support the new business. A few scattering big pictures now and then could not keep it alive.

The heads of Famous Players, Zukor, Edwin S. Porter, the director and Daniel Frohman conferred long and seriously. The condition appeared to call for a picture a week, fifty-two a year. This was a stupendous order.

"There's not enough picture talent in the world to make that many pictures in a year," Porter declared. He was right.

But out of the pressure of necessity Porter arrived at a schedule of thirty pictures planned for the ensuing year. The schedule was a compromise between the famous players idea and mo-

—620—

ADOLPH ZUKOR, who fought his way to mastery in the motion picture industry, as an Independent with the "feature picture" idea.

JESSE LASKY, the vaudeville producer who brought the cabaret to America, and later plunged into the new feature picture movement in 1913, thereby ultimately writing his
name into the Famous Players-Lasky Corporation.

tion picture practicality. Out of it the whole modern race of screen stars was to be born.

It was decided that there should be three types of pictures: ten Class A, strictly famous players in famous plays, fifteen Class B, made up of "well known picture players" in famous plays, and the rest Class C films to be made of odds and ends under the name of Famous Players Stock Company.

Porter added J. Searle Dawley, his assistant at the Edison studios, to the directorial staff. Zukor and Frohman went gunning for plays and players. For Class A they got Minnie Maddern Fiske, Lillie Langtry, Henry Dixey and John Barrymore.

And now for a nifty. They decided to head the second rate productions of Class B, with Mary Pickford, a "well known picture player," then playing with Belasco in *A Good Little Devil*. They acquired the rights and the cast of this production for the films for $15,000.

This rating of Miss Pickford shows that the stars were still the especial property of the speaking stage in 1912–13. The motion picture was still enjoying a feeling of inferiority, and recognized no stars of its own making.

Belasco's stage presentation of *A Good Little Devil* opened at the Republic theater January 8, 1913, and drew a considerable attention in the motion picture field because "Little Mary" headed the cast. The motion picture industry "pointed with pride" to one of its players honored by stage recognition. When Famous Players translated the play into a picture, David Belasco appeared with Miss Pickford in a bit of prologue. The name of Belasco has been borrowed and rented to lend dignity and importance to motion picture projects occasionally ever since.

The brightening dawn of the feature drama illuminated promises of opportunity to more and more adventurers in the realm of the new art as the months went by.

Among these interested observers of the new trend in pictures was Arthur Friend, a lawyer with some theatrical experience and connections in Milwaukee and New York. By the spring of 1913 Friend was enthusiastically telling everyone that there were great things ahead in the motion pictures and urging some sort of a venture. Among his friends were Jesse L. Lasky and Lasky's brother-in-law, Samuel Goldfish, now Goldwyn—which is yet another motion picture story.

The Laskys, the Goldfishes and the Friends gathered at Naples, Maine, a summer resort, in the season of '13. There Arthur Friend had a practically unlimited opportunity to pour out his excited anticipations concerning the motion picture business.

Samuel Goldfish was then a salesman for a glove manufacturing concern in New York. He had some other business projects in view, but he listened with a tolerant patience and a growing interest. Jesse Lasky listened, too, perhaps not so much interested.

Lasky had an eventful background of ups and downs. He had had experiences calculated to make him careful of the new and untried. He had started his working life as a cornet player in a San Francisco theatre and, for a time, enjoyed the distinction of being the only white man in the Royal Hawaiian band. Then came a few months of newspaper reporting and a try at prospecting in the gold rush at Nome. Back home and broke in San José, Lasky and his sister Blanche went in for music as a juvenile team, appearing at benefits and club performances. An offer from a vaudeville agent brought them east, where they took an engagement to play with Leon Hermann's show of magic. Leon was a nephew of Alexander Hermann, and on his uncle's death assumed the title of *Herrman the Great, Napoleon of Necromancers.*" Lasky became his manager.

With the rise of the vaudeville boom Lasky booked Hermann at a thousand dollars a week, an amazing salary for the time, and set looking about for more wonders to book. In Utica, N. Y., he found B. A. Rolfe, a cornetist, whom he promoted in vaudeville. The partnership of Lasky & Rolfe, producers of vaudeville acts, followed, with such numbers as *Colonial Septette* and the *Military Octette.* Soon Henry B. Harris, then a theatre manager, became Lasky's associate. Their vaudeville enterprises prospered and Lasky found himself the master of a fortune of $150,000. He went to Europe looking for ideas and found one—the cabaret.

The Folies Bergère, the Lasky-Harris introduction of the cabaret idea to America, burst on New York like a rocket the night of Monday, April 24, 1911. It was a sensation for a minute. Its admission price, $2.50, was the highest in New York outside of the Metropolitan Opera House. A hot wave came early in the season and New York left for the seashore. The Folies Bergère brilliantly and completely failed.

Lasky was broke. He thought of California and home again. Then he caught afire with a new idea, an operetta inspired by California. Looking for some one to write the libretto he consulted Mrs. H. C. DeMille, who then conducted a dramatic agency. Lasky wanted William DeMille, but William was busy with *Strongheart* and various Belasco affairs. Mrs. DeMille vigorously suggested her younger son Cecil, who was not so busy. Lasky was dubious. He did not know Cecil, but out of courtesy he had to talk to him. Cecil had winning ways. He talked Lasky into the deal and a one hundred dollar advance. The operetta succeeded and the Lasky-DeMille association was cemented.

Lasky was now beginning to recover from the shock of the grand collapse of the Folies Bergère. It was hardly to be expected that he would have an enthusiastic ear for another new project. He had bought about a half a million dollars' worth of pioneering experience in the cabaret. While Friend talked feature pictures, Lasky went fishing in Lake Sebago.

When the vacation was over and the Friends, Laskys and Goldfishes were again in New York, Friend was still talking pictures. He convinced Blanche Lasky Goldfish.

Finally at the luncheon table at the old Hoffman House, Goldfish surrendered to Friend's everlasting campaign. They would go into the motion picture business.

Jesse Lasky was still wary. He could be committed no farther than to participate by permitting the use of his name. So the Lasky Feature Play Company was born, with $26,500 capital.

At the Lambs club, Cecil DeMille and Jesse Lasky overtook Dustin Farnum and sought to decoy him into the motion pictures. They suggested that he might have a substantial interest in the concern for his services. They intended to make *The Squaw Man*, a stage success, purchased for $5,000, a thousand down and the rest on terms. Farnum was cautious. He opined that he would rather have $5,000 in cash. Farnum on this occasion missed a bet, but on the grand average of such propositions he was correct.

The Squaw Man was Indian and western. Cecil DeMille was to make the picture. The Lasky Feature Play Company looked over the map and elected to go to Flagstaff, Arizona, to make the first production. The name seemed majestic, lone, dignified as a cactus and sufficiently romantic to inspire a great picture.

When Cecil DeMille and Dustin Farnum got off the train at Flagstaff they looked about and saw absolutely nothing. There was nothing to see.

When the train was iced and watered to resume the long haul across the desert, the engineer whistled and the conductor highballed for a departure. Dustin Farnum and Cecil DeMille got on right behind the conductor, bound for Hollywood. They had heard that it was a good place to make films.

Shortly the New York office of the Jesse Lasky Feature Play Company, established in the Longacre Theatre building, was petrified with a wire reading

"We have rented a barn in Hollywood for two hundred dollars a week."

The barn stood, and still stands, at Vine and Selma streets, now a shipping room for the output of the adjacent acres of the Famous Players Lasky studios.

The Squaw Man was in due time photographed, developed and printed. Meanwhile the picture had been sold in advance to the states' rights market for $43,000, which promised the company a handsome profit. But disaster loomed right ahead. The picture when presented for screen examination wobbled and leaped and danced. Dustin Farnum's *Squaw Man* appeared to have acute St. Vitus. The purchasers complained in great violence.

"Defective film" someone whispered in the fevered home office conferences. In haste they drew up papers for the filing of a heavy damage suit against the Eastman Kodak Company, makers of film stock. They were out for revenge and indemnity.

They decided to consult experts for witness stand purposes. The negative was bundled up and taken over to Philadelphia to be submitted for diagnosis by the celebrated Sigmund Lubin, whose experience with "duping" and film manipulation made him the unquestioned authority. He was of course a member of the Patents Company group, but he could be approached diplomatically, even by Independents.

"Pop" Lubin ran a roll of the negative through his fingers rapidly and held it to the light.

"Terrible, terrible." Lubin shook his head sadly, like a surgeon called too late to operate.

"The negative stock was defective, wasn't it?" Arthur Friend demanded eagerly. As the lawyer he wanted to get action.

"No—the stock was good enough." Lubin was still shaking his head.

The assembled delegation was crestfallen, depressed and done. There was not even a hope of collecting from Eastman.

"Is there anything, anything at all—that can be done?"

They hated to hear the answer, but they had to ask.

"Well," Lubin began deliberately, enjoying the suspense, "you used two different cameras, didn't you?"

They had.

"That's why," Lubin went on, without relaxing the nervous tension, "your negative gets out of step with itself—two different frame lines—that makes the picture jump."

Lubin grinned at their woe.

"Maybe I can fix it for you—if I make the prints."

Lubin got the print contract right away. Then he re-perforated the film to put the frames back in step and proceeded to print *The Squaw Man*. It was saved and with it the Jesse Lasky Feature Play Company.

This first picture of the Lasky company was marketed under the publicity ministrations of Harry Reichenbach, subsequently to become the most famous of film press agents. Reichenbach gave early evidence of his peculiar genius in the production of synthetic news of sensational character. A year before he went to the motion pictures he perpetrated the promotion of *September Morn*, a painting by Paul Chabas depicting a comely young woman clad in the modesty of her pose and the autumn atmosphere.

A reproduction of the painting was placed on exhibition in the window of a Fifth avenue art shop. Reichenbach employed a gang of urchins and messenger boys to stand in front of the window and make remarks. He then telephoned the office of Anthony Comstock and let nature take its course in the newspapers. This campaign was supplemented with a cartoon for hand circulation depicting a censorial person in Puritan glasses sternly addressing *September Morn* with a command: "Hands Up!" Reichenbach was rewarded for his efforts with a fee of $25. Some years later, with advancing technique, Reichenbach duped New York with the story of *The Virgin of Stamboul* for Universal Pictures Corporation. He set the police to dragging a lake in Central Park for the virgin's body, and maintained a mysterious official Turkish high commission at a downtown hotel. The Turkish notables concerned were recruited from East Side coffee houses and sequestered in the Hotel Navarre while being trained in their parts. The largest item of expense in this campaign was $400 for French pastry served the Turks.

In recognition of Reichenbach's work on this picture the State of New York passed a law forbidding the giving of false information to the press. Reichenbach retaliated with a circular to the legislature threatening to prosecute the members under the act for broken campaign promises.

Reichenbach's publicity stardom took him to the lofty salary of $1,000 a week. In 1925, he transferred his valued attentions to the palms and profits of Florida in behalf of Addison Mizner's Boca Raton development.

Now back to Lasky and 1913. Adolph Zukor saw *The Squaw Man* and sent Lasky a message of congratulation. Then they met for the first time at luncheon at Delmonico's. It may have been all intended just by way of congratulations, and again it is possible that both of them wanted to size up the competition.

—627—

Zukor was anxious for the development of the feature picture idea in the mind of the public and the amusement world. He employed C. F. Zittel, then connected with the *New York Evening Journal,* to tell the story. Zittel showered the dramatic and motion picture trade press with the big picture idea and photographs of Zukor. The success of the campaign was proven when Arthur Brisbane, despite his deep-dyed dislike of the motion picture, editorized in the *Journal* with a warning to the stage magnates of Broadway that Zukor was a serious invader.

Now from out of the West came a tall solemn stranger, one W. W. Hodkinson, representing the Progressive film exchanges of Los Angeles, San Francisco and elsewhere along the Pacific slope. He was among the most important of the buyers of the new Independent feature pictures. He arrived in New York in January, 1914, to stay a few weeks making new contracts. He stayed for years and became the central figure in the new reorganization of the business of the motion picture.

Hodkinson's attitude and functions, important because of their influence, were the resultant of his earlier career. Only fourteen years before, in 1900, Hodkinson was a night telegrapher in the offices of the Denver & Rio Grande railway in Pueblo, Colorado. He was industrious and ambitious. He studied mightily at correspondence school courses in the hours when his sounder and key were idle. He hoped for a railroad career. When the Gould interests took over the D. & R. G., and Hodkinson's friends higher up were swept out, he left the telegraph office to become a salesman for the International Correspondence Schools.

To keep his customers sold Hodkinson labored with them to make their lessons intelligible to them. It worked and he became perhaps quite as much of a teacher as a salesman. When the panic of '07 arrived Hodkinson was established with a considerable organization at Ogden, Utah. As employment waned correspondence school selling grew harder. When he went to the Ogden post office each midnight to mail his daily reports to correspondence school headquarters he passed a noisy Mormon dance hall. He reflected considerably on human folly and the ease with which amusement was sold while advancement and education were so very hard to sell. Hodkinson was most seriously minded.

Then the movies came with nickelodeons, Ogden's *Dreamland* and *The Electric*, typical of their time. Hodkinson's neighbors complained of the dime novel notions that their children brought home from the movies. Hodkinson looked in at the screen and found himself impressed with what he sensed as its educational possibilities. Also Hodkinson had never seen the sea. Pictures of the sea and ships fascinated him.

It was in the pattern of destiny that years ahead he was to deliver to the public Elmer Clifton's *Down to the Sea in Ships*, the screen saga of New Bedford and whaling days. By the same token when affluence came, Hodkinson acquired a fishing camp cabin at Montauk Point, Long Island, and a place by the sea in Florida. The screen eventually took him to the sea.

Hodkinson and some neighbors acquired a movie show and made it a family theatre, with clean floors, clean pictures and— daringly enough, with a ten cent admission, double the standard movie admission.

In due course Hodkinson's quest of pictures made an exchangeman of him. When the Patents Company arose he sold to the General Film Company and became a district manager for the new efficiency régime under J. J. Kennedy. He established an amazing record. In his territory, Denver west to the Pacific, he fought for intelligent exhibition of better pictures for longer runs and higher admissions in better theatres. Someway he won for General Film twenty percent of its gross revenue from ten per cent of the population of the United States.

When Kennedy left the General Film Company, Hodkinson left too, to become an Independent exchangeman, and founded his concern, named the Progressive. In this he was secretly financed by Frank Marion and Samuel Long, of Kalem and the Trust. His methods had won their support.

Hodkinson was more than ready for the feature pictures when they came. They fitted his idea of progress and the uplift of the motion picture, both as business and as art.

Now Hodkinson had come to New York to buy more features. He had as well a feature to sell, *The Sea Wolf*, made in California from Jack London's story, by Hobart Bosworth, with a producing concern newly formed and financed by Frank C. Garbutt, a Los Angeles real estate operator.

Hodkinson entered into negotiations with Famous Players for their coming pictures. The stage was set for a new drama of personalities and struggle.

Hodkinson represented the machinery of motion picture merchandising and distribution. He had been schooled in the rigid discipline of the Trust. He had built upon it and applied it.

Adolph Zukor, head of Famous players, was the most significant single figure in the field of picture production. He was inwardly driven by Napoleonic ambition.

In the terms of these two personalities, production and distribution were due to meet—and clash.

There were endless negotiations.

Zukor was beset by his problems, and fear that distribution was going to control production.

When Zukor thinks he walks. There was a night in this period when he walked from midnight to sunrise. Twice that night in the streets of New York he saw Battery Park, and once he crossed One Hundred and Twenty-fifth street. When the Sioux started ghost dancing it meant trouble along the Big Horn. When Zukor starts walking it is time for everybody on the reservation to look out.

Hodkinson and distribution represented only one of Zukor's problems. Mary Pickford was getting expensive. The whole theory of "famous players" was undergoing revision. It seemed that "famous players in famous plays" was not the perfect idea after all. Zukor's Class A pictures, with the great names of the stage in them, were falling down, while his Class B with this little girl with a curl was getting the money—and she and her mother knew it.

Zukor got peace for a moment with an agreement to pay Miss Pickford a thousand dollars a week. In January, while the distribution pot was coming to a boil, Miss Pickford, with Edwin S. Porter in charge, went to California with a company to make *Tess of the Storm Country*, one of her greatest successes.

When that distribution contract with Hodkinson's Progressive exchanges was ready to sign Zukor had walked a lot of mileage. Hodkinson, in the offices of Zukor's attorney, Elek J. Ludvigh, read it. In his understanding of its terms it would have invaded his pending deal for the pictures of the Jesse Lasky company. It was aimed at control of the business by control of production.

"We'll take care of Lasky," they promised Hodkinson. He did not want Lasky "taken care of." Hodkinson had seen competition taken out of production by control in the Trust, and he had observed the consequences.

Hodkinson walked out, the contract unsigned.

Here was an impasse and a crisis.

Al Lichtman, sales manager for Famous Players, sent out a wire call for the rest of the big buyers of features. He planned to sell the pictures anyway.

Soon the five major exchangemen of the feature picture trade were assembled in New York. They were: Hodkinson, Hiram Abrams of Boston, W. L. Sherry of New York, Raymond Pawley of Philadelphia and James Steele of Pittsburgh.

Hiram Abrams, later the executive head of the United Artists, was then the partner of Walter E. Greene in motion picture distribution and theatres in New England. Greene began in the remote days of the little traveling picture show and followed the frequent pattern, with the successive steps to motion picture theatres and then an exchange system. Abrams joined later in the ascent, in the course of a business career that began in his school days in Portland, Maine. He was carrying a paper route, when his mother's complaint about watered milk put him in the notion of dairying and a milk route. The milk route led to a restaurant and near the restaurant was a music store. Through the music store Abrams became a collector of installment payments on pianos. The music business brought contact with song slides and singers appearing in the motion picture theatres. Abrams and Greene met through the Green Theatre in Portland. The threads of destiny joined. We shall soon see Greene again.

W. L. Sherry, the New York exchange factor in the situation, brings in a flash of the infinite drama of chance in the great human ant hill of Manhattan. Sherry, in 1912, was a salary loan agent in the downtown section. Scanning the "Business Opportunities" column of the *New York Times* one morning he discovered an intriguing advertisement:

WANTED—A man to put $5,000 into a promising, etc., etc.

It was a "blind" advertisement inserted by Al Lichtman, the new sales manager of the new Famous Players, trying this despairing last expedient to find a buyer for the first of their features, the historic *Queen Elizabeth*, with Sarah Bernhardt.

Sherry answered the advertisement, and was swiftly on the road to riches. In a few years he had amassed about a million dollars in motion picture profits.

The exchangemen, assembled in New York in 1914 found a leadership in Hodkinson. One day at his office at 110 West Fortieth street, a five part agreement and pact was formed. They decided to pool their power and Paramount Pictures Corporation was born. It was named after an apartment house sign that Hodkinson had seen that morning and the trade mark, now known to the world, was the picture of a mountain that he sketched on a blotter. The Rocky Mountains, through Hodkinson, had a good deal to do with picture history.

Now Paramount had the power. It was the market. For Paramount Hodkinson made contracts with Zukor, Lasky and Garbutt of the Bosworth concern. An advance of $25,000 a picture was to be made. The producer was to receive 65 per cent of the earnings from rentals and the distributor, Paramount was to take 35 per cent. The figures were based on Hodkinson's General Film Company experience. The 65–35 ratio remained a constant of picture distribution practise for many years.

It was all settled—almost.

Adolph Zukor was now one of three picture producers under contract to supply films to Paramount. And W. W. Hodkinson was boss of Paramount.

Zukor began walking again.

Consonant with Hodkinson's interest in education, growing out of his correspondence school experiences, Paramount early in its career made an effort at screen culture. Hugo Munsterberg of Harvard, a German psychologist, was retained in editorial and supervisory relation to a one reel "educational" release entitled Paramount Pictographs.

This release contained interesting bits of psychological tests calculated to intrigue the screen audiences, but pictures definitely aimed at making audiences think rather than feel have never achieved popularity. The editorial labors of the *Pictographs* passed to J. R. Bray, one of the earliest and ablest makers of the so-called educational pictures.

Not long after this association with picture production Dr. Munsterberg wrote a work entitled *The Photoplay*, with a slight historical survey, and a very considerable line of psychological discussion. This was the first serious discussion of the motion picture as an art to appear in book form. It followed, in some degree, the investigations of students of psychology at Harvard, among them Horace M. Kallen, then a student and now a professor of psychology in the New School for Social Research in New York, who wrote for the *Harvard Magazine* in 1909 what was likely the first consideration of the motion picture from a scientific point of view. The Munsterberg book was of decided service in its period by way of indicating to the intelligentsia that the lowly motion picture was worthy of attention.

CHAPTER SIXTY-THREE

"THE BIRTH OF A NATION"

THE explosive, spectacular successes of the early feature pictures, typified by *Quo Vadis* and *Traffic in Souls*, reacted tremendously on two of the motion picture's most vigorous personalities.

Harry E. Aitken, president of the newly promoted Mutual Film Corporation, envisioned new heights of promotional success.

D. W. Griffith, until now the admitted master of the art of the screen, was challenged to attain anew.

Griffith had found his ambitions halted that day when he got Biograph's decision to stick to the short pictures of the Trust's General Film program output.

Then one day Tony O'Sullivan, formerly of Biograph and now of Aitken's Majestic studios, said: "Mr. Griffith, meet Mr. Aitken." Aitken and Griffith shook hands, and again history was headlong on its way.

October 1, 1913, Griffith left Biograph, at the end of five of the most significant years of motion picture evolution. On October 29, trade journal advertisements announced that D. W. Griffith was "now with Mutual Movies."

Every motion picture patron of a decade ago will remember the famous slogan "Mutual Movies Make Time Fly" and the winged clock trademark. As a trademark the idea had some merit and the great demerit of offering the motion picture as a mere time-killer. It was too honest.

Griffith, with Mutual, plunged into a campaign of production with amazing speed and celerity. He was specifically in charge of the operations of the now amalgamated Reliance-Majestic studios. Griffith's contract called for a large salary, a stock participation, and the privilege of making two independent pictures of his own each year. He promptly discovered that if there was going to be any salary, he would have to make it quickly. *The Battle of the Sexes* went into production overnight and was ready for delivery in seven days. When the situation calls for pot boilers, Griffith is a fast cook.

The advertisements had announced that D. W. Griffith, the great Biograph director, was to supervise all Mutual productions. The type was large and clear.

A few weeks elapsed and this campaign penetrated as far as Los Angeles. Then another advertisement appeared announcing that, despite Mutual's Griffith proclamation, "he has nothing to do with Keystone comedies." The advertisement was Mack Sennett's signed declaration of independence.

Quite distinct and apart from the Mutual advertising of Griffith, a page broadside appeared in the *Dramatic Mirror* of December 31, 1913, proclaiming in part:

D. W. GRIFFITH
Producer of all great Biograph successes, revolutionizing motion picture drama and founding the modern technique of the art. Included in the innovations which he introduced and which are now generally followed by the most advanced producers are: The large or close-up figures, distant views as represented first in Ramona, the "switchback," sustained suspense, the "fadeout," and restraint in expression, raising motion picture acting to the higher plane which has won for it recognition as a genuine art.

A list of productions which took in practically every picture Griffith had made from *The Adventures of Dolly* in 1908 to *Judith of Bethulia* followed. The advertisement was signed by "Albert H. T. Banzhaf, counsellor at law and personal representative."

Griffith was getting relief after five years of anonymous labors at Biograph. No longer would he hide his light under a bushel. There was certainly nothing stingy about the credits which Banzhaf showered upon his client.

In a strict technical sense the claims can be disputed and early motion picture men have on occasion taken Griffith to task for them. The close-up, exemplified in *Fred Ott's Sneeze*, appeared in the Edison peep show pictures of 1894, and other bits of camera manipulation involving fade-outs, double exposures and the like figured in the early Melies magic pictures, all before Griffith's advent.

However, the broader and more important claim of raising motion picture acting to a higher plane was amply justified. While Griffith may not have originated the close-up and like elements of technique, he did establish for them their functions in screen narration.

And the while, affairs were much astir in the Mutual Film Corporation. It was troubled within itself with the issue between the rising importance of feature picture and the current grind of program output of short subjects. Mutual adhered for the moment to the same program idea which ruled the General Film. Meanwhile Aitken launched the allied Continental Features Corporation to sell big pictures, independently but linked to some degree with Mutual. The best of these bigger pictures came from the Reliance-Majestic studios under Thomas H. Ince.

Griffith, whose contract permitted him to make two independent pictures of his own each year, in addition to his work for Aitken, was now secretly preparing for his first big effort. February 14, 1914, Griffith arrived in Los Angeles, ostensibly to finish a screen version of *The Escape*, a drama by Paul Armstrong. But Griffith's chief activity was concerned with arranging for the services of extra people by the thousands, with uniforms and horses for whole armies. He was making picture preparations on a scale without precedent in motion history.

Griffith was deliberately setting out to make the world's greatest motion picture. He was hungry for recognition and success.

The story which Griffith had chosen for his purpose was based on *The Clansman*, a novel by the Rev. Thomas Dixon. A script for the speaking stage, dramatizing the Dixon novel, had been brought to Griffith's attention by Frank Woods, head of the Mutual's newly formed scenario department. Griffith's first casual attention had grown into a deep interest.

The Clansman story as Griffith visioned it for the screen, was a saga of the South, the Civil War, and the days of Reconstruction, all expressed in spectacular form with the sweep of battle lines and acute melodrama—a mingling of patriotism, hate, terror, suspense and mystery. The historic Ku Klux Klan gave the story its major movement and its title. No doubt Griffith's Kentucky nativity and early associations as the son of Colonel Jacob Griffith were an influence in the selection of the story and its production.

The novel which was Griffith's inspiration for *The Birth of a Nation* became in the same period the inspiration of Joseph Simmons, then attached to the national headquarters of the Woodmen of the World in Omaha, and looking for an order of his own to promote. Simmons originally designed that his new secret society be named "The Clansmen," and changed it to the Ku Klux Klan when he found the first title had been appropriated by a small western project of similar tenor.

The picture *The Birth of a Nation* and the K. K. K. secret society, which was the afterbirth of a nation, were sprouted from the same root. In subsequent years they reacted upon each other to the large profit of both. The film presented predigested dramatic experience and thrills. The society made the customers all actors in costume.

—638—

To tell all of the romance of ambition, politics, and finance involved in the making of *The Clansman*, would also require the space of a large volume. Half a dozen times the completion of the project was threatened when backers, terrified by Griffith's expenditures, refused to continue support. Griffith reached everywhere for money. His struggles are reminiscent of Bernard Palissy, the sixteenth century ceramic artist, burning his very home to keep the fires of his furnace going. In one desperate circumstance J. D. Barry, secretary to Griffith, obtained a loan from a Pasadena capitalist. Griffith, grateful, insisted that Barry keep the usual commission, some seven hundred dollars. Barry refused, taking stock in *The Clansman* to this amount to cheer his chief. Barry thought, of course, the money was gone. It was. But it came back, bringing a profit of $14,000.

The Mutual Film Corporation, through Aitken, the president, became an investor in the picture in the sum of $25,000. When this came to the attention of the directors there was a bitter session. They insisted that Aitken had acted without authority and that he must relieve the Mutual of this wild venture. He did. The insuing profits of that block of stock amounted, Aitken admits, to something more than a quarter of a million dollars.

The Clansman was to be released in twelve reels. As the time for its marketing drew near, the question of its distribution became a serious problem. It was such a product as could not be handled by any of the existing distribution machinery of the older concerns.

W. W. Hodkinson, with his various West Coast feature exchanges and various exchange affiliations in Paramount, was considered.

Famous Players then also had a big picture in work, *The Eternal City*, with Pauline Frederick in the leading rôle, under production by Porter in Rome. It involved some financial problems and many conferences with Paramount. Paramount was rapidly becoming what it had set out to avoid, a program concern, with ten reels a week in two features. The old problem of a consistent regular commercial supply from sources which should be governed by the often inconsistent and irregular course of art was reasserting itself. *The Eternal City* was costing large sums, possibly $100,000 in total, and it was going to require special selling and presentation on a level above the Paramount routine. This gave rise to a project for the formation of the Select Film Booking agency, as a Paramount special organization to place super-pictures in a super-market. It was an early step toward a solution of the problem which more recently has been met by the special road-show presentations of such pictures as *The Covered Wagon, The Ten Commandments,* and *The Hunchback of Notre Dame.*

This Paramount effort toward the bigger market brought thoughts of the great Griffith picture in that direction. An appointment was made to discuss distribution of *The Clansman.* Word of this went to the office of Famous Players. Then word went back that *The Eternal City* could never be handled by the same concern along with "that dirty nigger picture." So does gossip shape the course of history.

The production of *The Eternal City* was the valedictory effort of Edwin S. Porter, the director. When the picture was completed he sold his interest in Famous Players and withdrew from production. He may be called the screen's first director. His motion career began with Raff & Gammon in the remotely early days, and his fame began with the making of *The Great Train Robbery,* first of the story pictures. After his departure from Famous Players Porter entered into the affairs of the Precision Machine Company, makers of the Simplex projection machine. The Precision concern was financed by James A. Stillman of New York.

Griffith finally met the distribution problem for *The Birth of a Nation* by forming the Epoch Film Corporation to exploit it independently as a road show. The choice of the name "Epoch" indicated what someone thought about it.

The Clansman had its première at Clune's Auditorium in Los Angeles on the night of February 8, 1915. It was the greatest motion picture event of that motion picture city. Talk of the vast operation on the Griffith lot, talk of the theme, had the city agog. There were mutterings of race war because of the negro element. Politicians, scenting trouble with the dark vote, grew hostile. The police were massed against a possible riot. The picture was a sensational triumph before that first night audience. In Washington the picture was shown at the White House to President Wilson and his family, and at special showings for the justices of the Supreme Court and members of the diplomatic corps. In New York a special showing was given the night of February 20, 1915, at the Rose Gardens, at Fifty-third street and Broadway. Thomas Dixon, author of the basic story, as the final scene passed, shouted to Griffith, *"Clansman* is too tame—let's call it *The Birth of a Nation."*

On March 3, under its new title, the picture opened for the New York public at the Liberty Theater, with a top admission price of two dollars a seat. The motion picture had taken its place on a parity with the drama.

Because of the halo that *The Birth of a Nation* has conferred upon them, some of the now famous names from the cast must be recalled: Henry Walthall, Mae Marsh, Elmer Clifton, Robert Harron, Lillian Gish, Joseph Henabery, Sam de Grasse, Donald Crisp and Jennie Lee. Seven years before the producer then just Larry Griffith, an actor out of a job—found a chance to play a rôle in a little one-reel Edison drama for five dollars a day.

The Birth of a Nation broke all theatre records in various world capitals and became, as it remains today, the world's greatest motion picture, if greatness is to be measured by fame. It has ever since continued to be an important box office success. Early in 1924 *The Birth of a Nation,* then nine years old, played in the great Auditorium Theatre in Chicago, surpassing any previous picture audience record for that house. The patronage of the Ku Klux Klan was credited with giving this run its extraordinary success.

The Birth of a Nation followed up its metropolitan successes with a sweep of the country by twelve road companies under the direction of J. J. McCarthy, who with his associate, Theodore Mitchell, became conspicuous figures in a running war of censorship agitations which rose in the path of the picture. There were lawsuits, riots and political intrigues. McCarthy was drafted for the exploitation of the picture because of his success at the Chestnut Street Opera House in Philadelphia in the exploitation of the earlier feature film dramas.

A storm of opposition to the Griffith masterpiece swept across the United States, north of the Mason-Dixon line. The whole negro race and its white defenders rose in a clamor for the suppression of the picture, with local oppositions of serious strength developing in every community where there was a sufficient negro vote to influence the politicians and office holders. The voters were there at home, whereas the picture was merely "a movie from New York." The political attitude was inevitable.

D. W. Griffith became for the time an outraged, screaming pamphleteer, campaigning for the freedom of the screen on terms of equality with the press.

It is to be admitted that part of Griffith's ardor grew out of the fact that he had money at stake in the picture, but it would be unfair to believe that this was the source of more than half of his zeal. There is considerable evidence from time to time that Griffith would rather make pictures than make money. It was indeed this very fact which so early set him apart from the commonplace in motion picture production.

Griffith issued statements, made speeches and wrote letters proclaiming fundamental rights of expression which he held should be self evident. His fight for *The Birth of a Nation* was really a fight for the whole institution of the screen.

The Boston branch of the National Association for the Advancement of Colored People upheld the "Black Abolitionist" tradition of New England by issuing a booklet against *The Birth of a Nation,* broadcasting it to negro leaders in every part of the United States. The president of the Boston organization was Moorfield Storey, a white leader of the movement.

The Boston booklet, read after ten years have cooled the heat of controversy, appears somewhat lacking in the measured caution and poise to have been expected of the New England intelligentsia. From its pages one discovers that Dr. Charles W. Eliot, head of Harvard and trademark of the "five foot bookshelf," charged the picture with a tendency to perversion of white ideals. Jane Addams of Hull House, Chicago, was "painfully exercised over the exhibition." Francis Hackett in the *New Republic* lambasted the Rev. Thomas Dixon, author of the story, as a "yellow clergyman." Booker T. Washington wrote letters to the papers. It was charged that audiences were sprinkled with Pinkerton men to suppress demonstrations. If so it was wise management. Oswald Garrison Villard wrote that *The Birth of a Nation* was "a deliberate attempt to humiliate 10,000,000 American citizens and portray them as nothing but beasts."

These attacks helped mightily to make Griffith's picture great. The roaring denunciations from the high places sent the whole public to the theatre to see what the row was about. It has been estimated that more than $15,000,000 has been spent at the box office for admissions to *The Birth of a Nation.*

It is an interesting commentary that this storm over the Griffith picture, rising for two years, was at its height while Europe was aroar with the World War. The United States had to fight the Civil War and the negro question all over again while the world was coming apart next door.

The bitterness of the battle gave Griffith the text for his next great screen effort *Intolerance,* a tremendous endeavor to expose the absurdities of public opinion down the aisles of history.

The Birth of a Nation was a large influence of encouragement in the budding movement that was to supplant the factory grind production of mere movies with motion pictures.

Motion picture technique was developing and acquiring form. Griffith in his California studios was continuing and building upon the tradition of Biograph, the while training a new school of directors. The Griffith sessions with his company about him on the grass under the pepper trees of California are reminiscent of the garden schools of the old Greeks. Griffith sat discoursing his enthusiasms, wearing the ruins of a most disreputable straw hat, often letting his interest run on to the neglect of rehearsals. Elmer Clifton and W. Christy Cabanne were among the several directors trained and launched by Griffith in this period.

Experimenting his way along, Griffith began somewhat reluctantly to admit that the titling of films was of at least casual importance. Anita Loos, the girl who sent scenarios from San Diego, went to the Griffith studios to doctor scripts and sit in the councils of the cutting room. She was to become the founder of the modern art of film titling.

When D. W. Griffith was directing "The Clansman" in the hills of California, the picture which, a few months later under the title of "The Birth of a Nation," gave him world fame as the screen's foremost director.

CHARLES CHAPLIN editing films in the cutting
room of his studio in Hollywood, California.

CHAPTER SIXTY-FOUR

"CHARLIE CHAPMAN" GETS AN OFFER

ONE sultry afternoon in the late summer of 1913 Adam Kessel sat in his office in the Putnam building meditating on the prosperous affairs of the New York Motion Picture Company and Keystone comedies.

There had not been a new war in the film world for at least a week and Kessel yawned under the monotony of the moment. He took his feet off the desk and decided to step out on Broadway and get the air.

As Kessel strolled past Hammerstein's he paused for conversation on the weather with Mike Sullivan, the manager, who stood in the lobby.

A laugh rippled across the audience inside.

"Guess I'll go look the bill over," Kessel decided and entered. He was one of the familiars who did not require even the formalities of a pass.

A skit entitled *A Night in a London Club* was on.

A small man with big pants and a curious gait attracted Kessel's attention and wrung a laugh from him.

When the act ended Kessel went back stage. He had a notion to interview this young man. There was just a possibility that he might be useful in Keystone comedies. He was certainly a most amusing little cuss.

The young man was somewhat curious about his caller, with whom he chatted in deepest and darkest London accents on the subject of the kinema.

"What the blooming 'ell—no."

"I tell you, Mr. Chapman, we can give you $75 a week."

The young "Mr. Chapman" was entirely dubious. He had profound doubts about so rash a venture. He had had a bit of a hard time here and there along the line and things were better now. He was in the good graces of Alf Reeves, manager of Karno's Pantomime Company, and they were booked solid on the big time from coast to coast.

There were other conversations. This Kessel was getting persistent. He raised the offer to a hundred dollars a week.

No. The young Englishman was going to take no such chances. He had the caution born of bitter experience. He had been born with a traveling troupe of strolling British players at Fontainebleau in France. His early boyhood had been spent against the seamy side of life in London, a child laborer in a toy factory. It had been a fight against penury and want. He was doing well enough now; why take a chance?

The Karno company moved along. But Adam Kessel still had that little English comedian on his mind.

A Night in a London Club was playing at the Nixon theatre in Philadelphia when Alf Reeves got a wire:

> Is Charlie Chapman with your company? Have him call Saturday our office, Putnam Bldg.
>
> > Kessel & Bauman.

In response to that wire Charles Chaplin duly appeared in New York and Adam Kessel raised the offer to $150 a week.

Chaplin went back to Philadelphia to consult with Alf Reeves. "You had better take it," was Reeves' advice, "because you can't hope to get much more here with us than you are getting now."

Chaplin was in no haste. His contract was due to expire in November, at which time the company was booked to play at the Empress in Los Angeles. He notified Kessel that he would start work with Keystone in Los Angeles then.

Mack Sennett made a call on Chaplin back stage at the Empress and one day in November Charlie took his baggy old pants and shoes out to the Keystone lot.

"What the blooming 'ell" was ahead he did not know. When in doubt an actor always does his favorite business.

Chaplin's first Keystone appearance was a part in a one reel release entitled *Kid's Auto Races*. He wore the gait and mannerisms that had been most successful in his music hall appearances. It was a bit of a trick he had picked up in the toy factory days when he imitated a wretched old bar fly who hobbled about at the Queen's Head, a London "pub," to hold the cabbies' horses for them while they roistered inside.

Chaplin's mother had reproached him mightily for making sport of the old unfortunate and perhaps that had helped to burn it into the youngster's mind. Now it was to be the making of his world wide fame.

A screen examination of *Kid's Auto Races* discloses that apparently Mr. Chaplin had a most amusingly awkward time with the camera. That too was a bit of business gleaned on the other side. In the summer of 1912, on his first engagement under Alf Reeves' management, they played on the isle of Jersey. Jersey's annual fête, "the Carnival of Flowers," was in progress. Chaplin and Reeves among the spectators were vastly amused at a fussy and ostentatious official of the carnival who persisted in centering himself in every scene covered by the motion picture cameras. The Keystone camera revived that memory and made it a part of Chaplin's screen début.

The little man with the baggy pants was on his way, due in time to become a vital factor in the tangled course of screen finance as well as the world's greatest motion picture actor.

Keystone comedies began and saw their prime before the star age. Chaplin, along with Mabel Normand and all that merry company under Mack Sennett, were anonymously presented to the public. But the picture of Chaplin in his make up, characterized by pants, shoes and cane, gave the posters advertising Keystone comedies a new drawing power. Chaplin became famous before he was known.

Mack Sennett, now, inadvertently, and incidentally to his own ambitions, gave Chaplin a mighty boost to fame. Remember that when Griffith was appointed to the director-generalship of Mutual, Sennett had advertised that Griffith had nothing to do with Keystone comedies. And remember, too, that Griffith began his vast and mysterious preparations for the making of *The Birth of a Nation* on his arrival in Los Angeles the middle of February 1914.

Sennett was still making one reel Keystone comedies, good comedies to be sure, but just one reelers. If he were not to be passed on the road to fame by Griffith and Ince with their multiple reel features, something had to be done. And so we discover that in April, 1914, Sennett went into production of a six reel comedy, entitled *Tillie's Punctured Romance,* with Marie Dressler and Charlie Chaplin.

The world had never heard of a six reel comedy. It was as stupendous an undertaking in its field as *Quo Vadis* or that Griffith mystery, the coming *Clansman.*

The choice of Marie Dressler for the title rôle was, of course, a tribute to the "famous players" idea which had been espoused by Zukor.

Miss Dressler has her own version of the casting, as related in her book *The Life Story of an Ugly Duckling,* in which she says: "I went up on the lot and looked around until I found Charlie Chaplin who was then unknown. I picked him out and also Mabel Normand. . . . I think the public will agree that I am a good picker for it was the first real chance Charlie Chaplin ever had."

The original discoverers of Charlie Chaplin should form an

association and hold a convention at the Polo Grounds, if the seating facilities are adequate.

Sennett labored with *Tillie's Punctured Romance* for fourteen weeks. In view of the fact that Keystone produced its one reeler standard comedies easily at the rate of one a week it is apparent he was making a supreme effort.

Tillie's Punctured Romance was a proclaimed success at its première showings. And out of this success Charlie Chaplin appears to have gathered a courage which importantly supported him in negotiations now under way.

Gilbert M. Anderson, the famous "Broncho Billy" of Essanay, went down to Los Angeles to negotiate. He was amazed at the esteem which Chaplin seemed to put on his own services. Anderson was led on and on to more and more ambitious offers.

All this bidding came to the attention of Kessel and Bauman in New York. They were selling Keystone comedies containing the peerless Chaplin's antics to the Mutual Film Corporation for ten cents a foot for the positive prints. This was a part of the merchandising practise of the old program system. It took no cognizance of star values or costs. Now Chaplin's price was going up, about tenfold. Kessel and Bauman announced to the Mutual that the price on Keystones would have to be eleven cents a foot, if they were to hold that funny little chap with the bamboo cane. Mutual's board of directors thought this decidedly absurd. The answer was "No."

Meanwhile Broncho Billy Anderson was getting dizzy at the heights to which Chaplin was leading the bidding.

One November day in 1914 George K. Spoor in Chicago received a telegram from Anderson at Niles. He indicated that he thought he could get Chaplin for a thousand dollars a week, which same was a great deal of money, even for prosperous Essanay.

Spoor with the telegram in hand walked into the advertising office of his plant. He had never heard of Charlie Chaplin.

"Who is this fellow Chaplin with Keystone?"

Frank Suttle, a member of the publicity staff, looked the telegram over.

"Guess he's that funny little fellow with the baggy pants."

"Is he good?" Spoor waved the telegram casually.

"Sure, the best they've got."

Anderson, armed with the backing of his Chicago partner, went back at Chaplin with an offer of a thousand dollars a week.

Chaplin glowed inside. But he shrugged his shoulders and hesitated. He could just as well charge Anderson for the delay. They closed an agreement at $1,250 a week.

With a fanfare of advertising Essanay announced its acquisition of Chaplin on January 2, 1915. Chaplin started to work at the Essanay Chicago studio, on a comedy in two reel entitled *Charlie's New Job*. The comedian shivered in the winds that swept down the west shore of Lake Michigan and pined for balmy California. In three weeks he was through with his picture and Chicago.

Chaplin's second Essanay picture, *A Night Out*, his favorite theme, was made at Niles, California, where he continued to the conclusion of his contract a year later. The casts at the early Chaplin-Essanay pictures all included the now famous Ben Turpin. Turpin rose in screen favor because of his charming affliction of cross eyes. Turpin acquired them on the stage playing the grotesque rôle of *Happy Hooligan*, and has since spent his life resisting the efforts of well meaning oculists to cure him.

Chaplin's third Essanay picture, *The Champion*, is among the most famous of his productions.

In the course of his Essanay engagement Chaplin attended a party where he met a very fair young person from Reno, Nevada, Edna Purviance. She was as blond as he was dark, as

CHAPLIN'S BILLING for his last stage appearance, at the Empress theatre, Los Angeles, in November, 1913 — Chaplin appears third from the top and in the center at the bottom.

WHEN CHARLES CHAPLIN went to Essanay, lured away from
Keystone by "Broncho Billy," he made this scene for
"Charlie's New Job," with Ben Turpin in the cast.

placid as he was mercurial. Chaplin became pictorially interested. Here was a graceful feminine foil, his photographic counterpart. She was invited to meet the camera at Niles. Miss Purviance was cast for a part in the Essanay Chaplins and remained connected with the Chaplin organization, gaining no small share of renown by dint of her nearly continuous appearance on the screens of the world. A dozen efforts to take her from the Chaplin company to be starred on her own account failed. At last she gleaned her reward with the title rôle of *A Woman of Paris,* produced and directed by Chaplin, in execution of a promise of nearly ten years' standing. Incidentally this picture served to bring screen fame to Adolphe Menjou, who appeared in support of Miss Purviance.

The Essanay furor of publicity about Chaplin set his career well under way. He was from thence onward to set a pace in starland. The motion picture world was never to be the same after Chaplin shambled into it. Affairs began to revolve around him. Bigger events were coming.

CHAPTER SIXTY-FIVE

THE SCREEN AND PRESS CONSPIRE

IF you had been a luncheon hour patron of the old Union Café in Randolph street in Chicago in the summer of 1905 you might have observed the daily entry and meeting of a certain two habitual customers of a special significance in our story. The newspaper and the motion picture were plotting there.

There are many reasons why the place should have been Chicago, and Chicago's Rialto. Up the street stood the Masonic Temple, once the city's chief architectural pride, where the Edison peep show revealed the motion picture in 1894, and nearby was the Schiller theatre where Latham's Eidoloscope appeared in '95 with its feeble miracle of the screen. It was the street of the horror haunted Iroquois, the old Powers theatre and the historic Sherman House.

Our two men meeting there at noon entered with the feverish bustle of Chicago and then lingered hours over their coffee and conversation. One was Moses Koenigsberg, a spacious person with an organ voice, and a leonine head with a wavy forelock. The other was Colonel William N. Selig, whom we have seen in many chapters of this narrative, now rising on the wave of motion picture prosperity.

Koenigsberg was in charge of the news affairs of the most strenuous period in the evolution of the most strenuous newspaper in all the field of journalism, to-wit the *Chicago Evening American*, property of William Randolph Hearst.

In the normal course of events, on days and at hours when nothing especially happened, the *Chicago Evening American* went tripping out into Chicago's Loop district at the rate of an edition about every forty-five minutes. Under the external pressure of vivid events or the internal pressure of even more vivid Koenigsberg inspirations, the *American* erupted editions fifteen or twenty minutes apart until relieved, and until the adjacent shores of Lake Michigan were knee deep in the lava, scoriæ, ashes and hot mud of the current sensation. The normal schedule was seventeen editions a day, with a new whimsy, thrill or shudder roaring across the first page of each of them. This made it desirable for Koenigsberg to have or overtake an idea expressible in type of 480-point and upwards every few moments.

The *Chicago American* was striving for a foothold and circulation, against the unanimous opposition of the old line papers. The typographical excitement was only one of the phases of the strife. In time the struggle resulted in Chicago journalism seizing the motion picture as a weapon in the circulation war, with, as we shall see, considerable effect on the institution of the screen, creating incidentally careers for a sprinkling of luminaries from Mary Fuller to Marion Davies.

Colonel Selig's motion picture enterprise had received inspirational impetus from the transient attentions of G. M. Anderson, who carried west from *The Great Train Robbery* the "story picture" idea.

Selig and Koenigsberg talked stories and story pictures.

"This film business is coming so fast that there is going to be a shortage of stories to photograph pretty soon," Selig observed. "We are going to be hard up for ideas." This was in 1905.

Now a plot jelled. Selig and his motion picture confrères, George K. Spoor of Essanay and George Kleine, determined upon a plan to pool a hundred thousand dollars to corner the world's market on film story rights. It was also planned that Koenigsberg was to become the editor of a magazine, from the cover of which he was to shoot the writing birds into the movie pot.

However, the interest of Spoor and Kleine waned. So Selig went ahead on an independent scheme in the same direction. He employed John Pribyl, of experience with Street & Smith's publishing house in New York, as his buyer of motion picture material from the field of literary production. Through Pribyl, Selig acquired the work of James Oliver Curwood, Rex Beach and many other contemporary writers of star fame. The books and stories acquired by Selig in this period for trivial sums proved in subsequent years assets of vital importance, when, under the adversity of new conditions in the motion picture field, Colonel Selig realized thousands from the resale of stories that had cost him hundreds in the days of his early foresight.

Koenigsberg, when the magazine plan faded, continued at his post with the *Chicago Evening American*. Destiny was saving him for a career as the impresario of the comic strip heroes, as the head of the Hearst syndicate enterprise which has given the public such figures as Harry Hershfield's *Abie the Agent*, and George McManus' *Jiggs*, the strongest competitors the motion picture had ever known. Incidentally and significantly, the strip comic is the newspaper's nearest approach to the presentation of a motion picture.

But Koenigsberg's part in the motion picture affairs had not ended with the sowing of the seed of certain developments ahead, nor had Chicago journalism even yet well begun with its influences on the screen.

In the ensuing years sporadic but related events developed to bring the screen and press together. Edgar B. Hatrick was assigned by R. A. Farrelly, of the Hearst wire news service, to take up the task of organizing the photographic departments of the Hearst papers into a world wide picture syndicate service. In the autumn of 1911 Hatrick began to cast interested eyes on the possibilities of covering the news in motion pictures. He purchased a film camera and tentatively tried making news pictures, offering them to the Pathé Weekly. The Pathé concern did not want to encourage so formidable a possibility of competition, so the plan failed—for the time.

But in another quarter destiny was at work. Edward A. McManus and Gardner Wood, in the year of 1912, were engaged in promoting circulation for *The Ladies World*, a McClure publication. Out of the editorial department came a project for a continued feature to be built about a mythical heroine to be known as Mary, and to be introduced with a cover design by Charles Dana Gibson. There was to be an unfinished story and a prize of $100 for the best answer to *What Happened to Mary?*

McManus was inspired with a notion for a tie-up with a motion picture, released each month, showing on the screen *What Happened to Mary?* The project was arranged with the Edison studios.

Mary Fuller was cast for the rôle. Miss Fuller had begun her film career in Vitagraph pictures in 1907 when Fred Thompson took her from the stage to play in *The Ugly Duckling*. She was now a full fledged Edison star.

In June, 1912, *The Ladies World* delicately paved the way with an article entitled *The Photoplay, an Entertainment and Occupation*, by Sarah Helen Starr. Since they were about to cooperate with the movies they had to make them appear respectable first.

The Escape from Bondage, chapter one of the series, was released July 26, 1912. The story was by Bannister Merwin. The title for the next month was *Alone in New York*. It was that kind of a story. Each installment of the *What Happened to Mary?* series was independent and complete. It was not a serial. The magazine stories and the screen releases did not synchronize accurately, but it was none the less a successful promotion.

Meanwhile the motion picture news idea was still simmering in the mind of Hatrick of the Hearst service. He made, independently, a one reel news picture of the inauguration of Woodrow Wilson at Washington, March 4, 1913. It was distributed to the screen trade by arrangement with Harry Warner of Warners Features, one of the antecedents of the Warner Brothers motion picture project of today. The inauguration picture made the Hearst picture service a profit of $2,000. Farrelly began to take notice. Hatrick renewed his campaign for a news reel.

At this juncture the Selig concern issued a two reel picture on *The Burial of the Battleship Maine.* It was distinctly a news picture. Hatrick suggested an alliance with Selig.

Farrelly, recalling Koenigsberg's acquaintance with Selig, wired him in Chicago to get in touch with the film man on the project. Koenigsberg, now no longer an editor, was a salesman of the Hearst wire news and syndicate services.

Meanwhile some other important movements had taken place in the Chicago newspaper field. The most significant of them was in the fact that Max Annenberg, circulation manager of the *Chicago Evening American* in the days of its bitterest struggles, had moved over to the *Chicago Tribune*, at great price. Annenberg is a true son of dynamic Chicago. He arose as a newsboy from the West Side melting-pot democracy of Maxwell street, under the tutelage of a Jesuit mission godfather, growing in grace and knowledge of the world, day by day. He is today in charge of the business and promotional affairs of *Liberty*, the weekly magazine off-spring of the *Chicago Tribune* and one of the several journalistic consequences of events in this chapter.

In 1912 the *Chicago Tribune* was still of the old line orthodox school of newspapers published for readers. But the new motif in Chicago journalism was having its effect, developing competitive moves, and a new xanthic coloration of the whole field.

The circulation rivalries between the seven Chicago newspapers had led to the organization of armed camps. A complex conflict raged. The wagon bosses who delivered papers to the stands and the newsboys became remarkably persuasive.

Picturesquely capable personalities appeared in the service of the circulation departments. Among these knights errant of the striving press were such striking figures as "Boston Tommy," Gus Gentleman, Mossie Enright, the Delahunty brothers, "Blue Eyed Bill" and "Herman the Huffy." They were, to a man, virile exponents of the Chicago spirit and full of the zeal of the robust journalism they served. They certainly sold the papers.

It may be that the pen is mightier than the sword, but the rotary press found great cooperation in the Colt automatic, the dirk, the blackjack and other shelf hardware.

Chicago newspaper plant equipment now began to include emergency hospitals, day and night surgeon service and a motorized legal department for police court appearances.

The *Chicago Tribune* acquired as its city editor Walter Howey, a reporter extraordinary, who in his round of adventures had received training in the dynamic office of the *Chicago American*. Annenberg and Howey spoke the same language.

James Keeley, who had long been an impressive figure in Chicago journalism, was losing his power as the publisher of the *Tribune* and as his star declined the volcanic treatment of the news favored by the Annenberg-Howey school began to color the paper.

Somewhere between Howey and Annenberg, probably with Howey, the conception of a motion picture and newspaper serial to run synchronously on the printed page and the screen was born. It was a stronger, more closely knit evolution of the *What Happened to Mary?* idea.

The path of propinquity led to the Selig Polyscope Company's office in Randolph street, and the background of the old Union Café round table discussions with Koenigsberg had prepared the way in the mind of Colonel Selig.

Out of this came the now famous title, *The Adventures of Kathlyn,* a genuine serial story, not a series, written by Harold MacGrath, author of much popular fiction of the super-romantic type, translated into a motion picture scenario by Gilson Willets of the Selig staff. The newspaper and the motion pictures were to appear simultaneously. The *Tribune* wanted to garner circulation from the nickelodeon audiences. It had grown to dignity and glory on appeal to the upper classes, now it was out to take volume off the bottom where the volume always is.

The motion picture serial took its title from the name of Kathlyn Williams, a member of the Selig company, known to the Hollywood colony of today as Mrs. Charles Eyton, wife of a production executive.

Miss Williams' career is a bright little cameo of success. She was reared in Butte, Montana, the city of mines and smelters. At about the time she was leaving high school she was thrown largely upon her own resources and, having a flair for dramatics, made her début on the local stage, subsequently appearing in stock company productions in various parts of the West. The abilities of the comely Miss Williams aroused the enthusiastic interest of Senator Clarke, the Montana copper king, who was instrumental in her taking a course of instruction at the famous Sargent Dramatic School in New York. From the Sargent School, Miss Williams stepped into an important part in the William Morris production of *When We Were Twenty-one.* After the New York run she went on the road with the play

MARY FULLER, famous star of the historic "What Happened
to Mary?" series, the Edison-McClure picture progenitors
of the serial era.

KATHLYN WILLIAMS, who gave her name to "The Adventures of Kathlyn," the Selig serial which marked the adoption of the motion picture as a weapon by the Tribune in Chicago's newspaper circulation war.

and, in the course of its Chicago engagement, she was seen and employed by Colonel Selig.

Things were coming fast for Colonel Selig. He was sitting in the seats of the mighty and holding partnership conferences with the two overlords of Chicago newspaperdom.

Came the day, as the title writers say, when Colonel Selig went down to New York to close the contract with the Hearst organization for the production of the Hearst-Selig Weekly, with the news negative gathered by the Hearst photographers and the motion picture production and distributed by the Selig Polyscope Company through the General Film Company, the great combine exchange system.

Moses Koenigsberg and Colonel Selig met to close the contract with a luncheon appointment at the Café des Beaux Arts.

"Now, I'm about to hook up with Hearst on this thing, and it reminds me that I have had a deal on with the *Tribune* about a serial," Selig opened. He described *The Adventures of Kathlyn* plan in detail.

Koenigsberg's face clouded with anger. Here was the original idea of the Union Café conferences of years ago getting away from him and, worse, being delivered into the camp of the opposition. Selig, oblivious, went on.

"Now," Selig continued, "Annenberg insists that I put up $20,000 for billboard advertising of the thing in Chicago."

This was the breaking straw of the negotiations in Selig's mind. The proposition was tossed on the table before Koenigsberg. Here was the chance to seize an opportunity and to deal a blow back, a surprise blow, at the old Chicago rivals.

Koenigsberg glanced at his watch.

"Can I have forty-eight hours on this?"

"Yes."

They proceeded to the closing of the Hearst-Selig newsreel contract.

When Koenigsberg laid that executed document before R. A. Farrelly, of the International News Service, he also unfolded the great serial opportunity in Chicago.

Farrelly was interested, but he had not been a part of the Chicago conflict. He did not have the same fire of interest. Koenigsberg wanted the idea put before William Randolph Hearst right away. Farrelly objected.

"No, not now. Of course he'll like the idea and he may take it and stop me on this news-reel thing. We have been working on this a long time."

Farrelly was pleading for his pet project. The serial proposal from Selig did not get to Hearst, and Selig went back to Chicago to make his peace with the *Tribune*.

On December 29, 1913, timed just to escape the Christmas distractions, *The Adventures of Kathlyn* flared out upon the world through the columns of the Chicago *Tribune* and newspapers to which the *Tribune* syndicated the story, and upon the motion picture screens served with Selig pictures through the General Film Company.

The picture proved a large success in the theatres. New circulation came to the *Chicago Tribune* in thousands. The *Tribune* picked up fifty thousand readers on *The Adventures of Kathlyn*, and held permanently about thirty-five thousand of them. The significance of this figure must be measured by the terms of circulation in the pre-war days. It represented nearly ten per cent of the total circulation of the paper. It was tremendous.

Naturally, down in the Hearst building at Madison and Market streets, there were reports, explanations, analyses, charts, conferences and cursings.

Andrew M. Lawrence, then publisher of the *Chicago Examiner*, the morning Hearst paper and the direct competitor of the *Tribune*, busied the leased wires in communicating to Hearst in

New York the terrible details of the great motion picture circulation outrage.

Annenberg was loose again!

Instructions went post-haste to Morrill Goddard, editor of the *American Sunday Magazine,* in New York, the Hearst Sunday color supplement, to get into this serial thing. Goddard drafted Edward A. McManus, who had the credentials of success from *What Happened to Mary?,* the Edison-McClure project.

About then the serial idea began to break out like smallpox in an Indian village in midwinter. Consider the dates.

January 31, 1914, Edison released the first chapter of *Dolly of the Dailies,* syndicated to sundry newspapers. The pictures starred Mary Fuller.

April 4, 1914, the Universal Film Manufacturing Company released the first installment of *Lucile Love,* starring Francis Ford and Grace Cunard, with the story syndicated by James Keeley's *Chicago Herald.*

April 11, 1914, the Eclectic Film Company announced *The Perils of Pauline,* with Pearl White in the title rôle and Paul Panzer and Crane Wilbur in the supporting cast, the story presented in the Hearst newspapers.

A new war had broken out. "Eclectic" was a corporation name out of Pathé's archives. Pathé had seceded and gone to war with the General Film Corporation because it had dared to accept the Hearst-Selig newsreel for distribution. Meanwhile Pathé was making the exploitation of a Hearst serial its first independent project in the fight with General Film. The institution of Hearst was thus astride two film horses, galloping off in opposite directions at high speed. He rode them both successfully.

The Hearst Selig news reel was edited by Ray L. Hall, a wire news service editor and the first newspaper man to edit news pictures for the screen.

While the *Kathlyn* picture had added circulation for the *Tribune*, the *Perils*, despite a screen success, failed to contribute to Hearst circulations, to the surprise of the promoters. The reason is clear. The conservative *Tribune* used the motion picture to reach into the emotion-hungry nickelodeon audiences. The vivid Hearst newspapers, Brisbaned and comic-stripped, already had that class of following and the motion picture could add nothing to their pulling power.

Meanwhile the *Chicago Tribune* was afire with serial enthusiasm. All through the days of *The Adventures of Kathlyn* plans were being made for a follow-up.

Joseph Medill Patterson and Robert R. McCormick, heirs and representatives of the family fortunes controlling the *Tribune*, began to discover interest and diversion of high degree in the conduct of the paper after Keeley left. Patterson, more sociologically than socially inclined, found a study in the manner in which this aggressive Annenberg extended the influences of his high tension circulation psychology beyond his department into the making of the newspaper wares he was selling. Here was a new sport, gunning for readers in the jungles of Chicago. The young masters of the *Chicago Tribune* joined in with enthusiasm.

All of which has a bearing on the train of developments which finds that same circulation fight expressed in terms of the *Tribune's* eastern by-product, *The Illustrated Daily News* and Hearst's picture paper *The Mirror* in New York, both still digging down into the masses for volume sales.

All through the days of *The Adventures of Kathlyn* the *Tribune* was casting about for a follow-up. Joseph Finn, of the impressive Nichols-Finn advertising agency, himself a graduate of the volcanic school of journalism, was called into conference. Paul R. Kuhn, of the Finn staff, a merchandising expert, went to work to take the serial business apart to see what made it tick, and how it could be made to tick louder. He found that the *Kathlyn* picture, successful as it was, had been only half sold to the theatres. *The Adventures of Kathlyn* circulated only twenty-four prints, due to restrictions imposed by the General Film Company. Kuhn's digest proved that a serial project could keep a hundred prints busy and reach many, many more theatres.

There were conferences and a decision to make a detective story serial. They did not know what the story was to be about, but the circulation formula called for certain sure fire elements; wealth, mystery, love and adventure. They decided on the title, *The Million Dollar Mystery*, and let the matter of the story go to be taken care of as routine.

Two weeks later Finn fell into a smoking car conversation on the Twentieth Century Limited with the stranger in the next chair. He proved to be full of motion picture information, and admitted presently that he was Lloyd Lonergan, scenario chief for the Thanhouser Film Corporation at New Rochelle. He introduced Charles Hite, president of the concern. When the train reached Chicago the trio went to the *Tribune* office.

Now came the Syndicate Film Corporation, floated through John M. Burnham & Company of Chicago, to finance *The Million Dollar Mystery*, to be made by Thanhouser and promoted as a newspaper feature by the *Tribune*.

James M. Sheldon, famous football star in the days of his glory at the University of Chicago, a friend of Burnham's, became president of the Syndicate concern.

At New Rochelle, Hite put the picture into production with a cast which included Florence LaBadie, Marguerite Snow and James Cruze.

This same Cruze, who is today the world's highest salaried director, at $6,000 a week in consequence of his fame as the maker of *The Covered Wagon* was then a member of the Thanhouser stock. He began his career as an entertainer with Billy Bank's medicine show in Utah and rose to the relative heights of the vaudeville stage. He was "resting" in New York in the summer of 1911 when a booking agent sent him to the Pathé studio in Bound Brook, N. J., to play a part in *A Boy of the Revolution*. At Thanhouser's studio Cruze rose to fame with the success of *The Million Dollar Mystery*. Then ill-health and misfortune overtook him and he fell into obscurity. After futile efforts to rehabilitate himself in the East, Cruze borrowed the fare to California from William Russell, a friend of Thanhouser days, and went trudging about the studios of Hollywood seeking work as an extra. He was unknown and progress came slowly, but *The Covered Wagon* came and with it fame anew.

The Lonergan scenario of the *Million Dollar Mystery* and the serial version for the *Tribune*, written by Harold MacGrath to the formula of riches and romance, progressed neck and neck under high pressure production. Meanwhile promotional plans new to the screen were under way.

On the staff of the Finn concern was a nonchalant, freehanded and deft-spoken copywriter who signed his name Jay Cairns, in spite of the fact that the newspaper world knew him as "Casey." J. Casey Cairns had come into Chicago through the main gate, which is to say the Chicago Union Stockyards, wearing curly chaps, musical spurs and a pair of six-guns, chaperoning a train-load of chuck steak on the hoof. The great open spaces behind him were getting full of wire fences and bleating sheep, whereas the field of Chicago journalism seemed to offer the very flower of the sort of excitement the range was losing. This led him to Finn and advertising and now to the motion pictures and New Rochelle as the first special production press agent.

Jay Cairns of Chicago registered at the Pepperday Inn, sent for a copy of the script on *The Million Dollar Mystery*, and retired for religious meditation. The shades of night were falling

Personalities of "The Million Dollar Mystery" company at the Thanhouser studios in 1914 — upper row, left to right — James Cruze, Florence LaBadie, Sidney Bracy, Lila Chester, Frank Farrington — lower row — Marguerite Snow, Harold McGrath, author, Lloyd Lonergan, scenario writer, and Charles J. Hite, president of the Thanhouser concern.

JAMES CRUZE, then an actor, and Jay ("Casey") Cairns, author of the great "missing heiress" hoax, in the days of the making of "The Million Dollar Mystery" at the Thanhouser studio in New Rochelle.

on the village when a very sober-faced, worried-looking young man with a western manner, presented himself at the New Rochelle police station and asked private audience with the officer in charge.

"A very serious thing has happened—Miss Florence Gray—millionaire's daughter, you know, has disappeared—millions involved, and we suspect there may be foul play. Hate to call you into it, but I know you'll be careful, etc., etc."

Cairns was reluctant and hesitated often. But under the pressure of police questioning he decided to give the officer a written statement on the affair, which he chanced to have with him. It was a neatly typed synopsis of the opening chapter of *The Million Dollar Mystery*. The names were those of the fictional characters.

It took the "missing story" fully an hour to reach Park Row, New York City, and ten minutes more to get all over the United States. It was an otherwise dull night for news. The story flowed freely over the leased wires.

In the *Chicago Tribune* office that night as usual, E. S. Beck, the managing editor, was shrewdly scanning the telegraph news proofs as they arrived wet from the composing room. The "missing heiress" story brought him up with a start. He sniffed. There was something slightly familiar about that story, but he could not place it. It had something of the odor of fish.

The *Chicago Tribune* did not carry the missing heiress story. Nearly every other newspaper in the United States did, including the Chicago Hearst papers down Madison street. And they continued to carry it, with developments locally discovered and meager facts wrung from the silent Cairns of the Pepperday Inn.

On the third day Cairns reluctantly parted with "the only photograph in existence" of the missing heiress. It bore a striking similarity to the publicity stills of Florence LaBadie issued by the Thanhouser company. The Hearst pictorial news service got a scoop on this picture.

The sixth day of the missing mystery the New Rochelle police called Cairns from the Pepperday Inn to receive tidings of immediate importance. They had a wire from John J. Halpin, the Chicago chief of detectives, announcing the apprehension of the missing heiress. The identification was positive and the girl was held pending shipping instructions.

On the seventh day the Finn-Tribune-Serial advertising campaign was launched in neat cohesion with the missing mystery of the newspapers.

The final realization of the facts did not tend to warm up any newspaper friendships on Madison street.

This was the first of the great film press agent hoaxes.

The Million Dollar Mystery swept through the motion picture theatres with a success without precedent or parallel. The twenty-three chapters of *The Mystery* played in about seven thousand motion picture theatres in a period when there were probably about eighteen thousand such houses.

Production costs of *The Mystery* were in the vicinity of $125,-000, and the gross receipts for the picture were nearly $1,500,000.

Even tragedy came to add to the golden flood. Charles Hite, the executive in charge of film production of the serial, was insured in favor of the Syndicate Film Corporation for $100,000. The night of August 22, 1914, driving a new eight cylinder motor car, he plunged through the railing of a Harlem river viaduct to his death.

The stockholders of the serial concern received 700 per cent on their investment. Promoters have been quoting that record ever since in florid prospectus literature on oil, film and ginseng projects.

A part of the *Chicago Tribune* promotional campaign in behalf of circulation and the serial included an offer of a prize of $10,000 for the winning suggestion for a sequel chapter of *The Million Dollar Mystery*. This was the most effective of several contemporary contests which made the United States a nation of scenario writers.

Miss Ida Damon, a St. Louis stenographer, submitted the winning sequel suggestion, a ten thousand dollar document of about one hundred words, typed on a yellow second sheet, torn in two.

But the complications of the sequel had only begun. The studio had thoughtfully made the "winning" sequel in New Rochelle some weeks before the winning idea was selected in Chicago.

Some uncooperative spirit, down Madison street, inspired inquiry into the contest by investigators for the United States Post Office. The *Chicago Tribune* and the United States of America voiced a unanimous demand that the sequel chapter follow Miss Damon's script. The letter of the law had to be followed. The *Tribune's* rivals were seeing to that.

The director of the picture was convinced of the superior dramatic merit of the sequel already made. Besides, Miss Damon had chosen to end the story amid the snows of Siberia and the weather reports indicated that in the current season New Rochelle might expect about one snow a century. The wires between Chicago and New York spit blue fire.

"It must be done."

"It can not be done."

"Do it anyway."

Fleeing the pressure of making hourly reports, Jay Cairns went to New York to appear before the Knickerbocker bar in the case of Manhattan vs. Martini. When he stepped off an early morning train at New Rochelle station he was overwhelmed with an impression that the entire landscape was white. How wonderful if true and how terrible and cruel if not! He felt of it and tasted it. It seemed to meet all tests. But with the caution of the true reporter he awaited confirmation. A milk wagon on its early rounds rattled past. Cairns overtook the wagon and interviewed the driver. The driver was unequivocal and emphatic in his opinion. It had been snowing, he firmly asserted, since midnight.

"Are you sure?" Cairns demanded. "This is very important to the World's Greatest Newspaper, two film corporations, and the United States Government, to say nothing of my many personal friends."

"Giddap," said the driver.

The sequel was shot at sunrise. Cairns directed.

Miss Damon was presented with her ten-thousand-dollar check on the stage of a St. Louis theatre, by the mayor, while the orchestra played *Hearts and Flowers* with muted strings—and then was promptly dismissed by her employers, the Certainteed Roofing Company, itself a national advertiser, because of the motion picture publicity involved.

To follow the large success of *The Million Dollar Mystery*, the *Tribune* conducted a new scenario contest with another $10,-000 prize. This vast serial was to be thirty installments long, sixty reels. The conditions were made simple enough to admit any contestant who could approximate a sentence. Just 19,-003 scenarios were submitted. The contest was all but closed with no possible material in sight when the last mail bag before the closing hour arrived. It contained a corpulent envelope strangely streaked with red barn paint. A despairing editor, who, incidentally, is the author of this history, seized upon it. The script within was from the volatile typewriter of Roy L. McCardell of New Rochelle, author of the Jarr Family, an interminable syndicate feature for the *New York World*.

McCardell's script was the only professional óffering in the contest. He had to win.

It is of interest to recall that McCardell back in the peep show picture era was among the first to contribute scripts to the American Mutoscope & Biograph company, for the making of its tiny tabloid comedies.   McCardell is thereby the author of both the shortest and the longest pictures in the world.

McCardell's story was titled *The Diamond from the Sky* and the script was sent to the American Film Manufacturing Company's studio in Santa Barbara.   The ambitious plans for the picture contemplated Mary Pickford for the leading rôle. Mary refused an offer of $4,000 a week, with far reaching consequences to be considered in another chapter.   Meanwhile the serial makers insisted on having the valued name of Pickford for their advertising, so Lottie Pickford, sister of Mary, was employed for the leading rôle.   Irving Cummings played the hero.

The Diamond from the Sky was directed by William Dean Tanner, also known as Taylor, the picturesque English adventurer who became the victim of the celebrated unsolved mystery of Hollywood in 1921.

CHAPTER SIXTY-SIX

PANCHITO VILLA SELLS A WAR

Pancho Villa, Mexico's "man on horseback," bandit, rebel patriot, was riding, silver spurred and merry with conquest and sin, at the head of his tatterdemalion legions on to Juarez.

The dream of glory that ever rides ahead of the "man on horseback" rode with the bold, brave Pancho, friend of the people, military heir-apparent to the kingdom of oil and gold and tobacco.

"Viva, Viva Panchito!"

It was a day of triumph, drunk with the ardor of the Mexican sun and—*aguardiente.*

With Villa rode Ortega and Rodriguez, he that was known as "the butcher." Natera and Monclovio Herrera were on the way. Wondrous names of romance, these, the lieutenants and compatriots of Pancho, the rebel chief.

Villa was winning and he would let the wide, wide world know. He was one with prince and potentates, this Alexander of the chaparral. Villa, like every military conqueror, was a dramatist. It was the physical excitement and emotion of war which lured him on. Modern wars are won by bookkeeping and the strategy of maps on flat-top desks. But Villa's generalship was of the feudal age, when valor was efficiency. Villa rode to battle and conquest because he loved the vision of himself on horseback.

And Villa ahorseback, in consequence of his propaganda of glory, became a figure of striking dramatic interest in the motion picture. Never of the slightest importance to the screen, he lighted it for a moment with the flare of his ambition. He did not, after all, tell the world of the glories of the great Pancho, but he tried.

The year of 1914 had just dawned when agents of Villa in El Paso on the border let it be known that the conquestador could be approached for the motion picture rights of his war.

The Kings of Babylon graved their conquest of the Hittites in tablets of stone. Trajan had his column, and Pancho Villa would inscribe his glories in the living shadows of the screen and let the theatre proscenium be his Arc de Triomphe. Meanwhile, in an immediately practical sense, pictures of the success of Villa would make Villa more powerful in taking tribute of those foreign interests which could use the friendship of any Mexican government whatsoever.

The El Paso representatives of a number of motion picture concerns sent wires away to their home offices in New York. New York home offices in the motion picture industry usually let telegrams from such inconsequential persons as El Paso branch exchange managers ripen on the desk. Fate, however, entered.

And Harry E. Aitken, president of the Mutual Film Corporation, read his mail and messages that morning. There was an appeal to the ever-glowing imagination of Aitken in this daring idea. Saturday, January 3, 1914, Frank M. Thayer, acting for the Mutual Film Corporation, signed a contract with Villa in Juarez, taking over the screen rights to the Villa version of the salvation of Mexico by torch and Mauser. It was agreed that Villa was to fight his battles as much by photographic daylight as possible. He was to share on a percentage basis on the earnings of his pictures. He received in hand paid, in most excellent gringo money, $25,000.

The story leaked by way of the bars and *keno* parlors of Juarez across the Rio Grande to the hotel bars of El Paso where the correspondents were covering the Mexican civil war in comfort.

The story clicked into the office of the *New York Times* at midnight within the week of the contract making, and at one o'clock in the morning a reporter got H. E. Aitken on the telephone at his apartment. Aitken was solemn, dignified and surprised, according to his statement quoted in the *Times*. It seems also that he was perturbed at having gone into a sort of partnership with Villa, the outlaw—this despite the fact that Aitken had been in the motion picture business several years.

The Villa story went around in the newspapers.

Villa delayed his projected attack on the city of Ojinaga until the Mutual could bring up its photographic artillery. When the cameras had consolidated their position the offensive swept forward and Ojinaga fell to Villa and film.

When the pictures reached New York they were found to contain too much Villa and not enough war. The films were shown in the Mutual Film Corporation's projection room to various officials. Francisco Madero, Sr., the aged father of the murdered president of Mexico, was in the audience that January 22, 1914, exiled from his home.

When the victorious Villa rode, close-up, through the streets of Ojinaga, a handsome young officer was at his side. The elder Madero leaped to his feet and shouted his name, "Raoul! Raoul!" The motion picture had discovered for him his missing son. Raoul Madero was now riding to vengeance for the family, in the rebel army.

Down through Mexico with Villa the Mutual's special camera cars traveled on the military trains, bearing to the peons the trademark message, "Mutual Movies Make Time Fly." Villa became one of the worst of that genus described in camera vernacular as a "lens louse." He had to be photographed riding at the head of a column every little while whether he needed it or not. Villa was not one of those controlled souls who can take it or leave it alone. This waste of film annoyed one

FLORENCE LaBADIE, who played with the old Biograph and
rose to greater fame in "The Million Dollar Mystery,"
greatest of the early serial successes.

SAMUEL L. ROTHAFEL, who began his motion picture career with a Saturday night show in a village hall and won his way to fame as the Broadway impresario of the screen.

HUGO RIESENFELD, who rose with Rothafel in Broadway picture presentations, and achieved independent distinction with his musical endeavors in support of the photoplay.

photographer into an expedient of cranking an empty machine. "I fooled the greaser that time—there's no film in the old box," he remarked to his assistant. He was overheard by a Mexican who understood Americanese. The cameraman was put over the border with a blessing and advice that afternoon.

It probably would have been pleasanter to Villa to have shot the cameraman, but Villa was interested in the film business now. Business forces many good men into compromises like that.

For the benefit of the films Villa staged an excellent shelling scene with a battery of light field guns. The picture went from close-ups of the guns to telephoto long shots of the hillside under fire, with bodies of men flying in the air after the shell bursts. The ugly rumor got about that the hillside had been planted with otherwise useless prisoners as properties.

But the evidence of the films is not to be accepted entirely for that. After the battle of Torreon it became apparent that the war needed a director and a scenario writer. H. E. Aitken discovered then what others have spent a great deal to learn since, that the best place to make war pictures is on the studio lot. Aitken went south, and on March 10 returned from Juarez with a new contract for the making of *The Life of Villa*, as per a good snappy New York scenario.

A staff was sent into Mexico to get the atmosphere, data and certain important scenes of Villa in action and close-ups to match-in on the continuity. Then the picture making of the Mexican war was transplanted to Los Angeles, where it could have the masterful supervision of D. W. Griffith. For screen purposes Griffith can make much better war than all of the generals from Cyrus to Foch. Real war is drab, sodden, bloody routine. The public wants ornamental, romantic war.

The Life of Villa did not live into any conspicuous success on the screen. It went on the shelf. Ownership of the negative fell into dispute and the picture vanished.

CHAPTER SIXTY-SEVEN

"ROXY" COMES TO BROADWAY

THE Strand theatre opened on Broadway, April 11, 1914, and the nickelodeon age of the screen was ended.

The motion picture had risen from the peep show novelty to the status of a vehicle of pretentious drama, and now stepped forth to contest the supremacy of the speaking stage on "The Great White Way."

In the history of the Strand theatre we may trace the lineage of the films, complete in every step. The Strand was the project of the late Mitchell Mark, who began at the beginning. When the first Edison kinetoscopes appeared in 1894 Mark was conducting a phonograph parlor in Buffalo, N. Y., under the name of "Edisonia Hall." It presented several scientific and electrical novelties, and was a dime museum of curiosities of the dawning era of electricity. Mark was really engaged in starring "The Wizard of Orange."

The daybook of the Kinetoscope Company records the shipment of a battery of peep show machines early in 1895 to Estelle B. Mark, Buffalo. And when, next year, the Armat-Edison Vitascope projector appeared Mark hastened to negotiate for "a screen machine." Then after a time the firm of Mark & Wagner opened a picture show arcade in New York's Fourteenth street, an avenue to fame for many of the motion picture's illustrious names.

The opening of the Strand by Mark completed, in his single career, the entire evolutionary progression from the Edison laboratory machine of 1889 to the grandiose modern screen period. Moe Mark, a brother, and the Mark-Strand theatres, carry on the tradition today.

Other pretentious efforts in showmanship with pictures had been made, but they were sporadic, occasional and remote. The Strand was definitely a part of the institution of the motion picture, and it signified its importance by boldly invading Broadway, the heart and stronghold of the art of speaking stage.

The coming of the Strand also marked the arrival on Broadway of a new genus of showman, the screen impresario.

This first and foremost of picture showmen, the new managing director of the new Strand theatre, had come a long and roundabout way to Broadway. It was late in December of 1908, far back in the nickelodeon age, when a foot-weary traveller turned into a tavern at Forest City, in the mining belt of Pennsylvania.

The wanderer laid down his sample kit—a handsomely bound prospectus of Stoddard's Lectures—and warmed himself by the big cannon ball stove. He got a whiff of hot wieners from the lunch counter.

The book agent was presently seated at a round-topped table, close to the wiener stand, entirely surrounded by steins. This was comfort. The more he regarded his sample kit the less he thought of it and better the beer and weiners seemed to be. Through a door that led to the tavern-keeper's quarters the young book agent caught a fleeting glimpse of a very comely young woman, the daughter of the household. The book agent was growing very fond of Forest City, Pa. He decided in his impetuous way to make it his home, at once. He stepped up with his most ingratiating manner of salesmanship and extended his hand to the proprietor who stood behind the bar. "I'm Sam Rothafel—how about a job?"

The voice with the smile won. Very shortly, Samuel Lionel Rothafel, late of the U. S. Marine Corps, late travelling representative of the latest edition of Stoddard Lectures, full morocco bound and indexed, appeared in a white apron, wielding the scraper that cut the foam off the tall schooners.

This is a perfect "success" story. He got the job and married the girl.

Upstairs was a dance hall that found little use. Rothafel had seen some motion pictures and had a notion Forest City might enjoy them. He got permission to make an experiment.

Just before New Year's Day, Forest City awoke to find the village billed for a show. The showcards were handpainted with effects by Rothafel, the presentation was by Rothafel, the projection was by Rothafel, the music was by Rothafel, the tickets were sold and taken up by Rothafel, the janitorship was by Rothafel and everything was fine except that the first half of the one reel show was upside down. It is interesting to note that this show included light effects from a crude switchboard, also by Rothafel, controlling the red, green and pink lamps that illuminated the screen at the opening and close of the show.

This was the beginning from which the elaborate modern art of motion picture presentation sprang.

Rothafel pursued a rising career as an exhibitor of pictures in the Middle West taking in Minneapolis, Milwaukee and other points. In 1913, the year before the advent of the Strand he was called to New York by Marcus Loew, who was now a chain theatre magnate.

While Rothafel sat in the reception room he overheard conversation. Loew was giving somebody pieces of his mind. Some of the large jagged chunks came over the transom.

Rothafel reached for his hat, and left. He has not gone back yet.

On the street, leaving the broken appointment, Rothafel ran into an offer which made him the director of the Regent theatre uptown in One Hundred and Sixteenth street, New York, where he remained until the Strand project appeared.

Rothafel is the chief exponent of the art of super-added appeal in motion picture presentation. His personal stamp is upon every outstanding motion picture theatre development in Broadway. He successively opened the Strand, the Rialto and the Rivoli, and was called in to swing the giant Capitol from an initial disappointment into a success. At the Capitol, Roxy's radio broadcasting made him a national figure. As this chapter is written an even more pretentious project, the Roxy theatre, entailing an investment of millions, is under construction in New York.

Rothafel opened the Strand with *The Spoilers*, a nine reel production of the story by Rex Beach, made by Selig. *The Spoilers*, first and best of the screen flowerings of the Alaskan saga, is one of the landmarks of screen history. Its success was extraordinary.

The original production of *The Spoilers* conferred fame upon its cast, which included William Farnum, Besse Eyton, Wheeler Oakman and Thomas Santchi. The terrific fight scene, a high point of the picture, made Farnum more famous on the screen than all his years of stage drama. It also set a fashion in screen fights and scenario construction.

The making of *The Spoilers* must be attributed in part to Rex Beach. Beach dealt often with John Pribyl, the literary buyer for Selig. They dickered over the story for months. Beach was being most canny. He demanded $2,500 for *The Spoilers*. It was an appalling figure. Pribyl and Selig were shocked. Authors were going to get expensive. Beach was firm and insistent. Presently they compromised and gave Beach a royalty arrangement. This brought Beach something close to a fortune for his story. It is the first instance in motion picture annals of a royalty arrangement with an author. It has remained as probably the only one that proved entirely satisfactory to the author.

In the years that followed *The Spoilers* lived three lives, being periodically reissued and resold to the states' rights market. In 1923 the story was remade by Jesse Hampton with Milton Sills in the role of *Roy Glenister*.

The Vitagraph theatre, which was the Criterion under temporary rechristening, opened a few weeks before the Strand, on February 27, 1914, and is frequently indicated as the inception of the modern screen theatre. It was, however, more accurately a personal symbol and high tide mark in the career of the Vitagraph trio.

Eighteen years before, Jimmy Blackton, cartoonist and feature writer on the *New York World,* went over to West Orange to interview Edison on the wonders of the Vitascope. Now Blackton, and Albert E. Smith, his prestidigitator friend from the lyceum halls, and "Pop" Rock, the billiard hall magnate from Harlem, were millionaires, with the name of their company in the white lights of Broadway.

The stage setting of the Vitagraph theatre was a replica of the drawing room window of Albert E. Smith's Riverside Drive mansion and the view of the Hudson unfolded there. J. Stuart Blackton made an address that opening night. "Pop" Rock took his pleasure in the audience.

Vitagraph was seeking to keep pace with the new feature movement of the motion pictures. The theatre was maintained for a time as a Broadway "first run" to add prestige to Vitagraph pictures. It was the first of the promotional presentations to influence the hinterland, which later came to make up the preponderance of Broadway screen shows.

For sheer geographical reasons there were two manifestations of the movement toward the big screen theatre which antedated the Strand, but because of their remoteness did not directly integrate themselves with the main current of motion picture evolution in the United States.

One of these early obtrusions of the bigger screen theatre-to-be was observable in California over the other side of the great plains and the Rocky Mountains. There under the tutelage of W. W. Hodkinson and his associate, Herman Wobber, there were pretentious theatre presentations of motion pictures before the screen began its occupation of Broadway. Sid Grauman of Los Angeles, an outstanding exhibitor of California, began his rise as a picture showman in this period.

A more sharply defined expression of independent development growing out of geographical isolation is afforded in the big theatres of Australia. They arrived four years before the Strand. Their story centers about J. D. Williams, who figures in many subsequent phases of screen history.

About twenty-four years ago Williams was the assistant treasurer of the Opera House in Parkersburg, West Virginia, which means he sold the tickets through the little window on nights when there was a show. The great novelty of the living pictures percolated to Parkersburg and made a traveling showman of Williams. He took to the road with a black tent and a one reel film of McKinley's funeral in 1902.

Williams followed the swallow, showing in the North in the summer and in the South in winter. The autumn of 1908 found him at the northern limit of his migrations in Vancouver, British Columbia. There Williams had a nickelodeon type theatre.

The great ships docked in Vancouver with their cargoes from the Orient and the South Seas. It was a terminal of Romance Road with romance at the far end.

Williams had been in one place quite a while. Also with the coming of the Patents Company, in '08, he saw that the free lance showman was shortly going to be considerably less free. Some sea-faring patron of his show left an Australian newspaper in his seat behind him.

Williams was curious about this land of Australia, where the natives threw boomerangs, leaves grew upside down on the trees and everything improbable was true. He idled through the discarded newspaper. An advertisement of a picture show way down there caught his eye. He stiffened up at the discovery that the admission was two shillings and sixpence, the equivalent of seventy-five cents in New York or six bits in Parkersburg.

Williams had the usual nickelodeon accumulation of old films and junk pictures on hand, a heritage of the days when every picture show bought its film outright. He went to Australia.

The remoteness of Australia from the rest of the civilized world made the canned entertainment of the motion picture popular for exactly the same reason that canned vegetables are popular in Alaska. The white Australians were a long way from home and the arts of their race. The art-canning process of the pictures served them wonderfully.

Williams prospered in Australia with his old pictures, which were new there. Then he got the current epics of the screen from the United States, like *The Great Train Robbery* and an Australian sensation in three reels entitled *The Kelly Gang*. Ned Kelly, the hero of this stupendous feature, was an outlaw hero of the Australian bush, partaking of the same glamorous fame as our own Jesse James, and Robin Hood.

By 1910 the geographical forces which gave the motion picture such special value in Australia had resulted in big picture theatres, the biggest in the world. Williams had the Britannia with 1,200 seats in Melbourne.

Traveling homeward Williams paused in California and established a contact with Hodkinson in 1914, thence on to New York in an effort to book Bosworth's *Sea Wolf* to the Strand. The far-away Australian development was threading itself back into the main fabric of the film institution via California. In three years more Williams was to figure in a major movement.

Almost simultaneously with the arrival of the screen theatre in 1914 the motion picture attained a new status of recognition in the press. The circulation-serial promotions covered in an earlier chapter had made the *Chicago Tribune* especially aware of the large public following of the films. The *Tribune* now established a motion picture review column, installing Jack Lawson, a rewrite man, as the critic. Lawson soon after was killed in an accident at the Chicago Press Club. He was succeeded as the *Tribune's* picture critic by Miss Audrie Alspaugh, who for circulation reasons signed her column "Kitty Kelly."

"Kitty Kelly" by reason of being the first independent motion picture critic attained a remarkable power over pictures in *Tribune* territory. For the first time in the history of the business the theatre men found a published judgment of the wares they bought, written by some one outside sycophancy of the trade press. Kitty Kelly could make or break a picture in the Middle West. Her judgments were excellent, but her taste was above that of the masses served by the screen. Her column was a large success, and she became the best disliked name in the world of the film makers. She was succeeded by Frances Smith, writing under the name of Mae Tinee.

The Chicago *Herald* quickly followed the *Tribune's* example and installed a photoplay department with Louella O. Parsons, previously a member of the Essanay scenario staff, as editor and critic. The new race of motion picture reviewers grew rapidly and in 1925 the list of newspaper film critics totaled four hundred.

James Oliver Spearing, whose competent criticisms of the motion picture published in the *New York Times* had earlier led to studio connections, became the first newspaper critic to achieve directorship. In 1925 Spearing was made a director by Carl Laemmle of Universal Pictures Corporation.

The rise of *Photoplay Magazine,* founding a new line of periodical publication based on the screen, started in this same

1914. The magazine began as a theatre program in 1912 and in two years attained a small circulation and a large printers' bill. Robert M. Eastman of the W. F. Hall Printing company, called James R. Quirk, a magazine editor with a newspaper background, to the rescue. *Photoplay* has attained a circulation of more than a half million, and nearly a score of motion picture publications have followed it into the field.

Photoplay was instrumental in bringing the directors of motion pictures to the public's attention. It published the first stories of Griffith, Ince, Sennett and their fellow craftsmen of the megaphone. Previously the public had heard of no one save the players. Quirk's editorial patronage also founded a school of writers about the screen, including notably Julian Johnson, now a supervisor of production for Famous Players, Randolph Bartlett, Allison Smith, Adele Rogers St. John, Frederick James Smith, Delight Evans and Agnes Smith.

An assignment from Quirk to the author for the writing of a series of articles on the history of the screen for *Photoplay Magazine* laid down the foundation for this history.

The constructive interest of J. Stuart Blackton of Vitagraph at the dawn of the feature picture era led to the founding of *Motion Picture Magazine* as an enterprise supported by the members of the Motion Picture Patents Company group, by a joint stock ownership. Eugene V. Brewster was employed as the first editor and, with the decline of the Trust components, he acquired ownership, subsequently developing a number of other screen periodicals.

Street & Smith, New York manufacturers of magazines, launched *Picture Play Magazine*, eventually piloted to success under the editorship of Charles Gatchell, a pictorially minded cartoonist deft with the printed word.

CHAPTER SIXTY-EIGHT

WASHINGTON, LONDON AND THE TAJ MAHAL

W<small>HEN</small> the World War erupted in August 1914 the motion picture industry, just emerging into a career on Broadway, was not even slightly shocked. The institution of the screen was not yet closely enough organized to have a responsive nervous system. The films were aware of the war only from minor, casual and incidental effects.

The United States was probably about 75 per cent of the motion picture industry of the world, and the picture makers of America were just beginning to develop their business within their own territorial boundaries.

Foreign export contracts, especially those with Teuton territories, were rapidly cancelled. The motion picture turned automatically to intensive development of the home field. And when Europe came to buy munitions the wage earners became temporarily rich and extravagant supporters of the proletarian art of the screen.

This condition resulted in giving the United States a practical monopoly in the development of the feature picture through the years of the war with consequences only now in 1925–26 becoming conspicuously apparent—with American pictures dominating the world market with an efficiency of about 90 per cent and England, Germany, France and Russia seeking to create or rehabilitate their screen industry, by subsidies, embargoes and the like.

August '14 passed without screen manifestations in America. In September an avalanche of titles came: *War is Hell, The*

Battling British, The Tyranny of the Mad Czar, The Last Volunteer, The Kaiser Challenges, The Great War of Europe, European Armies in Action, England's Menace, Germania, and the like. They were mostly just titles. The pictures were largely assemblies of scenes taken in military maneuvers and parades of the pre-war days.

Old pictures, anything with a military tinge, were resurrected from the film vaults, among them Lubin's *Battle of Shiloh, Under Fire in Mexico* and *The Strife Eternal,* a drama based on the ancient War of the Roses.

The Warlords of Europe had not yet discovered the screen as a propaganda agent. That was to come, but meanwhile military censorships swiftly blinded the cameras of Europe.

The first important, and importantly authentic, pictures of the war came through the absurd luck and enterprise of a newspaper photographer, with a series of adventures which takes us back again to Chicago.

Edwin F. Weigle, a news photographer, was in the service of the Chicago *Tribune* in 1913 when open and avowed war with Mexico appeared to impend. Weigle wanted to go to Mexico. He haunted the editors seeking assignment. The *Tribune* did not take either Mexico or Weigle that seriously, then.

However Weigle proved resourceful. He had a large diamond ring, considerably too large for a photographer. He parted company with the ring at the Sign of the Three Balls, and borrowed a motion picture camera from a friend, Harold Brown of the *Chicago Herald.* Weigle headed south. He was a film war correspondent out looking for his war to happen.

Chance found Weigle shipbound at Tampico while he was determinedly trying to get to Vera Cruz, on that special and particular day when the United States Marines landed on the text of an insult to the American flag. There was a bit of street skirmishing and shooting, with some casualties and one marine from Chicago killed. Weigle photographed the proceedings in his calm matter of fact way. The Mexicans shot off some of his buttons, but Weigle was not worried about buttons.

He had come to photograph a war and this seemed to be it.

Emissaries of the competition met Weigle's ship at the dock in New Orleans with large offers for his story and pictures, especially the pictures, but the only idea in his mind was to get to the *Tribune* office, 7 South Dearborn street, Chicago, Illinois, with his negatives.

Weigle prospered mightily with his pictures. He had left Chicago an obscure cameraman on a wild goose chase and he came home with fame, laurels and a scoop.

When, in 1914, things began to get a bit thick in Europe, Joseph Medill Patterson, one of the editor-owners of the *Tribune*, set sail for the continent, taking Weigle along. Eddie Weigle had become Mr. Weigle now. The stars were with Weigle again. He was in Antwerp when the city fell before the German advance. He made pictures in the streets between shell bursts and he set up his camera on the Dutch frontier, photographing the mad rout of the Belgian refugees pouring into Holland. War was his dish and he was there with a spoon.

When Weigle went to Europe the second time he went into Germany. He visited relatives in the Fatherland, living over the Rhine, and made sundry motion pictures of war activities. Meanwhile came one Donald Thompson, formerly of Topeka, Kansas, and a great deal of elsewhere, an adventurer of the camera. Thompson went into Europe for a Montreal newspaper and came back for the *Chicago Tribune*, bearing some pictures that he had made and a great many more that he had bought or otherwise acquired while in Germany.

From these sources the *Tribune* in Chicago accumulated a considerable supply of war negative.

The picture, entitled *The German Side of the War*, opened September 20, 1915, at the Forty-fourth Street theatre in New York. It was an opening with a bang. No attraction before or since has the record of such a sensation in so short a time. The lines awaiting the attention of the box office extended for four blocks.

The mad rush to the German war pictures was so impatiently tense that ticket scalpers, unable to renew their supply from the box office, went down the long lines selling strip soda checks to the unsuspecting.

It was the first chance that the German population of New York had to see anything on the screen that admitted there were two sides to the war.

It was also the last chance.

The high adventures of war photography fell to Merle LaVoy, a stalwart youth from the tall timber of Tower, Minnesota. LaVoy started early on trails of adventure. He ran away from home, with his pet dog, and got a job as dishwasher in a lumber camp.

The ill-tempered cook kicked the dog. LaVoy discussed the matter so earnestly that the cook had to be rescued from the swaying top of a tall spruce with a block-and-fall. The dishwasher was fired.

LaVoy swore to be done with a country where the doctrine of free speech did not permit verbal justice to a Swede cook. When he alighted he was in Alaska.

LaVoy packed freight over the passes and saved his money. A pal borrowed the money, and, departing for the States in haste, left LaVoy a kodak to cover the debt. The kodak made LaVoy a photographer.

About 1913, LaVoy went around the world as the photographic accompanist of Ben Boyce, publisher of a Chicago mail order journal. LaVoy had a strong back and great pictorial zeal. He lugged a forty pound panoramic camera through the Orient. It was a ridiculous burden, but important.

The big panoramic camera enabled LaVoy to make a genuinely remarkable photograph of the famous Taj Mahal. No such picture of the classic tomb had ever been made before, because no other photographer was foolish enough to carry such heavy optical artillery into the depths of India.

Now it chanced that in Chicago LaVoy had picked up a trivial job of photographing Thomas Riley Marshall of Indiana to make a little movie trailer used to promote a Chautuaqua circuit.

When LaVoy decided to look into the rumor of excitement in the European war, he put a print of the Taj Mahal masterpiece under his arm and went to call on Marshall. Marshall had, to be sure, forgotten LaVoy, but the Taj Mahal and conversation made them acquainted again. LaVoy left with a letter of introduction to the world in general signed by Thomas Riley Marshall, vice president.

LaVoy took a bunch of prints of the Taj Mahal, which had proven so good a talisman, and marched on Washington. With Marshall's letter he got to the secretary of Josephus Daniels, Secretary of the Navy. He sent the secretary to Daniels with his card, his compliments and a print of the Taj Mahal. Daniels ordered the picture framed, and dictated a letter for LaVoy.

LaVoy invaded the office of Lindley M. Garrison, Secretary of War, now with a letter from Marshall, a letter from Daniels —and another picture of the Taj Mahal. Mr. Garrison admired the Taj Mahal. He also gave LaVoy a letter "to whom it may concern."

Now LaVoy tightened his belt, unfurled another print of the Taj Mahal and headed for the White House. Here luck changed. The magic of the Taj Mahal could not prevail over the fact that Woodrow Wilson was at that moment most displeased because a young remote relative of the family was using a White House letter to promote a boxing club in London. In the circumstances, while he did think well the Taj Mahal, he could not give LaVoy a letter. May we not assume LaVoy had letters enough.

LaVoy went to the war, blandished and bullied Frenchmen, frolicked along the British line and pictured the muddy excitements of No Man's Land. He rode lorries, slept in dug-outs and ate canned willie. He got his pictures and went to London to take a bath.

In London our photo-adventurer from Tower strolled around for a look at No. 10 Downing street. He felt that a few close-ups at that door would help his picture materially.

The police got curious about LaVoy and he found it necessary to stand a Bobby on his eyebrow while talking the matter over. They locked LaVoy up for that.

In the middle of the night the jail resounded with an outburst of Brobdingnagian, not to say Rabelasian, song, memories of the lumber camp troubadours of the American Northwest. These were followed by songs of the Yukon and Alaskan ballads. LaVoy was just getting around to selections from his repertoire gleaned from the *bêche de mère* traders of Rarotonga when it was decided to release him and let London sleep.

LaVoy took up his stand at No. 10 Downing street again. On occasion he went back and forth to Paris.

Scotland Yard got interested. LaVoy was escorted by a number of very plain clothes men into the presence of Sir Basil Thompson.

A stenographer came alongside. Two grim detectives took their seats nearby, and the sentry at the door came to attention.

Sir Basil Thompson entered, took his seat and fixed LaVoy with a glittering eye,—as nearly as LaVoy could be fixed.

"We have been observing you, Mr. LaVoy—it's all up—now out with it—what's your game?"

Sir Basil turned over the reports which traced LaVoy's movements between London and Paris in infinite detail. It was a grim set of facts. Such sessions opening in the office of Scotland Yard sometimes concluded with a firing squad.

The stenographer sat with poised pen. Anything that LaVoy might say was to be used against him.

LaVoy was up against it, and at his ease.

"If it may please your Lordship," LaVoy replied in deep and insincere humility, "I am photographing the war—that's my game."

There was some discussion. Thompson was skeptical. LaVoy was sarcastic.

"Come now, my man, make a clean breast of it."

LaVoy reached into the inner pocket of his vest and produced in sequence three letters, "to whom it may concern," signed: Thomas Riley Marshall, vice president of the United States, Josephus Daniels, Secretary of the United States Navy, Lindley M. Garrison, Secretary of War, U. S. A.

While Sir Basil regarded the letters LaVoy started absent-mindedly humming "The Star Spangled Banner."

The dignified Sir Basil was convinced at last.

"You may go now."

"Not yet," replied LaVoy. "Now it's my turn. You've been a lot of trouble to me, and I have come all the way over to make some pictures to help England on the screen. It's time you were helping me."

LaVoy had a plan and plot. With the acquiescence, not to say coöperation, of Scotland Yard, he set up his camera behind a screen at a window close to No. 10 Downing Street and shot telephoto close-up of the comings and goings of the world's war time diplomats. He bagged Balfour, Asquith, Lloyd

George and many another. The luck of the Taj Mahal held after all. LaVoy's pictures went to the American Red Cross.

The Germans began, somewhat belatedly, to plan for motion picture propaganda in the United States. The American Correspondent Film Co., of Bridgeport, Conn., a newly organized concern, in August of 1915 admitted a propaganda arrangement with Austria and Germany. Some few pictures were brought into America and offered for release. They were clumsily photographed and more clumsily edited. They attained no circulation of importance. They did, however, bring the concern under the attention of Allied agents in New York, and after the United States had gone into the war, in May, 1918, Felix Malitz, president, and Gustave Engler, secretary of the company, were sentenced to prison on conviction of violation of divers and sundry war laws. Other more craftily engineered projects escaped official attention, but none of them were of any important service to the German cause.

The French, with plans for the exploitation of loans on the American money market, were early in the field with films of the Allied side of the war, and Britain followed rather closely. None of the war pictures of this period or later are of any particular significance to the student of the art of the motion picture. The war pictures were all glorified topicals, embodying no technique beyond that of the everyday news reel.

Allied and German propaganda met on the screen in Switzerland, which was, of course, thronged with the agents of every combatant and many of the neutrals. On a screen in Geneva the agents of the Allies first saw *The Cruise of the Moewe*, a veracious camera record of the captures and sinkings of that famous sea-wolf. For more than three years spies, diplomatic agents and secret service men sought a print of this amazing picture. It had been made by deliberate plan of the Germans for use in internal propaganda, to give their own people courage by the sight of German triumphs at sea.

The showing in Geneva proved to be a mistaken, unpopular confession of *Schrecklichkeit*. The film was hastily recalled and secreted.

Late in the spring of 1920 Ariel Varges, a cameraman for Hearst's International Newsreel, got a scent of the Moewe film in an obscure corner of a European capital. This Varges had demonstrated considerable facility at doing things. When Great Britain put a ban and a frown on all things Hearst because the Admiralty denial of the sinking of *H. M. S. Vindictive* was met by Hearst's publication of a photograph of the sinking, Varges eluded the restrictions by becoming a captain in the British army, detailed on photographic and intelligence work.

Now Captain Varges, resplendent in uniform and the best British manner, went after *The Sinking of the Moewe*. It was in the possession of a German secret agent. The agent had an inamorata, fair but approachable. She had another gallant friend who was a chauffeur, and the chauffeur, naturally, had several friends, all fair. Captain Varges bought a lot of wine and displayed gold money.

One day in May, 1920, the diplomatic pouch received at the British consulate in New York included a considerable package under seal of Captain Ariel Varges, addressed to Edgar B. Hatrick, general manager of the International Newsreel Corporation, 228 William Street, New York. *The Cruise of the Moewe* had arrived.

The more sensational portions of *The Cruise of the Moewe* were inserted in the Hearst news reels, and wasted on the picture market merely because they were not specially proclaimed. The motion picture trade does not know screen news.

Second only to the *Moewe* picture was *The Log of the U-35*, a German propaganda picture also for internal use. Back of that cruel and beautiful one-reel gem of motion picture art is a real life plot of novel dimensions.

Back in 1870, in the Franco-Prussian war, one Captain de la Perrier of the French army was taken prisoner by the Germans and carried away to a camp in upper Lorraine. When the war was over he had forgotten the lilies of France for a German fräulein. They were wed and lived happily ever after in Germany. A son was born to them. He was christened Armand de la Perrier, French enough to be true, but reared a German on German soil. When the Austrian submarines put to sea in the Mediterranean, young Lieutenant Armand de la Perrier was in command of Unterseebote 35.

One member of his staff was a motion picture cameraman equipped and assigned to a recording of the feats of the U-35. The magnificent and terrible record of war and destruction at sea, made under the direction of Lt. de la Perrier, is a screen memorial to this Franco-Prussian's artistry. The screen has seen no more capable handling of the pictorial possibilities of the sea. De la Perrier's log and his pictures show that he maneuvered for days to get an enemy sailing vessel under full canvas and satisfactorily backlighted. Then he sank her against the sun of the dawn, ensign flying at the forepeak as it settled into the sea, gilded by the streaming low angle light.

The Log of the U-35 also came into the hands of the Allies, some months after the signing of the Armistice. One copy went to London and from the war office into the film trade through Sir William Jury. Copies came to the United States. A conflict of ownership of rights arose and complicated distribution. But it was of no consequence. The war was over.

CHAPTER SIXTY-NINE

JACK JOHNSON'S FILM KNOCKOUT

W HEN John Arthur Johnson, otherwise Jack Johnson or "Lil' Artha'," knocked out Jim Jeffries at Reno, Nevada, on July 4, 1910, he also terminated the prize fight picture for the United States.

The prize ring, as indicated in earlier chapters, was the inspiration and subject matter of the first developmental steps of the screen art. Major Latham tried to build a projector to put prize fight pictures on the screen. Enoch J. Rector increased the scope of the camera to record long fight scenes. Biograph essayed the first photography under artificial lights to record a fight. Now the prize fight had served and it was done.

With the rising tide of censorships and a new sense of obligation to the public the established leaders of the motion picture were now considerably less interested in the ring.

The rights of the Johnson Jeffries fight, the last to be lawfully offered on the screen, were acquired for the General Film Company by George Kleine.

"We were not so excited about making the fight picture," observed Kleine, "but we did not want some of the Independents to get them and do a lot of exploiting that would have been harmful to the business."

The negotiations were completed by Kleine in a dressing room conference with Johnson who was then appearing at a Philadelphia theatre. The deal was considerably complicated by Johnson's earnest participation in a crap game throughout the session.

J. Stuart Blackton, accompanied by William T. Rock, of Vitagraph, took charge of the photographic work at ringside and sped back to New York with the films. Strong agitations were in the air at once. Canon William Sheafe Chase of Brooklyn urged that Mayor Gaynor should take steps aimed at revoking licenses of theatres showing the pictures. The Mayor failed to attend a special showing of the picture to which he was invited to Vitagraph. Theodore Roosevelt wrote a denunciation of the fight pictures for *The Outlook*, and announced he would advocate a law against fight films in every state where fights were forbidden.

The Johnson-Jeffries film was offered for states' rights sales. It was given its premier in New York at the Alhambra Theatre, Seventh Avenue and One Hundred and Twenty-fifth street, July 16, close to the "black belt." No real disturbances resulted but there were race riots as the result of other showings. The picture profits were quoted at $300,000.

Johnson's subsequent conduct and spectacular affairs in Chicago added velocity to the movement. Johnson opened a saloon known as the Café de Champion in Chicago's black and tan region, ornamenting it with sterling silver cuspidors. He also gained first page attention and more racial dislike by marrying Lucille Cameron, a white girl, with a wedding feast which Marquis James writing in the *Chicago Inter-Ocean* described as "an indescribable orgy."

July 31, 1912, Congress enacted the Sims bill, making interstate traffic in fight films unlawful. Officially that was the end of fight pictures so far as the regularly constituted motion picture business of the United States was concerned.

When Johnson went down to defeat before Jess Willard, July 4, 1915, in Havana, Cuba, cameras recorded the battle and the films went into the European and South American trade. The negatives were developed and printed in a small plant in Toronto, Ontario. About ten prints sufficed for the world market, but south of the border was the great forbidden field of the United States which then represented about nine times as great a market for the films as all the rest of the earth.

If in some manner the fight film laws could be evaded, avoided or nullified, a fortune was waiting. Millions wanted to see just how the "White Hope" vanquished the "Big Smoke." An effort to bring in the pictures was as inevitable as a fringe of rum ships on a dry coast. Months passed with minds busy on plans.

A scheme of amazing cleverness was evolved. A method was invented to import the picture without bringing in the film. An ingenious motion picture mechanician built a device by which the picture could be projected from the Canadian side of the boundary in light rays which crossed the border and were recorded on another film under the Stars and Stripes.

On April 5, 1916, a party of motion picture experts left an automobile by the road close to the Canadian-American boundary in Quebec. They carried film cans containing the negative of the Johnson-Willard fight. With the most painful care they labored through woods, swamps and streams for more than a mile to keep a quarter of a mile, at least, north of the soil of the United States. They made rendezvous with a party from the States at the international boundary stone one mile north of the Delaware & Hudson railway station at Rouses Point, New York, U. S. A.

A tent was set up over the stone with its northern stakes pegged into Canada and its southern exposure in the United States. Richard Parr, a U. S. customs service officer, entered the tent and made careful observation, by pre-arrangement. The Canadian squad handling the negative of the fight pictures gingerly moved about placing it in the machine with careful steps that they might not touch by so much as a fraction of an inch the forbidden soil of the United States, at any time that the film was in their hands. The negative when in place in the machine was just twelve inches, or one good English and American foot, from the land of the free and the home of the brave.

The blank raw stock for the positive was threaded in the receiving side of the machine on the sacred soil of upper New York state and the patriots started up the mechanism. The great Willard victory came across in terms of light and shade.

When the operations had been completed the machine was dismantled and the negative went back the swampy trail to the waiting motor car, without touching the United States.

No effort was made to conceal the remarkable expedient. On the contrary it was announced to the world. The promoters of the project felt entirely secure in their ingenuity.

The positive film which went through the machine on the American side was promptly taken in custody by the customs, and the picture men started a line of contention by which they expected to prove its legality for all practical purposes.

It was expected that it could be proven that there had been no violation of the statute in projecting the picture into New York state, and that by similar methods it could be at least apparently so transported across each state line as the various territorial rights were sold.

Immediately the facts began to get hazy. It is said that the film which went through the American side of the international machine was taken in custody at once by the customs officials and that it was never developed, leaving the success of the effort a mystery until this day. But at any rate there was a private showing of the picture, presumably as imported by projection, on April 15, 1916, at the laboratories of the Duplex Motion Picture Corporation, 178 Fulton street, New York.

A man alleged to have a large influence in important places in Washington entered into the affair. A plan was evolved by which the picture was to be very freely handled in the normal and usual manner with the projection-importation method used as a mere publicity blind, an alibi to be used in explaining things to the Department of Justice.

The price set upon this extraordinary service was, so the inside story goes, $200,000—payable in full in advance. The counter proposition was $1,000 a state, when and as successfully invaded by the picture. The differences over price broke up the deal.

The complicated affairs of the picture project involved a large number of men of widely varying degrees of standing. Although many were named openly and some were whispered about, the master manipulators of the scheme remained in complete obscurity, escaping all publicity and subsequent official attention. The picture did not get to the theatre screens.

An indictment under the federal statute, charging unlawful importation of fight films for exhibition purposes, was returned against a list of names of no major consequence in the affair. An array of lawyers including George Gordon Battle, and Abel I. Smith, former U. S. district attorney, appeared for the defense when the case went to hearing at Syracuse, N. Y. The jury disagreed, July 13, 1916 and the case was over. Nothing has been heard of the pictures since.

But some aspects of the old scenario of arrangements were due to assert themselves again.

When Tex Rickard staged the bout between Jack Dempsey and Georges Carpentier at Jersey City July 2, 1921, the motion picture camera was at ringside. Presumably the pictures were being made for export.

Some months later the Dempsey-Carpentier fight burst forth on the screen in many parts of the United States, in obvious defiance of the statute.

Rumor began to trickle through. In time the Brookhart-

Wheeler Senate committee began an investigation of the institution then unpopularly known as the Department of Justice in Washington. The fight picture and the arrangements pertaining to its exhibition became a part of the complex aftermath of the Teapot Dome revelations.

It appears that there was a very special and private showing of the picture at Edward B. McLean's "little green house" with an audience of high officials. The testimony threaded the scenario of arrangements through the operations of Jess Smith, the same who killed himself in Harry Daugherty's apartment after occupying an unofficial desk in the Attorney General's office. Jap Muma who appeared to appertain to the McLean staff through newspaper connections was also mentioned.

Once again the identical figures of the old Johnson-Willard picture affair appeared—$200,000 general overhead, and $1,000 a state.

The wide newspaper publicity resulting was necessarily followed by prosecution. On March 30, 1925, Judge Bodine, in federal court at Newark, imposed a fine of $7,000 each on Tex Rickard, Jap Muma and Fred C. Quimby, a motion picture man concerned with the distribution of the fight films. There were lesser fines for lesser figures. Some appeals were filed.

It is significant to observe that the prize fight picture affair was not really a concern of the institution of the screen. The illicit fight picture promotions have been the projects of outside opportunists only incidentally using the film.

CHAPTER SEVENTY

BARA AND THE VAMPIRE

THE arrival of the long feature dramas produced a critical problem in the film affairs of William Fox. In spirit and fact an Independent, he had, by force of courts and politics, compelled the trust to supply him with film, letting him compete with the combine's General Film Company. The other Independents meanwhile waged patent wars, made their own films and rose with the feature pictures.

Now by 1913 Fox with his legal clutch on the short program films of the trust, found himself in the position of a man with a pass on a train that was not going anywhere. General Film was near the end of the line. Its trivial one reel pictures belonged to the nickelodeon age. Fox had both a film distribution business and a growing chain of large theatres to safeguard.

In the season of 1913–14 Fox announced the Box Office Attractions Company as a national distributor and advertised that he would purchase feature film negatives.

The first pictures thus acquired came from the studios of the Balboa Amusement Production Company, which had taken over the then abandoned Edison studios at Long Beach, California. This project was under the administration of H. M. and E. D. Horkheimer. Balboa pursued an adventurous career of picture making with many kinks in the prosperity curve. The high mark of Balboa attainment is immortalized in the episode of a day when the sheriff came with a writ of attachment in behalf of a creditors' judgment.

This was, by all signs and tokens, the end. But the urbane

and agile minded Horkheimers were going to be cordial gentlemen to the last. They invited the sheriff and his deputy to have a look about the plant and enjoy the novel sights of a studio before the fatal papers were served. Within the hour the sheriff and his deputy were at work in flatteringly heroic rôles before the camera. The papers were delayed until the crisis could be met, and Balboa was temporarily saved.

William Fox soon found that freelance production was not an adequate source of supply for a safe business structure. He was confronted with the necessity for making pictures, and turned to J. Gordon Edwards, who since 1910 had been in charge of the staging and stock plays for Fox at the old Academy of Music in Fourteenth street. Edwards was sent on a tour of Europe to study film production.

Edwards came thus to the threshold of the motion picture from a long stage experience. He was born in Montreal and educated at a military academy for a career in the British army. He went to England to a rifle match and came away with the conviction that officering in the British army was a rich man's pastime, not a career. Edwards was in an uncertain state about his future, when an idle hour spent in St. Lawrence Hall regarding paintings of famous actors, Booth, Irving, Barrett and their like, filled him with ambition for the stage.

Inspired by the pictures on the wall of St. Lawrence Hall, Edwards headed for New York and Broadway to carry the situation by direct assault. He got small parts with Harry Corson Clark, then better parts with Nat Goodwin. In time Edwards became a stage director.

As the producing manager of the Suburban Garden Theater in St. Louis Edwards became the sponsor of a daring policy of big stars for the summer shows. There he engaged Amelia Bingham, Wilton Lackaye, Cissie Loftus, James K. Hackett, Edmund Breese and Mabel Taliaferro. Edwards was on the road, playing Des Moines with Amelia Bingham one winter season, when Miss Marguerite Clark, then with DeWolf Hopper in musical comedy, visited backstage at a matinee and was engaged for the Suburban Garden summer shows. This was Miss Clark's first effort in drama, and led eventually to an engagement with Edwards at the Academy of Music where she was discovered and engaged by Famous Players.

Now Edwards was having his look around in Europe before the big plunge into picture production. In Copenhagen he engaged Betty Nansen, already famous in the United States for her work in imported pictures. He sailed just as the World War began. When he arrived in New York he was the supervising director of Fox pictures.

The first Fox production effort was *Life's Shop Window*, made on Staten Island under the direction of Henry Belmar at a cost of $4,500. It starred Claire Whitney and Stuart Holmes.

A weighty gathering of officials gathered for the screening in the projection room of the Box Office Attractions Company. The picture ran in silence. When it was off the audience turned and waited for Fox to speak. He was smoking fiercely, evidently laying down a screen.

"Let's burn the damn thing."

Edwards called for help and Winfield Sheehan came to the rescue.

"No, let's run it."

To the amazement of all hands *Life's Shop Window* became a hit. Edwards cheered up and the Box Office Attractions Company took on some new directors, including Frank Powell and Edgar Lewis.

Early in the busy producing schedule came *A Fool There Was*. Fox acquired the screen rights to the stage play, which had been evolved from Kipling's poem, *The Vampire*, which in turn had been inspired by a painting by Burne-Jones. Thus

was the interesting cycle of the idea, from the dead art of painting to the new living art of the photoplay, completed.

The direction of *A Fool There Was* fell to Frank Powell, a
graduate of Biograph. Powell had recently completed *The
Stain*, written by Forrest Halsey, for Pathé.

While Powell was making *The Stain* one Miss Theodosia
Goodman, of some stage experience under the name of De Coppett, applied for a part. Powell was impressed. The next day
he took her with the company to work in exteriors at the Petit
Trianon, Lake Ronkonkomo, Long Island. Powell pondered
deeply. He put her into the background away from the camera.
He did not want her recognized and classified as a mere extra.

When the casting of *A Fool There Was* began, Valeska Suratt,
Madeline Traverse and Virginia Pearson, all of whom later ap-
peared in Fox pictures, were considered for the vampire rôle.
Powell demurred and presented the unknown Miss De Coppett.
He evolved for her the name Theda Bara under which she was to
attain world fame, "Theda" being an obvious contraction of
Theodosia, while "Bara" was derived from a relative's name
of Barranger.

A Fool There Was became a box office hit of January 1915.
Theda Bara was made famous overnight. This success, true to
rule, ordained a career of screen vampiring for the demure
and circumspect Miss Goodman.

Thus began the building of the great Bara myth. Plotters
and compounders of iniquitous publicity fictions appeared in
the persons of Johnny Goldfrap and Al Selig, press agents.
Selig had been a confrère of Winfield Sheehan, now the Fox
general manager, in reporter days on the New York *World*.

Immediately Miss Goodman began to acquire a most amazing
atmospheric past. Conscienceless typewriters plied the motion
picture columns of the press with the announcement that Theda
Bara was the daughter of a French artist and an Arabian mis-

THEDA BARA in the pose and role of the *Vampire* in "A Fool There Was," with which the William Fox studio gave the screen a new type and the language a new verb.

tress, born on the sands of the Sahara. "Bara" was indeed a mere cypher, being Arab spelled backwards. That proved the rest of the story. "Theda" was just a rearrangement of the letters of "death." This deadly Arab girl was a crystal gazing seeress of profoundly occult powers, wicked as fresh red paint and poisonous as dried spiders. The stronger the copy grew the more it was printed. Little girls read it and swallowed their gum with excitement.

Bara spent days at the Underwood & Underwood studios, posing with skulls and crossbones, glass balls, and all the trademarks of Oriental desert mysticism.

The motion picture public went to the theater to see about all this promisingly snaky stuff and found that the effect on the screen was up to the advance notices. Theda Bara of the screen, working her willowy way with men, became the vicarious and shadowy realization of several million variously suppressed desires.

When Bara made her first trip to the Fox California studios there was a publicity pause in Chicago. Major M. L. C. Funkhouser, Chicago film censor, declined to meet Miss Bara.

The press agent arranged for the photoplay critics of the Chicago press to meet Bara at the Blackstone. She received in a darkened parlor draped with black and red, in the tone of her sweeping gown. She was white, languid and painfully polite. The air was heavy with tuberoses and incense.

The staging worked magic. The interviews were in hushed tones, and the results were columns. When the door closed on the last caller the windows went up.

"Give me air!" commanded Bara.

Bara wove her way through no less than forty pictures in her three years with the Fox concern. Which means more than one picture a month.

Within a few months of her first screen appearances the

"vamp" became an all too common noun and in less than a year it was a highly active verb, transitive and intransitive.

This verb may prove to be the only permanent contribution of the Fox-Theda barrage to the world.

In about the same proportion as the Theda Bara pictures made money at the box office they made trouble with the censors, then a rapidly increasing official race.

The early period of Fox pictures was strongly colored by the famous-players-in-famous-plays idea. Among the Fox stars of the time were Edmund Breese, Dorothy Donnelly, Wilton Lackaye and Bertha Kalich. William Farnum, with the glory of his success in Selig's *The Spoilers*, to top his stage fame, went to Fox pictures at $1,000 a week and rose to $10,000 a week.

A considerable share of the fame of Fox pictures grew out of the internal drama and resultant publicity relating to the production of *The Daughter of the Gods* with Annette Kellerman under the direction of Herbert Brenon, one of the motion picture's most spectacular and volatile personalities. He subsequently came to a second fling of fame for the making of a picture from J. M. Barrie's *Peter Pan* with Betty Bronson for Famous Players.

Brenon was born in London, son of a journalist. He arrived in New York on the merry fourth of July, 1896, and located in Pittsburgh. He dabbled in real estate selling, and in one meager period presided at a bargain counter retailing socks. In Johnstown, the city made famous by a washout, Brenon operated a nickelodeon theatre until competition took the profits away and he left for New York and the vaudeville stage. In the early period of Laemmle's Imp company he found employment as a scenario writer, and became a director.

One of Brenon's pictorial penchants is the filming of mermaids and sea-water fantasies. His last important work for the Imp was in the making of *Neptune's Daughter*, from a script by

Captain Leslie Peacock, with Annette Kellerman. The cast included Leah Baird, William Welch and William Shay.

When Brenon went to the Fox organization he had another moist story with him, *The Daughter of the Gods.* He pleaded and persuaded Fox into undertaking its production and sailed for Jamaica with a large company, including Miss Kellerman, cast for the title rôle. Brenon plunged in with tremendous energy and remodelled that end of Jamaica. He drained and restored an old Spanish fortification, Fort Augusta at Kingston, at a cost of $100,000. He built a Moorish city, a city of gnomes, and a great tower for the heroine's dive into the sea. He imported twenty camels for five minutes work at a cost of $7,000. It was spectacle picture making with a splash.

Brenon was charming publicity material. William Fox began to feel that he was being overshadowed in print. Then Fred B. Warren, publicity agent, formerly of the *St. Louis Star* and other journals, met the situation with an able news release entitled *King by Cable.* This related how Fox personally directed every inch of the picture, using the Western Union for his megaphone.

When the miles of negative were finally landed in New York and the picture was, as he thought, done, Brenon resigned. Fox was deeply unhappy about the picture. He considered it something less than a total loss. It was time to call a doctor. He recalled what he considered good editorial work on *The Honor System*, a picture made at his Western studios. The main title credited the editing to one H. G. Baker. Fox wired to have Mr. Baker sent on to New York. He was much surprised when H. G. Baker walked in, in the person of Miss Hettie Grey Baker, who became editor-in-chief of the Fox productions.

When Herbert Brenon learned of the re-editing of his picture, and heard that Fox had decided to leave him out of the credits on the film and advertising, the war started. The first move was an injunction suit, in which the application was denied in the New York supreme court August 25, 1916. Brenon contended unsuccessfully that his verbal contract had assumed full publicity credit. The hearing was ornamented with the exhibit of a letter, which Brenon said he received from Fox in Jamaica, reading:

> "Believe me, dear Herbert, I pray for you every night before I close my eyes, that God will spare you so that I will be able to be so proud of you, because I can just imagine how great a man you will be when this picture is assembled and shown throughout the world. . . ."

It is a reasonable presumption that if William Fox was doing any praying about *The Daughter of the Gods* it was with reference to the cost sheets.

Meanwhile, when he found that he did not legally have to give Brenon credit for the picture Fox decided to do it.

When arrangements for the premiere at the Lyric were made instructions were issued not to give Brenon an invitation and by way of special precaution guards were employed to keep him out.

William Fox was in the lobby that night of October 17, 1916, when one of his confidential employees approached with the news that Brenon was in the house.

The house was searched. They found Brenon, wearing a lovely set of false whiskers, in the best seat in the house, middle of the orchestra, on the aisle. Brenon stayed, and presumably enjoyed himself.

After the Brenon controversy, directors began to be cautious about credit clauses in their contracts.

Subsequently, when Brenon went to the Selznick organization to direct *War Brides*, Fox won an injunction preventing his use of any reference to *The Daughter of the Gods* or other Fox pictures on his letterhead. Also, the Fox Film Corporation proceeded to produce a picture entitled *The War Bride's Secret.* Brenon sought an injunction against the title and lost.

Fox spectacle picture making reached its high point in J. Gordon Edwards' *The Queen of Sheba,* which completely revealed Betty Blythe to the screen and made her a star. Edwards established himself as a creative historian by presenting King Solomon without a beard, on the ground that "no motion picture audience would stand for Sheba falling in love with a set of whiskers."

Edwards had eminent precedent for his decision. Years before Sigmund Lubin in Philadelphia cut General Grant out of a John Ince Civil War drama to be rid of a set of whiskers.

Here we see the confidence of two mighty influences, George Eastman's Film and King C. Gillette's safety razor reacting upon the institution of art. Verily not even the whiskers of Solomon may stand in the path of culture's triumphal march onward and upward.

CHAPTER SEVENTY-ONE

$104,000 FOR MARY

THAT $4,000 a week offer to Mary Pickford to star in *The Diamond from the Sky* serial, one of the incidental resultants of the Chicago newspaper circulation war, was the source of reactions which upset the motion picture industry in general—and Adolph Zukor in particular.

The week of November 21, 1914, was a highly anxious time for the head of Famous Players.

Zukor had been paying Miss Pickford $1,000 a week, and now this wild Chicago *Tribune-Mutual* serial project was offering to quadruple her salary.

Zukor went on his long, lone walks again, thinking it out.

The serial offer meant $208,000 a year, and they were ready with $50,000 to pay down when the contract should be signed.

Zukor's experience had shown him that Mary Pickford's pictures were the essence of his project. He gave up the bidding game and went to persuasive talking—the coming glory of Famous Players, the elevation of the screen and the like. On November 28 he announced a contract with Miss Pickford for the coming year at a salary of $104,000.

Famous Players was saved on that day and date. The fame of all the other famous players was nothing unless it was supported by Mary Pickford. She was the one player really famous to the motion picture exhibitors and their public.

The terms of the contract with Miss Pickford were given out rather freely. This was done for a most studied purpose. Adolph Zukor was not from the beginning merely a garrulous publicity seeker.

It seems that Miss Pickford was to appear in not less than

eight or more than twelve pictures in the coming year. Famous Players was to pay all the wardrobe required, from shoes to dresses. Mary was to have a voice in passing on the plays to be filmed.

The wardrobe details were thrown in for decoration. The essential fact to be borne thus gently into the mind of the exhibitors was that a well defined limit in the quantity of film from this premier star had been established.

It was announced also that Mary had been over-ruled in a demand for a clause in her contract providing that "all Pickford features must be sold at double the customary prices and that an exhibitor showing them must charge double admissions." This was paving the way for something, too.

Conditions had markedly changed from the time only five years before when Mary appeared in one reel a week, and sometimes more. Remember that only six years before she was just a little girl from a stock company walking down Fourteenth street looking for a job.

Gladys Smith of Toronto, and Adolph, the furrier's apprentice from Hungary, were getting along in the world.

Meanwhile the Famous Players exploitation of Mary sent Biograph and the Imp Company into the mothballs looking up the old one reel negatives in which she appeared. Re-issues of the early Pickfords came flooding on to the market, to the considerable annoyance of Adolph Zukor.

The little exhibitor in the nickelodeon storeshow with a vintage one reeler could fling a banner to the public gaze announcing "Mary Pickford—Today—5c."

This did not fit in with Zukor's plans for getting back his $104,000 and a margin. Caustic comments issued in the trade press.

Carl Laemmle, of the Universal, owner of the Imp's Pickford pictures, was moved to issue a defensive statement concerning his re-issues, saying that "instead of trying to mislead the exhibitors into thinking that his were the new pictures, he has taken pains to impress on the exhibitors that they were re-issues."

In 1923, to protect herself against various lines of re-issued pictures of other days, Miss Pickford purchased a large number of old negatives, including all of the Pickford-Biographs, for which she paid $10,000.

The follow-up to Zukor's announcement about Mary's high priced contract came from W. W. Hodkinson, head of the Paramount concern distributing Zukor's picture. On February 6, 1915, Paramount issued an announcement, saying that: "Owing to the enormous salary which it has been necessary to pay Miss Pickford in order to secure her services, all future releases will be first released to big city theatres charging a minimum price of twenty-five cents." This plan was also announced for the pretentious *Eternal City* made in Rome with Pauline Frederick.

The next week Zukor started something more significant than conspicuous. It was softly announced that the Waybroad Film Company, Adolph Zukor, president, had leased the Broadway theatre from Stanley V. Mastbaum of Philadelphia. The Broadway was located some two blocks up the way from the Metropolitan Opera House. So it was inevitable that the new policy of the theatre was announced to make it "the home of the grand opera of motion pictures."

Zukor there started his theatre control campaign which has been the focal activity of the motion picture business for the last decade.

Stanley V. Mastbaum of Philadelphia was the head of the Stanley Company of that city, which grew out of the purchase of theatres owned by Sigmund Lubin. The Stanley circuit, earliest of the important theatre chains, became a demonstration of the power of combination and a pattern to endless development of chain theatre combines to come. It continues under the ministrations of Jules Mastbaum.

The high price of Pickford put Zukor into picture exhibition on Broadway. He wanted to set a pace for the nation and give his pictures the glamour of "The Great White Way."

The announcement of Pickford's large salary went rippling through the studios and gave every aspiring player an itch to be mentioned in the big figures.

Players sought exaggerated salaries and gave out exaggerated reports of what they did get. In turn competitors began to announce bigger and bigger salaries, regardless of fact, to make their plays and players seem as important as Mary Pickford and her pictures. They started in thousands and got to millions in about two years.

Now the public began to acquire its impression of the motion picture as an institution of unlimited wealth and glorious extravagance. See what Mary did!

With the motion picture reaching up ambitiously toward higher admission prices and better theatres, there was an inevitable stirring among the commercial chieftains of the speaking stage. The Lasky deal for the production of Belasco plays was announced the last week in November of 1914, and was followed by some highly glorified interviews with Belasco on art, the stage and the screen. The Lasky company announced the engagement of Blanche Sweet, who had attained star status under Griffith at Biograph, and Edna Goodrich of stage fame as one of the beauties of the original "Floradora" company and one of the prettiest wives that the late Nat Goodwin ever lost.

Zukor's announcement of his Broadway theatre as "the home of the grand opera of motion picture" brought a swift reaction from the Lasky company. Through Morris Gest, negotiations

—711—

were opened with Geraldine Farrar, Metropolitan opera star. There appears to have been some rivalry—Famous Players was negotiating too.

Farrar, it was intimated, might prefer to make a trip to California and the Lasky studio, rather than to work at Famous Players in New York—if she were properly entertained.

Jesse Lasky and his then brother-in-law, Samuel, then Goldfish, met Farrar under the soft light of her drawing-room and were promptly swept into a contract. It stipulated three pictures, *Carmen, Maria Rosa* and *Temptation,* to be done in eight weeks, for a salary of $20,000, house, servants, groceries and motor car in Hollywood—and a special car for the rail journeys.

A terrific blast of publicity followed this announcement. Figured in terms of space rates it was a million dollar move for both Farrar and the Lasky company. Farrar was interviewed on everything from art to toothpicks while the motion picture was rediscovered by several imposing national magazines. The film folks who had started to lunch at Delmonico's began to speak of her as "Jerry" in their democratic sort of way.

Also, by striking coincidence, William Fox prepared for the production of a version of *Carmen* with Theda Bara.

As an earlier phase of the theatrical invasion of the screen, the Shubert theatrical interests and the World Special Films Corporation entered into a coalition June, 1914. In September Brady's plays were to be produced with original casts in so far as possible.

In February, 1915, the World Special Films concern became the World Film Corporation headed by Arthur Spiegel of Spiegel, May, Stern & Company, a mail order house. His motion picture activities were financed through Laddenberg Thalman & Co. The roster of financial houses with a finger in the picture business was beginning to grow. Lewis J. Selznick began to blossom in the trade press under the imposing title of vice president and general manager of the World. When in September of the autumn before, the Peerless company, a producer for World release, announced the acquisition of Clara Kimball Young, the Vitagraph star, emphatic notice was served that credit should be given to Lewis J. Selznick. Selznick was building hopes and laying plans.

Yet another sequence of realignments brought a new concern of note into the field. Al Lichtman, who had left Famous Players as one of the sequels of the formation of Paramount, had in 1914 formed the Alco Film Corporation. The Alco plan was to tie up with leading theatres in key cities. It was a forerunner of the idea expressed in the subsequent formation of the First National Exhibitors Circuit. Lichtman was backed in the Alco project by William Sievers of St. Louis, an exhibitor. Richard Rowland and James B. Clark of Pittsburgh, who had earlier sold out to the trust's General Film, were continuing in business as independents, now with an interest in Alco. They presented *Tillie's Punctured Romance*, the Sennett-Dressler-Chaplin feature comedy, and *Michael Strogoff* with Jacob Adler, *The Ragged Earl* with Andrew Mack, and introduced Olga Petrova, then a vaudeville artist, to the screen in *The Vampire*. The latter pictures were produced by Harry Cohen, first operator of the first nickelodeon in Pittsburgh, and George Cook of the Cook Lithograph Company, incorporated as Popular Plays and Players, a direct simulation of the Famous Players idea. Alco led a short and stormy life under the presidency of Walter Hoff Seeley, who flitted petrel-like through many film companies, promotions and publishing projects. Alco died in litigation.

Now Richard Rowland and the associated exchangemen found themselves without a film company. They had built the spokes of a distributing machine around the Alco hub and now the hub was gone. Late in January, 1915, they met in Parlor B of the Hotel Claridge to talk about it, and Metro Pictures Corporation, named after the Metro Lithograph Company, resulted. Richard Rowland became Metro's president, Joseph Engel, treasurer, and Louis B. Mayer of Boston, secretary. Petrova became their first star. Not long after they re-introduced Juliet Shelby to the films, this time as Mary Miles Minter. She received her eminent "M's" from Metro.

CHAPTER SEVENTY-TWO

TRIANGLE, FAIRBANKS AND RIESENFELD

THE issue between the costly new feature drama, personified by Mary Pickford, and the old nickelodeon type short picture of the program grind, typified by the "Broncho Billy" one reelers, was now in 1915 to be fought out in internecine strife in both the Mutual Film Corporation, oldest of the Independent federations and in the older Patents Company-General Film group, the Trust. Both Mutual and General were destined to suffer secession of their progressive elements—while the old guard lingered to a slow fade-out.

To the historian it is a moment of dramatic import. Here was the breaking of the chain of corporation lineages that began with the Kinetoscope Company of 1894, with a single peep show parlor in Broadway, and ran in continuous succession to the Trust and 1915, with 17,000 screen theatres in America—twenty eventful years of evolution. Now Fighting Jeremiah J. Kennedy, the steam-roller boss of the Trust, had retired with a fortune to Brooklyn and golf. The old dynasty was nearing the end because the men, minds and mechanisms of the pioneer period were weary and stretched to their elastic limit. They could not progress.

This breaking of the chain was precisely indicated in a conversation which took place in the office of Kalem, one of the Trust's producers. Frank Marion was talking to William Wright, general manager.

"This business is going into these long pictures. They tie up a lot of money and you have to take a chance. We will keep

—715—

Kalem going as long as the short pictures last, and then we'll quit."

Kalem started, a full-blown producer, in 1907 on $400 cash capital. Now in 1915 Mary Pickford's salary with Famous Players was $104,000 a year.

Kalem did quit. But some of the more hopeful of the old guard joined in a new endeavor. A combine of Vitagraph, Lubin, Selig, and Essanay was incorporated in New York April 13, 1915, known thereafter as "V. L. S. E." It distributed features made by its members, who also continued to contribute short pictures to the old General program. V. L. S. E. was a confession that the Trust had been "busted" by sheer growth of the art. It was also something of an anticipation of the decision in the case of the U. S. vs. the Motion Picture Patents Company on October 15, 1915, which commanded them to desist from their "unlawful acts."

The exact moment of the passing of the old order was three years ahead of that particular day and hour in 1918 in the Edison studios when Alan Crosland, directing *The Unbeliever*, a six reel drama, signalled "cut" to the camera man. The lights died on the last scene, and the stage hands came to strike the set. It was thirty-one years since Edison's dream in 1887 of "a machine which should do for the eye what the photograph did for the ear." Now the dust is drifted deep on the Edison stage in the abandoned studio in the Bronx and the only sound is the rowdy chatter of sparrows entering through broken panes to build their nests.

When in June, 1919, the last annual meeting of the General Film Company was held in the office of J. J. Kennedy at 52 Broadway the stockholders were not on speaking terms. Their interests were elsewhere and competitive. The old corporation which had brought them millions needed a loan of $20,000. It was refused. General died without enough friends to bury it.

The Motion Picture Patents Company, parent of the General, came to the end of its active career on April 9, 1917, when the United States Supreme Court in the case of the Patents Company vs. The Universal Film Manufacturing Company held that the patents combine could not enforce the use of licensed film on patented projectors in the theatres. Old Major Latham's "loop" was the patent concerned. That was the end of the wars Edison started May 13, 1898, in his suit against the Mutoscope.

In 1925 the Patents Company was still alive, consisting of a brass name plate at 65 Fifth avenue and a correspondence file in the office of H. N. Marvin. The Patents Company can not die until it settles its last suit—a litigation to collect an assessment on members for past litigation costs. The old warrior trust leans on a rusty sword.

The schism in Mutual, paralleling General's split, was marked with more action and excitement. Early in 1915 John R. Freuler and Samuel S. Hutchinson owners of the American Film Company, both Mutual stockholders, went on a European sightseeing excursion.

H. E. Aitken, president of the Mutual, was instituting a feature picture department under the brand name of "Master Pictures." This was apparently related to the fact that as the Griffith superman myth grew, the yes-men of his organization began to reverentially refer to him in hallowing tones as "The Master."

Now Freuler and Hutchinson's American Film Company studio had made and shipped a feature entitled *The Quest*, starring Marguerita Fischer, wife of Harry Pollard, director.

When the American's chiefs returned from Europe they

found that Aitken had left *The Quest* on the shelf. Meanwhile the Reliance-Majestic, Griffith and Ince features were going to the market.

It was Aitken's assertion that *The Quest* was not really a "Master Picture," or more simply that it was not up to standard.

Freuler and Hutchinson could not forget that Aitken was interested in those other features, the simon pure "Master Pictures" by the Master.

Action was had. *The Quest* was released. Also the American's advertising, spiritually governed by Joseph Finn of Chicago, began to designate Samuel Sheffield Hutchison as "The Master Producer."

Meanwhile Freuler went to converse with the Wall Street interests of the Mutual group. At the ensuing annual election on May 1915 Freuler was elected president to succeed Aitken. He brought in John Cecil Graham as general manager, the same J. C. Graham who has more recently represented the Zukor interests in acquiring domination of the British film world with results affecting world politics and trade. Freuler also acquired the services of Dennis J. Sullivan, previously of the sales board of the American Tobacco Company.

Aitken was chagrined and pleased. He was free to follow a new idea. He withdrew the Reliance-Majestic pictures, which meant Griffith, from Mutual, while his friends Kessel and Bauman withdrew the products of the N. Y. M. P. and Keystone, meaning Ince and Sennett.

After sundry financial conferences in New York, Aitken went mysteriously west. At La Junta, Colorado, out in the sheep and sugar beet belt, he dropped off the train. On July 20 at La Junta Aitken met with Griffith, Ince and Sennett in the Harvey house parlor and closed agreements on a new deal.

The Triangle Film Corporation, with Griffith, Ince and Sennett as the apexes, was announced with a fanfare of trumpets.

It commanded attention as a sensation by declaring for movies at two dollars a seat. This daring drew wide publicity attention.

Before long Triangle stock went on the curb and began to climb most profitably. The motion picture had at last joined up with American industry and the manipulation of the market. It was by this move "big business."

In Los Angeles the New York Motion Picture plant became the Fine Arts studio and D. W. Griffith began to outline a new line of productions for Triangle release.

This brought another influx of names. Triangle announced stars in imposing array: William Collier, De Wolf Hopper, Raymond Hitchcock, Sam Bernard, Eddie Foy, Weber & Fields, Dustin Farnum, Frank Keenan, Willard Mack, Forrest Winant, Henry Woodruff, Louise Dresser, Billie Burke, Mary Boland, Julia Dean, Sir Herbert Tree, Bessie Barriscale, Louise Glaum, William Desmond and W. S. Hart. There was still the powerful coloration of that famous players idea, the borrowing from the stage. Aitken had been watching Zukor.

Of all this array the most important, as the box office was to prove, was William S. Hart, who became, by reason of his own romantic interest, the screen's good-bad-man of the ornamentally Wild West. Pinto Ben, a docile pony, and Hart became famous together. Hart was of the stage. His last important appearance on the boards was in *The Trail of the Lonesome Pine* in 1913. He went to his old friend Ince in California to work in the pictures at $75 a week in 1914 and appeared in a two reeler entitled *Two Gun Hicks*, written by C. Gardner Sullivan. Hart began to attract attention with his later appearance in *On the Night Stage*, a Mutual Master picture, directed by Reginald Barker. Thirteen feature pictures made Hart world famous, and so prosperous that in 1922 he said he had to quit work to save income tax expenses.

While Griffith was busy in California the Triangle chiefs continued their scouting in New York. At the Knickerbocker grill, Adam and Charles Kessel and C. O. Bauman at lunch spied Douglas Fairbanks, then a Broadway stage star, at an adjacent table. They drew him into conversation and a contract with Triangle-Fine Arts. This was, they thought, a considerable stroke. Fairbanks had been sought for pictures before, when Daniel Frohman decoyed him into the Famous Players studio just to look around. Famous Players made a scene with Fairbanks then, a bit of action at a card table, in the hope of interesting him in the pictures. But this plan had come to nothing.

Fairbanks started West and Griffith got a wire to prepare for his coming with a story.

Griffith had plenty to do and no great enthusiasm at the prospective addition of this new player, to him somewhat unknown. While Fairbanks sped across the country toward Los Angeles, Griffith called a hurried council of Frank Woods and Mary O'Connor of his scenario department, and there evolved a plot entitled *The Lamb*. It appeared on screen titles accredited to "Granville Warwick," the name under which Griffith's story conceptions went to the public.

Signe Auen, whose name has since been metamorphosed into "Seena Owen," appeared opposite Fairbanks in *The Lamb*. Miss Auen had newly entered pictures as a result of a chance meeting with Marshall Neilan. Miss Auen had known the able Neilan when,—which is to say, when he was driving a motor car for Colonel I. N. Peyton, a Los Angeles magnate summering at Lake Coeur d' Alene in Idaho, where she, then a Seattle belle, appeared as a guest. When she next saw Neilan they met on the streets of Los Angeles. He was a director, presiding over Ruth Roland's screen performances, and Miss Auen was looking for a professional engagement. Neilan sent her to Griffith.

WILLIAM S. HART, first and most famous of the good-bad-men
of the screen, the classic exponent of the storybook Wild
West.

ANITA LOOS, first to make screen titles an art and the founder
of the film profession of "wise-cracking."

"Too cold for an actress," Griffith remarked bluntly, as he regarded the calm Scandanavian blonde.

"Then I'm an actress," she retorted, "because I'm trembling inside right now."

"You are engaged," replied Griffith. A year ahead he was to cast this cold lady for the fervid rôle of the *Princess Beloved* at Belshazzar's feast in *Intolerance*.

The Fairbanks beginning with Griffith, initiated with *The Lamb*, was most inauspicious. Griffith was not pleased with the new star's athletic tendencies. Fairbanks seemed to have a notion that in a motion picture one had to keep eternally in motion, and he frequently jumped the fence or climbed a church at unexpected moments not prescribed by the script. Griffith advised him to go into Keystone comedies.

The organization acquired John Emerson, actor and stage director, late of Charles Frohman, Inc. Emerson had made two screen appearances, the first one for Famous Players in the screen version of *The Conspiracy*, in which he had starred on the stage. He now took a motion picture assignment on condition he could range at will and study the works. In the scenario and editing department he found a considerable interest in the work of the petite Anita Loos.

"It seems," observed Emerson, reading a Loos script, "that you buy the kid's clever lines in the scenario and then throw them away. Why not put them on the screen?"

Clever titles did not mean a great deal to Griffith. He thought entirely in terms of pictorial action and it was not consistent with his view to build situations by action which were going to deliver their punches in titles.

Fairbanks, the player Griffith did not admire, Emerson the novitiate director and Anita Loos the writer of bright words, were pushed off together as a unit to work out their own destiny.

It meant fame for the three of them and the foundation of an improved technique of screen story telling. The Griffith development of action now picked up a lot of Loos words. The business of making wise-cracks became a new motion picture profession, and the photoplay became more completely a hybridization of the picture and the printed word.

Katharine Hilliker, a San Francisco and New York newspaper writer, built upon this technique in the jazz titling of educational and scenic pictures for C. L. Chester, and gave a new impetus to subjects of the sort. The screening of sheer beauty then came into vogue through the labors of Robert Bruce, cameraman producer, and Clyde E. Elliott, producer of Post Pictures. As the scenic market waned Miss Hilliker transferred her attention to the drama, and with her husband, Captain Harry Caldwell, translated the German *DuBarry* into *Passion*—the picture which made Pola Negri an American star.

It is evident that Fairbanks, starting at Triangle with his deep rooted notion that movies should move, has contributed importantly to screen technology. In an article in *Vanity Fair* of December, 1925, Fairbanks wrote:

> The art of the screen is almost purely emotional,—as a painting, an opera, or a church service is emotional. Without sacrificing this most important value, it can not teach, philosophize, too much, or, in short attempt to address itself, as words do, to the thought processes.

It is fitting to record here that in the offices of Thomas A. Edison, inventor of the motion picture, for many years there has hung a framed legend reading:

THERE IS NO EXPEDIENT TO WHICH A MAN WILL NOT RESORT TO AVOID THE REAL LABOR OF THINKING
—Sir Joshua Reynolds.

Edison has devoted his life to machines intended to make thinking unnecessary for the masses. Fairbanks is devoting his to pictures calculated to keep their minds off the fact they do not think.

The Triangle Film Corporation made good its advertising threat of two-dollar-a-seat pictures, with the opening of the Knickerbocker theater as its Broadway house. The night of September 23, 1915, all the motion picture personages of New York turned out to see what had been brought forth. The opening bill included Douglas Fairbanks' first screen appearance in *The Lamb*. The showing included the first Thomas Ince Triangle picture, *The Iron Strain*, with Dustin Farnum and Enid Markey, and *My Valet*, with Raymond Hitchcock.

It was the most ornate opening that Samuel L. Rothafel, now lured away from the Strand theater, could execute. Hugo Riesenfeld, directing the orchestra that night, began his motion picture career, which made him the managing director of the Rialto, Rivoli and Criterion theaters in Broadway for several years.

Riesenfeld's story begins in Vienna, considerably spangled with highlights and shadows. His musical career opened with a disappointment. When a child violinist with ambitions, he was taken to a famous Vienna instructor.

"You have no chance," the great man said, "because your little finger is too short for the violin."

Riesenfeld invested years of practice, training that abbreviated finger, and, marvel of marvels, it grew. The youngster became something of a protégé of the famous Strauss of Vienna, and in time rose to the position of concert master at the Vienna opera house.

Gustav Mahler, master of the Vienna opera, being a musician

and a whimsical one, observed with annoyance that this able young violinist was always smiling. It made Mahler peevish, then angry. It wore on him, while Riesenfeld kept smiling through. One day the explosion came. Mahler fired Riesenfeld and the smile.

Riesenfeld sought America, the land of promise. It did not seem to fulfill the promises very rapidly. He paced the board-walk at Atlantic City and wondered whether to starve or jump into the surf. Then a wisp of a chance came. A booking agent sent word he would hear Riesenfeld play. A young woman went along to play the piano accompaniment. Her playing was weak and thin, because of her nervous tension over this moment so important to Riesenfeld. To cover the shortcomings of the piano as much as might be Riesenfeld played his mightiest with the violin, "double stopping" for a wealth of tone.

He knew he had done well, and hoped the weakness of the piano might be overlooked. It was, entirely. Word came the next day that the agent had an engagement for the wonderful pianist. For the time being, he added, there was no prospect for the violinist.

But there came a turn in the tide, and Riesenfeld appeared as the concert master for Oscar Hammerstein at the Manhattan opera house.

From the Knickerbocker engagement for Triangle, Riesenfeld went with Rothafel to the new Rialto.

Riesenfeld's methods of interpretative musical treatment of the photoplay are to be counted a distinct contribution to the art of the motion picture theatre, extending a wide influence. Men trained in his organization have carried the technique far afield, among them Nat Finston who became the musical director of the Chicago Theatre, head of the big Balaban & Katz chain in the Middle West, and Erno Rapee with recent triumphs in Berlin.

An element of sheer whimsy entered into Rothafel's choice of Riesenfeld for musical director at the Rialto. Rothafel is certainly not superstitious, but he is just naturally fond of the letter R. Rothafel's ardent R's have rippled through all his theatres and their personnel: Rothafel, Riesenfeld, Regent, Rialto, Rivoli, Joe LaRose, Rapee, Ramsaye, and the radio—not to mention his interest in racing and romance. If it has an R in it, it is his oyster. There are also letters that Roxy does not like. His name was Rothapfel when he left the Rivoli and Rialto, but it was Rothafel when he reached the Capitol.

For a number of years Riesenfeld was known to Broadway as "Dr." Hugo Riesenfeld, which was a by-product of Rothafel showmanship. Firmin Schwinnen, an organist who enjoyed an array of degrees, including a Ph.D., appeared in the house program of the Rivoli with it on view, contrasting slightly with the unadorned name of Hugo Riesenfeld, listed as the musical director. This appeared disproportionate and displeasing to Rothafel. He was not moved to take away Schwinnen's doctorial honors, but upon discovering that Riesenfeld had been educated at the University of Paris he immediately conferred a doctor's degree upon him and ordered it into the house program and all publicity utterances.

This resulted in embarrassments to Dr. Riesenfeld when he was from time to time consulted on questions of personal health by stage hands and visiting picture stars.

CHAPTER SEVENTY-THREE

HENRY FORD ANSWERS A WAR CRY

ALTHOUGH the motion picture industry had been too busy to pay much attention to it, the World War had been in progress a year when the autumn of 1915 arrived.

But the pressure of political and economic events operating to draw America closer to the struggle began to make an impress. The first motion picture recognition that it might be America's war, too, came with Commodore J. Stuart Blackton's swift enthusiasm over Hudson Maxim's war inspired book *Defenseless America*.

Blackton read the book one night and dashed off a letter to Maxim asking for the motion picture rights and enclosing a check as first payment as material evidence of his earnestness.

Under the title of *The Battle Cry of Peace* the picture was pretentiously produced and duly presented in September, 1915, at the Vitagraph Theater in Broadway. The picture starred Norma Talmadge and Charles Richman. It was a preparedness preachment which won warm endorsement from the belligerently minded, most conspicuously from Colonel Theodore Roosevelt, then having a bully time with the Plattsburg training camp. National exploitation of the picture began.

Out in Detroit on November 18, 19 and 20 of this 1915, Henry Ford was listening to the pleas and representations of Rosika Schwimmer with reference to a large opening to sell some peace in Europe. Louis P. Lochner and the Peace Ship were in the offing.

Just when Ford had begun to put his mind on peace, December 1, 1915, Detroit was bombed by an airplane, laden with advertising matter for *The Battle Cry of Peace*. This was no time to litter up Ford's front yard with heralds on a war movie. He was positively annoyed. He promised to look into the matter and give it sincere attention, later. He was busy on the blue prints of a plan to get the boys out of the trenches by Christmas.

April 12, 1916, the *New York World* and other important newspapers all over the country carried a full page proclamation by Ford charging that *The Battle Cry of Peace* was plain propaganda for the professional war merchants and munitions makers. Ford delivered his broadside at Maxim's book and Blackton's picture quite impartially. He pointed out that Maxim munitions corporation stock was on the market.

After the always-to-be-expected exchange of denials and charges in the columns of the newspapers, the Vitagraph filed a damage suit against Henry Ford for just one round million dollars.

Ford was served with the papers in the lobby of the Biltmore Hotel as he was leaving for Detroit on the afternoon of August 21, 1916. A few legal motions were made and the suit was forgotten.

Screen gossip relates that a certain extra man cast as member of the mob in *The Battle Cry of Peace* under the name of Leber Bronstein, address the Bronx, was really one Leon Trotzky, a rambling journalist of slightly radical opinions, later of prominence in Russian politics. A Hollywood cameraman carries clips of film alleged to present the distant face of this "Leber Bronstein." Trotzky has not included this episode in writings about himself.

Out in California Thomas H. Ince of Triangle with characteristic shrewdness, was studying the pulse of the box office and the motion picture public's reaction to *The Battle Cry of Peace* and war propaganda. Ince decided there was a market for the other side of the situation.

Civilization, in which Ince presented an indictment of war, painted with a big brush, opened at the Criterion theatre June 2, 1916. It was in tune with the anti-war sentiment of the country.

The opening was made a signal event, calculated to start a wave of emotion. A first-class feature story for the newspapers was created when Billie Burke fainted in the audience, overcome with the thrill and suspense of the picture. Presumably the fact that Miss Burke had been working in a picture for Ince-Triangle release was not connected with this episode. Wild acclaim broke from the first night audience and Al Woods pulled the reluctant Ince on to the stage to take a bow and make a speech. The *New York Times* commented that Ince was refreshingly modest. Ince was a capable actor.

This was the year of the second Wilson campaign. Students of the political situation, including William Cochrane, press representative of the Democratic National Committee, averred that *Civilization* with its delineation of the horrors of war was a large influence in the Wilson victory at the polls. It put pictorial meaning into the slogan "He Kept Us out of War" on which Wilson was re-elected.

But *Civilization* was not made as propaganda for Wilson. It was made to make money, which it did abundantly. It was advertised as a million dollar spectacle. It cost approximately $100,000 and returned Ince $800,000.

A long record of such effective business attainments on the screen won for Ince a reputation among the critics of the motion picture for being utterly commercial and with only the genius of the commonplace. In 1924 Ince produced a screen version of Eugene O'Neill's *Anna Christie,* a vehicle neither commonplace nor "movie" in character. He sent it to the market without unusual promotion and awaited results. The critics acclaimed the screen *Anna Christie* as a triumph of art. Despite this acclaim the picture did not hit the box office stride of the typical Ince output.

Months later, Colvin Brown, vice president and New York representative of the Ince organization, looked up from the reports in surprise to announce to Ince that *"Anna Christie* may net fifty thousand."

Ince responded with a gesture of indifference.

"I wouldn't care if it lost a hundred thousand," he said. "I made that one for the highbrow critics—they say Tom Ince can't make anything but box-office movies."

The autumn of *Civilization's* success saw the last of the great serial picture projects. The Randolph Film Corporation was formed in Chicago, with George Kleine as the film component and the now standardized *Chicago Tribune* tie-up for syndication of the story. The new serial was projected to outshine every previous effort of the kind. The biggest available star was to be engaged. Many were considered and none chosen. It was a momentous and perplexing matter.

Still star hunting, Max Annenberg, the *Tribune's* circulation manager, came to New York. One night in Times Square he met his friend Florenz Ziegfeld, of the Follies. They strolled up Broadway together and turned into the Ansonia to continue the chat in Ziegfeld's suite.

While Ziegfeld was looking for the glasses, or something, Annenberg strolled about admiring the drawing room. On the grand piano was a most imposing framed platinum print photograph of Billie Burke, who was and is also Mrs. Ziegfeld.

When Ziegfeld returned the negotiating began. Billie Burke was on tour in the west. If pressed her manager, being also her husband, would in his managerial capacity communicate the offer which reached the interesting figure of $150,000 for thirty weeks' work in the films.

Mr. Ziegfeld finally prevailed on Mrs. Ziegfeld and was rewarded with a fee of $25,000. The entire sum of Miss Burke's salary was put up in advance with the Astor Trust Company in New York.

Rupert Hughes, a stellar writer of fiction for the *Red Book* magazine under Ray Long's editorship, was employed to write the story under the patrician title of *Gloria's Romance*, also for $25,000. All motion picture serials, before and after, have had dime novel titles. This was to be most de-luxely different.

The picture went into production on a lavish scale with real mahogany panelling in the sets and many ornamental details.

The Kleine selling forces amazed the industry with $850,000 in pre-release bookings. The picture went out with a flourish —and, in show parlance, "flopped." The great serial days were over with the passing of the nickelodeon age and the dominance of neighborhood theatres. The Ford car was making the movie goers nomadic amusement shoppers. Serial publication for screen or printed page is for the regular subscribers. The movie public now began to buy its shows like news-stand wares.

In 1919 a quartette of brave conspirators met to form the Supreme Pictures Corporation to rehabilitate the status of the serial with a master effort in mystery and detective story thrills. It was to be a million dollar corporation, etc. In electing officers they decided to leave the presidency to the toss of a coin.

Louis Grossman, the business man of the party, flipped a quarter in the air. It struck the desk and rolled off on the floor.

Then the august directors of that million dollar corporation spent a half hour on hands and knees searching for the missing twenty-five cents.

The baffled searching party included John W. Grey, mystery scenario writer, Arthur B. Reeve, author of complex detective tales, and—Harry Houdini.

The corporation has faded and the quarter is still missing.

Douglas Fairbanks distinguished among the great of the screen as the one actor who has made a career instead of having it happen to him — as he appeared in "The Black Pirate."

CHARLES CHAPLIN and
JOHN R. FREULER,
president of the Mutual
Film Corporation, pho-
tographed in 1916 after
the signing of the
$670,000 contract which
marked the recognition
of Chaplin as the great-
est box office attraction
in the world.

CHAPTER SEVENTY-FOUR

$670,000 FOR CHAPLIN

B<small>Y</small> the autumn of 1915 Charles Chaplin had become the biggest single fact of the motion pictures.

Developments of the next few months were to make him the most widely famous personality in the history of the world. Yet he had been on the screen only two years.

The peculiar, complex politico-commercial conditions within the plotting rivalries of the film corporations in New York now conspired to give Chaplin's amazing success an even greater scope.

Chaplin was nearing the end of his one year contract with Essanay, working in the studio at Niles, California. His Essanay pictures were as strikingly successful as the Keystone comedies which had introduced him to the screen the years before.

The old Keystone-Chaplins were working to the limit of the capacity of the supply of old worn prints in the exchanges of the Mutual Film Corporation. Mutual could get no more prints, because of the strained relations with Harry E. Aitken and Kessel and Baumann of Triangle, who owned the negatives.

As the Mutual's prints of such classics as *Dough and Dynamite* wore out they could not be replaced. At the same time the numerous states' right and independent exchange men were getting a bootleg supply of re-imported Keystone Chaplins. These were prints of the same subjects made for Mutual, sold by Keystone abroad for foreign consumption and shipped back into the United States. Also a large traffic in "duped" copies of Chaplin comedies, made by screen outlaws by the illegal process of making a negative from a positive print, gained large circulation. The "dupes" went out by the thousands.

No one, not even Mary Pickford in the days of her Biograph one-reelers, had been so often and constantly on the screen.

Some measure of the amazing Chaplin circulation may be gained from consideration of one single theater, the humble little Crystal Hall, operated in Fourteenth street, New York, in connection with a penny arcade. A Chaplin comedy went on the screen there with the release of his Keystone pictures in 1913. From that day until the establishment burned in 1923, ten years later, Chaplin was off that screen a total of one week. In those four days the management experimented with Chaplin substitutes in the form of comedies made by two of his best imitators. The experiment proved that Fourteenth street would accept nothing but the genuine. In two days the receipts of the film show would drop fifty per cent if the genuine Chaplin was missing.

The reports and letters from Mutual's sixty-eight exchanges brought this clamor for new prints of the Keystone Chaplins to the desk where John R. Freuler of Mutual sat in the Masonic Temple building, facing out toward the Metropolitan clock tower.

Other great film distributing concerns, and some that hoped to become great, sensed the same demand. Many deep plans were laid for the capture of Chaplin. His Essanay contract was not more than half fulfilled when these plans began to blossom into campaigns.

Essanay was soon alert. It became most difficult for strangers and emissaries from the East to see Chaplin. The guards at the Essanay West Coast studio tightened the restrictions and sight seeing parties were held at their distance.

Jay Casey Cairns, the press agent hero of *The Million Dollar Mystery* promotion, being in the West, was assigned to investigate the Chaplin situation. His approach to the Essanay studio at Niles by way of the office was repulsed.

Cairns appeared the next day at the Essanay corral attired in sombrero, chaps and spurs. He mingled with the cowboy extras and rode into the studio on an Essanay horse to see Chaplin. It was a victory for the cavalry.

The wire reports back to the seat of strategy at the Mutual offices in New York indicated that Chaplin would listen if the talk was in terms of money.

There was not only Essanay to deal with but the competition of every other large film concern in the business. Also every friend or remote acquaintance of Chaplin was trying to be his agent for a share in the profits.

The business of stalking Chaplin honeycombed the cafés and hotels of the coast with intrigue. Niles and Los Angeles were full of spies and special agents on the Chaplin situation.

The Mutual had relays of watchers, negotiators and emissaries. Harry Caulfield, of previous experience in film diplomacy in the service of P. A. Powers in the Universal war, was chief of the Mutual's agents.

Chaplin was extremely aware of the situation. When his work for Essanay was done he left for Chicago to see George K. Spoor, head of the company. Spoor offered a profit sharing contract, promising a minimum of $500,000 for the comedian's share in the next year.

Chaplin was amazed. He headed East to see if they would speak louder in New York. They would.

Chaplin's signature was not dry on the Plaza's register when the new campaign, bigger and better than ever, began.

Chaplin never suspected that he had so many, many warm friends. They kept getting warmer. All the delights of Manhattan, with considerable frankincense and myrrh, were laid before him.

The negotiations in behalf of the Mutual were conducted by John R. Freuler, who never shared in the extravagantly ostentatious play life with which many film magnates were fringing their careers. He was in the motion picture exclusively as a business. His discussions with Chaplin, for this reason, assumed a sensational contrast with the other campaigns. Freuler was pictorially, too, at an advantage. His imposing height, crowned with white hair and a benignly efficient manner, made his mere mention of a million sound like hard money in the drawer. He looked more like a millionaire than anyone else in the film trade.

Chaplin was not at all sure that there was any reality in this bombardment of offers in which verbal millions were seemingly tossed about like confetti in the standard cabaret scene.

After the parties began to pall on Chaplin and he had seen the bright lights turned off in the early morning, the Freuler campaign began to take effect. It carried to him more conviction of reality than the rest. He doubted everybody, but doubted Freuler the least.

Chaplin and Freuler came to an agreement one Wednesday night in February, 1916, at the close of a conversation session on the mezzanine floor of the Hotel Astor.

The price was $10,000 a week for Chaplin's services, for a year, payable each Saturday, and a bonus of $150,000 for the signing of the contract, total $670,000 for the year's work.

Freuler turned to a writing desk in the foyer and wrote Chaplin a check for $5,000 on the First National Bank of Milwaukee. The next day Chaplin received additional checks for $45,000.

Meanwhile Nathan Burkan, attorney for Chaplin, and Samuel Field, attorney for the Mutual Film Corporation, labored over the employment contract which was formally signed two days later at the Mutual offices. Burkan demonstrated his genius by selling his six dollar fountain pen, with which the contract was signed, to Freuler for thirty-five dollars. It seems that Billie Burke and sundry other stars had signed contracts with that same pen.

Chaplin on this day received another check from Freuler for $100,000, completing the bonus payment.

Chaplin turned to his brother Syd as they reached the street.

"Well, I've got this much if they never give me another cent. Guess I'll go and buy a whole dozen neckties."

It was a large moment in the emotional life of this young man who makes a joke of the world because it is so sad. A few weeks later, on April 16, Chaplin celebrated, or at least could have celebrated, his twenty-seventh birthday.

It is natural, meanwhile, to wonder why the Essanay concern let the profitable Chaplin pass into other hands so lightly. George K. Spoor calculated that the year of 1916 held promise of a profit of $1,300,000 on Chaplin pictures. Yet Spoor let him walk out the front door.

The "S" of Essanay was at odds with the "A."

With Chaplin picture profits pouring in G. M. Anderson's interest in the concern would have been both valuable and costly. Spoor executed a bear movement by letting Chaplin escape. Then he bought out Anderson.

So ended the screen career of *Broncho Billy*, star of *The Great Train Robbery* and with a record of 375 weekly one-reel Wild West dramas behind him.

This was also the beginning of the end of the greatness of Essanay. But Spoor had taken millions in profits, and now they were safely anchored in Chicago lake shore real estate.

Chaplin's salary with the new Lone Star Corporation, which was to make his Mutual pictures, began March 20, 1916.

The publicity announcement of the Chaplin contract and his $670,000 salary was a world sensation, setting the newspapers agog with new excitement about the screen.

Zukor's $104,000 contract with Pickford had been surprising enough. Now in the news writers' view this Chaplin salary was something between an outrage and a world wonder.

Chaplin started his Lone Star series with *The Floorwalker*, a scenario based on his observations of a department store escalator during the New York negotiations. The series of twelve two part pictures required occupied Chaplin eighteen months, half a year longer than was anticipated. He began to proceed more carefully, evolving his technique with vast pains. He often exposed as much as 120,000 feet of negative to get the 1,500 feet required for a subject. Many of his appreciative critics have held his *Easy Street*, made in this series, as his best work.

In this period Chaplin began to subdue some of the broader elements of his comedy. Meanwhile he was, by force of his work and the publicity attendant upon his new salary, coming to the attention of literary and artistic persons of authoritative name. Minnie Maddern Fiske wrote an appreciation of Chaplin which appeared in the moribund but still eminent *Harper's Weekly*. Heywood Broun, then with the *New York Tribune*, discovered Chaplin and discussed his comedies in approving words. Before long the little man with the baggy pants was being solemnly discussed in such dignified journals as *The New Republic*. The slap-stick star of the slum nickelodeons of 1913 had begun to be classic and a pet of the philosophizing literati by the end of 1916.

Chaplin's "fan" mail came from all quarters of the world, from Sweden to the Straits Settlements and from Punta Arenas to Pekin. His message of the ultimate triumph of Meek Inferiority won the world.

The "duping" of Chaplin comedies for domestic consumption and the world trade became a thriving outlaw industry now.

A Chicago darkroom bandit while engaged in counterfeiting Chaplin comedies, observed with appreciative interest the advertising which William Fox was giving to the Brenon-made Kellerman feature entitled *The Daughter of the Gods*. The "duper" made careful choice of scenes from several Chaplin comedies and a selection of mermaids, diving scenes and whatnot from Brenon's production. He doubled these subjects, superimposing Chaplin upon a Kellerman background. The composite product, in which Chaplin shambled and cavorted through the eerie Brenon fantasies, was issued to the underground trade entitled: *Charlie, Son of the Gods*.

Competitors who lost in the bidding for Chaplin engaged in propaganda campaigns aimed at impairing his value to the Mutual. Censorships were agitated. Scandals were circulated and imitators were launched, all to little effect.

The anti-Chaplin war was even waged overseas by the same unfriendly competitors. It was discovered that Chaplin's contract provided that he was not to pass beyond the borders of the continental United States. This was a simple safeguard against the war situation and the possible whimsicalities of some British draft officer. On this provocation an uproar was raised in the London press, intended to hold Chaplin up as a slacker and seeking to cast shame on him and the Mutual Film Corporation because he was not offered up for cannon fodder. In spite of this, however, the rights on the Lone Star Chaplin pictures for the British Empire were sold for a total which paid his salary.

The twelve comedies of the Lone Star series, including Chaplin's salary, cost approximately $100,000 each, which was considerably more than the average five or six reel feature of the period. It has been estimated with reasonable accuracy that the motion picture theatres of the world have paid $5,000,000 in film rentals for those pictures, which would mean that the public has spent perhaps twenty-five millions at the box office for them—nearly twice the box office price of *The Birth of a Nation*.

These comedies are however still working and their final total can not be estimated. The earning power of Chaplin pictures is apparently limited only by the physical life of the negatives. Theatres which paid fifty dollars a day for Lone Star Chaplins in the week of their issue in 1916 paid four times that price for the same pictures six or seven years later. The like is true of no other film product.

In sequel to Chaplin's rocket success came a chapter of mingled comedy and tragedy. George K. Spoor of Essanay, who had surrendered Chaplin to the market a few months before, joined in the last united stand of the Patents Company's surviving producers, Kleine, Edison, Selig, Essanay, known as the K. E. S. E. This concern now announced, in terms but thinly veiled, a rival for Chaplin, in the person of Max Linder. Linder, a Frenchman, was the screen's first famous comedian. He appeared in Pathé pictures in the pre-Trust days. Linder's fame was greater within the industry than with the public. His heyday had been nearly ten years before.

The advertising of the return of Linder and accompanying press propaganda was shot directly at Chaplin, and it was laden with innuendo. It inferred that Chaplin was sloppy, unclean and sordid on the screen, whereas M. Linder in his new Essanay comedies was to be revealed a Beau Brummel, a Chesterfield— and very funny.

Max Comes Across was the title of the initial effort, following the Essanay pattern laid down with Chaplin in *Charlie's New Job*. This picture was released February 6, 1917. Max came across, but he did not go over. Two more pictures were made and nothing happened at the box office. It was then given out that M. Linder was ill, and near unto death as the aftermath of wounds and hardships in the trenches of the World War.

Linder went to Hollywood and shook hands with Chaplin under an orange tree. He sailed for France. The Linder experiment cost Essanay $87,000.

In a hotel in Paris Linder and his wife, a beauty with whom he had eloped two years before, committed suicide October 31, 1925.

Among the screen comedians developing as contemporaries of Chaplin, Harold Lloyd is the most conspicuously successful. Lloyd began his theatrical career as a boy in Omaha, playing parts with the Burwood stock company, going thence to Chicago. In his travels Lloyd picked up a part as an extra with the Edison company and was inspired to move to Los Angeles to make a try for a screen career. Working in *Samson and Delilah* at Universal City he met Hal Roach, a young man with an ambition to direct.

Roach inherited $3,000 and plunged into production with Lloyd to play leads. *Just Nuts* resulted and from it a contract with Pathé. Lloyd began as an imitator of Chaplin, then rose in his pride and became original.

Lloyd was amazingly ambitious. He wanted to make enough money to indulge his fancy for striped silk shirts without limit.

The young comedian's first long stride came when he hit upon the notion of portraying the youth always wearing tortoise shell rimmed spectacles—one of the outstanding aspects of Young America.

This decision came near to ending Lloyd's screen career. The Pathé concern insisted on a continuance of his eccentric character of *Lonesome Luke*. Lloyd threatened to quit, and won.   In consequence his balloon tired spectacles are in a fair way to become as world famous as Chaplin's shoes.

In 1923 Lloyd became his own producer.   His comedies have attained gross figures comparing favorably with the million dollar successes of Chaplin.

CHARLES CHAPLIN and MAX LINDER — the day that Linder, vanquished in a war of comedy on the American screen, called at the Lone Star studio to say goodbye.

HAROLD LLOYD, comedian extraordinary, being most extraordinary for his commonsense and acute judgment of the humor of the "plain-boiled" American commonalty. He started to imitate Chaplin and suddenly became original and famous by burlesquing the young men with the balloon-tired spectacles.

CHAPTER SEVENTY-FIVE

MARY, QUITE CONTRARY, TAKES A MILLION

Just after New Year's Day in 1916 Mary Pickford and Adolph Zukor had a chat. The subject was salary.

Zukor and Pickford agreed on a new arrangement like that of the year before, a fifty-fifty participation in a Mary Pickford-Famous Players Corporation, but with the drawing account increased from $2,000 to $4,000 a week.

This was very nice and satisfactory—but, Zukor indicated that there were some special reasons why he chose not to sign such a contract just then and there. So Mary and Adolph shook hands on it, by way of sealing the deal.

There were many of those special reasons why Zukor did not want to sign that contract then, as was to be revealed in the ensuing excitements of 1916.

The newspapers of January 8 carried a one-paragraph announcement that Pickford and Zukor had closed a contract. This item made no mention of salary but it stressed the assertion that she received fifty per cent of the stock of a new company. It was intended to serve Famous Players' strategy by keeping bidders away from Miss Pickford. It might have served well, but the unexpected happened.

In February the exciting announcement that John R. Freuler of the Mutual Film Corporation had contracted to pay Charles Chaplin $670,000 for a year's work came to upset the scheme.

Mary had been in the films five industrious years before Chaplin started. Now she was getting a mere $4,000 a week while this stranger helped himself to almost three times as much.

Here and now there was a head-on collision between that Chaplin contract and Mary's pride.

It seems that Mary discussed her discontent with Cora Carrington Wilkenning. Mrs. Wilkenning had come into contact with Miss Pickford as a scenario agent. Also she had been instrumental in the making of an agreement with the McClure Syndicate for the selling of newspaper articles signed by Miss Pickford and written by Frances Marion, beginning the autumn before. This was Miss Marion's first motion picture contact, leading to an important career as a scenario writer and a share in the triumphs of *Abraham Lincoln* produced by Al and Ray Rockett.

That syndicate series was but one of the ways in which Miss Pickford realized upon the values of her valued name. She also leased her features and fame to the Pompeian Company, makers of a massage cream, heralded over the land with calendars picturing "America's Sweetheart." By another deal Mary arranged to collect royalties on a radiator cap for motor cars, and by yet another for the use of her name by a music publisher. The McClure Syndicate series paid Pickford $24,243.30 between October 31, 1915, and September, 1918, which was sixty per cent of the gross sales.

When Mrs. Wilkenning heard how Mary felt about it she went out to see what could be done. There has been a law suit pending nearly ten years to decide whether or not Mrs. Wilkenning was Mary's agent, which is another and an incidental story. At any rate she went out to sell Mary.

Naturally and immediately Mrs. Wilkenning went to see John R. Freuler of the Mutual, the man who had done so handsomely by Chaplin. It was an opportune call. Freuler was exceedingly aware that Mutual's old line producers were going to let the concern die the same death that was overtaking the General Film, and for the same uninspired reasons. If there were to be

Mutual pictures Freuler had to get them. He wanted Pickford.

Then Miss Mary went down to the Mutual offices with the green carpet and the red mahogany and sat right where Chaplin had sat before her. Inevitably that Chaplin deal came into the conversation.

"I think," observed Freuler with typical deliberation, as he reached to his breast pocket, "that we might make Miss Pickford happy, yet. You might sign a contract with this pen—it is the one Mr. Chaplin used."

Freuler flourished the big Waterman. Perhaps it was in preparation for this gesture that he had bought it from Chaplin's attorney.

"But before I offer any figures," Freuler continued, "I must consult our exchanges and some of the exhibitors to see how much your pictures would be worth."

Mary tapped the floor with a petulant foot. She did not like that. She felt the whole world knew what she was worth.

"You see," Freuler went on, ignoring the storm in Mary's eyes, "my investigation may show that you are worth a great deal more than I would venture to offer, off-hand."

This was a pacifying thought.

Freuler issued a "pink letter" to the Mutual's branch managers, making inquiry about probable earnings on Pickford pictures in all parts of the country. The Mutual's "pink letter" system derived its name from the color of the paper which denoted a confidential communication from the home office, to be kept under lock and key in a special binder. Unfortunately this made it very convenient for the spies of competitive concerns to locate important correspondence. The offices of all the major film concerns were in this time sprinkled with espionage agents, planted as employees. The fact that Mutual was investigating Pickford possibilities became known among the competing film chieftains immediately.

Mrs. Wilkenning, the agent, was still looking for a chance to stir up new bids for Pickford. The report came up Broadway by way of Wall street that 111 Fifth avenue, the office of the American Tobacco Company, was seething with millions and motion picture ambitions. It was reported that Benjamin B. Hampton, vice president in charge of advertising, was about to head a big money invasion of the film field.

Hampton was interested when Mrs. Wilkenning called. There were conferences in her offices. Pickford and Hampton met there. Mary seems to have been a bit hesitant, now that she was face to face with a step that might break her long and profitable connection with Famous Players. Hampton wanted to talk certainties and insisted on something tangible upon which to base his contemplated promotional efforts.

On that brave day, the seventeenth of March, in 1916, he received a tiny note on a bit of blue paper, reading:

I have positively made up my mind to leave Famous Players.
MARY PICKFORD

The next day Hampton achieved a real option, in a lengthy letter written by Mrs. Wilkenning and signed by Mary. Mary got a thousand dollars down on that option and gave Hampton thirty days in which to make his arrangements for a corporation which was to give her fifty per cent of the stock and a drawing account of $7,000 a week—not so big as the Chaplin deal but better than the Famous Players arrangement at $4,000.

With this option signed Hampton began looking about for capital and the creation of excitement generally in the inner and upper circles of the motion picture industry.

It was time to see how Zukor might react. Mrs. Wilkenning called on him with the tidings.

"He really questioned that she had signed with Mr. Hampton, and he said if he lost Miss Pickford then he intended to go out of the motion picture business, which he had no intention of doing," Mrs. Wilkenning quoted Zukor in testimony relating to that session in subsequent litigation.

Meanwhile the leaven of the Hampton promotional efforts was working. The motion picture industry was ripe for ferment. The old order of the nickelodeon age was sinking and the new dramatic feature period was uncertainly formative.

Within a week of the Pickford option, on March 23, to be exact, the rumors broke into print. The New York *Times*, without direct quotation of authority, discussed reports sufficiently comprehensive to indicate that anything, or everything, or both, would happen in the motion picture world. Mergers were hinted involving Lubin, Essanay, Selig, Triangle, Mutual, Famous Players, Lasky and Morosco and Pallas, the latter two being contributors to the Paramount program. The story included, too, the news that Benjamin B. Hampton was reported to have made a tentative offer of $500,000 a year to Mary Pickford. The *Times* was inclined to be cautious about the Pickford paragraph. A reporter called up Mary, who was quoted as saying she was then working under a temporary or tentative contract of the handshake with Zukor. There are of course such things as tentative handshakes.

The whole motion picture industry was tentative. Every thought or move of the day was filled with ifs, ands and buts. A banking syndicate, with an eye on a big promotional merger with Triangle, offered Zukor $1,500,000 for his control of Famous Players. Here was in the realm of the motion picture precisely what is meant by the term "psychological moment." The psychologist was Adolph Zukor.

" I knew then," Zukor remarked to the author ten years later, "what I could do with a million and a half dollars. It would have been a nice nest egg for the family. But I didn't know what I could do with myself. I didn't have any picture of retiring to run a shoe store or something like that. There I was with it all on one ace, you might say. I decided to stay in and play."

The lone ace was Mary Pickford. Zukor went to walking again, studying his strategies. A pedometer record of Zukor's mileage would reflect motion picture conditions as accurately as the barometic readings on a weather map.

The day after the story of the merger talk and the Pickford-Hampton deal, the *Times* carried a brief statement from Zukor to the effect that Miss Pickford was in fact under a contract which was a renewal of the 1915 at double the money. It was that handshake again, not so tentative in Zukor's view.

The fact was, in this great tentative situation in the film industry, whoever emerged from the situation in possession of a contract with Mary Pickford was going to hold the whip hand in the whole industry.

In some dim way every concern in the business realized this. The price of Mary Pickford became the price of supremacy.

Because it was the Chaplin contract with its reaction on Pickford which had become the source of the ferment in the industry, it is necessary to compare their places before the screen world. Pickford was obviously in this situation more important commercially. This did not mean she was the greater star. It did mean that she was a bigger leverage in the hands of a selling organization. She appeared in a rather continuous supply of five-part feature pictures, eight or more a year. Chaplin appeared in two-reel comedies. The big feature length comedy was not yet established. Relatively, Pickford appeared in larger packages. Pickford was a fancy staple, Chaplin was a rare spice.

Meanwhile the announcement that Chaplin pictures made by the Lone Star Corporation, although marketed through Mutual exchanges, were to be sold independently of the Mutual program, so that no theatre would be compelled to take anything else with them, had its effect on Pickford.

And still the angling for offers went on. William Randolph Hearst and Mary Pickford met in Mrs. Wilkenning's office. Hearst wanted a proposition. Pickford wanted an offer. It did not come to figures.

Hampton was seeking to place his Pickford option. He found Vitagraph over in Flatbush interested. A bright picture of an infusion of new capital and Vitagraph domination of the film business was painted.

The gloriously pictured prospect opened the way for a promotional reorganization of the Vitagraph company, which had stood unchanged since that remote day when William F. Rock with his handful of films joined J. Stuart Blackton, the cartoonist and lecturer, and Albert E. Smith, the spirit cabinet performer, with their "American Vitagraph" version of the Edison Projecting Kinetoscope. On May 5, 1916, a statement was issued over the names of Smith and Blackton announcing that plans had been completed for a new concern, Greater Vitagraph, with a capitalization of $25,000,000. B. B. Hampton and H. H. Vreeland were added to the board of directors.

But the Hampton-Pickford option had lapsed before any deal could be completed. Mary refused to extend that option. There were plenty of prospects for her now.

Albert E. Smith was still hopeful of capturing Pickford for Vitagraph. He opened negotiations with favorable prospects.

Smith and Pickford had become friendly. There was a new baby at the Smith household, and Albert E., the father, was as proud as fathers usually are in such circumstances. Considerable discussion of the world's most wonderful little Smith percolated into the Smith-Pickford negotiations.

A conference which was expected to complete negotiations was held at the offices of Denis O'Brien, of O'Brien, Malevinsky

& Driscoll, attorneys for Pickford. Smith, hat in hand, bowed his adieu for the day.

"And, now, when am I going out to see that wonderful baby?" Mary trilled.

Smith's mind was intense upon that contract which seemed right in his grasp. He hoped to close with Pickford at $10,000 a week.

"Just as soon as we get this business signed up and out of the way," Smith replied. Business was first in his thought.

"If that's it, I'll never see the baby," Mary tossed back at him, and turned away.

That was the end of Vitagraph's negotiations. In a flash Smith knew that Pickford had taken offense, as though the idea were to make a social visit a reward of the contract. But it was too late. Big business hangs on little threads.

Now John R. Freuler of Mutual returned from a tour of investigation and presented Pickford with a proposition which included the alluring terms of a fifty per cent interest in a new company, a drawing account of $10,000 a week, a bonus of $150,000 for her signature, and, over all, a guaranty of one million dollars a year.

Mary said "Yes."

Samuel M. Field, attorney for Freuler and Mutual, set about drawing a contract with a dotted line at the bottom to be decorated with the autograph of "Mary Gladys Moore, known as Mary Pickford."

Mary went back to Famous Players and the glad, glad news was broken to Adolph Zukor.

Zukor took another walk. Things were thickening up rapidly for him. A few days were to decide his fate and the order of events for motion picture history of the next ten years.

There were some late sessions and conferences of secrecy at Zukor's residence on Riverside Drive. It was a good place to walk. Al Lichtman, Hiram Abrams and Walter E. Greene, both of power in Paramount, which distributed Zukor's pictures, attended these sessions. There were a number of sequels.

June 13, 1916, W. W. Hodkinson was succeeded in the presidency of Paramount Pictures Corporation by Hiram Abrams.

Hodkinson, the organizer and master of Paramount, had controlled distribution, and distribution controlled the film business, simply by force of the fact that the distributing concern held the scepter of the biggest organized buying power. It was foreordained that Zukor and Hodkinson should come to issue and clash, from that day in 1914 when Hodkinson insisted on making an independent contract with Lasky.

This silent, adamantine Hodkinson from out of the West could not be brought under control. He might be eliminated, but not subdued.

Now Hodkinson was out—to form another concern, the Hodkinson Corporation, which after various readjustments and refinancing operations is now known as the Producers Distributing Corporation.

With the field clearing before him in the Paramount situation, Zukor was now ready to supplement that handshake with Mary Pickford by a written contract.

Samuel M. Field of Mutual, with the million-a-year contract waiting, received a telephone message stating that Miss Pickford would not sign it.

June 24, 1916, Mary Pickford signed again with Zukor. It was not for a million a year. But it sounded almost as good. Mary's new contract called for a guaranty of $1,040,000—but the term was for two years. It put the million in headlines, anyway. Technically the contract was with the Pickford Film Corporation, with Mary's compensation set at half the profits, with the guaranty paid in installments of $10,000 each Monday. In addition there was a bonus of $300,000, but payable, if, when and as earned by the pictures. This was to compensate for the fact that Freuler had paid Chaplin $150,000 cash for signing his one year contract.

Mary's new contract contained several prideful provisions. It was agreed that her name was to be in the biggest type and the only featured name in any advertisement of her pictures. She was guaranteed parlor car transportation for herself and her mother to and from California and a motor for services outside of Greater New York. The corporation agreed to provide a studio to be known as the Mary Pickford studio, in which no other pictures could be made, and in the event she made winter pictures in California, she was to have a stage to herself. She was to have a voice in the choice of stories, casts and everything else. Just by way of completeness Mary under this contract collected $40,000 for the time between May 29 and June 24, when she had not been on the payroll, this on the ground that the time was spent in examining scenarios.

June 28, fifteen days after the dethronement of Hodkinson in Paramount, and four days after the Pickford contract, Zukor announced a sweeping merger, the Famous Players-Lasky Corporation, which took in the Lasky Feature Play Company and various minor concerns, including Bosworth, Morosco and Pallas. Note also that Adolph Zukor was President.

Jesse Lasky continued to be the executive more especially concerned with production of pictures, with Zukor in business control. Samuel Goldfish, Lasky's brother-in-law, continued as manager of the Lasky studios in Hollywood.

Zukor had Mary Pickford—and he had consolidated production for Paramount distribution. He had put Hiram Abrams at the head of Paramount. Zukor was on his way, full speed ahead.

August 12, 1916, in the Moving Picture World Zukor ardently declared for the wisdom of program booking, Paramount's method of distribution, by which it sold its product "take all or nothing."

August 16, 1916, came an intended bombshell of mystery—Artcraft Pictures Corporation, formed to distribute the products of the new and costly Mary Pickford concern, in competition with Paramount. Walter E. Greene, previously of Paramount and former partner of Abrams, was Artcraft's official president. Lichtman was general manager.

Action was being had on all sides. Three weeks later, September 3, 1916, Samuel Goldfish was disconnected with Famous Players-Lasky Corporation. There were business and personal differences. It was reported that Goldfish received a million in cash for his interest.

A few weeks later Zukor swung again, and Paramount Pictures Corporation was acquired, for stock and cash, by the Famous Players-Lasky Corporation—a twenty-five million dollar concern, controlling pictures from the studio camera to the theatre. Zukor ruled production and distribution. It was just four years since he started with his feature picture idea, the term of a college course. He had taken his Master's degree. Zukor was certainly "The Doctor."

There were, however, a number of minor chores yet to be done along the path and around the premises of the citadel of control. There was William Sherry, for instance. Sherry was probably the largest single shareholder in the Paramount and in the merging process became an important holder of Famous Players-Lasky stock. This was in the nature of an inadvertence. It was unforeseen that this was going to happen when Sherry, a loan agent, answered Al Lichtman's blind ad in the classified "Business Opportunities" column of the *New York Times* and invested $5,000 in the New York rights on Zukor's *Queen Elizabeth* in 1912. Since New York proved to be, in point of revenue, about ten per cent of the United States, the rise of Paramount carried Sherry to fortune. He had the best corner lot in the new screen development. Sherry had $800,000 worth of Paramount and enough incidentals to rate him a millionaire.

Sherry got in by buying a picture. The way in is often also the way out. He has told the story on the witness stand. The great Famous Players-Lasky combine had a picture entitled *Joan the Woman,* starring Geraldine Farrar. It had a big title and a big star. But in some way it did not seem essential to the program. Sherry was offered some more bargain rights, this time on Joan, for $125,000. They compromised at $100,000.

Sherry, rushing for the bonanza, put up his new Famous Players stock with the Irving National Bank for collateral on a loan. The stock was still at 80, or thereabouts. He got Joan. Then Joan got him. His $100,000 investment returned $50,000. Meanwhile Famous Players discontinued dividends and its stock sagged off to about 30 or less. Sherry eventually had to sell his stock.

The Zukor absorption of Paramount also took Hiram Abrams, its president, into the Famous Players-Lasky Corporation as an employee, as well as a shareholder. Shortly a feud between Abrams and Zukor arose, with the inevitable result. Abrams left.

When Samuel Goldfish left the Lasky studios on the West Coast he headed East with a deep resolve to reassert himself. In affiliation with Edgar Selwyn of Selwyn & Company, dramatic producers, and Margaret Mayo, an author, Goldfish announced the formation of Goldwyn Pictures Corporation Christmas week, 1916. It is a stock joke of the industry that one of the tentative names was Sel-fish Pictures. Goldwyn Pictures Corporation indulged in some of the most profound announcing that the industry had heard. It was largely a reiteration of the Famous Players idea, with a close paralleling of pattern. Maxine Elliott was the Goldwyn equivalent of Zukor's first star, Sarah Bernhardt. Mae Marsh, signed by Goldwyn, carried some of the same glamour of Biograph that Pickford had brought to Famous Players. Mary Garden was the Goldfish ditto to Lasky's contract with Geraldine Farrar, and Madge Kennedy of the original Goldwyn group was an expression of the general "famous players" notion.

The famous players fetich did not prove a sensational success. Some elements of the trade were so ungallant as to refer to Goldwyn as "the old maids' home." The first picture, featuring Maxine Elliott, was stored away in the vault at Craftsman Laboratory for more than a year before it was thrust upon the market.

The Goldwyn concern experimented with a drive aimed at creating in the author a new order of stardom. "Eminent Authors" were imported by the Hollywood studio in quantity lots. They included Rex Beach, Rupert Hughes, Mary Roberts Rinehart, Sir Gilbert Parker, Eleanor Glyn and others of magazine glory. No new stardom resulted. The authors proved to be writers still, not picture makers.

The Goldwyn concern in its subsequent career underwent many struggles and reorganizations, incident to which Samuel Goldfish changed his name to Goldwyn. However, the corporation parted with him and later enjoined him against the use of his new name, unless accompanied by the phrase "not connected with Goldwyn Pictures Corporation."

For a time the Dupont interests, grown familiar with and callous to explosions in the dynamite business, entered into the affairs of the Goldwyn concern. Somewhere interwoven into the mixture and connected by an attenuated thread were the political ambitions of Coleman T. Dupont, who was once willing to accept the White House.

The only enduring mark of the Dupont invasion is the great Capitol theatre in Broadway, which passed with other interests into the ultimate Metro-Goldwyn merger control. Meanwhile the Duponts have been these several years engaged in experimental production of film stock, an incident of extensive chemical activities in Delaware. They may yet importantly affect the screen by technological developments.

The intrusion of the Goldwyn concern in the winter of 1916–17 was, however, only a casual matter in the campaigns of Adolph Zukor. He was frying fish on several fires.

CHAPTER SEVENTY-SIX

TWO MILLION ON BELSHAZZAR

WHILE the business of the motion picture was muddling through into its new alignments of 1916, D. W. Griffith dared forth with the most venturesome experiment in all the history of film technique—the picture entitled *Intolerance*.

This production earns a place in motion picture history sheerly on that element of technique. It was the first and only film fugue.

Intolerance is of interest to the student of the motion picture in its relation to the evolution of the art of screen narration under Griffith. *Intolerance* was the last word in a sequence of experiments which began in Griffith's Biograph period, in the course of which in 1910 he produced a version of *Enoch Arden* with cutbacks and simultaneous lines of action.

When Griffith returned to California from his presentation of *The Birth of a Nation* and its terrific tangle of censorship struggles his mind was occupied with reflections and calculations which inevitably were to color his subsequent work.

It must have been even then apparent to Griffith that the Triangle concern to which his ordinary and casual product was contributed was not going to afford him a major career. *The Birth of a Nation* by the effulgence of its success made it necessary for Griffith to contemplate some even more impressive film undertaking.

While Griffith was casting about for something which should be his pretext and inspiration for outdoing *The Birth of a Nation* he was reviewing the troubles he had had with that picture, and seeking half-consciously a solution of the problems presented.

Out of this was born the impulse to let the screen itself reveal the cruel, ridiculous and wasteful consequences of intolerance —censorships by the public will—by a presentation of social, religious and economic struggles down the aisles of history.

Griffith saw the picture in bits and splotches of action first and then cast about for some thread on which they could be strung to give cohesion, continuity and conviction to the whole preachment. Griffith found what he sought on a page of Whitman's "Leaves of Grass":

> . . . endlessly rocks the cradle,
> "Uniter of here and Hereafter."

The lines of the poet supplied Griffith with the pictorial suggestion he was seeking, the thread to join his tales of intolerance.

All through that night Griffith pondered and wrote piles of notes. By dawn he had the skeleton scenario of *Intolerance*. It was a conception of one mood and many tenses.

The Griffith idea, which he labelled for selling purposes *Love's Struggle through the Ages* was more actually a litany of human hates, to be told by the interweaving of four periods. For his contemporary sequence Griffith had a modern melodrama suitable to his purpose. It was *The Mother and the Law*, with Mae Marsh and Robert Harron in the leading rôles. The story was laid on a capital and labor background with tinges of plot suggestions from the Steilow case. This picture had been scheduled for release through the Mutual Film Corporation as a "Master Picture" only to be withdrawn with the secession of the New York Motion Picture Corporation and the formation of Triangle. The three historical periods chosen were to give occasion to picture on a grandiose scale the fall of Babylon before the hordes of Cyrus, the Christ legend of Judea, and the massacre of the Huguenots on St. Bartholomew's Eve in France All these were interwoven in the assembly of the picture with the time lapses covered by a mysterious, soft-focus, half-lighted picture of Lillian Gish rocking a cradle—or as Griffith's title said it: "A golden thread binds the four stories—a fairy girl with sunlit hair—her hand on the cradle of humanity—eternally rocking——"

With zealous abandon and capital, which came readily after his triumph with *The Birth of a Nation*, the Griffith lot on Sunset boulevard became a maelstrom of titanic construction. There rose Babylon with walls three hundred feet high, the architectural pretensions of old France, and the streets of ancient Judea. About it all was a hush of mystery. No one knew what Griffith was doing, but everyone learned that he was doing a lot of it.

Stupendous expenditures were incurred, setting new precedents in grandiose gesture for the motion picture. The influences of the glorification of dimensions in *Intolerance* have been discernible in screen spectacles ever since, down to *The Ten Commandments* and *Ben Hur*.

It has been given out that Griffith's payrolls for actors and extras in *Intolerance* for long periods ran as high as $12,000 a day. It is alleged that the banquet hall scene for the feast of Belshazzar cost a quarter of a million dollars.

The cast included many famous screen names, among them: Sam de Grasse, Joseph Hennabery, Tully Marshall, Elmer Clifton, Signe Auen, Bessie Love and Ralph Lewis. Count Eric von Stroheim, subsequently himself famous as a director, played the rôle of a Pharisee. Constance Talmadge played *The Mountain Girl*, a rôle which brought her attention and opened the way to a star career under Selznick auspices later.

When the shooting and shouting were over the cost sheets totalled the reputed figure of $1,900,000 and there were 300,000 feet of negative. *Intolerance* in the rough was so big that it took seventy-five hours to look at it. It was edited to thirteen reels. Let us recall in contrast that at the end of 1895, the first year of film production, the total studio costs of the industry were $1,110. *Annabelle the Dancer*, the master production of 1895, was thirty-five feet long.

Intolerance opened at the Liberty theatre in New York, scene of *The Birth of a Nation's* triumph, on September 6, 1916. It played in legitimate theatres in all the major cities, here and abroad. It was inevitably a sensation and a topic of considerable debate. It was mostly a debate about Griffith.

Griffith who above all others had evolved a screen technique of close-up and cutback to clarify plot movement, intensify emotional content and to make attention automatic and unconscious, had betrayed the motion picture public.

The concept denoted by the word *Intolerance* is an abstraction of thought. A motion picture which has to be thought about is in the same status as a joke which has to be explained.

Griffith sought by concrete emotional illustrations from history to create a dramatic appreciation of an abstract principle in the minds of the screen masses. If they had ever had the deductive capacity for digesting historical experience, the conditions of intolerance which gave him his inspiration would not have continued for the two thousand four hundred and fifty-four years between the fall of Babylon and *The Birth of a Nation*.

The public never goes anywhere to intellectualize. It went to *Intolerance* in just sufficient numbers to find out that it did not know what it was about. The consumers of the great common denominator of the emotional arts found themselves confronted by a specimen of screen algebra, ornate but confusing.

To Griffith the scenes of Lillian Gish rocking a cradle did mean "a golden thread" denoting the continuity of the human race and binding his fugue of period pictures. But to the movie audience a picture of a cradle is a hieroglyph meaning: "there is going to be a baby," "there is a baby" or "there was a baby." It does not mean the continuity of the race, and it does not suggest intolerance—rather the opposite. The introduction of a cradle in a motion picture is more likely to set the audience to counting back nine months on its fingers than it is to set it to reflecting on man's inhumanity to man.

Picture-wise exhibitors looked at the cradle scenes and deduced that Griffith was trying to put something over on the Pennsylvania board of censorship.

So, *Intolerance* was a magnificent failure.

Griffith's most dramatic gesture with *Intolerance* was never announced to the public. His backers went into the project expecting to get another *Birth of a Nation*. All they saw for their money was the cradle. They grumbled and after grumbling began to roar.

"Very well, I'll buy it," Griffith responded, and began the payment of installments on a million dollar item of experience. The experiment was worth the price, but it is unfortunate that Griffith had to pay it.

The month of the presentation of *Intolerance* brought an odd, faint echo of the name and fame of Griffith. With promises of an unsupported pretension a seven part picture entitled *Charity* was given a showing to the states' right market at Loew's Roof in New York. This picture was produced by Frank Powell, who had been a member of the old Biograph organization and who had brought Theda Bara to screen fame in *A Fool There Was*. *Charity* for a combination of reasons was a dismal thing. The scenario idea on which it was based came from Linda Arvidson Griffith, Mrs. D. W. Griffith, who had been living apart from her husband several years while he travelled the path to "The Master's" throne alone.

Now it may have been coincidence that Mrs. Griffith's picture drew a cold abstract title like *Charity* just when Mr. Griffith's picture attained the bald abstraction of *Intolerance*. It may also have been a coincidence that the keynote of *The Mother and the Law* part of *Intolerance* was struck by the experiences of Mae Marsh in the heroine rôle as a victim of a corrupt orphanage, while *Charity* devoted itself to an alleged exposure of corrupt orphan asylums. If so, the simultaneous presentations of the far separated Mr. and Mrs. Griffith seem most astonishing.

Charity was produced with the backing of a wealthy New York brewer, who presently withdrew from the project because of pressure from religious organizations which considered the production an attack.

The public heard a great deal of *Intolerance* but *Charity* remained in obscurity. It was drab and sordid, alarmingly faithful to the portrayal of slum life. The cast included Mrs. Griffith, Creighton Hale, Sheldon Lewis, Zena Keefe and others of equal ability and fame. Two years later the picture fell into the hands of the slowly decomposing Mutual Film Corporation. It had a Chicago premiere on Michigan avenue, opened with a profound, prayerful address by Bishop Samuel Fallows. Even prayer was unavailing. In 1920 *Charity*, re-edited and re-titled as a roaring melodrama, shorn of propaganda, made a third equally insignificant sally on the states' right market. There was a curse on it.

LINDA ARVIDSON, who played at Biograph in the years of its
glory — and long kept it a secret that she was Mrs. David
Wark Griffith.

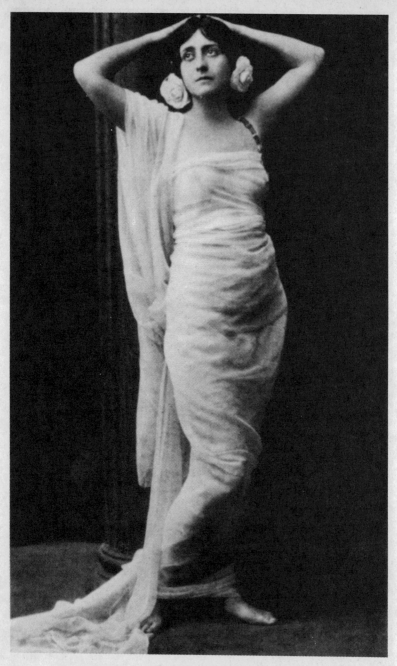

CLARA KIMBALL YOUNG, the star with whom Lewis J. Selznick set forth on the selling war that won him success and millions and a name in the electric lights.

CHAPTER SEVENTY-SEVEN

ZUKORED AND SELZNICKED

ADOLPH ZUKOR had little more than well begun to organize his feudal barony of the screen in 1916 when a jester, with cap awry and bells a-jingle, cartwheeled into the banquet hall to thumb his nose toward the head of the table and make impertinent remarks while he helped himself to the wine and meats.

This invader was the blond stranger from Pittsburgh, Lewis J. Selznick, whose entry into the films we have traced by a trail of salt herring and diamonds.

The motion picture industry which was being permanently Zukored, was now also to be transiently but utterly Selznicked.

Selznick was officially vice president and general manager of the World Film Corporation. He had also appointed himself the general disturbance of the motion picture industry.

When Carl Laemmle of Universal, who had "accepted a resignation" from Selznick two years before, signed a series of advertisements pleading with exhibitors to "use the brains that God gave you," Selznick issued the remark that the motion picture business "takes less brains than anything else in the world."

In the conduct of the World Film Corporation Selznick was hampered slightly by a board of directors, including some bankers. The bankers were in the World as a result of a pleasant bit of Selznickery. Early in the history of that enterprise Selznick found himself at the helm of the World Special Films Corporation, an importing concern acquired from Emanuel Mandelbaum and Philip Gleichman of Cleveland. Selznick had a company and wanted capital. He went looking for it where it is, namely Wall street. He had the American rights on a prophetically entitled drama, *Whom the Gods Would Destroy*." The picture cost him $4,250. Selznick ventured below the deadline into the financial belt and personally sold to ninety-nine bankers one share each at $42.50. He kept a share himself. It was easy for Selznick to find ninety-nine financiers so busy and impatient they preferred writing a small check to spending the week in argument. The investment made money and from the ninety-and-nine Selznick hand-picked backers for the World Film Corporation.

Selznick inaugurated the ornate special preview functions for motion picture promotions, now mentioned in screen trade parlance as "throwing a party." The Astor hotel was the scene of these operations, stimulated with cut flowers, corn and grape juice and dancing. The Ritz-Carlton has since supplanted the Astor as the scene of these rites.

One of Selznick's exploitation functions accidentally made a star. He had invited the Who's Who and What's What of Broadway to a Roman festival for the first screening of *The Seats of the Mighty*, a Canadian production of a story by Sir Gilbert Parker. The print did not arrive and at the last moment the only available World picture, *The Wishing Ring*, was presented. The picture made an impression, starting a career of stardom for Vivian Martin and success for Maurice Tourneur, the director.

Selznick often disagreed with the bankers in the World Film Corporation and usually triumphed. But at last one day he picked himself up outside, dusting himself off. The next week, January 29, 1916, *Variety*, a trade journal, contained this item:

"Clara Kimball Young left Monday for Havana, accompanied by Mrs. Lewis J. Selznick. Mr. Selznick leaves next week for Jacksonville."

Accurately interpreted this meant that Selznick was "going South" with the World Film Corporation.

Clara Kimball Young was the vital part of the World Film Corporation's program. Broadly, her pictures sold the rest of the output.

Shortly Selznick announced the formation of the Clara Kimball Young Film Corporation, with himself as president and general manager. It was proclaimed that exhibitors would now be able to book the profitable Clara Kimball Young pictures without swallowing a whole program of less acceptable pictures. The Young pictures were to come at the rate of one a month beginning the approaching October.

Selznick operated from the Hotel Claridge as a base and proceeded to evangelize the film industry with his new principle of star merchandising.

Selznick by super-salesmanship made his project finance itself. He sold franchises to exhibitors and collected advance deposits against rentals, enabling the making of the pictures. He started with an idea, rented a street number and got to a crest of several million dollars.

When, in August, the Mary Pickford Film Corporation announced distribution through Artcraft Pictures Corporation, Selznick seized opportunity. In Artcraft, Adolph Zukor was operating behind a light screen. His name did not appear in the slightest outward connection with the project. Selznick now punctured this screen with an open letter, published in the trade journals:

I congratulate you, Mary. You are a pretty shrewd, as well as a pretty *little* girl.

What stronger evidence could there be that the Clara Kimball Young Corporation is organized on the most progressive basis than your adoption in the Mary Pickford Film Corporation of the very idea and ideal that I have originated?

Will you please express to my friend, Mr. Adolph Zukor, my deep sense of obligation? It is indeed delightful to encounter among one's co-workers a man so broad-gauged that neither false pride nor shortsightedness can deter him from the adoption of an excellent plan, even though conceived by another.

Faithfully,

LEWIS J. SELZNICK.

Miss Mary Pickford,
270 Riverside Drive,
New York City.

This letter served to make the friendship between Zukor and Selznick a great deal warmer but not much thicker.

Meanwhile an electric sign, among the first to be used for general motion picture advertising purposes apart from a theatre showing, blossomed at Forty-sixth street and Broadway, at large expense, announcing Clara Kimball Young in *The Common Law*, to be distributed by Lewis J. Selznick Enterprises, Inc. The confused public, never having seen an electric sign except at theatres, tried to buy admissions to *The Common Law* at the drug store soda fountain below.

Selznick was busily and alarmingly financing his project by the selling of franchises on his product to leading exhibitors, including Jones, Linick & Schaefer of Chicago, A. H. Blank in Iowa, Stanley Mastbaum in Philadelphia and elsewhere.

This was making mighty inroads on the plans of his contemporaries, especially Zukor's Famous Players-Lasky-Paramount combine. Selznick's star series bookings broke into program schedules of all the other distributors. War started.

William A. Brady, who had taken up the leadership of the World Film Corporation, advanced to upstage, center, and addressed himself to the motion picture world with great feeling, warning exhibitors against, "adventurers, grafters and pettifoggers." He mentioned no names and he did not need to.

Nothing could have served Selznick better. Publicity by denunciation is still publicity.

Others were more practical. Selznick was ill at the Hotel Astor when Adolph Zukor went to call. He doubtless hoped there was nothing trivial the matter with Selznick. He wanted to end this disturbance. He was exasperated.

Zukor offered Selznick $5,000 a week for life if he would go to China and stay there. Selznick refused. Otherwise he would be emperor of China today.

One source of Selznick's strength was in an apparently remote part of the background. This was his friendship with Marcus Loew. Loew appears to have enjoyed both admiration for and amusement at the gyrations of Selznick, who was playing battledore and shuttlecock with the film game. Also there perchance lingered some of the atmospheric condition which had led Adolph Zukor to depart from the Loew concern in 1912. Selznick was heckling Zukor. Personal loans from Loew and aid at hard moments saved Selznick in crises.

This intimacy with Marcus Loew and the Loew organization added the Talmadges to the array of Selznick stars. Selznick had been in unavailing negotiation with Norma Talmadge, a lesser star of the Triangle constellation. When she married Joseph Schenck, booking manager for the Loew theatres, things were different. Selznick secured Talmadge and the Loew theatres booked her pictures. Of these ingredients came success and fame. The first Selznick picture with Norma Talmadge was *Panthea*, produced in the autumn of 1916 by Allan Dwan.

Again the Selznick enterprises scored with Alla Nazimova, famous Russian actress. She had been appearing in *War Brides*, a sensational skit playing the Keith vaudeville circuit. Selznick paid her $30,000, or about $1,000 a day, to appear in a picturization of her act, under the direction of Herbert Brenon, of the Herbert Brenon Corporation. Selznick organized a company for any star who wanted one. Certificates of incorporation made inexpensive but handsome premiums. Richard Barthelmess, who had been in vaudeville with Nazimova, made his screen advent in *War Brides*. The picture was a box-office triumph and earned a gross of $300,000.

Selznick built mightily and prospered upon his initial success with the Clara Kimball Young pictures. With the Talmadges in the height of star favor, sold on series contracts by themselves, Selznick was shooting large yawning holes in the solid program booking schedules of the Zukor-Famous Players policy.

One morning Selznick awoke to discover that the news headlines screamed of revolution in Russia and the overthrow of the Czar. Selznick wrapped a brocaded silken dressing gown about him, rang for Ishi and demanded tea from the samovar. A secretary came panting, pencil poised, to take dictation. It was a cablegram, sent paid, which, translated from the Russian read about thus:

NICHOLAS ROMANOFF
PETROGRAD, RUSSIA
  WHEN I WAS POOR BOY IN KEIV SOME OF YOUR POLICEMEN WERE NOT KIND TO ME AND MY PEOPLE STOP I CAME TO AMERICA AND PROSPERED STOP NOW HEAR WITH REGRET YOU ARE OUT OF A JOB OVER THERE STOP FEEL NO ILLWILL WHAT YOUR POLICEMAN DID SO IF YOU WILL COME NEW YORK CAN GIVE YOU FINE POSITION ACTING IN PICTURES STOP SALARY NO OBJECT STOP REPLY MY EXPENSE STOP REGARDS YOU AND FAMILY

SELZNICK
NEW YORK

Selznick was disappointed when he did not get a reply. If the Czar had arrived he would have got the job, and perhaps a percentage of the profits.

Selznick played the film game and all other games with a dash and zip intended to take away the breath along with the loose change. He was willing to stand pat on the lowest hand in the deck and bet five grand before the draw. He acquired Ishi, a Japanese major-domo, and instructed him in the art of marinated herring. He rode in a Rolls-Royce and in the velvety depths of his Park avenue apartment soothed his eyes with Italian marbles and great vases from the Orient.

Selznick was a rollicking film success, proclaimed to the skies of the night every kilowatt hour.

Whereat Adolph Zukor waxed exceeding wroth. Selznick was a buzzing fly in the cream pitcher.

There is an ancient political adage; "If you can't lick 'em, join 'em." Zukor decided to join and work from the inside. It is the old story of the wooden horse at the gate of Troy.

On March 15, 1917, there was an inconspicuous paragraph in the trade journals announcing that Aaron Jones of Chicago had arrived in New York for a visit. His name was the first one in the celebrated triumvirate of Jones, Linick & Schaefer, Chicago theatre magnates, proprietors of a local distribution system, known as the Central Film Company, and related enterprises. They had Selznick picture franchises.

It seems a bit roundabout, but Jones came from Chicago with messages from Adolph Zukor at 485 Fifth avenue to Lewis J. Selznick, 729 Seventh avenue, New York, N. Y.

Selznick has subsequently stated that Jones received a pleasant little $50,000 for his services as messenger.

Conferences between Zukor and Selznick ensued. Plans were evolved which promised to make Selznick Pictures even more profitable, accompanied by the acquisition of an exact 50 per cent interest in the Selznick concern by Zukor. Selznick was to remain president. Their pictures were to be made at the

Lasky studio of Famous Players-Lasky in Hollywood, with all of the vast facilities of that concern and sundry economies.

Also as a personal token, Myron Selznick, son of Lewis J., then growing up to the maturity of almost seventeen years, was to go into the studio to become a production authority, understudying Jesse Lasky and Cecil DeMille.

Of course there was to be no outward merger. The Selznick concern was to continue in vigorous competition on the market after the pictures left the studios. The brand name, however, was changed to Select Pictures Corporation. This was the joker, and the source of much subsequent action.

Now that he had become Selznick's partner, Zukor moved to eliminate the irritating sight of his name from the electric lights of Broadway, the film maintitles, and the billboards all the way from Eastport, Maine, to Point Loma, California. It was a city-beautiful movement.

Selznick sat back in silence and acute nyctitropism. A great obscurity fell on him. His name disappeared entirely, save for one shining spot. Some months before when the Schenck interests, for family reasons, set out to launch Constance Talmadge, sister of Norma, with Selznick pictures, Lewis J. was riding high in power. He was induced to lend the brilliance of his sibilant name by contracting that the maintitle of each of the new star's pictures should read: "Lewis J. Selznick presents Constance Talmadge in" etc. The contract held now and kept the name on the screen.

In some way the plan to have Myron Selznick go West to understudy Lasky and DeMille at the studios fell through. Probably there never was any real intention of letting a scion of the House of Selznick through those gates in Vine Street, Hollywood.

Also Lewis J. Selznick was prospering in discomfort. Select Pictures Corporation was making money for him as well as for Zukor, but Selznick wanted action. Then came the last straw, which made the camel buck.

There was a message from Hollywood stating that the Talmadges wanted the line "Lewis J. Selznick presents" dropped from Constance's pictures. Selznick's sleuths reported that the message had originated at a point geographically identical with the top of Adolph Zukor's desk at 485 Fifth avenue. These same reports indicated that the Talmadges had been offered inducements and favors for their subscription to the request for the elimination of Selznick's name.

"If they're going to do that, I'll put my own name on some pictures," exclaimed Myron Selznick. "They can't stop that."

"Boys will be boys," quoth Lewis J., father, as he helped himself to a gold tipped cigarette decorated with the doubleheaded eagle.

Young Selznick went shopping for stars and came back with a contract with Olive Thomas. It was a signal stroke for the youngster. He was still a minor, and his mother signed the contract as a measure of legal responsibility. Myron closed his contract with Miss Thomas at $1,000 a week against competing offers from established concerns at twice that figure. Behind that apparently strange decision of the star is one of the countless sentimental and pathetic real life stories which fill the shadows back of the tinsel of stage and screen.

Olive Thomas was clutching at romantic adventure and the play of a childhood she never had had when she chose the contract with this Selznick boy. He and his glowing plans made an appeal which was stronger than the larger offers of staid routine business.

Miss Thomas was fated to unhappiness. She was born Oliveretta Duffy, and grew up in a depressing, smoky Pennsylvania community. She married into that life of grime, labor and sweat.

The marriage was a desperately unhappy one. The girl fled to New York, taking refuge in a cousin's household in Harlem. She haunted the streets of uptown New York looking for work and found it at last behind a basement counter in a department store. She had escaped the grime of Pittsburgh for the grind of a shop-girl in Harlem.

Then came one of those bits of Aladdin magic which are the lure of New York. A newspaper bidding for shop-girl circulation announced that Howard Chandler Christy, the famous artist, was holding a competition for a perfect model, the supreme New York beauty. There were prizes to be awarded, and the glory of having one's picture in the paper.

Oliveretta Duffy had recovered a bit from the depressions of Pittsburgh, and there was a radiant Irish beauty just back of her eyes, ready to bloom. She took a chance, reported sick at the store and in her pathetic best clothes went downtown to the Christy studio to sit waiting with the throng of the ambitious. It was a convention of the piquant beauties of the New York shop girl. Every race of the metropolitan melting pot was represented in that array. Oliveretta Duffy won—the prize, the picture in the paper, the publicity, everything.

Over in Broadway Florenz Ziegfeld was engaged in his business of "glorifying the American girl" per the "Follies." His merchandise was and is feminine beauty, preferably famous beauty. Here was youth and beauty, with a brand new fame in the papers. Oliveretta Duffy went to the Follies and burst into fame as Olive Thomas. She was a sudden sensation, the toast of Broadway. Strong men grew dizzy under her eyes. She was overwhelmed with admiration and gifts of treasure, diamond necklaces, pendants, rings, parties, orchids, everything that the dreaming little shop girl might fancy on the screen of her imagination.

On this wave of adulation Miss Thomas was signed by Triangle Pictures Corporation for the screen. Her screen appearances were successful enough with Triangle, but Triangle was driven more with promotion than performance, and its decline had set in when her contract expired.

Olive Thomas had won the world, and still had not found happiness. Her triumphs were all in the desperate, hard, grown-up world. The Myron Selznick contract was a chance to be a kid. She wanted to play, not with the thrill of millionaires and diamond necklaces, but the simple fun of a couple of youngsters breaking into business.

Master Myron Selznick was now launched in redemption of the family name from obscurity. He took offices at 729 Seventh avenue, near the offices where his father presided as the suppressed head of Select Pictures. A new electric sign burst upon the gaze of Broadway:

SELZNICK PICTURES—OLIVE THOMAS

Now it was really a very good sign. But Adolph Zukor did not like it. He had been to a lot of trouble, not to say expense, to obliterate that name. Here it was sprouting up again, as vigorously persistent as a dandelion on the front lawn.

Furthermore, it was reported at 485 Fifth avenue that over at 729 Seventh avenue the office of the president of Select was filled with posters, sketches and advertising matter pertaining to Myron Selznick's enterprise. The young man seems to have been getting considerable fatherly advice.

This led to an open discussion and an open letter from Adolph Zukor in the trade press discussing the president of Select. It had become a public fight.

Selznick, holding half of the stock and being in office, successfully resisted efforts to dislodge him. Before long it was announced that he had purchased the Zukor interest in Select.

Some swift moves and developments ensued.

The Selznick organization began to lose its stars, all of them through the usual paths of departure except Olive Thomas. Tragic death from poison ended her career in Paris, where she had gone in an interlude between pictures. Probably all of that story has not been told and never will be told. She had won success, as it is called, beyond measure. She had money, adoration, yet another marriage, and it all was nothing.

Outwardly the House of Selznick continued strong, with a brave show of electric lights and advertising. But decline was under way.

Zukor launched a new concern, Realart Pictures Corporation, with Mary Miles Minter and a secondary line of stars, in pictures well designed to give Selznick direct competition. Realart drew to its service many members of the Selznick selling organization.

Selznick increased the effulgence of his advertising to support a product of waning star value. A heavy campaign of painted bulletins told the world that: "Selznick Pictures Make Happy Hours," an echo of the ancient "Mutual Movies Make Time Fly." Selznick picked the slogan out of a conversation with Al Lichtman, who was once again with Zukor as sales manager for Famous Players-Lasky.

Ostensibly as a lavish gesture of gratitude, Selznick presented Lichtman with a costly watch, the back of which flamed with inlaid diamonds illuminating the inscription:

TO AL LICHTMAN
from
LEWIS J. SELZNICK
In grateful appreciation of
SELZNICK PICTURES
MAKE HAPPY HOURS

Lichtman was properly pleased with the watch, and in his travels showed it in pride to the world of the motion picture.

Selznick was pleased with it, too. He felt that he had put a Selznick twenty-four sheet in the vest pocket of the opposing sales department. "Beware of the Greeks when they come bearing gifts."

Selznick's banking strength began to wane. Loans of millions were called with abruptness. Eventually the corporation fell from its effulgence into a receivership and ultimate liquidation. In the summer of 1925 Lewis J. Selznick, with more backers and a new bankroll, descended on Florida to investigate the real estate excitement.

Paralleling his pleasant diversions with Selznick, Adolph Zukor pursued his program with lengthening strides. Late in 1916 he announced the addition of George M. Cohan to Artcraft pictures in *Broadway Jones,* released in March, 1917. Cohan was not a motion picture hit. Zukor was still trying that old "famous player" idea. His last, and probably final, experiment with it was in 1918 when Famous Players made two pictures with Enrico Caruso. The first of these, *My Cousin,* went to its premier showing at the Rivoli theatre where the great Caruso sat in a loge box to regard it.

"It is good, not silly like the rest of the pictures," Caruso modestly commented to the author of this history.

But the box office results across the nation proved that Victrola fame has nothing to do with the screen. Caruso's second picture stayed in the can.

Following up the acquisition of Cohan in 1917, Zukor gathered into Artcraft all the major stars of Triangle when that aspiring concern began to expire. He took over John Emerson and Anita Loos, and Fairbanks, then Thomas Ince, D. W. Griffith and Mack Sennett. The Aitken triangle was absorbed into the Zukor polygon. Zukor was out to surround all the box office value in the world. Roscoe Arbuckle, a comedian who had risen in Keystone and Sennett comedies after Chaplin's departure, was acquired through a new company organized by the Schencks, and "Fatty" went into the Paramount pot.

Douglas Fairbanks had been driving himself upward into the top rank of stardom by dint of ability and crafty management. When Chaplin arrived in Los Angeles with the crowning fame of his great $670,000 contract in 1916, Fairbanks began to be seen about with the comedian a great deal. And when shortly Mary Pickford signed her million dollar contract with Adolph Zukor it happened that the three were often together, Douglas, Mary and Charlie. Usually there was a still camera about, and the pictures of the trio got into the papers. Benny Zeidman, an office boy of the old Lubin concern, now grown up into ruthless ingenuity, represented Fairbanks. A good deal of copy went forth along with those pictures containing the phrase "Doug will soon be in the same class with Charlie and Mary." Fairbanks occasionally grew offended at Zeidman's enthusiasm and fired him, but Benny paid no attention to that. He got the pictures in the paper.

The master stroke of this campaign was a result of an impromptu athletic match between Fairbanks and Chaplin alongside the studio fence. They frolicked and broadjumped and leap-frogged to Fairbanks' delight. On the other side of the fence was Benny Zeidman with a cameraman. They made a half reel of film which went into private non-commercial circulation among exhibitors and movie magnates. It carried ocular argument that Doug and Charlie were intimate, therefore inferentially box office equals.

And Benny probably got fired again for that. But it did not interfere with his salary. Fairbanks made good on his campaign. He was, indeed, soon in the same star class with Charlie and Mary. That got him into Zukor's Artcraft.

Excepting only Chaplin, Zukor had all of the topmost of the great names on the screen. May 1, 1917, he announced that

LEWIS J. SELZNICK, who entered motion pictures selling diamonds and stayed to play big hands for high stakes in the hectic game of the film trade.

GLORIA SWANSON, in the days of her service to Mack Sennett comedies of the early Ukelele Period — her robust friend in this scene is Mack Swain, comedian of Keystone origin.

Famous Player Lasky Corporation had acquired control of Art-craft. Now all of the eggs were in one very large basket.

Over at Vitagraph in Flatbush, J. Stuart Blackton, one of the founders, was growing unhappy as he grew obscure. Vitagraph, one of the first and once one of the mightiest picture concerns in the world, was falling behind with the rest of the old Patents Company group. Edison, Kalem, Lubin and Biograph, glorious in their day, had shut down and quit.

Blackton decided to leave the old home and seek a share of Zukor's place in the sun. He withdrew from Vitagraph and entered into a contract to produce independently for Famous Players. This arrangement was short lived.

When once again Sir Thomas Lipton came over to sail the *Shamrock* through the publicity seas of the newspapers, Commodore J. Stuart Blackton was a guest aboard the yacht on which Lipton enjoyed his tea and the races. William Dunn, formerly a Vitagraph actor and director, was in Blackton's retinue. Dunn had been Blackton's "idea man." Below decks, somewhere adjacent to the buffet, Dunn overtook a new idea. He beckoned his chief, Blackton aside.

"Say, if Lipton can get it for selling tea, and Lever for selling soap, and Dewar for selling whisky, then you ought to get it for making pictures!"

"Get what, Bill?"

"Listen, *Sir* Thomas Lipton, *Lord* Leverhulme, *Sir* John Dewar."

Blackton went back to watch the races.

A few months later Blackton sailed for London to launch a new film project, whether on Dunn's idea or not, it does not matter. He arranged for a spectacular effort, a long feature drama to be made in natural color by the Prizma process. *The Glorious Adventure,* a scenario of the days of King Charles and the great fire of London, was written by Felix Orman to give the camera color opportunity. Blackton scanned the peerage and cast Lady Diana Manners as the heroine. Promotional literature made note of the fact that Blackton was of British birth.

The picture was a fair success abroad, but an indifferent attraction in the United States. It marked the beginning of serious efforts with natural color in screen drama.

The Glorious Adventure paved the way for Lady Diana Manners' stage appearances in the United States in Morris Gest's presentation of *The Miracle*. Also Flora Le Breton and Victor McLaglan, introduced by the Blackton production, came over to join the Hollywood film colony.

Commodore Blackton, after a number of other productions, returned to the United States and Vitagraph, with which he remained until the sale of the concern to Warner Brothers, in 1925.

CHAPTER SEVENTY-EIGHT

WILSON, HEARST AND CREEL

W<small>E</small> have come to the place where the World War impinged upon the affairs of the motion picture in the United States. It is a chapter of sensational importance—because nothing of importance occurred. The United States government declared war on Germany April 6, 1917.

It was quite a large war. But it was all overseas. It was stupendously big and very distant. The war was not very personal to any of us unless we were required to attend with a musket. The public really was not inclined to pay much attention to it. It was a big show, but monotonous. It had delivered its entire dramatic and emotional punch when the world went to screaming at the top of its voice in 1914. By 1917 we had grown used to the shouting.

This perfectly understandable and honest public attitude was reflected more accurately and frankly in the motion picture than in any other institution.

We had elected Woodrow Wilson, the second time, because "he kept us out of war." And now in April '17 we were in the blamed thing. We went to mass meetings and applauded the band, but we did not enlist in conspicuous numbers.

For related and additional reasons, if you will turn to the published organs of the motion picture, April and May of that year, you will have difficulty discovering that there was a war.

One motion picture of the early war period became an international issue, deeply involved with world affairs with a history that has been held a secret of diplomatic records. It was the serial entitled *Patria*. The story is intricate, touching high places and famous names.

Edward A. MacManus was at the head of the International News Service and the International Film Service, both Hearst enterprises. It will be remembered that MacManus first invaded the pictures with his serial idea and the Edison-Ladies' World-McClure *What Happened to Mary?* series. MacManus was studying the war situation and looking for ideas to be capitalized in the autumn of 1916 when everybody but the public knew we were going into the big fight overseas. The newspapers and the atmosphere were full of preparedness propaganda.

By way of improving the scenery and giving accent to the Internationals' newsreel picture MacManus and fellow conspirators planted a most impressive Joan d'Arc, in glittering armor and mounted on a white horse, in a woman's suffrage parade on Fifth avenue. It was the first flowering of an idea of preparedness for women.

Presently this idea began to elaborate itself in the mind of MacManus and grew eventually into a full-blown outline of a motion picture serial which was to get aboard the trend of the day and capitalize at one and the same time the interest of the feminist movement and the patriotic wave. It was to be a motion picture written to a prescription.

Some elements of the history of the Dupont family of Delaware, famous munition makers for generations, suggested the basis for the story. John Blanchard Clymer started writing the piece. Charles Goddard also took a hand at the story and eventually it came under the pen and hand of Louis Joseph Vance.

The original purpose was to show the United States attacked by an imaginary nation, with the heroine, *The Last of the Channings*, saving the country, through great suspense.

This was, however, too good an opportunity to be lost from the point of view of the Hearst newspapers. It will be recalled that these papers had had a great deal to say about the Japanese, about a naval base in Magdalena Bay down the Gulf of Lower California, about the Mexican situation and the yellow peril in the West.

Also the American punitive expedition into Mexico with its hide and seek pursuit of Villa was fresh in memory as a bit of contemporary history. The stage was well set.

William Randolph Hearst became more than usually interested in this motion picture detail of his multitudinous public enterprises and interests. The opportunity was amazingly pat to make the screen story a harmonic chord in the newspaper and magazine symphony.

The imaginary foe of the United States in the serial story became an allied army of Mexicans and Japanese.

The serial was produced by the Wharton studios. Irene Castle headed the cast, which included Milton Sills, Warner Oland and Nigel Barrie.

There were two nations displeased most particularly with *Patria*—Mexico and Japan. We were not on speaking terms with Mexico. Japan was suave and indirect. Mr. Hanrihara of the embassy down in Washington continued to bow and smile as usual. But Japan had a treaty with Britain and some very direct diplomatic wires. From roundabout ways pressure began to build up against *Patria*. In various places about the country the picture was banned.

Then one day the International's home office received a tactful letter, reading:

Several times in attending Keith's theatre here I have seen portions of the film entitled *Patria*, which has been exhibited there and I think in a great many other theatres in the country. May I not say to you that the character of the story disturbed me very much. It is extremely unfair to the Japanese and I fear that it is calculated to stir up a great deal of hostility which will be far from beneficial to the country, indeed will, particularly in the present circumstances, be extremely hurtful. I take the liberty, therefore, of asking whether the Company would not be willing to withdraw it if it is still being exhibited.

With much respect,

Sincerely yours,

WOODROW WILSON.

Patria was called in for alterations. The Japanese and Mexican flags were cut out of the picture and it managed to squeeze by the censorship and back into the market, considerably crippled at the box office.

When anything is everybody's business it is nobody's business. In such cases we have a meeting and appoint a committee.

The war was a good deal of a committee affair.

The government—our committee at Washington—and its chairman, Woodrow Wilson, had to have some money and quite a bit of help to take care of this war job. They had to get it out of us.

But we were busy with "business as usual," living, working, playing and going to the pictures. Since we insisted on going to the picture show instead of going to war the committee decided to get to us by breaking into the screen. It was easier to go where we were looking than it was to make us turn around.

Naturally the first step was to appoint a committee. The picture business was assumed to be organized into the National Association of the Motion Picture Industry, with William A. Brady its president.

In a letter from the White House, President Wilson appointed Brady chairman of a committee which was to get the motion picture industry to do something about the war. One way or another the president of every motion picture corporation in the United States became the member of a committee which was to do something about the war. The result was a tremendous rush of publicity in the trade press about the wonderful recognition which had come to the industry. That was the only result.

The first real junction of the screen and war affairs came through the American Red Cross. The Red Cross had to grow tremendously and it had to get before the public fast. It started a bureau of pictures and sought to reach us with film pleas. The pictures were shown mostly at meetings. They were miscellaneous collections of foreign and domestic pictures pertaining to the war. They were not theatrical products in any sense, which is another way of saying they were amateur pictures without entertainment and a punch. In consequence they reached a very small audience.

About April 14, 1917, George Creel was appointed chairman of the "Committee on Public Information." It was his difficult assignment to be at once and the same time something of a censor and very much a press agent for the war. His job was defined as "selling the war to America." After the war Creel wrote a book *How We Advertised America*, which is a story of that selling campaign. It is rather clear that the war had to be sold to us. They are still collecting installments.

Meanwhile the motion pictures made by the Signal Corps of the army, which were the only American war films available, were going to the Red Cross. Their only important distribution was through the Red Cross bureau of pictures to the newsreels. The little one reel news releases had the burden of telling us all that was told pictorially about America's part in the war. The films were haphazardly made, haphazardly distributed and presented in the same way.

Creel, tremendously busy, began presently to see the screen a neglected medium. Looking back it seems a belated recognition. But the fact is that the Creel bureau had to get to work immediately and the long established institution of the press with which he was most familiar was a thousandfold more available for propaganda. The basic patterns of operation had all been worked out by long experience. In the realm of the screen they had to be pioneered—pioneered in a world of war.

Charles S. Hart, then an executive of the Hearst magazine organization, was drafted into the service of the Committee on Public Information and assigned by Creel to look into this picture matter. Hart reported shortly that Red Cross distribution was not giving America a pictorial message. It was not a criticism of the Red Cross, because it was not a propaganda organization. It was a mere incident of the jumbled make-shift rush of war moves.

In March of 1918, nearly a year after America's entry into the war, a meeting of Red Cross officials, headed by George Murnane, a New York banker, and the heads of the Creel organization was held at 10 Jackson Place in Washington, headquarters of the Committee on Public Information. As a result of that session the pictorial activities of the war were turned over to Creel. The Division of Pictures of the Committee on Public Information resulted.

Establishing offices in New York, Hart set about trying to connect the flow of war pictures available from the Signal Corps, and other sources, with the established channel of distribution to the theatres, the motion picture industry.

A curious problem existed. There never had been one like it. Distribution of propaganda to the press was relatively easy. The press is a commercial institution which gets its raw material, the news, by picking it up, free. Its editors are presumed to know news and what it is worth no matter where it comes from. The motion picture, equally but no more commercial than the press, pays high for its material and judges largely by price.

The government could hand a good story to the news associations and every newspaper reader would see it. If the government handed out a free motion picture nobody saw it. A free picture was not merchandise and could not go through a merchandising machine. The government through the Division of Films of the Committee on Public Information was thereby forced into the motion picture business, as a business.

The only avenue to the public was the theatre screen. The only route to the theatre was a selling route. A picture has to be sold to the distributor, sold to the exhibitor, sold to the public at the box office.

Theoretically the motion picture industry should have been permitted to send cameramen to the war, just as newspapers sent correspondents. But the motion picture enjoys no such status as the press. Military persons look on all cameras with suspicion. Few officers of the military establishment had ever heard of the motion picture. The idea of filming the war in the sense that it was covered for the newspapers was really beyond comprehension.

The Committee on Public Information went into the film business in New York. It also used all manner of suggestion and pressure to get cameramen to put into the photographic service of the Signal Corps.

When Hart went about New York to put government pictures into the established channels, the big distributing concerns, he came abruptly against the fact that there was no unity in the business. The film world was still a war within itself, recognizing no common interest.

"Hand your pictures over to me—you can't trust the other fellows," was the uniform statement up Fifth avenue and down Broadway.

It was sincere, too. That was the way the picture magnates felt about each other. Obviously the government could do no such thing. The principle was impossible.

The result was that the Division of Films fabricated and assembled its own war films, presented them for metropolitan first runs in the name of the United States of America and then contracted on a percentage basis for subsequent circulation through various distributors. The government had all the troubles which beset an independent producer.

Statistically the history of the government in the film business takes about four lines:

Title	Theatre bookings	Film rentals
"Pershing's Crusaders"	4,189	$181,741.69
"America's Answer"	4,548	185,144.30
"Under Four Flags"	1,820	63,946.48
"Official War Review"	6,950	334,622.35

Sundry other items brought the total receipts of the Division of Films up to $852,744.30. But the money is of no matter save as it indicates circulation. The war pictures reached about the same number of audiences as Chaplin comedies, about one third of the theatres, an excellent showing considering the slight entertainment value of the war. Dennis J. Sullivan, the same executive who had handled the distribution of the Chaplin comedies for Mutual, was in charge of the distribution of the government pictures through most of their active period.

The manner in which the war was photographed made it impossible to assemble a real production. The cameramen were under no central editorial control. The result resembled a story of the war about as a scrapbook resembles a historical novel. This was no fault of Hart or Creel. It was an incident of war.

The *Official War Review* was edited by Charles Urban, the

American-British pioneer of Kinemacolor fame, and Ray L. Hall, first editor of Hearst newsreels. The *War Review* was, however, not a newsreel. Censorships saw to that. The feature pictures of the Division got most of their emotional values from the attentions of Samuel L. Rothafel, the Broadway screen showman.

The Division of Films died before the same firing squad which executed the Committee on Public Information. The Creel organization was wiped out by congressional enactment June 30, 1919, without benefit of clergy. Creel had inevitably made many enemies in what could at best have been a thankless job. The newspapers blamed him for all of the annoyances of the war. The motion picture industry resented him as an intruder. The anti-Wilson politicians hated him because he was a peculiarly personal element of the Wilson institution.

The Committee of Public Information died intestate. The method of its taking off by congress did not even permit of burial, much less administration of the estate. Not a cent was available for closing its accounts and liquidating its extensive and farflung affairs. It was left in just such a tangle as any going business would have been if overtaken by a disaster which wiped out staff and payroll.

For this reason there were of course many unbanked checks, uncollected accounts and scattered assets, including costly pictures stored in film vaults all over the world. They blamed Creel for that and shouted scandal. He hired a watchman and made weekly trips to Washington at his own expense trying to rescue the claims.

The truth is that the Committee on Public Information's record is one of the best made by the government in the conduct of the war, considerably better than in certain matters of shipbuilding, aircraft, railroading and the like.

The anti-Wilson forces made their attack on Creel very personal and he, being a Quixotic Celt, took it that way to a dramatic degree. He was so thoroughly martyred that he was able to convert his troubles into current literature for several years. He is something of a professional under-dog fancier, always fighting for somebody or something. Even the title page of his *How We Advertised America* announces him as "Author of Ireland's Fight for Freedom."

The feelings involved are epitomized in the appreciation of Irish loyalty in the inscription which Creel wrote on the fly-leaf of a copy of that book, presented:

> To Charles S. Hart
> Companion of my travail, solace of my misery, source of my accomplishment, and a gay, faithful and unfailing comrade,—with the devotion of his friend
>
> GEORGE CREEL.

There is the pleasant dolorousness of the skirling pipes in that. It is a refrain from the same eternal tune theme as *The Lament of Douglas* or the poetic gloom of *Mollie Brannigan* as sung by John McCormack.

The peculiar fact for screen history is that the vast experience of the war contributed nothing whatever to the art of the motion picture.

D. W. Griffith went abroad during the war and renewed his pride of Welsh blood by shaking hands with David Lloyd George. Griffith, who had made so many excellent wars before the camera in the hills of California, made a war picture in France with the war left out. It was *Hearts of the World*, a tale of a village behind the lines.

Among the countless adventures of the war cameramen the exploit of Larry Darmour, in the Signal Corps photographic service, was unique. Darmour had served his film novitiate on the Gaumont Mutual Weekly, under the editorship of Pell Mitchell, who assigned the youth to the Ford "peace ship" excursion.

Darmour's next approach to Germany was in uniform via Château Thierry. He arrived on the eve of the famous advance. He strolled about to look over locations and completely lost track of the war. Darkness came on, and Darmour hesitated to blunder about lest he step on the war in the night. He rolled up in a shell hole and took a nap.

The most eventful morning of the war was announced by an exchange of barrages. Darmour awoke to find that he had been first over the top by several hours. He was in the middle of No Man's Land between the Lines. The American barrage and the German counter barrage swept over him. Darmour stayed by his shell hole and escaped unharmed. He returned from the war with an impression that its perils had been slightly exaggerated.

The war brought Sarah Bernhardt's last screen appearance in *Mothers of France* circulated in America in 1917. In this picture, Bernhardt, crippled and enfeebled, a sad relic of herself as the personification of Gallic emotion, sat through her scenes in a chair. Only five years before this same Bernhardt in her *Queen Elizabeth*, imported by Adolph Zukor, started the rise of feature pictures and the re-formation of the entire industry.

There was again a contact between the war and the motion picture in the use of stars to help sell the Liberty Loans. The Treasury Department sought the drawing power of many of the major personalities of the screen, including Pickford, Chaplin, and Fairbanks. They made personal appearances at meetings and little trailer pictures of them were added to theatre programs. This activity established acquaintance between the stars and William G. McAdoo, Secretary of the Treasury, and his publicity engineer, Oscar Price.

There was a confab around Price's big flat-top desk in the

U. S. Treasury building in Washington one day. It reached the chatty stage.

"Why don't you folks get together and distribute your own pictures—you are big enough to do that," Price remarked. It was a passing thought—and a disturbing one. A new company and a great deal of complication were to come out of that.

The Treasury Department under Carter Glass, successor to McAdoo, with Frank Wilson in charge of its publicity drives, circulated a pictorial history of the war on the screen, under the title of *The Price of Peace*, selling the Victory Loan, the last installment on our debt to LaFayette. Then Frank Wilson, grown accustomed to the dizzy altitude of big figures in the Treasury, went out to form a motion picture finance company.

CHAPTER SEVENTY-NINE

MARY, McADOO AND MONTE CARLO

EARLY in 1917, just when Adolph Zukor had bought a dubious truce with Selznick and was busy counting all the jewels of starland into the strongbox of his Famous Players-Lasky Corporation, the tocsin sounded again. He rushed to the battlements.

A cloud of dust was rising on the western horizon and there was the increasing thunder of hurrying hoofs. An uprising had broken out in theatredom and the foe was riding down on the citadel of Adolph-the-Aggressive.

The exhibitors were coming! Their lances gleamed in the starlight and their eyes lusted for treasure.

The leader of that menacing column had risen out of the sea and the other end of the world. J. D. Williams, former assistant treasurer of the Parkersburg opera house, was home again from Australia, looking for something to do.

It was late in 1916 when Williams, after parting with his large theatre interests in the Antipodes, set about trying to promote a big screen theatre project in Los Angeles. Right abruptly Williams found Los Angeles bankers and capitalists timid about such a venture. They had heard something. He sought the source of their timidity and found it was in the conversation and complaints of Thomas L. Tally, one of California's leading showmen and a pioneer from peep show days.

Tally, it seemed, was exceedingly annoyed because of the rising cost of big star pictures, more especially the pictures controlled by Adolph Zukor. Also the selling policy which had made him buy a whole program in order to get Mary Pickford was an embitterment. Tally was alarmed lest the increasing control of the producer interests should reduce the whole race of theatremen to serfdom.

Williams tried to win Tally's support for a big theatre project in vain. Tally had another, combative notion. It was time, he opined, for the exhibitors to pool their purchasing power and deal directly with the stars. Williams joined in the plan and together they started on a tour of the key cities enrolling the leading exhibitors as they went.

When Williams arrived in New York he had enlisted the co-operation of about twenty-seven of the principal theatre operators of the country, each in control of a pace-making house in an important center.

The First National Exhibitors' Circuit was announced in New York in the middle of April 1917.

Zukor broadsided with expressions in the trade press and signed a preachment in *Variety* on the question "Are you an Exhibitor or a Producer?"

Meanwhile Goldwyn and other picture chieftains were busy, everybody seeking to make a block-booking contract with the combined exhibitors, or to undermine their organization.

A new war was on.

The masters of the industry were out to wipe out this new menace of their supremacy before it could gather headway. Many and devious were the moves.

The most simple and direct steps started, as usual in the strategy of the picture business, over the luncheon table. J. D. Williams, as the organizing factor of First National, was invited to lunch with Lewis J. Selznick and Adolph Zukor, then partners in Select Pictures Corporation. They met at the Café Beaux Arts and when it got down to the coffee Williams was offered a large and handsome salary. It was pointed out to him that the First National idea would probably fail and leave him flat. He was prevailed upon to conditionally accept a sum in advance.

He put it in his pocket, playing safe. After awhile he returned it. The first significant move of First National was pursuit of Charles Chaplin. Chaplin was making his last picture for the Lone Star Mutual release. Mutual was a desperately sick company. Its decline had been steady and continuous from the day it lost Griffith, Ince and Sennett.

John R. Freuler, president of Mutual and the author of the big Lone Star deal with Chaplin, figured anew and bid a salary of $1,000,000 for another series of twelve comedies.

Chaplin was shopping about.

Syd Chaplin, representing his brother, met officials of the First National in Chicago at the Hotel Sherman. They offered to pay $1,075,000 for eight two-reel pictures, with a number of provisions for latitude in production which Chaplin wanted. Freuler's bid was in fact the highest, since it meant straight salary, with Chaplin assuming no production cost. First National's offer meant more liberty of expression. Chaplin had outgrown a job.

First National got Chaplin.

It was a pleasant bit of irony that Thomas L. Tally, the Los Angeles member of the First National group, who did not think Chaplin was funny, had to handle the details of the signing of the contract. Tally had never used a Chaplin comedy in his theatre.

Now First National threw down the gauntlet and went after Mary Pickford. Harry Schwalbe, First National official representing the Stanley theatres of Philadelphia, went to Los Angeles on this mission. It was an arduous campaign. He sought Mary and dined often with her mother, Mary's shrewd business counsellor. Schwalbe had the backing of the great theatre organization and the bidding mounted higher and higher. Eventually he agreed to give Mary a contract for three pictures at $250,000 each, if she would leave Artcraft, and to pay $50,000 to her mother for her good offices and good wishes.

Mary accepted the First National offer. She again was not going to be "second to Chaplin." By a later adjustment Mary got an additional $100,000 each for her pictures, making a total of $1,050,000.

First National reached about for stars and acquired among others the Talmadges and Thomas H. Ince with his increasing production plant.

In the period of his First National contract Chaplin's comedies evolved from the two reel calibre of his Lone Star-Mutual series into feature length dramas. This was in a degree a mechanical adjustment to the market, fitting his product physically to his star value and the major position on the program of the theatre.

Chaplin's greatest picture of the time was *The Kid*, which incidentally made a star of little Jackie Coogan. It is the tradition that Master Coogan stumbled into his screen career by winking at Chaplin in a Los Angeles railway station.

The Kid was completed in the midst of Chaplin's first domestic crisis, when attorneys were seeking a settlement with Mildred Harris, the first Mrs. Chaplin.

There was prospect that the negative of the unborn *The Kid* would be attached on an alimony claim and Chaplin hurried East with it. In New York the process servers pursued Chaplin and his comedy from hotel to hotel and up and down and about. Meanwhile the negative, for safe-keeping, was continuously in transit in a meandering taxicab, with Carlyle Robinson, Chaplin's press agent, riding on guard over the treasure.

When the chase pressed too close the film laden taxi leaped convenient state lines, into New Jersey, into Connecticut, up hill and down dale across bridges and ferries. Those tin cans contained a world of laughs and a fortune for Chaplin. They came to rest at last in far away Utah where the state laws prevented attachment. Chaplin there caught his breath and cut his comedy in peace while the lawyers negotiated in Los Angeles.

The Kid was worth the trouble. It was far beyond the anticipations of the original First National contract, which, after many squirmings and negotiations by Chaplin, was abrogated. On the new and special deal for *The Kid* Chaplin profited considerably more than a million dollars. The one picture was worth more than the original contract for eight pictures had contemplated. Chaplin's art and craftsmanship had outgrown contracts.

Meanwhile First National was a-whirl and agog with internal politics and external combat. The threat was noised about that Adolph Zukor was out to win a control of this troublesome independent manifestation by the purchase of component theatre interests. Williams fortified the First National by the formation of a voting trust. The moves were intricate, rapid and continuous. Famous Players began to launch into a theatre control campaign of its own with the purchase of many houses in dominant centers, leading eventually to the acquisition of several hundred theatres.

The war for motion picture supremacy had moved on to new battlegrounds. We saw it rise in the beginning over patent control, thence to market monopoly based on a patents pool or cross-licensing system, and then for a time center on a competitive struggle of picture production and stars, from which Zukor emerged with the stars. Now in its next phase it was becoming an issue of theatre seats, real estate investments and large scale financial operations. The fight started at the lens in Edison's first camera at West Orange and spread to the screens of the world.

Now that the inventors, cameramen, exchangemen, and exhibitors had taken their fling at motion picture control, it was the actors' turn.

The scene and setting for this new manifestation was the rose bowered veranda of a California bungalow. William G. McAdoo, son-in-law of President Wilson, also former Secretary of the Treasury and now Director General of the railroads, was there taking his ease and recuperating from the travail of government service under the stress of war. McAdoo had, on December 12, 1918, resigned effective January 17, 1919.

About January 7, when the Director General's private car arrived in the yards of Los Angeles, there was a band serenade under the auspices of Douglas Fairbanks, and a conclave of picture personages of high degree.

Remember that incident of Liberty Loan days when the stars in the drive were around the desk down in the treasury building in Washington? "Why don't you folks get together and distribute your own pictures?" Oscar Price had casually suggested. Price was the press agent of McAdoo's administration in the treasury, and now his assistant in administration of the government's railroad affairs. The idea behind that chance remark was now about to bear fruit. It was a notion that had been stirring into life in many minds.

Up at Santa Barbara at McAdoo's bungalow the old friends of the Liberty Loan campaigns talked it over. It was quite a gathering. Douglas Fairbanks, Mary Pickford, and Charles Chaplin and D. W. Griffith were there. There were several such conferences. The picture stars now definitely proposed that McAdoo should head an organization which would market their film wares. Both McAdoo's record and his fame, begilded with high office and Washington, made him an especially desired association. McAdoo declined.

"But, if you will get Oscar Price, I will help you organize and be your counsel," McAdoo suggested.

And so it was arranged at a meeting held at Fairbanks' home in Beverly Hills January 19. About the eighteenth of March, Price arrived in New York to begin operations. The United Artists Corporation of Delaware was incorporated in April, with Price as president and McAdoo its general counsel.

The announcement of United Artists was something of a sensation to the sensation-weary film world. The classic comment of the occasion came from Richard Rowland, then head of Metro Pictures Corporation. He received the interesting tidings from Arthur James, press and intelligence agent of Metro. Rowland meditated on the significance of the new move for almost a full second.

"So," he remarked, "the lunatics have taken charge of the asylum."

It should be added, lest there be an assumption that the comment sprang from snobbery, that Rowland has been philosopher enough to classify himself as "one of the accidentally successful."

The name of Hiram Abrams came early into the affairs of United Artists and presumably he had been something more of a factor in the formation of the organization than the outward moves indicated. Abrams' long association with Paramount and the Zukor enterprises gave him, in the eyes of the uniting artists, something of the atmospheric value that accompanied the comfortable assurances of the old Famous Players-Artcraft payroll with which they had parted not so long before. McAdoo and Price were a handsome new front, but they seemed to want some of the old back to lean against.

Meanwhile Abrams and Adolph Zukor had fallen apart with considerable depth of feeling. Therefore Abrams might well have been expected to make the competition of United Artists with Famous Players-Lasky decidedly snappy. Ben Schulberg, who had risen in executive function from his position as Zukor's first press agent, went along with Abrams.

Differences arose a little quicker than immediately between Price and the United Artists over issues which centered on Abrams' program and plans as general manager of the concern. There was a most animated debate in Douglas Fairbanks' bedroom in a New York hotel, and Price resigned, effective April 15, 1919. Shortly McAdoo also disconnected and sold his shares in the enterprise.

Incident to the McAdoo-Price withdrawal a vastly pretentious theatre project intended to assure the stars of United Artists a sure avenue to the market went by the boards. This scheme which Price had been engineering included the millions of the Dupont interests, James and Nicholas Brady, E. E. Smathers, a wealthy oil operator, Joseph Godsol, and a consolidation with the then still active Goldwyn concern.

This loss of the theatre project left the United Artists and their product to the open market, with only the box office value of big names to compete against the intricate machinery of control and theatre domination which the big corporations were building. The consequences were becoming evident as this chapter was written in 1925 when Joseph Schenck, a factotum in United Artists and a friend of the "big interests," all but consummated a plan to lead the big stars back to the fold by a merger with Metro-Goldwyn-Mayer. The deal was upset by Chaplin's refusal.

Meanwhile D. W. Griffith, departing from United Artists, entered in the service of Zukor again as a director for Famous Players.

With First National bidding for stars for its theatre machine, Zukor building a theatre organization and the great stars organizing themselves, Marcus Loew, theatre magnate, found it necessary to bestir himself.

Loew had continued prosperously as an exhibitor since the historically remote days when Zukor left Loew Enterprises to go his own gait. He was extending his theatre holdings widely. There appeared to be an excellent chance that he was going to be caught between the two sides of exhibitor-distributor warfare. As a counter move Loew acquired a control of Metro Pictures Corporation in January, 1919. Loew became a producer-distributor to protect his far-flung theatre chain.

Loew went into Metro at a fortunate moment. Metro's fortunes were at low tide. The concern was somewhat uncertainly recovering from the staggering blows of the influenza epidemic and its shutdown of the picture industry, coming on top of the post-armistice period when it along with every other motion picture concern was overloaded with war dramas. In those gloomy days Metro saw its weekly income drop from $108,000 a week to $6,000, while a weekly payroll for the distributing system alone was eating into the treasury at the rate of $30,000 a week. In addition Metro was at that time engaged in the costly production of *The Red Lantern* with Alla Nazimova.

The world was trying to find itself in the dull hush that followed the war. Loew got in on the ground floor.

Then strange fortune smiled on Metro. Richard Rowland, then president of the concern, is a person governed by a whimsical even if practical philosophy. War pictures had well near spelled the ruin of Metro, and yet Rowland followed with a fatal fascination the weekly advertisements of *The Four Horsemen of the Apocalypse* by Vincente Blasco Ibáñez. It was a novel of war, and through these months when all the world was trying to forget the war its circulation was mounting, mounting, mounting.

Here was a success which seemed to flaunt itself in the face of every index of the times. It was something to engage the attention of the busy-minded Rowland, alert in that game of chance and wits that is the motion picture. But, curiously typical of the world of the motion picture, Rowland's curiosity did not lead him to investigate the book, to read that rapid, cloying tale of horrendous glamours for himself. The book was nothing, but those weekly figures in the *Literary Section* of the *New York Times*—"fortieth printing—forty-first printing—forty-second printing" were enamoring and compelling. A dozen times he decided to order negotiations for the motion picture rights, and then one word, "War," intervened, and he did not make the step. It would be a folly against all experience. War pictures were dead.

An agent, a Broadway sharpshooter, vending motion picture rights, found his way into Rowland's office in his rounds.

"How'd you like to have the rights on *The Four Horsemen of the Apocalypse?*—ten thousand dollars advance against ten per cent royalty?"

Rowland sat like a man with a lone ace and a distrusted hunch against a pat hand. He decided to draw four cards.

"I'll take it," the president of Metro decided, wondering what to think of himself as he spoke.

A week passed and nothing happened. Rowland was almost glad it did not.

Then Jack Meador, press agent for Metro, strolled into the office.

"How would you like to buy *The Four Horsemen of the Apocalypse*—I know the Ibáñez representative."

Here was that hunch offering itself again.

"Yes, I want it," Rowland replied.

Metro paid a commission of $1,000 to the agent who could not deliver the story, and agreed to pay $30,000 to the representative of Ibáñez on the signing of the contract.

Meanwhile Ibánez came over to see this strange America which had gone so mad over his book. There were other bids for *The Four Horsemen*. It was winded that the Fox Film Corporation had offered $75,000. Ibánez thought the Metro deal, all but consummated, was inadequate. Rowland effected a compromise and paid an advance of $20,000 against ten per cent of the royalties. The story was Metro's.

"Read the *Four Horsemen*," Rowland wired Metro's west coast studio.

"Do not buy *Four Horsemen*, it will not film," the studio replied.

"Have bought the *Four Horsemen* and it is going to be filmed anyway," replied Rowland. Everybody in the Metro establishment shook their heads over this wild notion of the boss's.

Rowland called in June Mathis.

"Take this book and make a continuity. When you get one you like bring it to me. You've got to make good on this for me. Everybody in the world thinks I'm crazy."

When Miss Mathis delivered her script Rowland thumbed it over rapidly. It looked like a script and he had faith in Miss Mathis.

"Now about a director?"

Miss Mathis had a notion of her own.

"There's a young man out there who is more likely to see this than anyone else—Rex Ingram."

Rowland was taking chances all along the line on this wild war picture project now.

"O. K.," he ruled. "And how about Carlyle Blackwell for this *Julio* part you like so much?"

"There is an Argentinian dancer out there—Valentino—he is the part," Miss Mathis suggested.

Rowland deliberated. "Why deliberate?"

"Say, you take this script and go out there and make this picture—hire anybody you like. It's your job."

When the *Four Horsemen* came to New York and got its Ritz premiere the picture folk looked at it. "Great picture—but it's war," they said, and went away feeling a bit surprised, maybe even a little sorry for Rowland. He had many grave doubts himself. The picture represented $640,000 of what had been very good money before it was spent.

Then the picture went on at the Lyric theatre. The second day brought a capacity business and the great career of the production had begun.

Profits began to loom. Rowland was preparing to leave Metro and he had in mind a trip to Europe.

"It looks like we were going to have to pay Ibáñez a lot of money," he commented to Marcus Loew. "Let's buy him out."

Over in Mentone, by the blue, blue sea, Rowland visited Ibáñez. The Spanish novelist was building an expensive new home. He possibly could use some cash. The conditions looked auspicious for a deal.

Rowland and Ibáñez motored over to Monte Carlo and dined. In the after-dinner hour they strolled about the Casino.

Oblivious to the clustered groups over the roulette tables they walked up and down that hall of chance. Rowland had to have a pretext for his proposition. He sprang it.

"As long as you have an interest in that picture we shall have to handle it by itself to be fair to you. But we want to be free to deal with it as our own. We may want to sell it along with other pictures and make combination deals—so we want to buy your share. Now you might get more by waiting and riding through with the picture—and you might not. Anyway, we will give you——"

Rowland mentioned some figure in francs, many, many francs. Ibáñez grinned.

"Talk dollars," he answered.

"A hundred thousand American dollars," Roland responded.

"No."

They took another turn down the Casino. Fortunes were passing at the whim of the little ivory ball at the wheel.

"The best possible figure is $150,000," Rowland ventured.

"No, no," from Ibáñez.

They strolled back and forth, pausing idly and casually to glimpse the monotony of that endless drama of desperation at the wheels of Monte Carlo.

"One hundred and sixty thousand."

Ibáñez shook his head.

"One hundred and seventy thousand—and that is all."

Ibáñez looked at Rowland and decided it was indeed all.

"Si."

And so it was settled. Which made the total cost of the story rights on *The Four Horsemen* just $190,000 to Metro.

When Rowland came ashore in New York again the books showed that they would on that date have owed Ibáñez $210,000. The gross earnings up to the end of 1925 on the picture were about $4,000,000. Ten per cent of that amount is $400,000, so Metro's winnings on that night at Monte Carlo are nearing a quarter of a million.

The role of *Julio Desnoyers* in that picture of course made Valentino such a figure of such a quality of fame as would have fired the pride of the virile old centaur, *Madariaga*, himself, the fictional progenitor.

It was not, after all, a triumph of a war picture. It was a triumph of a new Don Juan of the screen, a victory for Latin love and suppressed desire among the movie millions. Valentino's fan mail mounted into hundreds of letters a day, on scented violet paper without outpourings of reverie fantasies about "dream visits." The box-office horde swallowed the *Four Horsemen* and the *Apocalypse* to get a sex thrill.

Not so long ago, Richard Rowland, now at the helm of First National, picked up the novel of *The Four Horsemen* to read it for the first time. He turned a few pages and then threw it under the radiator. He had had all the excitement there was in that story.

MARCUS LOEW, hero of one of those storybook careers, beginning at the age of six as a newsboy on New York's East Side and in middle life now the head of a hundred million dollar motion picture concern, the Metro-Goldwyn Corporation.

CHARLES C. PETTIJOHN of Indiana, Broadway and Fifth Avenue,
the lawyer who figured in the formative background of the
Motion Picture Producers and Distributors of America, Inc.,
becoming the chief field lieutenant of Will Hays.

CHAPTER EIGHTY

WILL HAYS GOES TO LUNCH

Down the years from the beginning of the screen it has been the original fancy of promoters, publicists, writers, educators, ministers and speakers generally to ring the phrase "the motion picture is only in its infancy."

For some twenty-and-odd years, while the quarrel raged about who was going to be the movies' papa, the infant continually kicked off the covers, knocked slats out of its crib, spilled its bottle and bawled for publicity, all the while accumulating bad manners and a lot of laundry.

About 1922, when Adolph Zukor, having taught the movie to say "Uncle," became its guardian *ad litem* and administrator *de bonis non*, it was time to get the infant a tutor.

The motion picture lives in a glass house, by, for and of exhibition. It is a decided exhibitionist. It intimately relates itself to the emotions of more people than any other art or industry. Its capital is personality and it is the personal affair of its millions of followers.

Fifteen years of the screen theatre and a considerable sprinkling of million dollar employment contracts sufficed to make the personages of the screen about the most thoroughly public figures in the world. Now a series of events pertaining to what would otherwise have been their private affairs, among important screen personages, contrived to shock the conventions and *mores* of the so-called American public. Most of these were commonplace matters, but being connected with the screen famous they became foci of national and world sensations.

In spite of the reluctance of the reading public to consider such material it becomes the painful duty of history to review a number of the choicer items.

The first of these sources of public agitation about the lives of the screen people to be considered must be the Pickford divorce, which by the misfortune of her fortunate position assumes an entirely disproportionate importance. As a divorce it was of no special importance. But neither was the apple shot by William Tell or the cherry tree chopped by George Washington. It depends on who does it. In this case it was "America's Sweetheart" who did it.

For some years it had been known and the subject of wide spread but unprinted comment that Mary Pickford's marriage with Owen Moore, a romantic episode of the old Imp picture days, had resulted unhappily. But mostly America had forgotten about it now.

About Saint Valentine's Day in 1920, Miss Pickford departed from Hollywood in quiet mystery. A remote ranchhouse on the outskirts of the obscure town of Genoa in Nevada became host to one Gladys Mary Smith Moore. Genoa is a proper spot for somber chapters of dead romance. It was settled by the Mormons, wanderers of the desert, in 1847, and has since become a lost town with scarce an inhabitant among its crumbling wooden shacks.

Nearby is the court town of Minden, not far also from Carson City. A lawyer filed suit in behalf of Gladys Mary Smith Moore for divorce from Owen Moore charging desertion.

Then like a figure in a melodrama, impelled by coincidence, Owen Moore and a camera man arrived in Virginia City. It was given out that Moore was there to make snow scenes for a coming picture. The title of the picture has not yet been announced. Now it chanced that he was unable to find hotel accommodations in Virginia City. So Moore drove on to Minden—fatal misstep! While he sat at luncheon in the little frame hotel, his mind busy on those snow scenes, an officer of the court surprised him and served the papers. Then Moore rode away in the snow—story book fashion. The sun sank in ruby and gold over the Sierras. It was a fade-out.

On March 2, Gladys Mary Smith Moore, accompanied by her mother, went into court at Minden before Frank P. Langen, judge, and gave testimony. A decree of divorce was granted.

The story was covered by a country correspondent of the Reno papers, in great simplicity of manner. It reached the newspapers of the United States couched in such gentle terms that they were several days discovering that it was a story. The first dispatches included this paragraph:

> Immediately after the decree Miss Pickford went back to the ranch where she had been living. She said she was seeking a quiet place to live and intended to stay near Minden for a long time and to make the state of Nevada her permanent home.

The pressure of queries from news editors in a few days had their effect on the correspondents at Reno and another wee trickle of a story came through quoting Miss Pickford as saying she would never marry again.

On Saturday, March 27, of the same year, 1920, being something less than a month later, Douglas Fairbanks gave a quiet but important party at his home in Beverly Hills. The party was in honor of Miss Pickford, the belle of Minden, Nevada. Now, incidentally, among the guests were the Rev. J. Whitcomb Brougher, pastor of Temple Baptist Church, and even more importantly one R. S. Sparks, who, it chances, was a deputy county clerk.

While Mr. Sparks was at the party he issued a license to wed to Douglas Elton Fairbanks, age 36, and Mary Gladys Smith Moore, age 26. This was more convenient than the red tape of the regular bureau at the court house, and, even less conspicuous.

The next day, Sunday March 28, Douglas and Mary were married by the Rev. Mr. Brougher.

So far so good. Sunday and Monday passed without events. Tuesday the story broke and went chattering over the wires. It was no sensation but it tended to confirm a report that Douglas and Mary were fond of each other.

Then something went wrong up in Nevada. April 16, Leonard B. Fowler, attorney general of Nevada, filed a suit to set aside the decree of divorce, charging collusion, fraud and untruthful testimony.

It began to be a national story. It was also something of a local disaster for Nevada's divorce industry. Several sojourners from the East found themselves annoyingly delayed in Reno by a wave of agitation against "short time divorces."

Eventually, in May 1922, the Supreme Court of Nevada sustained Pickford's divorce. Meanwhile it was frequently in the public prints, in news and editorial columns and on the public tongue. It was unfortunate for Miss Pickford and unfair. It was also unfortunate for the motion picture. The Pickford divorce was less open to question than thousands which passed unnoticed, but motion picture fame afforded a mark.

The flow of newspaper and grapevine comment on the life of the motion pictures was given a dash of much stronger stuff in 1921. On July 12 of that year an action was brought by Attorney General Allen of Massachusetts for the removal from office of Nathan A. Tufts, district attorney for Middlesex County. Among the specifications it was alleged there was some connection between the district attorney's office and the suppression of the social news of a motion party four years before.

It seems that a number of motion picture magnates of national prominence had attended a dinner to Fatty Arbuckle, given at the Copley Plaza March 6, 1917. The diners adjourned for coffee and pastry at Brownie Kennedy's roadhouse at Mishawum Manor, Woburn, Mass. A pleasant time was had by all and the check, when added up at 4 o'clock in the morning, totalled $1,050. Presumably the $50 was for hat checks. But the first cost was nothing to the upkeep.

Less than a month later the host of the evening got word from a friend in Boston that things were not so good. Some of the girls had talked and now there was trouble in the offing. There was a hurried conference of film magnates in the calm of New London, Conn., close to the Sound if any preferred to jump in. A fund of $100,000 was raised to deal with the situation. The money was presumed to be applied where it would do the most good in the least time. Details will be found in the newspapers of July 12 and 27, 1921. The affair and its revelations had a bearing on personal issues within the industry as to which the writer is charmed to be neutral.

This event breaking in the newspapers added to the velocity of gossip and ill-will against the motion picture industry. There have been steel parties, coal parties, banking parties, and even other motion picture parties, of greater ornamental merit than the $101,050 function of Woburn, but it got the publicity.

It was a decided misfortune that this Woburn morning reception should have been a sequel to a dinner to Fatty Arbuckle. Because that young man was in his ill-starred way to bring down on himself and the motion picture a crushing Keystone of disaster within a few weeks of the July disclosures.

Monday, September 5, 1921, there was a party at a San Francisco hotel, attended by a number of persons variously connected with the motion picture, including Fatty Arbuckle. Virginia Rappe, a screen actress, died following the affair. Details began to percolate, and, on September 11, Arbuckle delivered himself to the authorities in San Francisco.

The smouldering gossip of corruption in the films broke into flame. New York film offices were stricken with terror. There were endless conferences. Lawyers scurried about. Press agents tore at their hair and typewriters. Statements flew and the wires to San Francisco were overloaded. The set of facts was discouraging. It was difficult for even the ingenious scenario makers to fit the admitted circumstances into an acceptable tale. It was the hope to pull a miracle scene with Arbuckle as hero.

Arbuckle's comedies were banned from the screen in several communities and in haste they were nationally withdrawn in hope of quieting the storm. It is clear that the patrons take their pictures personally.

Elaborate plans for defense were laid. Minta Durfee Arbuckle, wife of the comedian, who had been estranged, was sent speeding to San Francisco. The slogan of the hour was "Stand by Roscoe." Several unreleased Arbuckle comedies and some millions in good will were at stake.

Two trials were had, resulting in disagreement of the juries. A third trial was more successful, resulting in an acquittal of Arbuckle on a charge of manslaughter. Minta Durfee Arbuckle later went to Paris and sued for a divorce.

With the hallowed decorations of a "peace on earth and goodwill toward men" movement an effort was made to release the Arbuckle pictures at a later Christmastide. The public rushed to the try-out showings in some remote towns, but an angry buzz from the uplifters caused a second retirement.

The affair had many of the aspects of accident. But while Arbuckle was acquitted of the somewhat technical charge against him, he and the whole motion picture business shared in a conviction at the bar of public opinion under a broader indictment.

By the time the Arbuckle affair was getting well worked into public ferment the motion picture chieftains began to admit that things were in an exceedingly bad way.

It was the autumn of 1921, and in the days of their trial there seemed to be no end of the pestilence and scourges. Woe was deep in the kingdom of the screen and the signs in the sky gave no promise.

But like the period of greatest suspense in a Griffith thriller, the lone horseman and champion of the right was even then galloping to the rescue. He had been on the way since the spring of 1919 at least. His coming had been forecast, not in letters of fire or stars or stars in the sky, but in very discreet whispers at discreet moments in directors' meetings, at luncheons all the way from the Ritz to the Astor.

The first public inkling, and it was a remote inkling, indeed, appeared on May 6, 1919, even before the motion picture sky had grown appreciably cloudy, in *Wid's Daily*, now the *Film Daily*, a motion picture trade journal. Page one of that issue presented an article from the graphic staccato pen of Joseph Dannenberg, editor, as follows:

MYSTERY LUNCH

WHO WAS THE LITTLE MAN AT THE IMPORTANT PARTY?

Scene, the Claridge, Parlor B.

Time, yesterday, about 12:30 P. M.

In the cast: Adolph Zukor, Arthur Friend, Famous Players; Pat Powers, Universal; Charles C. Pettijohn, and Wm. J. Clark of Exhibitors Mutual, and several others of the industry, AND, a little slender man who was probably of importance.

As the party arrived they quietly reached Parlor B, and for once no one would say what it was all about.

Investigation disclosed that Parlor B had been secured for a luncheon by Charles C. Pettijohn. Late yesterday, when Pettijohn was found he said: "Oh, my birthday falls on May 5 and I had a little party." But he smiled in a peculiar manner.

None of those attending the luncheon would discuss what took place. Interest is chiefly aroused in who the little man in the gathering was. He has not been a familiar figure in picture circles, at all events.

This story was accurate as far as it went except that Pettijohn is likely to have a birthday any time. The luncheon party in Parlor B, however, included also: William Fox, Robert H. Cochrane of Universal; Gabriel Hess and Samuel Goldfish of Goldwyn Pictures Corporation; Saul Rogers, attorney for the Fox Film Corporation; Percy Waters and Harry Berman.

Since this is not a nominating speech it is not necessary to hold out on the mystery of the mysterious little man "who was probably of importance." He was Will Hays, chairman of the Republican National Committee.

Now this was not at all the inception of the movement which today connects Hays with the industry, as might be hastily surmised. Hays was looking the motion picture over as a campaign manager. The motion picture industry did not know yet that it was looking for a deliverer and it little suspected Pettijohn of being a prophet. That is one of the important things about Pettijohn.

We must indulge in a film cutback to Indiana, a state famous for its output of fiction and practical politics.

Will Hays is from Indiana.

Charles C. Pettijohn is from Indiana.

When Will Hays was the chairman of the Indiana Republican organization, Charles C. Pettijohn was secretary of the Indiana Democratic organization.

Indianapolis centers on a Circle.

Hays and Pettijohn were friends as well as political enemies. Pettijohn is counted by those who know him well a first class friend and an able politician. No one will ever erect a cigar store behind him on the hasty assumption he is a wooden Indian. Pettijohn was also at this time a lawyer of some repute, due to his skill in defending some impetuous gentlemen charged with the promotion of the local death rate.

Among other things, Pettijohn, in political and other affairs operated in close and confidential capacity for Thomas Taggart, Democratic boss of Indiana and proprietor of Pluto's poignant waters and French Lick, where one can also play golf.

Pettijohn came into the motion pictures as attorney for Frank Rembush, an Indiana exhibitor, and then as the legal advisor of the state organization of exhibitors. When William J. Clark of Clark & Cornelius, Detroit brass founders, bought the bleaching bones of the Mutual Film Corporation in 1918, Pettijohn came to New York to render legal service. After a look around he joined the Selznick organization.

Pettijohn was and is, therefore, a person of experience. Politically he can observe the wealthy waddle of the Elephant quite as far as he can see the long eager ears of the Donkey. Which manifestly has nothing to do with the situation.

However, we may recall for the moment that hardly a block down Broadway from where Parlor B of the Claridge stood is Marcus Loew's theater, which was once Hammerstein's Music Hall, and that in the days of 1896 and the full-dinner-pail campaign the Republican National Committee held seven boxes at that palace of amusement. There, for the duration of the battle, the newly invented American Biograph presented the miracle of living pictures of Major William McKinley. By coincidence Abner McKinley, a brother, just before the campaign had become a stockholder in the American Mutoscope & Biograph Company. The Republican admiration for the screen began at the beginning.

Now, by 1919, the engineers of the Republican campaign had not forgotten the accidental disaster of the Ince anti-war picture, *Civilization*, which had played so large a share in the second Wilson victory. It was desirable, among other things, that no such accident be repeated. And May 5, 1919, was none too early to be thinking about November and election time in 1920. Hays wanted the screen for Harding.

It was October 14 when Pettijohn left Exhibitors' Mutual to take his desk in the Selznick offices. For a number of years Selznick had been thinking of squaring things with the World Film Corporation for the events of 1916 and remarks by William A. Brady. Brady had been succeeded at the head of World by Ricord Gradwell, a master salesman for the Oliver typewriter. Now in 1918–9 the World was in its dotage. Gradwell left and the corporation began to make a living selling its heirlooms, among them the screen rights to *Way Down East*, acquired by Griffith for $175,000. Selznick bought the feeble World and tied it out in his backyard, like a goat.

It chanced that the World was the distributing agent for Kinograms, a news reel. Kinograms was prospering for the moment on a burst of royal largess. British patriots had expressed a substantial appreciation of handsome attention given to one Edward Windsor, H. R. H. Prince of Wales, on the occasion of his first visit to Canada and the United States. The Prince was filmed freely, producing a profound flapper palpitation throughout America. An eight reel assembly of the news reel recordings by Tracy Mathewson, cameraman-to-the Prince, was edited by Charles Urban, now established in New York, and sent to London for British Empire consumption. On the strength of the able showing of the Prince, interests identified with the Canadian Pacific Railway invested a quarter of a million in a concern known as the Associated Screen News, which took in, for a time, Kinograms and the Gaumont News & Graphic. The Associated Screen News of Canada, a related enterprise, survives and flourishes in Montreal under the ministrations of Bernard E. Norrish, who as superintendent of publicity for Department of Trade and Commerce, had made Canada the first nation to engage officially in propaganda film production. Incidentally at about this juncture, the Hudson's

Bay Company made a large investment in Educational Films Corporation in New York, headed by Earl Hammons. The Hudson's Bay Company was the last furrier to go into the picture business. Now the Associated Screen News of the U. S. A. for various reasons, including Pettijohn, began the production of a twice-a-week reel entitled Selznick News.

The air was full of news reels, and the news reels were full of Warren G. Harding.

Will Hays made it a point to give the news reels the same recognition as the press. Harding posed willingly and often. Hays, the mystery man from the luncheon in Parlor B, was getting better and better acquainted in and about the film industry. Lewis J. Selznick had heard a great deal of him from Pettijohn and was proud of Hays' acquaintance as a genuine insider and man of affairs.

It became well impressed on the motion picture industry in several ways that Hays could be a friend worth having and the motion picture had never had any pals who knew telephone numbers in Washington. It was properly impressed. Quite a few little favors were done, done in that graceful open handed way that is bread-upon-the-waters. Just for example, Nicholas and Joseph Schenck had a Russian friend who was confronted with Ellis Island difficulties which prevented entry into the United States. A way around Ellis Island, perfectly lawful but dexterously managed, was found. Now the Schencks had Fatty Arbuckle comedies released through Zukor's Famous Players, and Talmadge dramas released through First National Exhibitors Circuit, and besides held an intimate relation with the Marcus Loew enterprises. It was a big tie-up of friendships. There were others.

The campaign, as need not be detailed, went through with such a success as to crown Hays with the largest wreaths of laurel ever issued to a campaign manager. Warren G. Harding and a Republican Congress went in with a roar like a Mississippi levee letting go under the June rise.

Then Hays took an office of his own and proceeded to wind up the far flung affairs of the campaign.

While Hays was so engaged some of his motion picture friends came to call. He was now a considerably bigger man than he had been at that luncheon in Parlor B.

William Fox suggested that he would like to have Hays join his organization at say about $75,000 a year. Some of the other motion picture concerns also thought they might be able to use a maker of landslides like the election of '20.

Hays was cordial and polite, but busy. He must have known perfectly well that all nice efficient Republican campaign managers become postmasters general. It is the traditional party method, time tried and proven. The post-office is the place for the organizer. It is sometimes good for the mails and it is always good for the party. This is something the Democrats have overlooked.

And never had the Democrats so overlooked the opportunity as when they installed Postmaster General Burleson. He had contrived to make the post-office, the one place where everybody gets a government contract, the most unpopular institution between Rainy Lake and the Rio Grande.

Hays naturally went to Washington and became Harding's postmaster general. Even more important, he became a vigorously effective postmaster general and restored the mail service which was beginning to be seriously missed, even in the telegraphically minded film business. Letters began to arrive on time. The post-office machinery picked up with a click and began to run with a steady purr. Drastic measures and burly marines in convoys discouraged mail robberies.

A serious crisis threatened in the impending rail strike. It is hard to visualize the demoralization of business that would likely have followed the cessation of mail service. Hays pictured it, and it is perhaps permissible at this late day to say that there were plans set ready to put the whole U. S. Army at moving the mails.

The post-office which had been intensely unpopular became popular. Even the dextrine on the back of the stamps tasted better after Hays got ahold.

Now by December, 1921, just when Hays was dashing from city to city and sitting up nights with the wires that told him the rail situation, the motion picture men were sinking deeper and deeper into the gloom of the industry's disgrace. They needed a friend, quickly.

The flow of scandal was telling at the box office. Censorship movements were acquiring new strength. Professional enemies of the screen were capitalizing opportunity.

The motion picture industry had made two slightly organized efforts to help itself. The first was the Motion Picture Board of Trade, born to a short and uneventful life under the auspices of J. W. Binder in 1915. The second was the National Association of the Motion Picture Industry of later date, headed by William A. Brady, a showman. The National Association could be of no help in the difficulties of 1921. It was weak from a lack of confidence and common interest. The motion picture men had to be driven by the most desperate necessity before they could unite for a common cause. They now knew they must unite and that the only effective aid must come from outside the industry. None of those who had participated in letting the motion picture fall into the Slough of Despond could be of use in pulling it out.

They remembered what baseball had done in a similar if not

quite so desperate a plight. Judge Kenesaw Mountain Landis had been plucked from his place of special eminence on the Federal bench to redeem the repute of the game.

The time was very ripe—over-ripe in fact.

Pettijohn discreetly mentioned the name of Hays to Selznick, and some others. Nicholas and Joseph Schenck had pleasant words to say. There were other nominations, among them Hiram Johnson of California and Herbert Hoover.

There was a conference at a lawyer's office down in the Wall Street district. "Not Hoover," they decided. "He's rich and independent." Johnson—well, Johnson was from California. Selznick was strong for Hays, for the reason, he says, "He was the biggest man I knew." The choice was Hays.

Hays had been injured in a train wreck. He was recovering under treatment in his suite at the Wardman Park Hotel in Washington. There Selznick and Saul Rogers went to interview him December 8, 1921.

They bore with them a roundrobin, under date of December 2, 1921, inviting Hays to the leadership of the industry. There were some touching phrases in that document. ". . . and are striving to have the industry accorded the consideration and dignity to which it is justly entitled, and proper representation before the people of this country. . . ." "We feel that our industry requires further careful upbuilding and a constructive policy of progress. . . ." One important passage read: "The compensation we are prepared to pay in the event of your acceptance is one hundred thousand dollars a year under a commitment satisfactory to you, for a period of three years."

The signatures included Adolph Zukor, William Fox, Samuel Goldwyn, W. E. Atkinson of Metro, Morris Kohn of Realart, Rufus S. Cole of R. C. Pictures, Lewis J. Selznick, P. L. Waters of Triangle, Carl Laemmle, and United Artists Corporation, by Hiram Abrams, president.

WILL HAYS, president of the Motion Picture Producers and
Distributors of America, Inc., called from the Harding
Cabinet to rescue the screen industry from the Slough of
Despond in 1921.

The roundrobin signed by motion picture chieftains inviting Will Hays, postmaster general, to head a new trade association.

Hays was properly surprised. It is, however, a safe guess that he was not entirely unprepared, and that some excellent information was coming from a reliable source in New York. Pettijohn had by this time cast loose from the Selznick concern and was officing for himself in Fifth Avenue.

Rogers and Selznick returned to New York and reported. December 17 there was a gathering at Delmonico's where Hays met the film men. He was going home to Indiana for Christmas. He said he would think it over some more.

Christmas morning the postmaster general was at his breakfast when a babble of small boy conversation arose around the bedecked tree in the next room. Three youngsters, Billy Hays, Jr., and his cousins, Charles Edward and John T. Hays, 5, 6 and 8, were exulting over their gifts, more especially a set of cowboy suits. They began to put them on, for a parade before their elders.

"I'll be Bill Hart."

"You won't, I'll be Hart."

"Won't either, I'll be him."

"Then I'll be Doug—so there."

Will Hays was listening. The politically acute are said to have their ears at the grass roots. Hays was this morning listening to the voice of the people expressing themselves with guileless sincerity at the foot of the Christmas tree. He decided the films were important.

The postmaster general's real decision about the scope and possibilities of that movie job appears to have been made that morning of December 25, 1921.

On January 14, next, the formal acceptance came and President Harding issued a statement from the White House, expressing appreciations of Hays and regrets at his approaching departure from the Cabinet.

In March, Hays opened the offices of the Motion Picture

Producers and Distributors of America, Inc., at 522 Fifth Avenue, and received the customary floral horseshoes.

A number of Democratic orators in Washington, including Senator B. P. ("Pat") Harrison of Mississippi, "viewed with alarm" and then the excitement subsided.   Hays went to work.

And there was work aplenty to do.

In the weeks while Hays was approaching his new and conspicuous post the motion picture scandal sensation wave had received a powerful new impetus.

William Dean Tanner, also known latterly as Taylor, an English soldier of fortune and of motion picture fame as a director, was murdered in his Hollywood apartment sometime in the dark hours between February 1 and 2.

Taylor was a person of more than commonplace studio calibre and the mystery of his taking off was of a nature to make him a national story, against the already highly colored background of the screen.

Developments in the Taylor case were taken by the newspapers as warrant for spectacular disclosures concerning the traffic in narcotics and the Los Angeles dope trade.

Newspaper correspondents from the East poured into Hollywood and wrote freely.   The nation's motion picture excitement was reaching its crest in March when Hays took office.

Evidences of a plan and directional skill now began to be apparent in the industry's dealings with correspondents.   The motion picture began to scream with outraged innocence.   It was a rather new rôle.

Writers, better known for their fictional contributions to the scenario departments than for their abilities as reporters, were brought in as a defensive army.   They reached Hollywood in the morning, and by night completed profound articles stating they had been unable to verify reports of wickedness.   These had the same importance as interviews on America with European celebrities who have just had their first look at the Woolworth building. But big names helped.

The second Sunday after the Taylor murder several Hollywood churches played to standing room only with many of the surprised regular attendants crowded into the back seats. An atmosphere of sweet piety pervaded the shade of the palms and pepper trees of Vine street.

Also those visiting newspaper correspondents became marked and observed men. They were run down, roped, hog tied and taken to lunch (without cocktails) and regaled with filtered facts.

Frank Woods, scenario chief at the Lasky studios, made daily reports in writing to Jesse Lasky on the movements of the correspondents. One item of annoyance was the pursuit of Edward Dougherty, robust and blue eyed son of a Chicago police captain, who was forwarding his exceedingly fervid literary impressions of Hollywood to the *Chicago Tribune* and its snappy little sister, the *Illustrated Daily News* of New York. It seemed impossible to get Dougherty to lunch.

The truth about Hollywood was really a pink compromise between its homemade whitewash and the red glow of the sensational press. The motion picture industry offered some rewards for the apprehension of Taylor's slayer—and trembled lest the solution should prove worse than the mystery. Gradually the sensation died, still a mystery.

Meanwhile, in New York, the Hays office was organizing, and teaching the motion picture industry not to be so self-conscious, so obvious and clumsy.

The right and left bowers of Hays developed to be Courtland Smith, formerly head of the American Press Association, incidentally a brother-in-law of Arthur Brisbane, and Charles C. Pettijohn, of Indiana and Fifth Avenue.

The Hays office set the motion picture industry an example in courteous, smooth operation and general diplomacy.

Since the coming of Hays the sensations of the motion picture world have not been sensational. A slight and normal sprinkling of scandal continues in the Latin quarter of the films yet, but they are no longer accepted symbols of the business.

Effective resistance has overcome a number of censorship movements, notably in Massachusetts, and the industry has found a meeting place for many of its common causes. The Hays office has prevented the production of some projected pictures carrying special peril of exciting agitations against the screen, and it has discouraged some of the excessive flamboyances of lurid movie titles and advertising. One of the important functions of the Hays office is to listen to people with a pain about the screen. It gives an outlet to shouting that used to be done in the newspapers.

Also because of the very considerable official and political acquaintanceship of Hays his organization has proven of important service to the American picture industry in many of its foreign relations.

An important service within the industry has been the establishment of standardized contracts, particularly between the distributors and the theatres, with a result of making such contracts valid documents instead of texts for fight. An extensive arbitration organization has kept several thousand minor film controversies out of court.

The Hays organization is supported largely by percentage assessments against the business done by its members. The cost to the industry, hence to the public, is somewhat above half a million dollars a year, about the cost of one good picture.

Charges of partisan service to "The Big Three," meaning Famous Players-Lasky, Metro-Goldwyn-Mayer and the First National, have been made by the new race of Independents, in the unending war of the "Outs against the Ins," which will always continue in the motion picture industry. However the major results of the Hays administration have been beneficial to the whole of the screen and its public.

A minority organization of film makers and dealers was formed in May, 1924, under the name of the Independent Motion Picture Producers & Distributors Association. I. E. Chadwick, a producer, who entered the motion picture industry as attorney for the Pathé-Eclectic concern in 1912, was elected the president, and Dr. W. E. Shallenberger, conspicuous in the new contingent of Independents, became chairman of the executive board. Dr. Shallenberger joined the motion picture as an investor with Charles Hite in nearly Mutual projects, including the celebrated *Million Dollar Mystery*. He flashed into the newspaper limelight in the autumn of 1925 with the announcement of a contract to pay "Red" Grange, football star, $300,000 to appear in a single picture.

Meanwhile the motion picture industry is now well out of its infancy, and the Hays office is teaching it how to wear long pants.

CHAPTER EIGHTY-ONE

TODAY

As this narration of screen history comes to conclusion in the latter days of 1925 the motion picture is engaging with increasing velocity in a new phase of development as a world industry.

The arrival of the World War in 1914 halted British and European production activities and left the evolutions of the art and the industry alike to America alone. The motion picture was thus delivered over to America at the beginning of its greatest development, the feature drama.

The world market for motion pictures is only now emerging from the war dust. For the ten greatest years of the motion picture's career, one third of the screen's existence, it has served but a fair fraction of its potential public.

Through this period, roughly 1914 to 1924, the American market was 80 per cent of the world market, and the American studios have maintained approximately a 90 per cent domination of the motion picture abroad.

Peace in Europe and rehabilitation of its affairs brings a rapidly widening field for the motion picture, with complex consequences to the American strongholds of the art. The foreign market which was formerly a 20 per cent incidental is rising in significance. In some instances it has contributed as much as 40 per cent of the world earnings of better pictures.

Three immediate consequences become apparent. The opening of the world market is carrying the American rivalries into struggles of exploitation overseas. Production policies formerly governed solely by the American tastes are tending to consider the world as the customer. The major foreign markets are each encouraging domestic production within their own territorial boundaries.

The American position is overwhelmingly strong with the foundation of uninterrupted growth and a continuously prosperous domestic patronage. Also, since the American producer has always served a polyglot and extremely diverse population, his products have automatically evolved with a certain innate internationalism, and a catholicity which tends to make them world market merchandise.

It is not an accident but rather a phase of screen evolution which finds the American motion picture industry, and therefore the screens of the world, administered rather largely by our best and most facile internationalists, the Jews, with those of Russian extraction slightly predominant over the Germans. This development has come by the same process and for many of the same reasons as the prior but similar evolution in the garment trade, so ably set forth by Abraham Cahan in his novel *The Rise of David Levinsky*. The most casual attention will discover that the motion picture and the garment trade have a psychology in common to a marked degree.

Many obscure but important ethnic and geographical factors have figured in shaping the destiny of the film art. The American motion picture theatre definitely took its rise out of the opportunity presented by the confusion of tongues and races in the Babel centers of concentration for imported labor, notably Pittsburgh, Chicago, Cincinnati, St. Louis, Milwaukee, and New York. From this beginning of service to seekers of fortune in the New World the motion picture took its still sustained keynote of ornate opulence and optimism. The screen chieftains of today are the industry's own elections from the store show and arcade exhibitors of the nickelodeon age.

It is of incidental interest that the Greeks have constituted the largest single racial group among picture showmen in the

United States. A hurried survey of a half a dozen years past found 1,400 Greek theatre owners in a total of perhaps fourteen thousand. The Greeks entered in the early nickelodeon days, mainly from small retail enterprises in the foreign and labor quarters, more frequently along the eastern American sector of the Athenian isotherm. Spyros Skouras of St. Louis, the head of Skouras Brothers Corporation, controls some thirty or more important theatres, and has made the Hellenic high mark of the industry.

In post-war development of the motion picture Germany is leading the foreign field, a fact of interest in view of the relative unimportance of German picture activity in the world market prior to 1914 when France and Italy vied for dominance. While the American product holds 90 per cent of the screen in Great Britain, Germany is making a vigorous effort to maintain control of her own screen, seeking to enforce a "kontingent" law forbidding importation of pictures save by German producers and one in a prescribed series of ratios.

A scheme of star transplantation between American and European studios is being evolved to hold the American control of the industry. And thus develops the trend toward further internationalization of the films. Meanwhile Famous Players-Lasky, long dominantly established abroad, has made some interesting pictorial penetrations of the foreign film situation with the production of such films as *Madame Sans Gène*, with Gloria Swanson in Paris, and more recently *Irish Luck*, with Thomas Meighan and Lois Wilson on the authentic old sod and literally kissing the Blarney Stone itself. Such is the diplomacy of art.

Some incidents of the production of *Madame Sans Gène* illuminate the French state of mind. Famous Players was induced to accept for American presentation the French produc-

Monroe

GLORIA SWANSON, the reigning "queen of the movies" as of
the days of 1925–6, at the crest of her wave of screen glory.

tion entitled *The Miracle of the Wolves*. Although Allan Dwan, Famous Players director, was ready to sail for the making of *Madame Sans Gène,* the French government discovered that it could scarcely entrust the filming of relics, monuments and national sites of historic memory to any other than a native director. So Leonce Perret, a Frenchman of transient American experience, was employed. Some hushed excitement resulted from a stealthy night excursion to make scenes using a bed, sacred to Napoleon and officially forbidden to the desecrations of the camera. The night watchman was using the Emperor's bed when the film party arrived.

Meanwhile Famous Players-Lasky's two major directors in December, 1925, set about the preparation of important foreign made productions for the next season. James Cruze is to make a picture now known as *Ironsides,* a story of the Tripoli pirates, D. W. Griffith is engaged on *The Sorrows of Satan,* from Marie Corelli's story.

Famous Players-Lasky interests, which dominate in the British empire and are well intrenched in France, are also strongly represented in Berlin. William Fox is said to be producing a series of pictures in Germany, arming to meet the "kontingent" ratio. Warner Brothers recently purchased a theatre in Paris, European equivalent of a Broadway first run for exploitation purposes. The movie wars of America are to extend their battle-lines to "over there." LaFayette, we come—again! *Vive le franc!*

Germany's present aggressive interest in a domestic film industry has a strong coloring of government support and suggests that the situation relates to some of the propaganda lessons learned in the war. It has been discovered with some alarm that the American motion pictures covering the screens of the world are also selling American merchandise with an influence on trade balances.

The trade situation and an agitation against Americanization in habits and speech is being made the text of discussion in Great Britain with speeches in Parliament and pleas for special legislation. Also the Prince of Wales, who was made a figure of world-wide screen acquaintance by American news reel photography, was recently sent on a tour to South America and elsewhere as an unofficial salesman. In other words, Britain's best screen star made a series of "personal appearances."

According to the Federation of British Industries only 5 per cent of the pictures shown in British theatres are of British production. In answer to the British excitement, J. D. Williams, of Parkersburg, Vancouver, Melbourne, Los Angeles, New York, etc., promoter of First National, and more recently Ritz-Carlton Pictures, employing Rodolph Valentino, in December of 1925 appeared in London announcing British National Pictures, Ltd., with a projected hundred acre studio, with all British capital and officers, and George T. Eaton, a retired Australian cattle man, at the head of the board.

In Italy Premier Mussolini issued an edict commanding that for one week in every two months Italian theatres must present Italian pictures exclusively. In Russia the Soviet Kino, while nominally a pure Russian monopoly, by lack of domestic production and force of demand, presents American pictures.

It is estimated that there are 50,000 screen theatres in the world, of which about 21,000 are in America.

Within the motion picture world of the United States the outstanding aspect of the industry in the post-war period has been the growth of theatre chains and booking combines, in part a sequel to the war for theatre and box office control which arose as a result of the First National Exhibitors' Circuit challenge to Adolph Zukor and the Famous Players-Lasky Corporation.

An estimate of about a year ago, credited to William A.

Johnston, editor of the *Motion Picture News*, calculated that some six thousand theatres were held by about eleven hundred ownerships in the United States. It is likely that rather more than less theatres are under chain control, because of a frequent policy of concealment.

Zukor's theatre control campaign got well underway in 1921 and has extended itself to several hundred houses. Early in this movement Famous Players took control of the Rialto, Rivoli and Criterion theatres in Broadway, dominating the street save for the Strand with First National affiliations and the Capitol of Metro-Goldwyn connection. Since that time every important Broadway showing has been in effect a trade showing for the promotion of the picture's bookings in the hinterlands. The Broadway theatres became important and acquired prestige in the days when Samuel Rothafel took his choice in an open market.

Zukor's film adversaries, using the tactics of Gustavus Rogers and William Fox laid down in the days of the Patents Company, inspired a complaint of conspiracy to develop a monopoly, by the Federal Trade Commission against Famous Players-Lasky and its many affiliated interests in 1921. In sequel there was a flurry of engagements for opposition pictures, including Universal's *Merry-Go-Round*, at Famous Players theatres on Broadway. After four years of sessions, at which most of the history of the industry was reviewed, hearings came to an end. In the event of a decision against Famous Players-Lasky another decade of court actions may be expected. Film litigants usually outgrow the cause of action before final judgments are rendered.

In what might be construed as an anticipation, Famous Players-Lasky on November 17, 1925, announced the formal separation of its theatre and production interests, and the formation of a new concern which would put its theatres—stated as 200 in number—into an amalgamation with the 500 theatres under the control of Balaban & Katz of Chicago, making an aggregation of between seven and eight hundred theatres in one chain, Public Theatres Corporation. The investment involved is estimated to range between $100,000,000 and $150,000,000.

The Balaban & Katz Corporation is a piece of Arabian Nights magic emerging from the kaleidoscope of Chicago's West Side and the push-cart markets of Jefferson street.

When Carl Laemmle, the Oshkosh clothing salesman, opened his first nickelodeon in Milwaukee avenue in 1906, Sammy Katz, a thirteen year old messenger boy, got a job playing the piano. Three years later Sam Katz had a theatre of his own with 144 folding chairs. He added a violin and 'cello to the musical equipment. After awhile he joined with Balaban Brothers, exhibitors, and with them later built the big Central Park theatre in Chicago on hope and a shoestring.

Katz with the aid of night schools and spare hours was acquiring an education on his way up. He finished high school, and went to Northwestern University and then took three years of night law school.

The Balaban & Katz motion picture operations swept onward to greater and greater scope, at last achieving domination of Chicago's "Loop" with the big Chicago theatre. Their powers grew with extending and ramifying booking combines into outlying regions until they were bounded on the north by Rubin & Finkelstein of Minneapolis and by Skouras of St. Louis on the south.

By the federation with the Zukor theatre interests, Sam Katz, Carl Laemmle's piano player, is now czar of a screen kingdom extending from the Atlantic to the Pacific. Through his dizzy rise to power Katz has taken precautions to keep his feet on the ground.

"That stuff about hard work and ambition is true, in a degree," he observes, "but you have to get the 'breaks.' Many a

time a little turn which I could not have controlled would have
wrecked me.

"Every little while I go down to the ghetto in Chicago and
have a good look at my father's old barbershop at Twelfth and
Jefferson. It says to me:

" 'Here's where you came from, Sam Katz. Now be yourself
and cut out the applesauce.' "

Katz is now 33 years old.

Marcus Loew, once a New York newsboy, now holding the
incorporated bouquet entitled Metro-Goldwyn-Mayer, taking its
name from two companies and Louis B. Mayer of Boston, is in
control of another growing chain, said to include more than 350
theatres. William Fox continues aggressively extending his
theatre interests. Laemmle's Universal is in the theatre market, and Warner Brothers are reported on the eve of a vast refinancing for acquisition of theatres.

The more recent campaigns of Famous Players-Lasky have
been under the direction of Sidney Kent, an exponent of the dynamic school of salesmanship, who has risen to power as Zukor's chief aide and general manager of the corporation.

Kent first appeared on the horizon somewhere out in the un-
fenced range country a-horseback, riding herd on wild beef,
according to tradition. At any rate he still wears spurs.

The town of Kent, Wyoming, is a footprint he left while in the
service of the Colorado Fuel & Iron Company. Later as sales
manager for the American Druggists' Syndicate he demonstrated
his skill at making them take it no matter how it tasted. He began his picture experience with the General Film Corporation
in the days of its last illness.

Shortly thereafter Kent entered the office of Adolph Zukor
and announced he had decided to go to work for Famous
Players-Lasky.

"At what salary?"

"Nothing a week—until we find out."

They gave him the Kansas City territory, which, because of Kansas, is the Great Desert of the film continent. He survived and took in the United States.

Many of the spectacular film titles which flash from the electric lights have taken their origin on Kent's desk as selling prescriptions to be compounded by the studios. This was the origin of *Manhandled*, a picture which became an important factor in the swift ascent of Gloria Swanson.

Miss Swanson happened into the pictures as a result of a sightseeing visit to the Essanay studios in Chicago. She went thence west to the Mack Sennett comedy factory in Hollywood. It is her solemn assertion that she appeared in only one bathing suit picture and that the costume in question was beyond question, consisting of three pieces and many ruffles. Miss Swanson later appeared in Triangle dramas. In 1919 she attracted the favorable attention of Cecil DeMille of the Lasky studio and was cast in *For Better or For Worse*. It proved to be for better. In the last discussion of salary bids Miss Swanson was quoted at $20,000 a week.

The Cinderella loving movie fans have an array of gossip stories of Miss Swanson's genesis. The favorite version places her as a sales girl in a Chicago department store. The official biography issued by the home office however states that she is the daughter of Captain Joseph Swanson, U. S. Army.

Cecil DeMille, after ten years of star directorship in the Lasky studios, departed from that connection in 1925, in sequel to disagreements said to have originated in the extraordinary costs of his spectacle *The Ten Commandments*, reported as $1,600,000, which was in turn his gesture of response to the surprise success of *The Covered Wagon* directed by James Cruze and costing, it is said, $800,000. DeMille then aligned himself with the new Independents as director general of Producers

Distributing Corporation, a rehabilitation of the Hodkinson corporation, under the general management of John C. Flynn, a one time publicity man and subsequently a member of Famous Players executive staff.

The motion picture industry is controlled by entirely automatic forces of growth by which it is evolving increasingly complex specimens of the so-called vertical trust. This is not the especially conscious plan of any one man or group of men but the following of basic laws of structure. It is as inevitable as the course by which the tree elaborates its organic processes complete from soil to nuts. The pattern, only slightly obscured by differing details, may be observed in all the arts, religions and other industries by which the alleged human race lives and reconciles itself to living. Everything that grows grows the same way. Nobody can do anything about it.

The elaborations of the motion picture structure tending toward a completion of the soil-to-nuts system even now include tentative discussions projecting an alliance with the Yellow Cab interests for a national motor film delivery system, at one end of the process, and a well formulated plan by which one of the big producers, in this instance William Fox, is about to engage in financing Broadway stage productions by way of fostering and controlling a source of raw material, the scenario.

The motion picture industry now contains within itself every important factor of its metabolism save the manufacture of the photographic raw materials, chief of which is the film. Figured in terms of area, which is the only basis of adequate comparison, the motion picture now consumes about one half of the photographic film produced.

The so-called raw stock or unexposed film is itself an extremely complex product, and its manufacture remains about the only important industry heavily safeguarded by secrets. Most of the secrets are George Eastman's. The film base is cellulose, nitrated and dissolved in an alcoholic solvent, coated with gelatine emulsified with photosensitive silver salts. The film's cellulose content consumes large quantities of cotton. One thirtieth of the world's output of silver goes into Eastman products alone, making the motion picture stand next to the United States mint, the world's largest single consumer of silver. The fine gelatine required is derived from young calves. It was formerly produced entirely in Germany but by war necessity the processes have been perfected in the United States.

When this history started we traced pictographic origins in the alphabet from the wild bull of the Sumerians and now we have come to the calf of the cinema—still wild.

Starting from the unexposed film the vertical trust administrations have all ready extended with considerable completeness over the whole route terminating with the seat in the theatre and the presentation of the shadows on the screen. The only actual merchandise is the emotional experience wrapped up and delivered to the occupants of the seats. Because of the tenuous and intangible character of the goods no saturation point is in sight for the industry.

A development of the general scheme appears in the announcement of December 15, 1925, that Publix Theatres is engaging in the construction of a "presentation studio" in Long Island City, adjacent to the Famous Players-Lasky film studios, for the preparation of the more important productions for the theatre showings. The pictures will acquire their complete mounting of incidental music, dance numbers, prologues and the like in the presentation studio.

The giant theatre chain will thereby escape dependence on the showmanship and artistic skill of local managements. The staff announced for the presentation studio includes Herschel Stuart, manager of production, John Murray Anderson, director of production, Nathaniel Finston, musical director, and Doris

Petroff, ballet master.   Nat Finston was evolved from the Roth-afel-Riesenfeld staff of presentation on Broadway.

This means that once again the local theatre managers across the nation will get all of the creative elements of their shows metaphorically out of a can, just as they did in the nickelodeon age.

Every element of the creative side of the industry is being brought under central manufacturing control.

This process in the world of the motion picture is spectacular and interesting, chiefly because it is the sole business of the motion picture to be spectacular and interesting.   It is however nothing to be alarmed about, to any greater degree than about the manufacture of Ford cars, delivered from ore mine to driver, or Socony gasoline piped from a mile under Texas to the back end of your car, or Armour's comprehensive business of converting the grass of the Argentine into tenderloins, fiddlestrings and thyroidin, for your nourishment, amusement and health.

Now that the vertical trust phase of development is making the motion picture magnate the principal theatre customer of his own studios he will be found to be reacting to a sense of more direct responsibility to the public taste.   The result will assuredly not lower the quality of motion pictures and likely it may improve them.

Business is business.

As the iris closes, a dispatch arrives from Hollywood announcing that William S. Hart, Jr., on the occasion of his third birthday, has received from his father a gift of a drum encrusted with gold and silver, with rosewood sticks to beat it, cost $650.

Evidently all's well in movieland.

We, like Sheherazade, have come to the end of our tales.

The story of *A Million and One Nights,* the romantic history of the motion picture, is told.

The genii have answered the Wish of the World with the Aladdin's Lamp of the camera and the Magic Carpet of the film. An empire built of shadow glories has prospered and its boundaries are the limits of Earth.

This empire of the screen has many subjects, slaves, magicians, sheikhs, dancing girls, princesses, grand viziers and emirs. Chief of them all is a certain philosophic little man from Hungary, silent and meek among his millions. His name is Zukor, first and last in the alphabet of screen fame. He has risen, for his day, even as Abou Hassan, from the bazaar to the riches and power of a Caliph Haroun Alraschid in a new Baghdad-on-the-Hudson, capital of Screenland, where dreams come true.

And what, do you fancy, is his rarest jewel, the symbol of his triumph and emblem of a life's success?

The answer stands on his desk by the window that looks down on the surge of Fifth Avenue. It is a bronze cast of a scuffled and worn pair of baby's shoes—the first shoes of "Buddy," his first grandchild.

> ". . . endlessly rocks the Cradle,
> Uniter of Here and Hereafter."

Which is the end of our story—and all the stories in the world.

APPENDIX

FIGURES—THEN AND NOW

The first annual statement of the first motion picture concern in the world, the Kinetoscope Company, conducted by Norman Charles Raff and Frank R. Gammon, in New York, preserved among the archives given to the author by Raff, is presented here. This statement gains a particular significance and interest when compared with the grandiose figures of the motion picture industry of today.

In 1925, the currently accepted general figures for the industry, all rough approximations, included:

Number of film theatres in the world	50,000
Film theatres in the United States	20,000
Persons permanently employed in the U. S.	300,000
Average number of feature films, annually,	700
Average weekly attendance in U. S.	130,000,000
Permanent investment in U. S. alone	$1,500,000,000
Annual U. S. expenditure for admissions	$ 550,000,000
Monthly U. S. output of raw film stock, in feet,	65,000,000

In contrast with these figures for the present status of the industry, consider the Kinetoscope Company's first report to its stockholders:

STATEMENT

Condensed Abstracts from the Books of the Kinetoscope Company at the close of business March 15th, 1895.

ASSETS

Cash in banks and on hand	$7,134.22
Bills Receivable	2,308.33
Higbee Contract	3,168.50

Sundry Accounts Receivable	3,329.40
Due from Thos. A. Edison	962.90
Invested in Negatives at Labor'ty	1,118.67
Furniture & Fixtures	356.50
Posters, Lithographs, Dickson Booklets, etc.	265.34
Sundry Supplies	64.52
Due from Exhibition Dept.	1,478.09
Stock on hand and paid for	9,255.80
	$31,379.37

LIABILITIES

*Bills Payable		$3,335.75
Current Accounts Payable (settled monthly)		1,033.02
Gross Profits—On Kinetoscopes	25,794.31	
On Films	2,870.91	
On Batteries	602.40	
	$29,267.62	

Operating expenses	7,283.37		
Divided # 1	5,000.00	12,283.37	16,984.25

Profits represented by Stock on hand (Kinetoscopes, Batteries, etc.)	8,089.25
	$31,379.37

Gross Receipts from Exhibition Department, from April 14, 1894 (date of opening first parlor) to April 1st, 1895.

NOTE: *Gross* Receipts are given, because during the first few months, a large amount of the receipts were used for purchasing Furniture and Fixtures, Stock, Electrical Devices, and in paying the *general* expenses of the Company. Therefore, a statement of the *net* receipts on our books would not be a fair indication of the actual results. In general it may be said that the necessary expenses of a first class exhibition parlor are about as follows:—

Rent, per month, say	$300.00
Manager and Attendants, say	140.00
Current and Light, say	75.00

* The original amount of this item was $17,940.00 and it covered monies originally put in by certain of our stockholders and has nearly all been returned to them. Balance is payable at our convenience.

Necessary incidentals are quite small, and the above items are less in some instances. At Chicago our Rent *and* Current have been $300.00.

Gross Receipts, New York Parlor, Apr. 14/94 to Apr.
1/95 .... $16,171.56
Gross Receipts, Chicago, May /94 to Apr. 1/95...... 7,409.84
Gross Receipts, Atlantic City, June 26/94 to Sept.
15/94 .... 8,098.05
Gross Receipts, San Francisco, June 20/94 to Oct.
26/94 .... 7,161.80
Gross Receipts, Washington & Balt., Oct. & Nov. /94.. 2,805.50
Gross Receipts, Sundry Exhibitions during period Oct.
say 1/94 to Apr. 1/94 .... 6,500.00

$48,146.75

Special attention is called to the item of negative inventory, listed among the assets, showing that the first year of motion picture production resulted in an investment of $1,118.67 in film subjects. Probably the most authentic figure for comparison available appears in the Department of Commerce data for 1923 when the total for all establishments engaged in the production of motion pictures was reported at $86,418,170.

THE FIRST FILM LIBRARY

Here is presented the oldest surviving list of motion picture films, the productions of 1894, for the Edison Kinetoscope, from the catalogue of Raff & Gammon, issued in October of that year. One copy of that catalogue was discovered by the author among the documents of the Kinetoscope Company.

This list of films represents the studio output for that first season of peep-show pictures, made at a total cost of less than a thousand dollars. This record is of importance in view of many conflicting and obviously erroneous claims of motion picture film production at earlier dates. These Edison pictures were the first motion picture films in the world and they, through the agency of the Kinetoscope, became the inspiration of all the many subsequent "inventors of the motion picture." The 1894 catalogue list follows:

Name of Subject	Films, Each.
THE COCKFIGHT	$12.50
WRESTLING MATCH, "Pettit and Kessler"	12.50
BERTHOLDI, The Marvellous Lady Contortionist	10.00
BOXING CATS (Professor Welton's)	10.00
A very interesting and amusing subject	
WRESTLING DOG (Wrestles with his trainer)	10.00
CAICEDO, The "King of the Wire" in his marvellous Slack Wire Performance	10.00
LAYMAN, The man of 1,000 Faces	12.50
GLENROY BROS., Boxing Bout (Burlesque)	15.00
GLENROY BROS., Farcical Pugilists in Costume	15.00
WALTON AND SLAVIN, "The Long and Short of It"	15.00
Comical and mirth exciting Burlesque Boxing Contest from Rice's "1492."	
LADY FENCERS (with Foils)	12.50
THE PICKANINNIES (3) Dance from "The Passing Show"	12.50
LUIS MARTINETTI, Gymnast and Contortionist, performing on the flying rings	12.50
SKIRT DANCE DOG Prof. Tschernoff's, from Koster & Bial's	12.50
SUMMERSAULT DOG Prof. Tschernoff's, from Koster & Bial's	12.50
BUCKING BRONCHO, An out-of-door scene	15.00
The men and horse of this subject are from "Buffalo Bill's Wild West."	
ANNIE OAKLEY, The "Little Sure Shot" of the "Wild West," Exhibition of Rifle Shooting at Glass Balls, etc.	15.00
MLLE. CAPITAINE ("The Perfect Woman") Exhibiting Trapeze performance	15.00
THE CARNIVAL DANCE, by 3 Dancers from the "Gaiety Girl" Company of London	15.00
Said to be among the best dancers in the world in this line.	
PAS SEUL No. 1 (Dance) By Miss Murray of the "Gaiety Girl" Company	15.00
PAS SEUL No. 2 (Dance) By Miss Lucas of the "Gaiety Girl" Company	15.00
TOPACK AND STEELE (Lively Political Debate, representing Cleveland and Harrison)	15.00
THE RIXFORDS, Acrobatic Feats (Head Balancing, a difficult and interesting feat)	15.00
FIRE RESCUE SCENE, Showing Fine Smoke Effects and Uniformed Firemen in Action	15.00
FINALE of 1st Act Hoyt's "Milk White Flag." Showing 34 Persons in Costume. The largest number ever shown as one subject in the Kinetoscope	15.00
BAND DRILL. Hoyt's "Milk White Flag."	15.00
DANCE. Frank Lawton and Misses Williamson and France. "Hoyt's Milk White Flag."	15.00
ELSIE JONES, No. 1, "The Little Magnet." Buck Dance	15.00
IMPERIAL JAPANESE DANCE. Three Japanese Ladies in the Costumes of their Country.	15.00

APPENDIX

ROBETTA AND DORETTO. Chinese Opium Den — 15.00

GRUNDY AND FRINT. Breakdown, from "South before the War." — 15.00

IN THE DENTIST'S CHAIR,—Administering Gas and Extracting a Tooth — 15.00
Dr. Colton, who first used gas for extracting teeth, is shown administering the gas in this film.

NEW BARBERSHOP (The old negative having worn out, we have had a new one taken which is superior to the old one.) — 12.50

BUFFALO BILL, The noted proprietor of "The Wild West." — 15.00

INDIAN WAR COUNCIL, Showing seventeen different persons—Indian warriors and white men—in Council. — 15.00

SIOUX GHOST DANCE (A very interesting subject, full of action and true to life — 15.00

VINCENTE ORE PASSO, Champion Lasso Thrower.
(This shows the wonderful skill attained by the subject, and is exceedingly interesting and popular) — 15.00

PEDRO ESQUIREL AND DIONECIO GONZALES—Mexican duel.
(Full of action, exciting and interesting) — 15.00

JOHN W. WILSON AND BERTHA WARING—"Little Christopher Columbus," Eccentric Dancers — 15.00

JAMES GRUNDY, Buck and Wing Dance — 15.00

JAMES GRUNDY, Cake Walk — 15.00
From "South Before the War." These are the best negro subjects yet taken, and are amusing and entertaining.

ROB ROY, A Burlesque Scotch Dance by Richard Carroll and the Jamies, from the Whitney Opera Company.
A success. Full of life and action. — 15.00

PADDLE DANCE, by Fiji Islanders, with Barnum & Bailey's "Greatest Show on Earth." — 15.00

DANCE OF REJOICING, by Samoan Islanders, with Barnum & Bailey's "Greatest Show on Earth." — 15.00

SILVER DANCE, by Cingalese, in Native Costumes, from Barnum & Bailey's Show. — 15.00

SHORT STICK DANCE, by Natives of India, from Barnum's Show. — 15.00

HINDOOSTAN FAKIR AND COTTA DWARF, from Barnum & Bailey's "Greatest Show on Earth." — 15.00

PROFESSOR ATTILLA. The World Famous Athlete and Strong Man Trainer. — 15.00

YOUNG WEIMER. The Champion Light-weight Dumb Bell Lifter of the World, pupil of Attilla. — 15.00

NEW BLACKSMITH SHOP — 12.50

NEW BAR ROOM, Showing a Quarrel in a bar room and a policeman taking a glass of beer on the sly. — 12.50

HORNBACKER AND MURPHY, Five Round Glove contest to a finish.
Price per set of five films, each showing one round. — 100.00
Or single rounds, each — 20.00

BILLY EDWARDS AND THE UNKNOWN, Boxing Bout in 5 rounds.
(This well known and prominent pugilist, with an antagonist scienced and skillful, gives one of the most, if not the most, spirited and exciting exhibitions of sparring ever taken for the Kinetoscope.
Price for each round — 25.00
(*We can furnish specially selected Musical Records for use on the Kineto-Phone, for nearly all of the films in the foregoing list. Price, each, $1.50*)

The naive advertising terms and recommendations of the period will compare favorably with the typical expressions of the trade advertising of the motion picture today.

INDEX

A

INDEX

INDEX

INDEX

INDEX

INDEX

Cook, George, 713
Cooper, Merian C., 600
Copenhagen, 515, 701
Copley Plaza Hotel, 806
Corbett-Fitzsimmons fight, 286, 287, 288, 289, 366, 377
Corbett, James, 110, 115, 281, 285, 366
Corelli, Marie, 825
Costa Rica, 342, 343
Costello, Maurice, 441, 443, 549
Cotton States Exposition, 139, 193, 194, 208
Count of Monte Cristo, The, 532, 533, 593
Course of True Love, 474
Courtenay, Pete, 110, 115, 281
Courtenay, William, 97
Courting of Mary, The, 577
Courtlandt, David, 511
Covered Wagon, The, 86, 134, 640, 664, 830
Cox, Clara, 89
Coytesville, N. J., 460, 492, 493, 506, 507
Craft, P. P., 516, 517, 518
Crafts, Rev. Wilbur Fisk, 482, 483
Crahan, Tom, 401
Crampton, Howard, 617
Creel, George, 611, 781, 784
Cremation of Sam McGee, The, 600, 601
Crescent Films, 423
Crisp, Donald, 641
Criterion Theatre (New York), 678, 827
Critics, 476, 681, 682, 729
Croker, Richard, 405, 406
Cromelin, Paul, 497
Crosland, Alan, 716
Crosland, Maggie, 84
Croy, Homer, 203, 204, 205
Cruze, James, 663, 664, 825, 830
Crystal Hall (New York), 732
Crystal Palace (London), 429
Cuba, 507, 532, 537, 540, 541
Cummings, Irving, 496, 669
Cunard, Grace, 661
Cupid's Barometer, 474
Curtius, Christopher, 181
Cushing, Jack, 109, 110, 115, 176
Cyclorama, lxvi, 16
Cyrus, xiv, lxi, 756
Czar of Russia, 766

D

Dædaleums, 14, 332

Daguerre, M. Louis Jacques Mandé, 15, 16, 69, 101
Daly, Augustin C., 382
Daly, Bob, 614
Daly, Dutch, 324
Daly's Theatre, 83, 84, 373
Damaged Goods, 613, 618
Damon, Ida, 667, 668
Daniel, xliv
Daniel, T. C., 138
Daniels, Harry, 342, 343, 346
Daniels, Josephus, 687, 689
Dannenberg, Joseph, 809
Danton, 182
Darkfeather, Mona, 534
Darktown Jubilee, 610
Darmour, Larry, 786, 787
Daugherty, Harry, 698
Daughter of the Gods, The, 704, 705, 706, 737
Davenport, Ia., 458
Davies, Marion, 461, 653
Davis & Sanford, 506
Davis, Harry, 429, 517
Davis, Robert H., 28
Davis, Sam P., 28
Davy Crockett in Hearts United, 491
Dawley, J. Searle, 441, 507, 621
Dean, Julia, 719
DeCoppet, Theodosia (see Bara, Theda)
DEFENSELESS AMERICA, 726
Defrauding Banker, The, 475
Delaware, Lackawanna & Western, 416, 417
Delgado, Don Jose Gil, 296
Delineator, The, 506
Delmonico's, 627, 817
Demeny, Georges, 145, 146, 198, 202
DeMille, Cecil, 249, 623, 624, 768, 830
DeMille, Mrs. H. C., 623
DeMille, William, 623
Democratic National Committee, 728
Dempsey, Jack, xv, 697
Denis, Ruth, 84
Denver & Rio Grande Railroad, 628
Denver, Colo., 326, 611
DENVER'S UNDERWORLD, 611
Depew, Chauncey M., 96, 97
Desmond, William, 719
Dessez, Elizabeth, 485
Desvignes, 14
Detroit, 361, 726, 727
Devil, 11, 179, 236, 242, 483
Dewar, Sir John, 775
Dewey Theatre, 479
DeWitt, Marguerite, lvii
Diamond from the Sky, The, 669, 708

—846—

INDEX

INDEX

INDEX

INDEX

INDEX

Levison, Wallace Goold, 47
Lewis, Edgar, 701
Lewis, Ralph, 757
Lewis, Sheldon, 760
Lexow Investigation, 612
Liberty Theatre (New York), 641
Lichtman, Alexander ("Al"), 597, 620, 631, 632, 713, 749, 751, 772
Lieber, Robert, 573
Life of an American Fireman, The, 415, 420
Life of Buffalo Bill, The, 517
Life of Moses, The, 516
Life of Villa, The, 673
Life's Shop Window, 701
Liggett & Myers Tobacco Company, xlviii
Lighting, 82, 186, 194, 400, 408, 440, 532, 572
Lillie, Major, 517
Lincoln, Abraham, 545
Lincoln, Fred, 426
Lindeman, Henry C., 184
Linder, Max, 445, 738, 739
Lindsay, Vachel, x
Lindsey, Judge Ben, 611
Lipton, Sir Thomas, 399, 775
Little Egypt, 337
Little Lord Fauntleroy, 511
Little Red School House, The, 501, 604
Littlest Rebel, The, 497
Little Teacher, The, 508
living pictures, 260
Livingston, Crawford, 580
Lloyd, Harold, 739, 740
Lochner, Louis P., 726
Lockwood, Natalie Dole, 180, 295, 296, 554
Loew, Marcus, 431, 478, 594, 676, 765, 797, 800, 829
Loew's New York Theatre, 323
Loftus, Cissie, 700
Lombard, Thomas R., 78, 79, 80, 81, 88, 380
London, 138, 147, 182, 229, 237, 238, 239, 240, 241, 299, 329, 414, 429, 646
London Film Company, 615
London, Jack, 402, 601, 630
London, Samuel H., 618
Lonely Villa, The, 503, 504, 505
Lonergan, Lloyd, 663
Lonesome Luke, 739
Lone Star Corporation, 735, 736, 737, 738, 746, 791, 792
Long Beach, Calif., 699
Long, Samuel, 459, 630
Loos, Anita, 513, 514, 644, 721, 773

Loos, R. Beers, 513
Lorne, Delores, 604
Los Angeles, Calif., 277, 425, 426, 507, 533, 534, 535, 568, 578, 630, 637, 646, 679, 719, 789, 794
Louis XVI, 181, 182
Love, Bessie, 757
Low, Barbara, lxix
Low, Dr. Seth, 98
Lubelski, Anthony, 426, 427
Lubin, Sigmund, 270, 272, 288, 377, 381, 384, 419, 420, 422, 466, 472, 495, 507, 527, 625, 626, 707, 710, 716, 738, 775
Lucas, Mae, 83, 84
Luchow, August, 582
Lucile Love, 661
Ludvigh, Elek J., 596, 631
Lumen, 159, 162
Lumière, Antoine, 243
Lumière, Auguste, xi, 163, 164, 165, 166, 167
Lumière, Louis, xi, 163, 164, 165, 166, 167, 205, 305, 318, 319, 348, 371, 530
Lure, The, 613
Lydig, Mrs. Philip, 296
Lyon, 163, 164, 165, 318

Mc

MacLaren, Gay, xlvi
McAdoo, William G., 787, 788, 794, 795, 796
McAlpin Hotel (New York), 529
McCardell, Roy L., 397, 668, 669
McCarthy, J. J., 642
McClellan, Mayor George B., 476, 477
McClure Syndicate, 742
McConaughey, Jack, 187, 188
McCormick, Robert R., 662
McCoy, Al, 465, 492, 493
McCutcheon, Old Man, 397, 421, 454, 456, 457
McCutcheon, Wallace, 422
McDougall, John, 61, 62
McDougall, Walt, 61
McGowan, John P., 507
McGowen, Hugh, 550
McGrath, Harold, 658, 664
McKinley, Abner, 216, 326, 811
McKinley, William, 99, 216, 275, 284, 323, 324, 325, 326, 329, 679, 811
McLaglan, Victor, 776
McLean, Edward B., 698
McManus, Edward A., 655, 661, 778
McManus, George, 654
McNally, John J., 378

—855—

INDEX

—856—

INDEX

My Cousin, 773
My Four Years in Germany, 495
My Old Dutch, 232
My Valet, 723

N

Nagipate, Chief, 601, 602
Nanook of the North, 600
Nansen, Betty, 701
Napa City, 28, 30, 31, 32
Naples, Me., 622
Napoleon, xv, 367, 545
Napoleon at Waterloo, 260
Nation, Carrie, 403
National Association of the Motion Picture Industry, 815
National Board of Review (see Censorship), 481
National Film Renting Company, 443
Navarre Hotel, 627
Navarro, Ramon, 463
Nazimova, Alla, 765, 766, 797
Nebuchadnezzar, xliv
Nederlandsche Biographe en Mutoscope Maatschappij, 329
Nehls, Richard, 427
Neilan, Marshall, 464, 575, 720
Nesbitt, Evelyn (see Thaw, H. K.), 475
Nethersole, Olga, 339
Netter, Raphael, 112
Nevada, 285
Newark, N. J., 350
Newcastle, Pa., 426
Newcomer, Sam, 29, 30, 31, 32
New Cook, The, 578
New London, Conn., 807
New Mexico, 544
New Orleans, 270, 271
Newport News, Va., 187, 188
NEW REPUBLIC, 643, 736
New Rochelle, N. Y., 498, 663, 666, 667, 668
NEWS, ILLUSTRATED DAILY (New York), 474, 663, 819
Newspaper Feature Service, 102
Newspaper War, 656, 657, 658, 659, 660, 661, 662
New Stenographer, The, 547
New York Celluloid Company, 164
New York Hat, The, 513, 514
New York Motion Picture Co., 533, 578, 581, 582, 645, 718
Niblo, Fred, 463
Niblo's Garden Theatre, 370
Nice, France, 264

Nicholas Sisters, 185, 187
Niépce, M. Joseph Nicephore, 16
Night in a London Club, A, 645, 646
Night Out, A, 650
Niles, Calif., 650, 731
Nipper's Lullaby, The, 232
Niver, Katherine A., 485
Nixon Theatre (Philadelphia), 646
Nome City, Alaska, 402, 622
Nomenclature, 551, 552
Nordisk (see Great Northern)
Norfolk & Western Ry., 468
Norfolk, Va., 184, 185, 186, 187, 190
Normand, Mabel, 506, 512, 583, 647
Norrish, Bernard E., 812
North America Phonograph Company, 78, 114
Northcliff, Va., 176
North Pole, 515
Northwestern University, 828
Northwest Transportation Company, 401
Notre Dame, 355
N. Y. M. P. (see New York Motion Picture), 534

O

Oakes, Ernest, 331
Oakland, California, 426, 427
Oakley, Anne, 83, 84
Oakman, Wheeler, 677
Oberammergau, xliii, 367, 372, 373
Oberholtzer, Ellis Paxon, 485
O'Brien, Malevinsky & Driscoll, 747, 748
Occident, 37
Ocean Grove, N. J., 375
l'Connor, Mary, 720
Odyssey, xlv, 516
Oes, Ingvald C., 515
Official War Review, 784, 785
Ogden, Utah, 629
Ogle, Charles, 441
Ojinaga, 672
Oklahoma, 543
Oland, Warner, 779
Olcott, Chauncey, 501
Olcott, Sidney, 459, 460, 461, 462, 464, 507
Oldenow, William, 592
Old Man's Darling, 474
Oliver Morosco Stock Company, 534
Olivier, Père, 355
Olympia (London), 239
Omaha, Nebr., 597, 638, 739

INDEX

O'Malley & Smith **Advertising Company**, 574, 575
One Exciting Night, 505
O'Neil, Eugene, 728
O'Neil, Nance, 453, 513
101 Bison pictures, 582
101 Ranch Show, 578, 579, **582**
O'Neill, James, 598
O'Neill, Rose, 179, 180, 295
On the Night Stage, 719
Ophir, H. M. S., 422
d'Orleans, Duc, 181
Orman, Felix, 776
Orpheum, Circuit, 265, 443, 601
Orpheum Travel Weekly, 601
Oshkosh, Wis., 446, 447, 448, 449, 450, 828
'Osler Joe, 456
O'Sullivan, Tony, 534, 635
Otero, 117
Ott, Fred, 57, 58, 59, 60, 79, 82, 238, 637
Ott, John F., 57
Ouspensky, 159
OUTLOOK, THE, 694
Owen, Seena, 720, 721, 757
Ox, liv, lv, 832

P

Page, Kerr & Cooper, 553, 554
Page, Parker W., 553, 555, 556, 557
Paine, Richard, 276, 277, 341
Palace Theatre (London), 364, 566
"Palacio del Carneado of Vedado," 541
Paley, William C., 370, 371, 390, 423, 424
Palmer, Mrs. Potter, 87
Palo Alto, 36, 37, 42, 46
Pan, 177, 180
Panchromatic film, 572
Panthea, 765
Pantoptikon, 128, 129, 131, 167, 176, 290, 367
Pants, 307
Panzer, Paul, 517, 518, 661
Papinta, 324
Paramount Pictographs, 633
Paramount Pictures Corporation, 496, 633, 639, 640, 710, 713, 749, 750, 752, 795
Paris, 138, 158, 182, 291, 296, 299, 353, 444, 445, 554, 566, 595, 601
Paris Exposition, 66, 401
Paris, John Ayrton, M.D., 11, 563
Paris Slums, 474
Paris, University of, 725
Parker, Sir Gilbert, 753, 762

Parkersburg, W. Va., 679
Parkhurst, Dr., 612, 618
Park Theatre (Brooklyn), 287
Park Theatre (New York), 618
Parr, Richard, 695
Parsons, Louella O., 681
Passion, 722
Passion Dance, 256
Passion Play, xliii, 291, 366, 367, 368, 369, 370, 371, 372, 373, 374, 375, 376, 377, 381, 382, 390, 396, 419, 474
Pastor, Tony, 252, 262, 263
Patents Company (see Motion Picture Patents Company)
Patterson, Joseph Medill, 662, 685
Pathé, Charles, 75, 151, 318, 348
Pathé, Emil, 444
Pathé Freres, 444, 445, 466, 472, 493, 518, 601, 661, 664, 702, 738
Pathé Journal
Pathé Weekly, 518, 655
Patria, 778, 779, 780
Patti, Black, 258, 342
Paul, Robert W., xi, 148, 149, 150, 151, 152, 153, 155, 157, 158, 160, 161, 166, 167, 205, 229, 232, 238, 239, 240, 241, 318, 348, 429
Pauncefote, Sir Julian, 99
Pawley, Raymond, 632
Pawtuckett, R. I., 476
Payton, William M., 381
Peacock, Capt. Leslie, 705
Pearson, Virginia, 702
Peckham, Charles, 426
Peerless Company, 713
Pelzer, William, 529
Pendegast, Wort W., 28, 29, 32
Pendleton, Ore., 611
Pennsylvania, 287, 312, 313, 482, 485, 759
Pennsylvania, University of, 43, 44, 45, 47
People's Institute of New York, 476, 477, 480, 481
Pepper Building (New York), 345
Pepperday Inn, 664, 666
Perils of Pauline, The, 661
Perret, Leonce, 825
de la Perrier, Armand, 692
Pershing's Crusaders, 784
Persistence of Vision, 2, 10, 11, 12, 13, 14, 17, 18, 19, 20, 40, 41, 71, 101, 122, 123, 141, 142, 143, 144, 145, 150, 151, 161, 162, 168, 169, 170, 171, 172, 173, 174
Personal, 421, 422
Persons, Tom, 521, 532

—859—

INDEX

INDEX

Rising, William, 492
Ritz-Carlton, 6, 762
Ritz-Carlton Pictures, 826
Rivoli Theatre (New York), 676, 773, 827
Roach, Hal, 739
Road of Anthracite, The, 416
Road to Yesterday, The, 551
Robbinston, Me., 545
Robespierre, 182
Robinson, Frederick H., 618
Robinson, Gertrude, 576
Rochester, N. Y., 62, 123, 199
Rock Creek Cemetery, 558
Rock, William T., 269, 270, 271, 272, 276, 349, 374, 393, 404, 412, 549, 566, 678, 694, 747
Rockefeller, John D., 301
Rockett, Al, 742
Rockett, Ray, 742
Roeber, Ernest, 185
Rogers, Gustavus A., 477, 479, 529, 827
Rogers, Saul, 479, 810, 816, 817
Rôget, John, 9
Rôget, Peter Mark, 9, 10, 11, 12, 162
Roland, Ruth, 464, 720
Rolfe, B. A., 623
roller photography, 61, 62
Romanoff, Nicholas, 766
Romantic Redskins, 575
Rome, Italy, 6, 236, 242, 463, 639
Romilly, Sir Samuel, 9
Ronkonkomo, Lake, 702
Roof Studios, 185, 210, 257, 328, 331, 404, 440, 533
Roosevelt, Kermit, 519
Roosevelt, Theodore, xv, 329, 337, 434, 435, 436, 437, 438, 439, 519, 520, 521, 522, 694, 726
Roscoe, Burton, x
Rose, Frank Oakes, 372, 462
Rose Garden Theatre (New York), 641
Ross, Duncan C., 185
Rotary lens Camera, 141, 142
Rothacker, Watterson R., 32, 536, 537
Rothafel, Samuel Lionel, 175, 249, 260, 675, 676, 677, 723, 724, 725, 785, 827
Rough Sea at Dover, A, 150
Rouses Point, N. Y., 695
Rowland, Richard, 573, 574, 713, 714, 795, 797, 798, 799, 800, 801, 802
"Roxy,"—see Rothafel
Royal Institution, 161, 238
Royal Northwest Mounted Police, 601
Royal Society, 10, 11, 162
Rubin & Finkelstein, 828
Ruggles, Charles, 534

Rulofson, William, 27
Ruskin, John, 45
Russell, Anne, 546
Russell, Frank, 368, 370, 371, 372
Russell, Lillian, 569
Russell, Sol Smith, 547
Russell, William, 664
Ryan, Joe, 611

S

Sage, Russell, 222
St. Bartholomew's Eve, lxi, 756
St. Catharine, 178
St. Denis, Ruth, 85
St. James Hotel (New York), 292
St. James Palace, 422
St. John, Adele Rogers, 682
St. John-the-Baptist, 247
St. Louis, Mo., 417, 429, 523, 524, 573, 667, 668, 823
Salaries, 434, 504, 512, 538, 624, 627, 663, 704, 708, 709, 710, 711, 716, 729, 733, 734, 736, 741, 744, 748, 750
Sales Company (see M. P. Distributing & Sales Company)
Salome, xiv
Salter, Harry, 504, 506, 511, 523
Salt Lake City, 606
Sampson, 324
Samson and Delilah, 739
San Diego, Calif., 513, 514
Sandow, Eugene, xv, 83, 255, 366
Sands of Dee, 536
San Francisco, 368, 426, 427, 535, 807, 808, 722
Sanger, 8
Santa Barbara, Calif., 669, 794
Santchi, Thomas, 677
Santiago, Battle of, 390, 391
Santley, Joe, 459
Sappho, xiv, 339
Saratoga Hotel, 601
Sarg, Tony, 424
Sarter, Baron, 182
Saved by the Juvenile Court
Sawyer, Laura, 441
Scala Theatre (London), 570
Scanlon, Rev. Charles, 484
Scenario, 288, 306, 421, 422, 423, 424, 455, 456, 462, 463, 509, 510, 512, 513, 653
Schenck, Joseph, 765, 796, 813, 816
Schenck, Nicholas, 813, 816
Schiller Theatre (Chicago), 305, 652
Schneider, Eberhard, 385
Schulberg, Ben, 796

—862—

INDEX

INDEX

Webster, Harry McRae, 606
Weigle, Edwin F., 684, 685
Wellauer, Emil, 208
Wellington, New Zealand, 278
Wells, H. G., 152, 153, 154, 157, 158, 160, 162, 265, 429
Welsh, William, 617
We Moderns, 619
Wenzell, A. B., 96
Werner, Lionel, 138, 163
Werner Brothers, 138, 163
West Orange, 138, 147, 150, 165, 218, 219, 220, 226, 228, 231, 244, 254, 256, 257, 274, 275, 280, 314
West Virginia, University of, 105, 106, 297
Western Film Exchange, 452, 595
Weston, Charles, 541, 578
What Happened to Mary? 655, 658, 661
Wheel of Life, 14, 17
When Knighthood was in Flower, 461
When We Were Twenty-one, 658
Where Are My Children? 618, 619
White, Abraham, 222, 223
White Horse Rapids, 600
White House, 275, 435, 439, 519, 780, 817
White, James H., 257, 403, 409, 414, 415
White, Pearl, 518, 661
White Rats, 407
White, Stanford, 336, 475
Whitestone Landing, N. Y., 533, 568
Whitford, E. P., 338
Whitman, Bert, 493
Whitman, Walt, 756
Whitney, Claire, 701
Whom the Gods Would Destroy, 762
Wickersham, George W., 529
Widow Jones, The, 257, 259
Wilbur, Crane, 518, 661
Wilde, Oscar, 133
Wilhelm, Kaiser, 133
Wilkenning, Cora Carrington, 742, 744, 745, 747
Wilkes-Barre, 312
Wilkes, John, 511
Willard, Jess, 694
Willard, O. H., 19
Willat, "Doc," 540, 541, 577
Willatowski, C. A., (see Willat, "Doc")
Willets, Gilson, 658
William Owen Dramatic Company, 458
Williams, Bert, 303, 609, 610
Williams, Brown & Earle, 391

Williams, J. D., 679, 680, 789, 790, 793, 826
Williams, Kathlyn, 658
Williams, Wilkes, 511
Williamsport, Pa., 517
Wilson, Ben, 441
Wilson, Frank, 788
Wilson, Harry Leon, 180
Wilson, Lois, 824
Wilson, Woodrow, 529, 641, 656, 688, 728, 777, 780, 785, 794, 811
Winant, Forrest, 719
Winik, Hyman, 518
Wisent, lv
Wish, xv, xxxviii, xxxix, xl, xlvii, xlviii, lxix, lxx, 74, 75, 834
Wishing Ring, The, 524, 762
Witmark, Julius P., 378
Wobber, Herman, 679
Woburn, Mass., 807
Woman of Paris, A, 651
Women's Christian Temperance Union, 287, 484
Wonders of Canada, 474, 475
Wood & Shephard, 324
Wood, Gardiner, 655
Woodmen of the World, 638
Woodruff, Henry, 719
Woods, Frank, 512, 513, 638, 720, 819
World Film Corporation, 712, 713, 761, 762, 763, 764, 812
WORLD, NEW YORK, 134, 274, 384, 702, 727
World Special Films Corporation, 712, 761
World War, 571, 683, 684, 685, 686, 726, 727, 728, 737, 777, 780, 781, 782, 783, 784, 785, 786, 787, 788, 797, 798
Wormwood's Dog and Monkey Show, 346, 349
Wright, William, 464, 715

X Y Z

Yankee Cruiser, The, 191
Yellow Jacket Mine, 27
Yip, Sam, 398
Young, Clara Kimball, 606, 762, 763, 764, 766
Young, James, 606
Zaza, 85
Zeidman, Benny, 774
Ziebarth, Charles, 575
Ziegfeld, Florenz, 255, 339, 729, 770
Zittel, C. F., 628

INDEX

ABOUT THE AUTHOR

Terry Ramsaye was born in Tonganoxie, Kansas, in 1885. He started his professional career as an engineer but switched to journalism when he joined the staff of the Kansas City Star and Times *in 1905. During the following decade he worked on newspapers in Leavenworth (Kansas), Omaha, St. Paul and Chicago.*

When Mr. Ramsaye joined the Mutual Film Corporation in 1915, the motion picture industry was still in its infancy. While at Mutual he produced some Charlie Chaplin comedies and founded Screen Telegram, *a newsreel which achieved conspicuous success during World War I. Subsequently, he was associated with Samuel L. Rothafel in the management of Broadway's Rialto and Rivoli theaters and launched and edited the newsreel* Kinograms.

In 1920 he retired to a farm on Long Island and devoted the next five years to writing this book along with many magazine articles. Then, after producing numerous adventure films and editing others, including Grass *(Paramount) and* Martin Johnson's African Hunt *(Paramount), he became editor in chief of* Pathé News *and* Audio Review.

In 1931 Mr. Ramsaye joined the Quigley Publishing Company as editor of The Motion Picture Herald, *a post he held until 1941. Subsequently he lectured on motion pictures and contributed articles about them to various encyclopedias and yearbooks. He continued his association with the Quigley Publications as consulting editor and author of a weekly column for the* Herald *until his death in 1954.*